Freedom and Criminal Responsibility in American Legal Thought

The first full-length study of twentieth-century American legal academics wrestling with the problem of free will versus determinism in the context of criminal responsibility, this book deals with one of the most fundamental problems in criminal law. Thomas Andrew Green chronicles legal academic ideas from the Progressive Era critique of a free will–based theory of criminal responsibility, to the midcentury acceptance of the idea of free will as necessary to a criminal law conceived of in practical, moral-legal terms, to the late-in-century insistence on the compatibility of scientific determinism with moral and legal responsibility. He traces the coinciding century-long shift from the Progressive attack on the criminal law's retributive premises to a modern version of retributivism that scholars believed could survive determinism. Foregrounding scholars' language and ideas, Green invites readers to participate in reconstructing an aspect of the past that is central to attempts to work out bases for moral judgment, legal blame, and criminal punishment.

Thomas Andrew Green is the John P. Dawson Collegiate Professor of Law emeritus and Professor of History emeritus at the University of Michigan. He served as editor or coeditor of Studies in Legal History, the book series of the American Society for Legal History, from 1986 to 2011. Green also has served as president of the American Society for Legal History, has been a Fellow of the Center for Advanced Studies in the Behavioral Sciences, and has held fellowships from the National Endowment for the Humanities and the John Simon Guggenheim Memorial Foundation. One of his previous publications, *Verdict According to Conscience: Perspectives on the English Criminal Trial Jury, 1200–1800* (1985), and the present volume together form the framework of his current project, a study of the relationship between ideas about the jury and ideas about criminal responsibility in the English and American past. That project will complete Green's work on two aspects of freedom in Anglo-American criminal justice history: political liberty and free will.

"A fascinating and illuminating study of the ways in which twentieth-century American legal academics (those concerned with both metaphysical truth and its implications for practical policy) grappled with the problems of free will and criminal responsibility. Green allows the authors he studies to speak for themselves, and thus brings out in admirably clear detail the contours and shifts of the debates within and between successive generations of thinkers." – Antony Duff, University of Minnesota Law School

"This deeply researched account of how twentieth-century legal thinkers have engaged with questions of freedom and responsibility is remarkable in its coverage and attention to detail. Green's close readings of the American texts – some well-known, many long-forgotten – and his careful explication of their contexts and meanings, vividly portrays how academic lawyers have struggled to make law's categories fit for practical use and also compatible with philosophical and scientific conceptions." – David Garland, New York University

Freedom and Criminal Responsibility in American Legal Thought

THOMAS ANDREW GREEN
University of Michigan

CAMBRIDGE
UNIVERSITY PRESS

CAMBRIDGE
UNIVERSITY PRESS

32 Avenue of the Americas, New York NY 10013-2473, USA

Cambridge University Press is part of the University of Cambridge.

It furthers the University's mission by disseminating knowledge in the pursuit of
education, learning and research at the highest international levels of excellence.

www.cambridge.org
Information on this title: www.cambridge.org/9780521854603

First published 2014

A catalogue record for this publication is available from the British Library

Library of Congress Cataloguing in Publication data
Green, Thomas Andrew, author.
Freedom and criminal responsibility in American legal thought / Thomas Andrew Green.
    pages   cm
Includes bibliographical references and index.
ISBN 978-0-521-85460-3 (hardback)
1. Criminal liability – United States.   2. Freedom.   3. Law – Philosophy.   I. Title.
KF9235.G74   2014
345.73'04–dc23   2014014938

ISBN 978-0-521-85460-3 Hardback

For Ruth
and for my brothers,
Chris and Steve,
in memory of our parents,
Alan and Gladys Green

Contents

Acknowledgments

I have incurred many debts over the long period during which this book evolved from a study of the criminal trial jury in the nineteenth- and twentieth-century United States to one on ideas about freedom and criminal responsibility in the twentieth-century United States, with the jury as no more than a leitmotif that appears, where relevant, at selected points throughout the text. Some of my student research assistants contributed to early stages, others to later ones, of this evolution. I express my gratitude to them all, whether or not their research help ended up on the cutting-room floor (to be recovered for use in future work on the relationship between the jury and ideas about criminal responsibility): Isabelle Antongiorgi, David Blanchard, Kelly Bozanic, Carolyn Frantz, Joseph Gonzalez, Jeffrey Jones, Jessica Lieberman, Kristin Olbertson, Matthew Perry, Adam Sloane, and Lu Zhang.

A second sort of evolutionary process took place during the later stages, when, over a number of years, I undertook a series of revisions of the original completed text. I could not have managed these revisions – and the major transformation they resulted in – without the help of two extraordinarily talented and hardworking research/editorial assistants, first Ellen Poteet and subsequently Merrill Hodnefield. Ellen and Merrill each came to know the entire subject matter of this work as well as I did: each was subjected to years of my lectures and musings, as well as, of course, to constant rereadings of successive versions of the manuscript. Each left her mark on the final manuscript. It is fair to say that many passages, especially in Part II, were talked out, reasoned over, and written jointly by Ellen and me; many others throughout the book – especially in Part III – were handled in the same way by Merrill and me. In addition, Merrill took the lead, working from my outlines (but often extending my envisioned coverage), in drafting substantial sections of the introductions to each of the three parts. Finally, Merrill composed the indexes.

Many colleagues, both here at Michigan and elsewhere, read and commented on one or another part of one or another version of the manuscript. I am grateful for their interest and insights: Susanna Blumenthal, Joshua Dressler, Antony Duff, Samuel Gross, Donald Herzog, Jerold Israel, Sandra Marshall, William Novak, Philip Soper, the late Eric Stein, and James Boyd White. A number read and commented on the entire manuscript: Hendrik Hartog, Elizabeth Kamali, Gerald Leonard, Michael Lobban, Martha Umphrey, and Ellen Unger. I thank Barbara Cain, Alan Gibbard, Douglas Husak, Sanford Kadish, Richard Lempert, Gabriel Mendlow, James Nickel, Alice Ristroph, David Rothman, Scott Shapiro, Jonathan Simon, Joseph Vining, and the late Herbert Wechsler for conversations on specific matters at crucial moments. And I am grateful to Susanna Blumenthal, Charles Eisendrath, Terrance Sandalow, and Rebecca Scott for many conversations over many years on one or another aspect of the freedom issue. Finally, for an academic lifetime of free will/determinism discussions, I am forever indebted to Peter Westen. (Peter advises me to stop thinking about the matter, but – please don't spread this around – he's a secret enabler.)

Generations of Michigan Law School and History Department students actually paid tuition to hear me talk about the subject matter of this book, as have students at the University of Nebraska College of Law, the Tel Aviv University Law School, and the University of Hawaii Law School. Collectively, these (and other) students have enriched my life and improved my work. That's true as well for students in several seminars in American Legal History at Princeton taught by Hendrik Hartog. I owe Dirk a very great deal for advice and encouragement, and for his use of successive drafts of the manuscript in his teaching.

Along the way, I have had much appreciated suggestions from David Hollinger and Edward Purcell regarding background reading in American intellectual history. At various stages I received valuable editorial help from Terre Fisher, Benjamin Friedman, Alexandra Gross, Brittany Harrison, and Ruth Homrighaus.

There cannot be a better informed, more efficient, or easier-to-work-with academic law library staff than that at the University of Michigan Law School. I very much appreciate everything that they have done for me over the years. Special thanks to Jocelyn Kennedy. And for wonderful faculty assistance over the years I thank Sharon Rice, Kimberley Latta, Rose Maten, and especially my current assistant, Dara Faris.

My editor at Cambridge University Press and longtime friend and professional colleague, Lewis Bateman, has offered excellent advice and extended great encouragement, for which I am greatly indebted. Thanks, too, for the abundant help given me by his assistant, Shaun Vigil, and for the insightful readings and advice of two anonymous readers for the Press.

I want also to recognize here the generous support I have received in connection with the early (American jury–based) stages of this long-range project from the Center for Advanced Studies in the Behavioral Sciences (and the Andrew Mellon Fund), the National Endowment for the Humanities, the John Simon Guggenheim Memorial Foundation, and the William W. Cook Endowment Fund of the University of Michigan Law School.

No words can express my appreciation to my wife, Ruth Brownell Green, whose love, support, and patience over the years have meant everything.

Introduction

The free will problem inherent in the acts of blaming and punishing is age-old and well-known. It has largely to do with the notion of just deserts. Conventionally, most of us tend to believe that the attribution of guilt and the imposition of punishment are deserved only if it may fairly be said that the actor exercised some degree of free choice, or – as it is often put – could have chosen not to do what he or she did. Yet most of us also believe there are limits to freedom of choice in particular circumstances, and some question whether it can be said that such freedom ever exists. That is, most of us engage in at least some degree of deterministic thinking: we believe free choice may be limited (or entirely precluded) by an individual's age, upbringing, or environmental influences; by mental illness and other psychological, genetic, or biological factors, or (as some would have it) by the inevitable hand of God or fate. We tend to conclude, consciously or otherwise, that at least some acts or choices are determined by forces outside the individual's control. Disagreements abound over the degree to which particular factors limit or preclude freedom, the meaning of free choice, and the question of whether the philosophical debate about the free will/determinism problem creates a false dichotomy – or identifies a real problem at all.

In the end, there is more agreement that the free will "problem" is not something worth worrying about as a general matter, however much it seems necessary on some occasions to consider it in relation to particular circumstances. This area of agreement is, of course, a significant aspect of human life. Those who are parties to the agreement have signed on for a variety of reasons. Some would say that it is obvious humans have free will, at least in most instances. Others would say that we have a powerful and ineradicable *feeling* of being free and could not make sense of our lives if we did not act in accordance with that perception of freedom. Still others would put it a bit differently, saying that life is meaningless – or that voluntary organization into "free" societies is impossible – unless either we are in fact free or can without too much moment-to-moment doubt proceed as though we are free; thus we simply ought to presume that we are. Some of these last persons are among those who would define "freedom" and "choice" in ways that do not depend on theories about true or metaphysically real "free will" as the phrase is colloquially understood.

The variations on this theme are endless and all too familiar. I need not dwell on them here. Most important is that the problem is always with us and that it arises in every part of our lives, even if we rarely expressly confront it. As a practical matter, we seem quite adept at living – and at evaluating our own and others' conduct – from a sort of midpoint that mediates between perspectives: we assign blame or explain away behavior (as essentially unavoidable), sometimes without conscious reflection, based on what we know about a particular person or circumstance. In fact, we even seem quite comfortable with shifts between these perspectives regarding a single event; we may insist in the heat of the moment that a particular person freely (and blamably) harmed us, yet we might come to think otherwise – to give more weight to the circumstances that influenced him or her – after cooling off.

The criminal law – my subject here – is only one of the very many contexts in which the problem arises and is resolved. But it strikes us as a critical one, both because the deeper discussion of human responsibility necessary to theories of blame and punishment requires direct confrontation with our doubts about the underlying concept of free will and because a good deal rests upon our resolution of the free will problem in this particular context. The liberty, or even life, of an offender may be at stake; the stigma of an assessment of criminal guilt certainly is. The safety of society and the vindication of the rights of those harmed by criminal behavior are at stake, too. Further, criminal adjudication is sufficiently public and deemed sufficiently important that we think its underlying presumption of free will sends a message to society at large about personal responsibility and our duties to each other.

It is therefore unsurprising that the history of criminal law has been intertwined with the free will problem. Nor is it surprising that, in this context, our conventional agreement about how to deal with that problem (that is, to set it aside) has come under some strain or – as a theoretical matter – that there have been disagreements about the resolution of the problem both as to the relevance of particular circumstances said to limit free will and as to the general question of whether the idea of just deserts (that is, of genuine responsibility for our acts) has any basis in truth at all. When we think about it, we quickly recognize that criminal law has been affected by the problem at every level: the definition of criminal offenses; the assessment of responsibility, including the practices we have adopted to reach such an assessment; and the way we deal with those found guilty, both in the formal sense of the institutions of punishment or treatment and in the informal sense of social views regarding the guilty. That is, when we do think about it, we are likely to think that the history of the criminal law (like the history of many aspects of human relationships and organization, only more so than most other aspects) has been in part the history of the free will problem. To be sure, the very concepts of "criminal law" and "criminal responsibility" have varied over time, and this conceptual history may be seen as overlapping with the history of ideas about free will.

Through the three essays that follow, I have sought to sketch the main contours of twentieth-century American legal-academic thought regarding the implications of the free will problem in criminal law. Hence the ideas are predominantly those of American legal academics, and specifically those of criminal jurisprudence scholars. Some such scholars were well read in philosophy or science (biological, social, psychological), and many others were more indirectly influenced by scholars in fields outside of the law. I draw attention to a few of the many philosophers, scientists, and others who investigated the meanings of free will and determinism in the twentieth century. But, in the main, I treat legal scholars within what has been termed their own "small world."[1] I focus on that cadre because they were distinctively, if not uniquely, a group devoted to a dual role with respect to criminal justice: that of truth-seeker *and* prescriptivist. This is to say, criminal jurisprudence scholars both wrestled with the question of the "true" scientifically, metaphysically, or morally correct bases for responsibility *and* sought to answer real-world questions about the practical attribution of criminal responsibility and the imposition of punishment. As is particularly significant to my work here, these questions required scholars to confront conventional notions of blame that often appeared to be incompatible with – or at least conceived of in very different terms from – scientific "truth." Some other academics and jurists played the sort of dual role I have described, but many of them were, in their professional lives, either mainly truth-seekers who did not take it upon themselves to prescribe, or prescriptivists who were not truth-seekers. In any event, whoever else might be said to have played this dual role professionally, most leading criminal jurisprudence scholars did; they self-identified as such, and they were understood by outside observers as playing that role.

Over the next few pages, I introduce some themes that appear throughout this book – and a few caveats – as context for my discussion of these

[1] Robert Weisberg, "Criminal Law, Criminology, and the Small World of Legal Scholars," *Colorado Law Review*, vol. 63 (1992): 521–68. Further, given my focus on legal scholars, my sparing consideration of evidence of the free will debate apparent in legal enactments or judicial opinions is particularly selective. Michele Cotton offers a much more comprehensive analysis of such evidence of the debate in practice, particularly in the latter half of the century, in "A Foolish Consistency: Keeping Determinism Out of the Criminal Law," *Boston University Public Interest Law Journal*, vol. 15 (2005): 1–48.

scholars and their work. It is perhaps most important to say that the writers I treat are center stage. To be sure, my voice enters, organizes, interprets, analyzes. But, more than is usually the case, I have allowed the writers to speak for themselves: it is the intellectual activity *itself* that I have chosen as my focus. Thus, this book is not aimed at presenting a traditional or fully contextualized argument on my part with regard to its themes; the themes move in and out of the narrative as scholars lived the experience of grappling with ideas about criminal responsibility, which these scholars did – or such is the perhaps fictive premise of my account – mainly in the context of their predecessors' and contemporaries' writings, rather than that of their own social and historical frameworks.

The book adopts a rough, three-Part periodization of twentieth-century American criminal jurisprudence: the 1890s through the 1920s (the Progressive Era), the 1930s through the 1950s, and 1960 to the end of the century. Each period provides the subject matter for each of three essays – or studies – in which I explore legal-academic writing of the time that implicates the free will problem and its relationship to criminal responsibility. Each essay, in turn, has its own distinctive approach, guided by the nature and breadth of the relevant writings. No single study is meant to exhaustively catalog every scholar of the period who meaningfully addressed free will, however. Encyclopedic comprehensiveness is not my aim. Rather, I give attention to particular voices that exemplify historical moments in the evolution of legal-academic thought on the free will problem as it relates to criminal responsibility. What I sacrifice by omission, I endeavor to make up for through an impressionistic narrative that places the writings I discuss in a broader frame.

The result might be best described as a mosaic. And, importantly, it has not been my goal to situate that mosaic in current meta-narratives, those of critical legal studies or of a Foucauldian sort coming most immediately to mind. Such interpretations have an undeniable relevance to my own concern with the relationship between law and freedom. For critical legal studies, the law safeguards the idea of individual autonomy insofar as it both undergirds and is the expression of capitalist economic relations; thus, even when the law is coercive, it seems to stand for free will and just deserts based on free will. For Foucault, too, freedom is a construct. In one version, the state endows people with an illusory freedom to win the trust of the governed and thereby insure state power. I do not take issue with either of these modes of analysis or with their convergence regarding the question of freedom, and I am ready to grant their validity (and that of many other perspectives) at a meta-level of historical analysis. That meta-level is not, however, the promontory upon which I stand. In fact, I have avoided "promontories" in order to enter into the intricacies of minds grappling with questions that, as they admit no simple resolution, have the power of refusing to die. There is something more. Meta-narratives, across the ideological spectrum, share this: a resistance to accepting an authority outside themselves. They posit their own determinism. I do not write a grand narrative because I do not want to fit these voices either into a conclusive historical proof or into an imposed pattern, whether progressive, circular, ascending, or otherwise. Regardless of the positions they argued for, the legal academics I present here thought themselves free enough to prescribe. To capture *that* spirit is to seize on the continuing vitality of legal academic thought in the world of the law.

THE FREE WILL PROBLEM AND THE CRIMINAL LAW

Consider the question whether, and to what extent, a criminal act requires a "guilty mind" or, instead, may be any act that, on its surface and without primary regard to the malevolence of the actor's intent, simply violates a legal proscription. Historically, some jurists, political theorists, and other commentators have asserted that the latter sort of act – that is, one that facially violates a previously enacted legal proscription – alone effectively meets the legality principle, *nullum crimen, nulla poena sine lege* (often abbreviated as "*nulla poena*") or (roughly) "no crime and no punishment without a pre-existing penal law." Of course, it is commonly assumed that such an act also has to be voluntary, in the very general sense that the offender acted on his or her own motion, not as the result of an external force (e.g., a physical push from someone or something else) or an internal one (e.g., epilepsy). But the actor's deeper motivation – his or her subjective intent to do wrong – might go unexamined. Other commentators, including most American jurists and scholars, have insisted that – particularly for the serious criminal offenses with which this book is concerned and which raise the free will issue most dramatically (homicide, serious assault, most forms of theft, rape, and arson) – a criminal offense requires both a voluntary act and the intent to do wrong. Such unlawful intent (or mens rea), in turn, presupposes cognitive capacity – in some jurisdictions also absence of an "irresistible impulse" – and the absence of duress or of other justifications, such as self-defense. It presupposes a desire to achieve an end, a belief that a specific action or actions would achieve the end, and the will to act upon the desire. The questions arise: Does an unlawful act accompanied by unlawful intent also have to be "freely" willed? And, if so, what does "freely willed" mean?

Issues surrounding what kind of intent an individual must possess in order for the state to justifiably take action against him or her under the auspices of the criminal law represent just one area, albeit a central one, where the free will question merges with questions concerning the overall goals and premises of the criminal law. As classically formulated, the law might serve various goals, or combinations thereof: crime prevention through incapacitation or deterrence of potential future offenders, retribution or moral condemnation for harms already caused, restitution for those harms, and opportunities for penance or reform of offenders. In simplified, abbreviated form, we might ask whether, in a particular time and place, the law is more concerned with (backward-looking) retributive punishment for morally culpable wrongdoing, or with the (forward-looking) consequential or utilitarian ends served by convicting and sanctioning (or reforming) offenders. The question of free will most obviously rises to the fore when the law forthrightly embodies moral condemnation or retribution, as both implicate judgment of the offender's intentional authorship of his or her harmful choices. Yet free will could also be viewed as an element of consequentialist goals, such as the reform of offenders, although perhaps more ambiguously: for example, is free will required for an offender to reform him- or herself from a lawbreaker into a law-abider? Or, perhaps, can the right reform regimen or moral education allow a lawbreaker who was previously (relatively) unfree because of determining forces, such as those in his or her home environment, to move beyond the influence of such forces and exercise a free will? Finally, of course, the law's aims are never singular, but are multiple, debatable, and, oftentimes, ambiguous or confused. Moreover, the aims and methods of the criminal law are intimately connected with a society's political and social arrangements; all elements – both the theoretical and the practical – necessarily inform the others, with the potential result being a patchwork of goals and ideals that are often impossible to sort out.

For these reasons, my consideration of the free will question unavoidably overlaps questions about the purposes and meanings of the criminal law over time. But it is important for me to stress that, although I touch on these latter complex questions when they are particularly relevant, such broad questions are not my primary focus.[2] Rather, the free will question is. Relatedly, I stress that my focus on ideas about free will is not meant to

---

[2] Of course, much has been written on the historical aims of the criminal law, albeit often without specific attention to the free will issue. One noteworthy exception is Gerald Leonard's important article, "Towards a Legal History of American Criminal Theory: Culture and Doctrine from Blackstone to the Model Penal Code," *Buffalo Criminal Law Review*, vol. 6 (2003): 691–832. Leonard draws a general distinction between what he labels as the "public" and "private" aims of the law. Public aims are largely consequentialist, with the goal of protecting social order. Private aims are more concerned with "individual moral and legal justice" (695). He aptly establishes that these "dual commitments" (804) or "double impulses" (733) of the law are each generally present, often overlapping, but just as often in tension. He also posits a strong relationship between the subjective intent requirement – along with its implication of an internal "choice to do evil" (726) – and the law's more condemnatory and retributive aspects. A central topic of Leonard's article involves the significant suspension of the intent requirement – even at times when such a requirement was generally thought necessary for serious offenses – found in statutory rape laws. Such laws illustrate a rare instance of strict liability (which was usually reserved for minor or regulatory crimes) for a serious crime; a man could be adjudged guilty of violating laws establishing an age-based requirement for consensual sex even if he reasonably believed that the girl was of age. Statutory rape laws thus embody one particularly stark point where the free will issue bleeds into questions concerning the purposes or meaning of the criminal law and the degree to which criminal

give the impression that scholars' resolution of the free will problem was the driving force behind the evolution of the criminal law theory and practice I canvass. Legal scholars' positions on the free will issue might lead them to favor certain purposes or procedures within the criminal law but, at any given historical moment, other factors are always at play, thus providing independent or intertwined motivations for the same prescriptions.[3]

The free will issue is just one element – and one that, although it touches everything, is remarkably elusive. Few legal scholars have put their thoughts about it into print, whether because scholars deemed it unimportant, uninteresting, or simply unresolvable; its influence on concrete changes in the criminal law and its administration is usually a matter of inference. This book expressly concerns the work of those scholars either who *did* confront the free will issue directly or whose thinking about criminal responsibility was most clearly shaped by the issue. That is, I seek to trace the ways in which confrontation with the free will problem *itself* evolved in American legal thought. Thus I have allowed the extant legal academic literature on free will to govern my main points of focus, essay by essay, and have been, for the most part, no more than suggestive about the influence on criminal justice administration of the academic ideas that I trace. Where some comment on the criminal justice system is nonetheless needed in order to contextualize views on the free will problem, I will refer the reader selectively to others' in-depth work on the subject. In other

responsibility depends on a knowing, subjectively intended or willed act. For just one other example, Michele Pifferi touches on themes germane to the free will issue in his comparative account of the aims of the English and American legal systems during the nineteenth and twentieth centuries, the two countries' divergent interpretations of the legality principle, and the resulting implications for how free will and moral responsibility affected the state's power to convict and punish its citizens. Pifferi, "Indetermined Sentence and the *Nulla Poena Sine Lege* Principle: Contrasting Views on Punishment in the U.S. and Europe between the 19th and 20th Century," in *Comparative Studies in Continental and Anglo-American Legal History, Vol. 31: From the Judge's* Arbitrium *to the Legality Principle, Legislation as a Source of Law in Criminal Trials*, ed. Georges Martyn, Anthony Musson, and Heikki Pihlajamäki (Berlin: Duncker and Humblot, 2013), 387–406.

[3] Take, for example, the consequentialist (as opposed to retributive) goals that dominated much discussion of the aims of the law during the American Progressive Era, where the story told in this book begins. One did not need to reject free will – or even to give much thought to it – to reject retributivism and to support consequentialism: one might simply conclude that retributivism, particularly when conceived of as sheer revenge, should be rejected as barbaric, wasteful, or simply counterproductive; and the alternative Progressive methods for crime prevention and the reform of criminals could be deemed enlightened, humane, and socially useful. Yet much of the selected criminal jurisprudence I will introduce from this period can be read as insisting upon an emphasis on the hereditary, social, and psychological causes of crime, and on rejecting the notion that crime is the product of a truly "free" will. Given the overlapping goals, concerns, and, indeed, silences of Progressive Era legal scholarship, it must remain an open question just how important the rejection of free will was *generally* to Progressive (and post-Progressive) legal scholars and, even for those who addressed the free will issue, whether it was foundational to their criminal jurisprudence, or largely incidental.

words, I seek to tell only a small part of the story of American criminal jurisprudence, which I hope will shed light on or contribute to other stories told from other points of focus, while also being an interesting and illuminating tale in itself.

THE FREE WILL PROBLEM IN TWENTIETH-CENTURY AMERICAN CRIMINAL LAW

Twentieth-century America provides fertile ground for exploration of scholarship on the free will problem for many reasons, an initial one being the broad currents of deterministic thought that, although hardly new, confronted American legal scholars with special force by the end of the nineteenth century.[4] Much criminal law theory of the Progressive Era reflected the influence of scientific-determinism, which was part of a fairly general scientific-positivist movement in the West, and which occasioned direct confrontation with what I will refer to as the "determinist critique" of free will. The Progressive iteration of determinism, in its most extreme form, accepted a universal determinism positing that all human choices and actions ultimately could be explained by a person's heredity, environment, or both. Less extreme (or "selectively deterministic") views suggested that, at a minimum, serious criminal acts were caused by undesirable background forces that impeded a freedom of will or ability to abide by the law that law-abiders – "normal" people – generally possessed. Thus, many scholars across various disciplines questioned the retributive aspects of the criminal law as unjust – and, potentially, as inefficient – because they implied the assignment of blame to actors who did not genuinely control, or freely will, their actions. This scientific-determinist mind-set would continue to influence legal scholarship throughout the century, augmented by the deterministic implications of advancing work in psychiatry and the developing behavioral and social sciences generally (and, even later, by neuroscience and gene sequencing) as well as by trends in academic philosophy. Much science and philosophy throughout the century seemed to agree that human thought and action merely occupied a place in the natural chain of universal causation. In accord, legal scholars commonly eschewed the separation, famously proposed by Kant in justifying criminal condemnation and punishment, between the "phenomenal" and the "noumenal" worlds, according to which the former – the natural world – is governed by physical laws of cause and

[4] See Susanna L. Blumenthal, *Law and the Modern Mind: Consciousness and Responsibility in American Legal Culture* (Cambridge, MA: Harvard University Press, forthcoming 2015) for a pioneering account of legal (mainly judicial) thought across the long nineteenth century. Blumenthal details the nature, and locates the influence, of deterministic ideas (both religious and secular) and examines the responses to them in relation to many areas of law, primarily – but not entirely – private law.

effect and the latter – the world of mind (or reasoning) – is not, but instead imports its own (first) cause.[5] Thus, at least for those legal scholars inclined to confront deeper questions bearing on criminal condemnation – that is, the group that I selectively draw upon in these studies – any discussion of criminal responsibility or penal theory inescapably required attention to the determinist critique.

But countervailing forces – theoretical, political, and cultural – were also at play, and legal scholars concerned about the determinist critique were uniquely positioned at the ever-negotiated intersection of determinist theory and the concrete application of the rule of law. As the century proceeded, the practicality of some hoped-for Progressive reforms (many of which were rooted in a deterministic mind-set) would be questioned. Concerns about excessive state power would receive heightened attention in the wake of both World Wars. And America's particular struggles with internal class and race divisions deepened the urgency of our insistence on individual rights – along with individual and state accountability. Indeed, particularly at issue for the twentieth-century American scholars I discuss was a second aspect of human freedom: political liberty. These two aspects of, or ideas about, freedom – free will and political liberty – interlace throughout our story in ways that might be viewed *either* as complementary or as in tension with each other, both theoretically and practically. On one hand, as is particularly important to the story told in these pages, political liberty might be understood to require adherence to a notion of free will underlying individuals' rights to self-determination and to freedom of action without state intervention or coercion. So understood, political liberty might restrict to exceptional circumstances progressive intervention into individuals' lives via scientifically informed therapeutics or other "benign" treatment for apparent criminal tendencies. On the other hand, political liberty might be conceived of as requiring the state to recognize the absence of free will by refraining from condemning and punishing, via the criminal law, those who could not have avoided criminality because their acts were determined by forces outside their control (including, some would say, by the environmental forces that arise directly from our social and political arrangements). This latter notion of liberty from unwarranted state condemnation might

---

[5] This is, of course, a very rough encapsulation. See Immanuel Kant, "Critique of Practical Reason," in *The Cambridge Edition of the Works of Immanuel Kant: Practical Philosophy*, ed. Mary Gregor (Cambridge: Cambridge University Press, 1996), 133–271 ("Critique of Practical Reason" originally published 1788). There are hints of this Kantian conceptualization of the free will problem, especially after 1960 when Kant's more familiar appeal to the right of every human to be conceived of as an autonomous being received fairly widespread acceptance. But only hints. In the main, the reception and forwarding of that "Kantian" appeal to a right was couched in relation to arguments for a merely hypothesized form of free will that did not require (or, in some cases, even allow for) a separate such "noumenal" sphere.

support on a wide basis the use of the very therapeutics or treatment (in lieu of punishment) that the former notion of political liberty would frequently call into question.[6]

Relatedly, where the legitimacy and efficacy of the law was at stake among the "free" people of a democratic nation, common views – or what I will generally refer to as "conventional morality" – could not be read out of the equation, no matter that determinist theories suggested that such views rested on wrongheaded and antiquated notions of human behavior. Legal scholars commonly – and likely correctly – assumed that conventional morality was rooted in a belief (or, perhaps, unself-conscious presumption) that human beings possess free will in the robust sense of a genuinely self-initiating power to think and act that justifies the attribution of moral and legal blame; that is, scholars assumed that conventional morality was premised on "true" free will, although it also incorporated selective deterministic thinking with regard to some people under some circumstances.[7] Hence the additional challenge: despite the commonness of deterministic (or quasi-

[6] The phrase "political liberty" generally relates to freedoms that individuals or groups possess with respect to participation in the creation of, or ongoing shaping of, government – its institutions, procedures, policies, etc. The rights to vote, to hold public office, or to serve on juries are three of many obvious examples. I am using the phrase broadly, however, to include also freedom from governmental coercion of a variety of sorts. Strictly speaking, this is a personal liberty interest (and sometimes referred to as such herein), although one relative to the state. Indeed, this latter aspect of political liberty (as I use that phrase) is the dominant one in this book. The "freedom-to" and "freedom-from" sides of political liberty are sometimes closely related. To illustrate, an individual's right to jury service, the jury's right to determine criminal guilt (whether by mere fact-finding or through a claimed right to find law), and the criminal defendant's right to trial by jury each also implicate the defendant's rights to be free from state condemnation and incapacitation that is considered unwarranted by a jury of peers.

[7] To be clear, my aim here is not to define the actual historical contours of conventional morality. Rather, I refer to "conventional morality" as imagined by scholars and as reflected in their thinking about the rule of law in the criminal context – including their thoughts about the extent to which the law could survive openly expressed doubts about the free will that they associated with conventional morality, and thus how their worries that law could *not* survive such doubts shaped theorizing about criminal responsibility. Thus, my focus is essentially on a critical perspective toward "conventional morality" that echoes H. L. A. Hart's distinction between conventional and critical views. See Hart, *The Concept of Law* (Oxford: Clarendon Press, 1961), 181: "it cannot seriously be disputed that the development of law, at all times and places, has in fact been profoundly influenced both by conventional morality and ideas of particular social groups, and also by forms of enlightened moral criticism, urged by individuals whose moral horizon has transcended the morality currently accepted." Most of the scholars I discuss indeed considered their own skeptical positions on free will more "enlightened" than that embedded in conventional morality. All this said, however, I myself do not mean to privilege the scholarly view in my work, but to take note of it as a historical fact. Moreover, I tend to think that this particular assumed aspect of conventional morality – this presumption of free will alongside a recognition of causal forces – is something of a universal; that is, I suspect that even those scholars who most adamantly rejected the conventional understanding of human behavior, and who wrote and taught in line with that rejection, nonetheless often unself-consciously hewed to the conventional view in their everyday lives.

deterministic) thinking across academic disciplines throughout the twentieth century, a legitimate, democratic rule of law could not unequivocally adopt the premises of determinism/universal causation – at least, it could not do so in an immediate and transparent fashion.

These historical tensions allow the free will problem, as it mainly presented itself in twentieth-century criminal law, to be fairly easily stated, at least in the abstract (and without the complexities that most scientists and philosophers have introduced). As truth-seekers, legal scholars seemed doomed to conclude that, at best, we do not know – perhaps can never know – whether a criminal responsibility–bearing version of free will truly exists. As prescriptivists, these same scholars seemed doomed to one of two fates. First, they could hypothesize the existence of free will in an attempt to maintain a somewhat traditional notion of responsibility. But, if they took this route, could they comfortably announce openly that the criminal law was based on mere hypothesis? Alternatively, they could define some form of criminal responsibility that did not rest upon even a hypothesized free will. But this path left them with the seemingly intractable question of how to prescribe a non–free-will-based form of responsibility for a political and social culture in which any such form was likely to be thought, at best, wrongheaded or unjust and, at worst, immoral or in derogation of basic human values. Indeed, those who eschewed proceeding by hypothesis – and who preferred instead to redefine criminal responsibility in keeping with their belief in determinism – still had to decide whether nonetheless to accommodate a widespread social belief in free will, at least pro tem. Much was at stake in proceeding either by hypothesis or accommodation: the possible sacrifice of unfree "criminal offenders" to practical needs or to prevailing beliefs (or, perhaps, to an enduring psychology, a consciousness of freedom). As truth-seekers, scholars might thus be inclined to search all the harder for a meaning of free will that shored up the hypothesis but, equally, as truth-seekers, they might be inclined to investigate their motives for doing so and to wonder whether their doing so was itself overdetermined.

Yet this is to state the problem in the abstract from the position of a legal historian. It is more difficult to discern precisely how twentieth-century American criminal law scholars actually understood the free will problem as they grappled with it. For those who acknowledged the core of the problem – the tension between the (at least supposed) unprovability of true free will and the pervasiveness of belief in it and in its relevance to criminal responsibility – few, it seems, considered it insurmountable. Their attempts to surmount the tension varied significantly and evolved over the course of the century alongside the evolution both of more general philosophical and scientific approaches to the free will question and of the politics, here and abroad, surrounding ideas of individual liberty and the role of the state in circumscribing that liberty. Some emphasized the age-old and much-cherished sense of personal freedom that, often alongside the law's commitment to political liberty and power to deter wrongdoing, they deemed sufficient to define a responsibility-bearing free will regardless of whatever scientific or philosophical doubts we might entertain about the ultimate springs of individual action. Others more generally emphasized the positive results of a legal system that assumes free will, regardless that we may question the existence of such a will on some deeper theoretical level. Still others concluded that the issue was not free will as such – or they endeavored to redefine the very concept of "free will" – based on their convictions that we should assume all acts and thoughts are determined but that this deterministic reality did not negate responsibility-bearingness, which consists of having had the (determined) capacity and opportunity to reason through the (determined) act before undertaking it. Thus might an individual be blameworthy, despite a lack of "free will" as that term was conventionally interpreted, by becoming a participant in the chain of causation that resulted in an act prohibited by law.

This last perspective amounts to saying that free will – in the sense of a responsibility-bearing will – is compatible even with a belief in complete determinism. Such philosophical compatibilism, variously defined, has a long history in Anglo-American criminal law theory that traces back to Hobbes[8] and especially to Hume.[9] And there are certainly hints of it in Progressive and midcentury American legal scholarship. But it was not until the last few decades of the twentieth century that compatibilism reemerged as a dominant response to the determinist critique, first in academic philosophy, then in criminal jurisprudence. By the end of the century, as is well-known, much legal scholarship had moved away from the strong responsibility-denying influence of the Progressive Era and toward acceptance (both formal and less formal) of philosophical compatibilism. And, for many theorists, compatibilism thus promised to put the free will/determinism debate to rest for the criminal law: if criminal responsibility survived determinism, the abstract notion of "free will" was, effectively, a nonissue.

NEGOTIATING DETERMINISM AND CONVENTIONAL
MORALITY: THE JURY, THE INSANITY DEFENSE, AND THE
BIFURCATION OF CRIMINAL PROCESS

Of course, resolving the free will problem was not really so simple for American legal scholars, whatever promise compatibilism may have held

---

[8] See Thomas Hobbes, *Leviathan*, introd. by A. D. Lindsay (New York: Dutton, 1950), esp. chap. 21, "Of the Liberty of Subjects" (originally published 1651).

[9] See David Hume, "Of Liberty and Necessity," in *A Treatise of Human Nature*, ed. David Fate Norton and Mary J. Norton (New York: Oxford University Press, 2000), bk. 2, pt. 3, sec. 1–2 (originally published 1739); and David Hume, "Of Liberty and Necessity," in *An Enquiry Concerning Human Understanding*, ed. Tom L. Beauchamp, (New York: Oxford University Press, 1999), sec. 8 (originally published 1748).

for scholars more purely inclined toward truth-seeking. Legal scholars concerned with the free will problem were faced not with a task of pure philosophy, but with resolution of the problem in the political and social context of our particular democratic legal system, in which not just political liberty, but also the conventional morality of the public, was a critical factor for both the law's enactment and its legitimacy. Thus, in their roles as prescriptivists, legal scholars became adept at compromise, using legal processes and institutions to mediate between the oft-conflicting premises of the determinist critique and of conventional morality. Accordingly, throughout this book, the reader will recognize repeated attention to several elements of the legal system that often occupied – or bridged – the space between the law's divergent philosophical and conventional premises. These elements include the role of the criminal trial jury, the definition and application of the insanity defense, and the bifurcation of the criminal process between the guilt assessment and sentencing stages, the latter stage merging with penological theory. Importantly, my intent is not to exhaustively examine these institutional elements. I treat these as themes, not subjects of study in their own right. But a brief introduction will illustrate their recurring connections to the scholarship on criminal responsibility that forms my subject.

The criminal trial jury, in particular, exemplifies the relationship between theories of criminal responsibility and conventional ideas about freedom. The jury is a direct representative of conventional morality during the trial process. The constitutional right to a jury trial is also, of course, a central guarantor of political-liberty rights within the criminal process; the jury trial implicates the jurors' liberty interest in relative independence when finding facts and applying the law of the state, as well as the defendant's liberty interest in being judged by his or her community. Ideas about the proper role of the jury were thus often coextensive with ideas about how conceptions of free will and political liberty were best expressed – or cabined – during the guilt attribution process.[10] And this remained true – that is, jury-based

---

[10] The relationship between the Anglo-American jury and ideas of human freedom is by no means a modern phenomenon. From its inception in the early thirteenth century, the jury exercised a significant degree of discretion; as arbiter de facto of both fact and law, it could acquit for many reasons, including because it believed the defendant was factually innocent of the crime charged, but also because it believed that the likely sanction for a crime was too harsh or because it rejected the wisdom of a particular law, at least as applied to the case at hand. These latter nullifying or "law finding" verdicts, which rejected some aspect of the formal law, were centrally exercises in political liberty. They also generally affirmed a rough notion of free will: a defendant was thought to have freely violated a law that the jury nonetheless believed was unjust or called for an overly harsh sanction. But juries also engaged in nullification that reflected deterministic thinking, albeit more rarely and less obviously; at least by the eighteenth century, there is evidence (particularly on the English side) that some verdicts reflected juries' perceptions of constraints on an actor's freedom arising from his or her external circumstances or internal state.

resolution of criminal responsibility remained a primary paradigm of legal theory regarding the responsibility issue – even though criminal charges, throughout the twentieth century, were increasingly resolved by plea bargains or bench trials.

Explicit commentary on the jury's notions of human freedom is often scarce. But, where such commentary exists, its nature – and, particularly, the inferences one might tentatively draw from it – adds to our understanding of scholars' views on the place of free will in the criminal law.[11] As we shall see, for example, in the early decades of the twentieth century, some scholarship oriented toward scientific-positivist reform criticized the jury as irrational and primitive in relation to the needs of an enlightened system of primarily consequentialist criminal justice: the jury, I infer, was deemed to render judgments on the basis of a belief in free will and therefore to reinforce the archaic, retributive premises that many scholars, within and outside the legal academy, thought no longer should occupy a central position in a legal system sensitive to scientific understandings of human behavior. Some other scholarship acknowledged jurors' selective deterministic thinking, which seemed evident when juries bestowed mercy (commonly in the form of acquittals or lesser verdicts) in apparent reaction to the social or psychological circumstances of the defendant – that is, in apparent reaction to matters of internal or external causation, as commonly understood, that suggested constraints on the defendant's free will. I infer from the limited commentary that such selective deterministic thinking by juries drew conflicting responses from determinists. They might embrace such thinking as

A fuller exploration of the Anglo-American jury's historical relationship, over the period 1200 to 2000, to ideas about free will and political liberty is a central focus of my ongoing work on the jury. The English jury was the subject of my prior book, *Verdict According to Conscience: Perspectives on the English Criminal Trial Jury, 1200–1800* (Chicago: University of Chicago Press, 1985). My ongoing study of the Anglo-American jury and its relationship to ideas about freedom is, in effect, aimed at bringing this prior work on the English jury forward in time and over to the American side, while bringing my instant work on twentieth-century American ideas concerning criminal responsibility back in time and over to the English side. I anticipate the themes of this study – which I hope will result in future scholarship by myself and others – in Thomas A. Green, "The Jury and Criminal Responsibility in Anglo-American History," *Criminal Law and Philosophy*, vol. 8 (2014): __-__ (also available at http://dx.doi.org/10.1007/s11572-013-9267-0). I have already touched on the scholarly view of the American jury – including the jury's role as a repository for ideas about free will – during the period 1900–1960 in Thomas A. Green, "Conventional Morality and the Rule of Law: Freedom, Responsibility, and the Criminal Trial Jury in American Legal Thought, 1900–60," chap. 15 in *Transformations in American Legal History: Law, Ideology, and Methods – Essays in Honor of Morton J. Horwitz, Volume II*, ed. Daniel W. Hamilton and Alfred L. Brophy (Cambridge, MA: Harvard University Press, 2010). I draw many of my instant informal observations on the jury from my past and ongoing research in this area.

[11] I am currently (as part of my larger project on the jury and ideas regarding criminal responsibility) assessing how far contemporary writings bear out the inferences mentioned here. I do not dwell upon them in this book.

a step on the road to a more enlightened law. Or, conversely, they might conclude that such ad hoc and unsystematic application of determinist notions made matters worse: I suspect that juries' selective determinism was thought, by some commentators, to operate as a kind of release mechanism that gave convictions based on a general belief in free will a greater degree of legitimacy, thereby overall reinforcing retribution; further, the resulting (and, some might say, sympathy-based) acquittals might exempt from the legal system those very "offenders" who many Progressive scholars thought most in need of incapacitation or treatment at the hands of the state. Indeed, some early-in-century academics, particularly those in the burgeoning field of psychiatry, therefore preferred an eventual narrowing – in some cases, even elimination – of the jury's role. Others, including some legal academics, hoped the jury could, over time, be "educated" and therefore led to reach verdicts more consistent with elite views of human behavior. But, on the whole, members of the legal field recognized that, even if the jury was inevitably linked with a popular (and wrongheaded) ethic of free will, the constitutional right to trial by jury entrenched, at least for the present, the jury's role in assessing guilt during trial.

The American jury's institutional position was further solidified by an influential early-twentieth-century decision of the Supreme Court of the State of Washington, *State v. Strasburg* (1910),[12] which interpreted the constitutional right to a jury trial to include a jury decision on the ultimate question of whether a defendant was legally insane. The court thus had entrusted to the jury a question that, for many legal scholars, epitomized the free will issue because it defined what was taken to be the most critical boundary between responsible and non-responsible behavior. The proper formulation of the test for insanity, and what scientific evidence was relevant to that inquiry at trial, raised the free will problem perhaps more than any other area of legal doctrine relevant to guilt assessment. How the *absence* of responsibility because of insanity was defined unavoidably implicated the personal qualities indicating the *presence* of responsibility; complete theories of the former required confronting the latter, and circumscribing those qualities that indicated responsibility directly begged the free will question. If one presumed universal causation, was legal insanity meaningfully distinguishable from the infinite number of other conditions that rendered the possession of a truly free will an impossibility? If such distinction is possible, and internal biological or psychological factors – or, indeed, external factors causing extreme psychic disruption – could be said to negate responsibility for an act because of "insanity," how does one draw the line between this lack of responsibility and the presence of responsibility despite other, arguably equally compelling internal and external forces, such as an extremely impoverished upbringing or an environment rife with crime? Do the former

---

[12] *State v. Strasburg*, 110 P. 1020 (Wash. 1910).

factors truly negate personal responsibility more than the latter forces – and, if so, does (or should) the distinction have anything to do with our estimations of the actors' relative abilities to exercise free will?

These questions rendered the definition of insanity a focal point throughout the century for many legal scholars concerned with the free will question. And the jury's constitutional role in making a final decision on insanity, albeit a separate (if related) matter, only complicated the issue; in addition to defining the presence and bounds of insanity, scholars often found themselves tasked with deciding what weight should be given to the testimony of experts in the behavioral and psychological fields. Such experts might be expected to import the latest scientific understandings of human behavior into the trial process, but with uncertain results: at best, they could influence the jury to adopt a scientifically informed view of the defendant's behavior; at worst, they could inappropriately usurp the jury's role or (perhaps of more concern to the experts) they could offend their own senses of truth by participating in a process that ultimately assumed at least *some* actors in fact freely willed their lawbreaking behavior.

Thus the jury's role and the definition of insanity often received attention from those scholars who sought to confront the determinist critique of free will while acknowledging the needs of a legitimate rule of law in a state committed to political liberty and the jury process. And when a scholarly commitment to determinism conflicted with those needs, scholars often took refuge in the bifurcation of criminal process between jury-based guilt assessment and the post-trial sentencing and penal phases.[13] Indeed, this bifurcation of process – which created distance between the publicly oriented trial stage and post-trial stages that were more hidden from public view – would be an important conditioning feature of twentieth-century academic criminal jurisprudence. (More generally, bifurcation is a central feature of the approach we take to the criminal law, one of those developments that tells us a great deal about who we are, or what we seek to be; the tendencies of mind it reflects are general to our jurisprudence, not special to the criminal law.) It was at the trial stage that the conventional morality of the jury had to be accommodated and when insanity – an imperfect label applied through an imperfect process – was adjudicated. Sentencing, on the other hand, was generally carried out by judges, who might be expected to exercise their legislatively bound discretion from the perspective of educated professionals, who were presumably more versed in the science and legal theory of the day than were ordinary jurors. Similarly, penology (ideally) could be carried out by penal officials according to policies that incorporated the latest in the sciences both of human behavior and of criminal justice administration. Thus,

---

[13] I refer to the phenomenon of bifurcation at the close of my study of the English criminal trial jury (Green, *Verdict According to Conscience*, 383). Others have noted the same or an analogous phenomenon.

sentencing and the penological theory that informed it could more directly engage the free will problem on scientific-determinist grounds in confronting questions concerning the aims and effects of punishment, and, of course, whether punishment per se – as opposed to treatment – was even a legitimate goal of the criminal law. Accordingly, for the early-American determinist scholar, these latter stages of the criminal process might compensate for the infirmities of a trial stage inevitably rooted in inaccurate notions of human behavior, thereby permitting the overall process to achieve some degree of theoretical soundness and, of course, to achieve justice and efficiency based on modern understandings of behavior. For these reasons, although I do not canvass legal-academic work centered specifically on sentencing and penology here, such work overlaps my primary subject and it will be touched on when it is particularly relevant.

Each of these aspects of the criminal law – the jury's role, the problems surrounding the defense of legal insanity, and the bifurcated criminal process – exemplified the confrontation between the largely deterministic bent of academic thought concerning the free will problem and the real-world application of a rule of law that, some would conclude, would always be inseparable from the conventional moral commitment to free will. And the relationship of each aspect to legal-academic free will scholarship evolved as the scholarship itself evolved. The jury's fortunes waned and waxed over the course of the twentieth century as the determinist critique matured and reformulated itself in light of changing understandings of the two ideas of freedom. Where some early-twentieth-century critics had been primarily concerned that the jury's institutional exercise of political liberty might reinforce unscientific notions of free will, for example, midcentury and later commentators more often acknowledged the jury's role in upholding a social idea of freedom that constituted both an important political liberty interest and a human dignity interest. Similarly, over the course of the century growing cultural, juristic, and theoretical commitments to just deserts brought sentencing and penology more in line with a retributivism that might be associated either with conventional morality or with the compatibilist, less–vengeance-based "neo-retributivism" favored by many legal scholars. Legal scholars' preferred formulations of the insanity defense, too, would often evolve in tandem with scholars' views not only of the true nature of free will, but of the necessities of political liberty and the value of both ideas of freedom to American society. Thus did these aspects of the legal system become points of negotiation between determinism and our societal commitments to free will and political liberty. Perhaps more often than not, academic theory employed them as vehicles for compromise, whether because individual institutions could separately embody distinct aims, resulting in an overall legal system that encompassed both scholarly and conventional views, or because any one institution might, from different points of view, be seen as furthering multiple aims at once.

THE FREE WILL PROBLEM AND THE SCOPE OF THIS BOOK

Twentieth-century American legal academics took many paths in attempting to define human responsibility in the face of the determinist critique; they sought to craft a workable rule of law from their commitments not just to theoretical soundness in light of doubts about free will, but to political liberty, to human dignity, and to respect for the law from the perspective of conventional morality. These paths form the subject matter of the essays that follow, in which I investigate legal academics' "small world."

It is important to repeat that I therefore offer only one small part of the story of twentieth-century American jurisprudence – and one that is significantly more descriptive than analytic. I present selected scholarly thought of the period, as best I can, on its own terms. The points of influence among this thought, politics, conventional views, and pragmatic concerns are complex, interwoven, and largely beyond the scope of this book. A good example of my limited scope of concern involves the renaissance of retributivist academic thought in the last decades of the century. This was a body of legal scholarship that I call "neo-retributivist" because it reinforced notions of responsibility and just deserts premised on the dignity and autonomy of the offender, rather than on true free will or revenge per se; it was most often roughly compatibilist in underlying approach, and thus was at least theoretically rooted in determinism. Because this scholarship nonetheless arguably reinforced real-world retributive and punitive practices, one might argue that, by the century's end, conventional morality – and its (presumed) retributive nature and implicit dedication to free will – had, in all-important *effect*, triumphed over determinist legal theory. Equally, one could posit that such theory, instead, had coopted conventional morality to its own free will–denying ends; it endeavored to harness that morality – often even to drain it of traditional vengeance – to support an essentially deterministic view of human action that scholars hoped would be ultimately borne out (albeit perhaps opaquely) in legal policy. But my aim is not to draw such definitive conclusions about these points of influence; indeed, undoubtedly there is truth in many different perspectives. Rather, my purpose lies more narrowly within the history of ideas; my primary subjects are the scholarly approaches themselves, some of which reflected on theory within larger social and political contexts, but many of which did not. Thus my main themes – the relationships between determinism and human responsibility, between free will and political liberty, and between conventional morality and the rule of law – are just that: themes, not coordinated as an overall argument, but presented as theorists encountered, recognized, and developed them or as the historian interprets theorists' ideas even where the theorists were not consciously focused on these themes. As I have indicated, I believe that much of the history of human relationships and society – not simply the history of ideas regarding criminal responsibility – can be seen from the perspective of my main themes here. Let the application of that claim to criminal responsibility theory in twentieth-century America stand as my argument, if one is needed, and let the several essays – or lengthy studies – be exercises in reading one's way into one important aspect of American legal thought.

Now a final caveat. Because I self-consciously present twentieth-century legal academic ideas concerning the free will problem simply as an aspect of the history of our criminal law, there is no intended message about the free will "problem," so far as I am concerned. I take no side with regard either to resolutions of the problem or, indeed, to whether meaningful resolution is possible. Although such a stance could seem to result in the "message" that in fact there *can* be no real message about this problem – about the meaning or truth of human freedom – the truth is that I simply do not know, and am unsure whether anyone can ever know with certainty, whether there can be any such message. That is as much as I say, for myself. If that is not enough – if the possibility of meaning must be more fully explored or more strongly affirmed – this book may not be for you.

PART I

FREEDOM AND CRIMINAL
RESPONSIBILITY IN THE AGE OF POUND

INTRODUCTION

The Progressive Era, when the story told in this book begins, evidenced the coalescence of an American academy of criminal justice scholars even before law schools paid much attention to the subject. A few scholars of criminal law – alongside many scholars and professionals from a variety of closely related fields, as well as penal officials and some judges – saw themselves as part of a transnational movement for an enlightened approach to the problem of crime in modern society. They revered science and the scientific method as applied to human behavior and to the design of social institutions including, of course, those regarding the prediction and prevention of antisocial behavior. They were, thus, a part of the forward-looking or consequentialist approach to criminal jurisprudence that had risen over the preceding century or more to challenge the more traditional backward-looking, retributivist (just deserts–based) account of the criminal law. Academics and practitioners in a variety of fields now joined to endorse the twin goals of deterrence and reform of individual offenders and to criticize the "primitive" retributivist ideas – premised on the concept of free will – that they claimed still underlay the doctrines and practices of American criminal law. They shared a largely deterministic, scientific-positivist view[1] that, at least as of the first meeting of the American Institute of

---

[1] American scientists began to develop deterministic theories of crime by the first half of the nineteenth century. The development of American psychiatry and the scientific exploration of responsibility, including the idea of moral insanity, is discussed in Susanna L. Blumenthal, "The Mind of a Moral Agent: Scottish Common Sense and the Problem of Responsibility in Nineteenth-Century American Law," *Law and History Review*, vol. 26 (2008): 99–160, and Charles E. Rosenberg, *The Trial of the Assassin Guiteau: Psychiatry and Law in the Gilded Age* (Chicago: University of Chicago Press, 1968), 61–74, 100–06, 243–58. See also Janet Ann Tighe, "A Question of Responsibility: The Development of American Forensic

Criminal Law and Criminology (AICLC) in 1909, seemed to them destined to usher in an age of progress.

Turn-of-the-century America provided fertile ground for Progressive reform, particularly in the area of criminal justice. As the country became more urban and grew increasingly nationally and internationally oriented, it faced a range of new concerns about crime and national security. Particularly in the years following the Great War, criminal activity seemed to skyrocket along with general concerns about political dissent. The immediate postwar year, 1919, was especially tumultuous, witnessing the pinnacle of the Red Scare, major race riots in several large cities, and the Boston Police Strike; the fears engendered by these events were intensified by the perceived rise in violence associated with Prohibition. In this atmosphere, alongside the federal government's growing regulation of various aspects of national life, federal influence was expanding through significant legislative incursions into crime control – including nationally orchestrated vice crusades against, among other things, prostitution, illegal drugs, and sedition – as well as through enforcement efforts including the creation of the Bureau

Psychiatry, 1838–1930" (Ph.D. dissertation, University of Pennsylvania, 1983, available at http://repository.upenn.edu/dissertations/AAI8406727), 25–68; Norman Dain, *Concepts of Insanity in the United States, 1789–1865* (New Brunswick, NJ: Rutgers University Press, 1964). British criminology exercised an enduring influence on American thought, and British developments are discussed in Martin J. Wiener, *Reconstructing the Criminal: Culture, Law, and Policy in England, 1830–1914* (New York: Cambridge University Press, 1990). Late Victorian British criminology and penology are the focus of David Garland, *Punishment and Welfare: A History of Penal Strategies* (Aldershot, Hants: Gower, 1985). Broadly speaking, the continental European influence centered on the Italian school's focus on heredity, stemming from the work of Cesare Lombroso, Enrico Ferri, and Raffaele Garofalo, and the role of environment, generally associated with the French school of Gabriel Tarde, Alexandre Lacassagne, and others. For a description of the development of each school and the relationship and tensions between them in Europe, see Ruth Harris, *Murders and Madness: Medicine, Law, and Society in the Fin de Siècle* (New York: Oxford University Press, 1989), 80–98; Robert A. Nye, *Crime, Madness, and Politics in Modern France: The Medical Concept of National Decline* (Princeton, NJ: Princeton University Press, 1984), 97–131; Gordon Wright, *Between the Guillotine and Liberty: Two Centuries of the Crime Problem in France* (New York: Oxford University Press, 1983), 119–28. For their influence in America, see Francis A. Allen, *The Decline of the Rehabilitative Ideal: Penal Policy and Social Purpose* (New Haven: Yale University Press, 1981), 40–44; Arthur E. Fink, *Causes of Crime: Biological Theories in the United States, 1800–1915* (Philadelphia: University of Pennsylvania Press, 1938), 99–150. Determinism was also sometimes applied to the study of race and other issues not directly related to crime. See, e.g., Stephen Jay Gould, *The Mismeasure of Man* (New York: W. W. Norton, 1981), 30–69. For a valuable recent analysis of a key difference between American and continental application of deterministic theory regarding penology, see Michele Pifferi, "Indetermined Sentence and the *Nulla Poena Sine Lege* Principle: Contrasting Views on Punishment in the U.S. and Europe between the 19th and the 20th Century," in *Comparative Studies in Continental and Anglo-American Legal History, Vol. 31: From the Judge's Arbitrium to the Legality Principle, Legislation as a Source of Law in Criminal Trials,* ed. Georges Martyn, Anthony Musson, and Heikki Pihlajamäki (Berlin: Duncker and Humblot, 2013).

of Investigation (later renamed the Federal Bureau of Investigation). As a general rule, governance on both the local and national levels was growing more centralized, bureaucratic, and administrative in nature. As part of this phenomenon, the nation's previously highly democratic, community-based *adjudicative* justice systems were becoming more centralized, bureaucratic, and *administrative* in nature; in one historian's words, our justice systems were increasingly entrusted to an "expanding professional-managerial class" that exercised a remarkable degree of discretion with regard to who should be arrested and prosecuted, for which crimes, and with what results with regard to treatment or length of imprisonment.[2]

Consistent with these trends, the 1920s marked the significant arrival of the modern crime commission, through which interdisciplinary conglomerations of Progressives brought their systematic approach to bear on gathering and studying real-world data that addressed the causes of crime and the administration of city and state justice systems. The first resulting major crime survey – the 1922 Cleveland Survey of Criminal Justice – included studies of police administration, prosecution, the criminal courts,

---

[2] On the rise of the administrative state and its effects throughout the criminal justice system, see, generally, Samuel Walker, *Popular Justice: A History of American Criminal Justice*, 2nd ed. (New York: Oxford University Press, 1998) (quoted material from 113 to 114); William J. Stuntz, *The Collapse of American Criminal Justice* (Cambridge, MA: Belknap Press, 2011) (the expanding discretionary power of administrative officials is a central theme for Stuntz, who associates overuse of official discretion with a collapse of the "rule of law" by the end of the twentieth century, see, e.g., 2–7). See also Elizabeth Dale, *Criminal Justice in the United States, 1789–1939* (New York: Cambridge University Press, 2011); Markus Dirk Dubber, *The Police Power: Patriarchy and the Foundations of American Government* (New York: Columbia University Press, 2005). On federal actions and legislation generally, see, e.g., Stuntz, *Collapse*, 132, 158–86; Lawrence M. Friedman, *Crime and Punishment in American History* (New York: Basic Books, 1993), esp. chap. 12, "A National System," and pp. 324– 69. On 1919 generally and the Red Scare, see Walker, *Popular Justice*, 148–52; Robert K. Murray, *Red Scare: A Study in National Hysteria, 1919–1920* (Minneapolis: University of Minnesota Press, 1955).
　Note that at times I refer, in the singular, to America's "justice system" – but most often only as a matter of convenience. America's criminal justice systems remained (somewhat uniquely among Western nations) predominantly local institutions despite a significant degree of homogenization and centralized federal influence. Dale discusses this point in *Criminal Justice in the United States* (see esp. 6–7, 143–45). Compare Friedman, *Crime and Punishment*, 461–63; Stuntz, *Collapse*, chap. 5, "Criminal Justice in the Gilded Age" (examining the historical geographic differences among local justice systems in the United States). Michael Willrich illustrates the turn toward a centralized, bureaucratic system on the local level in his book on Progressive Era Chicago and the creation of its municipal court system, *City of Courts: Socializing Justice in Progressive Era Chicago* (Cambridge: Cambridge University Press, 2003), esp. chap. 2, "A Managerial Revolution." Lawrence M. Friedman and Robert V. Percival also famously describe the shift from "*adjudicative*" justice to an "*administrative*" system inherently characterized by the discretionary (and often informal and unrecorded) decisions of "full-time crime handlers (prosecutors and police)," in *The Roots of Justice: Crime and Punishment in Alameda County, California, 1870–1910* (Chapel Hill: University of North Carolina Press, 1981) (quoted material from 193).

correctional and penal treatment, and the relationship of medical science to criminal justice. It would become a model for later surveys and reforms, which generally became aimed at increasing administrative efficiency and professionalism throughout the country's justice systems.[3] Nationalized Progressive efforts would not truly culminate until the 1930s, in the aftermath of the Great Depression.[4] But the early Progressive faith in a rational, informed bureaucracy laid the groundwork for this hopeful new era of professional administration dedicated to analyzing, controlling – and, ideally, ultimately rooting out at the source – antisocial tendencies.

This context marked the founding era of the modern American criminal justice system, which stretched from roughly the 1870s to the 1920s, with the Progressive Era (essentially the latter half of that period) constituting the chief moment of experimentation, advances, and overall consolidation. Progressive criminal jurisprudence fits well with the existing commentary on the rise of the administrative state in the late-nineteenth and early-twentieth centuries. The reformist writing of the early-to-mid teens ranged over every stage of criminal justice administration: investigatorial technique, prosecutorial bureaucracy, trial procedure – including, inter alia, the rules of evidence, the role of the judge, and the scope of the jury's authority[5] – and, most important, penology and the treatment of the insane, of the feebleminded,[6]

[3] See Roscoe Pound and Felix Frankfurter, eds., *Criminal Justice in Cleveland: Reports of the Cleveland Foundation Survey of the Administration of Criminal Justice in Cleveland, Ohio* (Philadelphia: W. F. Fell, 1922). For a brief background to the Survey, see Frankfurter's "Preface," v–ix. The Cleveland Survey's ambitious (but less impactful than many had hoped) federal counterpart was the Wickersham Commission, which issued its reports in 1931. On these and other crime commissions see, e.g., Walker, *Popular Justice*, 152–57; Friedman, *Crime and Punishment*, 273–74, 360–62.

[4] With regard to crime policy, the 1930s would see, for example, the greatest strides toward professionalization of police training and equipment as well as toward more national coordination in law enforcement, including initiation of the Uniform Crime Reporting system, which required local agencies to regularly report data to the FBI on seven index crimes thought to provide a picture of the state of crime and law enforcement throughout the country. The 1930s would also see, of course, the failure of some reforms and the abuse of power at many levels, including within the expanding FBI under J. Edgar Hoover. See, e.g., Walker, *Popular Justice*, 157–66; Friedman, *Crime and Punishment*, 271–72; James D. Calder, *The Origins and Development of Federal Crime Control Policy: Herbert Hoover's Initiatives* (Westport, CT: Praeger, 1993).

[5] E.g., Robert H. Gault, review of *The Public Defender: A Necessary Factor in the Administration of Justice*, by Mayer C. Goldman, *Journal of Criminal Law and Criminology* (hereafter *JCLC*), vol. 8 (1917): 315–16; Jesse L. Deck, "Some Needed Reform in Criminal Procedure," *JCLC*, vol. 8 (1917): 325–36; Edward J. McDermott, "Delays and Reversals on Technical Grounds in Civil and Criminal Trials," in *Proceedings of the American Political Science Association*, vol. 7 (Baltimore: Waverly Press, 1910), 97–110; Edson R. Sunderland, "The Inefficiency of the American Jury," *Michigan Law Review*, vol. 13 (1914): 302–16.

[6] E.g., George G. Battle, "The Problem of the Disposition of Insane Criminals," *Virginia Law Review*, vol. 1 (1913): 108–19; Bernard Glueck, "Psychiatric Aims in the Field of Criminology," *Mental Hygiene*, vol. 2 (1918): 546–56.

and of juvenile offenders.[7] Innovations continued with respect to the use of probation, the indeterminate sentence, and parole,[8] the recourse in some states to sterilization,[9] and the attempt to reform prison conditions to the standards of the rehabilitative ideal.[10] The guilt assessment stage, however, at least with regard to the more serious felonies, witnessed fewer initiatives: the substantive law remained largely intact, and, despite a great deal of scholarly agitation, trial procedure did as well.[11] If the guilt assessment stage saw significant change, it was in the ever-increasing number of defendants who forewent trial by pleading guilty.[12]

From outside the legal profession the dominant thrust continued to center on the causes of antisocial behavior.[13] Alongside notions of behavior based mainly on hereditarian influences, there had long since emerged an

[7] See, e.g., Steven L. Schlossman, *Love and the American Delinquent: The Theory and Practice of "Progressive" Juvenile Justice, 1825–1920* (Chicago: University of Chicago Press, 1977); David S. Tanenhaus, *Juvenile Justice in the Making* (New York: Oxford University Press, 2004).

[8] See, e.g., Walker, *Popular Justice*, 119–27; Friedman and Percival, *Roots of Justice*, 197–98, 224–33; Friedman, *Crime and Punishment*, 406–11.

[9] See, e.g., Mark H. Haller, *Eugenics: Hereditarian Attitudes in American Thought* (New Brunswick, NJ: Rutgers University Press, 1963), 133–41; Herbert Hovenkamp, "Insanity and Criminal Responsibility in Progressive America," *North Dakota Law Review*, vol. 57 (1981): 541–76, 563 n. 75.

[10] See, e.g., Walker, *Popular Justice*, 127–31.

[11] Transformation of trial practice did occur in the juvenile courts; this increased the pressure for reform of the regular courts, but to no avail. See Schlossman, *Love and the American Delinquent*. For a contemporary account, see John P. Briscoe, "Reforms of the Criminal Law," *JCLC*, vol. 8 (1918): 653–57. George Kirchwey, President of the AICLC, recommended in 1918 the extension of juvenile court practice to adult courts. George W. Kirchwey, "Proceedings of Tenth Annual Meeting of the American Institute of Criminal Law and Criminology: President's Address," *JCLC*, vol. 9 (1918): 327–40, 337.

[12] Plea bargaining was by no means a new phenomenon; it was common even as of the latter half of the nineteenth century. But criminologists addressed its pervasiveness as a potential problem in the 1920s. See, e.g., Walker, *Popular Justice*, 73–74, 153; Stuntz, *Collapse*, 73; Friedman, *Crime and Punishment*, 250–52; George Fisher, *Plea Bargaining's Triumph: A History of Plea Bargaining in America* (Stanford, CA: Stanford University Press, 2003). See also Friedman and Percival on the "twilight" of the jury trial and the rise of plea bargains in part as an element of a supposedly "more 'rational,' 'professional,' process" (*Roots of Justice*, 192–95).

[13] Discussions centered on the relationship between brain structure and behavior, the existence of physiological characteristics peculiar to criminals, the possibility of atavistic degeneration through heredity, and the consequent development of "born" or "instinctive" criminals. The varieties of American deterministic thinking displayed in these debates, and the generally deterministic assumptions of many scientists, are especially apparent in the *Medico-Legal Journal* of the New York Medico-Legal Society, the published annual proceedings of the National Prison Association, and in the increased participation of Americans in international congresses on crime, criminals, and penology. For more discussion of determinism in American studies of the causes of crime, see, for example, Merle Curti, *Human Nature in American Thought: A History* (Madison: University of Wisconsin Press, 1980), 273–312; Larry K. Hartsfield, *The American Response to Professional Crime, 1870–1917* (Westport,

environmentalist perspective. Scholars of the late nineteenth century added Freudian and other forms of psychoanalysis.[14] Classic studies in behaviorism soon followed.[15] Contemporary advances in behavioral science focused not only on the genesis of "crime" but also on the treatment of offenders. Although these advances grappled with the concept of responsibility generally, they paid special attention to the problem of legal insanity. In this context, behavioral science scholars took a leading role in recommending reform of trial procedure; alongside some legal writers, they criticized the prevailing insanity test, argued for revision of the rules concerning presentation of expert testimony, and took on the question of the roles of both judge and jury.[16]

There were significant fault lines below the surface of the Progressive movement, however, especially with respect to thinking about serious criminal offenses committed by adult offenders, including disagreements as to the following: Was *all* human behavior determined, or only behavior that signaled abnormality, such as "criminal" behavior?[17] Was the criminal law

CT: Greenwood Press, 1985), 149–88; Hovenkamp, "Insanity and Criminal Responsibility," 541–75; Tighe, "Question of Responsibility," 234–92. For more extensive background and scholarship on these issues – as well as additional notes and references relevant throughout Part I of this book – see my prior version of this Part, published as "Freedom and Criminal Responsibility in the Age of Pound: An Essay on Criminal Justice," *Michigan Law Review*, vol. 93 (1995): 1915–2053.

[14] See, e.g., Elizabeth Lunbeck, *The Psychiatric Persuasion: Knowledge, Gender, and Power in Modern America* (Princeton, NJ: Princeton University Press, 1994); Nathan G. Hale, Jr., *Freud and the Americans: The Beginnings of Psychoanalysis in the United States, 1876–1917* (New York: Oxford University Press, 1971); Jacques M. Quen and Eric T. Carlson, eds., *American Psychoanalysis, Origins and Development: The Adolf Meyer Seminars* (New York: Brunner/Mazel, 1978).

[15] E.g., William McDougall, *An Introduction to Social Psychology* (Boston: J. W. Luce, 1909); John B. Watson, *Behavior: An Introduction to Comparative Psychology* (New York: H. Holt, 1914); see also Ray Madding McConnell, *Criminal Responsibility and Social Constraint* (New York: C. Scribner's Sons, 1912); Maurice Parmelee, *The Science of Human Behavior* (New York: Macmillan, 1913).

[16] E.g., Frank H. Bowlby, "Insanity as a Defense in Homicide Cases" (pt. 2), *Case and Comment*, vol. 17 (1910): 554–60; Edwin R. Keedy, "Tests of Criminal Responsibility of the Insane," *JCLC*, vol. 1 (1910): 394–402; Edwin Keedy et al., "Insanity and Criminal Responsibility" (report of AICLC Committee "A," chaired by Professor Edwin Keedy), *JCLC*, vol. 7 (1916): 484–91; Carlos F. MacDonald, "Expert Evidence in Criminal Trials," *Proceedings of the Academy of Political Science in the City of New York*, vol. 1 (1911): 641–59. On criticism of expert witnesses in insanity cases, see the 1909 *Proceedings of the Wisconsin Branch of the American Institute of Criminal Law and Criminology* (published 1910), 30; Charles W. Eliot, "The Popular Dissatisfaction with the Administration of Justice in the United States," *Green Bag*, vol. 25 (1913): 65–73, 69; MacDonald, "Expert Evidence." On the jury, see Battle, "Disposition of Insane Criminals," 114–18; Bowlby, "Insanity as a Defense," pt. 2, 558; MacDonald, "Expert Evidence," 646; Maurice Parmelee, "A New System of Criminal Procedure," *JCLC*, vol. 4 (1913): 359–67, 361–62.

[17] Not all observers of crime were strongly deterministic, in the sense of believing that "normal" individuals were also determined. See, for example, Craig Haney's important article,

chiefly "utilitarian" – that is, aimed at securing overall social well-being by way of preventing criminal behavior through the most efficient form of deterrence? Or was it more concerned with "reform" – that is, aimed at the treatment and cure of those found to have committed criminal acts? That is, when the two main goals of consequentialism (deterrence and reform) were in conflict, which ought to prevail? What ought to be the relationship between criminal law and traditional widespread social understandings of "free" action; should a thoroughly "scientific" law premised at least in part on determinism stand in defiance of those understandings, or should a more moderate expression of scientific law work, in compromised fashion, to alter those understandings and thus only gradually become truly scientific? And how far should consequentialism of whatever sort accommodate commonplace political liberty concerns that presupposed limits to the reach of the state's implementation of the criminal law?

Indeed, consequentialist thought – which was often accompanied not only by determinist leanings, but by great faith in the rational benevolence of scientifically informed governance – raised new concerns about political liberty. Some deterrence-based academic scholarship, in embracing the notion that the chief aim of the criminal law was social defense, had at times endorsed forms of strict – or near-strict – liability.[18] Reform- (or treatment-) based scholarship further magnified political liberty problems: at times it appeared to put such emphasis on an accused's apparent need for treatment that it gave short shrift not only to the question whether the would-be offender had manifested a formal legally proscribed intent, but even whether he or she had committed a prohibited *act*. For these reasons, although both schools of consequentialism thus gave less emphasis to political liberty than did traditional desert-based theory, the treatment school was deemed to present the greater threat to the rights of the individual against the state. Its presumed excesses in this regard led the more deterrence-oriented theorists

"Criminal Justice and the Nineteenth-Century Paradigm: The Triumph of Psychological Individualism in the 'Formative Era,'" *Law and Human Behavior*, vol. 6 (1982): 191–235. Haney argues that the movement for individualization in the early Progressive period grew out of the long-standing focus in nineteenth-century America on individual responsibility. His account suggests that for many fin de siècle criminologists and penologists – and for psychologists as well – the ideology of "psychological individualism" maintained a belief in free will by describing criminal behavior as the product of a moral disease. These same criminologists and penologists, it seems to me, were nonetheless deterministic in their methodology and in much of their analysis.

[18] E.g., Charles Dudley Warner, "Some Aspects of the Indeterminate Sentence," *Yale Law Journal*, vol. 8 (1899): 219–24, 220; O. F. Hershey, "Criminal Anthropology" (pt. 3), *Criminal Law Magazine and Reporter*, vol. 15 (1893): 778–84, 778–80. See also Dubber, *Police Power*; Gerald Leonard, "Towards a Legal History of American Criminal Theory: Culture and Doctrine from Blackstone to the Model Penal Code," *Buffalo Criminal Law Review*, vol. 6 (2003): 691–832.

to correct for their own tendency to privilege prevention at the expense of due process.

These fault lines conditioned legal thought (and much practice) regarding criminal responsibility throughout the century. It is their emergence and unsettling of the early determinist influence on criminal law theory and administration that gives definition to the first period I discuss. Progressive Era scientific determinism impelled some American scholars to confront more directly the nature and reality of free will as well as its implications for the political liberty aspects of freedom.[19] The progressive[20] notion that those who have committed crimes have done so as a result of circumstances over which they had little or no control vied with the progressive concern that limits on state intrusion into the life of the individual quickly evaporate when human behavior is viewed in this fashion.[21] Freedom from the state traditionally presumed – even required – that the criminal law be premised upon the possibility of human freedom. There was no easy way

[19] Willrich has neatly shown the tensions among existing ideas about responsibility in his chapter on the Chicago Boys' Court, the arm of the municipal court system that informally extended something substantially along the lines of juvenile court practice to males just over the cutoff point for statutory juvenile justice (*City of Courts*, 208–40). As Willrich observes, "some social scientists, reformers, and jurists looked forward to the day when the states would adopt [the "socialized" juvenile court] model for the scientific treatment of *all* offenders," yet "most lawyers and judges, and, one suspects, most Americans, still expected the courts to treat accused felons *as if* their crimes were the product of nothing more than 'the inscrutable moral free will'" (210 [quoting from the AICLC's "General Introduction to the Modern Criminal Science Series," in, e.g., Raymond Saleilles, *The Individualization of Punishment*, trans. Rachel Szold Jastrow (Boston: Little, Brown, 1911), v–ix; I discuss the "General Introduction" in Chapter 2]). The Boys' Court required its judges to navigate the often narrow ground left for progressive experimentation, walking a fine line between their "socially interventionist ambitions" and their lack of power to formally suspend normal protections and rules of procedures for non-juvenile offenders (211–12). See also David J. Rothman, *Conscience and Convenience: The Asylum and Its Alternatives in Progressive America* (Boston: Little, Brown, 1980), esp. chap. 2, "Individual Justice: The Progressive Design."

[20] I use the term "progressive" (lower case) in its conventional sense. I use the term "Progressive" (upper case) to refer to the ideas associated with the Progressive Era (roughly, for my purposes, the 1890s through the early 1920s, although I refer to its early years as the fin de siècle), including those ideas as they persisted – or were revived – later in the century. Often, the ideas associated with the two terms overlap, but some "progressive" ideas were not so clearly in the mainstream of the Progressive program.

[21] Although I stress the scientific-positivist elements of the Progressive movement, of course "progressives" expressed a variety of concerns and approaches to the betterment of society. See, e.g., Daniel T. Rodgers, "In Search of Progressivism," *Reviews in American History*, vol. 10 (1982): 113–32. See also my discussion of the contrast between Progressive critiques of criminal law and of private law in Chapter 2. A central motivation was the creation of institutions that fairly and justly mediated between individuals and society. Progressives' obvious opposition to arbitrariness and corruption in government meant their faith in the state was far from blind or unqualified, despite their hopes for a new era of rational criminal justice administration.

to accommodate the conflicting ideals. Accordingly, those criminal justice scholars to confront the dilemma commonly took refuge in an increasingly bifurcated trial process: they entertained their doubts about the free will of an offender at the sentencing phase of the criminal process – where the ultimate issue of responsibility was less prominently involved and a more intrusive, treatment-based approach was less controversial – and allowed their "progressive" approach in that context to disguise from themselves how little they had confronted the implications of their doubts at the trial stage, where responsibility was most directly involved. This largely unself-conscious maneuver led to a substantial degree of incoherence in both the theory and the practice of criminal justice, even as it bore testimony to Americans' determination to uphold the underlying concept of free will.

This first essay (Part I) thus addresses attempts in American legal schol-arship (and some overlapping scholarship from other fields) to incorporate more rationally progressive science, and its influence on the concept of free will, into a legal system in which the presumption of free will was deeply – if not always consistently or logically – embedded. Modern American criminal law scholarship was, in many senses, still just emerging at the turn of the century. There were comparatively few law journals dedicated specifically to criminal jurisprudence. And few legal scholars wrote much of a sustained sort on the free will problem that scientific-positivism posed for the crim-inal law; generalizing from the random comments of the day is of limited help in this regard. In part for these reasons, this Part, which is mainly a (mildly) reduced version of an earlier article, is distinctive among my three studies: although I raise examples of the range of commentary by legal (and other) scholars on the free will issue, my route into and across the period 1900–1930 lies in large part through the work of one central figure, Roscoe Pound, and an important corner of Pound's voluminous writings. The most prominent legal academic of the era, Pound was broadly representative of Progressive thought. But his resolutely juristic stance led him to fear the implications for political liberty and for the idea of law itself of a purely treatment-based criminal law. Most important, although Pound's approach was certainly his own – guided by his own concerns and predilections – it thus encapsulated the range of issues that the determinist critique would pose for criminal responsibility scholars throughout the century. Truly both truth-seeker and prescriptivist, Pound actively brought behavioral science into the law, yet he continued to insist on the sovereignty of the law and rule by the bench rather than the clinic. He also moved toward a recognition of the social and political backlash that would result from a too-sudden adop-tion of a truly scientific criminal law.

The plan of this essay is as follows. I begin (Chapter 1) with a side-long glance at some features of fin de siècle criminal jurisprudence, which I approach primarily through a reading of a few papers written at the outset of his career by a little-known New York lawyer, Gino Speranza. Strongly influenced by the behavioral science of his day, Speranza reflected a radical perspective shared by relatively few contemporary practitioners – although decidedly by an increasing cadre of academic legal theorists and penologists, and even some members of the bench. I chose Speranza because he represents a movement that brought deterministic ideas from the behavioral and social sciences into law. In that respect he stood as a kind of missionary to lawyers from "scientists." But Speranza also soon discovered that the limits of common lawyers' own cultural traditions largely prevented the assimilation of determinism into law, and came to appreciate the conservative value of some of those traditions. He illustrated the limits beyond which few American lawyers of the day – who answered to the imperatives of widespread social views – would proceed in assimilating the social and behavioral sciences. He thus helps to define the scope of the problem that the legal profession confronted.

I turn in Chapter 2, the main section of this essay, to a lengthy odyssey: the evolution of Pound's criminal jurisprudence from 1905 to 1923. Born in Lincoln, Nebraska, in 1870, Pound was trained in both botany and law. He served first as a member, then as Dean, of the Nebraska law faculty and thereafter on the law faculties of Northwestern and Chicago. He moved to Harvard in 1910, where he was Dean from 1916 to 1936.[22] Pound continued to write until his death in 1964, although his truly creative period had ended by the 1930s. With respect to criminal jurisprudence, Pound is both a window into the more general characteristics of the period and a distinctive voice, the latter especially in his tendency to locate the free will problem in relation to Anglo-American history – particularly, to view an emphasis on free will as a species of American exceptionalism rather than to locate it in relation to social or behavioral-science universals. Most notable, he was an avowed assimilationist, and his writings reflect the strains that are the lot of the common lawyer who would join the insights of law and science. Although he began with a critique of Americans' exaggerated ideas about freedom (both political liberty and free will), Pound managed to retain a resolutely juristic perspective, always keeping a safe distance from the hardcore determinism of much Progressive Era criminology and penology. In his own way, Pound sought to meet the challenge of the fin de siècle, to resolve what Speranza had deemed unresolvable. The evolution of Pound's approach was gradual, however. He looked forward to, but never clearly articulated, cautious reform over time of all aspects of criminal justice administration that would meld the principles of social and behavioral

---

[22] On Pound's background and career path generally, see David Wigdor, *Roscoe Pound: Philosopher of Law* (Westport, CT: Greenwood Press, 1974); Paul D. Carrington, "The Missionary Diocese of Chicago," *Journal of Legal Education*, vol. 44 (1994): 467–518, 503–11; John Fabian Witt, *Patriots and Cosmopolitans: Hidden Histories of American Law* (Cambridge, MA: Harvard University Press, 2007), chap. 4.

science with the imperatives of legal science, and yet maintain respect for the *claim* of human freedom. This claim seems to have inhered in the individual's own consciousness of freedom, Pound's recognition of which perhaps signaled a modest acceptance of the idea of free will even as he continued to view criminal offenders as mainly constrained by social and psychological factors.

Pound's approach – eclectic, unsystematic – overlooked inherent contradictions, unself-consciously adopting an evasive approach to the most difficult problems. More history, impressionistic sociology, and commentary on contemporary legal practices than analytical jurisprudence, Pound's contribution to modern criminal justice study has been largely forgotten – mined for aphorisms but not appreciated as the fine tapestry that it is. I tell Pound's story both for its own sake and as an introductory foray into the history of early-twentieth-century academic criminal jurisprudence. For the most part, I let Pound speak for himself. (Indeed, this entire first essay is largely devoted to recovering voices that have long since drifted away or have been recorded over by our own idiom as we have addressed the same issues.) Although I remain agnostic as to just how far Pound was truly representative, I see him as part of the progressive juristic vanguard and as a true Progressive.

Finally, Chapter 3 recreates some high points of what might be called a conversation among a number of commentators on criminal justice from 1923 to 1930. By the mid-to-late 1920s, the differing approaches to an overall scientific-positivist perspective on criminal law had announced themselves fairly clearly. From our own perspective, it would appear that by the 1920s the Progressive optimism of the inaugural 1909 AICLC meeting had been substantially tempered, that early unity had given way to division, and that "scientists" outside of the legal academy were marching to a different drummer than were most of those scholars and practitioners within it. Most, but not all – for the scientific-positivists of the legal academy persisted and were themselves divided, or perhaps strewn out all along a consequentialist spectrum that ran from prevention through punishment for "repression" to prevention through "treatment" and "cure." Thus this "conversation" of the 1920s centrally serves to introduce what I see as the beginning of a new era, one marked not so much by new issues as by the new energy and increased attention to those issues already within the legal academy; this energy and attention – toward the inherent tensions of a scientifically informed law, toward the most appropriate role for science to play in legal administration, and toward the law's unique cultural and political roles – would manifest in burgeoning scholarship on criminal responsibility through the rest of the century.

This conversation also brings Pound's story to a close and puts him in perspective. Viewed, now, from the beginning of the twenty-first century, Pound's story matters because his work dealt with problems pressed on lawyers by "scientists" that remain at the foundation of our thinking about criminal justice. As is evident in Parts II and III of this book, despite all that has happened since the mid-1920s, Pound's story remains, in a special sense, largely our own. Our analyses of the persisting questions go far deeper, and we are attentive to ultimate contradictions that Pound seems not to have confronted. Nonetheless, we build on the same shaky foundations, partly recognizing that it is the best we can do; partly, but only indirectly, taking the infirmities into account; partly forgetting along the way how much we rest matters of life and liberty on theories that resist verification – indeed, that invite strong skepticism.

I

Prologue

The Fin de Siècle: Speranza

Writing in 1901, in the pages of a legal magazine, *The Green Bag*, a young member of the New York bar named Gino Speranza stated: "Law is one of the humanities."[1] So it is, but what caused Speranza to say so in such an insistent tone in his article, "The Medico-Legal Conflict over Mental Responsibility"? Perhaps Speranza's intended audience was scientists whose specialization was the study of human behavior and its application to the treatment and cure of criminal offenders. Many of them had trained abroad or at home on the writings of late-nineteenth-century European criminologists and penologists, thus joining a large phalanx of students of human behavior whose approach was decidedly deterministic. For many of these scientists, all behavior – like all events in nature – had its causes, and the will itself, whether it gave in to desires or resisted them, was the plaything of forces that it did not ultimately create or control. For these strong determinists, whatever value the concept of free will had in more speculative areas of life, everything that science could know about human behavior could be understood without invoking that concept.

There was nothing new about the concept of determinism. Men had reasoned their way to it long before the late nineteenth century. For some, the concept of an omniscient God had rendered the notion of human free will logically impossible or even downright blasphemous. For others, the general concept of cause and effect led to determinism long before modern science reinforced that view. Indeed, a deterministic, or "naturalist," position characterized various currents of thought regarding criminal justice in the

---

[1] Gino C. Speranza, "The Medico-Legal Conflict over Mental Responsibility," *Green Bag*, vol. 13 (1901): 123–26, 125.

United States since at least the late eighteenth century.[2] What was new in fin de siècle America was the pervasiveness of deterministic theory among practitioners of applied behavioral science, and few areas of social policy were so profoundly affected as were the fields of criminology and penology. From these fields, the influence of determinism spread to other domains of the law, although – as we shall see – the law ultimately fought off the worst ravages of the disease.

In Speranza's day, behavioral science was recognized by the legal profession – as by educated Americans generally – as a breakthrough of considerable importance. It held out the possibility of a solution to the problem of criminal behavior that greatly concerned both Europe and America. Its principles, many thought, would lead to the rehabilitation of those criminals who were not biologically, or otherwise, beyond salvation: if one understood why people behaved as they did, one might then design an environment that would reform the behavior of most – perhaps even the majority – of those persons with criminal tendencies. The implications of the new penology that took root in the Gilded Age and flowered in the Progressive Era were many, however, and among them was the message that humans were not responsible for their behavior, a message that the legal profession and society at large were unwilling to accept. I hazard the guess that, for most Americans, Progressive Era penology came to stand for the idea that rehabilitation involved a process of strengthening the inherently free will of persons who, by reason of one or another social influence, had been unable to resist the temptation to break the law.[3] Thus, for society as a whole, the new concepts of human behavior were made compatible with the traditional notion of free will – a marriage that provided a lasting, if uneasy, conceptual framework that has survived the decline, closer to our own day, of the rehabilitative ideal.

The lay conclusions that most Americans wanted to draw about the relationship between free will and rehabilitation seem not to have concerned

---

[2] Some of these currents are reflected in, for example, David J. Rothman, *The Discovery of the Asylum: Social Order and Disorder in the New Republic* (Boston: Little, Brown, 1971), 59–78. See also David Brion Davis, *From Homicide to Slavery: Studies in American Culture* (New York: Oxford University Press, 1986), 18–26; Arthur E. Fink, *Causes of Crime: Biological Theories in the United States, 1800–1915* (Philadelphia: University of Pennsylvania Press, 1938), 1–19; Jon Pahl, *Paradox Lost: Free Will and Political Liberty in American Culture, 1630–1760* (Baltimore: Johns Hopkins University Press, 1992), 6–9; Francis A. Allen, *The Decline of the Rehabilitative Ideal: Penal Policy and Social Purpose* (New Haven: Yale University Press, 1981), 3–16.

[3] Compare, e.g., David J. Rothman, *Conscience and Convenience: The Asylum and Its Alternatives in Progressive America* (Boston: Little, Brown, 1980), chap. 2, esp. p. 50. Rothman does not venture the precise supposition I have made in my generalizing account. See also Craig Haney, "Criminal Justice and the Nineteenth-Century Paradigm: The Triumph of Psychological Individualism in the 'Formative Era,'" *Law and Human Behavior*, vol. 6 (1982): 191–235. Haney would, I believe, apply a version of this perspective to many of the new scientists as well.

most behavioral and medical scientists. But, in Speranza's circles, optimism regarding the new penology was guarded. At the time that Speranza wrote, the major elements of Progressive Era penology were still largely in the theoretical stage. Questions remained concerning whether the principles of treatment were headed for general acceptance and for the political support crucial to obtaining funds for institutions and properly trained personnel.[4] Speranza's 1901 article, however, had to do not so much with penology as with a related matter: legal insanity. The principles of the new science applied to one as they applied to the other, but the two matters differed in what proved to be important ways. For law, for lawyers, and for the public at large, the science of human behavior posed far greater problems with regard to the insanity defense than with regard to the punishment – I should say, the treatment and cure – of convicts, even though the insanity defense involved far fewer persons. The reasons for this relate to the fundamental bifurcation between the trial and punishment stages of the criminal process that had long been emerging in Western jurisprudence. Progressive Era penology was to further this split.

At the level of theory, the bifurcation of criminal process reflected the differing ways in which jurists and behavioral scientists conceptualized criminal responsibility. Despite determinism's inroads elsewhere, at the trial stage the traditional concept of guilt – mens rea premised on free will – retained most of its force for intent-based crimes. At least, this appears to have been true for most legal commentators.[5] The defendant might have been buffeted by forces over which he possessed little or no control, but he had – so the theory ran – retained sufficient determination over his behavior to be thought of as having acted freely. In his influential *Treatise on Criminal Law*, Francis Wharton put this pact with the angels as follows:

---

[4] See generally Rothman, *Conscience and Convenience* (discussing the political dynamics behind the rise of the treatment ideal); Michael Willrich, *City of Courts: Socializing Justice in Progressive Era Chicago* (Cambridge: Cambridge University Press, 2003).

[5] Not all commentators who were swayed by the new sciences ultimately compromised on the free will issue with regard to the guilt assessment stage. Representing both the potential influence of science on the law and the range of responses among the legal community, a few legal writers recommended that the jury determine solely whether the defendant committed the "act" with which he had been charged. Charles Curry, for one, would then have had a group of experts classify the defendant "as a mad, born, habitual or occasional criminal, or a criminal of passion, and then the court should sentence him for an indefinite time, or suspend his sentence according to the nature of the case, and the history, condition and character of the offender." "Criminals and Their Treatment," *American Law Review*, vol. 36 (1902): 10–35, 22. Ethan A. Dausman would then have had the jury answer a second question: whether or not the defendant could "be safely permitted to remain at liberty without injury to the welfare of society." If the jury found that the defendant could not be safely released, the court would sentence him for an indefinite period. "Crime and Criminals," *American Law Review*, vol. 36 (1902): 661–80, 678. Possibly, both Curry and Dausman were building on suggestions for jury-based determination regarding the "act" that had long been part of the debate over use of experts to determine the "criminal" element in legal insanity cases.

To responsibility (imputability) there are, we must remember, two constituents: (1.) capacity of intellectual discrimination; and (2.) freedom of will. If there be either incapacity to distinguish between right and wrong as to the particular act, or delusion as to the act, or inability to do or refrain from doing the act, then there is no responsibility. The difficulty is practical. *No matter what may be our speculative views as to the existence of conscience, or of freedom of action, we are obliged, when we determine responsibility, to affirm both.*[6]

Wharton added, by way of a significant footnote:

The controversy which divides theologians as well as metaphysicians as to the freedom of the will is not involved in the discussion in the text. It may be possible that, from a high metaphysical point of vision, all acts are necessitated. With this, however, jurisprudence, which is a practical science, has nothing to do. There have been indeed leading jurists, such as Feuerbach, who have adopted the principle of necessity as a basis, and have invoked the fear of punishment as a counterweight to the temptation to crime.... But this, as is well said by a leading German author ... takes not only from jurisprudence, but from life, its moral dignity, making the former a mere marshalling of mechanisms, and the latter, a mere mechanism of necessities.[7]

Wharton, likely speaking for many in his field, thus affirmed the traditional view of guilt assessment in strong terms that reflected deeply rooted reasons for the preservation of traditional ideas of mens rea at the trial stage, even long after those ideas had begun to give ground at the post-trial stage.

The potential distance between the premises of the two stages could be great because of the clear conservatism inherent in the legal definition of criminal responsibility, that is, in its broad presumption in favor of freedom. Consider the narrowness of the two legal categories that constituted the main defenses of unfreedom: duress and insanity. Duress required a threat, or reasonable belief in the threat, of direct and dire physical harm – a gun-

---

[6] 1 Francis Wharton, *A Treatise on Criminal Law* (8th ed., 1880), 51–53 (emphasis supplied).

[7] Wharton, *A Treatise on Criminal Law*, 53 n. 1. Wharton's formulation was retained into the 1930s in the 9th edition (1885), vol. 1, p. 53; 10th edition (1896), vol. 1, p. 49; 11th edition (1912), vol. 1, p. 65; and 12th edition (1932), vol. 1, p. 70. An editorial note in the *American Law Review* put the matter rather differently while neatly summing up the conflict that the law was confronting by the end of the nineteenth century:

In the most general sense, no man can refrain from doing what he does. In an absolute sense, no man is a free moral agent, any more than a grain of sand which drifts in the wind is a free moral agent; but every act which a man does is, when done, the result of a series of causes which have existed throughout all time. When men get sense enough to understand this, then the right to punish crime will rest upon a different ground from that upon which it is now placed.... The sheet-anchor in this conflict of opinion is this: the foundation of will is intelligence, – knowledge, or the power to know; when that is possessed, the law must conclusively presume that the power of self-restraint exists along with it, and must act and punish upon this assumption. (*American Law Review*, vol. 19 [1885]: 765)

to-the-head example would overstate the case, but not by much.[8] Legal insanity generally required lack of knowledge of what one was doing or of the fact that it was wrong, although, by Speranza's time, a fair number of states allowed recourse, under some circumstances, to the so-called irresistible impulse test, the classic formulation of which required a causal nexus between a preexisting mental disease or defect and the suspension of the defendant's control over his behavior.[9] At least as a matter of law, longstanding diseases of the brain that did not obliterate one's cognitive capacities, result in severe delusion, or destroy self-control did not meet these tests, nor did many other mental states that medical scientists generally classified as insanity in the context of civil commitment. If prevailing rules regarding legal insanity typically excluded, for example, the kleptomaniac, a fortiori they excluded the great mass of defendants who had been indicted for property offenses and whose only claims in mitigation – had they been allowed to make them – would have been based on poverty, lack of education, influence of evil associates, or other essentially social circumstances.

The criminal trial thus represented a first stage in the criminal process at which the law, reflecting general social mores, insisted on the existence of free will despite the fact that, increasingly, those found guilty were immediately turned over to a sentencing process wherein their relative unfreedom might be widely construed and they were often viewed in part as victims of biological or social circumstances. At this second, "individualized" stage of the criminal process (at least according to the ideal), information about the convicted defendant's background, upbringing, associates, and so on – matters rarely formally admissible during the trial – became relevant. Progressive Era penology aspired to the creation of a large bureaucracy dedicated to gathering, sifting, and analyzing such data and to a bench prepared to pass judgment regarding sentences case by case on the basis of that information.[10] It bears comment that juries, aided by clever lawyers or the

---

[8] See, e.g., 1 Wharton, *Treatise on Criminal Law* (8th ed.), 130 n. 11; see also 10th ed., p. 117 n. 1. For the contemporary English rule, see Sir James Fitzjames Stephen, *A General View of the Criminal Law of England*, 2nd ed. (London and New York: Macmillan, 1890). Stephen describes the rule as "narrowly limited and somewhat capricious" (69). He states that it does not cover a murder defendant who shows that his own life was threatened if he did not commit the act, for if it did: "Criminals might commit offences with impunity by threatening others." He noted, however, that "the fact of compulsion may always be taken into account in reduction of punishment" (70).

[9] See *Parsons v. State*, 2 So. 854 (Ala. 1887). On the law of insanity at the end of the nineteenth century, see 1 Wharton, *Treatise on Criminal Law* (10th ed.), 49–73.

[10] Compare Rothman, *Conscience and Convenience*, chap. 2. Rothman's account reports contemporary ideals rather more than actual practices. One leading criminologist of the 1930s both criticized the halfhearted application of the new penology and commented sardonically upon what I have termed the "bifurcation" of trial and sentencing:

And so we witness the strange spectacle of a defendant being indicted and tried for a specific *offense*, the only issue being whether or not the crime was committed, for

defendant's demeanor, sometimes drew their own inferences regarding such matters even during the trial stage, achieving a kind of "individualization" that leavened the law and tracked the new penology in a rough-and-ready fashion – serving unself-consciously, one might say, to mediate the conflicting paradigms of criminal justice. Nonetheless, the point remains: the law of evidence regarding guilt or innocence reflected one concept of human behavior; the new penology – ideas about the appropriate treatment of offenders who have run the gauntlet of our blaming instincts and have satisfied our need that they carry the stigma of criminal guilt – reflected quite another.

The complex juristic reaction to the intellectual currents of the late nineteenth century can be witnessed in microcosm in a three-part article that appeared in the *Criminal Law Magazine* in 1893. Here Omer Hershey, a practicing lawyer, addressed the subject of "Criminal Anthropology."[11] Hershey's response to the new learning was, overall, sympathetic. But, presaging themes in both Speranza and Pound, he initially criticized the overreach of some of its practitioners and concluded that, in any case, its practical application to criminal responsibility remained a matter for the future. "Criminologists," Hershey asserted,

fail to recognize the difference between a purely scientific treatment of crime and the practical treatment which it must receive under the law. Science and law cannot afford to be hostile, but neither can they hope to move arm in arm. Science moves rapidly; its mistakes are easily corrected and its consequences are remote. Not so law. It changes slowly and carries immediate responsibility. It must be certain, and, therefore, more or less arbitrary.[12]

Nonetheless, Hershey went on to observe that the new science had much to contribute to current penal practice, if not to the concept of guilt.[13] And then – most striking – despite his seeming recognition of entrenched traditional ideas, Hershey proceeded to reject utterly the subjective intent requirement, urging that a "man without any intention to commit a crime,

which the legislative prescribes a definite punishment, and a history of the background of the offender furnished by the probation department which is generally irrelevant and may not be introduced at the trial. The stark inconsistency in spirit between the criminal law seeking to punish for guilt and the administrative device of probation seeking rehabilitation of the offender is blurred by slipping the probation report to the judge before sentence is imposed. (Nathaniel Cantor, "Conflicts in Penal Theory and Practice," *JCLC*, vol. 26 [1935]: 330–50, 334)

11 O. F. Hershey, "Criminal Anthropology" (pts. 1–3), *Criminal Law Magazine and Reporter*, vol. 15 (1893): 499–504, 658–63, 778–84.
12 Hershey, "Criminal Anthropology," 778.
13 Hershey, "Criminal Anthropology," 783–84:

If criminal anthropology is not likely to have much influence on the great body of criminal jurisprudence, its value in the larger question of crime and criminals cannot be over-estimated. … An anthropological examination is to determine the *status* of the criminal, his proper treatment and the time and conditions of his liberation. If the science can do this, criminal law has no fault to find. Whether it can do more, time will show.

may, nevertheless, have the criminal intent, the *mens rea,* necessary to make his act a crime. Criminal intent is determined from acts alone and not from any psychologic tests." (If the legally insane are not punished, he claimed, it is "because they have no *mens* at all.") This conclusion, in turn, was drawn from his consequentialist position on the "penological criterion" of the criminal law that, he asserted, was "social necessity; its measure of justice the safety of society."[14] Thus did Hershey seem to advocate, on some level, for a traditional view of responsibility, but one that was so informed by consequentialism that the notion of the will underlying a criminal act became largely irrelevant. This was a move that would become familiar to many in the legal sphere during the Progressive Era and beyond: the scientists' charge of irrationality would be blunted by invoking the aims of the law; the relevance of individual blame (and thus of free will) would be minimized by denying the relevance of retribution and stressing instead the purely utilitarian side of criminal justice as a social defense, which had long been one element in classical criminal jurisprudence.[15]

Still, one suspects that even many late-nineteenth-century, deterrence-oriented social defense jurists would have rejected a strong theory of determinism – which they probably viewed as, at best, no more verifiable than "free will" – and, like Wharton, defended the law's underlying "presumption" of human freedom. In truth, we do not yet know what most jurists thought regarding all of the questions Hershey had raised. The legal profession as a whole may well have mirrored society at large, translating the presumption of free will regarding responsibility into the justification of retribution regarding punishment. Some judges, law-trained penologists, and legal academics reflected varying levels and aspects of the "scientific" perspective. Yet wisdom counseled against head-on confrontation.[16] Sometimes wisdom even counseled an exaggerated insistence on true orthodoxy: to take

---

[14] Hershey, "Criminal Anthropology," 778–80.

[15] See, e.g., Charles Dudley Warner, "Some Aspects of the Indeterminate Sentence," *Yale Law Journal,* vol. 8 (1899):219–24, 220.

[16] Witness Holmes's circumlocutions of the preceding decade. Oliver Wendell Holmes, *The Common Law,* ed. Mark DeWolfe Howe (Boston: Little, Brown, 1963) (Holmes originally published in 1881). I read Holmes as skeptical about human autonomy. He recognized (with some diffidence) the widespread notion of relative degrees of freedom, as when he suggested: "If punishment stood on the moral grounds which are proposed for it, the first thing to be considered would be those limitations in the capacity for choosing rightly which arise from abnormal instincts, want of education, lack of intelligence, and all the other defects which are most marked in the criminal classes" (38). But an inherent determinism seems to underlie an earlier passage, which supports reading the later apparent allusions to the true freedom of *some* persons as mere lip service: "The desire for vengeance imports an opinion that its object is actually and personally to blame. It takes an internal standard not an objective or external one, and condemns its victim by that. The question is whether such a standard is still accepted either in this primitive form, or in some more refined development, as is commonly supposed, and as seems not impossible, considering the relative slowness with which the criminal law has improved" (35). For an important related discussion of Holmes,

the most obvious example, law tended to follow general social perspectives on freedom of the will in the context of the trial of the assassin Guiteau.[17]

It may suffice to say that, from this remove, it is difficult to tell just how polarized the worlds of law and science were in the last decades of the century. What we can discern in at least a general way is that, at the fin de siècle, some medical and behavioral scientists were greatly agitated about what they deemed to be the atavism of the law. In their view, Americans hewed to an outdated notion of human behavior, premised criminal law on a false concept of guilt, and based punishment on primitive feelings of revenge. For many medical scientists, this posed a special problem: as expert witnesses in insanity cases, they were confronted with legal definitions that did not match medical conceptions of human behavior.[18] Criminal guilt assumed free will, and for the scientist – who was trained to ascertain the causes of mental states and acts – that concept of criminal responsibility was, at best, problematic. Why distinguish *among* causes; why deem only some symptoms relevant? What *was* – in a world of causes and effects – "free" agency?

THE NEW CENTURY: GINO SPERANZA

In this heated atmosphere, Gino Speranza was less equivocal and more optimistic than were most legal scholars in demanding a closer dialogue between law and medicine. Born in Connecticut in 1872 to Italian immigrants, the young Speranza was something of an anomaly: an American lawyer with a continental background, through his family and his studies, and with a powerful continental jurisprudential disposition. His early writings dealt mainly with criminal jurisprudence and penology. His later work focused on crime and immigration. By the end of his career, he extolled the virtues of Americanization,[19] but his perspective was not a characteristically American judicial one. He was a lawyer in league with behavioral scientists and, to a significant degree, at war with his own American profession, even though many in that profession admitted the importance of penal reform.

see Richard A. Posner, *The Problems of Jurisprudence* (Cambridge, MA: Harvard University Press, 1990), 168–69.

[17] See Charles E. Rosenberg, *The Trial of the Assassin Guiteau: Psychiatry and Law in the Gilded Age* (Chicago: University of Chicago Press, 1968).

[18] See Janet Ann Tighe, "A Question of Responsibility: The Development of American Forensic Psychiatry, 1838–1930" (Ph.D. dissertation, University of Pennsylvania, 1983, available at http://repository.upenn.edu/dissertations/AAI8406727), 203–26, 234–92; James C. Mohr, *Doctors and the Law: Medical Jurisprudence in Nineteenth-Century America* (New York: Oxford University Press, 1993), 176–79, 197–212, 234–36.

[19] Speranza's endorsement of assimilation and Americanization has been described as an act of "self-denial." Louis C. Anthes, "Race or Nation: An Italian-American's Critique of Immigration" (unpublished manuscript, September 28, 1994, on file with the author), esp. 27. I am grateful to Mr. Anthes for allowing me to cite his essay.

Speranza's 1901 article, "The Medico-Legal Conflict over Mental Responsibility," was meant to console, to induce patience and understanding. His words – at greater length than I have as yet given them – were as follows:

There is one barrier, however, that appears insurmountable, as to which, while it stands, law and medicine may declare a truce, but can agree to no terms of peace; I refer to that most ancient and greatest of questions – the freedom of the will.

The study of man from the physiologic standpoint has an undoubted tendency to make him, in the eyes of his investigator, a creature of forces beyond its control. Man in this aspect ceases to be a free agent in the eyes of the student....

It will hardly be denied that the tendency of psycho-physical study of man must be towards a denial of spirit.

Law, on the other hand, stands pre-eminently for the freedom of the will. Without this as a foundation-stone juridic science has no existence, for the very test of juridic responsibility is man's power of choice. To this the juridic philosopher brings the sentiment of humanity, the teachings of metaphysics and the experience of history, which are repugnant to the physical measurement of the soul; he contends that after you have taken man's brains to pieces you have not yet found his mind; that molecular interaction may be demonstrated as the physical counterpart of thought, but it is not thought....

Medicine is essentially a positive science: it is based on the observation of physical phenomena. Law is one of the humanities: it is [in Holmes's words] the "witness and external deposit of our moral life. Its history is the history of the moral development of the race." The doctor and the jurist too often forget the many-sidedness of man. The mental pathologist is dazzled by the discoveries regarding the physical basis of mind and his mental equation thereupon blinds his judgment. On the other hand, lawyers make too much use of logic, forgetting that [Holmes again] the "life of the law has not been logic, but experience." ...

Can these opposing forces be turned into a common stream of usefulness? Can this medico-legal conflict be brought to a settlement which will be neither a mere working truce nor a concession to eclecticism, but an agreement based on reason and scientific data? ...

Let neither the doctors nor the lawyers draw an impassable and inflexible line around their respective fields of investigation, but let them work in common for a common end. No mere doctor, and no mere lawyer, will be the one master that will solve the problem of mental responsibility in law.... The Great Pacificator in this medico-legal conflict will be he who ... will serenely and persistently strive for the study of man as he is in his many aspects ... it will be he, who, knowing the dangers and impracticability of endeavoring to solve human problems by adhering to theories and ideals, is nevertheless confident that without theories and ideals the hope and certainty of progress are idle and vain boasts.[20]

---

[20] Speranza, "Medico-Legal Conflict," 125–26. Speranza's phrase, "The Great Pacificator," was, of course, derived from the popular reference to the Antebellum master of political compromise, Henry Clay.

Are you consoled? Was Speranza? These are noble thoughts elegantly stated, but that should not deter us from asking: Was Speranza being sincere? At first blush, we may harbor doubts. There is perhaps too much poetry and too little rock-hard meaning in Speranza's plea for reconciliation, tolerance, and cooperation. What light can we shed on his "Medico-Legal Conflict" article from an examination of his other writings?

Two of Speranza's earlier writings – one from 1899, one from 1900 – are of special interest in relation to the later piece. The first and the more scholarly of the two was a paper read before the Society of Medical Jurisprudence, entitled "Natural Law versus Statutory Law."[21] By "natural law" Speranza meant the laws of nature that are discoverable through scientific observation and analysis – not the more traditional natural law of religion and philosophy that for centuries had been defined as the moral laws designed by God and knowable to man through God-given powers of reason. By "statutory law" Speranza meant the principles of juridical science – historically based and time-tested principles that either had been embedded in statute or had retained force as non-statutory common law. Over time, some of the discoveries of natural science had accounted for incremental changes in the law. In the main, however, Speranza seems to have believed that legal science remained traditional and precedent-based: natural science had been assimilated by juridical science only to the extent that it could be made to conform to the latter's precepts.

Speranza's impression of the resulting state of the law was clear – his attack on juridical science was unrelenting: "Venerability is its pride, stare decisis its demigod. It is conservative almost to the point of stagnation."[22] It bases

its decisions on antiquated and discarded theories ... finding justice not so much in the appreciation of facts in a new and modern light, but in the decisions of judges, dead or living, whose claim to authority at times arises from the fortuitous circumstance of having occupied the bench of the highest tribunal of the land![23]

Speranza's critique turned in the direction of a fairly conventional plea for an utterly positivist approach to criminology and penology.[24] His optimism and his confidence in the new sciences of the day were nearly unbounded, as were those of his audience, the members of the Society of Medical Jurisprudence. But Speranza struck a more original note than most other critics in his treatment of the legal profession's "bias against innovations":

[21] Gino C. Speranza, "Natural Law versus Statutory Law," *Albany Law Journal*, vol. 59 (1899): 400–05.

[22] Speranza, "Natural Law versus Statutory Law," 400.

[23] Speranza, "Natural Law versus Statutory Law," 401.

[24] Speranza claimed: "I am not here to defend [the 'Positive School's'] theories or to attack its critics, but merely to state its method of research and to describe its field of activity" (Speranza, "Natural Law versus Statutory Law," 402). He quickly dropped this pretense of neutrality.

"If you touch our courts," cry the lawyers, "you will destroy the bulwarks of our liberties; if you change our laws you will endanger our most cherished principles!" But these are not arguments; they are the repetition of those wails of despair which well-meaning but narrow-minded men raised during the so-called conflict between science and religion.[25]

The "wails," the appeals to "the bulwarks of our liberties," were simply not to be taken seriously.

Nor would they be. The "Positive School of Criminal Jurisprudence" would carry the day. For, Speranza now asserted: "Justice ... is *truth, absolute truth*." And, although the "conflict between science and jurisprudence, between natural law and statute law, is unavoidable and irrepressible," no "prophetic power" is required "to predict that such conflict will have but one radical though salutary result – it will establish the fact that it is *Truth* and not the *King* that can do no wrong, thus substituting an *axiom* for an *assumption* as the cornerstone of juridic science." "Science has destroyed empires of venerable theories," he boldly concluded, "let us hope that the kingdom of scientific law is at hand!"[26] This does not sound like the consoling counsel of compromise that Speranza wrote for the benefit of a mainly legal audience two years later. Of course, the later paper had in fact envisioned a *near total* victory on the part of science; only the one irreducible problem of free will could never truly be solved – save by mutual agreement not to agree – and there is no sign that Speranza had seen this point before 1901. But it was as though the scientist-lawyer, in 1901, stood before his legal colleagues, chastened by new insight, and appealed over their heads to the scientists to join him in his campaign to make peace with the juristic tradition. What was the source of this insight that brought Speranza to his Canossa?

Not long after he addressed the Society of Medical Jurisprudence in April 1899, Speranza published an article in the February 1900 issue of *Popular Science Monthly,* in which he addressed an educated public on "The Decline of Criminal Jurisprudence in America."[27] His subject was not simply the conflict between law and science, but the difference between the continental, or "Latin," approach to criminal jurisprudence and that of England and America – the "Anglo-Saxon" approach. The article reflected Speranza's admiration for the great advances in criminal jurisprudence of the Italian and French schools of the preceding decades. But it reflected, too, a grudging appreciation of the Anglo-Saxons' great contributions to law and justice. The readers of *Popular Science Monthly*

---

[25] Speranza, "Natural Law versus Statutory Law," 401.

[26] Speranza, "Natural Law versus Statutory Law," 403–04. Speranza understood that science still had a long way to go: "Criminology is still in its infancy" (403).

[27] Gino C. Speranza, "The Decline of Criminal Jurisprudence in America," *Popular Science Monthly,* vol. 56 (1900): 466–73.

were no doubt pleased to hear at the outset that the "rights of personal security, personal liberty, and private property have been called the 'rights of the people of England,'" and "while, in a certain sense, they belong to all civilized people, yet, in their practical application, they are peculiarly the creation of Anglo-Saxon common sense and love of order." Speranza pointed out that on the Continent the attempt to vindicate these rights – "clothed by the Latins in the seductive garb of *Liberté, Egalité, Fraternité*" – "gave us a Reign of Terror, a Commune, and finally a doubtful republicanism," whereas the Anglo-Saxons – employing "the less dazzling formula, 'That no man shall be deprived of life, liberty, or property without due process of law,'" – achieved "more enduring democracies 'of the people, by the people, and for the people.'" The Anglo-Saxons found in courts of law "the highest safeguard for their ancient rights" against the threats posed by a "partisan Legislature and a tyrannical Executive." It was natural, then, "that it has become a belief, having the force of faith, that in our courts will be found the bulwark of those liberties which we consider essential to the full enjoyment of life."[28] We may wonder how many of Speranza's readers had read his address to the Society of Medical Jurisprudence, which had just been reprinted in the pages of the *Albany Law Journal,* where the author mocked the notion of judicial bulwarks of liberty as a fraudulent excuse for not embracing a more properly scientific approach to the law.

To be sure, as in the earlier paper, Speranza criticized Anglo-Saxon justice as too slow to put law on a scientific footing. He issued a report card on Americans' progress in basing the criminal law – the branch of law on which "we must rely for the enunciation of what acts shall constitute a breach of the right of life, liberty, and property" – on the "highest dictates of human knowledge."[29] Our record, Speranza confided to his readers, was poor. Law schools, for example, devoted little time to teaching criminal law, and faculty members who taught the subject did not specialize in it. Both young lawyers and the community at large were cynical about criminal courts, criminal defendants, and the criminal bar. On the Continent, "where less boast is made of inalienable rights," the situation was the reverse: "it is the ambition of all lawyers to get a reputation at the criminal bar."[30] The Anglo-Saxons – and here Speranza meant mainly Americans – were failing in their duty to safeguard the fundamental rights for which they were famous. It was a gentle and respectful, but thorough, scolding.

---

[28] Speranza, "Decline of Criminal Jurisprudence," 466.

[29] Speranza, "Decline of Criminal Jurisprudence," 466–67.

[30] Speranza, "Decline of Criminal Jurisprudence," 469. Cf. Hershey, "Criminal Anthropology," 780–81 (contrasting the "antagonism" between scientific and judicial standpoints in England and America with the embrace of medicolegal scientific investigations by many prominent lawyers and judges on the Continent).

The transition from Speranza's Society of Medical Jurisprudence address to his 1901 article in *The Green Bag* was well under way by the time he wrote the intermediate *Popular Science* article. No doubt the intended audience had something to do with the changed tone and perspective. But the conclusion seems irresistible: Speranza was – perhaps because of a rethinking occasioned by the forum for which he wrote – taking the Anglo-American rights-oriented tradition more seriously. There were costs to society from hidebound adherence to tradition, but that adherence had, after all, prevented sudden radical innovations that might have concentrated too much power in a single person or in an institution beholden to popular passions of the day. Conservatism and basic freedom had, roughly speaking, been blood brothers in the Anglo-Saxon tradition. The problem, as Speranza now saw it, was that the Anglo-Saxons were in danger of sacrificing on the altar of mindless traditionalism all they had achieved. Some sensible accommodation between modern science and traditional rights must therefore be reached, especially in criminology. Speranza noted that, under the prevailing American system of criminal justice, many defendants were sentenced to prison who ought to have received psychiatric treatment under conditions of civil commitment, and many others who ought to have gone to prison were acquitted on "technicalities" that "save scoundrels."[31] The more rational system of the Continent, where the new sciences were respected within legal circles, was a guide to be followed. But, Speranza seems to have been saying, its lessons in tyranny should not thereby be overlooked.

Thus, Speranza sought a middling, best-of-both-worlds position, one that both accorded the realities of nature their due and respected the deepest yearnings for human freedom. Irrational treatment of criminal defendants he would not abide; yet, in the service of liberty, the concept of free will ought to retain a place at the core of the legal – not the scientific – conception of human behavior. Let me recall his words, or those of Edward Payson, whom he quoted. Law, Payson wrote, with respect to the Anglo-American tradition, had "'shunned many a quagmire, detected many a false light and stood fast against an onslaught of ism and ology on the road of human progress.'"[32] Yet Speranza himself was cautious in his approach to this emerging rationalization of the American legal profession's perspective; he balanced it against the injunction that "'to set up a legal test or standard of insanity which is not in harmony with the teachings of medical science ... is a disgrace to jurisprudence and a travesty upon justice.'"[33] Although we may conclude that Speranza's consoling compromise was

---

[31] Speranza, "Decline of Criminal Jurisprudence," 472.
[32] Speranza, "Medico-Legal Conflict," 126 (quoting Edward P. Payson, *Suggestions toward an Applied Science of Sociology*).
[33] Speranza, "Medico-Legal Conflict," 126 (quoting Dr. Carlos F. MacDonald, *American Journal of Insanity*, vol. 56 [1899]).

sincerely meant, we must also recognize that it was more wishful thinking than a practicable or coherent program. Where would one draw the line between the reforms that science demanded in the defense of fundamental rights and those repugnant to the concept of human freedom, also crucial to the defense of those rights? For all one could say, the American system of criminal justice already drew the appropriate line. Who could ever say whether we paid a higher cost for our concept of freedom than the market-place of human ideas actually required?

From the perspective of history, we can draw some conclusions. We know that the movement of which Speranza was a part fed into the larger, more politically based, movement for the reform of American institutions, including those of criminal justice. Indeed, as of 1901, Progressive Era penal reform was already under way. As it turned out, there *was* room for change, even dramatic change. But we can also now see how much – from the scientific point of view – was compromised along the way. Americans made some significant attempts to reform penology, but they stood fast with regard to the criminal trial and the legal definition of criminal responsibility, thus deepening the bifurcation of the two main stages of criminal process and increasing the appearance, at least, of irrationality.

THE NEW SCIENCE AND "INCORRIGIBLES"

The rejection of a thoroughgoing "scientific" approach – in the name of defending both the concept of free will and the principle of political liberty – exacted costs and accrued benefits that can never be weighed and evaluated, save through the lens of our own political preferences. We can, however, identify one benefit of the traditionalism pervading Progressive Era penology that many would count very heavily on the positive side. I mention it because it both brings us to another of Speranza's deepest concerns and reminds us of an enduring aspect of the Anglo-Saxon approach to human freedom and social justice.

The new schools of behavioral science remained divided on the practical applications of their theories. Among the matters on which there was disagreement was the question: What to do with incorrigibles? Indeed, who *were* "incorrigibles"? According to the new scientists, heredity or environment or disease of the brain could produce a propensity to engage in behavior that the state defined as criminal. In *some* cases, this propensity was reversible, in others not; scientists differed in their assessment both of the pathology involved and of the likelihood of response to currently available treatments. All agreed that some persons would never respond in the manner implied by the concept of "cure," but the universe of such incorrigibles varied for different students of human behavior. Moreover, incorrigibles themselves were thought to differ: some incorrigibles lacked the cognitive processes necessary for cure, whereas others possessed those capacities but were so lacking in social conscience that nothing could be done. Should all be treated as insane and "humanely" cared for until they died? Should some be so treated and others not?[34]

Americans had long been exposed to the doctrine that criminal law ought not to be based on revenge or retribution, but ought instead to look to a mixture of cure and prevention. If cure was impossible, prevention might still be an option. Permanent incarceration was one form of prevention, but, as Americans came to see over the course of the nineteenth century, it had two drawbacks. First, it was expensive; second, it was strong medicine for recidivists whose crimes were relatively minor. The threat of this degree of incapacitation (which immediately resulted in individual or "specific" deterrence of the offender) might deter others (and thus achieve "general" deterrence), but the proportionality between the harm a convict had caused society and the hardship visited on him might offend one's sense of justice. Just how thoroughly "scientific" ought one be in the name of general crime prevention?

By 1900, a few American scientists who studied criminal behavior were coming to share an extreme and "therapeutic" form of the social defense position that some continental criminologists and penologists had introduced into the transatlantic literature of the late nineteenth century. Some favored "benign" (non-retributive) execution or "elimination"; others counseled permanent incarceration of recidivists, however minor their recurring crimes. In Anglo-American circles, the proponents of this form of the social defense concept could be found among those who had been influenced by Herbert Spencer's social Darwinism.[35] Should we be entirely surprised, then, to find in the *American Law Register* of 1904 an article by Gino Speranza

[34] Generally speaking, an author's views on the existence of incorrigibles and the possibility of reforming or curing them were linked to beliefs about the causes of crime. Strict hereditarians, although rarely suggesting that all criminals were born criminals, usually supported the notion that incorrigibles required permanent segregation or even execution. E.g., W. Duncan McKim, *Heredity and Human Progress* (New York: G. P. Putnam's Sons, 1900), esp. chap. 5, "A Remedy"; address by Henry Hatch, "Crime and Criminals, and What Shall Be Done with Them," in the 1904 *Proceedings of the Annual Congress of the National Prison Association* (Pittsburg: Shaw Bros., 1904), 302–07. Environmentalists could express support for the possibility of curing some criminals, with indeterminate sentences to deal with possible incorrigibles. E.g., Henry Maudsley, "The Moral Sense and Will in Criminals," *Medico-Legal Journal*, vol. 2 (1885): 1–9. Most often, as Frances A. Kellor noted in 1901, American criminologists drew on both the Italian (hereditarian) and French (environmental) schools in thinking about the causes and, hence, treatment of crime. *Experimental Sociology, Descriptive and Analytical: Delinquents* (New York: Macmillan, 1901), 1–5. See also Francis Wayland, "Incorrigible Criminals," *Journal of Social Science*, vol. 23 (1887): 140–44; address by Francis Wayland, "The Incorrigible – Who He Is, and What Shall Be Done with Him," in the 1886 *Proceedings of the National Prison Congress* (Chicago: R. R. Donnelley and Sons, 1887), 189–93.
[35] E.g., Henry M. Boies, *The Science of Penology* (New York: G. P. Putnam's Sons, 1901); G. Frank Lydston, *The Diseases of Society* (Philadelphia: J. B. Lippincott, 1904).

that criticized American penology under the title of "The Survival of the Weakest as Exemplified in the Criminal"?[36]

Speranza's 1904 article reflected a mixture of compassion and severity, of treatment and repression. He asserted that prison was inappropriate and, indeed, counterproductive for those persons who were merely "mistaken," having been temporarily led astray by social conditions or circumstances. A system of probation or, at least, early parole was needed, and Speranza took the opportunity to berate American penology for its backwardness in this regard. Such reforms were only slowly coming into existence in most states, although they would soon come, quite universally, with a great rush. As for the true "criminal class," which was much smaller than most Americans recognized,

it deserves most repressive measures against it for the social good.... The truly criminal are a danger, and the hope of reforming them is almost a negligible quantity....

The whole juridic framework must be erected on the modern lines of the social defence. The conception of punishment as a defence to crime has gone into bankruptcy: it neither defends nor deters. Criminal therapeutics must take its place; that is, where a cure is possible, let the remedial agencies suggested by criminologic and sociologic science have full scope. But where juridic therapeutics fail, let there be no mistaken altruism to perpetuate the unfittest.[37]

What Speranza most feared was that the new penology, when it came, would serve to condition the truly criminal to act as though they were reformed although in fact they were not, and so make those least fit for social existence the most adept at negotiating the conditions of existence in modern society. A proper system of scientific evaluation of human behavior would facilitate the separation of the treatable from the incorrigibles – that is, from the "truly degenerate," and thus the "truly criminal," in the scientific, not moral, sense – but it would have to be "based on more reliable, tangible, and positive tests than the somewhat vague and uncertain theory of the forces of good and evil in man and their control by the spirit or the will."[38]

Thus, in the end Speranza chose science over free will in this particular context. The compromise he had recommended three years earlier regarding *assessment of responsibility* had given way to the exigencies of social defense against serious crime regarding *determination of treatment*. American penology, however, was to prove only partly responsive to the non-retributive social defense theorists – whether of the strictly utilitarian

---

[36] Gino C. Speranza, "The Survival of the Weakest as Exemplified in the Criminal," *American Law Register*, vol. 52 (1904): 159–66.

[37] Speranza, "Survival of the Weakest," 163, 165–66.

[38] Speranza, "Survival of the Weakest," 166. Speranza was by no means alone among lawyers in his views regarding penology. See, e.g., Charlton T. Lewis, "The Indeterminate Sentence," *Yale Law Journal*, vol. 9 (1899): 17–30, 27; see also Warner, "Some Aspects of the Indeterminate Sentence." Both Lewis and Warner were leading penologists.

or of the more treatment-oriented, scientific-positivist stripe. Progressive Era reforms were to reflect a mixture of new and traditional concepts of human behavior. Many Americans favored retention of capital punishment or long-term incarceration for serious felonies and were skeptical of the naïve optimism on display in the new system of probation, indeterminate sentences, and parole as it applied to less serious felonies; they resolutely held to a notion of retribution. Serious offenders – even incorrigibles – were morally evil persons who refused to obey the law and who therefore deserved the worst. In effect, there resulted a shaky alliance between those holding traditional views and the deterministic-social-defense theorists – an alliance of the sort that, in France, had created a "politics of social defense."[39] But this alliance was based solely on agreement regarding results, and only with respect to incorrigibles. With regard to treatable offenders, and with respect to the premises upon which criminal responsibility rested, the two camps could not have been farther apart.

Americans – or American society as a whole – took a middle road, mixing the rhetoric of social determinism with the language of free will and drawing lines accordingly, if irrationally. But it was primarily resistance to the new science and to its deterministic premises, I believe, that led Americans at large to reject a strictly therapeutic version of social defense. The scientific concept of the "incorrigible" would remain subject to question; relatively few convicts would be thought of in that way.[40] Most criminals, we seemed to believe, had chosen to do wrong and, if they possessed cognitive abilities, both deserved punishment and were probably reformable: under the right conditions, they would choose, freely, to do right. Although actual conditions of imprisonment typically made a mockery of our ideals, most Americans remained convinced that the inalienable "Anglo-Saxon" rights to freedom and due process required both the opportunity for rehabilitation within a system of reasonable punishment and constant adherence to the concept of free will. Whatever the social benefits, the social and personal costs of an openly deterministic social defense theory were too high. They

[39] See Robert A. Nye, *Crime, Madness, and Politics in Modern France: The Medical Concept of National Decline* (Princeton, NJ: Princeton University Press, 1984), 171–226.
[40] There were, however, sixteen states that passed some form of a sterilization law between 1907 and 1917, although most such laws were aimed at the insane or feebleminded even if they often included habitual criminals, drunkards, and sex offenders as well. See Haller, *Eugenics*, 133–41; see also Allen, *Decline*, 41 (referring to the eugenics movement as a whole, Allen notes that "for the first three decades of the present century [it] rivaled the rehabilitative ideal in its appeal to the educated and influential segments of the community"). Hovenkamp notes that between 1907 and 1926, twenty-three states enacted such sterilization laws ("Insanity and Criminal Responsibility," 563 n. 75). See also Kenneth M. Ludmerer, *Genetics and American Society* (Baltimore: Johns Hopkins University Press, 1972); and, for a brief retracing of American attitudes toward eugenics, criminal anthropology, and sterilization laws, see Lawrence M. Friedman, *Crime and Punishment in American History* (New York: Basic Books, 1993), 335–39.

offended both the prescript of political liberty against restraints imposed by
the state and the deeply held faith that human worth and free will were, in
the last analysis, one and the same.

More practical considerations also entered the mix. Progressive Era peni-
tentiaries had much less capacity to rehabilitate than their enthusiasts hoped
or expected. And, as I will touch on again in later chapters, this reality –
and its impact on both public perceptions and elite theory – would continue: more recent penologists have rejected indeterminate sentences as
ineffective and even fraudulent devices whereby many offenders are incarcerated far longer than they need or ought to be. Rather than reform and
achieve parole, many offenders quite predictably stagnate and remain under
lock and key. The position of rehabilitation's critics has been strengthened
through the colorable claim that, from the perspective of traditional principles of legal and human rights, the resulting long-term incarceration is
unjust. Thus, although criminal law has never fully recovered from the fin
de siècle critique launched by the new scientists, social disillusionment with
criminal justice administration has shadowed attempts at reform each step
of the way.[41]

FREE WILL AND THE JURY

But the post–Progressive Era crisis in penology is not the whole story. Less
noticed, perhaps, was the gradual de facto breakdown of the bifurcation of
trial and punishment on which the traditional concept of criminal responsibility had come to depend. The deterministic language of penology inevitably fed back into the earlier guilt determination stage of the criminal
process. Or so some commentators thought – including, as it happens,
Speranza, who was among the first to address the question of jury behavior
in this fashion. We do well to conclude our discussion of the fin de siècle
with a brief return to Speranza's writings, this time to his comments on the
criminal trial jury.

As I observed in the Introduction to this book, historically, the Anglo-
American jury exercised a significant degree of independence through
nullifying or "law finding" verdicts, which rejected some aspect of the formal law in favor of the jurors' view of justice in a particular case. The late-
nineteenth-century American jury rarely had a formal *right* to "find law."
Any such right certainly had been largely, if not quite entirely, rooted out

---

[41] See Allen, *Decline*, 32–34, 44–49. Allen provides a subtle assessment of the many kinds of
claims regarding the failure of rehabilitation attempts, and notes how modern supporters
of a "just deserts" doctrine have pointed to these failures in their criticism of the use of
long-term and indefinite incarceration (51–52, 57–58, 66–69). David Rothman discusses the
vicissitudes of modern penology, including the critique of the rehabilitative model, in "The
Crime of Punishment," *New York Review of Books*, February 17, 1994, 34.

of American jurisprudence across the middle decades of the nineteenth century.[42] Still, a limited power of nullification unavoidably remained: the jury's rights to find facts and apply the law of the state, combined with its right to finality in criminal cases ending in acquittal, undergirded a de facto power to "find law" and thus to skirt the formal law (at least in favor of the defendant). As the law-finding doctrine declined, some writers on the jury process turned their attention to the "science" of fact-finding, and in doing so they often criticized jurors as unintelligent, too sympathetic, or otherwise guided by their emotions.[43] For a time, optimistic reformism accompanied the endemic cynicism. Some commentators looked forward to a new era of jury deliberations characterized by rational decision making in accordance with existing legal rules.[44] But, by Speranza's day, doubts about the possibility of a truly rational jury process matched – or outweighed – optimistic impulses.

All the same, few lawyers responded favorably to some behaviorists' call for replacing the lay jury with a panel of "experts," even in legal insanity cases. Perhaps lawyers were coming to see the principles of the new science as even more threatening than the worst excesses of jury behavior. Indeed, it may be that some of the lay jury's most severe juristic critics still saw that institution as the last line of defense against the scientists' attack on the orthodox approach to criminal responsibility – that is, on the rule of law itself. Thus, although lawyers and scientists agreed that criminal process ought to be made more rational, and although both singled out the jury and the myriad "technicalities" of the law that recourse to the jury entailed as a prime site for reform, there were distinct limits to this area of agreement. If the two camps were destined to remain apart – especially regarding use of a lay jury to determine the issue of legal insanity – within the legal world

---

[42] The most comprehensive account of the demise of the law-finding doctrine remains Mark DeWolfe Howe, "Juries as Judges of Criminal Law," *Harvard Law Review*, vol. 52 (1939): 582–616. For discussion of the criminal trial jury in the late nineteenth and early twentieth centuries, see, e.g., Lawrence M. Friedman and Robert V. Percival, *The Roots of Justice: Crime and Punishment in Alameda County, California, 1870–1910* (Chapel Hill: University of North Carolina Press, 1981), 182–95; Albert W. Alschuler and Andrew G. Deiss, "A Brief History of the Criminal Jury in the United States," *University of Chicago Law Review*, vol. 61 (1994): 867–928; David Millon, "Juries, Judges, and Democracy," review of *The American Revolution in the Law: Anglo-American Jurisprudence before John Marshall*, by Shannon C. Stimson, *Law & Social Inquiry*, vol. 18 (1993): 154–57. See also Stanton D. Krauss, "An Inquiry into the Right of Criminal Juries to Determine the Law in Colonial America," *JCLC*, vol. 89 (1998): 111–214.

[43] On the (lack of) intelligence issue, see, e.g., "Trial by Jury," an unsigned comment from the *Chicago Legal News*, reprinted in *Albany Law Journal*, vol. 2 (1870): 159 ("Our jury quit their shops for the courts of justice; they march straight from the weighing of cheese to the weighing of testimony; from dealing in candles and bacon, to dealing with the lives, properties and liberties of men."). On the emotions of jurors, see, e.g., J. Kopelke, "Criminal Law Reform," *Albany Law Journal*, vol. 29 (1884): 148–49.

[44] E.g., Charles E. Grinnell, "Beyond a Reasonable Doubt," *Green Bag*, vol. 9 (1897): 97–102.

itself a similar form of disagreement was bound to make itself felt. The more "scientific" the jurist, the more the jury required reining in – but, then, only to a point. At that point, the more fundamental difference between lawyer and scientist kicked in.

Speranza's comments on the jury are scattered throughout his work. What mainly must be kept in mind is that, among lawyers, Speranza's attempt to make sense of de facto law-finding was unusual, for he spoke from the perspective of behavioral science. Like most true behavioral scientists, Speranza favored top-down reform; the conscience of the community had its place, but it could not bear the entire burden of remaking an outmoded and irrational process of criminal justice. His earliest remarks were conventional: like many others, lawyers and behavioral scientists alike, he criticized the "emotional and hysterical acquittals of persons guilty of taking the law into their own hands to avenge their honor." Speranza applied this criticism to his observation that there was a widespread "social complicity with crime" that undermined the principle of the social defense.[45] Yet, at some point – it is not clear just when – he came to see jury behavior as a response to new ideas, and in that sense as *positive,* albeit also as confused and born of frustration. He appears to have traveled a path that some others were taking during the first decade of our century, one that even some other lawyers trod, but – once again – his behaviorist and deterministic perspective led him to a solution that had both the virtue of consistency and the defect of total impracticality.

Speranza did not settle entirely for the generalities about misplaced "pity" or "sympathy" so common in the period. In his 1903 article "Criminality in Children," he appears to have taken a further step:

Careful study will show that the tenderness of the law in its provisions regarding special cases, and more especially the tenderness in its application in given cases, has its reason not so much in the unfitness of the punishment to the crime as in its unjust and unfair application to those who are not the real culprits. Thus the theft of bread is larceny, and larceny should be under the ban of the law; but the hungry man who steals a loaf would probably go free because the trial jurors would say: "It was not he who stole – but the Social Conditions that let him get hungry." And more clearly, if a child kills his playmate, the jury will almost instinctively attribute the child's malevolence to the indifference or maliciousness of the parents.[46]

Nearly a decade later, Speranza had begun – as had some others – to suggest even more clearly that jurors sometimes reflected progressive notions; they were not always simply, and habitually, "sympathetic" or "sentimental," but were occasionally ahead of the law in grappling with the social origins of

[45] Gino C. Speranza, "The Coefficients of Impunity," *American Law Register*, n.s. vol. 39 (1900): 647–55, 652–54.
[46] Gino C. Speranza, "Criminality in Children," *Green Bag*, vol. 15 (1903): 516–20, 516.

crime. In 1912, Speranza opened his brief essay "New Horizons in Penal Law"[47] with the assertion that "public opinion is growing restless over the administration of the criminal law." In noting that jurors registered this discontent he suggested: "The fact is that *the popular mind has come to make part of its convictions the reforms contended for by penologists for over a century* regarding the basic principles of the function of the state towards the criminal." But at times jurors, in exercising lay judgment, risked breaching social defenses. Thus did Speranza, in this, his final article on criminal responsibility, explain nonetheless how "reformers and laymen have, under the impulse of such discontent, carried their protest beyond just bounds, by extending sympathy where it was not deserved – resulting often in hysterical verdicts – and thereby exposing themselves to the just charge by conservatives of a desire to override the law."[48]

Speranza concluded with the observation that the "old saying that 'the punishment must fit the crime' is but the precursor of the modern principle that the discipline must fit the criminal"; if the fit was proper, "juries would not acquit against their oath." Presumably, absent the prevailing tension between their increasingly scientific understanding of crime and the traditional retributive approach to penology, jurors would accept the exigencies of the concept of the social defense. Speranza noted that "public opinion revolts against [an offender's] elimination by death," but opined that "it would approve perpetual exclusion from society in a penal colony."[49] In accord, he called for the "swift application of suitable discipline," which in most cases would be work.

> I call it discipline for want of a better word; for it is not punishment and it is not mercy, but a social means to a social end. Such end is that society shall be protected; and such protection modern penal law must attain by different means, varying from the simple fact of conviction, with no other penalty ... to the absolute elimination of the transgressor from society.[50]

Such "basic principles" of the "new penology" that Speranza invoked might, he said, be called "more humane," but he preferred to style them "more just because ... more rational."[51]

Speranza's insight was, of course, just that: his own way of understanding a form of jury behavior that might otherwise have been described, without more, as foolish sympathy. Nonetheless, there is reason to believe that Speranza – and a few other commentators – were not far off the mark. Indeed, from the perspective of our own day, it would be surprising if the

---

[47] Gino C. Speranza, "New Horizons in Penal Law," *Case and Comment*, vol. 18 (1912): 745–46.
[48] Speranza, "New Horizons in Penal Law," 745 (emphasis added).
[49] Speranza, "New Horizons in Penal Law," 746.
[50] Speranza, "New Horizons in Penal Law," 745.
[51] Speranza, "New Horizons in Penal Law," 745.

rhetoric of determinism had not gradually affected the understanding of society at large as popular journals, newspapers, and novels referred more and more to the factors that conditioned criminal behavior. One might conjecture that, increasingly across the decades of our century, the ritual of the trial stage has been thoroughly adulterated. We have gradually come to reflect our often subconscious ambivalence regarding the doctrine of mens rea, our underlying doubts about the criminal law's general presumption of free will. Although we know that rehabilitation rarely works, we accept much of the behavioral science analysis of crime and we thus often intuitively balk at assigning a full measure of guilt. Fortunately, we are not often tested in this way, as most cases end in guilty pleas on a "bargain": if the defendant "freely" chooses to plead guilty, doubts about her having freely chosen to commit the underlying offense are paved over – or simply not addressed.

For Speranza's part, he wrote little on the problem of criminal justice after 1904. His 1912 parting shot, "New Horizons in Penal Law," bears the influence of the widespread concern with penology of the early years of the American Institute of Criminal Law and Criminology, an organization in which Speranza played a minor official role from 1911 to 1913.[52] But the issues the young Speranza struggled with have, of course, remained central to criminal justice. And Speranza's advice in his 1901 paper – that "law is one of the humanities" – has proved prophetic. Proponents of a strictly scientific approach to criminal responsibility have made little impact upon the daily life of the law; attempts at a middle ground have dominated, melding the insights of behavioral science with a lawyer's perspective.

[52] Speranza served as chair of the Committee on Crime and Immigration. See *JCLC*, vol. 1 (1911): 680; *JCLC*, vol. 4 (1913): 523–27.

2

The Progressive Era: Pound

The AICLC and the 1909 Rapprochement

Gino Speranza's serious acknowledgment of determinist scientific principles – expressed *alongside* his informed dedication to a uniquely American concept of freedom – presaged the delicate task of balancing science and free will that legal practitioners and scholars would confront throughout the twentieth century (and beyond). Most immediately, as more legal thinkers accepted the potential relevance of progressive science to the law, support for a middle ground such as that envisioned by Speranza would soon reach a high point, particularly with regard to penological theory. The tensions and anxieties of the fin de siècle gave way to the more optimistic reformist perspective of high Progressivism, and to an attempt – albeit temporary – at rapprochement between scientist and lawyer.

Legal thinkers could not help being affected by the "scientific" ideas that lay all about them. If the great bulk of them affirmed ideas that were more or less compatible with the conventional understanding of criminal responsibility, many nonetheless followed the scientists' lead in approaching penology in decidedly behaviorist terms. The most famous manifestation of the early-twentieth-century program in criminal justice and the interchange between scientists and lawyers was the formation – by Roscoe Pound and others – of the AICLC in 1909.[1] The Institute's publication – the *Journal of*

---

[1] The AICLC was an outgrowth of the National Conference on Criminal Law and Criminology held in Chicago, June 1909. See American Institute of Criminal Law and Criminology, *Proceedings of the First National Conference on Criminal Law and Criminology* (Evanston, IL: Northwestern University, 1910) (hereafter *Proceedings*). For a brief discussion of the Chicago conference and the creation of the Institute, see James W. Garner, "Editorial Comment," *JCLC*, vol. 1 (1910): 2–5. See also David Wigdor, *Roscoe Pound: Philosopher of Law* (Westport, CT: Greenwood Press, 1974), 142–45.

the American Institute of Criminal Law and Criminology, later renamed the *Journal of Criminal Law and Criminology*[2] – aired all the leading issues of the day, matters of practice as well as more theoretical concerns. The work of the Institute was carried on primarily through committees,[3] whose endeavors intersected with national and state bar association committees, state legislative commissions, subgroups of medical and psychiatric associations, associations for prison reform, and state crime commissions. From these organizations there came a deluge of writings that, together with the state and municipal criminal justice surveys of the 1920s that Pound helped to organize, form the foundation for modern criminal justice scholarship.

Legal scholars and scientists addressed reforms at every level of the criminal justice system and shared a particular interest in the insanity defense, which occasioned some of the more intense debates about the proper overlap between science and law. Legal scholars and practitioners continued to seek reform of, but nonetheless to work within, the prevailing system of jury trial. In part, they were responding to the 1910 decision of the Supreme Court of the State of Washington in *State v. Strasburg*,[4] which invalidated legislation that abolished the insanity defense – and instead provided for post-conviction mental examination in cases in which state officials thought it appropriate – as an infringement of the constitutional right to a trial by jury. In reaching this decision, the *Strasburg* opinion commented along the way on the limited implications of the new criminological theory for the traditional social and legal concepts of guilt.[5] The movement for such

---

[2] The journal's title – which I consistently abbreviate as "*JCLC*" – was called the *Journal of Criminal Law, Criminology, and Police Science* during the period 1951–1972, after which it regained the name *Journal of Criminal Law and Criminology*.

[3] See *JCLC*, vol. 1 (1911): 677–82 (listing the various committees).

[4] *State v. Strasburg*, 110 P. 1020 (Wash. 1910).

[5] The Court held that, to "take from the accused the opportunity to offer evidence tending to prove [insanity] is in our opinion as much a violation of his constitutional right of trial by jury as to take from him the right to offer evidence before the jury tending to show that he did not physically commit the act." In arriving at its decision, the Court also addressed the "very able and ingenious argument" to the contrary, which was "based upon the seeming assumption that the modern humane treatment of those convicted of crime practically removes them from the realm of punishment" (*Strasburg*, 110 P. at 1024–25). The court quoted extensively from counsel's brief on this point:

"The central idea upon which the whole fabric of criminal jurisprudence was formerly built was the idea that every criminal act was the product of a free will possessing a full understanding of the difference between right and wrong and full capacity to choose a right or wrong course of action.... A better understanding of crime and the science of criminology now convinces us that this theory is wholly wrong – that a dominant percentage of all criminals are not free moral agents, but, as a result of hereditary influences or early environments, are either mentally or morally degenerate." (*id.* at 1025)

The brief, as quoted by the court, then asserted that older forms of punishment "are giving way to workhouses, reformatories, and asylums, the purpose of which is to instruct, educate, and reform rather than further to debase the individual, and the modern systems of criminal

legislation had reflected an odd marriage of interests among scientists; some jurists who considered the jurisprudence of insanity archaic; and many other jurists, politicians, and members of the public at large who sought to eliminate recourse to the "insanity dodge" via overly susceptible trial juries. After 1910, most legal scholars accepted the courts' negative responses to such radical reform as a fait accompli and adhered to the traditional common law understandings of defendants' rights, political liberty, and the concept of mens rea. At the same time, juristic criticism of the more egregious features of jury trial was intense.

But the potential still remained for a more deterministic legal-academic perspective on criminal responsibility – as distinct from penology – as was signaled by a brief but important flagship statement that appeared under the auspices of the AICLC. At the National Conference on Criminal Law and Criminology's 1909 Chicago meeting, the Conference resolved to establish a series of modern continental criminal-science studies in translation.[6] The committee charged with selecting and preparing the works was – more so than the Conference itself – dominated by legal academics, all from the "Chicago School." The Chair was John Henry Wigmore, Dean of the Northwestern School of Law, and under whose auspices the 1909 Conference had been held. Pound, who shortly after the conference migrated from Northwestern to the Chicago Law School, and his new colleague at Chicago, Ernst Freund, served under Wigmore – as did William Smithers of the Philadelphia-based

---

classification and segregation are themselves a recognition of the fact that every criminal is a concrete problem" (*id.*). The court responded:

The argument seems to be in its last analysis that, because of modern humane methods in caring for and treating those convicted of crime, there is no longer any reason for taking into consideration the element of will on the part of those who commit prohibited acts.... Learned counsel's premise suggests a noble conception, and may give promise of a condition of things towards which the humanitarian spirit of the age is tending; yet the stern and awful fact still remains, and is patent to all men, that the status and condition in the eyes of the world, and under the law, of one convicted of crime, is vastly different from that of one simply adjudged insane. We cannot shut our eyes to the fact that the element of punishment is still in our criminal laws. It is evidenced by the words "shall be punished." (*id.*)

One concurring opinion responded to the novel argument more abruptly:

The argument that persons are no longer punished for their crimes is illusory and unsound.... The man who is deprived of his liberty is also punished, and you cannot change the fact by changing the name.... [W]hy should we attempt to uphold the statute on humane grounds, when it is an apparent and palpable attempt on the part of the Legislature to punish those whom it fears the tribunal created by the Constitution will acquit? (*id.* at 1027, Rudkin, C.J., concurring)

This discussion bears an obvious relationship to the issues raised by the General Introduction to AICLC Modern Criminal Law Series, discussed later in this chapter.

[6] See *Proceedings*, 16–17, 204, 219.

American Bar Association (ABA), and two non-jurists, the sociologist Maurice Parmelee and Robert Scott, a political scientist.

The Committee's "General Introduction,"[7] which appeared in all of the Series publications until the late teens, was behaviorist in tone and substance. But just how deterministic was it? Its language, not uncommon among the progressive jurist caste of the 1910s, was that of negotiation and compromise; its generally positivist approach to the free will problem nonetheless preserved a basis for something like the traditional notion of criminal responsibility. Yet this was not a clear revival of the true compatibilism that had arisen in earlier Anglo-American theory[8] and that was present, but comparatively rare, in turn-of-the-century America.[9] Rather, the General Introduction may be read, in places, as irresolvably ambiguous, and thus it stands as a testament to the opacity of all but the most explicit early-twentieth-century juristic ideas regarding criminal responsibility.

The General Introduction began with a rehearsal of the early path of medical science, in which conceptions of the causes of disease and notions of treatment were primitive and undifferentiated. Modern medical science progressed by recognizing the individual characteristics of different diseases. "The same truth," the Committee stated, "is now known about crime; but the understanding and the application of it are just opening upon us."

---

[7] "General Introduction to the Modern Criminal Science Series" in, e.g., Raymond Saleilles, *The Individualization of Punishment*, trans. Rachel Szold Jastrow (Boston: Little, Brown, 1911), v–ix (hereafter "General Introduction").

[8] See Thomas Hobbes, *Leviathan*, introd. by A. D. Lindsay (New York: Dutton, 1950), chap. 21, "Of the Liberty of Subjects" (originally published 1651); David Hume, "Of Liberty and Necessity," in *A Treatise of Human Nature*, ed. David Fate Norton and Mary J. Norton (New York: Oxford University Press, 2000), bk. 2, pt. 3, sec. 1–2 (originally published 1739); David Hume, "Of Liberty and Necessity," in *An Enquiry Concerning Human Understanding*, ed. Tom L. Beauchamp (New York: Oxford University Press, 1999), sec. 8 (originally published 1748).

[9] Some early-twentieth-century legal thinkers indeed appeared to embrace a more complete compatibilist stance, allowing for a comparatively unworried affirmation of criminal responsibility – and, often, of a notion of "free will" itself – alongside scientific determinism. Perhaps the most significant strain of such thinking was represented by Edward Lindsey, a member of the Pennsylvania Bar (as well as of the American Anthropological Society) and an Associate Editor of the newly founded *JCLC*. Lindsey published an article in the first volume of the *JCLC* in which he stated: "An act of free-will is as much determined by conditions as any other event, but the decisive factor in an act of free-will is not any extraneous circumstances, but the character of the acting person. To state it briefly, we define free-will as a will unimpeded by compulsion." Edward Lindsey, "Penal Responsibility and Free-Will," *JCLC*, vol. 1 [1910]: 695–97, 696. Lindsey drew on a recent article by Dr. Paul Carus, "Person and Personality," *Monist*, vol. 20 (1910): 364–401. "Dr. Carus," wrote Lindsey, "thus clearly shows that we need give up neither our notions of causality nor of freedom of will" ("Penal

The old and still dominant thought is, as to cause, that a crime is caused by the inscrutable moral free will of the human being, doing or not doing crime, just as it pleases; absolutely free in advance, at any moment of time, to choose or not to choose the criminal act and therefore in itself the sole and ultimate cause of crime. As to treatment, there still are just two traditional measures, used in varying doses for all kinds of crime and all kinds of persons, – jail, or a fine (for death is now employed in rare cases only).[10]

The modern approach by contrast would recognize that crime, like medical disease, has "natural causes, – that is, circumstances which work to produce it in a given case." Thus the Committee characterized the prevailing *legal* view regarding the causes of crime as an absolutist version of the concept of free will and appealed instead to the "natural causes" that "work to produce" crime. Although the Committee quite self-consciously, and almost adamantly, stated, "it need not be asserted for one moment that crime is a disease,"[11] it accommodated the notion that crime was the product of deterministic "natural causes."

Certainly the Committee's recommendation for studying the causes of crime left little scope for human freedom, at least on the part of those who were criminals. In calling for "new efficient measures" in dealing with offenders, it insisted on the collection of "all the possible data that can be causes of crime, – the man's heredity, the man's physical and moral make-up, his emotional temperament, the surroundings of his youth, his present home, and other conditions, – all the influencing circumstances." And it prescribed the study and comparison of "different methods of treatment, old or new, for different kinds of men and of causes." It further compared American criminal law unfavorably with European practice – because of the American public's conservatism and the legal profession's myopia.[12]

The Committee glided over the questions inherent in the use of such individualization, however, including whether it ultimately rendered the law a mere instrument of non-retributive social defense – itself a euphemism for "repression" – or of "benevolent" cure in the offender's and the social interest. Just as significantly, could not the Committee's seeming message of non-responsibility actually undermine the social defense by preaching a sermon that would weaken the resolve of potential offenders? Or could the focus on the offender rather than society at large lead to early release of "cured" offenders and thus detract from the general deterrent capacity of criminal administration? Might a retreat from harsh punishment – even were it replaced with "benign" long-term incarceration – itself be a potential "cause" of criminal behavior?

Responsibility," 696). As we shall see, such affirmative compatibilism received little explicit attention in the writings of criminal justice scholars until its revival in the 1970s.
[10] "General Introduction," vi.
[11] "General Introduction," vii.
[12] "General Introduction," vi–vii.

Over the course of the Progressive Era, such questions increasingly challenged the rapprochement of 1909. In part they resulted from the Great War and its immediate aftermath, which saw heightened concern with crime and national security. But they were also the product of the intensive study by psychologists and penologists of incarcerated offenders; the results of such studies, allegedly revealing large numbers of "insane" and "feeble-minded," held challenging implications both for traditional approaches to guilt assessment and for hopes of addressing crime through successful treatment or examination of social conditions.[13] The growing importance of psychiatry further intensified conflict between lawyers and behaviorists. Even those lawyers disposed to view criminal behavior as determined increasingly concluded that the psychiatric school undermined the social defense. In its own ambiguity, the General Introduction to the Modern Criminal Science Series papered over the competing strains of Progressivism, as represented by the varying perspectives of individual criminal justice scholars. The General Introduction was, after all, written by a committee. More to the point, it was written by a legal culture at war with itself.

Private Law and Pound

The deterministic rhetoric of the Progressive Era, then, made inroads on the presumption of free will in the criminal context, portraying *will* and *context* in constant competition. But an examination of contemporary noncriminal jurisprudence further reveals determinism's only tenuous grip on American legal thought. Deterministic criminal jurisprudence had originally come from outside the legal academy and had penetrated it in more than a modest way, while accommodating a residuum of the traditional concept of mens rea and a freedom-affirming view of the rehabilitated offender. With respect to noncriminal jurisprudence, the implications of deterministic thought seem to have played out rather differently. In that context, a more conventional message of Progressivism held sway, one that largely avoided the tensions and darker themes of Progressive Era criminal justice. Here, the vanguard of the new, anti-classical jurisprudence – from Pound's early sociological jurisprudence down to the realism of the 1920s and early 1930s – more comfortably adopted

---

[13] On this point, note George Kirchwey's 1918 President's Address to the AICLC. Kirchwey had been Dean of Columbia Law School, then warden at Sing Sing. In his address, Kirchwey told his audience about Dr. Bernard Glueck's studies in Sing Sing:

> Of the population of Sing Sing prison apparently nearly 60 per cent ... were not normal, were either abnormal or subnormal, half of them probably mentally defective in such degree as to be practically irresponsible, twelve years of age and under mentally; the other half divided unevenly between those whom the psychiatrist classes as psychopathic and those whom he classes as insane, were all of them either continuously or occasionally quite irresponsible for their acts. In other words – let us be conservative – upwards of one-half of the population of Sing Sing prison is made up of persons who are *non compos*. They should not

a relativistic approach to human autonomy. As in criminal jurisprudential writing, the enemy was an exaggerated view of autonomy. In the context of private law, however, jurists conceived the problem in light of the perceived imbalances in bargaining power in the marketplace and in society at large. Given this crucial difference in setting, the remedy, reflected in writings both on private law and on the main currents of constitutional doctrine, was an adjustment of the balance of power among individuals or between individuals and collective entities. Noncriminal jurisprudence focused, then as now, more directly on the problem of equality of opportunity than on the problem of free will per se.[14]

The modern critique of criminal law in the main preceded that of private law. Although the latter, too, had roots in the late nineteenth century,[15] it did not become widespread until the 1910s and 1920s, by which time the late-nineteenth-century behavioral and medical science attack on the principles that underlay criminal law already had led to movements for juvenile justice and reform in penology, intense conflict regarding the insanity test, and some tellingly defensive commentary regarding the concept of mens rea. The critique of private law, by contrast, began early but matured slowly, largely out of attempts to limit the reach of private law concepts as they were embedded in constitutional law. In its origins, this critique of private law bears significant relation to the attack on traditional concepts of criminal responsibility. But outside of criminal law, the critique of human freedom

be held responsible by the law for their acts on the presumed ground of their capacity to choose between the right and the wrong. ("President's Address," 333–34)

[14] The point I want most to make is that a gentler – and perhaps the *true* – spirit of Progressivism informed the early *private* law–based critique of classical jurisprudence. Like most of the reform projects of the day, this side of sociological jurisprudence called for direct confrontation with the facts of social existence and a flexible, efficient use and manipulation of the environment (both physical and mental) to make good on America's promise of (relatively) equal opportunity for personal autonomy and development. Like other programs, it viewed governmental institutions as instrumental, recognizing their creative shaping power; it rationalized this reforming role for institutions as a necessary counterforce to those aspects of social and economic life that distorted, corrupted, or suppressed fundamental American values. This mainstream Progressivism – and sociological jurisprudence as well – was founded on a soft, albeit definite form of behaviorism. It recognized the fragility of the human will and the limitations on autonomy in a complex industrial society. In general, and in the context of private law, Progressivism emerged as the first wave of modern revisionism; it was dedicated to using the new sciences as instruments for recovering the *old* values, to optimistic and only very partial exploitation of the techniques of science, and to systemic repression of the new scientists' bleak implicit message. The drift within Progressivism toward a harsher, more deterministic social control ethic – as in the case of some forms of penology – was a drift out of the mainstream, and perhaps in its most "progressive" forms, out of Progressivism altogether. For an excellent treatment of Progressivism (which is not responsible for the tenor of my own brief account), see Daniel T. Rodgers, "In Search of Progressivism," *Reviews in American History*, vol. 10 (1982): 113–32.

[15] See Morton J. Horwitz, *The Transformation of American Law, 1870–1960: The Crisis of Legal Orthodoxy* (New York: Oxford University Press, 1992): 33–143.

was always somewhat muted and emerged more clearly from economics, sociology, and political science than from behavioral and medical science.[16]

Traditionally, many jurists and scholars had come to see the rights to liberty, property, and freedom of contract as natural to man, in the sense of fitting his own purposes and inclinations. Many thus unavoidably saw human nature and potential as bound up with the phenomena of human reason, autonomy, and enjoyment of the fruits of the free exercise of human faculties. Some found Spencer's social Darwinism plausible: human development and competition accorded with nature's inevitable sorting out of the fit from the unfit, so interference with natural processes was socially regressive. Others may have continued to believe that God intended man to be an autonomous and self-realizing being. Still others, no doubt, saw social and economic well-being and productivity as the beneficiaries of this autonomy-based conception of human nature and activity. Most jurists indulged a combination of these notions, a curious blend that made classical jurisprudence complicated and compelling.[17]

[16] For an important account of late-nineteenth and early-twentieth-century developments regarding deterministic perspectives in the social sciences, see Thomas L. Haskell, *The Emergence of Professional Social Science: The American Social Science Association and the Nineteenth-Century Crisis of Authority* (Urbana: University of Illinois Press, 1977), 234–56. My point here is that those private law jurists who were influenced by developments in the social sciences seem not to have moved beyond episodic concern with aspects of environmental causation to holistic conclusions of a deterministic sort.

[17] Noncriminal classical jurisprudence of the late nineteenth century was, of course, more epiphenomenal than often appears from conventional historical accounts. It did give heightened emphasis to general tendencies of mind, and thus it provided a target for critics oriented toward the social context of individual thought and action. But today we see classical jurisprudence through the lens of, among others, Holmes, who exaggerated formalism in order to set off his own deeply skeptical views. See Mathias W. Reimann, "Holmes's *Common Law* and German Legal Science," in *The Legacy of Oliver Wendell Holmes, Jr.*, ed. Robert W. Gordon (Stanford, CA: Stanford University Press, 1992), 72–114. Pound, too, may have exaggerated the typicality of classical jurisprudence – but largely because, by nature, he simplified matters in order to think more clearly about them. He still aptly epitomized the main thrust of the conventional legal thought of his day and, indeed, nicely mocked the often-unstated assumptions of fin de siècle jurists and legal academics. His prewar writings evidenced a refreshing candor about the jurisprudence of the times – and a degree of simplification on his part does not suggest he was anything but a learned, wise, and important legal scholar. His historical and philosophical writings were perhaps overly schematic, but his reach was impressive – even extraordinary – and he used his ability to create schemas and taxonomies to good advantage. For relevant accounts of Pound, see James E. Herget, *American Jurisprudence, 1870–1970: A History* (Houston, TX: Rice University Press, 1990), 164–70; Paul Sayre, *The Life of Roscoe Pound* (Iowa City: State University of Iowa, 1948), 312–80; Wigdor, *Roscoe Pound*; N. E. H. Hull, "Reconstructing the Origins of Realistic Jurisprudence: A Prequel to the Llewellyn-Pound Exchange over Legal Realism," *Duke Law Journal*, vol. 1989 (1989): 1302–34, 1306–11; G. Edward White, "From Sociological Jurisprudence to Realism: Jurisprudence and Social Change in Early Twentieth-Century America," *Virginia Law Review*, vol. 58 (1972): 999–1028, 1004–12. For a valuable discussion of the complexities of "Victorian Legal Thought," see Daniel R. Ernst, "The Critical Tradition in the Writing of American Legal History," review of *The Transformation of American Law, 1870–1960:*

By Pound's day this worldview had encountered searching criticism for several decades from political scientists, sociologists, and historians, among others; most of the attack had not been aimed at the law, as such.[18] Pound contributed to this scholarship by deploying the new criticism in his attack on classical formalism.[19] He styled his foray "sociological jurisprudence," and indeed established himself as the leading exponent of the subject; his 1908–1909 essays, "Mechanical Jurisprudence"[20] and "Liberty of Contract,"[21] lay at the cutting edge of the legal-academic Progressive critique of the formalism and the exaggerated view of human autonomy deemed prevalent in noncriminal classical jurisprudence. He attacked on two fronts: first on the obsession with formal rights at the constitutional level that, as he saw it, rationalized the striking down of social legislation on grounds that such legislation limited autonomy in the domains of property and contract; and second, on the Langdellian formalism in private law that gave unrealistic primacy to the ideal of autonomy. In reality, Pound parried, man was a social being: his actual autonomy was relative to his social context; any fair-minded attempt to accord all people some semblance of their basic rights required constant attention to their social situation.

That Pound wrote extensively in both noncriminal and criminal jurisprudence made him a rare bird in his day. It is perhaps instructive that he brought differing emphases to bear on his concern about human freedom in the two domains. In his criminal law writings, to which scholars have paid scant attention, Pound gave significantly greater emphasis to his skepticism regarding the concept of free will – which in itself says something important about the difference between the two fields of concern. Yet even in his criminal justice studies, at the cost of coherence – and by skating on the surface – Pound fashioned a relatively untroubled accommodation of the

The Crisis of Legal Orthodoxy, by Morton J. Horwitz, *Yale Law Journal*, vol. 102 (1993): 1019–76, 1037–46.

[18] See, generally, Haskell, *Emergence of Professional Social Science*; James T. Kloppenberg, *Uncertain Victory: Social Democracy and Progressivism in European and American Thought, 1870–1920* (New York: Oxford University Press, 1986); Dorothy Ross, *The Origins of American Social Science* (Cambridge: Cambridge University Press, 1991), 53–142; Morton White, *Social Thought in America: The Revolt against Formalism* (Boston: Beacon Press, 1957), 11–106. White focuses on the law on pages 59–75, using Holmes as a link between the larger, non-juristic movements and the beginning of a juristic critique.

[19] David M. Rabban, *Law's History: American Legal Thought and the Transatlantic Turn to History* (New York: Cambridge University Press, 2013), superbly details the widespread and non-formalist historical approach taken by many leading legal academics of the "Classical Era." He shows that Pound's portrayal of the historical school was superficial at best and often misleading or inaccurate. See, esp., pp. 430–32. Pound's more plausible targets were discrete examples of judicial formalism that emptied out the complexities of contemporary legal-academic scholarship.

[20] Roscoe Pound, "Mechanical Jurisprudence," *Columbia Law Review*, vol. 8 (1908): 605–23.

[21] Roscoe Pound, "Liberty of Contract," *Yale Law Journal*, vol. 18 (1909): 454–87.

determinist critique; he envisioned fundamental change over the long term and settled, in the short run, for reforms that mixed discordant elements. Throughout the remainder of the century, criminal law scholars concerned with the free will problem would attempt to sort out many of the same questions that Pound faced – indeed that Pound helped to define. Some would take up the charge to reduce over time the discordance he identified within the law's aims and methods through incremental reform. Others, we might say, sought through theory to redefine the supposed discordance, and thus to bring a semblance of philosophical unity to the law as it traditionally existed even in the face of lingering doubts about free will.

POUND'S EARLY CRIMINAL LAW SCHOLARSHIP: 1905–1915

Pound's criminal law writings, from almost the fin de siècle down to his 1923 Colver lectures – which were delivered at Brown University and published, with only slight revisions, seven years later as *Criminal Justice in America*[22] – repay consideration because they reflect the thinking of a moderate realist of pronounced social science bent, a *juristic* Progressive of large vision. Pound's criminal law jurisprudence – as it evolved across the Progressive Era – reveals those understandings of history, politics, and society that reflected the tensions that one of the most influential and widely read early-twentieth-century academic common lawyers experienced regarding the interrelated problems of political liberty and free will. In retracing Pound's steps over two decades, we witness the final – yet, as we shall see, inconclusive – act of the fin de siècle drama with which we began.

Pound, like Speranza, was a lawyer. But whereas Speranza had fully embraced a version of the behavioral science theory of his day, Pound (although originally trained as a botanist) remained a jurist through and through. Still, Pound – here a true Progressive – resisted the idea of an unbridgeable gulf between the law and science. If Pound perceived the most intractable problems that the new science presented, he chose to avert his gaze; for the most part, he tended to write as though they did not exist.[23]

---

[22] Roscoe Pound, *Criminal Justice in America* (New York: H. Holt, 1930).

[23] This is at least mainly the case, as my study of Pound will suggest. See also Sheldon Glueck, "A Memoir in Appreciation of the Dean of American Legal Scholars," in *Roscoe Pound and Criminal Justice*, ed. Sheldon Glueck (Dobbs Ferry, NY: Oceana Publications, 1965). Glueck provides a comprehensive overview of Pound's criminal justice writings, covering many areas that I do not treat. He correctly notes that Pound paid little attention to the substantive law, noting that "he left to others the baffling issue of mixing the oil of ethically based 'responsibility' with the water of science-influenced determinism" (23). For two other discussions of the general characteristics of Pound's approach to criminal justice, see John Griffiths, "Ideology in Criminal Procedure, or, a Third 'Model' of the Criminal Process, *Yale Law Journal*, vol. 79 (1970): 359–417, 391–95; Louis H. Masotti and Michael A. Weinstein, "Theory and Application of Pound's Sociological Jurisprudence: Crime Prevention or Control?," *Prospectus*, vol. 2 (1969): 431–50.

Also like Speranza, Pound believed that the Anglo-American tradition had spawned a concept of rights that was artificial but highly useful as a brake on the overweening power of the state. Pound produced a mini-history, from classical times forward, into which the Anglo-American experience neatly fit. The history of the West, he asserted, exemplified a cyclical pattern. Periods characterized by the unrestrained and arbitrary power of the state were followed by periods that saw an accent on the rights of the individual. Nineteenth-century America, in the second part of the cycle, celebrated a concept of natural rights founded, in part, on a reception of English resistance theory, itself a reaction against the royalist hegemony of the preceding centuries. Such ideas accorded well with our own early political and social experience, or what Pound termed our "pioneer attitude"[24]: freedom-loving Americans manifesting individualism in their desire to govern themselves, to take law into their own hands, to shake off the yoke of common law formalities.

For Speranza, the century's turn was the new age of behavioral science, whose methods and concepts directly countered the free will–based ideas of the nineteenth century. For Pound, at least well into the 1920s, the new age was the age of collectivism; the demands of modern life made the nineteenth-century concept of individualism, to put it mildly, an inconvenience. But Pound, unlike Speranza, looked mainly to sociology and political science, rather than to behavioral and medical science, perhaps as a result of his early focus on noncriminal law. Pound understood that behavioral and medical scientists had attacked – he came to say they had "routed" – the concept of free will in criminal law. But he paid only intermittent and relatively minor attention to that fact, from which, as we shall see, he never drew truly deep or disturbing conclusions. It did not blunt his optimistic belief that law and science were ultimately headed in the same direction. For Pound, scientific notions were functional, instructive – the keys to administrative efficiency. Science was above all a means to mediate between the individual and the collective order. The new learning made plain that the reification of rights in common law theory – as well as their constitutionalization in some important instances – threatened paralysis and threatened to undermine the position of those individuals whose social and economic circumstances rendered their possession of those "rights" a cruel artifice.[25] Yet, as he would comment in 1920, in "The Future of the Criminal Law,"[26] the age also witnessed a drift back in the direction of unrestrained authority; once again, insistence on "individual freedom" and on individual rights,

---

[24] Pound, *Criminal Justice in America*, 132.
[25] See, generally, Pound, "Liberty of Contract."
[26] Roscoe Pound, "The Future of the Criminal Law," *Columbia Law Review*, vol. 21 (1921): 1–16 (from an address delivered before the semicentennial session of the American Prison Congress in October 1920).

in the form of the procedural guarantees of the *criminal law,* had to be maintained up to a point, in order to achieve the proper balance.

What, then, of the new behavioral science? Pound repeatedly rejected the essentials of what he called the "orthodox" common law theory of crime: the retributive theory, the necessary joinder of act and intent, and the notion that the offender had possessed free will. But Pound never spelled out an alternative system of criminal justice, aware that dismantling the orthodox approach posed dangers for political liberty. He deferred problems to the future, seeking temporary refuge in the bifurcation of trial and penology. Too much the jurist to follow the implications of the free will critique to their logical ends, he adopted his own middling position, one that recognized offenders were at least largely the product of social or other determining conditions, but that sought to accommodate this perspective within the existing system. He urged a de-emphasis of the concept of individualism and, above all, a reform of legal institutions. That reform, together with a gradual erosion of the doctrine *and practice* of retribution, would, Pound thought, cure the worst infirmities of criminal law and its administration while allowing for retention of necessary protections against the state. If tensions remained, they would disappear in time, as law accommodated itself to developments in science. The underlying theory of crime would itself eventually be reformed – the assumption that the offender possessed a truly free will would disappear – but the rest of the criminal law would evolve from reforms already under way. The administration of criminal justice would change, perhaps dramatically, but it would remain in its essentials the administration of justice by jurists and as jurists understood it.

The logic of Pound's reformist position would be clear in 1909, when he reviewed Maurice Parmelee's well-known *Principles of Anthropology and Sociology in Their Relation to Criminal Procedure*.[27] But before examining Pound's remarks in that year, I turn my attention to a series of articles from 1905 to 1908 in which Pound had already marked out a distinctive position on the state of criminal justice administration in America.[28] Pound's 1903 *Outlines of Lectures on Jurisprudence* reflects both his interest in Thomas

---

[27] Maurice Parmelee, *The Principles of Anthropology and Sociology in Their Relations to Criminal Procedure* (New York: Macmillan, 1908).

[28] Pound's earliest criminal law writings reveal the influence of his student days and of his early teaching and practice in Nebraska, where he was attentive to problems of procedure that he always understood as more than matters of machinery. He quickly saw the interplay between judge and jury and the manner in which each filled out the law on the books. See Wigdor, *Roscoe Pound*, 98–99. From his legal education at Harvard under the tutelage of John Chipman Gray he absorbed an appreciation of the judge's lawmaking role (89), and in his Nebraska professorial capacity – through exposure to, among others, the prominent sociologist Edward Ross – he developed his understanding of the social importance of creative exploitation of the judge's role (111–13). Frontline practice, mostly in the private law arena, taught him the subtleties of jury-based law-finding.

Holland's *Elements of Jurisprudence* and, perhaps more importantly, his attraction to Sheldon Amos's discourse on criminal law.[29] Amos contributed a modern perspective on criminal jurisprudence, including elements that folded over easily into the embryonic sociological jurisprudence that Pound borrowed from fashionable German legal scholarship.[30] But Amos influenced Pound in other ways as well: in lengthy passages that Pound prescribed for his students,[31] Amos preached the necessity of a fit between the mandate and theory of the law and deep-seated social norms. Nowhere was this more important than in criminal law. As Pound saw it, sometimes this meant legal reform could proceed only so fast; sometimes it meant devices were required to correct for the inflexibility of law. But the attention to the necessity of creating a "fit" was always present. This strain of thought ran through Pound's publications during his Nebraska days – down to 1907 – and thereafter, through his final days in the mid-1960s at Langdell Hall.[32]

To his earliest criminal law work, then, Pound brought the same elements that have been studied by scholars of his noncriminal jurisprudence. The extraction of Pound's specific ideas on criminal jurisprudence from his more general frameworks of sociological jurisprudence, organicism, instrumentalism, and Progressivism works some scholarly injustice, but helps in the task of retracing Pound's thinking about the role of freedom in American *criminal* justice. In any case, one has to sneak up on the issue of freedom in Pound, for that, in a sense, is the route he himself took. He rarely focused on the issue systematically. Rather, he most often resorted to anecdotal accounts of actual on-the-ground experience to make his points about the role of the ideal of human agency in the description and assessment of the law in practice. From a historically and sociologically informed empiricism, one in which the issue of freedom – first political liberty, later free will – played an increasingly important role, Pound drew his observations and prescriptions.

[29] Roscoe Pound, *Outlines of Lectures on Jurisprudence, Chiefly from the Analytical Standpoint* (Lincoln, NE: Jacob North, 1903), 66 (noting Thomas Erskine Holland, *The Elements of Jurisprudence*, and Sheldon Amos, *The Science of Law*).

[30] See James E. Herget, "The Influence of German Thought on American Jurisprudence, 1880–1918," in *The Reception of Continental Ideas in the Common Law World, 1820–1920*, ed. Mathias Reimann (Berlin: Duncker and Humblot, 1993), 203, 215, 221–23.

[31] Pound, *Outlines*, 66.

[32] Paul Carrington notes that Dean Wigmore enticed Pound to leave his post at Nebraska and come to Northwestern, where Wigmore encouraged his criminal justice reform scholarship and where Pound organized the 1909 national conference on criminal law and criminology ("Missionary Diocese," 503–11). Pound was active as well outside the law school, having joined various interdisciplinary organizations. But, in 1909, much to Wigmore's dismay, Pound accepted a position at the University of Chicago Law School, probably in order to gain greater access to the likes of John Dewey, Ernst Freund, Hull House's Jane Addams, and the prominent sociologist Albion Woodbury Small, his recent collaborators. Pound put these credentials and connections to good use. He leapt into the vanguard of the national campaign for judicial law reform.

From his first essay on criminal jurisprudence in 1905, Pound associated popular discontent concerning both private and criminal law with the American adversary system's "exaggerated respect for the individual."[33] In light of the widening gulf between the law and contemporary attitudes – resulting from a period of dramatic social change that spawned diverse interests and conflicting groups – the existing law's focus on "individualism" could no longer achieve "justice." That is, it could not "adjust the relations of every man with his fellows so as to accord with the moral sense of the community." When law fails, the "individual looks at cases one by one and measures them by his individual sense of right and wrong";[34] juries were tempted into ad hoc, extra-legal decision making. Pound's remedy for this problem appeared initially in his 1907 article, "The Need of a Sociological Jurisprudence." The article asserted that a widespread disrespect for law engendered "appeals to the so-called unwritten law ... appeals from the clear and settled law to the individual feelings of the citizen."[35] But Pound considered these antinomian attitudes temporary, the consequence of a period of social upheaval. In articles published in 1908, he optimistically asserted that, once stability returned, the judicial process would again be a bedrock of law rather than an opportunity for lawlessness.[36] During the transition (echoes of Speranza), jury behavior was unpredictable for a reason: "Juries are conscious that the law in some way does not accord with the general sense of right, and find verdicts which are crude attempts to vindicate half-grasped conceptions of social justice."[37]

On the whole, however, Pound was ambivalent about the role of the jury, as was evident in his most comprehensive prewar study of criminal administration, "Inherent and Acquired Difficulties in the Administration of Punitive Justice," a speech delivered to the American Political Science Association in December 1907 and published the following year.[38] There,

---

[33] Roscoe Pound, "Do We Need a Philosophy of Law?" *Columbia Law Review*, vol. 5 (1905): 339–53, 346–47.

[34] Roscoe Pound, "The Causes of Popular Dissatisfaction with the Administration of Justice," in *Report of the Twenty-Ninth Annual Meeting of the American Bar Association* (Philadelphia: Dando Printing and Publishing, 1906), 399.

[35] Roscoe Pound, "The Need of a Sociological Jurisprudence," *Green Bag*, vol. 19 (1907): 607–15, 607.

[36] Pound claimed that

this friction between ethical and sociological theory and legal theory is a temporary phenomenon. When the shifting to the new standard of justice is accomplished, when education and the labors of sociologists have brought about the internal conditions of life measured by reason, the judicial machine will run normally once more and law will speedily take care of the external conditions. (Roscoe Pound, "Enforcement of Law," *Green Bag*, vol. 20 [1908]: 401–10, 403)

[37] Pound, "Enforcement of Law," 403.

[38] Roscoe Pound, "Inherent and Acquired Difficulties in the Administration of Punitive Justice," in *Proceedings of the American Political Science Association*, vol. 4 (Baltimore: Waverly Press, 1908), 222–39.

he expressed regret concerning the "extravagant power conceded to juries," but conceded that, given the absence of a codified criminal law, juries – quite humanly – "[took] the law into their own hands." The popular sense of a derailment in the justice system translated into a popular call for greater efficiency. For Pound, however, the "inefficiency" was less the result of administrative breakdown than of the tension between the need for reform and popular retributivist assumptions. He noted that the "public desire for vengeance" was deep-seated and that juristic commentators were divided between those who sided with "moralists or sociologists" in their condemnation of it and those who regarded it "as a legitimate as well as practically necessary end." Pound conceded that "to prevent self-help and to meet the demands of the moral sentiment of the community, it is necessary to retain much that is purely retributive." But, he added, this same emotion played havoc with the administration of criminal justice, producing serious inconsistencies: "One jury is stern, applies the revenge theory as like as not; another is soft-hearted. And so the fact that *we are not all agreed, nor all of us in all our moods, upon the end of punishment,* infects both legislation and administration with uncertainty, inconsistency, and in consequence, inefficiency."[39]

These insights went to the heart of Pound's account – indeed, they governed it perhaps more than he himself realized. They bridged "inherent difficulties" – such as the desire for revenge, the problems of controlling the inevitable need for discretion, and the ties between criminal law and politics – with "acquired difficulties," which were at once embedded in our inherited common law adversary system and given a special turn by the American historical experience. Americans' attraction to natural law theory and ultra-individualism flowed from our resistance to English legal and political oppression. This latter resistance to governing magistrates exacerbated common law "jealousy" of legislation, procedural complexity and delays, and, most important, the exaltation of juries over judges that interfered with efficient, accurate, and consistent administration of criminal justice. Pound understood that the ("inherent") retributive theory was related to the ("acquired") unbridled powers of the American jury, but he sketched the essentials of that relationship in only vague terms. We must abandon the retributive theory, he now counseled – adding almost derisively that it was "taught as among the *fundamental* of law."[40] He predicted that "general improvement will come through better general education in sociology,

---

[39] Pound, "Inherent and Acquired Difficulties," 225–27, 232 (emphasis added). As my emphasis is meant to indicate, I read this statement as poignant and self-revelatory, not as one of Pound's commonplace observations. I sense that it reflects a lifelong personal perspective that Pound normally did not allow to rise to the surface in his writing.

[40] Pound, "Inherent and Acquired Difficulties," 230–35.

leading the public to abandon the retributive idea and the man in the street to desist from his demand for revenge."[41]

Pound nonetheless remained vague about what the "retributive idea" involved. As to free will and the conventional doctrine of mens rea, he was almost silent. Although he opposed the requirement of intent as an element – particularly for many statutory offenses – his opposition appears essentially instrumental; it does not appear to have been a direct rejection of retributivism's inherent acceptance of the relevance of intent.[42] Rather, the intent requirement forestalled attempts at rational social control. Further, if Pound believed the intent requirement was premised on a false conception of human behavior, he had not said so. He may have accepted the criminologist's view that "'crime [was] a disease'"[43] and assumed his audience would understand all of the implications of that view. But his chief point was that sociological and criminological education would stem the desire for revenge and so make possible rational and efficient procedures for determination of responsibility as well as intelligent and effective means for reforming convicted offenders. Pound sought a rational, sociologically informed ordering between liberty and social needs, but not – at least not explicitly – an entire rejection of the conventional notion of mens rea or a retreat to a system of criminal justice premised upon a deterministic theory of the social defense. It was, all and all, an elaborate, even beautiful construct, evasive on the critical issue of underlying premises as, one might suggest, any socially acceptable *juristic* account of criminal justice must inevitably be.

Finally, Pound's somewhat ambiguous call for a reduction in the powers of the criminal trial jury requires further comment. He continued to evidence sympathy regarding some forms of jury "lawlessness" that responded to the gulf between individualistic legal conceptions and the social conception of justice, yet again suggesting that the jury was not always retrograde, but sometimes, rather, progressive: "In a crude way, juries are continually attempting to apply a newer standard of justice, but half-grasped, and the

---

[41] Pound, "Inherent and Acquired Difficulties," 239.

[42] Pound, "Inherent and Acquired Difficulties," 234.

[43] Pound acknowledged the criminologists' complaint that the law deals with offenders as "normal" persons although crime had been demonstrated to be a "disease" (Pound, "Inherent and Acquired Difficulties," 222). Two years later, when he addressed the first meeting of the National Conference on Criminal Law and Criminology (June 7, 1909), he stated: "[The criminologist] complains that whereas it is demonstrated that *in many cases* what we call crime is a disease, the law persistently deals with *every* offender, unless he is of unsound mind, as a normal person, and as a reasoning being who has wilfully gone wrong" (*Proceedings*, 1 [emphasis added]). Of course he also signed on to – perhaps coauthored – the 1911 General Introduction to the Modern Criminal Science Series, which rejected the notion that crime should be understood to be a "disease," albeit in terms that left room for the conclusion that crime was nonetheless the product of "natural causes" outside the individual's control ("General Introduction," vii).

result is shown in many otherwise inexplicable verdicts."[44] But he vehemently opposed the official law-finding doctrine where "such absurd legislation" continued to exist and he railed against the practice of allowing juries to set punishments: "They will be lawless enough without encouragement," he remonstrated. He noted instances of inconsistent jury verdicts, which resulted from the variable influences of "sentimentality" or from varying reactions to the "unwritten law," which flourishes in one place as it withers in another.[45] In closing, he prescribed "limiting the jury to their proper function of finding facts, and giving the court power to hold them to it," by which he seems to have meant giving judges the power of "fair comment on the evidence" and of alerting jurors to the "sophistry and buncombe addressed to them by counsel."[46] Pound seems to have believed that immediate procedural corrections would eliminate, or at least limit, the tendencies of juries to respond variably and outside the strict rule of law to the vagaries of retributive or merciful impulses.

True jury reform would also come, but it awaited the advent of sociological jurisprudence. That new day would bring forth a rational and consistent form of criminal justice, wherein retribution and the intent requirement would have given way to – what? A criminal jurisprudence that did not depend upon a concept of free will? If so, was Pound prepared for the implications of so fundamental a transformation of law? Of culture? Of human psychology? Unlike Speranza, Pound had not yet gone to the heart of the matter. He had avoided the Scylla of despair and the Charybdis of utter "science." But, then, he was only getting under way. So far as one can tell, he had not yet truly confronted the challenge to will theory that science posed for law in the fin de siècle.

A seemingly unavoidable occasion for such a confrontation presented itself when, in 1909, Pound reviewed Parmelee's *Principles of Anthropology and Sociology in Their Relation to Criminal Procedure*.[47] Parmelee, a social scientist with strong interests in criminal anthropology – and, a year or so later, a co-signer with Pound of the General Introduction – supported the scientific-positivist school of criminal jurisprudence and argued in favor of a limited form of the social defense theory of criminal justice. Parmelee's critique of the classical school's reliance on the concept of free will was trenchant:

We have already indicated that [the positive school] does not accept moral liberty as a basis for penal responsibility. This does not mean that the existence of a free will is

[44] Pound, "Inherent and Acquired Difficulties," 231.
[45] Pound, "Inherent and Acquired Difficulties," 236.
[46] Pound, "Inherent and Acquired Difficulties," 239.
[47] Roscoe Pound, review of *The Principles of Anthropology and Sociology in Their Relation[s] to Criminal Procedure*, by Maurice Parmelee, *American Political Science Review*, vol. 3 (1909): 281–84.

necessarily denied. As a matter of fact some representatives of this school deny it and others do not. But they all agree that *even if it exists it is something so incalculable in its character that it cannot be considered in developing a science of criminology and in the practical treatment of crime.*[48]

Parmelee paid only intermittent attention to the dangers that an emphasis on social defense might pose for political liberty. At times he wrote quite broadly: "by carefully studying the criminal himself, his rights as an individual are abridged only to the extent that social welfare demands."[49] Elsewhere he was more guarded, although perhaps less so than he himself recognized: "A positive [criminal] procedure must retain every guarantee of individual liberty ... for the criminal so that restrictions placed upon him shall not exceed those demanded by social defense."[50] Not surprisingly, Parmelee was hostile to the institution of jury trial. He conceded, in much vaguer terms than Speranza would employ three years later, that juries kept "judge and justice in touch with the public"[51] and that they tended to "individualize punishment," but he stressed that this form of individualization "has not always been on a rational basis."[52]

Responding to Parmelee, Pound endorsed a modern criminology with the caveat that the law must, in the short term, stand its ground. He proceeded upon the understanding that the scientist "refuses to define crime," noting that, by "criminal procedure," Parmelee meant a "'process by means of which the class called criminal is separated from the rest of society.'"[53] But "the law," Pound asserted, "must proceed from defined crimes and from a definite, settled theory. Hence, for the lawyer, the analytical view of crime, that it consists in doing what the State has forbidden under sanction of public prosecution, in violating a public duty, imposed, for whatever reason, by the State, is the only tenable one." Pound termed the practice of "deal[ing] with the criminal rather than with crime" the "criminologist's strongest point," but he insisted that "to minimize the dangerous possibilities of magisterial caprice, corruption or ignorance," the law required "generality, uniformity, and to a considerable degree mechanical action" – an inhospitable environment for individualization. The defense of political liberty required a cautious approach to implementing behaviorist doctrines and procedures. The power to legislate crimes and punishments carried with it the possibility of "dangerous forms of oppression of one class or one portion of the community by another"; thus, "one form of criminal procedure for all causes involving grave penalties will remain an indispensable protection to the individual."[54]

[48] Parmelee, *Principles of Anthropology and Sociology*, 20–21 (emphasis added).
[49] Parmelee, *Principles of Anthropology and Sociology*, 122.
[50] Parmelee, *Principles of Anthropology and Sociology*, 130–31.
[51] Parmelee, *Principles of Anthropology and Sociology*, 381.
[52] Parmelee, *Principles of Anthropology and Sociology*, 363–64.
[53] Pound, review of Parmelee, 281–82 (quoting *Principles of Anthropology and Sociology*, 7).
[54] Pound, review of Parmelee, 282.

Pound recognized the tensions that his prescription entailed, here again invoking the jury's role:

Undoubtedly our law has carried protection of the individual much too far. Undoubtedly American criminal procedure has developed a sort of jury lawlessness. But the history that led up to the constitutional and common-law guaranties of individual rights and to the power of juries to render general verdicts may repeat itself, and is by no means to be ignored.[55]

Thus he continued the dualistic approach to the jury as both necessary leavener and dangerous obstruction to justice that had characterized his earliest writing. Perhaps he was acknowledging the reach of behavioral science in 1908 when he suggested that, "in a crude way, juries are continually attempting to apply a newer standard of justice."[56] Indeed, Pound seems to have anticipated Speranza's 1912 insight that juries were influenced by the rhetoric of penological reform. But whereas Speranza doubted the jury's ability to apply wisely the new science before its basic principles were embedded in official legal practice, by 1909 Pound – in the interests of political liberty – appeared to accept ad hoc, jury-based applications of such ideas as, for the time being, the better part of wisdom.

In his review of Parmelee, Pound granted the importance of behaviorist research from Europe, but he remained skeptical of its ability to travel: "our criminal law is so rooted in theological ideas of free will and moral responsibility and juridical ideas of retribution, and both criminal law and procedure are so thoroughly mechanical, that we by no means make what we should of our discoveries."[57] Pound's writings on criminal justice in the following years often continued to situate free will in a religious frame. It is unclear whether he approved or eschewed a divine notion of free will existing in a sphere distinct from the practical realm of legal administration. But he can be read as calling for a concept of *criminality* that would exclude the element of free will almost entirely. Recall his assertion that "for the lawyer," crime must "consist[] in doing what the State has forbidden under sanction of public prosecution, in violating a public duty, imposed, for whatever reason, by the State."[58] Due process and other essentially political considerations required clear and pre-fixed definitions of criminal offenses. Yet, applied literally, this still would allow for rejection of the application of only a very limited concept of free will to offenders and make possible legislative abandonment of simple intent in cases in which the state so desired. Pound thus appears to have subscribed to the procedural due process aspects of political liberty while accepting some version of behavioral science's view of the person.

[55] Pound, review of Parmelee, 282–83.
[56] Pound, "Inherent and Acquired Difficulties," 231.
[57] Pound, review of Parmelee, 283–84.
[58] Pound, review of Parmelee, 282.

Yet, all told, Pound's overall stance with regard to free will remained ambiguous. His writing in the area of civil law did not lay siege to the general concept of autonomy as did his writing on criminal jurisprudence, at least as of 1909. Rather, here, he seemed to stress *relative* degrees of autonomy. In "Liberty of Contract" – exhibiting a sociological bent – Pound referred to "practical conditions of inequality"[59] and complained that justice had, in the nineteenth century, come "to be regarded as a device to secure a maximum of individual self-assertion." "Puritan theology," he claimed, problematically "gave rise to ultra individualism."[60] He criticized one court for failing to "consider that laborers in mines may be in a continual condition of poverty, and, that, as Lord Northington put it: 'Necessitous men are not, truly speaking, free men, but, to answer a present exigency, will submit to any terms that the crafty may impose upon them.'"[61] He further noted: "It is said that statistics show the great majority of accidents happen in the last working hour of the day, when the mind is numbed and the operative has *ceased to be the free agent* which our law contemplates."[62] As to the remedy for such *situational* unfreedom, Pound supported legislation that comported with a newly emerging "moral sense of community," and "the custom of the people, the expression of their habits of thought and action as to the relations of men with each other." He also contrasted "the direction of popular thought" – as evident in jury verdicts in some kinds of private law cases involving egregious imbalances in bargaining power – with "the older individualism" still embraced by courts.[63] Yet, surely these popular habits of thought and action did not embrace a rejection of the notion of free will! Pound thus reflected potentially opposing attractions to both an anti–free will view and a more relativistic position. His constant reiteration of the need to reform the orthodox theory of criminality was in powerful tension with his desires to maintain protection of the individual and vindicate political liberty.[64]

This tension also persisted in Pound's evolving, prewar impressions of the trial jury. The jury generally had fared well in Pound's 1909 review of Parmelee. It upheld the moral sense of the community in adjusting the mechanical legal rules that could not be altered suddenly in a society devoted

---

[59] Pound, "Liberty of Contract," 454.

[60] Pound, "Liberty of Contract," 459.

[61] Pound, "Liberty of Contract," 471–72 (criticizing and quoting *Vernon v. Bethel*, 28 Eng. Rep. 838, 839 [1762]).

[62] Pound, "Puritanism and the Common Law," *American Law Review*, vol. 45 (1911): 811–29, 823 (emphasis added).

[63] Pound, "Need of a Sociological Jurisprudence," 612–15.

[64] See, however, Pound's remarks at the 1909 National Conference on Criminal Law and Criminology, when he was drawn into a heated discussion of the possibility of scientific determination of the "criminal type" and ultimately spoke quite favorably about the possibility of a more thoroughgoing scientific view of criminality (*Proceedings*, 89–98). Pound began quite tentatively:

to political liberty. And its virtues, as Pound portrayed them, exposed the dangers of a trial in which the jury was restricted to a mere determination of whether the defendant had committed an "act" that the state had defined as a crime. But that was Pound playing defense against the overreach of the new science. Between 1909 and 1911, Pound came to view the criminal trial jury with increasing skepticism. In his introduction to the 1911 English translation of Raymond Saleilles's classic work, *The Individualization of Punishment,* Pound was downright negative. Far from serving as a needed countermeasure, jury intervention had made it difficult for courts "to procure convictions at all in cases of homicide."[65] As a result, many jurisdictions had left the penalty to the jury only to find that this produced wild inconsistencies. Pound concluded:

Obviously the crude individualization achieved by our juries, and especially by leaving the assessment of penalties to trial juries, involves quite as much inequality and injustice as the mechanical application of the law by a magistrate. Unchecked jury discretion upon the whole is *worse* than the unchecked magisterial discretion from which the classical school sought to deliver us.[66]

Although Saleilles himself addressed the problem of responsibility as well as that of punishment – and, indeed, offered a middle position, albeit an opaque one, that saved something akin to conventional theory[67] – Pound

I don't think that any criminologist now claims that probably we shall ever be able to look at a man and say that he is necessarily a criminal. On the other hand they do believe, and they seem to have a good deal of warrant for believing, that there is to a certain extent – just how great that extent is we cannot tell – a physical type of person who is born with anti-social tendencies, which we call criminals; that is, his physical make-up is such that he has the tendency to do those things which are anti-social. (92–93)

He noted that such study was proceeding in Europe, where "they have a freedom of dealing with criminals ... which we do not have in this country. In this country, in accordance with the requirements of due process of law, very little can be done beyond what any person may voluntarily submit to." Pound now warmed to his subject:

If we are to accomplish anything in this country we have got to have general laws providing for some such mode of investigation. I do not know how far at present it is practicable, but that in the future something of the sort will have to be done, I really have not much doubt.... It runs somewhat counter to our Anglo-Saxon notions, but it will come. As to how far it is an immediately practical question, I confess my mind is still open. (93)

Pound did not address the question of the use of the results of such (future) studies.

[65] Roscoe Pound, "Introduction to the English Version," in Saleilles, *Individualization of Punishment*, xvi.

[66] Roscoe Pound, "Introduction" to *Individualization of Punishment*, xvii (emphasis added). Pound was friendlier, however, to the civil trial jury (see p. xv).

[67] Saleilles, *Individualization of Punishment*, chap. 6. For an excellent discussion of Saleilles's views, see David Garland, *Punishment and Welfare: A History of Penal Strategies* (Aldershot, Hants: Gower, 1985), 186–89. Garland addresses Saleilles's concept of the "subjective reality" of free will (Saleilles, *Individualization of Punishment*, 158–59). As I shall argue, Pound came to a similar position a few years later; possibly, he was influenced by Saleilles in this regard, but neither his "Introduction" nor his later writings specifically suggests that he was.

seems to have been paying increasing attention to the sentencing stage, when a better educated judge should apply the new learning and (although perhaps Pound did not consciously think of it in this way) make up for the inevitable infirmities of the guilt assessment stage. Clearly, Pound's patience with the criminal trial jury had worn thin.

A similar shift occurred in Pound's thinking about the jury's application of the insanity defense. When, in 1910, Pound had reflected sympathetically on jury intervention, he singled out, inter alia, the tendency of the jury to correct for the mechanical nature of the law of insanity.

> Jury lawlessness is the great corrective of law in its actual administration.... [W]here in a particular cause there are peculiar considerations of mitigation or circumstances requiring exercise of a dispensing power, the power of juries to render general verdicts needs only a little help from alienist theories of insanity to enable a verdict to be rendered which will accord with the moral sense of the community. Here the law is often too mechanical at a point requiring great nicety of adjustment.[68]

But a year later, in the wake of the *Strasburg* decision, which Pound characterized as just another unfortunate victory of "classical theory" over "modern legislation,"[69] his tolerance had largely evaporated. "Exercised in homicide cases," Pound wrote, the power of juries to render general verdicts "led to the situation Mark Twain satirized when he called upon the legislature to make insanity a crime."[70] Where, earlier, he had trusted juries to react to constraints on an individual's free will not yet formally recognized by the law, he now appeared in part to question the resulting exemption from the legal system for an indefinite class of relatively "unfree" offenders. Better to convict, I assume, on the act itself and let post-trial specialists determine treatment. In other words, in a twist on the progressive notion that criminal acts often were not freely willed – and with a result that merged with the prescriptions of those scholars more purely interested in the social defense – Pound urged an even lower bar for "responsibility" in order to afford treatment for those offenders who, although arguably "unfree," otherwise might be released despite their dangerous natures or lack of reform.

Pound was commencing an important transition. Specific examples of progressive criminal trial jury responses – reflecting emerging social customs and embodying "newer standards" that were "half-grasped" – would, within a decade, become little more than a part of frontier justice, reflecting "pioneer ideas" or embodying "unwritten law." And, significantly, new tensions would also set in. On the one side, Pound responded to the seduction of massive, government-sponsored social reform that began to render

---

[68] Roscoe Pound, "Law in Books and Law in Action," *American Law Review*, vol. 44 (1910): 12–36, 18.

[69] Pound, "Introduction" to *Individualization of Punishment*, xi.

[70] Pound, "Introduction" to *Individualization of Punishment*, xvi (referring to Mark Twain, "A New Crime").

mediating institutions such as the jury unnecessary intrusions rather than necessary evils. On the other side, Pound still recognized the incipient dangers of too much reform, especially the threat of a criminal law dominated by the collective – and administrative – state. Basic protections would remain necessary; the new theory would have to be assimilated carefully and, as always, gradually. Individual liberty, once too great, would now have to be protected against the needs of organized society. The cycle was changing. Human freedom would now have to be redefined as itself a social interest and as valid as such. And, as such, jurisprudence would have to insist on it. But Pound would not refer to the orthodox theory of free will in the criminal law, nor would he refer to the "corrective" powers of the criminal trial jury. For a new age, Pound would postulate a new version of an unstable mix of ideas.

POUND'S FUTURE OF THE CRIMINAL LAW: 1916–1921

Pound's 1916 speech, "Juristic Problems of National Progress,"[71] represents the first stage of Pound's mature work on criminal jurisprudence. The years of work on his tripartite study of sociological jurisprudence[72] and on many briefer succeeding essays had served him well. So, too, had the prewar era of high Progressivism influenced Pound's thought – deepening it and producing an attractive self-consciousness. Pound continued to believe that the role of law – of society in general – was the "satisfaction of a maximum of wants with a minimum of sacrifice of other wants" rather than, simply, the maximizing of individual self-assertion.[73] He had grown increasingly convinced, though, that the moral and social life of the individual and, indeed, the preservation of what he would now term "free individual action," were among the most basic wants and, hence, were themselves central social interests. This turn of thought – Pound's application of social-interest theory[74] – accompanied his fear that the drift toward centralization, the eclipse of the

---

[71] Roscoe Pound, "Juristic Problems of National Progress," *American Journal of Sociology*, vol. 22 (1917): 721–33.
[72] Roscoe Pound, "The Scope and Purpose of Sociological Jurisprudence" (pts. 1–3), *Harvard Law Review*, vol. 24 (1911): 591–619; vol. 25 (1911): 140–68; vol. 25 (1912): 489–516.
[73] Pound, "Juristic Problems," 724.
[74] On the derivation of Pound's theory of social interests, see Wigdor, *Roscoe Pound*, 210–14. Wigdor emphasizes Pound's attraction to "organicism" and to the idea of "relation." Wigdor traces the idea of organicism to late nineteenth-century thought (see, esp., 325–26, 326 n. 11), and concludes that, with respect to his social-interest theory, Pound was influenced first by Rudolph von Jhering, but more importantly ("directly") by Albion Small. Wigdor states that "Pound hoped that this theory would replace the conventional preoccupation with 'rights' as the basis of law" (213). Herget, *American Jurisprudence*, 167–69, establishes the relationship between Pound's theory of social interests and the ideas Pound gleaned from Jhering, Josef Kohler, and William James. Herget states that, for Pound: "To have a chance of being accepted, these claims [i.e. "interests"] must be more than mere personal demands;

judicial process by newly minted administrative agencies, and the sheer mass of legislative mandates would undermine political liberty, overall social efficiency, and, especially, individual freedom. This new emphasis on "free" or "spontaneous" action significantly heightened the tension that plagued his criminal jurisprudence. But operationally, what did this language of "freedom" mean? I start by considering the role this new language played in his 1916 speech.

Pound began the speech by criticizing the old theories of lawmaking as "necessitarian." In the seventeenth and eighteenth centuries, he asserted, "men conceived they were finding law while making it. To these centuries all law was inevitably determined by the nature of man." The nineteenth-century jurist "came to doubt whether he could do more than observe the processes by which legal rules and doctrines took their predestined shapes."[75] But now "the time," Pound announced, "calls for voluntaristic theories of lawmaking on the part of jurists and judges," or what he called an "engineering interpretation of jurisprudence." The watchword of such an interpretation would no longer be efficiency, but, in the military fashion of the day, "organization and preparedness"; the new legal science would be one that "constructs as well as observes ... that observes in order that it may construct." He anticipated objections to such a "voluntaristic philosophy of lawmaking," the most serious coming from the "political and philosophical individualist," who will "say that the grain of truth in the nineteenth-century theories of juristic and legislative futility is in the necessity of safeguarding this spontaneity of individual action, this individual initiative in thinking and acting which is the mainspring of progress." But Pound rejected this argument as failing to take account of the "ever-widening recognition and securing of social interests." The essentially eighteenth-century perspective on justice "as a problem of reconciling government and liberty" had given way to "a problem of reconciling organization with spontaneous individual effort; of reconciling social control with individual initiative."[76] The formulation was not entirely new for Pound,

---

they are asserted to be morally right, accepted by society, and generally applicable to some particular class or group of persons" (168). Pound's attention to social interests was becoming a dominant theme in his criminal-justice writings at least as early as 1913. See Roscoe Pound, "The Administration of Justice in the Modern City," *Harvard Law Review*, vol. 26 (1913): 302–28. For further discussion of the background for Pound's social interest theory – and the claim that Pound gave these ideas a distinctive turn – see Sayre, *Life of Roscoe Pound*, 359–64.

[75] Pound, "Juristic Problems," 723. Pound asserted: "The irresistible movement of the ethical or political ideal to realize itself, the inevitable operation of natural forces as completely beyond human reach ... the relentless working out of biological laws as hard and unyielding as those that shape animal and vegetable life – these ... convinced men that the most that legal science could do for us was to teach us to observe nature's machine in operation" (723–24).

[76] Pound, "Juristic Problems," 724–27.

but it was more elaborate and uttered with greater urgency; as an element of his focus on the proper balance of systemic change, something very like a language of free will was becoming a staple of Pound's social theory and jurisprudence.

To illustrate the objectives of an "engineering interpretation of jurisprudence," Pound chose the criminal law, labeling it "a well-understood body of tradition proceeding on one theory on which we have grafted an overgrown mass of legislation proceeding on many diverse and conflicting theories," and claiming that "it is no one's business to put the whole into even the semblance of order, much less to survey the whole, trace its different constituents with reference to the ends to be attained, and seek to make it more effective toward those ends."[77] Pound had initially encouraged the proliferation of interdisciplinary writings under the auspices of the AICLC as a route to greater comprehension.[78] Now, seven years later, he vainly but optimistically struggled against the centrifugal energies that – one might have thought, predictably – had been released, depicting criminal law as fragmented into a "medical view in which the criminal law is thought of in terms of the insane and the epileptic"; a "psychological view in which it is thought of in terms of the feeble-minded"; as well as the perspectives of penologists, social workers, and the police.[79]

Pound soon integrated his insistence upon the need for system and coordination with his newfound attention to "individual freedom and individual initiative." In 1919, in one of his least known, yet most revealing essays, "Society and the Individual," he stated that individual interests lay side by side with "public interests," which are "the claims which the state may make simply as such," and "social interests," which included, inter alia, "the social interest in the individual human existence."[80] Individual interests, then,

---

[77] Pound, "Juristic Problems," 728.

[78] *Proceedings*, 3.

[79] Pound, "Juristic Problems," 728–29. Pound's focus on system and overall coordination – in the "military" style or otherwise – dominated his later writings generally. It simultaneously reflected his deep skepticism that mind, man, or society could be understood from any one particular perspective and his perhaps naïve faith in a holistic approach to solving problems, one that melded the best of all available ideas. His skepticism also had a larger dimension, that of the historicist. No age found final answers but only solutions suitable to itself. This aspect of his skepticism – a species of relativism – left room for belief in the existence of general social mores, of ideas, attitudes, and practices that, at any one time, bound a society together and provided the basis for consensus despite the presence of competing interests. This blend of elements that underlay Pound's engineering interpretation of jurisprudence eventually separated him from the postwar realists, whose private law writings typically denied the existence of pervasive, society-wide moral conventions and stressed the arbitrary quality of judicial decision making. See, e.g., G. Edward White, "From Sociological Jurisprudence to Realism," 1010–21.

[80] Roscoe Pound, "Society and the Individual," in *Proceedings of the National Conference of Social Work* (Chicago: Rogers and Hall, 1920), 103–07, 104–06 (conference held June 1919).

received both separate treatment and a place within social interests. Pound was attempting to redress a movement in the direction of the collective state to which, he may well have feared, his own early writings had contributed. His argument, stated in generalities that failed to make clear the nature of the "freedom" he was now attributing to the individual, extended ideas that he had expressed at least as early as 1910 and that seem to have crystallized steadily in the 1913–1919 period.

In "Society and the Individual," Pound at first briskly denounced the classical view of "society and all social groups as products of individual agreement," and – perhaps surprisingly, at this point of his scholarship's evolution – produced the most comprehensive deterministic account of human thought and behavior that, to my knowledge, he ever set forth:

Metaphysically the individual conscious ego may, if you will, be the unit. But it is a profound mistake to take that ego for the *ultimate reality* in the social world. You and I are born into the great stream of society. We die out of it. But it went on before us and will go on after us, and if some of us are able to do something to shape some part of its course, yet how much more will it have shaped us, molding our thoughts by fixing the conditions under which and words by which we think, controlling our actions by bonds of convention, fashion, general opinion, of which we are hardly conscious, which we can resist only here and there, and then often but feebly, and forming our very personality by the pressure day and night of a thousand points of contact with our fellows in the stream. So true is it that the individual is a social product or a social outcome rather than society an individual product.[81]

Pound did not say how long he had held this general view, which had long been fashionable in social science – but not, so far as one can tell, in legal-academic – circles.[82] Nor can we know how much leeway the power to "resist only here and there, and then often but feebly" allows. But, most important, Pound rushed on, observing:

a few years ago all this was, one might say, trite. But a reaction has set in. Men have come to fear that in this emphasis on the social stream the interests of the individual in the stream will be overlooked and neglected – as it has been said, that our social

---

[81] Pound, "Society and the Individual," 104.

[82] Pound read voraciously (see Herget, *American Jurisprudence*, 164–65), but he often reduced many variations on a theme to an effective (and affecting) monovocal synthesis. Pound had been influenced by James, Dewey, and a great many others with respect to both pragmatism as a general matter and an interest in consciousness and experience more specifically. (For an excellent study of will, consciousness, and "pragmatic truth" in late-nineteenth and early twentieth-century thought, see Kloppenberg, *Uncertain Victory*, 64–94.) I have not attempted to associate specific Poundian formulations with specific social science or philosophical writings. Pound's "methodology" makes it difficult to do so; his lack of philosophical depth (which is *not* to say lack of learning and wisdom) makes it a bit beside the point. I have sought to show how Pound applied his learning; others will shed more light than I can on the specific sources of that learning.

thinking would abolish the individual. Thus there is coming to be a marked revival of the abstract individualism against which we were all in revolt a decade ago.[83]

Then, moving from his tentative, distancing phrase of two years earlier – "the political and philosophical individualist ... will say that [there is a] grain of truth in the nineteenth-century theories"[84] – Pound proposed a compromise directly conceding the value of individual interests as at once self-standing and an aspect of the social interest:

I submit the way to meet this reaction is *to recognize the kernel of truth in the old individualism* – that is, that one of the chiefest of social interests is that each individual have an opportunity to lead a human life; to recognize a social interest in the moral and social life of the individual, and to recognize that one of the chief agencies of social progress is individual freedom and individual initiative.[85]

This pragmatic approach to human freedom allowed for restraints on freedom on essentially utilitarian grounds, even as it recognized that freedom as being a central feature of human existence, of what it meant to be human.[86]

Thus Pound had revived a concept of "individual freedom" in his work, but he would remain supremely vague about the underlying nature of that

---

[83] Pound, "Society and the Individual," 104. It is not clear what Pound is referring to here; his comment might reflect ongoing trends in "domestic" political and social thought or it might reflect the reaction against either Marxist ideas or certain strands of German thought that emphasized the community over the individual.

[84] Pound, "Juristic Problems," 726.

[85] Pound, "Society and the Individual," 104 (emphasis added).

[86] It is possible that Pound was influenced by Parmelee, or that they mutually influenced one another. Parmelee had in 1916 defined "normal life" as "the spontaneous expression of human nature," and had concluded: "Now it is evident that in any organized society the spontaneity of the individual must be limited at least a little by the need for a certain amount of social control." Maurice Parmelee, *Poverty and Social Progress* (New York: Macmillan, 1916), 452. Pound had referred to "spontaneous individual effort" in his 1916 speech in a similar context: "We may restate [the matter] as a problem of reconciling organization with spontaneous individual effort; of reconciling social control with individual initiative" (Pound, "Juristic Problems," 727). Two years later, Parmelee wrote: "But the progress of science has destroyed for all practical purposes the theological and metaphysical doctrine of a free will." He warned that "fear," as an aspect of the penal function, while useful, "stands in the way of many changes which will prove to be beneficial, and thus impedes social progress. Furthermore, it prevents the highest possible degree of free activity on the part of human beings, and thus hinders the spontaneous expression of human nature which should be the principle object of civilization and of human culture in general." Maurice Parmelee, *Criminology* (New York: Macmillan, 1918), 379, 384. Pound and Parmelee appear to have tracked one another. Pound expressed his views regarding "spontaneous individual effort" within the context of his theory of the social interest. Parmelee led more from the perspective of achieving progress while not sacrificing social control.

In one important particular, Parmelee seems not to have influenced Pound. In his 1918 book, Parmelee adopted a view that, he said, reconciled the problem of responsibility:

freedom. He seems to have defined it as the *consciousness* of freedom, rather than as an ultimate reality. Still, he sometimes sounded as though individual freedom was indeed a reality. He, himself, might have thought of it as sometimes one, sometimes the other. The slipperiness of his idea of freedom is evident in his application, in 1920, of social engineering to private law, when he advocated for balance between "free and spontaneous self-assertion" and law that "secure[s] a maximum of interests with a minimum sacrifice of interests to leave such persons free to contract as they choose."[87] Here he found room for a significant measure of "individual freedom and ... initiative" in property and contract, although, of course, he did not refer to it as the exercise of free will. And although the "freedom" he here described probably did not reflect ultimate reality, in private

> while it is true that the human organism and human nature have been determined by all the forces which have acted upon them, it is also true that this organism is a complex mechanism and center of energy from which radiates stimulations and impulsions which may have far-reaching consequences. Furthermore, as an organism it is highly self-directing, more so, indeed, than any other organism. Consequently, we have every reason to regard the human organism as an efficient cause of the deeds which emanate from it, and the consequences of those deeds. In this positive and scientific sense, then, we may regard the individual as responsible for his conduct. (*Criminology*, 380 [compare this view with Parmelee's statement of a decade before, in *Principles of Anthropology and Sociology*, 20–21, quoted in the section of this chapter on Pound's early criminal law scholarship])

> Parmelee, the sociologist, drew here upon Ray Madding McConnell, a Harvard ethicist, who expressed a fairly straightforward form of classical compatibilism: drawing on Hume and Spinoza, McConnell urged that to act out of "free will" – as the concept is generally understood both by compatibilists *and* by the general public – is simply to act in accordance with one's will while unimpeded by unwanted obstruction or compulsion; it is irrelevant that one's willings are, nonetheless, ultimately determined along with all natural events (McConnell, *Criminal Responsibility and Social Constraint*, chap. 12, "Freedom as the Absence of External Constraint"). As I discuss further in the text, Pound (the lawyer), however, avoided this level of philosophical inquiry and often appears to have rested his views on the mere consciousness – if not the reality – of freedom. Note, however, that, as I outline in Chapter 3, Pound's protégé, Sheldon Glueck – a lawyer *and* behavioral scientist – expressed views similar to those of Parmelee.

[87] Roscoe Pound, "A Theory of Social Interests," in *Papers and Proceedings of the American Sociological Society*, vol. 15 (Chicago: University of Chicago, 1921), 16–45, 27–28 (conference held December 1920). Note that, here, Pound quoted William James: "'Must not the guiding principle for ethical philosophy ... be simply to satisfy at all times as many demands as we can?'" (28 n. 1, quoting James, *The Will to Believe*, 205). Some thirty years later, Pound would modify this view:

> Thinking of the civil side of the legal order, I have come to feel that instead of putting the task of law, as William James did, in terms of satisfying as much as we can of the total of human demands, we do better to speak of providing as much as we may of the total of men's reasonable expectations in life in civilized society with the minimum of friction and waste. Free self-determination is a much prized and eminently reasonable expectation which must ever be weighed in adjustment of relations in and by politically organized society. (Roscoe Pound, "The Role of the Will in Law," *Harvard Law Review*, vol. 68 [1954]: 1–19, 19)

law matters Pound saw the ideal Progressive legal order as adjusting for genuine imbalances in the practical ability of persons to exercise the freedom they *imagined* they possessed in some ultimate sense. Social engineering recognized competing interests – indeed, "real" interests – among them the *claim* to human freedom as an aspect of human consciousness that engendered both social progress and the individual's sense of well-being. Inherent tensions remained among the strands of thought about individual freedom in Pound's private law writings, but on the whole, in *that* context, his open references to compromise and coordination papered over those tensions.

With respect to criminal jurisprudence, the matter was very different. In that setting, Pound was convinced that attributing true autonomy to criminal offenders was factually wrong, productive of retributivism, and detrimental to the social interest in dealing intelligently with the underlying causes of crime. Inevitably, his references to free self-assertion – heuristic or otherwise – seemed to clash with his continuing critique of the role of free will in the orthodox theory of criminality. Any contradiction was often obscured, however, by his focus on the need for a rational, coordinated, functional system of criminal administration. When Pound focused specifically on the underlying theory of criminal responsibility, he carried over his comprehensive-sounding rejection of the nineteenth-century concept of free will. But when he wrote about criminal justice as the balancing of the social interest in public order and the social interest in the individual, he was not concerned with arriving at first principles regarding human freedom; here his language was ambiguous. All of Pound's major writings of the early 1920s on the criminal law and its administration manifest these ambiguous tendencies.

Pound's most important application of his theory of social interests to criminal justice appeared in "The Future of the Criminal Law," a paper he gave at the American Prison Congress in the fall of 1920. In this setting, though, where one might expect sustained attention to the enduring problems that the new science presented for an underlying theory of criminal responsibility, Pound addressed instead the issues of political liberty and the place of criminal law – mainly those procedural aspects that reflected its highly charged political role – in the story of the West and, finally, in the story of modern America. It is here that Pound suggested most strongly that collectivism might, in some spheres, have gone too far.[88] He gave great scope to his long-standing concern about the use of administrative agencies rather than the common law courts to resolve issues of criminal justice, referring, inter alia, to boards of probation and parole, whose role reduced the court's

Pound restricted himself here to the private law, expressly "say[ing] nothing of the role of the will in criminal law" (ibid.).

[88] Pound, "Future of the Criminal Law," 9–16.

participation in sentencing to a mere formality. In other contexts, judicial determinations were being preempted by preliminary reports by "alienists or psychiatrists" or by "boards and commissions" that resolved matters through "inspectors and secretaries and agents."[89] Avoidance of regularly constituted judicial tribunals meant loss of protections against governmental overreach. But even in those courts, there was overreach: "American prosecutions today are coming to be conducted with a ferocity without parallel in common-law trials since the Stuarts."[90]

Pound's essay presented in brief compass his pendulum-swing schema for criminal justice history. Periods of repression were succeeded by periods of relaxation of authority. The exaggeration of individual freedom in eighteenth- and nineteenth-century America had given way to a social perspective – Pound had himself campaigned for that change – but there were signs that, in some respects, the pendulum had now swung too far. As Pound saw it, the institutions of Progressivism threatened the very values that Progressives had sought to restore and to protect. The post–World War I war on crime – including, one supposes, the Red Scare – severely compromised political liberty and the due process of law. Pound identified the emerging problem of overemphasis on the state as a failure on the part of jurists and others to perceive that the moral and social life of the individual was itself a central social interest. This problem was especially pressing in criminal justice, where the implications for political liberty lay on the surface.

Once again reform of the criminal law required compromise: "Compromise of such claims, for the purpose of securing as much as we may, is peculiarly difficult. The far-reaching nature of the interests involved calls for the best of which the science of law is capable." And, once again, Pound addressed the need to value an offender's "free will" without making clear whether he had embraced the concept as true, or, merely as a claim, apparently valuable in

---

[89] Pound, "Future of the Criminal Law," 1. A harbinger of Pound's criticism of the displacement of the regular judicial process by administrative process can be seen as early as 1913 in his cautious approach to juvenile courts (see Pound, "Administration of Justice in the Modern City," 322). In 1914, Pound again revealed some significant ambivalence when describing reforms in criminal justice:

> Even in criminal causes, which we think of as *par excellence* the domain of the common law, juvenile courts, probation commissions and other attempts to individualize the treatment of offenders, and the endeavors of the medical profession to take questions of expert opinion out of the forum and commit them to a sort of medical referee, bid fair to introduce an administrative element into punitive justice which is wholly alien to our inherited ideas. (Roscoe Pound, "Justice according to Law" [pt. 2], *Columbia Law Review*, vol. 14 [1914]: 1–26, 14)

Pound's essay, "Juristic Problems of National Progress," also makes the point with evident force. Horwitz argues that Pound was friendly toward administrative processes until his "about-face" on the matter in the late 1930s (Horwitz, *Transformation of American Law*, 217–20). This appears to be true with respect to noncriminal matters, but not as to the criminal law.
[90] Pound, "Future of the Criminal Law," 9.

itself. Pound continued to complain that, "instead of intelligent compromise, our juristic theory of the past has sought to proceed on the basis of one of the two contending elements exclusively." Thus, in the seventeenth and eighteenth centuries, American "theories of natural rights exalted the social interest in the individual life at the expense of the social interest in the general security." The criminal law infringed those rights; thus "it had to be justified by deriving its rules, its sanctions and its authority ... from the free will of the offender himself." The problem was intensified in the nineteenth century, when "the fashion of juristic thinking sought to make the individual free will, as an ultimate metaphysical *datum,* the starting point of all legal obligation." From this experience it followed that "limitations on magisterial enforcement of the prohibitions imposed to maintain the general security ... should receive the whole emphasis."[91]

As he had before, Pound then softened this standard critique of an overemphasis on individualism with the phrase he had employed in his 1916 address on "Juristic Problems" and in his 1919 remarks on "Society and the Individual": "I concede that there is a kernel of truth in these traditional legal theories." Crucially, however, given the context, he appeared to have aimed the concession, this time, directly at the "ideas of free will" in the criminal law. Thus the concession *seems* especially far-reaching. At first glance, one might even wonder: Could free will be the true kernel, with our exaltation of it to the expense of all else being the real problem? Had the perceived threat to political liberty engendered a belief in the kind of human freedom that the orthodox common law presumed to exist? Apparently not. For Pound immediately returned to wholly instrumental considerations and, then directing his attention to the benefits of modern understandings, he observed that the same legal profession that needed to be warned about executive overreach "still adheres either to the eighteenth-century idea of natural rights as qualities of human beings ... or to the nineteenth century will-philosophy, with its ideas of free will, vicious will and abstract will, which modern psychology has wholly undermined." Indeed, next he appeared to go further than ever before in his call for cooperation among lawyers and social and behavioral scientists: "Scientific study of law," he now urged, "is no less important to the community than scientific study of medicine. Few *diseases* threaten civilization more persistently than the manifold forms of antisocial action that we *call crimes.*"[92] The caution of the 1911 General Introduction – "it need not be asserted for one moment that crime is a disease"[93] – seems to have weakened. From there Pound moved on to his long-standing trademark, all-purpose prescription for the future of the criminal law: "continuous intelligent bringing to bear upon the fundamental

---

[91] Pound, "Future of the Criminal Law," 11–12.
[92] Pound, "Future of the Criminal Law," 15 (emphasis added).
[93] "General Introduction," vii.

problem and its applications in detail of all that legal and social and medical science have worked out."[94] Pound's recognition of "individual freedom" and of "free mental activity" had not, I infer, truly altered his conviction that the most important part of the "fundamental problem" was the concept of "free will" as the basis for criminal responsibility.

Pound aptly entitled his essay "The Future of the Criminal Law," for it struggled with many of the problems that have played havoc with criminal jurisprudence down to our own times. Pound himself, of course, thought that the best minds, the grandest efforts of all scientists, legal and otherwise, would resolve these problems. Unlike Speranza, he counted law as a science and looked forward to eventual integration of the insights of all the sciences. His reaction against the furthest reaches of executive justice in wartime and its immediate aftermath led him to stress the importance of the *consciousness* of human freedom and to insist that this consciousness – when nurtured by social programs that limited barriers, governmental as well as private – gave full sway to human potential as well as to social well-being.[95] Yet, each time he appeared to finally answer the question, it seemed to arise once more: Was mere *consciousness* of freedom really all that was at issue? Witness the dramatic denouement of his chapter, "The Rights of Englishmen and the Rights of Man," in *The Spirit of the Common Law*:

> The chiefest of social interests is the moral and social life of the individual; and thus individual interests become largely identical with a social interest.... Although we think socially, we must still think of individual interests, and of that greatest of all claims which a human being may make, the claim to assert his individuality, to exercise freely the will and the reason which God has given him. We must emphasize the social interest in the moral and social life of the individual. But we must remember that *it is the life of a free-willing being.*[96]

The language of "claim" appears – and then, just as Pound describes humans as "free-willing beings," is eclipsed. Pound's theory of social interests captured – and domesticated – the element of human freedom, but gave it a place so prominent that it is sometimes difficult to see precisely what his comments on the scientific renunciation of the concept of free will amounted to. Still, Scylla and Charybdis had once again been avoided; Pound had safely reached the beckoning shores of deeply humanistic ambiguity.

CRIMINAL JUSTICE TODAY: POUND IN THE EARLY 1920S

That ambiguity – or perhaps better, dualism – marked Pound's two most important writings on criminal justice: his "Summary" concerning criminal

---

[94] Pound, "Future of the Criminal Law," 16.

[95] See, generally, Roscoe Pound, *The Spirit of the Common Law* (Francestown, NH: Marshall Jones, 1921).

[96] Pound, *Spirit of the Common Law*, 110–11 (emphasis added).

justice in the American city in the 1922 Cleveland criminal justice survey[97] and his lectures, the following year, on *Criminal Justice in America*. But the two works display other, not unrelated tensions as well. Pound's Summary contained a belated attempt to come to terms with the implications of the new sciences for the prospects of a reformed system of criminal justice; his valedictory lectures, on the other hand, retreated to a mainly historical perspective on current conditions. Ultimately, the historical account that had served Pound so well for so long trapped him, reinforcing his tendency not to probe deeply into matters for which history was a poor guide and analysis of theoretical underpinnings a necessary next step.

Pound's masterful 1922 Summary integrated insights tracing back to his 1908 piece, "Inherent and Acquired Difficulties in the Administration of Punitive Justice," with more recent reflections on the role of the individual interest as an aspect of social interests and empirical information drawn from the Cleveland project. The Summary remains Pound's fullest and most cogent account of the problems inherent in criminal administration; its most original aspect is his discussion – engendered, no doubt, by the Cleveland Survey itself – of the relationship between the new sciences and the criminal law. He opened the essay with a brief but considered discussion of the problem of free will:

Not the least significant discoveries of modern psychology are the extent to which what we have called free will is a product, not a cause, and the extent to which what we take to be reasons for actions are but rationalizings of what we desire to do and do on different grounds. In the administration of justice there are many subtle forces at work of which we are but partially conscious.[98]

Pound warned that one must understand that human beings, legal machinery, and the "complex environment" were formed by "tradition, education, physical surroundings, race, class and professional solidarity, and economic, political, and social influence of all sorts and degrees." Complexity reigned: "we must insist on plurality of causes and plurality and relativity of remedies." The critique that emerged was not, for Pound, the conventional thrashing of the Puritan notion of free will, but the rejection of a reductionist attempt to match cause and cure one-on-one. Both individuals and sciences had succumbed to mono-causal explanation: "Neither the science of law nor the science of politics has escaped this struggle to master complex facts by giving them a fictitious appearance of simplicity."[99]

The language of freedom reappeared when Pound turned from this causal morass back to the criminal law. Here Pound concluded that compromise was necessary between the general security and – familiar phrases – "free

---

[97] Roscoe Pound, "Criminal Justice in the American City – A Summary," in Pound and Frankfurter, *Criminal Justice in Cleveland*, 559–662 (hereafter "Summary").
[98] Pound, "Summary," 561.
[99] Pound, "Summary," 561–62.

individual initiative" or "free mental activity." These were "claims" that deserve protection as social interests in the individual life.[100] Nothing in the Summary suggests that for Pound such claims stood for actual aspects of human nature rather than states of mind. Nor did Pound repeat his characterization of human existence as "the life of a free-willing being,"[101] a phrase whose short life in his work perhaps simply paid fleeting homage to the mysteries of human behavior.

Indeed, when we turn to Pound's reflections upon the implications of the new sciences for criminal law we no longer even encounter the language of "free individual initiative." Rather, we find the assertion that, although traditional criminal jurisprudence "thinks of the offender as a free moral agent who, having before him the choice whether to do right or wrong, intentionally chose to do wrong,"[102] the theoretical basis for such traditionalism had been washed away. Here – hopeful about the prospects for change, but less sanguine about the best process for it – Pound achieved his most sustained assessment, and most implicit endorsement, of the implications of the new science:

We know today that the matter is much more complicated.... We know that criminals must be classified as well as crimes. We know that the old analysis of act and intent can stand only as an artificial legal analysis and that the mental element in crime presents a series of difficult problems. We recognize that in order to deal with crime in an intelligent and practical manner we must give up the retributive theory. But this means that we must largely make over our whole criminal law, which was rebuilt around that theory in the last two centuries, and that work is going on slowly all over the world.... We shall achieve lasting results neither by some analytical scheme or rigid system worked out logically in libraries on the sole basis of books and law reports, as some lawyers seem to hope, nor by abandoning the experience of the past, preserved in the law reports, and turning exclusively to administrative, non-legal, expert agencies, which is the hope of many laymen.[103]

Finally, Pound addressed the new sciences more directly:

Medical science has all but undergone a rebirth within a generation. Within a generation psychology has risen to a practical science of the first importance, with far-reaching applications on every side. Psychopathology has overturned much that the criminal law of the past had built upon. Indeed, the fundamental theory of our orthodox criminal law has gone down before modern psychology and psychopathology. The results are only beginning to be felt. One result is a just dissatisfaction on the part of the medical profession with what they observe in judicial administration of justice and legal treatment of criminals. In prevention, in criminal investigation as a preliminary to prosecution, in the trial of issues of fact and in penal treatment

---

[100] Pound, "Summary," 576–77.
[101] Pound, *Spirit of the Common Law*, 111.
[102] Pound, "Summary," 586.
[103] Pound, "Summary," 586–87.

we have much to learn from the physician and psychologist and psychopathologist. But during the period of transition in which we are learning it and are learning how to use it there will be much experimenting and some fumbling and much dissatisfaction.[104]

In other words, as of 1922, the *real* challenge had to do with altering the traditional habits of American democratic thought and behavior that had long since been ingrained in current administrative practices. Just how much progress, and of what sort, had Americans so far made? Pound approached these final questions in his 1923 lectures, which constitute his great summing up on the question of criminal justice. The central message of the lectures was not that the idea of a determined or compromised will might undermine the conscious belief in human freedom that Pound so highly valued. Rather, the message was that Americans still gave freedom *too much* rein, in practice as well as in theory, to suit the conditions of modern life. Pound pleaded for institutional development and new habits of behavior, individual freedom in accordance with self-restraint. As to deeper philosophical and psychological issues, they played little role in *Criminal Justice in America*.

Pound commenced his first lecture by observing that, just as crimes should be seen in their specific rather than their general natures, so too were the sources of law specific.

Hence, today jurists approach the law from psychology rather than from metaphysics. They think of the scope and subject matter of law from the standpoint of the concrete desires and claims of individual men in civilized society, not from the standpoint of the abstract qualities of the abstract individual, nor from the standpoint of the logical implications of the abstract individual free will. They consider the desires or claims found to be involved respectively in the individual life.[105]

But the claims of individuals could clash, and the purpose of the law was to balance competing claims, whatever might be said about the psychology that accompanied, or generated, those claims. In this, the 1923 lectures are by no means original; Pound had been saying as much for years, as his concept of social interests took hold, evolved, and came to reflect a settled and inspiring confidence. Yet his focus in 1923 was, in a sense, increasingly practical – albeit more aspirationally than concretely so. His assessment of where things stood as of the 1920s was rooted in the relationship of political liberty to the needs of the modern state, and lay against a background assumption that the law's mission was eminently achievable. And this mission – of practical adjustment between the individual and the social order – left little room for consideration of the theoretical basis for a notion of criminal responsibility. Free will was now a metaphysical question apart.

[104] Pound, "Summary," 588 (for additional discussion of these themes see also 645–48).
[105] Pound, *Criminal Justice in America*, 4.

In his final lecture, "Criminal Justice Today," Pound looked back over America's past to show the tensions between individualism and the striving for order that had obstructed a viable institutional basis for America in its current stage of transition: a new balance had to be achieved in light of modern conditions. The open frontier was not the modern city, and the democratic ideals the frontier had fostered must be tempered to suit the times and pruned back for overzealousness. Still, they should not be jettisoned. Ever haunted by the specter of Marxism, even in calling for more training and organization at all stages of the criminal justice system, Pound emphasized that scientifically designed institutions could preserve – rather than threaten – American ideals. Americans need only achieve an understanding of those ideals appropriate to the contemporary context.[106]

Pound was not entirely negative in his assessment of current conditions. Recent advances in penology drew his praise:

> It is enough to say that the prospect here is much more immediately hopeful than at any other point in American criminal justice. We are less in a rut here. A body of trained workers has been growing up which thoroughly understands the problem, its history, and its present status. We are less hampered here than elsewhere by the pioneer tradition and by pioneer institutions. Penal treatment is not unlikely to continue to be characteristically the American field of progress in criminal law and administration.[107]

Alongside these supposed successes of Progressive Era penology, however, Pound noted that judges at their own discretion often failed to utilize the resources of the police and social agencies.[108] Moreover, he observed:

> Penal treatment in America today raises specially difficult questions because the time calls for individualization and the traditional spirit of our law calls for generalized penalties; because our ideas, inherited from the last century, are characteristically humane and stress the individual life, while the times demand greater regard for the general security.[109]

Significantly, Pound chose not to address the darker aspects of the new penology, specifically the concept – strongly supported by some deterministic jurists and criminologists of the 1920s – of permanent segregation or "elimination" of "incorrigibles" in the "social defense."

To the successes in penology Pound contrasted the deficiencies of prosecution and trial. He combined a well-informed critique of an outmoded and disorganized prosecutorial bureaucracy with a scathing attack on the politics that produced bargained pleas. To this Pound added the conventional complaint that convictions too often led to appeals and the further

---

[106] Pound, *Criminal Justice in America*, 214–15.
[107] Pound, *Criminal Justice in America*, 198.
[108] Pound, *Criminal Justice in America*, 33–35.
[109] Pound, *Criminal Justice in America*, 197.

claim that the judge "in too many states ... is made quite powerless to control the trial, and the jury becomes an independent tribunal with large scope for disregarding or nullifying the law." Here, the vestiges of pioneer justice were deeply embedded and a protective ideology made them resistant to reform: "Distrust of judges, lay magistrates, free rein to counsel in the forum, *extravagant powers of juries,* an uneducated, unorganized, deprofessionalized bar are urged as democratic, and *their supposed democratic character is expected to make up for their manifest inadaptation to the demands of justice today.*"[110] Pound's history of criminal justice in America thus contains a striking portrayal of the distorting impact of the individualistic ethic in our newly industrialized social and economic order. He both saw and exemplified the predicament of modernity. The tensions he uncovered were structural and permeated every institution in society. Yet Pound maintained a rationalistic view that pioneer justice and pioneer attitudes would pass: they were the product of a historical phase, and the necessities of the present would eventually overwhelm current attempts to accommodate them.

Pound's understanding of the "democratic" spirit of his own day had its limits. As I have observed, Pound associated that spirit with traditional concepts of political and human freedom, and he assumed that newly gained knowledge regarding the place and role of the individual in the modern social order would eventually reduce what he saw as held-over, and thus immature, strivings for "self-assertion." We have seen too that the dangers of the new kinds of knowledge regarding the individual largely escaped him. By 1923, moreover, Pound no longer appears to have considered whether some of the manifestations of the "democratic" spirit that plagued the administration of criminal justice issued from distinctively modern ideas. In particular, consistent with the general direction of his commentary over time on the criminal trial jury, the jury ultimately became one of Pound's principal targets. Where, in the beginning of his career, he had often balanced criticism of the "lawless" jury against the observation that the jury had long operated as a useful safety valve that sometimes even applied *progressive* notions in the face of overly traditional legal doctrines, in 1923, Pound's Progressivism was more to the fore. His position was that the recent modest reform of penology reflecting a more enlightened perspective on the nature of criminal behavior lessened the need for jury intervention in criminal cases. He appears not to have considered the possibility that this Progressive rhetoric itself took a toll on jurors, who, at the guilt assessment stage, were being asked to stigmatize as "criminal" defendants whose "guilt" was increasingly seen as problematic. Although jurors no doubt adhered to the conventional view that, in principle, most defendants possessed the capacity to act freely, they can hardly always have escaped the sense – subconscious though it may

---

[110] Pound, *Criminal Justice in America*, 199 (emphasis added).

often have been – that, in reality, the particular defendant before them was a victim of circumstances beyond his control.

In short, Pound failed to see that the rhetoric and to some extent also the practice of modern criminal justice depended upon an increasingly artificial bifurcation between guilt assessment and sentencing. His mature writings on criminal justice do not advert to the possibility that the modern jury, in its role as a safety valve, might sometimes have intuitively drawn lines, outside the formal rules of law, that allowed the concepts of the new criminology to coexist with more traditional notions of criminal responsibility.[111] The jury was, in a sense, simply continuing to behave as it had for ages; only now, theory had come to provide a more "scientific" rationale for what the jury had earlier done on the basis of its own rough understanding of justice. Pound's concerns about the dysfunctional character of jury power fit well with the concerns of others in the late Progressive Era, when the "irrationality" of jury decision making became a common theme in realist writing. But Pound failed to consider whether particular instances of ad hoc acquittals – or convictions on lesser-included charges – resulted from the influence on the jury of popularized notions of behavioral science, weakening his analysis of the very problems of modern criminal justice he sought to address.

---

[111] Contrast, e.g., the comments of Dean Henry Ballantine of the University of Illinois College of Law in an address delivered at a meeting of the Illinois State's Attorneys Association:

> The law has failed to take sufficient account of the possibility of different degrees of accountability of those not altogether innocent. At present, the jury fills up the gaps existing in the law of responsibility, and takes into consideration the moral elements and motives of crime. Those who as a result of hereditary taint and unfortunate environment, are mentally and morally degenerate, have not full penal accountability with normal men any more than little children, and if punishable at all, are punishable in a much less degree. (Henry W. Ballantine, "Criminal Responsibility of the Insane and Feeble Minded," *JCLC*, vol. 9 (1919): 485–99, 498)

Ballantine nonetheless preceded this observation with a statement adopting the conventional paradigm: "The positivist theory is neither practical nor convincing.... [F]or practical purposes the law must accept the common-sense postulate of free will upon which we all act. We assume in normal persons moral responsibility. They are accountable for their acts, and may justly be punished if they fail to control their conduct" (494). Ballantine thus seemed to offer his own somewhat middling stance, recognizing the possibility of lesser responsibility but, overall, strongly speaking for the traditional view (and in favor of the jury). Considered alongside Pound's scholarship, Ballantine's statements remind us that the legal academy certainly was not of one mind on how strong a view of free will the law should take. Presumably many – including among them a great deal of scholars (and jurists) who were not moved to write or speak at all about the subject – were generally content with the traditional view, particularly in practice, despite the widespread influence of the new sciences. Ballantine (like Pound) further shows, however, that any given scholar to touch on the criminal responsibility question was often, at least to some degree, of two minds. It simply is not clear how many legal scholars of the era adopted more radical Progressive views, in part because there is more historical work to be done on the subject, but also because of the scholars' own silences and ambiguity.

Indeed, in Progressive America – and beyond – "pioneer justice" could imply two very different meanings. Pound's relegation of the jury solely to the old frontier was a mistake, but it was an easy one to make, for – then as now – jurors themselves may have translated modern questions of responsibility into archaic ones, or unself-consciously moved back and forth between new and old: from one perspective, the slayer of his wife's lover vindicated his honor; from another, he had been out of control, which is to say he lacked the capacity for mens rea. There had been a shift over time from use of the oldest category, self-defense, or the next oldest, manslaughter, to that of legal insanity as a fictive device for mediating tensions between formal rules and widespread social attitudes – this was a development qualitatively different from any that had preceded it. Public outcry over the new convention confirmed that it posed an especially serious threat to traditional concepts of responsibility. The insanity defense thus provided new theories for old attitudes, but also a vocabulary and set of ideas that blended easily with those surrounding the new penology that may well have infected the assessment of responsibility in a very wide range of cases. Jurors likely negotiated the distance between old and new ideas, or mixed them together, applying them willy-nilly and not always self-consciously. The jury took its place on the new frontier of justice even as it acted out its place on the old one.

CONCLUSION: POUND UNRESOLVED

Pound believed that the remedy – the element that was most needed to improve the administration of criminal justice – was a better educated, less political, and more dominant bench. Armed with knowledge of the new sciences, the judge would oversee a process that met the imperatives of a modern industrial society, one that balanced the needs of order and individualism. The latter would be stripped of unjustifiable and intrusive elements of "self-assertion," but would retain a substance and vitality that accorded with the social interest in the deepest aspirations of humankind and served as a barrier against an all-powerful state. But how did the new sciences and the guilt assessment function of criminal process fit with Pound's particular concept of individual freedom? Was Pound clear in his own mind about the relationship between this uplifting consciousness of "freedom" and the potentially bleak message of the new sciences that the judge was to learn and apply? Listen one last time to Pound's oft-stated exhortation, in this case the closing lines of his final 1923 lecture:

The juristic thinking of today must transcend both nineteenth-century individualism and nineteenth-century socialism.... Instead of valuing all things in terms of individual personality, or in terms of politically organized society, we are valuing them in terms of civilization, of raising human powers to their highest possible unfolding – toward which *spontaneous free individual action* and collective organized effort both contribute. As this mode of thinking becomes general, the paths of criminal justice will be made straight.[112]

If Pound ever suspected that the contradictions among the various ideals that he himself espoused might not be resolvable, he never let on. His focus on the larger social order and on the role of the individual in that order largely, although not entirely, diverted his attention from the individual qua individual – from the problems inherent in the concept of human freedom.

The tensions and ambiguities that appear in Pound's thought do not admit of resolution within his own writings. Pound believed that science had seriously undermined the concept of free will, and he was among the most prominent in juristic circles openly to proclaim that law should (gradually) abandon that concept as a core requirement for criminal responsibility. Yet, although he emphasized the consciousness of, or the claim to, human freedom, he never brought that recognition together with his position on the mens rea doctrine. Moreover, Pound never outlined what a non–free-will-based system of criminal law would look like; he never assayed how in such a regime the reach of the social-defense or therapeutic state would be limited by traditional ideas of due process. He did not speculate about the impact of the open renunciation of *true* free will on the consciousness of human freedom that, as he saw it, was critical to political liberty, self-realization, and overall social progress. Pound wrote about freedom mainly in the context of procedural guarantees, not substantive law or underlying theory. History was his guide and perhaps his constraining master, political liberty remained his central focus, and the task of balancing the needs of society and the claims of the individual remained his conception of the ultimate goal of criminal justice. The key to achieving this goal, he thought, was adherence to judicial – not administrative – process alongside the empowerment and improvement of the bench, which would draw upon, without being superseded by, behavioral science experts. Given the immaturity of virtually all forms of scientific theory, the integration of legal and behavioral science would come slowly, but meanwhile progress would be manifested by a resettling of the relationship between judge and jury. He seems not to have considered that such a resettlement might itself be frustrated by the impact of behavioral science, which the law had not yet formally assimilated, on the popular imagination.

Pound's private thinking on the most intractable problems of criminal jurisprudence is similarly elusive.[113] Publicly, he settled for the platitudes that he was writing in a "period of transition," that "we are learning" the

---

[112] Pound, *Criminal Justice in America*, 214–15 (emphasis added).
[113] I have reviewed Pound's pre-1930 papers, including much of his correspondence, but have found nothing that sheds a light different from that indicated in his published writings on

message of the new sciences as well as "learning how to use it." He disguised his true thoughts – whatever they were – with the concluding observation that the road to reform would not be smooth: "there will be much experimenting and some fumbling and much dissatisfaction."[114]

In this moment, Pound sounded not a little like the Speranza of the "Medico-Legal Conflict," who had appealed for calm and for a melding of the best of the scientific and the legal traditions. As Pound put it, "the experience of the past, preserved in the law reports" – some undisclosed distillation of that experience – would have to inform, or be made to fit with,

> the issues with which I am principally concerned. Pound's published writings after 1930 do not reveal substantial attention to these problems or significant development in his thinking about them. In 1965, a year after Pound's death, Sheldon Glueck offered his assessment of Pound's views:
>
> > because [Pound] ... recognized the ethical element in law, he would not have been satisfied with a purely behavioristic criminal law, which removed such concepts as intent, motive, deliberation, premeditation, "malice," and the defense of insanity from the substantive law definitions of crimes and assigned them, as mental concepts, exclusively to psychology and psychiatry. (Glueck, "Memoir," 22)
>
> (Of course, Pound's criticism of the *Strasburg* decision suggests that, at least as of 1910, he countenanced legislative abolition of the insanity defense, at least when a convicted person retained the right to examination while incarcerated and, if found insane, could be transferred to an asylum.) Paul Sayre recounts a colloquy between Pound and several students during a seminar held at some point in the mid-to-late 1920s (Sayre, *Life of Roscoe Pound*, 170–78). Pound stated: "Claims are made by human beings; this I consider objective fact. Now the psychological forces in which those claims can also be stated is another matter. Doubtless an important matter and part of the whole juristic picture." He continued: "We necessarily deal with approximations in law and as such they are true." He told his students that the law had to deal with "actual claims," stating that: "All science constantly deals with conventional approximations," and asking: "Are you going to preclude the law from dealing with approximations as every other science does?" He added:
>
> > If you will permit me, I would like to add this: Where is the moral element in all this psychology of yours or do you think it's just a question of deterministic psychology and that morals are outmoded and there is no such thing as morals anymore? It's matters like this that worry me with the psychological approach as I have seen it developing recently. (175–76)
>
> It is possible that Pound was conceding here that even the concept of mens rea ought to be based on the human "claim" to freedom, but that matter appears not to have arisen. It appears from Sayre's account that Pound was discussing affirmative claims (e.g., the claim to the right of free speech; the claim to the right to be free from harm) and the reasons the law ought to respect them. I do not believe that Pound truly confronted here the problem of basing criminal responsibility on the fact that humans made general claims to freedom, that is, of holding a person criminally responsible on grounds he had acted "freely." In *that* context, I believe, Pound himself doubted the wisdom of recognizing the "freedom" that the law presumed.
>
> [114] Pound, "Summary," 588. The issues that Pound left unresolved should not detract from the fact that, as others have recognized, his observations were indeed relatively advanced, coming as they did from a legal scholar, despite the fact that he tended to skate over the dire implications of the new sciences for the concept of criminal responsibility. See, for example,

the new learning of the "expert[s]."[115] Like Speranza, Pound suggested here that the deepest problems of the substantive criminal law could be resolved only by a combination of law and science. Unlike Speranza, however, even at this isolated moment of insight, Pound seemed to believe that law and science could meld completely, speak with a single voice. Law was different from the behavioral sciences, but it *was* a science and one that could be perfected by rational selection from among the principles of the two domains. Pound seems never to have doubted that law and science could achieve ultimate unity, never to have conceded that the principles of the latter would always play havoc with those of the former, that the ultimate demand of the human project was adjustment to the reality that, law is, indeed, "one of the humanities."[116]

comments by Arthur Wood, a Professor of Sociology at the University of Michigan, who reviewed Pound's essay in the Cleveland Survey and concluded that Pound's "philosophic spirit, historical perspective, and scientific insight make it a landmark in American criminological jurisprudence." Arthur Evans Wood, "Methods of Criminological Inquiry," *JCLC*, vol. 16 (1925): 437–52, 443.

[115] Pound, "Summary," 587.

[116] Gino C. Speranza, "The Medico-Legal Conflict over Mental Responsibility," *Green Bag*, vol. 13 (1901): 123–26, 125.

3

Pound Eclipsed?

The Conversation of the Mid-to-Late 1920s

INTRODUCTION

For a time, many of those who wrote on criminal justice quoted Pound. His influence was considerable throughout the interwar period. But increasingly it was his sheer presence that drew attention, rather than his historical perspective and general ideas associated with sociological jurisprudence. Pound was well aware of the new currents of the immediate postwar years, including the marshaling of forces for our first great war on crime.[1] His late writings on criminal justice reflected his concern that individual liberties might be lost – that coordination of the social order might go beyond reasonable limits. Although he himself had been central to the first of the great crime surveys and had drawn to some extent upon the mass of data it provided, in the main, Pound was backward looking. He wrote generally – and in generalizations. He was indefatigable in promoting empirical research,[2] but in his own writings he rarely looked at matters up close. New facts were made

---

[1] Pound was a leader among the academics who responded to the heightened concerns about crime and the enforcement of public order. As I observe in Chapter 2, he was instrumental in the development and proliferation of crime commissions, which met with varying degrees of success. He was a central figure behind the Cleveland Survey, which brought the pervasive practice of plea bargaining and discretionary enforcement to the attention of the populace and became a model for subsequent reforms.

[2] Pound sought to continue the tangible work of the Cleveland Survey through the fairly successful Harvard Crime Survey of 1926 and his work on the Wickersham Commission's 1929 national survey. From his bully pulpit at Harvard, Pound attempted to create an atmosphere in which legal scholars would take the need for criminal justice reform seriously. He encouraged the development of fellowships for students and professors in the area of criminal law, and was a force behind the creation of Harvard's Institute of Criminal Law in 1929 – an innovation that fell victim to the Depression by 1935. See David Wigdor, *Roscoe Pound: Philosopher of Law* (Westport, CT: Greenwood Press, 1974), 246–48.

to fit ideas he had formed over two decades, and those decades themselves were treated as part of a *longue durée*. So, in due course, was Pound.

The social, political, and legal ferment of the war years – and the intellectual movements that resulted – are largely missing from Pound's work. They can be found in the writings of those who were influenced by his many contributions, but these are as often as not writings that pay him homage as they pass him by. The true point of departure in criminal jurisprudence and criminal justice studies was the mid-twenties, just after Pound's audiences had straggled home from his yet-unpublished lectures. It manifested itself in a new school of criminologists who fed on the data of the Cleveland Survey and of the many other studies that followed, and in a number of legal academics who reflected increasing interest in criminal jurisprudence and criminal justice administration. It showed also, of course, in continued concern among medical-jurisprudence scholars – both in and outside of the academy – with the long-standing problem of legal insanity. Although all of these groups are traceable to the great cooperative enterprise of the AICLC, the mid-twenties were nonetheless the beginning of the halcyon years, the era of geometric increase in new initiatives.

The first stirrings of the new era give more perspective to Pound's part in the story. But the characters I have chosen to illustrate the beginnings of this historical chapter were closer in spirit to the young Speranza, for they struggled in earnest with the problem of law and science rather than holding it at bay and wishing it well for the future. Much of what they wrote in the twenties continued discussions that dated from the late nineteenth century, matters that Pound had recognized but largely skirted: the psychology of vengeance, the problem of criminal responsibility, and the principles of an enlightened penology. Among those who took up these themes were the veteran psychiatrist William A. White and the neophyte behavioral scientist and legal scholar S. Sheldon Glueck.

I first consider a few central aspects of their work from the mid-twenties and then sketch in the outlines of what I treat as a "conversation" among them and others at the dawn of a new era. This early conversation would more clearly circumscribe the increasingly informed and deliberate debate among criminal jurisprudence scholars – which would continue throughout the twentieth century – concerning the proper relationship between science and criminal responsibility. Although science's deterministic insights into human nature began to seem beyond debate, commentators would also acknowledge what they saw as the law's unique role in human life. Dean Wigmore came to champion one version of the claim that, should sheer science pervade all areas of the law, it would erode the law's central purposes, which – at least for the time being – were utterly in conflict with the notion that the lawbreaker merely requires a "cure." The early terms of the debate thus also opened up larger questions, which would be addressed with more philosophical sophistication over the remainder of the century, concerning the proper purposes of the law and their relationship to our deep attachment – whether psychological or political – to ideas of personal freedom.

WILLIAM A. WHITE

By the time William White wrote *Insanity and the Criminal Law* in 1923,[3] he had practiced as a psychiatrist for more than thirty years and had become a leading figure in legal-insanity reform circles. White was appointed super-intendent of the Government Hospital for the Insane (Saint Elizabeth's) in 1903 and became an early American supporter of Freudian psychoanalysis. By the late 1920s, his interest in legal questions resulted in his push for coop-eration between the American Psychiatric Association and the ABA.[4] White adopted the psychiatrist's typical compromise position. He recognized the constitutional obstacles to the preferred reform – which was the substitu-tion of medical or psychological experts for the lay jury in the determina-tion of legal insanity – and argued instead for independent expert witnesses alongside those called by opposing parties and for a liberal test that did not import "artificial" – that is, legal as opposed to psychiatric – definitions of insanity. White nonetheless signed onto the 1916 "Keedy" report – a report by the AICLC committee on Insanity and Criminal Responsibility that included a recommended legal definition for insanity, and thus fell consider-ably short of White's real preferences – because he believed some reform was better than none at all.[5] But, in his independent writings, he pressed his more extreme views in the hope that he could effectively go over the heads of jurists and appeal directly to the educated public. He achieved, unwittingly, the ultimate irony: he analyzed jury behavior in terms that made the consti-tutional right to jury trial seem not merely an aspect of political liberty, but an enlightened response to the deep tendencies of human behavior.

From his psychiatric perspective, White began by describing crime in primitive society as "infantile" antisocial behavior that "tends to stir similar tendencies in the herd which are under severe repression in the service of civilization and culture." The member of the "herd" who is directly offended rationalizes his punishment of the criminal as getting "rid of sin," but "he is trying to get rid of that sin which he feels is resident in himself." Thus, the criminal "becomes the handy scapegoat upon which he can transfer his feel-ing of his own tendency to sinfulness"; he "deludes himself into a feeling of

[3] William A. White, *Insanity and the Criminal Law* (New York: Macmillan, 1923).
[4] See Janet Ann Tighe, "A Question of Responsibility: The Development of American Forensic Psychiatry, 1838–1930" (Ph.D. dissertation, University of Pennsylvania, 1983, available at http://repository.upenn.edu/dissertations/AAI8406727), 436–500.
[5] Edwin Keedy et al., "Insanity and Criminal Responsibility" (report of AICLC Committee "A," chaired by Professor Edwin Keedy), *JCLC*, vol. 7 (1916): 484–91. The story of AICLC Committee "A," and White's role on that committee, is recounted in great and telling detail in Tighe, "Question of Responsibility," 310–81.

righteous indignation, thus bolstering up his own self-respect and serving in this roundabout way, both to restrain himself from like indulgences and to keep himself upon the path of cultural progress." From these "crude beginnings" came modern "concepts of crime, criminals and criminal law."[6]

The original negative impulse in response to an offense is vengeance, which is not constructive, but tends "only to prevent disintegration by destroying the disintegrating factors." Punishment in accordance with the prescriptions of society permitted the expression of personal vengeance.[7] Most significant, this process was transformed over time – to civilize the impulse – by formal institutions designed to determine responsibility, such as the criminal trial jury. The jury "becomes society," or "the herd, in miniature, reduced in size to the minimum number of constituent units that conceivably may adequately reflect its opinions and feelings." Its judgments, White asserted, "can only be understood as biological forces operating as selective agents in a practical manner ... in accordance with the standards prevailing at the time." The substitution of the jury for the individual who had been offended "makes for a better organized, more closely knit, and highly integrated structure"; vengeance recedes into the background, although it remains the underlying motive.[8]

The central purpose of White's book was to argue for reform of the legal insanity defense. The argument was not for the full-blooded reform he preferred wherein the jury would find whether the defendant had committed the act and experts would determine whether he had been sane at the time of the act. Nevertheless, White could not resist pointing out that, under his preferred approach, the "antipathic emotions of the herd" could still be assuaged. Then science could take over:

After the prisoner was condemned and the key turned upon him, so to speak, the public would promptly forget him, as now, and any constructive scheme of social therapeutics could then be worked out in peace and quiet and free from the emotional strains that now not infrequently greet an effort on the part of the accused to effect his acquittal by way of the plea of insanity.[9]

But White conceded that his preferred scheme was unconstitutional, an objection he regarded as "incontrovertible" given "the standpoint of crime as now conceived, as an offense against society which must be punished."[10] He turned instead to realistic consideration of how the law of insanity ought to be administered, and he produced a strikingly original suggestion

---

[6] White, *Insanity and the Criminal Law*, 13–14. For a discussion of White's views, see Herbert Hovenkamp, "Insanity and Criminal Responsibility in Progressive America," *North Dakota Law Review*, vol. 57 (1981): 541–76, 656–66.

[7] White, *Insanity and the Criminal Law*, 16–19.

[8] White, *Insanity and the Criminal Law*, 183–85.

[9] White, *Insanity and the Criminal Law*, 168.

[10] White, *Insanity and the Criminal Law*, 169.

manifested (by his lights) in the 1916 Criminal Responsibility Bill proffered by the AICLC committee on legal insanity.

Two of the most important features of the Bill were its adoption of an eminently flexible insanity test and its provision for court-appointed experts in addition to those called by the parties. The two reforms interacted in a significant fashion, according to White: the independent expert, unconstrained by service to one of the parties and, therefore, far more credible than the presumed partisan experts, would serve to get *all* of the real psychological facts before the jury. As a result, the

> verdict will reflect such sympathy as the added facts may warrant, sympathy being understood to stand for that quality which enables one to put himself, in his feelings, in the place of the other fellow and so to appreciate, at first hand, his position with reference to all of the facts, his temptations, his weaknesses, his disappointments, desires, ambitions, wishes, tendencies and all that sort of qualities which make him a human being at one with others.[11]

The jury, "free from the impedimenta of artificial and static tests to which they are required by law to adjust their findings, will find the law and the custom much more accurately.... The jury needs ... to be left as free agents through which the law as it exists in the popular consciousness may flow to free expression."[12]

Thus did White seek to harness the true and organic role of the jury to the cause of reform. At least with respect to the insanity defense, but implicitly in all serious criminal cases, White endorsed the law-finding that he viewed as inevitable and argued for a transformation of the vengeance impulse into an unobstructed flow of human sympathy – a close cousin of both age-old empathy and modern deterministic psychology. Indeed, White went on to claim that the progress of criminal procedure had been away from personal vengeance and toward an "impersonal meting out of justice." Here, White invoked history: "early in the jury system juries were chosen who knew the contestants or the defendant," whereas now jurors are chosen for lack of that very knowledge "on the theory that they will thus bring a judicial attitude of mind to bear upon the questions at issue." This made it possible to proceed yet further, "to get at the real merits of the broader, and more particular social issues, unhampered by the distorting effects of prejudice or of powerful emotions."[13]

It is worth remarking upon the differences between Pound's and White's accounts of criminal justice administration. Pound wrote as an amateur, although accomplished historian and professional common lawyer; White wrote as a professional psychiatrist and amateur anthropologist. Pound

[11] White, *Insanity and the Criminal Law*, 209.
[12] White, *Insanity and the Criminal Law*, 209–10.
[13] White, *Insanity and the Criminal Law*, 210–11.

conjoined deep respect for the "claim" to free will with both a call for reasonable restraint on individual assertion and a professed acceptance of the behavioral scientists' denial that "criminals" in *fact* freely chose to commit unlawful acts; White was a dyed-in-the-wool determinist. Both envisioned a future in which those convicted of criminal behavior would receive treatment rather than punishment. Pound placed trust in a bench educated in the principles of human behavior: better to leave the sentencing power in the hands of the court, which would be vigilant with respect to convicts' rights, than to surrender convicts up to a cadre of experts employed by the bureaucratic state. White put his faith in experts, who he imagined would exercise independent judgment. White was sanguine about long-term, even permanent, civil commitment of convicts when required by the severity of their illnesses. Pound skirted that issue, assuming, presumably, that most convicts were treatable well within the time frames already employed in criminal justice administration.

Although Pound looked to a future in which scientific principles of treatment would dominate, it remains doubtful that he fully accepted White's bleak theory of human behavior. For Pound, the consciousness of freely willed expression, creativity, and self-control remained basic, and his focus on this sunnier side of human psychology leaves his reader to suppose that, by Pound's lights, the incurable were few and far between. One infers from Pound's account that most offenders were the product of social forces that were subject to change by an educated public. If change did not come easily, it was because the conditions of a modern industrial order were difficult to alter; political will failed. There is little in Pound to suggest he took seriously either White's view of crime as the product of deeply embedded antisocial urges or White's view of criminal justice as the group's collective sublimation of its own similar urges. Pound viewed humans as far more rational and malleable than did White, despite the fact that his historical perspective led him to emphasize the influence of "holdover" attitudes.

We have seen that, for Pound, the jury reflected the common view, in both a social and a political sense. It had once played a vital role as a brake on tyrannical authorities and had then served usefully to leaven the overly mechanical common law. The jury had provided discretionary justice in communities that lacked a well-articulated governmental structure. In all of these instances, the jury had exercised an independence that was rationalized through an ideology of personal freedom. In Pound's early accounts, the jury had just as often protected the defendant against the "social group" as it had acted out group vengeance against an offending individual. Yet, in writing about the insanity defense, Pound focused on the problem of the unwritten law, railing at the jurors' often wrongheaded sympathy for the defendant.[14] He ultimately regarded the continued

---

[14] See Roscoe Pound, *Criminal Justice in America* (New York: H. Holt, 1930), 125–28.

"extravagant" power of juries as an aspect of cultural lag, explicable in terms of American history and the now-outmoded extreme ideology of freedom that it had inspired. All this would pass: "General improvement will come through better general education in sociology, leading the public to abandon the retributive idea and the man in the street to desist from the demand for revenge."[15]

In White's account of typical jury practice, on the other hand, the desire for vengeance dominated, despite his also recognizing instances of juror empathy. He ultimately capitulated to a full jury trial in legal-insanity cases in the name of constitutionalism; political liberty now would have its day. But he argued for independent witnesses on the ground that their setting forth *all* the circumstances surrounding an unlawful act would lead the jury away from vengeance, toward understanding and sympathy. White sought to employ his principles of psychology to produce verdicts of "not guilty by reason of insanity," by virtue of which defendants would be turned over to medical experts for treatment. Thus White hoped to make scientific use of the very sympathy that Pound identified with the sham of the "insanity dodge" and the unwritten-law acquittal. According to White, modern psychology and the jury trial could be made to go hand in hand in this second-best manner.

This tour de force argument for unrestrained testimony to the jury found little support in interwar writings. White's 1923 prescription for reform remained sui generis and one wonders whether he himself had produced it only as a *reductio ad absurdum*. Nonetheless, his stress on the enactment of vengeance and on jury psychology left its mark on the post-Poundian era. White produced an account of criminal justice based upon allegedly universal and deep-seated human motivations rather than upon Pound's relatively local history of the sociopolitical struggle among individuals and between the individual and the state in mainly the Anglo-American tradition. White's account by no means entirely displaced Pound's, but as a rival theory it perhaps garnered as much support among criminologists as did Pound's more tepid sociological jurisprudence among legal scholars.

S. SHELDON GLUECK

Sheldon Glueck was among the most important of those scholars who drew on both Pound and White in exploring the more fundamental issue of criminal responsibility and bringing the behavioral science perspective into the legal academy. Although he was essentially a behavioral scientist, Glueck possessed a law degree and, by virtue of Pound's sponsorship, would ultimately

---

[15] Roscoe Pound, "Inherent and Acquired Difficulties in the Administration of Punitive Justice," in *Proceedings of the American Political Science Association*, vol. 4 (Baltimore: Waverly Press, 1908), 222–39, 239.

join the Harvard Law faculty.[16] Glueck's 1925 book, *Mental Disorder and the Criminal Law*,[17] was at once a stunning synthesis of the insights of his elders and an original contribution to the legal insanity debate. The originality of his work can easily be missed, for Glueck was the paragon of the balanced, pragmatic, common-sense scholar. Although in the 1930s he moved toward a more determinist stance, for the moment I seek to capture him as of 1925, when he attempted to shore up Pound's sociological jurisprudence by converting Pound's consciousness of freedom into something like a true free will–based position.

Glueck's important study recommended reforms of the legal insanity defense that worked within the basic structure of the AICLC proposal but incorporated a series of judicial instructions embodying the view that the cognitive, affective, and conative aspects of the human mind were interdependent.[18] He believed that this approach to avoidance of the rigid and unscientific cognitive test would allow for more accurate jury responses, although he fully recognized that the jury would never be a scientific institution. But, for Glueck, that hardly made the jury system second best.[19] From his perspective – at least as of the mid-1920s – science could go only so far. Indeed, Glueck sought to breathe life into the traditional legal position on the relevance of free will to criminal responsibility. He effectively glossed the ideas of those jurists more commonly associated with legal orthodoxy and, by applying the principles of mentalist psychology, he took those ideas to a new level of sophistication. Still, it is not easy to pin down what Glueck meant by human freedom. He tended to circle round the concept, focusing

---

[16] Glueck emigrated to the United States from his native Poland in 1903. By 1924 he had earned several degrees, including two in law from the National University Law School in Washington, DC, and an AM and PhD from Harvard. Glueck taught criminology in the Harvard Department of Social Ethics for four years before joining the law faculty in 1929. Two years later he became a full professor, and he was named the Roscoe Pound Professor of Law in 1950.

[17] S. Sheldon Glueck, *Mental Disorder and the Criminal Law: A Study in Medico-Sociological Jurisprudence* (Boston: Little, Brown, 1925); see also S. S. Glueck, "Ethics, Psychology and the Criminal Responsibility of the Insane," *JCLC* 14 (1923): 208–48. For an excellent, more comprehensive discussion of Glueck's ideas, see Tighe, "Question of Responsibility," 382–435. I agree with Tighe that Glueck believed that "man's choices and actions in life were both free and determined" (393). I have sought to expose Glueck's struggle to make sense of this view.

[18] Glueck, *Mental Disorder*, 118–22, 264–66.

[19] See Glueck, *Mental Disorder*, 465–66:

> Taking it all in all, the jury of laymen from all decent walks and stations of life, provided, always, that honest and intelligent men do their share of jury service, is as good a device, in our opinion, as could be evolved, for the difficult task of arriving at conclusions on the basis of frequently conflicting testimony. A jury of experts is not pliable enough mentally for the quick and, on the whole, efficient group mind process ... for experts are liable to be dogmatic, too onesided, each clinging to those theories borne out by his own particular experience ... less tolerant of the views of others.

more on the problem of moral responsibility and remaining ambiguous about just how it depended on freedom. We may briefly trace his steps.

Glueck began with a description of the subjective notion of responsibility, which "arises from the general opinion, based upon life's experiences, that a person possessed of the ordinary human faculties to an apparently normal degree is capable of acting, and therefore, must, and is by us expected, to act according to an accepted, socially required standard of morality." Of such a person, Glueck continued, "we say that he has a free will ... that in the ordinary affairs of life, he is able to choose the good and avoid the evil."[20] But is this illusory? Glueck initially conceded that humans could hate, love, forgive, and attribute blame, all without a belief in human freedom.[21] Yet he continued:

they do these things because, on the one hand, their innate, instinctive nature prompts them to it, and, on the other, their intelligence and experience teaches them that most human beings have some *capacity for purposive, creative activity,* albeit under the influence of innate, psycho-physical dispositions, or "instincts," and their emotional accompaniments, or "motives." ... If, therefore, we would use the expression "free-dom of will" at all, let us employ it – as some writers of the Mentalist School of Psychology do – as describing man's capacity to act with consciousness of purpose, albeit on the basis of his instinctive nature.[22]

Glueck thus pragmatically defined responsibility on the basis of empirical observations of human behavior, our common practical beliefs, and our experiences of ourselves and others. It appears that Glueck not only allied himself with the mentalist school against the most deterministic "modern radicals," but that he believed that purposive conduct in fact involved choice and creativity in the sense of "some self-direction." In his next pass, however, he sided with the mentalist school over the behaviorist school on strictly *instrumental* grounds, critiquing behaviorism's failures: "It is difficult to see, on the other hand, how, under a purely behavioristic (mechanical-materialistic) conception of the human organism, there is any room for belief in even a shred of free, self-directive, purposive, and to that extent responsible, activity."[23]

In his discussion of the criminal trial jury, Glueck produced a somewhat different account of responsibility that took account of the psychology of responsibility that characterized society at large, thus melding his approach to responsibility with a description of social psychology that had much in common with White's. He appears to have attempted to harness White's insights to his own less deterministic views. The result was a justification for jury trial that overlapped White's at points, but that departed from it in

---

[20] Glueck, *Mental Disorder,* 89–90.
[21] Glueck, *Mental Disorder,* 93–94.
[22] Glueck, *Mental Disorder,* 94 (emphasis added).
[23] Glueck, *Mental Disorder,* 96.

critical ways. In later portions of *Mental Disorder and the Criminal Law,* Glueck reiterated his view that the "presence of mechanism does not mean that human beings have not some spark of capacity for consciously and creatively guiding their conduct in conformity with legal sanctions,"[24] once again seeming to commit himself to an objective conclusion about human behavior. He presented this view as a response to deterministic behaviorists, but then dismissed the debate over free will as largely irrelevant in the face of group psychology:

as we have repeatedly said, it is our belief that praise and blame, the urge to hurt in retaliation, the instinct to self-protection, – these are all concepts that have their tangible illustration and sanction in the psychology of human nature; and, similarly, society's right to self-protection is found in group psychology, in the primitive urge of the group to maintain itself against those inimical acts of individuals that threaten its very existence. This *psychological* basis of responsibility is primary; the rest is mere addition, refinement, sublimation, and rationalization.[25]

This appears to give away the store, but Glueck was prepared to argue from the "psychology of human nature" – even from the "primitive urge" – to a concept of responsibility that accorded with the presumption of "educability," by which he meant that if the offender "was able to profit by experience to a more or less normal degree, then he is responsible both morally and to the group, for violating the laws of the group." The test for educability depended, of course, on what the "offender's life history and mental examination disclose."[26] But did this mean merely that the individual could be affected by the threat of punishment, or instead that the individual possessed a capacity for actual self-direction? Taken as a whole, Glueck's work seems to imply the latter.

For Glueck announced two important principles of justice: first, the primary right of society to social protection; second, recognition of the personality of the offender. Those principles brought together the many strands of his thinking on criminal justice. Sounding like White, he noted the dangers that attended the first: "particularly atrocious acts stir the group mind, as they do the individual, with hatred, disgust, fear, and a deep sense of outrage," forcing "Justice into a mésalliance with Vengeance." Glueck argued that "some toll must be paid to revengefulness and the desire for blood." Then sounding much like Pound, he asserted: "This is one of the inherent weaknesses in all social institutions; and only the solvent of liberal education can aid in its reduction." And here we have the link to the second principle: we have a "duty to suspend judgment upon the actor until we have made an effort to examine into the 'natural history'

---

[24] Glueck, *Mental Disorder,* 444–45.
[25] Glueck, *Mental Disorder,* 445.
[26] Glueck, *Mental Disorder,* 445.

of [the defendant's] act." Why? Because "our anger soon cools when we learn that a certain offender *really could not have avoided the act.*"[27] But what does this mean? When we come to *believe* he could not? Or when we learn he *actually* could not? Glueck seems to have meant the latter – and in fact to have believed, although he never attempted to illustrate, that sometimes one could, and sometimes one could not, have "avoided the act." True responsibility – and the group's (presumably, the jury's) assessment thereof – depended on the defendant's capacity for purposive action, on some degree of "self-direction." Whereas White imagined a jury process that allowed for empathy in the context of totally deterministic premises, Glueck envisioned a jury-based determination along lines that complied with, or at least could be understood in terms of, traditional notions of responsibility. Glueck believed that "fulfillment of all these purposes" required resort to "modern scientific instrumentalities" and attention to the "more or less conflicting social interest in the general security, on the one hand, and the social interest in the welfare and opportunity for freedom of individual self-expression, on the other."[28] Here, he again sounded like and cited Pound, whose sociological jurisprudence – really, social engineering – he sought to exemplify.

Glueck's integration of Pound's sociological jurisprudence and White's psychology of vengeance was masterful rhetorically, if bereft of philosophical rigor. Although superficially Glueck seemed to track White more closely, adding only a much deeper psychology of freedom, the relationship to Pound's work is intriguing. Like Pound, Glueck pushed the abstract doctrine of free will to the side. Unlike Pound, however, Glueck seems to have treated the freedom he associated with conscious purposive action as an ultimate reality, even though it might appear to us to be a close relative of Pound's "conscious ego" or the mere consciousness of freedom. Nonetheless, whatever internal incoherence Glueck's mid-1920s theory of responsibility might have possessed, its translation into specific terms of group judgment – of jury behavior – filled a critical gap in Pound's account. Pound's work exhibited a superficial form of pragmatism, a Progressive Era functionalism. Glueck revealed a deeper philosophical pragmatism that took Pound's notion of the consciousness of – or "claim" to – freedom a further step, that coordinated it with group psychology, and that sought to ground justice and responsibility on the overlap among actual capacity for self-direction, the objective fact of "educability," and the social desire to seek retribution. What was most attractive and ultimately influential in Glueck's account was the protean aspect of his thought. It was open to adaptation to a degree that White's was not. And it had, more than anything else, the *ring* of common sense.

[27] Glueck, *Mental Disorder*, 446–47 (emphasis added).
[28] Glueck, *Mental Disorder*, 447.

JOHN H. WIGMORE AND THE ONGOING CONVERSATION
OF THE 1920S

The conversation of the mid- and late 1920s that White and Glueck helped to initiate soon dissolved into a cacophony of discordant voices. The debate over criminal responsibility, to which the issue of free will was central, had increasingly become conflated with the debate over the goal of penal intervention: Was it cure of the defendant, protection of society, or both? Little wonder that Pound, who had long before noted the disagreements among the new scientists, as well as between scientists and jurists, resolved to remain above the fray. Safely ashore, out of the dangerous currents, dominating the littoral: so stood Pound. Not so his erstwhile colleague, Northwestern's Dean Wigmore, the first President of the AICLC and, you will recall, chair of the Institute's Modern Criminal Science Series Committee that, in 1911, had called for a scientific approach to the causes and treatment of crime. Flush with enthusiasm, the committee had endorsed individualization within a treatment model, not committing itself to a single perspective – utilitarian, scientific-positivist, or otherwise – nor, for that matter, referring specifically to the goal of deterrence. The latter, no doubt, figured as an important aspect of "penal or remedial treatment," but it was "remedial treatment" that seemingly reflected the spirit of the General Introduction to the Series.[29] By the mid-1920s, however, Wigmore's own emphasis had fallen upon the goal of deterrence: he now pointedly distinguished the "point[s] of view" of "remedy or repression," which "in recent years ... have been dimly seen to be destined to lead to more or less conflicting conclusions and results."[30] For Wigmore, among the results was the adoption of more or less conflicting language regarding human freedom.

The occasion for Wigmore's entry into the post-1923 conversation was a symposium on Judge John Caverly's sentencing of Richard Loeb and Nathan Leopold to life imprisonment, rather than execution, on grounds of their youth, for their confessed slaying of Robert ("Bobby") Franks in 1924. At the sentencing hearing, Clarence Darrow, representing Loeb and Leopold, famously introduced extensive psychiatric testimony concerning his clients' mental condition to urge that they were not fully responsible for their acts.[31] Wigmore protested that "the reports of the psychiatrists called

---

[29] See "General Introduction to the Modern Criminal Science Series," in, e.g., Raymond Saleilles, *The Individualization of Punishment*, trans. Rachel Szold Jastrow (Boston: Little, Brown, 1911), v–ix, vii.

[30] John H. Wigmore, "The Relation between Criminal Law and Criminal Psychiatry," *JCLC*, vol. 16 (1925): 311.

[31] For the hearing before Judge Caverly, see Alvin V. Sellers, *The Loeb-Leopold Case, with Excerpts from the Evidence of the Alienists and Including the Arguments to the Court by Counsel for the People and the Defense* (Brunswick, GA: Classic Publishing, 1926). Under Illinois law, the punishment for murder ranged from fourteen years in the penitentiary to death. If the defendant were found guilty by a jury, then the jury would determine the

for the defense, if given the influence which the defense asked, *would tend to undermine the whole penal law.*" He attacked the psychiatrists' views as "sheer Determinism," which implied that there was "no choice for us, because all human acts are predetermined." Wigmore alleged that psychiatrists believed determinism would "eliminate moral blame, and therefore eliminate penal consequences." This, he stated, was a mistake – and one that even the early positivist, Enrico Ferri, had recognized: "The measures of the modern penal law," said Wigmore, "are not based on moral blame, but on social self-defense. When there is a weed in your garden, and you cut it down, you do not do this on any theory of the moral blame of the weed, but simply on the theory that you are entitled to keep weeds out of your garden." Wigmore's central point was that "the kingpin of the criminal law" was deterrence theory and that the psychiatric approach would "lessen the restraints on *the outside class of potential homiciders.*" "Society," he claimed, "is entitled to use appropriate measures to repress antisocial acts. Society's right of self-defense is equally valid even when the human weed was predetermined by nature and environment to do just what he did."[32]

sentence; if the defendant pled guilty, then sentencing would be fixed by the court. Darrow entered a guilty plea in order to avoid a jury's outrage and to gain a forum at which time the defense could "offer evidence as to the mental condition of these young men [and] to show the degree of responsibility they had" (11). At the sentencing hearing, Darrow called a number of psychiatrists who testified, inter alia, that Leopold was a "paranoid personality perhaps developing into a paranoid psychosis" and Loeb suffered from a "disordered" or "split" personality (23–24). The boys were in the grip of a peculiar "king-slave compulsion" in which "each boy felt inadequate to carry out the life he most desired unless he had some one else in his life to complement him, to complete him. Leopold, on the one hand, wanted a superior for a companion. Loeb, on the other, wanted some one to adulate him for a companion. The psychiatric cause for this is not to be found in either boy alone, but in the interplay of their two personalities caused by their constitutions and experiences" (30–31). Judge Caverly sentenced Leopold and Loeb to life in prison, with the recommendation that they never receive parole. Caverly acknowledged the impact of the medical testimony, stating:

the careful analysis made of ... the defendants and of their present mental, emotional, and ethical condition has been of extreme interest and is a valuable contribution to criminology. And yet the court feels strongly that similar analyses made of other [defendants] would probably reveal similar or different abnormalities. The value of such tests seems to lie in their applicability to crime and criminals in general. Since they concern the broad questions of human responsibility and legal punishment, and are in no wise particular to these individual defendants, they may be deserving of legislative but not of judicial consideration. For this reason the court is satisfied that his judgment in the present case cannot be affected thereby. (319–20)

Caverly eventually grounded his decision to incarcerate the defendants on their youth, stating that "the court believes that it is within his province to decline to impose the sentence of death on persons who are not of full age" (321).

[32] John H. Wigmore, comments in "The Loeb-Leopold Case: A Symposium of Comments from the Legal Profession," *JCLC*, vol. 15 (1924): 401–05. Wigmore's views regarding the importance of deterrence are stated more fully in John H. Wigmore, "The Judge's Sentence in the Loeb-Leopold Murder," *Illinois Law Review*, vol. 19 (1924): 167–71. See also John

Wigmore cautioned that a deterministic theory could excuse not just serious crimes, but all deliberate breaches of the law. Finally:

It is an excellent thing that these scientists have had their day in court thus publicly, because their theories have been going about in books and articles and have begun to affect public opinion. It is time that the issue be squarely faced in the open, before the whole administration of the penal law is undermined. Let public opinion look into the literature on this subject, and learn to discard that false sympathy and dangerous weakening that is apt to arise on first acceptance of the biopsychologic doctrine of Determinism.[33]

Wigmore's comments drew a response from Dr. H. I. Gosline, Director and Chief Psychiatrist of the Dallas Child Guidance Clinic, who declared that the deterrence theory was wrongheaded because, even if it deterred in the short run, it

does not cure, because it only represses, and because it dams back and causes to fester in the body politic.... Of course [the psychiatric view] is Determinism (with a capital "D," as our good friend spells it). But the psychiatrist, who is the determinist, is going to do much more for "social self-defense" than the "measures of modern penal law" now do.[34]

Gosline argued that psychiatrists did not beg indulgence for dangerous criminals, but humane treatment, which in many cases meant psychiatric care. This, he asserted, would mean that "most of them would stay for life – there would be very little more of this three to five year business"; that, he concluded, would be the "greater deterrent to crime."[35]

Wigmore's response to Gosline was somewhat heated. Under the "Cure theory," as Wigmore termed it:

Morality has gone to the bow-wows, and [the] community has passed into a state of drab, cool, materialistic unmorality which would make Life a chill, scientific grave-yard and laboratory combined. Let the sociologists speculate as much as they will on the primitive origin and evolution of the Moral Conscience. The great fact remains that it IS.[36]

H. Wigmore, "Juvenile Court vs. Criminal Court," *Illinois Law Review*, vol. 21 (1926): 375–77.

[33] Wigmore, "Loeb-Leopold Case," 405. Perhaps Wigmore also had Clarence Darrow in mind. Darrow was a "popularizer" of determinist ideas; even worse, he made them accessible to jurors. See Clarence Darrow, *Crime: Its Cause and Treatment* (New York: Thomas Y. Crowell, 1922). It seems likely, at any rate, that Wigmore had concerns about the impact of the new science on jurors.

[34] H. I. Gosline, letter to the editor, "The Loeb-Leopold Case Again," *JCLC*, vol. 15 (1925): 501–05, 504–05.

[35] Gosline, "Loeb-Leopold," 505.

[36] John H. Wigmore, "Comments on Dr. Gosline's Comments," *JCLC*, vol. 15 (1925): 505–08, 507.

Wigmore repeated his claim that the psychiatric approach addressed the individual offender but failed to deter the "outside mass." Moreover, he posited, that approach was "suicidal." He imagined Dr. Gosline "face to face" with a "thug": "What is Dr. Gosline going to do about it now? 'Let me cure you, my sick fellow'? Why, before our worthy doctor has a chance to utter the sentence, the thug will fill him fatally full of lead." The "Cure theory," Wigmore concluded, should be "restricted" to "the very limited and feasible field of, say, juvenile offenses, until it can demonstrate its right to a safe and gradual enlargement."[37]

Wigmore's invective had been intended, no doubt, for White, who had testified for the defense in the Loeb-Leopold case as a preeminent representative of the psychiatric point of view, a role he played with relish.[38] But where Wigmore was sardonic, White was condescending. His review of Glueck's 1925 book is a case in point. White greeted *Mental Disorder and the Criminal Law* with a mixture of congratulation and caution. It is not clear that he correctly assessed the true purport of Glueck's project, which he appears to have taken as a tactical concession on the question of human freedom as well as on the matter of procedural reforms relevant to the insanity defense. It comes as little surprise that White termed Glueck's recommendations for reform "conservative." At the same time, White deemed Glueck's book to have "the double advantage of being written by a lawyer who has a humanistic point of view." He continued (with Wigmore in mind?):

[37] Wigmore, "Comments," 508. One legal scholar representing the contrasting view was Yale Law School's Robert Maynard Hutchins, who commented in "The Law and the Psychologists," *Yale Review*, vol. 16 (1927): 678*ff*:

> One of our leaders [i.e., Wigmore] has lately repudiated the efforts of social scientists to aid us in dealing with crime and punishment, saying that we can determine the preventive effect of jail sentences, fines, and executions by searching our own hearts; no statistics are necessary. Yet his own masterly treatises [on the law of evidence] show on every page that after searching our hearts for centuries we have utterly failed in the hunt: its result has been a mass of conflicting rules, of metaphysical doctrines, of methods of concealing the truth now sanctioned in our courts. (689–90)

> Hutchins added: "To say that, when the psychologists have anything to offer, the law is ready for them is not enough. If we of the legal profession wait until the psychologists have something to offer us, we may never have it offered" (689). It is not clear whether Hutchins was referring to Wigmore's commentary on the Loeb-Leopold proceedings or to comments by Wigmore on a different occasion.

[38] See John H. Wigmore, "To Abolish Partisanship of Expert Witnesses, as Illustrated in the Loeb-Leopold Case," *JCLC*, vol. 15 (1924): 341–43. Wigmore complained that the "voluntary adoption of the endearing, attenuating epithets 'Dickie' and 'Babe' to designate the defendants reflects seriously on the medical profession. The whole evil of expert partisanship is exemplified in this action of these eminent gentlemen." He claimed they were "adopting epithets calculated subtly to emphasize the childlike ingenuousness and infantile naivity of the cruel, unscrupulous wretches in the dock" (341). White, the first witness for the defense, employed these "epithets." See Sellers, *Loeb-Leopold Case*, 15–18. White, of course, was a strong proponent of nonpartisan expert witnesses.

This humanistic point of view is not needed in order to get over suggestions in line with it to the physician. He is accustomed to it; but the lawyer is by profession and tradition almost without it and he will not be nearly so apt to pay attention to recommendations coming outside of his profession.[39]

White attributed Glueck's "conservative" strategy to his being a lawyer and suggested that Glueck intentionally eschewed "radical" ends in favor of moderation. "Whichever method of procedure is advocated, the conservative or the radical," White conceded, "is probably a matter of temperament almost entirely." Perhaps reflecting on his own recent book, White concluded that "there seems to be no way of telling when to advocate one and when the other."[40] White nonetheless felt compelled to respond to Glueck's lengthy discourse on responsibility in frank terms:

The reviewer is rather inclined to believe that we can never solve the question of responsibility, about which so many of the pages of this book are written.... [R]esponsibility is a conclusion based upon a feeling attitude rather than upon an intellectual one. It is a rationalization of the jury's wishes.... The fact that it is a fiction may or may not be significant.... Perhaps a more important question is whether as a fiction it has or has not survived its usefulness.... Society is not, or I might perhaps better say should not be, interested in responsibility but only in social assimilability. The simple thing which I have always advocated is to do away with all these inquiries into responsibility, insanity and the like, and merely remove anti-social offenders from society and keep them as long as they remain anti-social.[41]

Of course, White had *faute de mieux* fashioned his own compromise two years earlier, imagining a process through which the jury – properly informed by psychiatric experts – would make the inquiry that was constitutionally required. As we have seen, however, White's vision of this process was consistent both with an entirely deterministic perspective – on that he would *not* compromise – and with rejection of the vengeance motif. Nonetheless, he clearly believed that his preferred reform program would meet the requirements of retribution and general deterrence: for the "herd," long-term incarceration and treatment would serve roughly the same ends as incarceration and punishment.[42]

Indeed, like Gosline, White almost certainly assumed that most serious offenders would be confined for longer periods than was the case under current sentencing practice; they would undergo a "constructive scheme of

---

[39] William A. White, review of *Mental Disorder and the Criminal Law*, by S. Sheldon Glueck, *Yale Law Journal*, vol. 35 (1926): 779–81, 780.

[40] White, review of Glueck, 780.

[41] White, review of Glueck, 780–81.

[42] In this regard, White foreshadowed later treatment-oriented legal scholarship, which was increasingly attentive to public conceptions of the law and which would defend the aim of "curing" offenders as most acceptable to the public because the accompanying confinement would be perceived as sending traditional messages of retribution and deterrence.

social therapeutics," and the problem of release by psychiatric experts of sane but antisocial offenders whom juries had found not guilty by reason of insanity would be avoided altogether. But these effects were incidental; cure through "treatment" was the true goal. White noted that this was also Glueck's intention; he evidently considered Glueck's concept of responsibility a mere buying of time until society was ready to dispense with that particular "fiction."[43] For White, "responsibility" and "vengeance" were correlatives, and he mistakenly read Glueck to think the same. White termed his own views "radical": he was well aware that they flew in the face of constitutional protections and the juristic theory of responsibility.

Some "radical" reforms for which both pure social-defense enthusiasts and treatment-oriented psychiatric experts campaigned found favor among some legal academics, who nonetheless recognized them as too radical to be implemented. John B. Waite of the University of Michigan, for example, referred to

yet another theory of the objective of criminal prosecution which is coming to the fore and, consummation devoutedly to be desired, may some day be adopted. This theory is, that prosecution seeks no punishment at all, but that it aims to ascertain those who have shown themselves presumably unfitted to mingle in society, with the object that they may thereafter be segregated from society either forever, or until such time as they become fitted for readmission.... But this theory is wholly inconsistent with present practices, is at variance with the judicial point of view, is a criminological and penological rather than a legal theory and cannot properly be here considered.[44]

Unfazed by such warnings from even the more receptive of legal academics, White carried the campaign against the judicial point of view into the heart of the enemy camp in August 1927. "Law and medicine," White stated at the annual meeting of the ABA in Buffalo, share common aims, but "have come to talk[,] as it were[,] different languages"; "they have thus far been unable to get together largely because they do not understand each other." Many in his audience may well have felt that they understood each other only too well, but White, who had begun by noting the importance of the fact that

---

[43] White, *Insanity and the Criminal Law*, 168. "Fiction" was, of course, White's term.
[44] John Barker Waite, "Irresistible Impulse and Criminal Liability," *Michigan Law Review*, vol. 23 (1925): 443–74, 454. Waite's overall position is nevertheless difficult to pin down. Leaving aside theories that he deemed premature (although "devoutedly to be desired"), he adopted the view that even in (or especially in) a deterministic world, nearly all people could indeed be determined in their behavior by the fear of punishment (470–71). As to the "desired" theory, Waite seems to have stood somewhere between White and Wigmore. Wigmore's deterrence-based view was premised on punishment in the social defense, if not on the basis of retribution. It certainly went beyond mere "segregation" of the offender. White favored "segregation," but on the basis of a theory that does not seem to reduce to what Waite termed a purely "criminological and penological" view. For a discussion of Waite on some of these points, see Hovenkamp, "Insanity and Criminal Responsibility," 572–74.

the ABA had "set aside a session to be devoted to psychiatry,"[45] proceeded to lecture his lawyerly audience as though it was yearning for instruction on where it had gone so wrong.

At the center of White's criticism of the practices of the criminal law was his observation that "the vengeance motive ... still functions but under a disguise, namely the disguise of deterrence, which makes it seem like something else."[46] Thus lawyers might say – and believe – that the law looked to the welfare of society rather than to the punishment of the morally culpable offender,[47] but they only deluded themselves. Everything pointed to this conclusion: the language of the law; the nature of trials; the failure to examine each individual offender in a detailed fashion; the prevailing approach to penology. The *claim* that the end of the law is simple deterrence, and not vengeance, was a mechanism familiar in psychiatry: "traditional beliefs and methods of procedure ... in order to be retained are given the odor of sanctity." White went so far as to characterize the convicted offender as a "scapegoat":

He is an individual whose personality has been built up in a way to explain the crime with which he is charged, and of his personality only the more superficial things ever get into the picture. In fact it becomes necessary to build up such an artificial personality if the emotion of vengeance is to be loosed against him. If one really knew the personality of the average criminal, how pitifully inadequate it was to cope with the situation in which he found himself and how logical and understandable his conduct under all the circumstances of the situation really was, it would be very difficult to get oneself into a state of mind that permitted the severity of punishment which the law often requires.[48]

White was careful to remind his audience that he endorsed society's right to segregate dangerous antisocial actors, which meant "largely ... doing away with fixed sentences." In counseling the "elimination of punishment as a vengeance motive," he justified "its retention only if used for definitely constructive ends for conditioning conduct."[49]

White's speech drew a mocking response from Wigmore. In an editorial in the *JCLC,* Wigmore noted the psychiatrists' "favorite attitude": "Punishment is mere revenge, atavistically perpetuated in our law; all that mere terminology should be abandoned." Had psychiatrists studied the philosophy of the criminal law they would have learned that it was no longer based on revenge. Wigmore listed its five purposes: to "*treat* the committer – thus if possible to cure or improve him"; to "*segregate* the committer – so as

---

45 William A. White, "Need for Cooperation between Lawyers and Psychiatrists in Dealing with Crime," *ABA Journal,* vol. 13 (1927): 551–55, 551.

46 White, "Need for Cooperation," 554.

47 White, "Need for Cooperation," 552.

48 White, "Need for Cooperation," 554.

49 White, "Need for Cooperation," 555.

to protect possible other victims"; to "*reaffirm publicly the moral code* for the community"; to "*frighten other potential committers* of similar deeds"; and to "*satisfy occasionally the crude public demand for revenge* – this in those few cases only where there would be danger of lynching if courts did not act." Reiterating his point that deterrence was aimed not at the individual who has already committed a crime, but at the large unarrested public, Wigmore scornfully adjured his intended audience – "Search your own memory, Mr. Psychiatrist!" – to consider why they did not speed, or why they did not follow through on the thought that they might try to bribe a policeman who stopped them for speeding. "It was the *Deterrence theory* working on your normal and respectable mind ... deep down in your Freudian sub-psyche. It was Fear! It was Deterrence!"[50] Wigmore clearly did not think that the law's admitted willingness to "*satisfy occasionally the crude public demand for revenge*" rendered its aims vulnerable to White's critique. Nor did he appear to think that the law's formal, theoretical aims were undermined by this acknowledgment that the popular view (at least "occasionally") was still that the proper aim of criminal punishment was vengeance.

Nothing Wigmore said on this occasion was necessarily inconsistent with a determinist perspective. He equated the "moral code" with the "moral emotions of conformity to the social principles of good and bad," but he adduced no particular basis for these.[51] Rather, he attacked psychiatrists generally, and White in particular, whose charge that vengeance functioned under "the disguise of deterrence" infuriated him; it also indicated to him that White did not truly believe in holding antisocial offenders for so long as necessary to cure them as a *general* deterrent. Wigmore must have read White to mean that the law looked *only* to revenge, hence only at the "committer," and he overlooked the possibility that White thought society at large would learn a lesson from the "conditioning" of offenders until they were cured. In light of Wigmore's diatribe of three years earlier, however, it is tempting to think that Wigmore also objected to the psychiatrist's call for effective decriminalization, believing that such a perspective undermined specific *and* general deterrence, not least because it destroyed the true basis of the "moral code," the foundation of conventional morality: the *belief* in free will. Of course he did not state – and very likely found irrelevant – whether a genuine, or at least *possibly* genuine, free will was a necessary predicate for such a belief. Again effectively separating the law's formal aims from the views of the public at large, it seems Wigmore was content simply for the law to send the apparent (and thus determining/deterrent) message

[50] John H. Wigmore, "Doing Away with 'God and Other Religious Terminology,'" *JCLC*, vol. 18 (1928): 493–95.
[51] Wigmore, "Doing Away," 493.

that individuals are, indeed, capable of self-determination and will be held responsible for the manner in which they exercise this capability.[52]

Wigmore's response to White drew its own response from the former Columbia Law School Dean and veteran criminologist, George Kirchwey. Kirchwey described Wigmore's editorial as "a vastly amusing exercise in logomachy," but opined that "it may be doubted if he was entitled to all the fun he got out of it." For "if punishment under whatever name survives, whether for the avowed purpose of deterrence or, as Dr. White would have it, as 'a definitely constructive' means 'of conditioning conduct,' will it not still and with the same effect teach the lesson that the way of the transgressor is hard?"[53]

There was, however, more to the disagreement between Wigmore and White. Kirchwey allowed that

---

[52] Wigmore affirmed the importance of belief in the "moral code" in "Juvenile Court vs. Criminal Court," 376:

> [Social workers and the psychiatrists] are going wrong. They are ... virtually on the way to abolish criminal law and undermine social morality.... Every day, in a thousand American courts, the judge is voicing the law, which says in thunder tones that go far beyond the courtroom walls: "Thou shalt not kill; for killing is wrong. Thou shalt not steal; for stealing is wrong. Thou shalt not cheat; for cheating is wrong." And the rest of the Commandments. The courtroom is *the only place in the community today where the moral law is laid down* to the people with the voice of authority. The churches do not do it. The clubs do not do it. Public opinion has no concrete and authoritative organ. The court alone does it, through the criminal code.
>
> ... But the social workers and the psychologists and the psychiatrists know nothing of crime or wrong. They refer to "reactions" and "maladjustments" and "complexes."

In a later editorial, Wigmore returned to the theme of deterrence; one must distinguish between those who are deterrable and those who are not. One school of psychiatry ("a loud and powerful one") viewed "all crime [as] analogous to a disease ... and that therefore the penalties of the criminal law are psychologically futile." This school failed "to reflect on the psychology of the normal person – those who constitute 99% of the population." Of these persons, "some ... are so made that they would execute this anti-social self-will *sometimes* only. And some persons are so made that they would execute this self-will *every time*. That is, they would if a motive still more powerful did not come in to restrain them, viz., the fear of the law's penalty." John H. Wigmore, "'Better Not Park There! You're Liable to Get Pinched,'" *JCLC*, vol. 22 (1931): 5–7, 6. Wigmore's language is consistent with the view that the "selfish will" is a biological or psychological fact. His references to how even normal individuals are "made" seems to affirm further his underlying determinist predilections.

[53] George W. Kirchwey, "Punishment and Other Penal Terminology," *JCLC*, vol. 19 (1928): 6–7, 6 (Kirchwey's contribution seems to have been untitled; the title I have employed appears as a column header under which Kirchwey's comments were placed). As previously noted, Kirchwey was temporary warden of Sing Sing in 1915 after his tenure at Columbia as Dean. He also served on the New York Prison Association's executive committee in 1907 and the New York State Commission on Prison Reform from 1913 to 1914. After retiring from Columbia in 1916, he joined the New York School of Social Work, heading its Department of Criminology from 1918 to 1932.

we can sense a profound conflict of policy [moving beneath the "topmost froth of" their "thought"]. The slogan of modern penology is the individualization of punishment – a parlous doctrine, *fons et origo* of the hopes and fears that underlie the controversy. Everyone accepts the doctrine in principle as a matter of justice and of social expediency. Applied, as the principle, for the most part, has been, casually, sentimentally, ignorantly, it has nevertheless been accepted as a necessary mitigation of the stern justice of the law. But what will become of the stern justice of the law when the principle of individual treatment comes to be applied intelligently, systematically, *in all cases?*[54]

Kirchwey insisted that "Dr. White and his fellow psychiatrists" aim at just such a goal. Moreover, he supposed that they might "end by persuading us all – all of us, at least, who have the courage to face the facts and the intelligence to apprehend them – that there is no crime without its extenuating circumstances and no criminal who is not, in a real sense, the victim of his fate." "At any rate," he said, "it will spare us the sentimentality which goes side by side with the cruelty of the present system." Kirchwey understood – or perhaps merely chose to gloss – the psychiatric perspective as a form of social defense, and this he thought a good exchange for the prevailing approach to individual responsibility. Kirchwey concluded his response to Wigmore with a clear endorsement of White: "This may be cold-blooded, it may not be 'justice,' but it should be far more effective as a social policy than our present system of 'justice tempered with mercy.'"[55]

Shortly after Kirchwey's brief note appeared, Pound took the stage once more, this time to deliver the main address – entitled "Science and Legal Procedure" – at the annual meeting of the American Psychiatric Association in 1928. Although nothing in the lecture proves definitively that Pound was aware of the interchange between Wigmore and White, it was relevant to White's address to the legal profession the preceding year in several ways. The paper was vintage Pound. It reveals his hostility to the idea of "the vicious will," once again historicizes the emergence of will theory, and says nothing about deep-seated retributive urges. In it Pound returned to the theme that characterized his earliest work and that, I believe, largely conditioned the cautious tenor of his subsequent writings. Echoing the perspective of Sheldon Amos, to which he had accorded prominence in his 1903 *Outlines,* Pound instructed his audience:

We may not expect to have a system of criminal justice far in advance of what the public can and will understand and believe in. We must make the demands of science clear and familiar to the public before we may, in deference to science, tear down much to which men are accustomed or build up much that is new.[56]

---

[54] Kirchwey, "Punishment," 6–7 (emphasis added).
[55] Kirchwey, "Punishment," 7.
[56] Roscoe Pound, "Science and Legal Procedure," *American Journal of Psychiatry*, vol. 8 (1928): 33–51, 36.

Science, Pound said, was advancing rapidly and in a state of flux. This made it "difficult to make an adjustment of legal conceptions and legal institutions and legal practices to scientific knowledge ... which will at once be intrinsically sound and commend itself to public understanding." Pound reminded the psychiatrists that "most people were brought up with certain ideas about criminals which speak from the society of the past," by which Pound meant "a pioneer or rural society." He now alleged that even the great Progressive Era advances in penal science and institutions had come before "the public had ... [been] taught what such things mean." The result, Pound said, was "a reaction in the last decade which threatens to do not a little injury to some of these new devices and to retard greatly the development of others."[57] Pound stressed his lifelong vision of the law's imperative: in the interests of "certainty, uniformity and equality, to do in the next like case what it did in the one before." Thus, he said, Aristotle had noted the great difference between the legal and medical practices: in law, the method of trial and error was greatly limited; if medicine followed the law, the physician would be required to "prescribe from a book, designated by the state, and according to rules laid down in that book." Experimentation of the sort expected of physicians is precluded for trial judges by the needs of "the general security."[58]

Was Pound replying to White's critique of "the present system," with its short list of remedies and stereotyped conceptualizations of behavior? Perhaps. But he came little closer than he had in 1922 and 1923 to addressing the difficult questions of vengeance and responsibility, and their relationship to principles of penology. When, at the close of his address, he turned to the problem of individualization, he stressed the importance of the role of the judge over that of the behavioral scientist.[59] This reaffirmed his belief that the traditional principles of political liberty that governed the law would, even in an enlightened and reformed system of criminal justice, continue to limit science's encroachments on jurisprudence. Pound thus continued to straddle the domains of the traditional common lawyers and the new behavioral scientists, invoking the latter's central claim but tempering it with a gradualism that would shield the former from the

[57] Pound, "Science and Legal Procedure," 36–37. Pound sounded the same note a year later:
    Men have come to fear that in our zeal to secure the individual life we may relax the hold of society upon the anti-social, impair the fear of the legal order as a deterrent upon anti-social conduct, and release habitual offenders prematurely to resume their warfare upon society. On the other hand, it has seemed to threaten the security of the individual life by committing too much to the discretion of administrative officers. (Roscoe Pound, foreword to "Predictability in the Administration of Criminal Justice," by Sheldon Glueck and Eleanor T. Glueck, *Harvard Law Review*, vol. 42 [1929]: 297–99, 298)
[58] Pound, "Science and Legal Procedure," 36.
[59] Pound, "Science and Legal Procedure," 47.

drastic consequences of determinism's full victory. A man for more seasons than most, Pound achieved only the semblance of a coherent, practicable program, satisfying himself that his principles of gradualism would hold in place the conflicting urges of the day, self-consciously shielding his chosen profession from the dangers of the looming abyss. His recognition in 1928 that the growth of penal science had occasioned a divide between scientific ideas and the understandings of the common man occasioned an important partial retreat from the cover of bifurcation. The principles of sentencing should not, he now counseled, depart too radically from those of the traditional assessment of guilt.[60]

Within months of Pound's address to the American Psychiatric Association, Judge Benjamin Cardozo spoke in somewhat different terms to the New York Academy of Medicine. Cardozo discussed New York governor Alfred Smith's 1928 legislative message, in which Smith recommended that the New York Crime Commission study the reform put forward by many "students of criminology": that, in Cardozo's words, "the whole business of sentencing criminals should be taken away from the judges and given over to the doctors. Courts, with their judges and juries, are to find the fact of guilt or innocence."[61] Smith had endorsed such a reform, which, of course, aligned him more closely with Glueck than with Pound. Cardozo, himself, remained agnostic about the project[62] which, in itself, placed him well beyond Pound, who religiously guarded the bench's control over sentencing. Cardozo registered agnosticism as well about the deterministic premises of some reformers[63] but that, he said, did not "detract from the fullness of [his] belief that at a day not far remote the teachings of the biochemists and behaviorists, of psychiatrists and penologists, will transform our whole system of punishment for crime."[64] In the then and there, though, Cardozo cited Glueck's view that humans had "'some spark of capacity for consciously and creatively guiding their conduct in conformity with legal sanctions,'" and endorsed the view, similar to Wigmore's, that punishment was necessary to deter both "the man who is criminal at heart" and "others

---

[60] Pound, "Science and Legal Procedure," 37. It is difficult to say just how strongly Pound felt about this. In his Preface to *Criminal Justice in America*, dated November 7, 1929, Pound noted that "in the years that have intervened [i.e., since 1923] much has happened, but little, I think, to change the main lines of the picture or important details" (xxiii).

[61] Benjamin N. Cardozo, "What Medicine Can Do for Law" (address before the New York Academy of Medicine, November 1, 1928), in *Law and Literature and Other Essays and Addresses* (Littleton, CO: F. B. Rothman, 1986), 70–120, 79–80.

[62] Cardozo, "What Medicine Can Do for Law," 84 ("I have no thought in all this to express approval or disapproval of the project of withdrawing from the court the sentence-fixing power.").

[63] Cardozo, "What Medicine Can Do for Law," 84 ("One may see a wise reform there without acceptance of the creed that virtue and vice are not spiritual essences, but high-sounding synonyms for the hormones of the body.").

[64] Cardozo, "What Medicine Can Do for Law," 86.

who in our existing social organization have never felt the criminal impulse and shrink from crime in horror."[65] He concluded this section of his address to the members of the Academy of Medicine in terms that resonated with the language of Speranza and Pound:

The methods, the humane and scientific methods, that have thus prevailed will spread to other fields. This is your work, I am persuaded, as much as it is ours. Your hands must hold the torch that will explore the dark mystery of crime – the mystery, even darker, of the criminal himself, in all the deep recesses of thought and will and body. Here is a common ground, a borderland between your labors and our own, where hope and faith and love can do their deathless work.[66]

Were they consoled? Was Cardozo?

Precisely at this moment, Pound's protégé and quasi–fellow-legal-traveler, Glueck, began the journey that was to move him ahead of Pound and Cardozo – on the road to the behaviorist abyss. Glueck did not entirely renounce his concept of human freedom, but he now began the task of severing the question of free will from the domain of criminal justice. In 1928 he proceeded only so far as to emphasize the importance of the sentencing stage, which would be dominated by the personnel and principles of behavioral science.[67] In 1930, at the moment of publication of Pound's increasingly backward-looking Colver lectures, Glueck reaffirmed his faith in bifurcation, perhaps seeking to assure his behavioral-science colleagues that the fact-finding process would, in practical effect, serve to determine only that an offender had committed the act, for which the appropriate form of "treatment" would later be determined.[68]

Some six years later, Glueck moved a crucial step further along the way from law to science. While reiterating his belief in humans' capacity for purposive behavior, he now conceded that "society has not yet invented an instrument for diving into a man's mind and determining the exact capacity for self-direction, self-control, and selective introjective power that he or the fictional 'reasonable' man of the law possesses."[69] More to the point, Glueck now argued, a criminal act indicated that the actor had *at that moment* lacked such a capacity:

[65] Cardozo, "What Medicine Can Do for Law," 88.

[66] Cardozo, "What Medicine Can Do for Law," 94–95.

[67] Sheldon Glueck, "Principles of a Rational Penal Code," *Harvard Law Review*, vol. 41 (1928): 453–82, 475. Glueck also stressed the importance of differentiating the "guilt-finding phase" from the "treatment (sentence-imposing) feature of proceedings." This article both struck a note that appears to rebut White – "No thoughtful person today seriously holds this theory of sublimated social vengeance" (456) – and explicitly endorsed White's view that the "criminal thus becomes the handy scapegoat" (458).

[68] Sheldon Glueck, "Significant Transformations in the Administration of Criminal Justice," *Mental Hygiene*, vol. 14 (1930): 280–306, 297.

[69] Sheldon Glueck, *Crime and Justice* (Boston: Little, Brown, 1936), 180–81.

Thus the criminal act occurring at any given time is the outcome of constitutional and acquired personal and social forces. It shows that the individual's power of resistance, or self-guidance, or selective choice and introjection of bits of the environment, has been overbalanced by the strength of the other circumstances.[70]

Glueck concluded that for all criminal cases, not just those involving insanity, these overmastering forces could be discovered and taken into account during the second stage of the process. Glueck made it clear that under his proposed scheme the jury would still determine the mental element of the crime; but the sentencing function, "different in methodology and aim," should be "entrusted to a tribunal to be composed, say, of a psychiatrist or psychologist, a sociologist or educator and the trial judge."[71] Almost all the way from law to science, but not quite. While renouncing the relevance of free will to the problem of criminal responsibility Glueck had nonetheless maintained the jury for determination of guilt, which from the *jury's* point of view might well involve the presumption of human freedom. Even as a scientist, Glueck had – wittingly or otherwise – vindicated the true imperative of the law through a consciously embraced prescription for formal bifurcation of the criminal process.[72]

---

[70] Glueck, *Crime and Justice*, 180.

[71] Glueck, *Crime and Justice*, 225–26.

[72] A full three decades later, in Glueck's 1965 memoir of Pound, he enlisted Pound as a full fellow traveler on the journey to a new system of criminal jurisprudence. If Pound actually ever made the trip, as opposed to envisioning such a system in prospective terms, he never said so in his writings. See Glueck, "Memoir," 22–23:

> It is probable that Pound's practical position on the role of the substantive criminal law in a society of advancing scientific knowledge and humanitarianism was to regard the objective of the proof of "guilt" as a strictly technical legal one, without any necessary implication of moral guilt. This would lead to the ascertainment of legal liability under existing methods of trial before the traditional criminal court; but once the legal status had been determined, the defendant would be turned over for sentence and determination of a correctional and treatment plan in the individual case to a board of specially qualified experts in the behavioral disciplines, presided over by a judge. Always, there would be careful legal protection of the convicted offender against arbitrary treatment and for the purpose of prescribed periodic review of the case to determine progress and to guarantee release from legally controlled custody when the offender had sufficiently improved in attitude and predictable future behavior to be no longer reasonably deemed a threat to society.

All in all, Glueck's speculation here seems plausible but more akin to what he himself espoused than to what Pound – given his more traditional common-lawyer's stance on political liberty – seems to have been able comfortably to accept. Perhaps Glueck's remarks reflect Pound's views as they developed after 1930. If anyone knew what the post-1930 Pound really thought, it ought to have been Glueck. But Glueck's memoir provides little sense of the early Pound and none at all of Pound's development. Pound's earlier views remain murky on the problem of guilt assessment, though his rejection of free will might be taken to imply the scheme Glueck outlines. As to sentencing, Pound jealously guarded the position of the judge. The "board of specially qualified experts" presided over by a judge was Glueck's idea, although he might over time have brought Pound around to it. See Glueck, *Crime and*

CONCLUSION

Whatever the virtues of the varied attempts of White, Glueck, and others more squarely within the legal academy to resolve the long-standing problems of freedom and criminal responsibility, their mid-1920s contributions had clearly commenced an era of greatly heightened concern within the legal academy regarding the implications of the new sciences for the administration of criminal justice. Over the several following decades, legal academics became more active participants in the ongoing debate over criminal responsibility, moving outward from their long-standing contribution to the problem of reforming the insanity defense. In doing so, they participated in an exchange both among themselves and with behavioral scientists – including the new cadre of deterministic criminologists – that produced the first returns from the endeavors for which, in their differing ways, Speranza and Pound had called.

The jurists' side of the early years of this exchange – from 1923 to 1937 – thus witnessed vigorous debate over the aims and purposes of the criminal law, including, at long last, focused legal-academic discussion of the relevance of the concept of free will to the problem of criminal responsibility. The influence of this debate would leave its mark on what became for a time one of the true foundation stones of modern American criminal jurisprudence, Herbert Wechsler and Jerome Michael's 1937 article, "A Rationale of the Law of Homicide." That study, which I address in detail in Chapter 4, famously adopted a utilitarian approach to criminal law focused on deterrence. Although it by no means utterly excluded the Progressive ideals of individualization and rehabilitation, it contributed to a clearer divide between the two main camps of the ongoing movement for reform of the criminal justice system: where Wechsler, Michael, and others would centrally use utilitarianism as the touchstone for defining the desired aims and processes of the law, another loose coalition of academics and practitioners still called for a focus on the treatment and reform of offenders. The perceived affirmation of – or threats to – ideas of human freedom by both camps brought

---

Justice, 226. As to a completely open-ended period of "legally controlled custody," nothing in Pound's pre-1930 writings clearly adopts this essentially positivist, treatment- and social-defense–based position. Glueck might have underestimated Pound's intuitive resistance, on due process grounds, to the kinds of reform that Pound's views on free will *seemed* to imply. He did not make sufficient room for Pound's very powerful endorsement of the consciousness of freedom and thus failed to appreciate the tensions in Pound's (at least pre-1930) criminal jurisprudence. Finally, Glueck appears to have been misled by Pound's optimism about the eventual accommodation between law and science; Glueck mistook a fundamental inability to face the future seriously for a merely *pragmatic* decision to leave the future to others. In short, whatever Pound became (or was willing to agree with in private), the Pound of the Progressive Era was a more complicated, more interesting, and more skeptical figure than Glueck captured in his otherwise effective *tour d'horizon* of Pound's contributions to criminal justice studies.

questions of free will and political liberty further to the fore and occasioned Wechsler and Michael's brief but clear statement of compatibilism; theirs appears to be the first such direct assertion of long-known compatibilist principles in a major twentieth-century American legal-academic work on criminal jurisprudence. At least, it appears to be the first such assertion in a widely read – and widely addressed – publication. And, for the moment, the assertion would largely be epiphenomenal; the legal academy as a whole still would not seriously take up philosophical compatibilism as the answer to the free will problem in the criminal law until the last few decades of the century. Thus, even in the generation of scholarship immediately succeeding Wechsler and Michael's contribution, although the free will question would more often be faced more or less directly, it would continue to be touched on, worried, and often evaded in ambiguous or idiosyncratic terms.

Still, the work of the mid-1920s to late-1930s, particularly including that of Wechsler and Michael, achieved a depth, a degree of internal coherence, and a clarity of overall system that contrasts markedly with Pound's corpus of criminal justice scholarship. This contrast existed partly because Pound wrote before the theoretical groundwork had fully developed, partly because he thought that society was not ready for a major departure from its "hold-over" habits of belief and action, and partly because he took relatively little interest in the substantive law. But it existed largely, I suspect, because Pound never fully accepted the implications of what he termed the rout of the free will doctrine for the traditional juristic approach to political liberty and the claim to human freedom. Pound invoked the new sciences and readily recognized, even claimed to welcome, their role in the future of criminal jurisprudence, but he never could bring himself to imagine what that future would look like. He rejected retributivism and said much else that could have led in the direction of one or another genre of the "social defense." But something – perhaps his particular form of belief in the human spirit, or his way of understanding old Progressive values, or his own brand of worldly wise common sense – kept him from ever openly endorsing that potentially stark penal theory, much less coming to terms with its increasing prominence in scholarly circles in the mid-to-late 1920s.[73]

As a result, Pound's Progressive account of the state of criminal justice in America soon began to show its age. Indeed, not so long after publication of his lectures in 1930, the final chapter, "Criminal Justice Today," had, so to speak, become history. And the preceding historical chapters – masterful by any measure and all the more impressive when it is considered that Pound

[73] John Fabian Witt, in *Patriots and Cosmopolitans: Hidden Histories of American Law* (Cambridge, MA: Harvard University Press, 2007), chap. 4, offers a fascinating portrait of the post-1930 Pound, the period of Pound's conservative (antistatist, anti–New Deal, and anti–much else) turn. What I have termed the fifty-something Pound's "own brand of worldly wise common sense" bore rather bitter fruit in the later decades of his long life.

had worked on American criminal justice history in relative isolation – were left to gather dust. *Sic transit:* the legal and behavioral science writings of the mid-1920s and beyond tested, as never before, the possibilities for a true integration of the insights of the new sciences with those of law, politics, and history. They tested, too, Americans' resourcefulness in interpreting the place of the crime problem in modern society, as well as in assessing the place of the conceptualization of criminality in modern social, political, and legal thought. The results – as we now know only too well – bore out Pound's prediction that "there will be much experimenting, some fumbling and much dissatisfaction."[74] But all of that is a story for another day.

---

[74] Roscoe Pound, *The Spirit of the Common Law* (Francestown, NH: Marshall Jones, 1921), 588.

PART II

CONVENTIONAL MORALITY AND THE RULE OF LAW

Freedom and Criminal Responsibility in the Forgotten Years: 1930–1960

INTRODUCTION

In 1926, historical sociologist Harry Elmer Barnes announced the triumph of determinism: "We have given up the notion of man as a free moral agent," he proclaimed.[1] Barnes did not explain to whom "we" referred, however, and there is scant evidence that legal scholars, in particular, shared his unequivocal confidence. Certainly, the 1930s did see progress toward reform in criminal justice administration throughout the United States, including a broad commitment – at least in theory – to rehabilitation-based penology. But the influence on legal and penal theory of strong determinists such as Barnes would face pragmatic, political, and philosophical challenges from all sides throughout the 1930s, 1940s, and 1950s.

These middle decades of the twentieth century constitute a "period" for criminal jurisprudence in only the loosest sense. Mainly, they simply lie between the formative era that is the subject of Part I and the late-twentieth-century turn back toward desert theory – and away from the primarily forward-looking (or consequentialist) perspective of legal-academic thought that dominated the first six or seven decades of the century – that I discuss in Part III. Accordingly, this somewhat impressionistic second essay, presented in three chapters, treats the 1930–1960 period as involving a series of alterations of perspective that reflect the increasing dissolution of the Progressive legal-academic worldview. This Part continues my exploration of the free will problem in twentieth-century criminal jurisprudence. But – like the other two Parts – it is also a freestanding, distinctive study guided by the writings of the period as necessarily circumscribed by my own specific research aims and limitations. Whereas Part I was organized around a few

---

[1] Harry Elmer Barnes, *The Repression of Crime: Studies in Historical Penology* (New York: George H. Doran, 1926), 24.

particularly identifiable voices both within and outside the legal academy –
with Pound as a central figure – that illustrated the free will issues posed
by Progressive Era law, Part II requires an approach designed to encompass
the growing chorus of voices that arose to address, often to further compli-
cate, and sometimes effectively to obscure, these issues. The figures I have
selected to highlight by no means exhaustively represent the scholarship of
the period. Instead I focus on scholars whose work exemplified important
midcentury ideas about the meaning of criminal responsibility – and the
place of free will and conventional morality – within the rule of law.

A significant element that separated scholars of the 1930s from their
predecessors was the development of an American school of criminology,
which came of age in conjunction with the criminal justice surveys commenced in the 1920s. To some degree, the earlier scholarship represented by
figures such as Speranza and Pound enjoyed the luxury of ignorance: they
envisioned some marriage of law and the new sciences in idealistic terms,
and, at least initially, they shared the optimistic view of behavioral scientists that the justice system ultimately could be molded from the top down
in accordance with Progressive ideals. Later scholars were all too aware of
the real state of criminal justice, as evidenced by the surveys and reports
of local and national crime commissions. Such studies discovered local
systems still dominated by political graft, parole schemes utterly divorced
from their originating treatment principles, and perceived failures of police
and prosecutors generally to ensure the conviction and punishment of
clearly guilty offenders. Further, although progressive reform efforts would
gain support in connection with New Deal programs and continue to rise
until their peak in the 1960s, the realities of indeterminate sentences, treatment efforts, and the administration of parole and probation programs initially often posed new problems instead of providing hoped-for solutions.
Indeterminate sentencing, for example, which permitted authorities to keep
an offender imprisoned until he was deemed adequately reformed, contributed to burgeoning prison populations because of slow moving (and, in
some prisons, still totally lacking) treatment programs. Prison conditions
overall also had failed to improve despite attempted reforms; many prisons became less humane, likely in part precisely because of rising prison
populations.[2]

Thus, although progressive reform efforts would gain support in connection with New Deal programs and continue to rise until their peak in the
1960s, the initial incarnations of attempted reforms often posed new problems instead of providing hoped-for solutions. Embedded in these realities
were also, of course, racial disparities and tensions at all levels of the legal

[2] For an overview of these on-the-ground challenges faced by reformers, see, e.g., Samuel
Walker, *Popular Justice: A History of American Criminal Justice*, 2nd ed. (New York: Oxford
University Press, 1998), 152–57, 164–65, 175–78.

system, epitomized in the 1930s by the Scottsboro cases.[3] The issue of race was still largely obscured, and the civil rights revolution vindicated by the Supreme Court under Chief Justice Earl Warren would not blossom until the 1960s, but the stage was set by a mounting awareness of the complex intersection between race and justice, which illustrated the importance of checks on the state's ability to intervene into the lives of individual citizens. Finally, it is worth remarking that, from the vantage point of society at large, no doubt the progressive picture of a treatable, "determined" offender often stood in stark contrast to the nation's ongoing War on Crime – and in particular to fears about organized crime, which did not dissipate with the end of Prohibition in 1933. Thanks in part to the media savvy campaigns of J. Edgar Hoover and the Kefauver Committee, Americans of the interwar and postwar periods perceived a growing threat from offenders whose intentional crimes epitomized conventional blameworthiness and summoned unapologetic retributive urges.[4]

This is not to say that scholars of criminal responsibility always engaged in direct confrontation with such factual, political, and social contexts. But it is certainly not mere coincidence that the historian begins to see an increasingly realist orientation to reform, that, among other things, was more sensitive to the presence of social attitudes toward crime and the justice system as well as to the needs for limits on the system. The newer generation of scientific-positivist scholars, although they generally did not waiver in their fundamental commitment to a scientific understanding of individuals and society, were increasingly united in recognizing the need to work with and alongside conventional attitudes – including traditional retributive urges and political values of freedom and equality – even in order for the law to move forward scientifically. This sensitivity would also lead to an

[3] In the South, the Alabama Scottsboro cases – in which eight young African American men were sentenced to death for raping two white women, and which were widely believed to have rested on highly suspect evidence – brought continuing racial bias in the legal system to the Supreme Court's attention. In the North, the post–Civil War urban migration of African Americans continued and, by the 1930s, African Americans were being convicted and imprisoned for major crimes in far greater numbers than whites. See, e.g., William J. Stuntz, *The Collapse of American Criminal Justice* (Cambridge, MA: Belknap Press, 2011), 18–20, 193–94. Race riots of the early 1940s, moreover, exposed the apparent inabilities even of increasingly professionalized police forces to control urban racial conflict – indeed, in many cases police only exacerbated violence. See, e.g., Walker, *Popular Justice*, 170–74. For general encapsulations of the vast racial disparities in the American criminal justice system throughout the twentieth century, see, e.g., Stuntz, *Collapse*, generally and esp. chap. 2, "The Wolf by the Ear"; Lawrence M. Friedman, *Crime and Punishment in American History* (New York: Basic Books, 1993), esp. 374–82.
[4] See, e.g., Stuntz, *Collapse*, 187–91; Walker, *Popular Justice*, 158–59, 168–70. The early-1950s Kefauver Committee was born of the presidential aspirations of Senator Estes Kefauver, who initiated a very public, McCarthy-esque investigation of the Mafia, which he vividly portrayed as a foreign-influenced, anti-American crime syndicate.

increasing division between behavioral scientists and legal scholars, as the latter became more concerned with the political and social limits to a workable rule of law.

Later in the middle years came the influence on American scholarship of political events surrounding the Second World War. The despotism threatening to spread from Germany, Italy, and the Soviet Union occasioned heated debates – and apparent deep rethinking – among many positivists of both the scientific and legal stripe.[5] The rise of Europe's totalitarian regimes had been premised in part on the very ideals of a scientific, administrative state that many American Progressives had sought to establish on their own soil. More controversially, even among U.S. scholars, determinist principles and the growing body of empirical evidence regarding human behavior had undermined the notion that the general public could rationally participate in popular democracy. The abuses perpetrated by European regimes occasioned American thinking both about the workability (and potential manipulation) of the scientific ideal in practice and about the desirability of democratic law, no matter how imperfect. By the 1940s and 1950s, scholars both in and outside of the legal field were rediscovering a language of values – as opposed to one of scientific objectivity – and increasingly positing the law as a moral, democratic institution that could not be described in the pure terms of science.[6]

The shift was most identifiable in debates about political organization – and the bounds of political liberty – among social and political theorists. But the more value-laden (as opposed to objective/scientific) concept of law inevitably infected the thinking of those attempting to make sense of the criminal law's relationship to conventional notions of free will. Thus, although few of these scholars explicitly discussed the influence of the postwar political

---

[5] Hereafter, as I hope will be clear from the context, I often use the term "positivists" to refer to those scientific-positivists who were interested in incorporating determinism and the new psychological and behavioral sciences into the law. This group overlapped with legal positivists generally; I do not focus on the legal positivist movement as a whole, but only some components of it as they relate to my inquiry into legal responsibility and free will. As will be further explained, my specific use of the label "positivist" in this way is also intended fairly narrowly: it distinguishes those "positivist" reformers who emphasized treatment and rehabilitation of offenders (in keeping with the latest behavioral science) from those "utilitarians" who privileged overall social welfare (while also often expressing determinist/scientific views).

[6] These themes are central to Edward A. Purcell, Jr., *The Crisis of Democratic Theory: Scientific Naturalism and the Problem of Value* (Lexington: University Press of Kentucky, 1973). With regard to their effect on jurisprudential theory, see especially chap. 9, "Crisis in Jurisprudence." Elizabeth Dale offers a related perspective on the practical and philosophical tensions between a state-imposed rule of law and the right to popular (and potentially extralegal) justice associated with sovereign citizens in *Criminal Justice in the United States, 1789–1939* (New York: Cambridge University Press, 2011). See, especially, her summaries, pp. 1–7, 132–37, and bibliographic essay, pp. 139–41.

and social climate, that climate exposed seemingly intractable dilemmas for those who hoped a scientifically informed notion of criminal responsibility could coexist with social and political ideas of freedom. In reemphasizing the law's defense of *political* freedom, positivists risked backing into a corner: Did valuing political liberty and democracy require also accepting a counter-scientific notion of freedom of the will? Could a state premised on political freedom and sovereignty of the people make criminal responsibility judgments – and, consequently, deprive individuals of their rights – on anything *but* the notion of freely chosen action? Similarly, if the sovereign people *believe* in free will, could a rule of law that questions this belief ever be popularly viewed as legitimate? Theoretical legitimacy was also critical, however. Much of the Progressive movement had been driven by an awareness of the injustice and (nonscientific) elitism of the existing system – and the progressive interest in criminal justice was aimed, in part, precisely at allowing individuals to reach their highest potentials to contribute, if possible, to the flourishing of human society. Progressive scholars would have a hard time accepting a legal system that purported to value individuals in freedom-affirming language if that meant ignoring the empirical, freedom-denying realities that, in their view, created real injustice.[7]

As I have suggested, those midcentury legal scholars to address criminal responsibility largely focused on practical concerns and only barely touched on these larger political and social questions; their published work, at least, most commonly expresses their small and focused world of theory and reform. But a significant shift began to seem evident, particularly as of the 1940s, as the internal debates centered on penology in part gave way to the recognition of a need for different language – and a way of describing what I have called a "moral-legal" idea of responsibility – that could present the legal system in conventionally acceptable, freedom-affirming terms while nonetheless maintaining a scholarly commitment to the underlying scientific realities of human behavior. The reorientation toward political liberty concerns, moreover, can be seen to have created a related subtle but crucial shift in emphasis from the overall needs of society and the social defense, to the individual actor as the locus of criminal "responsibility," however defined.

The result, when middle period writings are viewed in historical hindsight, appears as an unfolding of perspectives that, to a large extent, mirrored the gradualist approach to a more enlightened law that, in essence but with few specifics, had been urged by Pound. The positivist reform tradition was increasingly a compromised tradition, tempered by pragmatism

---

[7] Compare Purcell, *Crisis*, e.g., 93, 106–07, 113. In charting the apparent clash between progressive behaviorism and the ideal of rational, "free" participation in popular democracy, Purcell illustrates the essential motivations of many Progressives and legal realists, who sought to expose the role of powerful interests and remedy injustice in the existing political and legal systems.

and by a sometimes grudging acceptance of the role of conventional social understandings of human behavior and of just deserts. For some legal academics, the (supposed) social view was anathema – and the long-standing reflection of it in criminal law doctrine and practice was still to be rooted out. For others, it was an unfortunate social view that, they concluded, must be taken into account by the rule of law, if that rule were to survive intact; at the same time these scholars cautioned that law must also work to undermine such conventional understandings and steadily work to bring about a more enlightened social view. Still others concluded that the very pervasiveness and resilience of conventional morality suggested that it accorded with a species of truth that the law ought itself to reflect. These differing perspectives were sometimes stated outright, at least within the confines of scholarly exchange. They were often illustrated – sometimes explicitly, sometimes implicitly – by scholars' conceptions of the jury's proper role, particularly in judging legal insanity: for obvious reasons, the degree to which the jury's traditional guilt assessment role was affirmed coincided with the degree to which the conventional belief in free will was accepted (albeit, often on somewhat fictive terms) as an element of criminal responsibility; and the perceived value of conventional beliefs relative to scientific views was often expressed by scholars' positions on the place of scientific experts in trials involving the insanity defense.

Central to my subject, then, are the varying meanings of, reactions to, and attempted manipulations of the disjunction – or possibility of disjunction – between scientific-positivist/determinist elite academic understandings of human behavior and those free-will-based understandings still generally supposed to exist in society at large. And, true to the focus of many legal scholars of the middle years, my study initially charts academic discussions concerning construction of legal doctrines (such as the law circumscribing the insanity defense) and procedures (particularly those related to sentencing and penology) most apt to achieve progressive goals over time. These discussions necessarily included, or at least implicated, views about the place of notions of free will in a workable legal regime. But the central theme was pragmatic: how to construct a principled (and thus scientifically enlightened) legal system that was legitimate and effective in light of conventional political and social views. For the most part, deeper philosophical questions about the debated human capacity for free will would not be approached directly by legal scholars until later in the century.

Indeed, this general lack of deep inquiry into the question of free will – even by my subjects here, those who touched upon it at least in some way – marks the historical division between the middle period discussed here in Part II, 1930–1960, and the last four decades of the century discussed in Part III. The division is rough; similar themes cross my fictive line, and some later scholarship that is particularly agnostic about, or deflective of, the free will issue might appear equally at home, thematically, in this middle section. Yet the division is not arbitrary. In the 1960s, a more robust notion of personal desert, heralded in 1958 by Henry Hart's "The Aims of the Criminal Law,"[8] would reenter the academic discussion of criminal responsibility. Although this notion of desert – and Hart's version, in particular – initially emerged from political liberty concerns to function as a constraint on mainly consequentialist goals, it begged the question of free will in a way, it seemed, that the purer consequentialism of the middle years simply did not. Scholars that forthrightly incorporated personal desert – for criminal acts, and for the consequences of those acts imposed by the law – and not just social protection, scientific rationality, or even individual treatment, had a hard time avoiding the connotations of criminal condemnation that Progressive Era commentators had pushed aside, at least in theory: blameworthiness, moral responsibility, and retribution – all potentially implicating subjective intent or the personal "will." Thus, my presentation emphasizes that, where legal scholars of the middle years continued to address free will irresolutely and in large part as an aspect of their accommodation of conventional views, those of the 1960s and beyond more often found it necessary to directly acknowledge the potential questions posed for criminal legal theory by the free will problem, even if actual answers to those questions were rarely clear.

I begin this Part (Chapter 4) in the 1930s, before the battle lines occasioned by the political upheaval of World War II were drawn. I note that the early 1930s marked a scientific-positivist high point for some outside of legal academia, one that quickly became a point of departure for some within the world of criminal jurisprudence. Their scholarship suggests that, as in the preceding generation, many legal academics to touch on the free will problem believed that the trial – or guilt assessment – stage of the criminal process was bound to be widely understood in terms of a conventional, free-will-based morality. And, like their predecessors, they appear to have concluded that the disjunction between the social meaning of the law and the law's potential "true" meaning (still largely consequentialist and explicitly or implicitly determinist) was best managed through the ongoing bifurcation of the guilt assessment and treatment stages. Most continued to accept that the threshold for invoking the criminal law necessarily must acquiesce to common notions of blame, at least for the time being. And some theorized their reasons for doing so, albeit usually in connection with their broader conclusions about the proper disposition of offenders once convicted. Thus, much scholarship ultimately centered on the sentencing stage.

Still committed to a scientific, rehabilitative penal regime, behavioral scientists and legal scholars alike engaged in an important debate about the primary ends of that regime. They largely differed only on the priority of individual rehabilitation relative to punishment-based general deterrence of

[8] Henry M. Hart, Jr., "The Aims of the Criminal Law," *Law and Contemporary Problems*, vol. 23 (1958): 401–41 (discussed at the close of this Part in Chapter 6).

prospective offenders. Of course, most were concerned with a combination of overlapping goals. And all were generally consequentialists invested in the positivist view of crime. But, for purposes of discussion, I distinguish the two primary camps by labeling those who put treatment and rehabilitation of the offender first (or where rehabilitation was impossible, permanent incapacitation) as "scientific-positivists" or "positivists," and those who privileged maximizing overall social welfare through a prevention-based system of law and non-retributive punishment (alongside, but ahead of, rehabilitation) as "utilitarians." Both advanced what they viewed as the best program of legal reform, theoretically and practically; both also thought their scheme best suited to reforming the social view of the causes of crime and, in turn, to reducing the distance between guilt assessment and post-conviction treatment of offenders.

All consequentialists, then, sought to lessen the gulf between their particular approaches to responsibility and punishment and what were – probably rightly – deemed to be conventional social ideas and practices. Positivists evidenced the greater degree of this kind of disjunction, at least in the short term. Accordingly, they made the most vigorous attempts to show that a scientific approach would wear down free-will-based social impulses for revenge, thus reducing disjunction in the long term. Utilitarians, by taking social passions into account within the overall calculus, more clearly reduced the distance between the rule of law and conventional morality. But they did so at the risk – as the positivists saw it – that "non-retributive" punishment would be understood socially simply as traditional retributivism, thereby reinforcing the association between criminal responsibility and free will.

Chapter 5 sketches some elements of the continuing evolution of both positivism and utilitarianism alongside the reemergence, in the post–World War II years, of the idea – in part generated by concern for political liberty – that free will unavoidably had some role to play in the criminal law. This idea, to one degree or another, invoked an older retributivist, just-deserts tradition. Yet its proponents – illustrating the enduring strength of positivist influences – also increasingly, if often only implicitly, conceptualized human freedom as a mere "as if" proposition; although they did not accept free will as *true*, they accepted it as integral to the legal system. In this sense, although consequentialist scholars of the middle years only began to experiment with new individual-oriented justifications for desert, they forwarded the shift away from an overarching social-needs-based approach to criminal justice and toward an approach re-centered on the individual citizen.

Finally, in Chapter 6 I follow the middle years to their culmination in a period of debate over legal insanity provoked by the *Durham* case (1954)[9] and played out to some extent in relation to the drafting of the Model Penal

[9] *Durham v. United States*, 214 F.2d 862 (D.C. Cir. 1954).

Code (begun in the early 1950s and promulgated in 1962). Even more explicitly than before, this debate took up the question of the relationship between criminal law and the idea (or convention) of free will. The focus on guilt assessment also redirected attention to the jury and, particularly, to the proper balance between the jury's views and those of behavioral or psychiatric experts – a balance that, in many ways, encapsulated the law's answer to the free will question in practice. This significant debate evidenced both continuing divergence and some significant convergence among the various schools of thought on how free will should be conceived and where it should find a place in the law – of course, these questions would persist and be reformulated in the years to come.

Overall, post–World War II traditionalism – to the extent it infected legal-academic thought – further reduced the distance between conventional ideas of free will and the rule of law. But there were limits to this effect, owing largely to consequentialists' narrow, mainly instrumental use of the free will concept. The newly emergent language of freedom extolling the virtues of a "moral-legal" conception of responsibility most commonly resided within consequentialist approaches that transmuted social understandings of free will as a reality into academic notions of very possibly fictive, but psychologically necessary or appropriately human, ways of thinking about one's self and others. Thus, elite theory mainly provided a way of conceiving of free will (or of manipulating belief in it) that was positivist in essence. Accordingly, I am inclined to think that the middle years – despite the diversity of views they ultimately brought forth – remained a second (albeit, quasi-utilitarian) stage in the Progressive, positivist transformation of criminal jurisprudence. The reemergence during that second stage of open recourse to a species of a language of human freedom – something beyond the mere accommodationism of the period's first decade – bore testimony to the gravitational pull of conventional morality regarding both the idea of free will and the closely related ideal of political liberty. But the orbital change in academic thought about a desert-based criminal law, and about the free will problem, still lay around an important corner.

4

Scientific-Positivism, Utilitarianism, and the Wages of Conventional Morality: 1930–1937

INTRODUCTION

The legal academic writings of the 1930s that I employ to chart the path of post-Progressive Era scholarship reveal quite disparate attempts to achieve a workable treatmentist approach while taking a retributivist conventional morality into account. These attempts were closely related to Pound's approach. Yet they proceeded well beyond Pound, sometimes by grappling more specifically with the question of responsibility and usually by attempting to systematize the relationship between conventional morality and reform that carried forward the ideals of the Progressive program. For most legal scholars, the objective was to provide a more nuanced account of the manner in which conventional morality could be contained and even eroded. The important goal was to work out a general system of criminal law that would be "Progressive" – in the sense of preserving the core values of the Progressive movement – yet make room (at least temporarily) for traditional impulses. Indeed, even those scholars who did not expressly accommodate traditional retributivist drives often incorporated notions of vengeance or blame into their prescriptions for systemic reform, consciously or not, by recasting such notions in language that better complemented the Progressive ideal. In this sense, the 1930s presaged an apparent truth that would rise further to the fore in the 1950s: truly eliminating retributivism from the law proved to be a significantly more complex task – and perhaps a less desirable one – than many early Progressives envisioned. Certainly any early, optimistically framed hopes – that the "friction between ethical and sociological theory and legal theory is a temporary phenomenon" that might simply disappear once education "brought about the internal conditions of life measured by reason"[1] – were eclipsed by the realities of real-world reform.

---

[1] Roscoe Pound, "Enforcement of Law," *Green Bag*, vol. 20 (1908): 401–10, 403.

A central, emerging idea concerned the inability of the vocabulary of
the behavioral and social sciences to deal with the law's moral aspects.
Thus, in the 1930s the prevailing winds of Progressive (scientific-)positivism
coincided with a growing separation between legal academics and behavioral scientists. Legal academics continued to be critical of a criminal law
founded on the idea of free will, but they accorded the social view on that
issue greater respect. This was but a part of the law's making good on the
wages of conventional morality.

And, as lawyers, they paid greater attention to the political liberty issues
that Speranza had identified and that Pound took seriously. Glueck, whose
training bridged the fields of law and science, would even continue to advocate for a limited concept of true free will, although he concluded that most
criminal activity was evidence that the offender's freedom had been compromised. Psychiatrist William A. White, on the other hand, held fast: he
denied the existence of free will and, although he would continue to make
pragmatic concessions about the extent of reform, he preferred a revolution
even in the guilt-assessment process to account for the realities of determinism. The other, more purely legalist, positivist-leaning scholars I introduce
here tended toward a traditional mode of guilt assessment based on criminal intent or mens rea. Sometimes ambiguous with regard to their true
feelings toward free will, they commonly turned to carefully circumscribed
discretion – whether of judge, jury, or penal authorities – in order to balance
the demands of a functioning legal regime with either conventional attitudes
(via jury discretion), scientific realities (via judicial sentencing and penal discretion), or both. But some, such as Jerome Hall – at least initially, during
this still-rising moment of Progressive effort – saw in past and contemporary
developments a dialectical movement toward eventual use of the highly discretionary and individualized juvenile court model at the guilt-assessment
stage even for adult offenders.

With regard to the more publicly insulated – and thus scientifically accessible – sentencing phase, jurists were more commonly of one mind with
regard to the need for consequentialist reform, albeit not with regard to the
preferred reform. A debate was unfolding within the legal academy concerning penological methods for reaching what, in fact, might be claimed were
common ends: it was not clear that the distance between the incapacitation for treatment favored by the declared positivists and incapacitation for
the "common good" emphasized by the utilitarians was so very great. Both
sides saw themselves as scientifically minded; both wished to minimize if
not overcome criminality. What divided them was a choice of means: individual or specific deterrence, on the one hand, and general deterrence on
the other. The more positivist-leaning legal scholars of the 1930s opposed a
general-deterrence–based utilitarianism that invoked "non-retributive" punishment. They believed that imposing punishment – for whatever nuanced
reason advanced by scholars – would reinforce an undesirable retributivist

understanding of criminal law in society at large. At the same time, they often accommodated the approach they criticized by stressing the general-deterrence effects of the therapeutic approach they favored. The story of positivist-leaning scholarship, then, is one of an ongoing Progressive inspiration diverging into various positions that compromised or adulterated the ideals of behavioral science by accommodating both social understandings (conventional morality) and the goals of general deterrence.

Despite this accommodation, the positivist-leaning scholarship of the 1930s also provoked a reaction in the form of a systematic analysis and approach founded on explicitly utilitarian principles. Central to this reaction was Jerome Michael and Herbert Wechsler's 1937 "A Rationale of the Law of Homicide," in which they remained true to treatmentism but sought to prioritize general deterrence and cure along utilitarian lines. They paid some homage to conventional morality, but did so within the confines of utility. For them, responsibility depended on intentionality in its varying degrees, and they accepted the compatibility of responsibility with the human capacity for deliberation, deliberation being critical to intent. But this responsibility was strictly dependent upon deterrability, which itself could exist in a determined world. This essentially compatibilist position implicitly allowed them to be unconcerned that the traditional free will problem posed a true dilemma for criminal responsibility. But their resulting idea of *non-retributive* punishment kept them from having to articulate the sort of philosophically complete compatibilism that some members of a later generation of legal scholars – who expressly considered desert and, later, even retribution, as valid elements of the law – came to embrace.

As is illustrated by the representative writings from this period I have attempted to capture here, there was no simple resolution or conclusion to the debate, which introduced a broad range of potential solutions for merging progressive reform with conventional views on responsibility. But these scholars of the 1930s took seriously their task of defining the means and ends of the legal system in what they saw as a new, modern era; indeed, they did so with studied regard both for the new sciences and for the history of the law as an institution. And the debate did shape legal thinking about criminal responsibility – including thinking that led directly to significant judicial opinions and practical reform – in the years following. The utilitarians did not win the day, but they did put before the positivists the challenge of providing a logic for when the law could justifiably take hold of people for purposes of reform or incapacitation. The challenge was essentially moral.

SCIENTIFIC-POSITIVISM

The Behavioral Science Critique of Free Will

In their continued critique of the law's reliance on notions of free will, many social and behavioral scientists pulled no punches. With regard to the assessment of guilt, for example, Harry Elmer Barnes's confident announcement that the era of the free moral agent was over was based on his unqualified assertion that there "is not the slightest iota of freedom of choice allowed to either the criminal or the normal citizen in his daily conduct." He thus recommended the "repudiation and elimination, once and for all, of the theological and metaphysical interpretations of criminal conduct and responsibility."[2]

With regard to penal reform, the starting point for many behavioral scientists was the more practical failure, as they saw it, of punishment to function successfully as a deterrent. According to sociologist Edwin Sutherland, in his 1924 text *Criminology*, punishment – regardless of aim – embittered offenders, made them more cautious in their criminal activities, and rendered those activities more exciting. Reform through medical, psychological, or other nonpunitive forms of "penal discipline" was thus both the ideal goal and a pragmatic necessity.[3] Karl Menninger put it this way:

> The psychiatrist seeks for the subject of his study, not retributive action, but diagnosis and scientific attempt at therapy, plus the protection of society. This, in a sense, is an "inhuman" attitude in that it is a departure from the instinctive mechanism that rules most of humanity; the clamor for vengeance is more "human." But treatment may sometimes be as painful as the sacrifice prescribed by the legal ritual.... [T]he psychiatrists, too, may prescribe painful treatment, but it is never retributive punishment, and never a program basing its efficacy on the fallacy that fear is the sole determinant of human behavior.[4]

The presumption of free will, which was the rationale for punishment, was also its Achilles' heel. On this radical positivists stood firm, rejecting what sociologist John Gillin termed the "absurd postulates" of a compromise-based neoclassical criminal jurisprudence. In Gillin's view, jurists and legal theorists quested for a hopeless grail in seeking a resolution between quasi-deterministic neoclassical ideas and more absolutist scientific principles. The seeming advance in neoclassicism took account of only the most obvious limits to the concept of free will, embracing mitigation in degree of guilt and, hence, in degree of punishment for those whose conditions were supposed to "ma[k]e it impossible for [them] to exercise free will." But because the concept of free will was *entirely* a fiction, the neoclassical system of partial responsibility rested upon fictive distinctions that introduced "an impossible basis for the actions of judges, juries, and experts."[5]

[2] Harry Elmer Barnes, *The Repression of Crime: Studies in Historical Penology* (New York: George H. Doran, 1926), 24.

[3] Edwin H. Sutherland, *Criminology* (Philadelphia: J. B. Lippincott, 1924), esp. chap. 15, "Ethics and Economy of Punishment."

[4] Karl A. Menninger, "Medicolegal Proposals of the American Psychiatric Association," *JCLC*, vol. 19 (1928): 367–77, 375.

[5] John Lewis Gillin, *Criminology and Penology* (New York: Century, 1926), 330–32. Worse, neoclassical theory "as a makeshift ... introduces the question of premeditation as a measure

Nathaniel Cantor, following Menninger and William A. White, asserted: "Our views of an individual, the language by which we describe human worth, our standards of praise and blame, our general moral values are saturated with theological traditions centuries old." Like Gillin, Cantor cited the by-products of this irrationalism: "strange concepts in the form of 'partial freedom', 'quasi-responsibility', 'limited responsibility' are employed in the futile attempt to reconcile scientific fact with practical procedure." Cantor would have none of it. "Man is responsible or he is not." He himself concluded that, for purposes of the law, man is not:

There is no intelligible universe of discourse for the concept of 'freedom of the will.' The whole discussion as traditionally carried on is hollow and verbal. Even when restated by such students as Professor Herrick and John Dewey, confusion results from employing the older terms to convey the newer implications. But whatever one's convictions, the whole question of individual moral responsibility is simply irrelevant in the discussion of penal philosophy. As a matter of fact, any reformative scheme involves the assumption of determinism in behavior.[6]

White similarly examined outdated notions of guilt that appeared empty in the light of modern scientific understandings. In *Crime and Criminals* (1933), he built on his more famous work of a decade earlier, tracing the origins of the conventional view of mens rea:

The idea of responsibility grew up in connection with the belief in freedom of choice when it was believed that a person in order to be responsible must of necessity have been able to have chosen differently, that as a matter of fact, he elected to choose the evil way rather than the good way and that he did so intentionally and knowingly and that this state of mind therefore constituted what is termed in law as *mens rea* or guilty mind.[7]

It followed, White stated, that "if the mind is so diseased that it is incapable of forming criminal intent, or understanding the nature and quality of the act performed," the law holds such a person not guilty. This was "simple enough" and completely understandable at the time of its formulation, for there was then "no question about man's ability to do or refrain from doing as he chose." White claimed that, at origin, this doctrine reflected the equation of crime and sin, of crimes as offenses against God. In current times, however, "responsibility" thus bore the albatross of a medieval past in the

of the freedom of the will." This made it logical that a first offender "who hesitates and can choose, deserves the heavier punishment, whereas the hardened offender, less likely to hesitate by reason of his habits, should escape with less punishment" (331). Gillin did not attempt to show whether this "logical" result was mirrored in actual practice.

[6] Nathaniel F. Cantor, *Crime, Criminals and Criminal Justice* (New York: H. Holt, 1932), 267–70. Cantor's deep interests in criminology and penology were informed by his degrees in both law and anthropology. He taught at the University of Buffalo, where he later would become chair of the department of Anthropology and Sociology.

[7] William A. White, *Crimes and Criminals* (New York: Farrar and Rinehart, 1933), 118.

scientifically informed present. Further, in practice this legal concept was applied in yet "another instance of human conduct being controlled by the emotions," rather than by reason and knowledge. The jury, "shedding all of the dialectics of the court-room," in reality finds a defendant insane, thus non-responsible, when upon hearing the "circumstances under which the forbidden act was committed and to some extent how those circumstances evolved," its "sympathy and pity" are excited. Conversely, if such evidence and the demeanor of the defendant provokes "hostility, anger and hate," the jury finds the defendant guilty. "Responsibility" had thus simply become "functionally a legal fiction."[8]

With the publication in 1936 of *Crime and Justice*, Sheldon Glueck, as both sociologist and legal scholar, was more sensitive to the dilemmas posed by the confrontation of scientific humanitarianism with conventional morality. He offered one of the more informed and long-considered articulations of positivist determinism, recognizing that the "introduction of humanitarian ideals of reform, together with the increasing call for participation of the biologic and social sciences in the administration of justice, and the resultant internal conflict of the criminal law, have rendered the problems much more complex than they were in the past."[9] Glueck did not abandon his earlier conviction in freely willed action,[10] but he now argued that punitive action had to be calibrated according to degrees of free will, with the warning coda that "human ingenuity has … not yet invented a machine for measuring this." The seeming implication was that criminal law was at an impasse. Glueck, however, would not have theory close off, rather than lead the way, in such matters of social necessity. Rather, he granted that some offenders were responsible in terms of traditional jurisprudence and he concluded that the jury effectively functioned to distinguish those who so qualified from those who did not. Of course, there remained the class of offenders who lacked a degree of responsibility as a result of more subtle determining factors: "Beyond being victims of defective intelligence and mental diseases, many criminals are more or less victims of the poverty and other unwholesome social influences over which they have little control."[11] But, critically, although the law did not always take such determining influences into account, it was *capable* of doing so. On this point he criticized the prevailing insanity tests as not giving wide enough purview to the host of independent factors bearing down on an individual's behavior.

Thus, Glueck was optimistic but, at least initially, avoided the seeming reductionism of the criminologists (e.g., Barnes and Cantor) and, for that

[8] White, *Crimes and Criminals*, 119–21.
[9] Sheldon Glueck, *Crime and Justice* (Boston: Little, Brown, 1936), 4.
[10] E.g., Sheldon Glueck, *Mental Disorder and the Criminal Law: A Study in Medico-Sociological Jurisprudence* (Boston: Little, Brown, 1925), 444–45.
[11] Glueck, *Crime and Justice*, 97–98.

matter, of the psychoanalyst White (who had sounded a note of displeasure at Glueck's devoting "so many ... pages" to "the question of responsibility" in his otherwise very favorable review of Glueck's 1925 book). For White, the solution was to recognize candidly that free will did not exist.[12] Glueck, on the other hand, believed he could make his point without entirely denying the existence of free will – and did so. But, as we have seen, in a later chapter he went a further step in denying the relevance of free will to *criminal* behavior, concluding that

the criminal act occurring at any given time is the outcome of constitutional and acquired personal and social forces. It shows that the individual's power of resistance, or self-guidance, or selective choice and the introjection of bits of the environment, has been overbalanced by the strength of the other circumstances.[13]

In other words, wherever one drew the line between the "free" and the "unfree," *criminal* behavior was on the "unfree" side. The point of "education" (i.e., reform in the therapeutic sense) was to fan "into flame [this] precious spark of creative self-direction despite the biologic and social ashes that are always tending to smother it."[14] Thus the "unfree" would be redeemed – made "free," a process that in no way altered the fact that they had been "unfree" at the moment they committed the forbidden act. Part behaviorist, part jurist, Glueck embodied the tensions that characterized relations between legal and extralegal academic elites.

Positivist-Leaning Jurisprudence

In general, twentieth-century American criminal law scholars increasingly accepted the idea that much – or even all – behavior was determined. Yet there was also a growing rough consensus that, for pragmatic purposes – indeed for a democratically rooted rule of law to function in any meaningful way – the law had to accept free will as an ineradicable psychological reality. As a whole, progressive jurists remained optimistic about the potential and workability of legal reform. But their prescriptions drifted from those of the more strictly deterministic social and behavioral scientists. Time had eclipsed Speranza's turn-of-the-century hope that "the kingdom of scientific law is at hand!"[15] Instead, jurists' mounting understanding of the realities involved in melding law and the new sciences cast a predictive quality on

---

[12] William A. White, review of Glueck, *Mental Disorder and the Criminal Law*, *Yale Law Journal*, vol. 35 (1926): 779–81, 780. Here White also stated that he himself was "rather inclined to believe that we can never solve the question of responsibility" but, even in recognizing this, never went so far as to imagine "some spark of capacity" for self-direction, as did Glueck (see Glueck, *Mental Disorder*, 444–45).

[13] Glueck, *Crime and Justice*, 180.

[14] Glueck, *Crime and Justice*, 180.

[15] Gino C. Speranza, "Natural Law versus Statutory Law," *Albany Law Journal*, vol. 59 (1899): 400–405, 404.

earlier observations, such as by Francis Wharton in 1880, that "no matter what may be our speculative views as to the existence of conscience, or of freedom of action, we are obliged, when we determine responsibility, to affirm both."[16] Indeed, the legal field could not openly announce that the free will presumption rested only on instrumental or utilitarian terms, lest the disjunction between legal theory and lay understanding become transparent to more than an elite; the very legitimacy of the rule of law was at stake.

This did not mean, however, that the legal field itself was united. Still drawing more or less on the behavioral sciences, jurists engaged in a heated debate regarding the goals and methods of reform – particularly penal reform. Positivists and utilitarians were divided on whether rehabilitative treatment or deterrence-oriented punishment should be the primary aim, regardless that the results of particular sentencing processes would often ultimately be the same in practice. All (or enough to divide the academy) depended on whether treatment or punishment was the defining term: the most desirable social order sometimes seemed to hang on a choice of words.

In 1933, University of Colorado law professor Henry Weihofen reflected this state of affairs in his comprehensive review of the insanity defense. Although Weihofen favored an emphasis on individual rehabilitation, his analysis had the potential to hold together, rather than rent, the academy. At base, it would seem, science's primary impact had been to unite reformers in rejecting retributivism:

The point is that the criminologists would inflict hardship and suffering only in so far and in such cases as they tend to confer a benefit, and not for their own sake. Penal discipline and incarceration would be things unpleasant to endure, but inflicted upon persons because it is necessary for their own well-being or for the well-being of society, and not as punishment for transgressions.[17]

Implicitly, if both unpleasant remedial treatment and deterrence-based punishment escaped the opprobrium of retributivism, the same penal discipline advocated by utilitarian deterrence theorists could appeal to positivists, at least if that discipline was not defined as traditional punishment. Indeed, Weihofen distinguished four "varieties" of deterrence-based punishment theory that complemented each other and incorporated the primary aims of both camps: reformation, disablement, example, and prevention. The varieties assumed: first, "that punishment makes men good"; second, that in some instances reformation is not possible; third, that the event of punishment will "deter others from committing the same crimes"; and, fourth, that the "threat of punishment ... [will] deter all persons from committing the

[16] 1 Francis Wharton, *A Treatise on Criminal Law* (8th ed., 1880), 52–53.
[17] Henry Weihofen, *Insanity as a Defense in Criminal Law* (New York: Commonwealth Fund, 1933), 440.

punishable act."[18] Reformation and disablement upheld specific deterrence; example and prevention aimed at general deterrence.

Positivists such as Weihofen distinguished themselves through their preference for the primacy of specific deterrence, via individual treatment and therapy, out of which would come, over time, the effects of general deterrence. This approach, they maintained, permitted greater flexibility to respond to criminal behavior based on possibilities for remediation and social reacclimatization. Significant support already existed for an expert-dominated tribunal at the sentencing stage that could advise on treatment's many forms. Glueck endorsed such a turn, Governor Al Smith advised the New York Legislature to consider it,[19] and Jerome Frank[20] wrote favorably of the procedural maneuver. Most jurists, however, remained vague about the implications of such a reform for the trial and for criminal responsibility itself. Rather, they accepted some version of existing practice, which affirmed criminal guilt and punishment for moral transgressions.

Thus bifurcation of the criminal process into separate guilt-assessment and sentencing phases continued to permit an ad hoc melding of conventional beliefs and positivist reform. Positivist jurists of the 1930s tended to have a more sophisticated assessment of social attitudes than earlier legal academics had achieved, however. Although they denigrated the urge for vengeance, they saw retributive feelings as relatively natural, and a more "objective view" as evolving gradually. Only a few positivist legal scholars renounced free will in toto, and most recognized the importance of conventional ideas about "just deserts" as a bulwark against unrestrained state-enforced therapeutics. Accordingly, the positivist commentators of the 1930s, confronting the dilemma of the disjunction between law's professional side and its lay interpretation, found a place for conventional morality in their prescriptions for reform: allowing the notion of free will to persist at the guilt-assessment stage enlisted conventional beliefs as a limiting force on the determinism-based state intervention that would be prescribed upon sentencing. Although such compromised reform thus maintained the tension of disjunction, the interplay between the two stages of process could also become a mechanism for the law's evolution. That is, penal policy was not only a form of positivist compensation for concessions made at the guilt-assessment stage, it was also a potential means by which society might be educated and thus by which conventional guilt assessment might eventually be altered or abandoned. Such a process of alteration or abandonment was

---

[18] Weihofen, *Insanity as a Defense,* 339.

[19] See Benjamin N. Cardozo, "What Medicine Can Do for Law" (address before the New York Academy of Medicine, November 1, 1928), in *Law and Literature and Other Essays and Addresses* (Littleton, CO: F. B. Rothman, 1986), 79–80.

[20] Jerome Frank, *Law and the Modern Mind* (New Brunswick, NJ: Transaction Publishers, 2009), 190 n. 10 (originally published New York: Bretano's, 1930).

understood as a matter of normal social evolution embedded in the history of law. Hence, positivist-leaning legal academics were, by and large, content to be gradualists, accommodationists, and compromisers.

Social Passions and the Rule of Law

In recognizing a need for some sort of synthesis between progressive goals and a legitimate rule of law, virtually all legal commentators on criminal responsibility now positioned themselves in some way in relation to social passions and understandings. Some openly counseled (at least within academic circles) that the law must rid itself of the "myths" of free will and responsibility – the "metaphysical jargon of the criminal law," as Weihofen put it.[21] Albert Harno, the staunchly positivist Dean of the University of Illinois College of Law, echoed those sentiments, complaining that the doctrine of criminal responsibility was "based on a preconceived conception of freedom of the will," which "involves a metaphysical question," and declaring that if the law focused instead on dangerousness, "the whole problem would become rational and there would no longer be any complicated question of moral responsibility."[22] Still, even Harno noted that although "it would be preferable to give no consideration to the retributive theory" in the rationale for a criminal code, "the desire for vengeance is so deeply rooted in human psychology that it would be a serious mistake for the drafters of a code not to grapple with it."[23]

Many legal academics did grapple with the problem of retribution, or "vengeance," whether or not they discussed the free will problem that was generally assumed to inhere in it. Law Dean Justin Miller of Duke University outlined the various ways in which the social urge for vengeance intruded on the law. He chided reformers who, he wrote, sometimes forgot Holmes's warning that law "'should correspond with the actual feelings and demands

[21] Henry Weihofen, "The Metaphysical Jargon of the Criminal Law," *ABA Journal*, vol. 22 (1936): 267–70, 267.

[22] Albert J. Harno, "Rationale of a Criminal Code," *University of Pennsylvania Law Review*, vol. 85 (1937): 549–63, 558. Harno made the issue of dangerousness central to a reformed code (see Albert Harno, "The Plan of the Criminal Code," *Illinois Bar Journal*, vol. 24 [1936]: 144*ff*) and was skeptical of deterrence theory: "We can be fairly certain that the doctrine of deterrence cannot be made the central theme of a modern code" ("Rationale of a Criminal Code," 552); rather, segregation and, where possible, "treatment" were central (558–59).

[23] Harno, "Rationale of a Criminal Code," 552. Harno's secondary acknowledgment of traditionalism alongside his clear commitment to positivism illustrates that, as of the late 1930s, progressive scientific values were still on the rise for many within the legal academy. Contrast, for example, the 1919 comments of Henry Ballantine (previously quoted in Chapter 2, p. 92, n. 111), who preceded Harno as Dean at Illinois and whose acknowledgment of positivism's insights into criminal guilt remained secondary to the necessary practical primacy of the traditional view: "For practical purposes the law must accept the common-sense postulate of free will upon which we all act. We assume in normal persons moral responsibility. They are accountable for their acts, and may justly be punished if they fail to control their conduct"

of the community, whether right or wrong.'"²⁴ It did not follow, Miller
hastened to add, that no improvement was possible. Through education
of society, as well as through better trained lawyers, something could be
accomplished. Miller looked favorably upon recent developments: juvenile
courts, probation, and psychiatric and medical clinics. There was hope, but
"development of criminal law must take place, in considerable measure,
subject to the limitations of local understanding and capacity."²⁵ Still for
Miller, not unlike Pound, the law remained in spirit opposed to the social
ethic. Although the law must take that ethic into account, the law need not
internalize social attitudes. The law stood outside and apart from the society
it sought to reform.

According to University of Maryland law professor John Strahorn, the
law was *itself* constituted by social passions, including vengeance. But this
fact did not necessarily pose insurmountable barriers to reform. For example, reforms aimed at curbing recidivism served the consequentialist goal of
specific deterrence – the law's concern solely with the antisocial tendencies of
a particular offender. Such reforms – including probation and parole – could
also be consistent with a demand for vengeance: incarceration remained,
at least as a threat, and this sufficed to "check the tendency to private vengeance." "What is needed is to educate the public to the extent that the
demand for vengeance will be satisfied by societal action of an intelligent
sort and not necessarily by incarceration alone."²⁶ This was a classic juristic
positivist move: it privileged reform of the individual offender over general
deterrence, stressed the consideration of dangerousness, and avoided direct
engagement with the issue of free will.

I focus here in more depth on a group of scholars – Raymond Moley,
Francis Sayre, Jerome Hall, John B. Waite, and Alfred Gausewitz – who
offered a range of positivist approaches to the law that incorporated, in one
way or another, the social passions bound up in conventional ideas of blame
and responsibility. For some, such as Moley, an underlying conventional
assumption of free will seemed to survive relatively intact, albeit in part
because of the limitations of science in practice. Others, such as Sayre – who
warned against a total determinist co-optation of law – would emphasize
the political and historical salience of blameworthy intent. Waite, in contrast, exemplified attempts to transmute conventional retributive urges into
a sort of vengeance-free psychology of contempt more equipped to achieve
progressive consequentialist ends. All carried forward the Progressive hope

(Henry W. Ballantine, "Criminal Responsibility of the Insane and Feeble Minded," *JCLC*,
vol. 9 (1919): 485–99, 494).
²⁴ Justin Miller, "Criminal Law – An Agency for Social Control," *Yale Law Journal*, vol. 43
(1934): 691–715, 713 (quoting Holmes, *The Common Law*[[1881], 41).
²⁵ Miller, "Criminal Law," 713–15.
²⁶ John S. Strahorn, Jr., "Probation, Parole, and Legal Rules of Guilt," *JCLC*, vol. 26 (1935):
168–79, 172.

that some significant transformation of the criminal law was still possible alongside the limitations posed by convention and history.

Raymond Moley

Raymond Moley was a Professor of Law at Columbia who, as a former Director of the Cleveland Foundation, had been intimately involved in various criminal administration surveys. Moley had also acted as an advisor to President Roosevelt on New Deal programs. As a scholar and policy maker, he was both intellectually attuned to the theoretical currents of his time and professionally sensitive to the political and historical workings of the criminal law. Like others in his field, he recognized the need for a thoughtful synthesis of science and tradition. The nuances of his particular practical approach illustrate how the various potential modes of synthesis created different implications for notions of free will and responsibility.

Science, for Moley, had persuasively shown that the law needed to adapt to "greater individualization of treatment."[27] But science could never appropriate entirely to itself the domain of human relations. Success depended upon the extent "to which the diagnosis of human nature can be reduced to scientific accuracy," and Moley was not convinced of that eventuality, however far displaced into the future. The application of science required realms of analysis and insight – from the individual subconscious to actuarial statistics – that were themselves evolving. And the psychiatrist's "guess," Moley insisted, "is much more in the nature of an expression of artistic insight than a scientific analysis."[28]

Moreover, argued Moley, convention died hard. He would not dismiss out of hand authoritative tradition regarding human nature in political society. "To view crime with the behaviorists," Moley wrote, "is to strike at moral and religious values very precious in the eyes of most of those who rule the world."[29] Those "impetuous friends of psychiatry," who would "ascribe practically all crime to mental defectiveness and who have proposed to substitute mental therapy under the direction of psychiatrists for the present processes of law," saddled psychiatry with "a task regarded by the law and public opinion as essentially a proper subject for the action of statecraft and jurisprudence."[30] And, even if convention's foundation was slight, the evolving theoretical alternatives were no less inchoate:

Psychology now teaches the importance of mental age, and "responsibility" in the face of this new synthesis, must be conditioned to a new meaning – perhaps no meaning at all. In the face of the devastating sweep of newer conceptions in psychology

[27] Raymond Moley, *Politics and Criminal Prosecution* (New York: Minton, Balch, 1929), 236.
[28] Raymond Moley, *Our Criminal Courts* (New York: Minton, Balch, 1930), xvi–xvii.
[29] Moley, *Politics and Criminal Prosecution*, 222.
[30] Moley, *Criminal Courts*, 135–36.

the basic assumptions of criminality are vastly altered. It is hardly sound to assert, as some of the "socially minded" persist in doing, that "a criminal law based upon vengeance must yield to criminal law based on" – something or other-else. "It" is based upon little that has not changed since it was formulated. It was based upon little when it was formulated. It can not be adjusted to a "new" conception because apparently a "new" conception has not yet formulated itself.[31]

In the interim, Moley looked at the glass as being half full. The new professional was there to compensate for limitations in traditional criminal jurisprudence. By drawing from current scientific knowledge, the law might absorb positivism's contributions without devaluing the criminal trial process. The great development of the Progressive Era had been to enlist discretion for treatment of the individual violator in the interests both of the person and society. Accordingly, Moley focused on the legal system's discretionary reliance on scientific input where it was most salient. Ideally, prosecutors and judges (and especially the latter), when armed with new knowledge regarding human conduct and "guided by the best of intentions," could use their roles – for example in charging, conducting bench trials, and sentencing – with an eye toward "treatment most likely to benefit the defendant and the state." Thus, the element of discretion, which had always been present in the legal system, could be harnessed for more enlightened ends.[32]

Moley achieved his compromise between science and convention by largely abstaining from the ultimate question of responsibility – around which, he observed, there was waged a "fierce and apparently indecisive battle."[33] Moley himself would not be drawn in. At least not directly. For he weighed in implicitly at the margins where the issue of voluntary wrongdoing clearly informed whether a traditional or scientific approach served the most desirable (and perhaps most realistically achievable) ends. He had no problem, for example, concluding that deterrence remained the best approach to professional crime. One must, he said, "make it clear to the potential professional criminal that he has more to gain by obeying society's laws than by breaking them."[34] On the other hand, he was impatient with standard tests for legal insanity; this was an area where "psychiatry ought to loom very large," and where the "rationalistic mode of accounting for many crimes … dissipates, in the practice of social welfare and mental therapy, even if not in the law and in the popular mind, the hopelessly irrational notion of free will as applying to all forms of misconduct except that of the 'mania.'" Here, "nothing is gained by those who argue the value of deterrence. Supervision and control are needed," and the issue raised by the

[31] Moley, *Criminal Courts*, xv.
[32] Moley, *Criminal Courts*, xv–xvi.
[33] Moley, *Politics and Criminal Prosecution*, 223.
[34] Moley, *Criminal Courts*, 139.

traditional right-wrong[35] test (whether a mental defect or disease caused the actor to be unaware of the nature of his act or of the fact that it was wrong) "ought to be and must be subordinated."[36]

In sum, the capacities of science, the public understanding of human nature, the appropriate place of "statecraft," and the practical necessity of achieving public security all deserved consideration. Science opened new horizons for the practice of discretion and thus enlarged the roles of prosecutor and judge. But science and political-legal rationalization did not always dovetail; their disjuncture would (and should) shape the future of the positivist initiative. So Moley followed Glueck in appealing to reasonable accommodation. But where Glueck sought to integrate criminal justice into the perspectives of criminology, Moley made criminal law the touchstone. The implications for scientific understanding of responsibility and free will consequently differed. Glueck, as we have seen, judged the criminal to be "un-free"; Moley essentially accepted the notion of voluntary intention to engage in wrongdoing and insisted upon the criminal being judged free, as distinct from the mentally defective who abided and acted outside the circle of moral responsibility. The criminal was not therefore to be made free, but had to bear the responsibility of his freedom. Perhaps most centrally, for Moley a scientifically informed concept of the person could widen the scope of judicial discretion to the extent that, in effect, the court could address, along with wrongdoing, the proof of moral responsibility. Significantly, Moley thus shared with his contemporaries – criminologists and jurists – a concern with the administration of the law that deflected more philosophical investigations. He did not probe the question of whether any person was truly free if human freedom *could* be left to judicial discretion. The authoritative hold of the legal language for responsibility, as well as convention (of which that language formed a part), was a buffer not simply against the unchecked forays of psychiatry, but also against metaphysical anxieties.

Francis Sayre

Francis B. Sayre of Harvard, one of the foremost legal academics writing in these years, also took up the language of voluntary intention although, again, not to directly question its philosophical underpinnings. Rather, he endeavored to demonstrate how, historically, our changing thresholds for acts that invoke the jurisdiction of the criminal law absorb the social priorities and expanding knowledge of successive periods. "Intention," "guilty mind," and mens rea referred to relative truths about responsibility with more or less salience – and with somewhat differing implications – for given

---

[35] With regard to terminology, I – and most of the writers I discuss – generally treat the "right-wrong," "cognitive," and "*M'Naghten*" tests interchangeably despite that the "right-wrong" label is also sometimes used to describe a somewhat different test predating *M'Naghten*.

[36] Moley, *Criminal Courts*, 130–34.

historical moments. Where Moley had focused on the opportunities for accommodating evolving understandings of criminality and blame through judicial discretion, Sayre was bent on demonstrating that accommodation was already an integral element of the criminal law's substance, in its defining terms. He cautioned, however, that the modern trend toward defining criminal acts with more regard to resulting social harm than to individual blame – a trend buttressed in part by legal- and scientific-positivist principles emanating from both legal and behaviorist circles – accorded to the state unchecked power and threatened fundamental political liberties.

Through his historical account of Anglo-Saxon law, Sayre demonstrated that, although punishment did not always "hang upon proof of any guilty state of mind," the later influences of Roman law and particularly of canon law on the common law were responsible for the requirement of "proof of a guilty intent." Blameworthiness was premised upon moral guilt, which was "essentially dependent upon one's state of mind."[37] "Blameworthiness thus came to be and still remains the foundation of the conception of criminality," although characterizations of blameworthy intent or mens rea may shift – and, indeed, although the modern law featured "no single precise state of mind common to all crime" but, instead, "the new conception of *mentes reae*."[38]

Thus, in more recent times, although the social defense had come further to the fore, blameworthy intent – albeit somewhat reformulated – was still the touchstone. We now

think of the function of criminal administration as, not the awarding of punishment to wrongdoers in proportion to their offenses, but the protection of social and public interests; and the criminal intent thus becomes not the desire to do wrong but the intent to do that which causes social injury.[39]

If the protection of social interests is taken to the extreme, however, criminality could be disengaged from intent and defined merely as a harmful "'act … *not* an act plus an intent.'"[40] On one hand, such "modernization" of law – and its implied expansion of strict liability – could be seen simply

---

[37] Francis Bowes Sayre, "The Present Signification of *Mens Rea* in the Criminal Law," in *Harvard Legal Essays*, ed. Roscoe Pound (Cambridge, MA: Harvard University Press, 1934), 399–417, 401. Sayre observed that, in early Anglo-Saxon law, "the objective of criminal justice was primarily to … suppress the blood-feud"; intent was "primarily material in so far as it rendered the conduct more provocative."

[38] Sayre, "Present Signification," 402–04. Sayre traced enduring "special defenses," such as "insanity, infancy, compulsion, coercion, mistake of fact" to "the same general conception of lack of moral blameworthiness," each developing "a substantive law of its own." Interestingly, with regard to legal insanity, he posited that "an arbitrary fixed formula was developed under which the task of determining criminal responsibility could in effect be handed over bodily to a jury, who might be expected to apply to the determination rough common sense" (403).

[39] Sayre, "Present Signification," 402.

[40] Sayre, "Present Signification," 400 (quoting Albert Levitt, "Extent and Function of the Doctrine of *Mens Rea*," *Illinois Law Review*, vol. 17 [1923]: 589).

as traducing the legal heritage of evolution through accommodation of our changing understandings of blame and of the purposes of the law. But Sayre criticized the modern realism that linked the heightened play of social interests in the law to the potential total elimination of mens rea.[41] Citing Albert Levitt, G. H. T. Malan, Robert Maynard Hutchins, and J. F. Dashiell, all writing between 1923 and 1931, Sayre argued that modern psychology abetted this movement.[42] Levitt had banished criminal intent entirely, asserting: "In the criminal law of England and the United States there is no place now for a doctrine of intent as a necessary ingredient of a crime."[43] Others had more ambiguously written of intent that it was "wholly and solely a matter of inference from behavior,"[44] that it was "imputed to persons who have conducted themselves after certain fashions," its meaning being "derived from theorizing about the significance of acts."[45] For Sayre these statements and others comparable, amorphous as they might be, gave momentum to arguments originating in legal positivism – whereby the state had the preeminent right to determine criminality – and in mid-nineteenth-century justifications for strict liability based on act not fault.

With respect to "true crimes," Sayre insisted, "no system of criminal administration can conceivably function based upon acts alone." He argued that strict liability's pertinence would remain "confined to a fairly definite group of offenses" that "in their fundamentals ... essentially differ from the traditional crimes of the classic law" and constituted a "new type of twentieth-century regulatory measure involving no moral delinquency." He referred here to the sphere of "public welfare offenses," in which might be descried a pendulum's swing, but not a total shift in the way we conceive of the law. He granted that criminal law represents a "compromise between the eternally conflicting interests of the individual defendant on the one hand and of the general public on the other." After a long focus on the individual, the criminal law was now moving, *under specific conditions*, to that other magnetic pole of the public interest. Thus, if the offense "involves widespread or serious injury to the public and if the penalty involved is no more than a light fine, we are willing to convict in some cases without proof of any guilty intent." But the shift in "emphasis" from the individual to the public was not – nor should it be – a renunciation of earlier tradition: "It bears no promise of a time when *mens rea* will cease to be a general prerequisite of the criminal law."[46]

---

[41] Sayre, "Present Signification," 410.
[42] Sayre, "Present Signification," 400.
[43] Levitt, "Extent and Function," 588–89.
[44] G. H. T. Malan, "The Behavioristic Basis of the Science of Law" (pt. 2), *ABA Journal*, vol. 9 (1923): 43–48, 44.
[45] Robert Maynard Hutchins, "The Law and the Psychologists," *Yale Review*, vol. 16 (1927): 678*ff*, 687.
[46] Sayre, "Present Signification," 405–09. Contrast, however, Markus Dirk Dubber's appraisal of Sayre's scholarship in his important book, *The Police Power: Patriarchy and the Foundations*

Sayre justified the critical relevance of intent by reference to deterrence theory: intent motivated the criminal to repeat the injurious act. He added that, for law to be effective, it "must reflect with more or less accuracy the popular opinion and conscience of the time and place." Here he returned to history in order to rebut those who lauded a coming age of *purely* nonpunitive law in service of the social defense. The root passions of the criminal law were "vengeance and retribution"; these gave way to the "churchly notion of punishment of evil doing," and "it is still the punitive element which assumes large importance in the popular consciousness."[47] Utilitarians, in particular, must recognize this reality: "In so far as the fear of punishment deters, it must be utilized in criminal administration."[48] The converse was also true: to "punish" (or, presumably, to subject to "non-retributive" sanctions that the public would nonetheless view as punishment) one severely who "caused injury through no fault of his own, by sheer accident or through a mistake of fact ... would so outrage the feelings of the community as to nullify its own enforcement."[49] Abuse of strict liability would teach the lesson that "innocent" men (as socially understood) were subject to conviction, and when "it becomes respectable to be convicted, the vitality of the criminal law has been sapped."[50]

Thus Sayre appeared, from a superficial perspective, to advocate for a fairly conventional view of the law. It is of interest, however, that he never justified the intent doctrine or criminal responsibility directly on the basis of moral wrongdoing, but only indirectly on the *effectiveness* of law. He criticized the positivist position – implicitly both that of legal positivists, generally, and of those more specifically oriented toward scientific positivism – for its tendency to undermine the law in the here and now. His defense of the intent requirement was premised on its application to cases of substantial punishment where society demanded it: social attitudes required a response. Whether Sayre would have deemed such punishment as properly retributive from the *official* point of view is difficult to say. But surely he recognized that is how it would be understood socially. The implication was that, as with intent, so with punishment: one might strip it largely of moral

---

of American Government (New York: Columbia University Press, 2005), at 167–75. Dubber suggests that Sayre's true aim to support a modern criminal law privileging the protection of social, rather than individual, interests rendered his proposed limits on the elimination of mens rea "naïve at best, if not hypocritical." Dubber claims that Sayre's proposed distinction between true crimes and public welfare offenses drew only a "vague," "thin" line that even Sayre recognized could be easily abused by authorities (169–71). Gerald Leonard questions Sayre's criteria for strict liability in "Towards a Legal History of American Criminal Theory: Culture and Doctrine from Blackstone to the Model Penal Code," *Buffalo Criminal Law Review*, vol. 6 (2003): 691–832, 817–19.

47 Sayre, "Present Signification," 410.
48 Sayre, "Present Signification," 415 n. 31.
49 Sayre, "Present Signification," 411.
50 Sayre, "Present Signification," 409.

content as a theoretical matter, but such a move must remain a matter of internal legal or penal theory; it did not – was not supposed to – reflect social understandings. It thus seems that Sayre would accept a radical disjunction between the true meaning of law and the law in practice, but resisted too great a disjunction between legal conventions (that is, the law in practice) and conventional social perspectives. Most important, he gave the social (and distinctly free will–based) view a prominence that raised the stakes for both those (scientific-) positivist-leaning legal scholars and those utilitarians who sought to establish a progressive legal regime without taking account of deeply ingrained traditions of conventional morality. Sayre challenged assumptions of a strict *legal* positivism while sharing with its contemporary advocates a social view of the law.

Jerome Hall

Like Sayre, Jerome Hall approached the possibilities of reform from the long view of the history of criminal jurisprudence. Unlike Sayre, however, Hall's touchstone was not the law's effectiveness. Rather, Hall focused directly on the role of public passions, which he believed were a crucial element that both encouraged reform and defined its limits. Thus Hall would bring his well-known historical study of jury discretion, *Theft, Law and Society*,[51] to bear in considering the scope and methods of modern reform.

In the early 1930s, Hall was setting out on what was to be a long academic career. After studying sociology at the University of Chicago under then Dean Albion Small, Hall moved on to Chicago's law school and, after practicing law from 1923 to 1929, began teaching at the University of North Dakota. Further teaching and studies took him to the law schools at Columbia, Harvard (during Pound's tenure as Dean), and Louisiana University. In 1939, he joined the Indiana Law faculty, where he remained through his retirement in 1970. Part Progressive and part traditionalist, in ways Hall's path would exemplify the shifting ground occupied by scholars examining issues of criminal responsibility and punishment throughout the twentieth century. At the outset, where Moley, Sayre, and the more determinedly "scientific" of legal academics discussed here commonly worked from the basic model of the criminal law for their recommendations, Hall advocated an experimental revamping of the criminal trial process. Following Pound's early 1920s optimism, Hall entertained (as would others) an alternative model: the juvenile court. But he left open the ramifications of doing so. When historical events and perhaps his own private reflections motivated his turning from the administration of law to its underlying principles, the implications of his early Progressivism became all too clear – Hall's traditionalism would overcome and he would decry Pound for advocating social engineering. But this is to get ahead of myself.

---

[51] Jerome Hall, *Theft, Law and Society* (Boston: Little, Brown, 1935).

Hall launched his career with "Social Science as an Aid to Administration of the Criminal Law,"[52] "Law as Social Discipline,"[53] and a review of Franz Alexander and Hugo Staub's 1931 book *The Criminal, the Judge and the Public*.[54] These studies and Hall's inquiry, "Has the State a Right to Trial by Jury in Criminal Cases,"[55] all composed during his years on the North Dakota law faculty, preceded publication in 1935 of his most important early work, *Theft, Law and Society*. In "Social Science," Hall insisted upon the value of social and behavioral science research for criminal justice administration, in part precisely because of the inescapable reality of public passions. He cited the vigilante lynching of Charles Bannon, an accused murderer whose "crime ha[d] many earmarks of an abnormal mind," suggesting that, if the results of Bannon's mental examination had been known, "it is reasonable to assume that [the] public ... would not have felt itself outraged."[56] Open then to psychiatry's insights and contributions, Hall supported the spirit behind William A. White's challenge to the American Bar Association, holding up the innovations of the juvenile court, which had "'boldly cast aside all the usual methods of procedure and developed a program in absolute contradiction to the established traditions, inasmuch as it does not use its machinery for fastening a crime upon someone and then meting out a seemingly appropriate punishment.'"[57]

Hall did not pretend "that the psychiatrist and the lawyer see all problems eye to eye," and so he did not take issue with an American Psychiatric Association committee report recommending "'the exemption of the psychiatrist from the necessity of pronouncing upon concepts of religious and legal tradition in which he has no authority or experience, such as ""responsibility," "punishment," and "justice.""'[58] Still, his stance toward psychiatry remained favorable overall. Reviewing Alexander and Staub's classic study urging abandonment of the concept of responsibility based upon free will and moral blameworthiness, he wrote: "Intimate contact with offenders whether for the prosecution or the defense produces the feeling in practically every case that if everything were known about the defendant, his

---

[52] Jerome Hall, "Social Science as an Aid to Administration of the Criminal Law," *Dakota Law Review*, vol. 3 (1931): 285–98.

[53] Jerome Hall, "Law as a Social Discipline," *Temple Law Quarterly*, vol. 7 (1932): 63–83.

[54] Jerome Hall, review of *The Criminal, the Judge, and the Public: A Psychological Analysis*, by Franz Alexander and Hugo Staub (New York: Macmillan, 1931), *Illinois Law Review*, vol. 26 (1932): 942–45.

[55] Jerome Hall, "Has the State a Right to Trial by Jury in Criminal Cases?," *ABA Journal*, vol. 18 (1932): 226–28.

[56] Hall, "Social Science," 286.

[57] Hall, "Social Science," 292 (quoting William A. White, "Need for Cooperation between Lawyers and Psychiatrists in Dealing with Crime," *ABA Journal*, vol. 13 (1927): 551–55, 553).

[58] Hall, "Social Science," 294–95 and n. 19 (quoting Menninger, "Medicolegal Proposals," 376).

motivation and his complete life-history, a fuller measure of justice would be achieved."[59] Under Pound's influence, Hall saw the lines of psychiatry and the law running in parallel – separate but complementary.

Theft, Law and Society was Hall's most sustained work of positivist assessment and recommendation. While advocating caution about how far and fast rational reform could and ought to proceed, Hall endorsed the scientific approach to criminal justice. Historians recall Hall's book as a pathbreaking study of English criminal justice administration in the eighteenth century. It brought together a great deal of information on jury mitigation in theft cases; although it was not the first such account, it was the most systematic. From his study, Hall drew lessons regarding modern reform of penal sanctions. He observed that social attitudes, in part as expressed through jury verdicts, dictated actual enforceability and thus must be considered in defining viable offenses and penalties. Those same attitudes dictated the extent to which the harshness of the law could be ameliorated, and thus limited the reach of legitimate reform. It was not Hall's point that the best law was that which mirrored social prejudices, but rather that which recognized the importance of public attitudes in the dynamism of legal reform moving toward the ideal.

Hall was convinced that vengeance would persist; it was a by-product of "the biological constitution of man." The lesson of the eighteenth-century English experience was that workable reform coincided with "a more refined expression" of such basic human feelings – not total circumvention of them. Thus, the individualization desired by positivists should work in tandem with deterrence, the role of which was "*creating and enforcing moral sanctions*," an important goal often overlooked by proponents of individualization.[60] Brought together within the frame of modern penology, deterrence and individualization allowed for release of common emotions, on the one hand, and the education of social passions, on the other. "Social attitudes," Hall wrote, "must be considered not only to limit present methods of treatment, but also to point the way to progressive utilization of individualization as technique to modify these selfsame attitudes. But it should be clear that no such attack can be undertaken on the whole front at once."[61]

Hall paid due respect to the community's "'sense of justice,'" declaring that the introduction of individualization within the rule of law should begin "*with the crimes which allow least public emotion, and [ascend] from that point only as rapidly as experimentation and an educated public opinion permit.*"[62] Here he raised the prospect of using petty theft cases as a laboratory for the future. Hall illustrated that public emotions regarding much

[59] Hall, review of *The Criminal, the Judge, and the Public*, 944.
[60] Hall, *Theft, Law and Society*, 294.
[61] Hall, *Theft, Law and Society*, 296.
[62] Hall, *Theft, Law and Society*, 297–98.

larceny allowed for non-penal treatment, as both history and current mores revealed.[63] In this regard conventional morality was ahead of the rule of law. Indeed, it was "generally believed that a huge number of minor thefts are caused by unemployment and poverty." Thus, the number of property offenses generally, and petty thefts in particular, "may be decreased by the amelioration of social and economic conditions." It followed that "skillful individualization of treatment [in this area] will show measurable results," and this practice "would go some distance toward setting the basis for its wider use at a later time." Hall suggested that, in petty theft cases, "administrative boards composed partly of psychiatrists and vocational experts" could "supervise the treatment of persons who are referred to them by all the criminal courts." Through such "specializing out the area of most promise and least difficulty," reformers could create "the most hopeful field for experiment in rehabilitation," setting the stage for future expansion.[64]

Within limits, juvenile courts also offered models of reform that could avoid breaking with the social "sense of justice" while enlisting scientifically enlightened jurisprudence. "The whole treatment of youthful offenders," he claimed, "shows what is involved psychologically in the administration of the criminal law, while the juvenile court development evidences the conditions that must exist before a wide individualization of treatment is possible." Hall defined individualization as treatment "required by [one's] own social and psychic needs" and suggested that "*carried to its limits*, it would mean that no other considerations should affect the treatment of offenders." There were, however, "limits": "It will be recognized that complete individualization of treatment conflicts with present public opinion and with the demand for infliction of punishment upon an offender who has aroused considerable anger or indignation."[65]

Hall's account of modern criminal law thus built upon Pound, Glueck, and Moley, but his particular contribution was to integrate the various elements of the criminal process rather than merely identify and analyze those elements as separable parts. Like Moley, Hall recognized the importance of discretion for any reform of the law where questions of blame, responsibility, and punishment were at issue. But Hall studied more intently than Moley the modernization of discretion from the perspective of the jury and not exclusively that of the bench.

Indeed, discretion was one important link between Hall's historical discussion of eighteenth-century English jury mitigation practices in felony cases and his analysis of twentieth-century American practice in petty larceny. The jury had been a central – perhaps originally *the* central – component in a recursive relationship between lay and official practice. Historical

---

[63] Hall, *Theft, Law and Society*, 304.
[64] Hall, *Theft, Law and Society*, 311–13.
[65] Hall, *Theft, Law and Society*, 292–93.

evidence for jury nullification, Hall saw, could be united first with the modern approach to prosecutorial discretion and then with all other sites for discretion. The modern jury's creative role was decidedly less extensive than that of its ancestor by virtue of the legal precision its ancestor had helped to create; discretion had come increasingly to be concentrated in the hands of judge and prosecutor because of the ever greater complexity of the criminal law. At the same time, legislation achieved an integration of new understandings that had been absent from earlier formal rules. New rules of law were thereby established to suit the changing needs of society. But this did not mean that discretion, particularly as it embodied evolving social understandings, would ultimately be eliminated. Rather, the process was cyclical, with one end of the circle opening onto a new stage whereby social understanding, legal knowledge, and formal rule once more drew closer together.[66]

Hall preserved the modern jury's place within the cycle by relegating it to three principal areas of activity. First: resistance to "unpopular law," which almost certainly referred to the recent phenomenon of nullification in prohibition cases, a common point of reference in the 1930s, and as well to other instances of true rejection of the underlying law. Second: so-called unwritten law cases (where, for example, husbands killed their wives' lovers), which might involve the jury's rejection of the formal law or might rest instead on sympathy for a particular defendant in particular circumstances. Hall noted that, here, conventional morality was changing and the rule of law was moving toward reversal of the older "unwritten" rule. But juries of course continued to find ways to mitigate the law in this area, some of these cases falling into the third category: "verdicts based upon evidence in mitigation introduced by psychiatrists under pleas of insanity."[67]

With respect to this last area, however, it is difficult to say exactly how Hall perceived the jury's role. The *modern* domain of legal insanity would not appear to exemplify the dynamic between the jury and legal officials that had governed the evolution of the rule of law. With regard to that dynamic, one imagines that Hall thought the early jury responded to legal rules, and especially to the law of sanctions, partly emotionally and partly on the basis of a kind of folk wisdom regarding punishment. The process was also occasion for jury education – and thus social education – as jurors had to clarify or reevaluate their moral assumptions about guilt according to evolving principles of a reformed penology (often as embodied by the sanctions imposed for particular crimes). Incrementally, but with advancing momentum, jury verdicts would thus align themselves with evolving elite notions of criminal jurisprudence. In modern legal insanity cases, however, testimony of a much more technical sort than that introduced in other cases

---

[66] Hall, *Theft, Law and Society*, 119.
[67] Hall, *Theft, Law and Society*, 112 n. 66.

came directly from medical scientists, and it might proceed well beyond an advancing folk knowledge or even the understanding society won from the principles of the new penology. Science led – and, Hall apparently believed, should lead – in this domain. Perhaps it was here that the model of the juvenile court was most crucial for wedding science and reformed penology in a context that schooled the layman without unduly compromising either professional expertise or the place of conventional morality.

So, generally, the criminal process incorporated conventional mores through discretionary judgments that remained within the purview of the jury and that, at times, influenced the evolution of the formal law. But the modern system also functioned – and evolved – through the discretion of officials. Through written enactments, the public "sense of justice" defined the scope of possible individualization by criminal justice authorities. Yet, just as the jury exercised discretion within *and* circumvented the written law in some cases, official practices both manifested the formally allowed discretion *and* avoided the prescribed constraints. The practices – by officials and the lay public alike – that circumvented formal limits were the most crucial:

From complaint to parole, the process of applying the criminal law deviates from the written enactment. Compromise, restitution, followed by modified or withdrawn complaints, dismissals, waivers, judicial interpretation, complete nullification by failure to apply laws, verdicts at odds with the facts – these and a score of other practices of both laity and officials characterize the modern administration of the criminal law. *Despite abuse, there is no doubt that this is the mark of an advanced system.*[68]

History showed that such "technicalities and practices which secure desired ends by indirection" can be eliminated only by incorporating within the written law the means for achieving those very ends, and that meant the further legal inscription of discretion through, for example, fully indeterminate sentences. Like Moley, Hall concluded that legal reform, therefore, lay "not in the direction of eliminating discretion," but "in the direction of securing a wiser use of it by intelligent delegation of authority, a more competent, honorable personnel, and careful checks."[69] What had often been characterized as haphazard and dysfunctional in criminal justice administration now emerged as rational refinement in procedure and principle. Legal machinery could evolve to bring into alignment the rule of law and social change.

Perhaps truest to Pound's original optimism – and despite growing awareness of the political and social complexities occasioned by attempts to integrate positivism into existing legal institutions – Hall showed that a young legal academic of the early 1930s could still embrace with few reservations

---

[68] Hall, *Theft, Law and Society*, 120 (emphasis added).
[69] Hall, *Theft, Law and Society*, 121.

the possibilities behavioral science presented for the interrelated reforms of the person (via individualization), the law (via a more scientifically efficient administration), and society (via the training of social reason to command social passions). The European example, notably the penal code experiments of Italy and Germany, was not yet a negative reference point. The Depression and war's absence (the Great War had ended global conflict) focused Progressivism's quixotic confidence on the broad sweep of social reform, as if the frontiers of society had at last been gotten the other side of and tamed. As he would continue to do throughout much of the twentieth century, Hall wrote very much to his time.

John B. Waite

The temptation of course is to seek in the writings of Hall and his contemporaries certain statements for or against traditional criminal responsibility. They wrote, after all, with a great deal of certainty regarding what needed to be reformed and even regarding the ways of going about reformation. What we have to seek instead are the niches where Hall and others sought and found certainty when the destiny of criminal responsibility, and hence of free will under a rule of law, was not at all sure. Where that supreme doubt entered – in the gaps between law and science, between treatment and social passions, between the criminal trial and the criminal administrative bureaucracy – the response for the period, before other certainties gave way, was to close the gaps.

　　John B. Waite, Professor of Law at the University of Michigan, is a case in point. Waite, who placed general deterrence within the penumbra of positivist treatment, took up the hiatus between individual deterrence and social deterrence. Like Hall, he insisted upon the relevance of a popular retributivism. Where Hall had appealed to gradualism, however, in transcending retributive punishment, Waite both demonized retributive punishment and attempted to transform it by way of an ambitious argument that vengeance could be replaced with (renamed?) social or moral condemnation. He argued that therapeutic reform of individual offenders provided the moral tuition that would separate the useful psychology of contempt from the harmful one of retribution. Along the way, his enthusiasm for the therapeutic approach – and his apparent wholesale trust in the wisdom of positivism – led him nearly to depart from traditional notions of legalism. The contrast to Hall was palpable and well illustrates the diversity of approaches among positivistic legal scholars who believed there might eventually be a dissolution of the disjunction between the law as it ought to be and present realities of social attitudes and political imperatives.

　　In his 1934 book *Criminal Law in Action,* Waite sounded the positivist refrain that a retributive theory of punishment obfuscated the criminal law; it focused sentencing unduly on vengeance toward the offender rather than on the moral education of society. Convinced that "while people talk of deterrence, the deeds of legislatures and judges indicate that the real purpose of punishment is satisfaction of the desire for vengeance,"[70] Waite concluded that this true aim of the law undermined both its administration and its effectiveness in protecting society. In attempting to prescribe reform that would genuinely promote deterrence, he veered back and forth between a non-retributive theory of punishment in the name of therapy and a fully nonpunitive approach.

A central element of Waite's approach was his rejection, as unfounded in fact, of the notion that mere threat of physical punishment deterred the impulse to commit crime. The law should aim, rather, at "indirect deterrence," which he described as "the creation of inhibitions based upon ideas of repugnance, or self-condemnation, or fear of public disapproval, rather than fear of physical discomfort." Condemnation and "punishment," he urged, ought to instill in every member of society an instinctive self-reproach at the thought of committing a similar act against the general good: deterrence resulted "only from the inhibitions set up in individuals by the characterization, through punishment, of the act as contemptible and of the actor as unfit for social acceptance."[71]

Like Hall, Waite found a model in juvenile justice. Juveniles might be taken under control and rehabilitated even though they had not actually committed an offense. Thus, the juvenile system modeled an appropriate effort to prevent crime through segregation while also recognizing that "those who have already committed crime *ought to be reconditioned, rehabilitated, reformed, and returned to society as no longer dangerous.*"[72] When it came to adult offenders, however, society rejected this sort of treatment because of what Waite believed were overwrought or outdated notions concerning both political liberty and the goals of punishment. Accepting that safeguards to protect the liberty of innocent citizens are unquestionably necessary, Waite nonetheless concluded that overzealous protection of liberty rights led to "disregard" of "the need of society for protection against crime."[73] Indeed, the "process of the criminal law" was not properly thought of as "the attempt of society to protect its members from harm, but rather as an effort of 'the state' to punish a recalcitrant individual."[74] Accordingly, because of our overzealousness about individual rights – and "because in the concrete case people are rarely interested in the imposition of punishment," possibly because of "an unconscious repugnance to punishment, in the abstract" – "rules and practices have come into law enforcement" that

---

[70] John Barker Waite, *Criminal Law in Action* (New York: Harcourt, Brace, 1934), 22–23, 26.

[71] Waite, *Criminal Law in Action*, 26–27.

[72] Waite, *Criminal Law in Action*, 18–19.

[73] Waite, *Criminal Law in Action*, 43–45, 58.

[74] Waite, *Criminal Law in Action*, 28.

subvert the overall legal system. Appellate judges, for example, took their otherwise laudable resistance to executive tyranny too far, "revers[ing] convictions on incredibly hyper-technical grounds" and "ma[king] fetishes of rule and form." Trial judges, in part because they therefore feared reversal, went to "absurd extremes" in enforcing procedural safeguards, often resulting in clearly guilty offenders going free.[75] Juries, despite their often-commendable role as "bulwark[s] against harshness and oppression," similarly were "an obstacle to the progress of justice and the imposition of deserved punishment" because they were inclined to acquit even murderers whose crimes – particularly those involving passionate reactions, such as when a husband discovers infidelity – aroused sympathy.[76]

Nor did the public at large escape his censure for the failures of the law. Waite asserted, for example, that the public "*does not seriously scorn and condemn law breakers.*" Citing the fascination with figures from Billy the Kid to Al Capone, he observed that the public commonly "respects rather than despises particular criminals." This "negatives the possible efficacy of punishment as a deterrence, because it takes disgrace out of penalty and leaves only physical inconvenience, pain, or death"; such "physical consequences," absent the necessary moral condemnation, "have never in the length of history deterred men or women from courses that promised honor or profit."[77] Further, and critically, the public's fear of the "overzeal and oppression" of police and prosecutors led to widespread support for the exaggerated protection of rights that resulted in under-enforcement of the law by judges and officials.[78] On this point, Waite admonished:

So long as [the public] acquiesces in an unnecessarily technical and obstructive attitude of a judiciary harking back to an era of different political conditions and an obsolescent theory of the purpose of punishment – just so long will it continue to be itself to blame in large measure for both the laxity and the difficulties in enforcement of the criminal law.[79]

This reference to "an obsolescent theory of the purpose of punishment" returned to the heart of Waite's account. The antiquated, but still widely held, notion that punishment effects retribution "explain[s] the present attitude of the public toward criminal procedure." For, "if the objective of the

---

[75] Waite, *Criminal Law in Action*, 56–58, 212.
[76] Waite, *Criminal Law in Action*, 69–71. In the context of his overall prescriptions, Waite's reference to "deserved" punishment does not appear aimed at invoking a robust notion of "desert" traditionally associated with retributive punishment for freely willed acts. Rather, I read this as a reference to factually "deserved" liability for objective wrongdoing – such as murders that are clearly and reasonably not excused by law – for which a functioning legal system should express (deserved) contempt, but which juries excuse from sheer lawlessness or emotionality.
[77] Waite, *Criminal Law in Action*, 272–74.
[78] Waite, *Criminal Law in Action*, 276–81.
[79] Waite, *Criminal Law in Action*, 288.

proceeding be retribution, the people as a whole have no vital interest in its success." No "real harm results if prosecution often fails," because "if retribution be not exacted in this case or that, the public as a whole is not injured." This state of affairs had led to the "quibble, casuistry, [and] technicality in the fabrication of 'rights'" that so undermined the law; "the effort at revenge is a struggle between an abstract government and an individual," and "the public looks on with interest, amusement, partisanship, but without any feeling of participation or social concern." Divorcing punishment from the notion of retribution, on the other hand, would allow punishment to function both as an element of individual reform and as a general deterrent: "Isolation, segregation, compulsory rehabilitation as a consequence of crime, are threats, whatever be the reason for their use"; further, punishment would still deter through its expression of "scorn, contempt or ridicule of those whose conduct fails to conform to social requirements."[80]

Despite his careful articulation of what he believed was the proper way to frame punishment, on occasion Waite simply dropped his distinction between rehabilitative/deterrent punishment and vengeful punishment, denouncing punishment in toto. In his chapter on the insanity defense, he recommended a jury of experts or, better yet, abolition of the defense on grounds that "an insane killer is quite as dangerous to society as a sane one." Neither reform was possible "so long as the accepted purpose of criminal prosecution is *punishment*. Punishment necessarily presupposes wrongdoing, and the wrongdoing cannot exist without consciousness of wrongfulness." Hence the general conclusion that insane actors should not be held liable, regardless that society – and some insane offenders themselves – would benefit from their being segregated or treated. This state of affairs also preserved the inconsistent criteria for defining non-culpable mental states, which indicated the hopelessness of the prevailing theory of criminality and practice of the criminal law: the insanity defense might apply to irresistible impulses, for example, but not to other circumstances in which we logically question whether vengeful punishment for conscious wrongdoing is appropriate, such as intoxication, "stupefaction" resulting from drug use, or, "transitory emotional surcharges which are not the product of 'disease.'"[81] Waite concluded his critique of the insanity defense by observing that when the purpose of the law aims "no longer at punishment, but instead at protection of society by segregation or elimination of provedly dangerous persons ... as it ultimately will [be] ... 'insanity' will become a liability instead of an asset."[82]

Thus Waite's deep social defense aims came to the fore. Once the true end of the law was "protection of the public peace," rather than "punishment of a wrongdoer," he asserted, its administration would be more efficient and

---

[80] Waite, *Criminal Law in Action*, 318–20.
[81] Waite, *Criminal Law in Action*, 31–36.
[82] Waite, *Criminal Law in Action*, 41.

effective.[83] It was here that he stepped to the very edge of traditional notions of legality. Because mere physical threat was futile, the proper goal was to "*eliminate from society* those individuals who were *known* to be dangerous." The reformability of the felon, *not* the apportioning of just deserts for moral wrongdoing, would determine the method of elimination. Punitive measures were to aim at reintegrating the individual into society. "It may be by rehabilitation," Waite wrote, "by education, training, discipline, therapeutic punishment, supervision, or whatever else will so recondition the particular individual as to justify his eventual return to society." Those who "can not be reconditioned," would not be returned to society, but would be kept in segregation. "In a harder society," or perhaps in a "progressive" society of the future, "all such useless members would be eliminated, permanently, by euthanasia"[84]:

We do not "punish" mad dogs, nor rattlesnakes, nor rats when we exterminate them. Nor shall we punish intolerably dangerous human beings. We simply shall refuse to accept the risk of their continued existence. Without rancor or animosity, not as revenge or retribution, but solely as a necessary measure of public safety, *we shall effectively and permanently eliminate them by death.*[85]

The key was that the weight of the law had to fall on *social* deserts instead of retribution and just *individual* deserts. And that end could be achieved only when the positivists' therapeutic methods – perhaps including benign elimination – were understood as the only appropriate forms of penal treatment. Hence the need for a didactic evolution of the language used to describe the law's aims. The goal of sheer punishment conjured up "the consciousness of wrongfulness," or subjective intention to do wrong, and connoted retribution. But deterrent segregation and treatment of those whose objective "wrongdoing" (or dangerousness) "fails to conform to social requirements" – alongside the "public scorn, contempt or ridicule" that followed from conviction – avoided the retributive connotations that had hamstrung the law.

Waite counseled using the law to stimulate a particular social response, without deeply examining whether most people might nonetheless then justify that response in free will–based retributivist terms. Perhaps he thought that "contempt" would be balanced by acceptance of "therapeutic treatment" in such a way that it really could exist in the absence of conventional moral judgmentalism – of retributivism. Like Sutherland a decade earlier, Waite attempted to construct a theory of non-retributive contempt. Unresolved was whether his critique of punishment and his particular positivist response in the name of deterrence and society's defense posed a contradiction or, like Hall's very different approach, proffered an open dialectic.

---

[83] Waite, *Criminal Law in Action*, 58.
[84] Waite, *Criminal Law in Action*, 312–14.
[85] Waite, *Criminal Law in Action*, 318.

Alfred Gausewitz

Alfred Gausewitz, professor at the University of Wisconsin Law School, made more direct use than Waite of existing retributive attitudes, including social assumptions of free will, in his study of the ends of the criminal law. The purpose of Gausewitz's 1936 article, "Considerations Basic to a New Penal Code,"[86] was to advise the State of Wisconsin with regard to creation of a new criminal code. In the article, he addressed the divergent aims of individualization and general deterrence. Employing a review of history somewhat differently than had Sayre and Hall, Gausewitz considered how a modern treatmentist model would affect the substance, as well as the procedure and administration, of the criminal law. His recommendations for reform privileged individualization and the integration of new scientific views of crime prevention, but without overly compromising the goals of retribution and general deterrence where such compromise contravened the public sense of justice. Indeed, although Gausewitz pointedly declared that a new, not a revised, penal code was at stake,[87] his recommendations followed the line of revision, lest the link between the substantive law and "justice" be lost. Moreover, his position that the rule of law should not depart too far from conventional morality's sense of justice was grounded in more than instrumental concerns regarding the law's effectiveness: he was expressly concerned with the social interest in individual liberty, the defense of which he concluded must remain a central goal of the law. Among his contemporaries, he arguably came closest to a position that bridged general deterrence and the positivist focus on individualization. His analysis also dealt more directly with both bifurcation (of the phases of criminal process) and disjunction (between elite views and pervasive social views). Yet Gausewitz still could not fully resolve the relation between the rule of law and conventional morality along the shifting boundary between individualization and general deterrence for the common good.

As background to his analysis, Gausewitz began his study by reviewing the "aims and methods" of the criminal law, the history of thought on the subject (here drawing on Pound), and present conceptions of the law. With regard to the origins of crime, the movement of history was away from the notion of "free moral agency" and toward the scientific study of the causes – at first reductionist, then more plural and complex – of criminal behavior. With regard to the purposes of criminal justice, the two central aims could be simplified as "punitive" – that is, retributive – and "utilitarian," which Gausewitz centrally associated with the goal of preventing future crime. The methods one might use to achieve this latter goal were: (general) deterrence – either by threat or by moral education, "the latter being by way of

---

[86] Alfred F. Gausewitz, "Considerations Basic to a New Penal Code" (pts. 1 & 2), *Wisconsin Law Review*, vol. 11 (1936): 346–400, 480–542.
[87] Gausewitz, "Considerations Basic to a New Penal Code," 346.

punishment as an expression of the moral disapproval of the community" – incapacitation, and reformation, the last through either "moral regeneration by expiation and penitence" or "education of intellectual faculties."[88]

But little attempt had been made to discriminate between the possible motives of utility and punitiveness. Further, although the state allegedly rejected retribution, Gausewitz questioned the genuineness of this stance. Like Waite, he pointed to the law of attempts and to "legislative, as well as judicial, efforts to make the punishment fit the crime." At bottom, he asserted, Anglo-American law lacked a directing aim; its central premises were varied and sometimes inconsistent. Therein lay the initial problem. For a penal code to be rational, Gausewitz claimed, it "must aim to be consistent with some theory of the purpose and method of the criminal law." And, if the prevention of crime is the ultimate aim, this was "but another way of saying that [a code] must be consistent with some theory of the cause or causes of criminal behavior." He acknowledged that a prior lack of knowledge of the causes of such behavior practically necessitated some lack of consistency or "consciousness of aim or method." But, more recently, research had shed much light on the subject. Indeed, it had confirmed that there is no one cause of crime, but, rather, multiple causes affecting different individuals in differing ways. This was the "thesis of the modern school of criminology," with which Gausewitz identified himself, and the thesis led "logically" to a central focus on individualization. That is, it led to individualization unless one were *not* concerned with an offender's future conduct. But, Gausewitz asserted with a promise of later elaboration: "we are necessarily [so] concerned."[89]

Gausewitz primarily discussed deterrence theory from the public's point of view. He had observed that the traditional retributive and deterrent aims of the law were in line with the neoclassical school of criminology, according to which the law accepted individual responsibility incurred by free will, save for those with a defective will, in infancy, under "justifiable passion," or the legally insane.[90] But, beginning with the 1909 AICLC conference, he asserted,

criminological materials have become increasingly available and sociologists and psychiatrists have persisted in their attacks upon the retributive-deterrent theories of punishment and the underlying theory of freedom of the will until the law has had to give their demands for individualization partial recognition.[91]

Still, despite the importance of the modern understanding of the will, he urged that "deterrence cannot be ignored as a method of crime prevention; it is too

[88] Gausewitz, "Considerations Basic to a New Penal Code," 352–54.
[89] Gausewitz, "Considerations Basic to a New Penal Code," 356–59.
[90] Gausewitz, "Considerations Basic to a New Penal Code," 357.
[91] Gausewitz, "Considerations Basic to a New Penal Code," 358.

deep-seated to be changed."[92] Thus, he emphasized the traditional commitment to deterrence associated with retribution and, accordingly, sought to
distinguish between a purely repressive utilitarian theory of deterrence and
one that bridged deterrence, reformation-based, and retributive aims.

Gausewitz's resulting prescription countered Wigmore's scheme, where
prevention by general deterrence ("repression") was primary, individual
incapacitation and reform were subordinate aims and, as Gausewitz put it,
with "satisfaction of the instinctive popular demand for revengeful punishment as a useful by-product." Instead, in keeping with his focus on individualization, Gausewitz asserted that individual incapacitation ("disablement")
should be primary, reformation secondary, and general deterrence a highly
valuable by-product. To this last end, he observed that incapacitation and
reform would themselves act as deterrents ("the degree of restraint ... and
the regimen necessary ... are unpleasant") and, further, would engender "a
sense of retribution," noting:

The fact that the ordinary individual cannot discriminate between a distasteful regimen imposed for the purpose of reformation and one imposed for the purpose of
deterrent or retributive punishment is just as true when one of the aims is made primary as when the other is.[93]

In this way, general deterrence would be "an unofficially recognized or extra-
legal purpose, to the same extent and in the same way that retribution now
occupies that position." And the Wisconsin statute providing that the state
prison should serve "for the punishment and reformation of all offenders,"
should be amended to read: "for the restraint and reformation." Thus, for
Gausewitz, the penal law should be, first and foremost, preventative in the
specific-deterrence sense: incapacitation was primary. Until reformation had
been achieved incapacitation would be "by segregation, except so far as the
protection of society could be accomplished by immediate incapacitation, as
for example, by castration or by execution."[94]

Gausewitz remained agnostic about the best approach to reformation;
he primarily advocated flexibility in sentencing where treatment was concerned. But he was confident about the benefits reaped from it. First, reformation and release served social ends: offenders were costly to "restrain"

---

[92] Gausewitz, "Considerations Basic to a New Penal Code," 358.

[93] Gausewitz, "Considerations Basic to a New Penal Code," 360–61 (responding to Wigmore's
schema as noted in John H. Wigmore, ed., *The Illinois Crime Survey* [Chicago: Illinois
Association for Criminal Justice, 1929], 743). Gausewitz conceded, however, that deterrence "would have to be recognized as the sole method in occasional cases," where release
(or failure to restrain) "solely because [the offender] is no longer likely to commit a crime
would 'outrage the sense of justice of the community'" (361 [quoting Gillin, *Criminology
and Penology* (1935 ed.), 507]).

[94] Gausewitz, "Considerations Basic to a New Penal Code," 363–64. I have preserved
Gausewitz's precise language on this last point; it is unclear, exactly, what circumstances

and, presumably, useful when fit to return to society. Second, reform was in the interests of the individual offender. Interestingly, Gausewitz's concern for the individual offender went well beyond that of typical positivists, although this point was sometimes lost in his discussion of the "aims and methods" of a new criminal code. Early in the 1936 article, he stated – albeit, surprisingly, merely by way of a footnote – his belief that "the principal function of the criminal law is to protect individuals from arbitrary action by public officials and others who may attempt to punish or treat them as criminals." He noted, in language redolent of Pound, that those who invoked the "protection of society" failed "to realize that there is a social interest in the individual."[95] Here, indeed, Gausewitz sided with Pound regarding the mutuality of interests between society and the individual. The defense of individual political liberty most surely guaranteed social justice. Thus, Gausewitz grounded his view not on utility per se, but on principles of "justice," the desire for justice being "so powerful and so deeply rooted in our culture that it cannot be flaunted [*sic*] or ignored." Hence Gausewitz counseled that there be "certainty in the definition of crimes" and urged that "to the ordinary individual [justice] means equality of treatment as between individuals … and treatment proportional to fault."[96] If he thought this brought "justice" and individualization into conflict, he did not say so. But he observed:

Thus, there is raised up in the deterrent purpose of punishment the requirement that it be *retributively* justifiable. The public would not tolerate punishment of an individual deemed undeserving, regardless of the social value of that punishment for deterrent purposes; and the converse is at least equally true.[97]

One begins to see the importance for Gausewitz of deterrence being secondary to individualized incapacitation and reformation. Initially drawing from Pound, he had moved beyond Pound's concept of "social interests" to

he envisioned as best addressed by immediate incapacitation via castration or execution. I suspect his reference to when society "could be" protected in such ways was meant to invoke (or perhaps, to encourage) laws allowing for castration or execution of those offenders, mentioned earlier in his paragraph, who were not reformable and thus "could never be given complete freedom." At times he hinted at more extreme views that might make us question his preference for treatment, as when he observed that, because the protection of society requires "that prisoners be confined or otherwise restrained until reformed, or for the entire period of their lives," then "*economy, if nothing else, would suggest that some effort be made to reform them*" (363 [emphasis added]). But his later commentary on the value of the individual and of "treatment proportional to fault" (375) suggests that his preference for treatment did not arise merely from concerns for economy. Thus I do not believe he should be read to advocate castration or execution even of offenders who were reasonably reformable, even if such extremes "could be" legislated.

[95] Gausewitz, "Considerations Basic to a New Penal Code," 354 n. 8.
[96] Gausewitz, "Considerations Basic to a New Penal Code," 375.
[97] Gausewitz, "Considerations Basic to a New Penal Code," 375 (emphasis added).

a stronger insistence on accommodating human values and psychology.[98] Moreover, he had effectively linked the defense of political liberty to a more traditional view of blame and punishment.

Gausewitz nonetheless labored to show that deterrence, even while only "incidental," would still operate "at least as effectually" in a system governed by "disabling and reformative methods" as in a system where deterrence was the primary aim. He clearly conceded the importance of deterrence, and the concession had of course important implications for the insanity defense and the theory of "responsibility." "If deterrence and retribution were entirely eliminated as a method of protecting society," the insanity defense could be abolished (perhaps Gausewitz's preference) and "criminals truly treated as sick individuals." But that, he knew, was impossible, given "the popular mind." As *State v. Strasburg* had counseled, "as a practical matter, punitive and deterrent punishment was actually still a part of the law."[99]

By the same token, the doctrine of responsibility would have to be retained, although "an integration of the treatment agencies would permit [that doctrine] to be ignored in the treatment [of] the great majority of cases." This reliance upon bifurcation of process reflected Glueck's influence and, as we shall see, distinguished Gausewitz's approach from that of Wechsler and Michael. As for the appropriate insanity test, ironically perhaps, the "right and wrong" test would suffice: "responsibility" was a social concept ("retribution and deterrence are intended to satisfy the public") and "the jury's determination is simply *ex post facto* legislation that certain types of persons under certain circumstances ought not to be punished, and all that is needed is a formula sufficient to make the jury take an objective, social attitude."[100] Here, Gausewitz put White (among others) to his own use (without explicitly adopting White's deterministic views). His critical insight was that a system where treatment dominated at the sentencing stage could more easily afford an insanity test that accommodated the social need for retribution – the exception to criminality upholding the principle of criminal responsibility. Guilt assessment would assuage much social passion, and the "incidental" message of punishment that accompanied what was often in fact (i.e., from the *official* perspective) nonpunitive treatment would both further assuage that need and supply a measure of general deterrence. This embrace and manipulation of the disjunction between juristic and social views would not have appeased either White, who opposed a policy of assuagement, or a strict utilitarian, who feared that the message of individualized treatment

---

[98] Gausewitz, "Considerations Basic to a New Penal Code," 375 n. 26. Gausewitz noted that a "psychoanalytical explanation" for this move could be found in Alexander and Staub's recent book.

[99] Gausewitz, "Considerations Basic to a New Penal Code," 393–94.

[100] Gausewitz, "Considerations Basic to a New Penal Code," 394.

would undermine the element of general deterrence. But no one writing in the 1930s came closer than Gausewitz to integrating the oft-conflicting aims of positivism, deterrence-based utilitarianism, and retribution. His positivism took account of the needs of deterrence and social demands regarding criminal responsibility less as opposed schools of thought than as coordinated elements in a rational administration of criminal justice.

With regard to the idea of free will, Gausewitz neither banished the concept nor employed it merely as a necessary concession to the "popular mind." Even were deterrence and retribution abolished "as *officially recognized* purposes of punishment," the concept would not lose its persuasiveness for the rule of law and for conventional morality.

Rather than deny a freedom of the will, reformation as a purpose of treatment is predicated upon the theory that one can order his life along socially acceptable lines. Since all our affairs of life are based upon a belief in some freedom of the will, surely the criminal law cannot divorce itself from that theory.[101]

The idea of free will was a universal, whatever its underlying reality, and modern treatment theory must accept the *consciousness* of freedom. Thus, strategies of treatment theory paved over the potential disjunction between the academic theorist and the general public, without eliminating the disjunction.

Less directly, Gausewitz invoked free will when he challenged the view that "the traditional legal analysis of a crime into act and intent is no longer significant or real." He first noted that it was difficult to determine whether Pound and others who "attacked these concepts" thought that act or intent or neither was the "real thing." Pound, Gausewitz supposed, looked to the mental element. But Levitt, Dashiell, Cantor, and perhaps Strahorn seemed to regard the act and, saliently, its effects upon society, as determinative.[102] Gausewitz conceded that intent "is not immediately knowable to anyone other than the actor"[103] – which he deemed to be "the thought of those who would ignore intent" – but, he argued, "intent" was nonetheless "a useful, though artificial, concept." Its absence signified "the type of act which does not indicate a personality sufficiently dangerous to require segregation or rehabilitation." This justified "retention of the intent concept" for purposes of treatment in a nonpunitive system, but beyond that (here the important, if indirect, invocation of free will):

---

[101] Gausewitz, "Considerations Basic to a New Penal Code," 384 (emphasis added) (citing Sheldon Glueck, *One Thousand Juvenile Delinquents* [1934], 247).

[102] Gausewitz, "Considerations Basic to a New Penal Code," 385.

[103] Gausewitz, "Considerations Basic to a New Penal Code," 386 (citing, inter alia, Hutchins, "Law and the Psychologists," and Robert M. Hutchins and Donald Slesinger, "Some Observations on the Law of Evidence – State of Mind to Prove an Act," *Yale Law Journal*, vol. 38 [1929]: 283–98).

it must be retained as a factor in the determination of whether there is to be any treatment, not only because the expression of the moral disapprobation of the community and the necessity of not outraging the public sense of justice make it true that "crime in general always has depended and always will depend upon deep-lying ethico-psychological concepts," but also because at least a prima facie indication of criminal propensity should be found in the act that sets the machinery of the law in motion.[104]

Thus did Gausewitz side with Sayre regarding the relationship between "intent" and social ideas of blameworthiness and simultaneously hold – in good utilitarian fashion – that "even under a naturalistic jurisprudence, it would be a social waste to treat other than those persons actually showing anti-social tendencies." "Psychic facts" were not mere "metaphysical jargon," but often signaled the presence or absence of those tendencies.[105]

Having established the "aims and methods" of a penal code and the implications of those aims for the substantive law, Gausewitz turned to problems of procedure and implementation. Individualization of treatment – both restraint and reformation – would require significant changes in trial and post-trial stages, for the latter especially with regard to his preferred use of indeterminate sentences. Gausewitz early on in his article had conceded that "to avoid swamping the treatment agencies with minor offenses," one would have to reserve the indeterminate sentence for felonies. He observed that Hall, to the contrary, would "utilize the indeterminate sentence only for the lesser offenses because they arouse the least public resentment."[106] This was no small difference: although both Hall and Gausewitz shaped their programs with the public "sense of justice" in mind, Gausewitz saw the indeterminate sentence as a deterrent and was therefore less concerned about public resentment of a "treatment" philosophy. The public, he maintained, would be educated by the entire system; if all elements of administration were reformed, the conclusion would be irresistible that offenders were under restraint until they could safely be returned and that restraint and reformation were unpleasant enough, as well as potentially permanent.

Gausewitz's program was the most sophisticated attempt of the interwar period to present remedy as repression, and repression as both individualized treatment and social deterrent. His *announced* purpose was to promote prevention, but by putting disablement first he appeared to be supporting the reverse, that is, repression as remedy. The indeterminate sentence could be seen as the threat of permanent incarceration; like Waite he even countenanced, where necessary, benign execution. But whereas Waite had charged

---

[104] Gausewitz, "Considerations Basic to a New Penal Code," 386–87 (quoting Francis B. Sayre, "Mens Rea," *Harvard Law Review*, vol. 45 [1932]: 974).

[105] Gausewitz, "Considerations Basic to a New Penal Code," 387.

[106] Gausewitz, "Considerations Basic to a New Penal Code," 365–66 (citing Hall, *Theft, Law and Society*, 298).

that retributive punishment was the villain of the piece – and had sanctioned, instead, both social contempt for the offender's behavior and the offender's own experience of self-contempt – Gausewitz sought a (mainly) non-retributive penal law while recognizing that the deterrence that was its by-product would itself be understood socially in retributive terms. Still, Gausewitz himself conceived of his approach as remedial. He believed that the wholly indeterminate sentence would lead, in the vast majority of offenses, only to fairly early release. And release would most often depend solely upon reform, not upon the practical necessities of general deterrence. In his conclusion he first rehearsed the mixed ends of the criminal law and then put the heart of the matter bluntly: "Considerations of humanity and economy require that the period of restraint be made as short as possible by efforts at rehabilitation as long as there is any reasonable prospect of success."[107]

Much of the second half of Gausewitz's article was given over to a detailed discussion of the administrative and procedural needs of a reformative system. The case for reform was practical as well as humane; the entire scheme explicated his view that the "criminal law should be used positively as an instrument for the prevention of crime as well as negatively to protect individual freedom by restraints upon official action."[108] By "prevention" Gausewitz meant many things, but specific deterrence through temporary disablement and reform loomed very large. In his prescriptions, he never strayed too far from the importance of public opinions of fairness and justice. Even with regard to treatment, he emphasized the lack of public support, in individual cases, for a system thought (sometimes wrongly) to employ fixed penalties. He optimistically concluded that "the public as jurors, as prosecutors, as judges, and as police," – albeit perhaps after the education that he assumed would result from systemic reform – "would be more willing to convict if they thought their conviction would merely subject the individual to treatment justified by requirements of reformation."[109] Hardheaded idealism might be the best way to describe Gausewitz's quasi-utilitarian, but mainly positivist, perspective.

THE UTILITARIAN REACTION: JEROME MICHAEL AND HERBERT WECHSLER

As we have seen, juristic positivists rarely challenged the idea of free will head-on. Progressive rhetoric – encapsulated in the 1909 statement of principles[110] and carried forward in 1920s and 1930s behavioral science – largely

---

[107] Gausewitz, "Considerations Basic to a New Penal Code," 540.
[108] Gausewitz, "Considerations Basic to a New Penal Code," 540.
[109] Gausewitz, "Considerations Basic to a New Penal Code," 494.
[110] See the AICLC's "General Introduction to the Modern Criminal Science Series," in, e.g., Raymond Saleilles, *The Individualization of Punishment*, trans. Rachel Szold Jastrow (Boston: Little, Brown, 1911), v–ix.

formed a backdrop that was reflected in juristic positivists preferring treatment to non-retributive punishment for general deterrence. But the various lines of juristic positivism, which was never a single project, were marked by attempts to compromise science and social convention, sometimes in order to eventually erode the latter, and sometimes not. Hall provided a historical and theoretical basis for a gradual incorporation of the scientific perspective that Pound had so often invoked in purely practical terms. Waite focused on the general deterrence effects of a treatment-based approach. Gausewitz constructed a system that found a place for Moley's skepticism of overly ambitious reform, as well as for the social realities – including conventional morality's attachment to free will – recognized by Sayre. Whereas Hall exemplified the Progressives' tendency to stand apart from conventional morality – to describe, manipulate, and thereby (it was hoped) to transform it – Gausewitz sought to embrace it as one of many features of positivist criminal law. Nonetheless, Gausewitz only hinted at free will's place within a legal – as opposed to social – concept of criminal responsibility. The articulation of a *legal* idea of free will came from the leading general-deterrence-based scholars of the 1930s, Columbia Law School's Jerome Michael and his former student and eventual colleague and coauthor, Herbert Wechsler.

Michael and Wechsler viewed themselves as heirs to a utilitarian tradition in criminal jurisprudence: the aim of the criminal law was prevention of crime in the name of the common good. Assertively consequentialist, the utilitarian perspective shared the Progressive critique of a vengeance-based retributivism. Although utilitarians deemed retributivism counterproductive specifically for its stress on desert over the end of prevention, they could support a treatmentist approach on some level because it was humane and accorded with prevention; to this extent, Progressives for a time presented a united front. But the logic of utilitarianism – prevention for the common good – decidedly privileged general deterrence over specific deterrence: hence the growing divide among consequentialists to which Wigmore had pointed in the 1920s in his distinction between the ends of "cure" and "repression." Wigmore's response to the Progressives' critique of free will in relation to criminal responsibility was arguably more aspirational than reasoned, however, and it perhaps lent credence to the common charge that the utilitarian appeal to punishment in the name of general deterrence masked an underlying vengeance.

Michael rebutted this charge in his 1935 address to the New York Neurological Society and the Section of Neurology and Psychiatry of the New York Academy of Medicine, in which he endeavored to explain the reasons for the divide between lawyers and medical specialists regarding criminal law and its administration.[111] Michael's address is of special interest

---

[111] Jerome Michael, "Psychiatry and the Criminal Law," *ABA Journal*, vol. 21 (1935): 271–76, 285.

for its own species of accommodation of conventional morality; it is also notable because Michael himself seemed to reorient the accommodationist approach he described there almost immediately thereafter. He began his address by using the occasion to state in summary form the bare utilitarian precepts of his 1933 book, *Crime, Law and Social Science,* coauthored with Mortimer Adler,[112] but he proceeded by venturing out more broadly onto difficult terrain by highlighting the multiple values inhering in the common good. Significantly, he posited that, insofar as the prevention of crime was a common good, it also had to account for social understandings. Retributivist urgings had a place, despite the fact that, as he and Adler had earlier stated, the "punitive theory" was downright fallacious.[113] So long as those retributivist urgings, he now elaborated, served the purposes of prevention for the common good, the social practice of retributivism was as useful as the legal theory of retributivism was wrong. Psychiatrists (and, Michael implied, juristic positivists as well) had failed to see this distinction. For positivists, accommodation amounted to a somewhat piecemeal toleration of conventional morality pro tem. For Michael, it meant something in the nature of its principled absorption.

Michael declared that the purpose of the criminal law was "the good of the state," where "state" indicated the body of social members more than the governing power over the same.

Laws are just if they serve the common good; they are unjust if they do not. A just law is not an end in itself but one among many means of achieving the ultimate political end of the state's welfare. From this point of view, the infliction of pain upon criminals is justified to whatever extent it protects society against criminal behavior, and not as an instrument of retribution.[114]

Yet the social defense was not the sole end of the criminal law. In aiming at the common good, the criminal law "defended" multiple values, including "social judgments regarding the final purposes of political and social organization," which were necessary to the law's own coherence.[115]

Michael also asserted that the medical profession misconstrued the nature of the criminal law when it launched its criticisms of retributivism and the associated unscientific idea of free will. On two accounts was the challenge unfounded. First, the underlying rationale of the criminal law was not retributivist. Second, even so, retributivism's dependence upon the idea of free will posed no problem, for the law found no incompatibility between determinism and (non-metaphysical) free will.

---

[112] Jerome Michael and Mortimer Adler, *Crime, Law and Social Science* (New York: Harcourt, Brace, 1933).

[113] Michael and Adler, *Crime, Law, and Social Science,* 341.

[114] Michael, "Psychiatry and the Criminal Law," 272.

[115] Michael, "Psychiatry and the Criminal Law," 273.

Determinism means the absolute rule of cause and effect in the physical order, – that nothing happens which is not caused. Freedom of will is a psychological and not a metaphysical concept, as so many medical men have supposed, and it is not a denial of determinism in the physical order. It means only the rule of deliberation in the psychological order, – that some human acts result immediately from a rational process of deliberation and are not involuntary in the sense that they are instinctive. To act voluntarily or with a free will is thus only to act after deliberation. The law assumes only that normal men, being normally rational, have freedom of will in the sense of the capacity to act deliberately; it does not assume that their behavior is without cause or antecedent conditions.[116]

This abbreviated statement of philosophical compatibilism (well known at least since Hume and occasionally appearing in early-twentieth-century American scholarship on criminal responsibility[117]) was not likely to be reassuring to the "medical men" to whom it was addressed in the context of their concerns about retributivism. It probably seemed to them to provide no basis for the assignment of *deserved* criminal responsibility other than that offenders were presumed to be participants in the regime of cause and effect.

For Michael, then, the human capacity of deliberation preserved criminal responsibility in the face of a scientific reordering of conceptions of human behavior. The insanity test determined whether the defendant had possessed the ability to deliberate or the "capacity to choose between doing and not doing the act." Where the defendant did not possess that capacity, he "cannot be said to have been a full moral agent or to have exhibited a vicious will." Hence the soundness of the right-wrong and irresistible impulse tests, the former being virtually universal throughout the country, the latter being "applied in many" jurisdictions. Michael conceded that the criminal law was open to criticism for not everywhere accepting the irresistible impulse test; here medical men had a point – something to teach lawyers.[118] Irresistible impulses precluded behavior *based on deliberation* – even among those possessed of the requisite reason and knowledge to generally know the difference between right and wrong – and that *nondeliberative* behavior was, ipso facto, outside of the domain of legal responsibility.

Michael was also speaking to fellow legal academics seduced by current fashions in reformation. He himself looked forward to the day when scientific knowledge made reformation a more practical means of achieving the common good, but until then he advocated the careful consolidation of knowledge, using the reform of juveniles as one opportunity for "the creation of a public opinion which will be sympathetic to the high purposes of

---

[116] Michael, "Psychiatry and the Criminal Law," 273.

[117] See, e.g., Edward Lindsey, "Penal Responsibility and Free-Will," *JCLC*, vol. 1 (1910): 695–97 (noted in Chapter 2, p. 58, n. 9); Maurice Parmelee, *Criminology* (New York: Macmillan, 1918), 380 (noted in Chapter 2, p. 81, n. 86).

[118] Michael, "Psychiatry and the Criminal Law," 273.

the psychiatrist and which will make possible the utilization of psychiatric knowledge and techniques throughout the whole range of the criminal law."[119] "Public opinion" was a central concern for Michael, just as it had become for most reformation-based positivists. Michael and Wechsler were later to claim that the distance between the positivists and their own position was not very great: both perspectives viewed the criminal law as a means of prevention in the name of the common good and both shared essentially deterministic premises. All that separated them was a disagreement over the priority of reformation and deterrence. But Michael's discussion of "public opinion" in his 1935 address suggests that – at this stage of his thought – he considered the differences more complicated than that.

Having defended a deliberation-based principle of criminal responsibility even in relation to retributivism, Michael observed that it "might be supposed that the concept of criminal responsibility has no place in a non-retributive system of criminal justice." That is, one might conclude that criminal responsibility in a non-retributive system is simply a matter of the "effect [of behavior] upon the social welfare," and it is therefore "just to inflict pain upon criminals to the extent that to do so will prevent crime."[120] Indeed, these were points that Michael and Adler had made in the 1933 book.[121] Now, however, Michael claimed there was more to be said, for "the average man does not so easily distinguish between inflicting pain upon criminals in order to punish them and inflicting punishment upon criminals in order to prevent crime; and not only is the retributive theory a philosophical position, but it represents popular notions of justice." Popular notions of desert and blameworthiness ran deep and must be taken into account. Here Michael, after quoting both F. H. Bradley and Justice Holmes, concluded: "This is a striking illustration of what I have already said, that a criminal law which serves the common good must necessarily attempt to achieve other values than the prevention of crime."[122]

The criminal law as it then existed was, he claimed, "ambiguous in character."[123] It could be viewed as serving the end of punitive retribution and it could also be viewed as serving the common good. In fact, it was both, and appropriately so. Whereas only two years earlier Michael and Adler had complained of "basic inconsistencies"[124] that frustrated the goal of necessary legislative reform, Michael now – albeit arguably only heuristically – defended the retributive aspect of the law that inhered in the social understanding of non-retributive punishment because the common good

[119] Michael, "Psychiatry and the Criminal Law," 285.
[120] Michael, "Psychiatry and the Criminal Law," 274.
[121] Michael and Adler, *Crime Law and Social Science*, 340–52, 359–61.
[122] Michael, "Psychiatry and the Criminal Law," 274 (citing, generally, Holmes, *The Common Law*, and F. H. Bradley, *Ethical Studies* [1876]).
[123] Michael, "Psychiatry and the Criminal Law," 274.
[124] Michael and Adler, *Crime, Law and Social Science*, 375.

could not be achieved without satisfying deep social attitudes. Michael's great contribution was thus to retrieve for the 1930s what he took Sir James Fitzjames Stephen's point of a half century before to mean: that conventional morality must for the time being have a place within a deterrence-based *utilitarian* perspective.[125] In doing so, Michael had aligned accommodationism with general deterrence rather than with incapacitation and reformation, and had positioned general deterrence as an important intermediate stage that would operate until reformation-based science had proceeded far enough to be effectively employed for the common good. Reformation, he challenged the positivists, would not by itself guide public opinion.

In 1935 Michael thus implicitly introduced a minimalist defense of the social idea of free will, recognizing the social and pragmatic value of accommodating conventional morality. Theory had its place, but also its limits. Of course, ironies resulted. Most significant, Michael's compatibilist explication of the law's idea of free will barely replicated social understandings of free will that underlay the blameworthiness to which Stephen, Bradley, and Holmes had referred. He neither noted that the free will of conventional morality was different from the legal notion he had himself propounded as compatible with retributivism nor investigated the implications for a system of criminal law that made use of (perhaps even encouraged) the prevailing nonlegal understanding of responsibility. On the other hand, his 1935 statement achieved the greatest possible "fit" between a utilitarian theory of criminal law and empirical social reality. It did not reimagine society in terms of that theory, divorcing the true law and its ends from the law in actuality. The partial execution of that task was left to his well-known collaboration with Wechsler, "A Rationale of the Law of Homicide,"[126] which appeared two years later.

The 1937 "Rationale" – Michael and Wechsler's classic two-part article in which they applied utilitarianism both to substantive legal theory (Part I) and to the treatment of offenders (Part II) – implicitly absorbed the shortcomings of Michael's 1935 approach. Here, concessions to conventional morality were few and mainly banished to incidental asides or footnotes, the more easily captured thereby within the overarching end of the common

---

[125] Michael, "Psychiatry and the Criminal Law," 275 (explicating Sir James Fitzjames Stephen, *A History of the Criminal Law of England* [London: Macmillan, 1883]). Compare Stephen J. Morse, "Thoroughly Modern: Sir James Fitzjames Stephen on Criminal Responsibility," *Ohio State Journal of Criminal Law*, vol. 5 (2008): 505–22. Morse, a compatibilist legal scholar who would write prodigiously on the issue of free will in the modern criminal law, himself concluded some seventy years after Michael's address that Stephen "presciently understood and almost always correctly resolved the debates about criminal responsibility that still bedevil us" (Morse, "Thoroughly Modern," 506).

[126] Herbert Wechsler and Jerome Michael, "A Rationale of the Law of Homicide" (pts. I [signed: Wechsler and Michael] & II [signed: Michael and Wechsler]), *Columbia Law Review*, vol. 37 (1937): 701–61, 1261–325.

good. Indeed, "Rationale" carried forward the project that Michael and Adler had begun. As had the earlier work, it looked forward to a rational and unified code, exemplifying the principles of "classical" criminal jurisprudence – that is, the Anglo-American utilitarian tradition of the nineteenth century. Championing those principles, "Rationale" yielded nothing to positivist assumptions either about the law or about the (supposed subconscious) intentions of utilitarians who premised punishment upon general deterrence. One infers that the authors were particularly irritated by the tendency of the more radical positivists to "psychoanalyze" the deterrence school and to conclude that deterrence was no more than a mask for the exercise of subconscious retributive impulses. The division between "repression" and "cure" that had destroyed the rapprochement of 1909 had led directly to that charge; Wechsler and Michael's two-part article was, in some measure, a reaction to a reaction.

"Rationale," Part I, displayed – contrary to Michael's 1935 address – a purifying, non-accommodationist overall thrust. The authors dealt first with "the problems involved in distinguishing criminal from non-criminal homicides," stating that persons evidencing "criminal" behavior should be defined as those whose behavior "it is desirable and possible to deter" and/or whose behavior "usually indicates that the actor is more likely than the generality of men to behave in undesirable ways in the future."[127] Their definition of a "criminal" thus reduced the word to a "strictly legal term": it included both those who were deterrable and those who posed significant danger to society, even if they were not deterrable. Accordingly, it included the "legally irresponsible" – that is, the legally insane. For, the article explained, when bringing individuals under the purview of the law at the guilt assessment stage, there was "no reason why the behavior of non-deterrable persons should not be made criminal to precisely the same extent as the behavior of deterrable persons." Society is equally threatened by both classes; the distinction between them "is significant only for the purposes of treatment."[128]

The authors recognized that in both legal and popular language, "the behavior of the legally irresponsible is usually denominated 'non-criminal.'" They saw some virtue in this: "the words 'criminal behavior' normally carry an implication of moral disapproval that can be put to practical use by reserving the words to designate behavior that is undesirable and possible to deter." But they would have none of it: the identification of "criminality" and "responsibility" was "practically undesirable because it leads to a misunderstanding of the function and effects of the rules governing responsibility,"[129] which is to say, it deflected attention from the more general end of "prevention," an end to be sought with respect to the non-responsible as

---

[127] Wechsler and Michael, "Rationale," Part II, 1261 (discussing Part I).
[128] Wechsler and Michael, "Rationale," Part I, 758–60.
[129] Wechsler and Michael, "Rationale," Part I, 758 n. 190.

well as the responsible, although by different means. That identification also led, they observed, "to preconceptions as to what the purposes of treatment should be," which is to say, it pointed in the direction of retributive punishment for criminal behavior, or to criticism of deterrence as retributively based – in any case, away from the central idea of sheer "prevention." What Michael alone before an audience of psychiatrists had portrayed as useful synergy between legal and social ideas, Wechsler and Michael writing to a legal academic audience characterized as dysfunctional.[130]

The purpose of the penal law, Wechsler and Michael unequivocally asserted, was prevention of behavior that was "inimical to the common good."[131] This meant that the future behavior of society at large (potential offenders) counted as much as – indeed, even more than – the future behavior of any particular offender. They turned first to behavior "desirable and possible to deter" in the law of homicide. At every step, they were attentive to the question of the plausibility, wisdom – even justice – of holding that an actor was responsive to the threat of a legal command. Intention and knowledge of harmful results were required for deterrability; a mere act that did not raise the presumptions of intent and potential for awareness was not sufficient. Here, however, they parted company from Sayre, who, when similarly arguing for the necessity of not divorcing act from intent in determinations of mens rea, had taken an accommodationist position regarding free will. In their system, the socially understood idea of free will was legally irrelevant.[132]

Rather, the law's focus was deterrability and, significantly, the legal definition of insanity came within that focus. Michael and Wechsler used the example of the right-wrong test to argue their position: "Those who do not know the nature and quality of their acts or do not know that their acts are wrong are, in the only intelligible meaning of those words, those who must be unaware of any threat of punishment that the law may make." Those "who, suffering from a delusion, believe that the facts are such that their acts would be lawful, must be unaware of the applicability of the legal threat." In such cases as these, punishment did not figure, for it could not fulfill the basic function of the law to deter. If the layman understood the incapacity of the defendant to shoulder responsibility for his or her actions, punishment would lose its deterrent effect by promoting sympathy for the criminal rather than a learned self-discipline that internalized the check of the law in matters of criminal behavior. As for the idea of a non-punishable act being caused by an "irresistible impulse," this test too must be measured in

[130] I do not exclude the possibility that one can learn from his student. As noted, "Rationale," Part I (unlike Part II), was signed: "Wechsler and Michael."
[131] Wechsler and Michael, "Rationale," Part I, 730 n. 126.
[132] Wechsler had earlier endorsed Glueck's suggestion that "'if ... we would use the expression 'freedom of will' at all, let us employ it ... as describing man's capacity to act with

terms of deterrability: it must refer to "an impulse that an individual would uniformly not resist regardless of the presence or absence of a legal threat." Although such impulses no doubt existed, Wechsler and Michael concluded that identifying individuals subject to them on particular occasions was no easy task. Given the "present state of knowledge," such identification "must obviously encounter tremendous difficulty"; moreover, it was "commonly known that the distinction is obscure," and "to sanction the inquiry at all holds out hope to potential offenders," and would likely "weaken the deterrent effect of the law upon those whom it is possible to deter." Thus, although the authors conceded that "rejection of the … test is open to objection," they departed significantly from Michael's unguarded endorsement of the test in his 1935 address. They added, however, that the "problem" of identifying those who were genuinely subject to irresistible impulses "will be simplified … as the development of psychiatry augments our knowledge of the characteristics of the non-deterrable class and *strengthens the case for eliminating the lay jury as the agency for determining* whether or not a particular individual is a member of that class.[133]

Wechsler and Michael were not proposing a rationale for the law of homicide so much as explicating the rationale they believed (pace Michael's 1935 address) was already embedded in the law. They brought it forward and cleansed it of impurities (i.e., misconceptions) that had resulted from both traditionalist and positivist adulterations. The law of homicide, they contended – indeed, all of the criminal law – was premised on deterrence, not on retribution, or on dangerousness (which was a residual category), or on the capacity or need for reformation. That is, the rules themselves had taken shape in light of the goal of the common welfare; deterrence had long been understood as the best means of achieving prevention. Critics of the utilitarian position had only to look at the history of the law itself. It remained to consider the logic and limits of deterrence *as treatment* in the modern world.

"Rationale," Part II, examined the problem of treatment in light of "two competing normative hypotheses which merit serious attention." These

consciousness of purpose, albeit on the basis of his instinctive nature.'" Herbert Wechsler, review of *Crime and Justice*, by Sheldon Glueck, *Columbia Law Review*, vol. 37 (1937): 690 n. 15 (quoting Glueck, *Mental Disorder and the Criminal Law*, 94). There is no indication that Wechsler thought of this as more than a capacity to respond, perhaps through deliberation, to stimuli. Although he doubtless had in mind a complex reasoning process and a consciousness that made humans different from, say, mice, that difference does not appear to be significant as a matter of actual "freedom." Something very close to Michael's earlier compatibilism was surely intended, but was less artfully put. Wechsler and Michael employed the word "choice" at several points (e.g., "Rationale," Part I, 734, 739, 752, 754), for example they referred to the individual's being "left free to choose his own course" (739). But their concept of choice appears to be a matter of consciousness consistent with a notion of caused deliberation; their language was more revealing at points, for example, "risks most men *feel* they can discover they are making" (749 [emphasis added]).

[133] Wechsler and Michael, "Rationale," Part I, 753–57 (emphasis added).

were the "so-called classical hypothesis which dominated nineteenth-century English thought, that the dominant purpose of treatment should be the deterrence of potential offenders," and the "positivist hypothesis which dominates contemporary penological thought, that incapacitation and reformation should be the dominant ends."[134] The "opposition" between these hypotheses was genuine but not, they stated, so great as commonly thought. Positivists, Michael and Wechsler claimed, had obscured – and magnified – that seeming opposition:

> Taking the false position that punishment is *necessarily* retributive in purpose, they have attributed to all Classical theorists the position that it *should* be retributive. Taking the position that retribution pre-supposes freedom of the will in the Kantian sense [rather than in the Humean deterministic yet compatibilist sense barely sketched by Michael two years earlier], they have assumed that all who defend the institution of punishment believe in such freedom. Thus the impact of the Positivist attack is on the ethics of retribution and the metaphysics and psychology of freedom.[135]

This attack, appropriately directed against writers in the Kantian and Hegelian[136] tradition, did not pertain to other writers, including the originators of classical ideas, for example, Cesare Beccaria, Jeremy Bentham, and Edward Livingston. Indeed, it was "in flat contradiction" of the fact that these latter commentators

> regarded punishment primarily as a means to deterrence, deterrence as a means to prevention, and prevention as a means to the social welfare, which is strictly equivalent to the Positivist conception of social defense. They regarded deterrence as possible because they believed that the behavior of human beings is frequently motivated by the desire to avoid threatened pain, a view which implies determinism in the psychological order quite as fully as the view that humans are educable.[137]

Here the authors had moved seamlessly from a rejection of the "Kantian" view to a deterministic position without spelling out the minimalist interpretation of free will that Michael had stressed two years earlier in his explication of the logic of retributivism. Michael, of course, had not sided with retributivism, but had seemed to allide the social understanding of criminal responsibility and what he claimed was, in fact, a utilitarian-based criminal law. Precious little attention to that social understanding made its way into "Rationale."

Michael and Wechsler apparently held a particular view of deterrence-through-non-retributive-punishment that, as they saw the matter, need not

---

[134] Wechsler and Michael, "Rationale," Part II, 1262.
[135] Wechsler and Michael, "Rationale," Part II, 1263 n. 7.
[136] Hegel's notion, drawing on Kant, that retributive punishment is preferable to deterrence and reform because retribution honors individuals as "rational beings," originates from his 1821 *Philosophy of Right*. See *Hegel's Philosophy of Right*, trans. T. M. Knox (Oxford: Clarendon Press, 1942), esp. § 100.
[137] Wechsler and Michael, "Rationale," Part II, 1263 n. 7.

be very different in method or effect from the positivists' concept of incapacitation and reformation. A practical divide remained, however, rooted in two main – and linked – considerations: how one viewed incapacitation, on which both deterrence-theorists and positivists relied; and when that incapacitation should end. The question of when incapacitation should end was the key point. From the positivists' perspective, sentences should be indeterminate, depending on the time required for reformation. But this might prove either too long or too brief from the point of view of general deterrence. How one viewed incapacitation also had to be considered. From the perspective of deterrence theorists, the message sent by reform-oriented incapacitation might ultimately reduce the general-deterrence impact of incapacitation. Incapacitation for reform might indeed be "unpleasant" – as positivists themselves noted in defending their position – but its main message might nonetheless be too benign, or might, as a later generation came to put it, erode the sense of personal responsibility. The same might be said about the specific-deterrence effect of reform-based incapacitation: much would depend upon how odious a particular offender found the process of "reformation." Yet how could one test for this, other than by means of the doubtful process of assessing recidivism rates, when, in any case, it would be too late? Conversely, mere non-retributive punishment during incarceration might fail as a specific deterrent where reformation would have succeeded; but this effect, too, would come too late and be too hard to draw conclusions from. Such problems were implicit in the authors' analysis,[138] which emphasized gaps in the present state of knowledge regarding reformation and recidivism. Still, Michael and Wechsler imagined a workable marriage between a dominant non-retributive punishment and a subordinate reformation during the period of incapacitation – and they implied that clinical understanding and methodology, perhaps alongside more study of the causes of crime and recidivism, had the potential to improve that marriage over time.

"Rationale" II explored at length the implementation of non-retributive punishment for general deterrence. At every point, Michael and Wechsler demonstrated an impressive command of the literature that bore upon their subject, reclaiming much of it for the logic of their own system after decades of use as justification for the positivist cause. Deterrence incorporated incapacitation and even reformation. The divergences between general deterrence and incapacitation as aims were unavoidable as the latter focused on the "future behavior of actual offenders" and the former on the "future behavior of potential offenders, that is, of the entire population." But the methods to achieve deterrence and incapacitation would coincide: execution and imprisonment. Gradation of punishment would be necessary, by the logic of deterrence theory, and should take account of the socially

---

[138] Wechsler and Michael, "Rationale," Part II, 1322–24.

required element of mitigation to avoid nullification. Incapacitation theory would take dangerousness into account to a greater extent as "incapacitation requires only that dangerous offenders be incapacitated and that they be incapacitated only so long as they are dangerous." Under both regimes, however, "efforts must be made during the period of their incarceration to reform offenders who will some day be given their liberty."[139] Without that as a central objective, both specific and general deterrence dissipated.

Still, although reformation must play a role either in a deterrence-based scheme or in one based on incapacitation, Michael and Wechsler argued that role should be subordinate to considerations of ultimate repercussions for society. Reformation as the chief end "required that efforts be made to reform offenders as soon as possible" and to release them "as soon as they have been rendered capable of living non-criminal lives." Problems were sure to follow from such a system: loss of general deterrent effect, difficulty in distinguishing between dangerousness and corrigibility, overreliance upon administrators, vulnerability to abuse of discretion leading to inequality in treatment and to nullification, and exorbitant costs neither the state nor its citizens were ready to pay.[140] The most idealistic positivist could not avoid these objections. Hence:

The problem is not whether the compromise shall be made but what its terms shall be. There is no answer to this problem for all times and places if, indeed, there is one for any time and place. To a considerable extent the conflict between deterrence and incapacitation, on the one hand, and reformation on the other, as ends of the treatment of criminals, represents a genuine antinomy in the government of men. No one who values humanity can fail to desire that reformation, broadly conceived, be made a more important end of treatment than it now is or be too fearful of the consequences of doing so.[141]

This was a powerful and humanistic argument regarding human needs, human capacities, and the dangers involved in too quickly translating humane ideals into human institutional forms. In their determination to counter the positivists, Michael and Wechsler had coopted much of the reformation position, while promoting general deterrence on behalf of the common good over the individual good. The authors drew lessons from contemporary expressions of positivist thought that conceded that the needs of the state limited the reach of theoretical abstractions, and that endorsed "prolonged"[142] or permanent incapacitation – even "extermination"[143] – for those not likely to reform.

[139] Wechsler and Michael, "Rationale," Part II, 1315–18.
[140] Wechsler and Michael, "Rationale," Part II, 1323–24.
[141] Wechsler and Michael, "Rationale," Part II, 1325.
[142] See, e.g., Winfred Overholser, "The Place of Psychiatry in the Criminal Law," *Boston University Law Review*, vol. 16 (1936): 322–44, 326.
[143] E.g., Waite, *Criminal Law in Action*, 318; Gausewitz, "Considerations," 363–64.

But the positivist drift was not so easily brought under control by compromise or co-optation. Michael and Wechsler's program hardly closed the contemporary debate. In the first place, the claim that positivists misunderstood the classical school's position on free will was overdrawn. The authors did not specify which positivists they had in mind. Perhaps they referred to early positivist writers, for more recent American ones – including White, whom Wechsler peremptorily dismissed in his 1937 review of Glueck – claimed only that the deterrence argument veiled subconscious motivations. Wechsler upbraided Glueck for failing to distinguish between legal rules that "were designed, or are retained" for a retributive purpose, that is, between those that "are adapted to serving those purposes," and those "adapted to serving *only* these ends."[144] This was fair enough but, from the positivists' perspective, rules that could be thought by society at large to have a retributive purpose were problematic quite apart from intentions, surface or subsurface, or compatibilities, whole or partial, with other dominant ends. One could – as had Hall – argue that the retributive impulse would eventually yield to the non-retributive understanding. For Hall, however, the agent of change would be a new conception of behavioral principles rather than a utilitarian theory regarding the reason for punitive penal treatment. Unsurprisingly, the utilitarian notion of achieving the "common good" struck positivists as an unpromising source of *non*-retributive social understandings.

Positivists preferred to confront the issue of human behavior directly. Fairness had to obtain: nonpunitive treatment was appropriate for persons who, after all, could not have helped (as positivists understood the matter) acting as they had. "Punishment," however theorists conceived of it, directed society's attention away from the factors that were responsible for the offender's failure to respond to the law's command and seemed to suggest that it was a personal failing in the offender that justified society in employing repressive treatment as a means of increasing his capacity – and that of prospective offenders – to respond appropriately in the future. Reformation went directly to the defects in the offender for which the offender was not truly responsible and ideally operated over time to induce the socially beneficial response not only from the offender, but from potential offenders as well.

Michael and Wechsler were not inattentive to this "fairness issue," which they addressed in "Rationale" in utilitarian terms:

we do not, of course, imply that we think the threat of punishment is nearly as effective a means to the prevention of criminal or otherwise undesirable behavior as the creation and promotion of those social conditions which make it easier for men to lead good lives, such, for example, as a just distribution of external goods, economic security, health, education and recreation. It should not be forgotten that the same

---

[144] Wechsler, review of *Crime and Justice*, 689–90.

hypothesis which justified the conclusion that undesirable behavior may be deterred by the threat of punishment also justifies the conclusion that desirable behavior may be encouraged by the promise of reward.[145]

"Rationale," moreover, must be read in light of Wechsler's 1937 article, "A Caveat on Crime Control," where he voiced skepticism of the hard-line crime-control approaches recommended by Tom Dewey, Herbert Lehman, and J. Edgar Hoover and argued more generally for the morality of social reform:

Man becomes good socially by being good individually and the general means to individual goodness are education, freedom from economic and physical handicaps, and the opportunity to function and be of service. This much follows from an understanding of men as a rational animal and it is unnecessary to point for collaboration to the findings of empirical research that most criminals are the under-privileged off-spring of under-privileged parents....

That the problems of social reform present dilemmas of their own, I do not pretend to deny. I argue only that one can say for social reform as a means to the end of improved crime control what can also be said for better personnel but cannot be said for drastic tightening of the processes of the criminal law – that even if the end should not be achieved, the means is desirable for its own sake.[146]

Michael and Wechsler never doubted that their utilitarian "rationale" for penal law fit with a liberal approach to economic and social policy generally. Nor did this liberalism clash, as they saw it, with an essentially deterministic understanding of human behavior. The possible tension between a social theory of the origins of criminality and a punishment-based response was, in their view, relieved by the concept of non-retributive punishment. Positivists were not so readily persuaded: the problem for general deterrence advocates remained how to educate society regarding the need for social reform even while employing a means of preventing undesirable behavior that *seemed* (to society at large) to rest on individual moral fault. Although Wechsler and Michael did not purport to resolve this issue, they nonetheless deemed their own solution the best that one could construct in an imperfect world.[147] It avoided unproven theory and the dangers of the "clinic" – the therapeutic state – even as it made room for reformation and parole after giving pride of place to deterrence. It struck a balance among evils, opting for the principle of treating people in terms they could

[145] Wechsler and Michael, "Rationale," Part II, 1264 n. 10 (also citing Alfred C. Ewing, *The Morality of Punishment* [1929], chap. 5). See also Wechsler, review of *Crime and Justice*, 691–92: "We may subscribe to a view which [Glueck] would share, that the justice of extensive reliance upon punishment and fear is dependent *at least in part* on the 'extent to which the social organization in which a criminal has lived and acted is one that has given him a fair chance of not being a criminal'" (quoting T. H. Green, *Lectures on the Principles of Political Obligation* [1927 ed.], 190).
[146] Herbert Wechsler, "A Caveat on Crime Control," *JCLC*, vol. 27 (1937): 629–37, 636–37.
[147] Wechsler, "Caveat," 634:

understand and, to that extent, in the terms of "fairness" dictated by conventional morality, if not those of what they themselves identified as the underlying theory of the rule of law.

Their theory departed from conventional understandings of the free will ethic. Although that departure was undisguised – non-retributive punishment being explained in utilitarian terms that were not intended to rely on a concept of true free will – their approach was bound to be understood *socially* in light of just such a concept. Like Hall, Gausewitz, and others, Wechsler and Michael constructed a system of penal justice that presumed a disjunction between purely juristic and broadly social understandings of the system's underlying principles. In the case of Wechsler and Michael's "Rationale," however, the disjunction was complete, whereas for at least some positivists the system was only *temporarily* internally disjunctive (i.e., premised upon bifurcation of guilt assessment and sentencing), and the relationship between theorist and public again only temporarily so. Pound, Hall, and Gausewitz argued that a positivist understanding of behavior should be clearly articulated and should govern treatment so far as public attitudes allowed; conventional principles would elsewhere apply, in what they thought would be an ever-diminishing sphere of criminal behavior. The "Rationale" provided no such clear lesson. Placing deterrence not only ahead of reformation of offenders, but also ahead of "education" of society as a whole, Wechsler and Michael sought to found modern American criminal jurisprudence on an academic theory that – as Michael had (at least implicitly) admitted but the "Rationale" did not – courted ongoing social misunderstanding.

"A Rationale of the Law of Homicide" was thus a thoroughgoing utilitarian account. It set the baseline for liability at capacity to respond to the threat of the law. It presented a utilitarian argument – not an independent limiting moral precept or a purely constitutional limitation – for the requirement of a due-process-based conviction of a criminal offense,[148] it

> Policemen argue for stern penalties and shout down parole. Humanitarians and social workers plead for light or indeterminate sentences and efforts to reform. Psychiatrists seriously maintain that they know how to separate the harmless from the dangerous and the corrigible from the incorrigible and to reform the corrigible. At the same time that they deny that morality can be distinguished from the mores, they denounce the moral preoccupations of the law as unjust, preach the theological virtue of charity in scientific disguise and urge that the criminal courts be turned into psychiatric clinics.
>
> In spite of much profession of cooperation and mutual esteem, one group does not really understand any of the others and this for the excellent reason that they all overstate their knowledge and take only a partial view of the problem. The unwelcome truth may be that there is no genuine solution to the ultimate dilemmas of treatment, because there is no knowledge sufficient to guide a rational choice.

[148] See, especially, Wechsler, "Caveat," 752–57. For H. L. A. Hart's criticism of Wechsler and Michael's sheer utilitarian approach, see my note in Chapter 7, n. 22.

counseled punishment-as-deterrence, and it endorsed reform of the convict warmly – but *only insofar* as the practice and rhetoric of reform did not interfere with either specific or general deterrence. The "Rationale" also recognized that social justice to a certain degree conditioned sentencing guidelines and their application, as well as the rules for liability. But its authors attempted to capture all of the contrasting perspectives on the responsibility question via a complex assessment of utility. *Omnia vincit utilitas* might well have been their motto: in principle, there was nothing that could not be factored into common-good theory, provided it *was* factorable. On their own terms legal rules could accommodate society's deeming most offenders responsible and justly deserving of punishment for freely chosen acts. The utilitarian legislator's perspective would continue apart, discerning the *true* meaning of the law. But could the legislator speak openly to the public about the law's true meaning and about the distance between that meaning and social understandings of criminal responsibility? Was the answer to *that* question also guided by utility? Wechsler and Michael did not address this problem. In this regard, the "Rationale" reflected, but did not analyze, disjunction.

The utilitarian legislator could take account of the positivists as well. Positivist teachings – or the ideas that underlay them – influenced public attitudes, which, as always, combined the contradictory impulses of a free-will-based retributivism and a relatively unself-conscious (and age-old) sympathy – or excusing syndrome – now increasingly understood in terms of ad hoc responses to the "causes" of criminal behavior. Michael and Adler – and one must suppose Wechsler as well – understood the juristic inclination to adopt, albeit partially and unmethodically, the implications of the positivist perspective. That, after all, was the concern that gave "Rationale" II its underlying rationale. Could Wechsler and Michael talk judges (and academic jurists) out of making room in particularly pressing circumstances for positivist understandings simply on the grounds that those judicial moves undermined a purely utilitarian approach? Could they persuade judges (and other jurists) to address social attitudes – retributive or positivist – solely from *within* the perspective of the utilitarian calculus? Or was the code-drafter left to devise a perfect code in the face of judicial, academic juristic, and legislative retributivist and positivist "*mis*understandings"?

CONCLUSION

In the end, perhaps unsurprisingly, late-1930s utilitarian thought did not so much supplant positivist-leaning jurisprudence as it produced a dualistic utilitarian/positivist mentality among most legal academics of the succeeding decades. And that dualism was further complicated by a recrudescence, in some quarters, of a species of free will theory. Utilitarianism was here to stay – sometimes dominant, but rarely unadulterated, and often accepted only so long as it accommodated both the scientific morality of positivist reform and the traditional morality of human autonomy.

In its own day, however, the "Rationale" was a breath of fresh air. Wechsler and Michael had presented an internally consistent system and had confronted the fact that the current state of knowledge did not allow for truly definitive answers to the deepest philosophical questions. What irritated the two authors most was the presumption that positivist-inspired reform necessarily should direct criminal justice.[149] The greatest weakness of the positivist position was not its scientism, but its failure to elucidate scientifically what it was that the law really *did*. Wechsler and Michael were bold enough to declare that a scientific analysis yielded a utilitarian rationale. In the following years, however, when legal scholars would have to

[149] This mind-set had become fairly general by the time Wechsler and Michael published their "Rationale." It sometimes was announced casually by legal academics as though all roads led – ultimately – in the direction of a reformationist approach. See, e.g., Livingston Hall, "The Substantive Law of Crimes – 1887–1936," *Harvard Law Review*, vol. 50 (1937): 616–53. Hall cited "indications of an impending readjustment in the underlying theory of penal treatment," referring to a future move away from a focus on "specific criminal acts and the criminal intent demonstrated by the crime," toward "a number of factors which bear on the problem of protecting society from anti-social aggression," and also toward the view "that the imposition of fines or imprisonment by way of revenge upon a 'vicious' will has no place in penology" (652–53). On this all consequentialists could agree. Hall then confirmed his place in the moderate positivist camp, signaling his acceptance of a degree of gradualism that reflected an understanding of the disjunction between elite and popular views and openly embracing bifurcation of the criminal process:

> It is possible that some state will boldly redraft its entire penal code on new lines, and make much of the present law obsolete. It is more likely that the near future, at least, will see the new principles put in *after* conviction; perhaps a disposition tribunal of experts to determine the length of penal treatment, under an even more indeterminate sentence than we are now accustomed to, will be established to take over the sentencing function only. If this is done, the existing penal codes will change only by degrees. [Here citing Sheldon Glueck, "Principles of a Rational Penal Code," *Harvard Law Review*, vol. 41 (1928): 453–82.]
>
> But modification of the law cannot do much more than to keep up with the social and economic movements of civilization in its selection of conduct to be regulated or prohibited, and justly to discriminate between the blameworthy and the innocent on the basis of act and intent, until reforms in personnel, in prison management, and in correctional treatment make it possible to apply the knowledge of other criteria of criminality which is accumulating under the leadership of scientific-minded investigators. (653)

For a contrastingly somber assessment of the vicissitudes of the movement for reform in criminal justice administration – and mainly in penology – see Sam B. Warner and Henry B. Cabot, "Changes in the Administration of Criminal Justice During the Past Fifty Years," *Harvard Law Review*, vol. 50 (1937): 583–615, esp. 598–603. The authors treated "reform" in terms of the treatment model of the juvenile court and noted how much remained to be achieved. They wrote against the background of increasing crime rates and increasing rates of recidivism. They did not – on the eve of Wechsler and Michael's seminal article – give attention to reform in the sense of a rationalization of criminal justice along lines of the deterrence model. The world of criminal justice, as they portrayed it, was divided between traditionalism and positivism.

negotiate rationale and reform in light of a stronger insistence on the moral context of the idea of criminal responsibility, the positivist frame would prove itself more elastic than either the positivist or utilitarian legal thinkers of the 1930s foresaw.

And a half century later, determinist legal academics would marry a *desert*-based retributivism and a revived Humean compatibilism, largely under the influence of the academic philosophy of the day. In doing so, they would entirely reverse the trends in criminal jurisprudence of the first two-thirds or more of the twentieth century. This juristic reversal, long in maturation, had its roots in developments of thought within and outside the legal academy of the 1940s and 1950s. These developments were, themselves, as I view the matter, in large part organic to what had gone before – in particular, to the accommodation of conventional morality that had from the very outset constrained the fullest flowering of the positivist side of the Progressive enterprise.

5

Entr'acte

Intimations of Freedom: 1937–1953

INTRODUCTION

Schools of thought, like the theoretical formulae they hold forth, can be as much conceits as encampments. They crystallize in abutting up against each other, which is to say that they may be the successors to, rather than antecedents of, disagreements within a common frame. For that reason, as the conversations of the 1930s illustrated, the "systems" of retributivism, positivism/reformationism, and utilitarianism were, for many legal scholars, not systems, in the sense of entirely coherent separable entities; they sustained mutual or at least crossing interests and ends. Both positivist and utilitarian legal theorists accepted the law's special obligation to defend political liberty, while attempting to accommodate what they viewed as progressive reform. Both admitted the recalcitrance of retributivist notions. Both left the free will question open for practical reasons and, in truth, theoretical precision with respect to that issue was not their ultimate aim: the persuasive authority of the law in society and for the individual was. Given such general premises to much of the discussion of the 1930s, as that decade neared its end, the schools of thought were nearing a stalemate. Their proponents had had their say.

By the 1940s, however, both schools of thought were confronted with a nascent resurgence of a kind of pragmatism regarding the basis for attributing criminal responsibility. The mid-1940s till the mid-1950s I take as a distinctive period in this regard, as it interjected into criminal law theory realist notions of free will that were, no doubt, in part an instance of the rethinking of American democratic practices in light of events abroad. Among criminal jurisprudence scholars, this pragmatism consisted in a recognition that responsibility – and, indeed, "free will" itself – was a moral-legal idea, rather than a supposed reality that ran counter to informed understandings of human behavior. This "as if" orientation to free will – that the law by its nature does, and should, proceed as if individuals freely will their actions – was not new. And it had received grudging recognition from some positivists and been accorded a place in their accommodationist enterprise. But it now increasingly became an actively embraced legal principle. The principle, once admitted, took varying forms and received varying degrees of affirmative acclamation. The more determinedly consequentialist granted its necessity mainly as a guarantor for political liberty. For others, the principle was distinctly broader and sometimes followed upon investigative questioning about their own assumptions regarding the sources and ends of human behavior. For them the idea of free will gained force, rather than losing credibility, by its very derivation from social practice – an inversion of the original Progressive perspective – and so acquired increasing importance. This stronger "as if" position crested in the 1960s and beyond, but there are intimations of that ascent in the voices of the 1940s and 1950s.

I outline the period 1937–1953 with a few particularly distinctive writings, including the ever-evolving scholarship of Jerome Hall, who remained at the forefront of the changing times, both as bellwether and foil. Hall took a sharp turn away from some of the positivist premises of his earliest work and became perhaps the most strident voice of this period to insist on the critical relevance of free will for the law; he came to reject sociological positivism as inconsistent with criminal law, which, as he now saw it, existed apart as a historical social institution that inherently concerned itself with morality. At this particular time, Hall still represented a relatively extreme view. But others, including fellow legal scholar Wilber Katz, increasingly were coming to the conclusion that, whether free will is merely a subjective experience or an as-yet-explained existential mystery, a strict determinist approach removes from law its central social function of encouraging and reinforcing individual personal responsibility, whether that responsibility is viewed in pragmatic, existential, or even spiritual terms.

I have chosen 1953 as the chapter's endpoint based on the release, in the following year, of *Durham v. United States,* the landmark case on the insanity defense that epitomized postwar attempts to acknowledge the necessary contributions of both science and conventional morality to the criminal law. The *Durham* test, to which I turn my attention in Chapter 6, was itself short-lived. But the test – along with mid-to-late 1950s reactions to it, including by the drafters of the American Law Institute's first Model Penal Code – marked the culmination of the middle years, which I present primarily as bridging the developments of the 1930s and those of the 1960s. I employ this comparatively short chapter as an entr'acte that provides (an admittedly internalist legal) context for the *Durham* decision and illustrates how the legal-academic thought of the middle years regarding the free will issue and related matters emerged as a mosaic of new departures from, and modifications of, well-worn views. There were to be sure points of convergence, but there were also divergences and even, from the perspective of what followed, culs-de-sac. And yet much of what the period produced was organic to that which preceded it, the new intimations of freedom having roots in the thought of those who largely had pushed the free will issue into the background.

Overall, the strains of positivism evident in high Progressivism and increasingly adulterated in the juristic thought of the 1930s morphed into something new in the postwar years: the conventional morality that had, perforce, been the object of a reluctant accommodation, now yielded, as some came to believe, an irreducible kernel of deep moral truth. This truth had the potential for a recrudescence of retributivism. But the truth might also be understood in mainly consequentialist terms, as the legal translation of society's moral condemnation rendered largely in the language of a moralized form of the rehabilitative ideal – Progressivism's ultimate bequest to midcentury criminal jurisprudence.

TRADITIONALISM REDUX: JEROME HALL AND THURMAN ARNOLD

Jerome Hall

As we have seen, in the early 1930s Jerome Hall embraced the turn toward social science in criminal jurisprudence – that is, the sociological jurisprudence represented by Pound.[1] But, by the close of the 1930s, his gradualism-turned-intransigence revealed that "traditionalism" was still one theoretical challenge from within the academy. In the late 1940s, his denunciation of sociological positivism or the "likening of human society to a biological organism" – and his suggestion that such thinking "recommends itself to the efficiency engineer, the mechanist, the dictator"[2] – reveals that Pound was now, by implication, a negative model. And, by 1952, Hall had let go of his previous embrace of the juvenile court: his revised and expanded *Theft, Law and Society* dropped the section on that court and its ideal, relative to all criminal cases.[3] Hall's evolution was effectively at the forefront of the greater shift in legal theory – toward acceptance of more full-blooded, or at least more fully theorized, ideas of free will and retributivism – that would occur later in the century. For the time being, however, his rebarbative tone may well have prevented his work from becoming a point of coalescence among his contemporaries.

[1] Jerome Hall's 1936 article, "Criminology and a Modern Criminal Code," *JCLC*, vol. 27 (1936): 1–16, 14–16, continued the approach taken in *Theft, Law and Society* (Boston: Little, Brown, 1935). Hall stressed the importance of taking social values into account in a "humanitarian" form of penology, one that was based on a "sociology of criminal law" and that would maximize individualization where possible.
[2] Jerome Hall, *Living Law of Democratic Society* (Indianapolis, IN: Bobbs-Merrill, 1949), 64.
[3] Jerome Hall, *Theft, Law and Society*, 2nd ed. (Indianapolis, IN: Bobbs-Merrill, 1952).

In 1937, Hall was responding to developments in the Soviet Union and Nazi Germany: his important article, "*Nulla Poena Sine Lege*," challenged authoritarian and – not incidentally – positivist moves that questioned or dismissed the threshold requirement of conviction of a preestablished criminal offense.[4] Due process – as guarantor of political liberty – dominated Hall's early suspicion of radical positivism; the words "free will" had yet to appear. His critique of the political liberty implications of positivism was soon followed by his insistence on recognition of the principle of retributivism. In his 1940 article on criminal attempts, Hall linked the requirement of an objective harm to "one basic premise of the common law of crimes ... that it is right that punishment be proportioned to the extent of harm done."[5] In itself, Hall argued, this hardly conflicted with the main ends of consequentialism: "Punishment should be inflicted because it is right to do so. But punishment may also have useful effects. It may effect reformation" and "it may also deter."[6] Nonetheless, he now insisted, the retributive element was primary:

The utilitarian argument, as sometimes advanced, seems little short of savagery – "punish the innocent so that the guilty may prosper." The common law approaches the problem from the other end. Is punishment just? If not, reject it, come what may.... So long as the proponents of utility agree that punishment should not be inflicted upon the innocent, they also espouse retributive justice. So far as it is agreed that rehabilitation and deterrence should be sought, utility is admitted.[7]

In 1941, Hall directly criticized "sociological positivism" in "Prolegomena to a Science of Criminal Law," boldly asserting: "We know of course that the vast pretensions of originality have been largely exposed."[8] He stressed the failure of sociological positivism to pay attention to "positive criminal

---

[4] Jerome Hall, "*Nulla Poena Sine Lege*," *Yale Law Journal*, vol. 47 (1937): 165–93.

[5] Jerome Hall, "Criminal Attempt – A Study of Foundations of Criminal Liability," *Yale Law Journal*, vol. 49 (1940): 789–840, 829. Hall claimed that the requirement that "there must be an act 'moving directly towards the commission of the offense'" (822) was more than simply an evidentiary matter, more than a rejection of assignment of criminal liability merely for thoughts. Nor did just any act suffice, "but an act that was harmful, that caused resentment, that ought to be put down, prevented," hence one that was a "harm" (819–20).

[6] Hall, "Criminal Attempt," 831.

[7] Hall, "Criminal Attempt," 830. For Hall, the defense of retributivism rested on what he took to be self-evident truths:

all human living is experience of values, of goodness, truth and beauty. This ultimate end of maximum value transcends all others. As a result, even when it is impossible to establish any deterrent or reformative effect of punishment, one may still insist upon appropriate treatment, that correctly reflecting the value involved. Such treatment may be defended not only intrinsically but also from a utilitarian viewpoint – as providing benefits resulting from instruction in the hierarchy of values. (831)

[8] Jerome Hall, "Prolegomena to a Science of Criminal Law," *University of Pennsylvania Law Review*, vol. 89 (1941): 549–80, 572.

law," and thus its failure to understand the criminal law as "social facts integrated in the moral attitudes," possessing "origins, histories, and observable effects on human conduct." For his part, Hall endeavored to work out a "sociology of criminal laws" that avoided the errors of both legal formalism and sociological positivism, the "distinctive phenomena" of which would be *"those penal laws which are part of (integrated in) the mores."*[9]

Developing this theme, two years later Hall insisted that crime "means an act which is both forbidden by law and revolting to the moral sentiments of society."[10] These notions were manifested in the administration of the law and confirmed the continuing importance of moral culpability. Drawing on his own earlier work, *Theft, Law and Society,* Hall noted that, in the actual administration of the criminal law, "stipulations for mitigation" often prevailed, fostering "infinite degrees of liability." This "process of administration," he asserted, Holmes had ignored; yet such individualization, by which "individual differences, inhering in the particular temperament, understanding and social situation of each defendant are to be considered," countered Holmes's "objective" view and pointed to the importance of moral culpability.[11] Thus, the individualization that had appeared in Hall's earlier text as a fairly standard version of the Progressive ideal now reappeared in an inquiry into criminal responsibility expressed in traditional moral-culpability terms that left positivism far behind.

Such an inquiry directly encounters some of the most ancient ideas of western culture, and especially that view of human nature which regards man as a being endowed with reason and able, within limits, to choose one of various courses of conduct. Intelligence, will, *together with the corollary of freedom of action*, are the traditional connotations which have persisted, more or less challenged, throughout the entire history of civilized thought.[12]

By 1943, Hall had subordinated the utilitarian intent that Wechsler had identified as the *true* meaning of the common law. He had taken his stand on traditional values and the traditional interpretation of the common law.

[9] Hall, "Prolegomena," 575–80 (emphasis in original). Hall was committed to a thick understanding of harm in the criminal law, and of its elements, particularly culpability. But "Prolegomena" did not create a link between legality and autonomy – or criticize "sociological positivism" for its deterministic assumptions. Hall launched a searing critique of "deterministic" "sociological positivism" several years later in Jerome Hall, "Criminology," in *Twentieth Century Sociology*, ed. Georges Gurvitch and Wilbert Moore (New York: Philosophical Library, 1945), 342–65.
[10] Jerome Hall, "Interrelations of Criminal Law and Torts: I," *Columbia Law Review*, vol. 43 (1943): 753–79, 770.
[11] Hall, "Interrelations," 772–73 (discussing Holmes, *The Common Law*).
[12] Hall, "Interrelations," 775 (emphasis added). Hall now espoused a merely partial form of bifurcation where positivist ideas influenced sentencing but did not establish a full contradiction between post-conviction treatment and guilt-assessment. "The major alteration by modern social science in this regard is quantitative, i.e., the degree of individual freedom is now widely regarded as much more limited than the tradition had it, and the effect has been

Hall turned to the insanity defense in his 1945 article "Mental Disease and Criminal Responsibility."[13] In Hall's view, the cognitive or *M'Naghten* (or "right-wrong") test – precluding liability if the accused, due to mental defect or disease of the mind, did not know the nature and quality of the act he was doing, or, if he did know it, did not know he was doing wrong – properly understood and applied, was sufficient. The separate "irresistible impulse" test was unnecessary because reason and will were conjoined in such a way that one who truly was unable to control his or her behavior could not be said at that moment to know the difference between right and wrong – and thus such an actor was already eligible for excuse under *M'Naghten*. Further, use of the "irresistible impulse" test (for which many in the psychiatric community advocated) was an invitation to conclude (wrongly) that what had not been resisted could not have been; because it could apply to otherwise sane (rational) actors, it undermined the common sense conclusion that rationality itself signified the power to choose one's course of action.[14]

Here Hall adverted to the psychiatrists' theory of the "integration of the self," noting that even they did not understand irresistible impulses as "non-voluntary," in the sense of "movement caused solely by physical force," but saw them as voluntary, that is, as "a movement of the (whole) self in which intelligence has participated." Thus, even they must conclude that a so-called irresistible impulse results from impairment of the intelligence. So how could psychiatrists insist on both the notion of "integration of the self" and a separate irresistible impulse test?[15] Hall's answer lay in the inconsistencies he attributed to the psychiatric critics of the law who, he claimed, relied not on "any established body of empirical knowledge," but on "a philosophy whose chief tenet is determinism."[16] Hall noted the critics' inconsistencies: they claimed that the concept of responsibility was meaningless and yet attempted to define it; they claimed that "psychiatry cannot share this responsibility" but concluded that "the psychiatrist is within his moral and scientific right to disregard the psychiatric excursions into the law." With evident frustration, Hall observed:

Thus "responsibility," reduced to a futile, metaphysical archaism when employed in the criminal law, in a sense as old as western civilization, is resurrected and embraced when the critics forget their special pleading! Rather obviously it has never occurred to them to "determine" what determines their Determinism, or to consider whether

to bring numerous sociological factors into any estimate of an offender's conduct and thus to modify and adapt his punishment accordingly" (776).

[13] Jerome Hall, "Mental Disease and Criminal Responsibility," *Columbia Law Review*, vol. 45 (1945): 677–718.

[14] Hall, "Mental Disease," 704–05.

[15] Hall, "Mental Disease," 707–09. For criticism of Hall's views in this regard, see Abraham S. Goldstein, *The Insanity Defense* (New Haven, CT: Yale University Press, 1967), 75.

[16] Hall, "Mental Disease" (1945), 710–11.

any significance whatever could be attached to their criticism of the criminal law or, for that matter, to any other problem-solving, if that dogma were consistently maintained. ...

Accordingly, if the psychiatric-critics of the criminal law assert their chief objective has been to demonstrate the invalidity of the fundamental principles of that law, and especially those concerning responsibility, this may be granted. But it is obvious that these principles represent basal value-judgments, and that, consistently with their own philosophy, these psychiatrists can do no more than assert that they prefer their own "attitudes" – they cannot, on their premises, even attempt to invalidate the ethical principles that support penal responsibility.[17]

The law's founding "basal value-judgments" here represented not a purely metaphysical "as if" but a historical reality that was denied at the cost of individual liberty, legal freedom, and the law's moral force. Hall took a sardonic delight in the contortions of logic, as he saw them, of the psychiatrist Gregory Zilboorg, whose critique of the legal concept of responsibility lay side by side with the claim: "'We [physicians] are singularly radical and free ... I must admit that we are the freest group in the world.'"[18] The internal contradictions of the psychiatrists' declarations offered the most compelling case in defense of the moral responsibility they strove so mightily to dislodge from centuries of Western thought.[19] Hall did not oppose reform as such, but rather reform that exempted the criminal act from the laws of moral gravity. To be sure, he conceded that psychiatric treatment must – and, frequently did – go hand in hand with punishment. But he valorized the "wisdom" of Western ideas regarding criminal responsibility and lauded "the complexity of the criminal law and its administration, where norms

---

[17] Hall, "Mental Disease," 712 and n. 176.

[18] Hall, "Mental Disease," n. 175 (quoting Gregory Zilboorg, *Mind, Medicine, and Man* [1943], 279).

[19] Hall also rebuffed William White's claim that the criminal law represented "'vengeance [that] still functions but under a disguise, namely the disguise of deterrence'" (Hall, "Mental Disease," 714–15 n. 187 [quoting William A. White, "Need for Cooperation between Lawyers and Psychiatrists in Dealing with Crime," *ABA Journal*, vol. 13 (1927): 551–55, 502]). He similarly excoriated the psychiatrists Zilboorg and Karl Menninger for their view of crime as a disease, the penologist Wilfred Overholser for adopting (allegedly) a "Lombrosian" social defense theory on the basis of a deterministic understanding of human behavior, and psychoanalyst A. A. Brill for recommending "dangerousness" as a substitute for guilt as the determinant of the "kind, and duration of the treatment." Alexander and Staub's instrumentalist argument that punishment was required for "'the public sense of justice'" – an argument that Hall had previously embraced – received kinder treatment, but nonetheless was found wanting (715). Hall further suggested that the positivists' push to divorce criminal acts from moral condemnation hindered adoption of the very reforms they favored:

in the philosophy of just punishment, the influence of strong temptation, neurotic constitution, and unfortunate environment are potent reasons for considerable mitigation of punishment. The probability is, therefore, that many desirable reforms, now delayed because they are coupled with fallacious theories that challenge the very foundations of criminal responsibility, could be achieved in large measure if they conformed to basic legal principles. (717)

of justice" still prevail, although they may "coalesce with the objective of deterrence and an unremitting search for rehabilitation."[20]

Hall's voice, sounding in the mid-1940s, was a cry from the wilderness. His own polemics heightened his legal isolationism, an ironic underside to his desire to broaden the American legal theorist's political vision to include a philosophy whose chief was the free individual in tests for insanity and in remedial treatment. The abrasive critiques perhaps alienated him from his contemporaries, who might otherwise have ceded to him a grudging respect for his quixotic forays against the windmills of destiny. Yet the distance thrown between him and the legal academy more generally stemmed from another rift, that between consequentialist legal theory and an illusive conventional morality that was made the more abstract the more looked upon as uniting in itself one heart and will, however fatefully determined.

Had Hall in fact said that free will was a reality? Or was it only a necessary and appropriate presumption? Hall certainly believed criminal law mirrored understandings that were organic to human life and consciousness. Yet he had not openly counseled founding criminal responsibility upon mere subjectivity. Instead, he treated subjectivity as corresponding to something like a scientific fact. If, in his 1945 article, Hall meant no more than that the "tradition" of *belief* in free will provided a basis for retributive justice, he nevertheless started from the strong position that free will was an inevitable aspect of human life and, especially, of human thought: addressing the first clause of the *M'Naghten* rule, he mused that it "reflects the traditional, common-sense doctrine that man is a moral being, that he is 'sufficiently' autonomous to render moral judgments by him and about his conduct defensible and useful." Moral responsibility was not "a 'hoary superstition' nor an adventitious phrase, spontaneously coined, but an abiding insight into what is paramount in human nature."[21] Thus had Hall come closer than almost any other prominent academic jurist of the 1940s to alliding "as if" and "as is" and – not incidentally – to avoiding disjunction.

Hall's *General Principles of the Criminal Law* (1947) brought together the explorations into the fundamental problems of the criminal law that he had undertaken in the decade following publication of *Theft, Law and Society*. In the final chapter, "Criminal Law and Criminology," he was intent on showing that criminologists, in their zeal for objectivity, had dismissed as irrelevant the moral life of the person. They quantified the quantifiable: behavioral symptoms. The ethical lay outside of, or was too deep for, their "simplistic mechanics," which failed to deal with the "inner realm of personal experience." Hall conceded that, in light of current knowledge, a scientific critique of moral values was justifiable. But the very domain of the criminal law was how persons reckoned the "right" and the "good." And,

---

[20] Hall, "Mental Disease," 717.
[21] Hall, "Mental Disease," 692.

however persuasive positivist assertions about criminal behavior might be, human nature remained *qualitatively* unique. The person was rational (could think for himself), and his actions were his own insofar as "human conduct embodies degrees of autonomy and self-control." Critically, even if personal autonomy and self-control were "hypotheses,"[22] as *necessary* hypotheses they presumed free will and thus raised the question (which Progressivism had never entirely erased) of whether the criminal law was to counsel a belief or a suspension of disbelief. In either case, a reorientation of focus was called for not only with regard to administrative reform and education of the popular mind, but also with regard to the fundamental elements of a moral-legal rule, where the law (and not just the criminal) was at stake.

Hall's chosen role was that of an ambassador between conventional morality and scientific objectivity. His perspective, even if distinctly his own without a groundswell of support behind it in the academy, was important in closing the opposition between conventional morality and the rule of law. He could speak the language of those who concluded that, in the substantive law, free will might function as no more than an "inevitable limitation on the precision of existing scientific methods and knowledge, and hence ... a mere margin of error." But he urged even them to see that, without a recognition of free will and of "the dynamism of the thinking, aspiring, problem-solving personality," no science and no law would carry human force. Judgments about criminal behavior could proceed forward on bases *other than* scientific analysis of observable phenomena, and Hall's position now was that they *should*. For more or less "correct" answers to human problems are "discoverable" as the "explanation of criminal behavior moves from the sphere of description to that of criticism on the basis of objective standards of truth and morality. More precisely, the description is itself largely influenced by such criticism."[23]

---

[22] Jerome Hall, *General Principles of the Criminal Law* (Indianapolis, IN: Bobbs-Merrill, 1947), 561, 564–66.

[23] Hall, *General Principles*, 563–65. For a vigorous critical (and positivistic) response to Hall, see Thomas A. Cowan, "A Critique of the Moralistic Conception of Criminal Law," *University of Pennsylvania Law Review*, vol. 97 (1949): 502–18. Although Cowan welcomed Hall's "most enlightened plea that the criminologist ... realize that he is dealing not with a mechanism, an automaton," he concluded that the overall lessons Hall drew from this were wrongheaded. "The moral foundation of the criminal law is taken by Professor Hall to be *force*, and the object of the criminal law is taken to be *punishment*" (rather than the "lofty one of treatment"). Force "can hardly be dignified by the term 'moral duty,'" and the (retributive) theory of punishment "is degrading." Hall, Cowan concluded, "lends his authority to present day mystical opponents of a sound empirical and scientific foundation for penal liability" (514–18). Hall responded to Cowan briefly in *Living Law*, 72–73 and n. 70. For a more approving (natural-law-based) response to Hall, see Miriam Theresa Rooney, "Law without Justice – The Kelsen and Hall Theories Compared," *Notre Dame Law Review*, vol. 23 (1947): 140–72.

Thurman Arnold

The mid-1940s saw another move toward a moral-legal rule with Thurman Arnold's opinion in *Holloway v. United States*,[24] a Court of Appeals (D.C. Circuit) legal insanity case and precursor to Judge Bazelon's 1954 *Durham* decision. As a member of the Yale law faculty in the 1930s, where he was brought on board by Dean Robert Hutchins's scheme for a marriage of law and the social sciences, Arnold had cast an anthropologist's eye upon politics and the law, including the exotic workings of the jury trial, which he described as a morality play giving vent to folk beliefs that the law held in good keeping. Despite its obvious partialities and irrationality, "the [jury's] claim is on our emotions, rather than our common sense."[25] Less diplomatic observers had castigated Arnold, whose early scientific objectivism and commitment to cultural relativity they derided – more or less astutely – as a rejection of morals that justified an antidemocratic, elite ruling bureaucracy.[26] In *Holloway* however, *Judge* Arnold's Progressive preference for a scientific approach to penology and his own mocking critique of the ethic of free will gave way, at least heuristically, to a positive approach to the belief in free will – or, as he then put it, "moral responsibility" – as a social fact. Arnold affirmed not only the trial court's conviction, but also his own move from a descriptive realist account to a (perhaps reluctant) prescriptive statement about the virtue of adjusting legal rules to the realities of conventional morality.

The defendant in *Holloway* had been convicted of rape and appealed on grounds that the conviction was unreasonable in light of the psychiatric evidence presented at trial. Two psychiatrists testified that the defendant could not tell right from wrong at the time of the offense; one testified that he could. Arnold first asserted that the "application of [the right-wrong and irresistible impulse tests], however they are phrased, to a borderline case can be nothing more than a moral judgment that it is just or unjust to blame the defendant for what he did." And then he stated more broadly: "Legal tests of criminal insanity are not and cannot be the result of scientific analysis or objective judgment ... they must be based on the instinctive sense of justice of ordinary men." According to this sense of justice,

there is a faculty called reason which is separate and apart from instinct, emotion, and impulse, that enables an individual to distinguish between right and wrong and endows him with moral responsibility for his acts. This ordinary sense of justice still

---

[24] *Holloway v. United States*, 148 F.2d 665 (D.C. Cir. 1945).

[25] Thurman W. Arnold, *The Symbols of Government* (New Haven, CT: Yale University Press, 1935), 145, 14–15.

[26] See, e.g., the discussions of Arnold's work on political and legal theory – and reactions to it – in Edward A. Purcell, Jr., *The Crisis of Democratic Theory: Scientific Naturalism and the Problem of Value* (Lexington: University Press of Kentucky, 1973), 111–14, 159–60, 197–99.

operates in terms of punishment. To punish a man who lacks the power to reason is as undignified and unworthy as punishing an inanimate object or an animal. A man who cannot reason cannot be subject to blame. Our collective conscience does not allow punishment where it cannot impose blame.[27]

Arnold distinguished the approach of modern psychology, "which proceeds on an entirely different set of assumptions. It does not conceive that there is a separate little man in the top of one's head called reason whose function it is to guide another unruly little man called instinct, emotion, or impulse." Instead, mental science sees reasoning as a "rationalization of behavior"; psychiatrists "probe behind what ordinary men call the 'reasoning' of an abnormal personality" in a process that "tends to restrict the area of moral judgment to an extent that offends our traditional idea that an offender who can talk and think in rational terms is morally responsible for what he does." Although his language (and especially the "little man" image) was sardonic, Arnold sincerely (if regretfully) insisted upon the difference between the "therapeutic standards" of psychiatry and the "moral judgment" of the criminal law. "Complete reconciliation" between the two was not possible; their purposes and assumptions were different. Thus the psychiatrist's own "moral judgment reached on the basis of his observations" was not binding on the jury "except within broad limits," that is, when "the verdict shocks the conscience of the court." Arnold's emphasis on "moral judgment," not only in borderline cases but in the criminal law more generally, and his insistence that the "institution which applies our inherited ideas of moral responsibility to individuals prosecuted for crime is a jury of ordinary men,"[28] would greatly influence Bazelon in his (very different) *Durham* opinion of a decade later.

Arnold's understanding of the public sense of justice, as of 1945, was more than a matter of the moral aspect of blame. In *Fisher v. United States*,[29] Arnold considered the trial court's instructions at a murder trial, which had given the jury substantial leeway in its consideration of all testimony, including psychiatric testimony. Arnold noted that "modern psychiatry has given us much scientific information which disturbs the former certainty of our judgments of individual responsibility and moral guilt," but stated that the "principal place for the application of such a therapeutic point of view" was the sentencing process. So far as the trial stage was concerned: "In the determination of guilt age old conceptions of individual moral responsibility cannot be abandoned without creating a laxity of enforcement that undermines the whole administration of criminal law."[30] In other words, a person incapable of reason "cannot be subject to blame"

[27] *Holloway*, 148 F.2d at 666–67.
[28] *Holloway*, 148 F.2d at 667.
[29] *Fisher v. United States*, 149 F.2d 28 (D.C. Cir. 1945).
[30] *Fisher*, 149 F.2d at 29.

but, short of that, science must not offend common beliefs regarding that capacity, both for moral reasons and to prevent "laxity of enforcement." Hence, relative to *Holloway*, one infers there was little reason to tamper with the traditional test for insanity, which left sufficient and appropriate space for the application of conventional morality. Indeed, it would be dangerous to do so.

Arnold's stance in 1945 remained akin to that of the realist who fashioned his prescriptions for the law in light of his observations of ordinary human behavior. Arnold's opinion in *Fisher* further reveals a commitment to bifurcation, but not of the typical positivist kind, where conventional morality at guilt assessment was deemed unfortunate but too strong to challenge, and at sentencing still a partial drag to be accommodated even as it was disrespected. Rather, Arnold had driven accommodationism to its endpoint; he had accepted, if only heuristically, what must be accommodated as central to the idea of justice for which the criminal law stood. His language regarding free will differed from Hall's, which invoked the "inner realm of personal experience" as yielding insights that could be tested "on the basis of objective standards of truth and morality." Sensible guilt assessment for Arnold meant giving appropriate scope to the ordinary view as represented by the jury, not to a set of retributivist principles shared by judge and theorist regarding the mysteries of human behavior. Moreover, unlike Hall, Arnold did not argue for retributivism other than as a moral-legal policy that was necessary for the public sense of justice, given ordinary men's views. He may well have believed – as he came later to say – that a judge's faith in free will was necessary to sustain belief that judicial decisions constituted the rule of law.[31] But there is no reason to conclude that he then – or ever – thought that the judge must believe, as did "ordinary men," that the criminal defendant who had employed reason had ipso facto, either as a scientific fact or as a testable moral "truth," acted with free will.

Thus, although Arnold gave the views of ordinary men a significant role, it is doubtful that he came close to Hall's own particular form of belief. Instead, he lent himself to a kind of suspension of disbelief, one that was largely a matter of strategy – situational and subject to change. That very suspension, of course, yielded its own form of belief and limits. A decade later, Arnold could accept Bazelon's melding of science and law in *Durham* as consistent both with his personal Progressive views and with the postulate that the law must bear the traffic of the views of ordinary men; Hall, as we shall see, viewed *Durham* in entirely different terms.

---

[31] Thurman Arnold, *Fair Fights and Foul: A Dissenting Lawyer's Life* (New York: Harcourt, Brace and World, 1965), 61.

POSITIVISM AND THE CONSCIOUSNESS OF FREEDOM:
ROBERT KNIGHT

Jurists such as Arnold who counseled no more than a suspension of disbelief regarding the traditional concept of criminal responsibility had, of course, some precedent for their position. In the late nineteenth century, we have seen, Francis Wharton insisted that jurisprudence was a "practical science," and that the "principle of necessity" – when applied to punishment-as-deterrence – robbed both jurisprudence and life of "moral dignity."[32] Relative truth had a greater hold on the law than absolute truth. The concession in 1901 of Gino Speranza that "law is one of the humanities" was yet another way of saying one must act on faith.[33] But was acting on faith denying an objective truth? Progressive Era positivists forced the issue, mocking the notion that the criminal had freely chosen to do wrong, and sometimes seeking to expose punishment imposed for deterrence as subconscious vengeance. Wechsler and Michael had responded by arguing that punishment, rightly interpreted, unveiled the utilitarian intent of the law. It required no act of faith, much less a suspension of disbelief, although their rationale obscured the place of individual "moral dignity."

Strict utilitarianism failed to dominate the juristic mind of the late 1930s and the 1940s, even as Wechsler became preeminent among criminal law scholars (and even as the 1940 Wechsler and Michael criminal law casebook[34] became the foundation stone for the emergence of criminal law as a mainstay of the American law school curriculum). Rather, the period saw an uneasy truce among positivism, utilitarianism, and traditional principles. For many jurists, positivist principles – still viewed mainly in terms of *penological* practice – remained the eventual ideal. But the European experience had revealed the dangers of unrestrained positivism and, at home, the practical difficulties of institutionalizing a due-process-based positivism perhaps increased many American scholars' tendency to seek a gradualist approach.[35]

For some jurists, pragmatism had long since offered a solution: morality might rest solely upon the universal consciousness of freedom. Pound, for one, had found this approach attractive, but had balked at basing the

---

[32] 1 Francis Wharton, *A Treatise on Criminal Law* (8th ed., 1880), 53 n. 1.

[33] Gino C. Speranza, "The Medico-Legal Conflict over Mental Responsibility," *Green Bag*, vol. 13 (1901): 123–26, 125.

[34] Jerome Michael and Herbert Wechsler, *Criminal Law and Its Administration* (Chicago: Foundation Press, 1940).

[35] Practical considerations certainly dominated in Yale law professor George Dession's warnings of the dangers and difficulties of holistically applying positivist ideas in criminal justice. George H. Dession, "Psychiatry and the Conditioning of Criminal Justice," *Yale Law Journal*, vol. 47 (1938): 319–40.

ascription of criminal responsibility upon that mere consciousness[36] – and had ended up in temporizing compromise. Psychoanalytic principles similarly recognized a consciousness of freedom and, perhaps ironically, by midcentury here the yield for a moral-legal rule was greater. Central to the psychiatric-psychoanalytic critique of the traditional rules of the criminal law had been the contention that their survival reflected a deep-seated need for the belief in one's own "freedom." Based on this very principle, the more "advanced" medical jurisprudence of the late 1930s and the 1940s thus sometimes conceded that the criminal law was founded not solely on primitive urges of vengeance, but also on the responses of normal and adjusted human behavior – that is, behavior indicative of a sense of personal, responsibility-bearing agency. The ascription of responsibility was thus itself productive of psychic health. The result placed a positivist-endorsed notion of freedom on surprisingly strong comparative footing. The strident Hall, for example, had committed himself to a necessary but somewhat abstract notion of freedom that could appeal to true believers in free will and those who had, following Pound, employed the language of the *consciousness* of human freedom. But now, among behavioral scientists that same consciousness of freedom was emerging as more than an abstract individual interest. It was a "fact" that only professional negligence ignored. The language of positivism might hold, much to Hall's chagrin. Yet the meaning of language could shift as it allowed for new understandings and alignments.

The president of the American Psychopathological Association, Robert Knight, illustrated this particular evolution of the psychiatric perspective regarding criminal law in his 1946 presidential address to the Association, "Determinism, 'Freedom,' and Psychotherapy." Knight began by rehearsing familiar strains, none of which could have come as a surprise to his audience: "Determinism is a fundamental tenet of all science.... In such a deterministic science of human behavior there is no place for the fortuitous, nor for free 'will' in the sense used in philosophy."[37] But the subject of the occasion was more nuanced. Knight was responding to a special committee of the ABA on the Rights of the Mentally Ill, which itself was reacting in part to comments by psychoanalysts on Arnold's opinion in *Fisher v. United States.* Observing that "the doctrines of psychoanalysis tend toward determinism," the committee had questioned whether psychiatrists holding such

---

[36] Little had changed about Pound's view on the subject even as of 1954. Recall his assertion that, on the "civil side of the legal order," "free self-determination" must be weighed as an aim of the law because it is "a much prized and eminently reasonable expectation" distinct from the "psychological question how far there is such a thing as individual free will." He expressly declined to apply the same reasoning to the other side of the legal order, however, specifying that he "sa[id] nothing of the role of the will in criminal law" (Roscoe Pound, "The Role of the Will in Law," *Harvard Law Review,* vol. 68 [1954]:1–19, 19).

[37] Robert Knight, "Determinism, 'Freedom,' and Psychotherapy," *Psychiatry,* vol. 9 (1946): 251–62, 251.

views were competent to serve as expert witnesses regarding questions of legal responsibility.[38] "They fear," Knight explained, "that the deterministic view implies an encouragement to irresponsibility.... They wonder how it can be decided which human acts are 'free' and therefore punishable, and which acts are 'determined' and therefore unpunishable."[39] Such fears, he continued, called for patient exposition.

The key to Knight's response was his point that the antithesis to determinism was "indeterminism – pure chance, chaos," *not* free will. The reality of determinism thus did not negate the quality of free will. Rather, as humans had long concluded – here crediting thinking on the supposed determinism/free will antinomy ranging back not just through Hobbes and Hume, but to Plato, Aristotle, and Socrates – the human sense of freedom coexists with the deterministic nature of our acts. In the language of his own day and field, free will referred to "a subjective psychological experience" that exists and (at least ideally) can be quantified. And, although free will is entirely influenced by deterministic forces, "compar[ing free will] to determinism is like comparing the enjoyment of flying to the law of gravity." Knight illustrated psychiatry's understanding of the range of freedom subjectively experienced by humans in making choices – from the healthy, integrated person who experienced a sense of freedom despite his or her awareness of internal determinative forces, to the unhealthy person who acted from compulsion or "conflicting urges and aims" and rarely experienced "harmony and freedom."[40] Most important, this "freedom" had nothing to do with literal "free will." Rather, it was "a subjective experience which is itself causally determined"; one's capacity for achieving this experience depended upon the integration and development of one's total personality, and thus was "causally determined in accordance with the psychological laws governing the inherited endowment, biological drives, etc."[41]

---

[38] "Report of the Special Committee on the Rights of the Mentally Ill," *Annual Report of the ABA*, vol. 70 (1945): 338–42, 339; and see Wilber Katz, "Responsibility and Freedom: A Difficulty in Relating Christianity and Law," *Journal of Legal Education*, vol. 5 (1953): 269–85, 274–75 (commenting on the committee report and Knight's response), discussed more generally in this chapter's section on Wilber Katz.

[39] Knight, "Determinism, 'Freedom,' and Psychotherapy," 252.

[40] Knight, "Determinism, 'Freedom,' and Psychotherapy," 255–56, 259. When mentally healthy people make simple ("trivial") choices, Knight explained, they have "the subjective sense of complete freedom of choice." "In weightier matters," on the other hand, "the healthy person has a combined feeling of freedom and of inner compulsion. He feels that his course is determined by standards, beliefs, knowledge, aspirations that are an integral part of himself and he can do no other; yet at the same time he feels free." "In a negative sense," such freedom "means absence of anxiety, of irrational doubt, and of those inhibitions and restrictions which paralyze both choice and action. In a positive sense it connotes feeling of well-being, of self-esteem, of confidence, of inner satisfaction based on successful use of one's energies for achievement that promotes the best interests of one's fellow men as well as one's own" (255–56).

[41] Knight, "Determinism, 'Freedom,' and Psychotherapy," 258.

Acknowledging that "normality and harmonious integration" were not evenly distributed, Knight accepted that the capacity of individuals to adhere to "man-made restrictive rules (laws)" varied greatly. "In spite of these imperfections of civilization," he nonetheless concluded, "society must expect of its members personal responsibility for their acts." The question remained, case by case, how best to deal "with those whose unlawful acts indicate that their sense of personal and social responsibility is insufficient to hold their behavior within the law." Here Knight cited the difference between lawyers, who "declare that when laws have been violated the culprits must be convicted and punished," and psychiatrists, who counsel "that many would be more likely to become rehabilitated through treatment and reeducation than through punishment." Knight, of course, was among those who preferred "treatment" (rather than "punishment"), associating it with development of the "sense of personal and social responsibility" that coincided with both mental health and the subjective experience of free will.[42] But he refrained from dismissing punishment on grounds that it was premised on an incorrect understanding of human behavior, as had so many positivists before him. Punishment was not ipso facto wrong. Nor was it necessarily right; Knight's acceptance of responsibility alongside determinism did not go so far as that of later, more expressly compatibilist thinkers, who would conclude that the coexistence of determinism and some form of individual freedom justified desert in retributivist terms. Rather, the relevant question for Knight (which he answered in the negative) was: Is punishment the best means for assuring and promoting psychic health and, from there, to individual acceptance of responsibility? Although the means to his ends thus differed from that of some positivist-leaning jurists, we might conjecture that many welcomed the idea of "psychic health" as an endorsement of the legal wisdom in suspending disbelief.

EXISTENTIAL PERSPECTIVES: SIR WALTER MOBERLY AND WILBER KATZ

By the early 1950s, there had emerged new ways of talking about responsibility – and of responding to the determinist critique – that accorded with prevailing standards of wisdom. Scholars demonstrated that the determinist critique could be rebutted head-on, or could be met with confession, *arguendo*, and then avoidance on practical grounds, or, yet again, could be characterized as inappropriate in the context of *criminal* responsibility. One need not dismiss the critique entirely: to a point, after all, it reflected a truth. Some took this theme a step further, offering consideration of determinism

---

[42] Knight, "Determinism, 'Freedom,' and Psychotherapy," 259. Knight did not go so far as to claim that acceptance of responsibility was a prerequisite for psychic health; rather, that acceptance was evidence of psychic health.

from the vantage point of its potential positive meaning for human life and psychology. The idea was to use determinism's lessons, to build upon it, to work with its ultimate unworkability. That humans did not – could not – fully assimilate determinism was the important point. Positivism, itself, had thus revealed certain truths intimately related to man's deep understanding of "the mystery of it all." As was true of Knight's approach, these truths could be translated into prescriptions for psychological well-being, for normality. They could also underlie a redescription of the concept of responsibility: humans were meant to come to grips with certain mysteries, and consciously to shoulder a degree of responsibility in the face of doubts about the conventionally rational basis for doing so. In other words, meaningful responsibility inhered precisely in the paradox of accepting responsibility *despite* the base scientific reality of universal causation. Of course, such arguments, being premised on determinism, could never shift entirely from an argument for imposition of moral and legal responsibility to the conclusion that one had been the true author of the act in question. The best they could do was to get one to *think* of oneself in that way, in the sense of *accepting* that way of thinking about oneself. Importantly, however, the law's imposition of responsibility did not depend upon the offender's *actually* thinking that way. It depended, rather, upon a confident conclusion that we all *ought* to think of ourselves in such a way and that the very imposition of responsibility helps us to do so. In treatment terms: the imposition was part of the therapy; successful therapy resulted in acceptance of the imposition.

In this vein, I offer the accounts of English ethicist Sir Walter Moberly and American law professor Wilber Katz. Although each approached the paradox of responsibility from a Christian perspective, their insights recast the idea of responsibility within a determined world in ways that influenced legal philosophy and that could help the law to incorporate a more complete picture of the individual psyche. Moberly in particular – along with his countryman, C. S. Lewis[43] – provided some American jurists with a new moral frame for their own legal analysis. His lectures were carried forward in the United States, first in Christian existentialist terms by Katz, and then along the lines of a classic secular and pragmatic reading by, respectively, Wechsler and Henry Hart.

Sir Walter Moberly

Sir Walter Moberly encapsulated the tensions between science and the legal concept of responsibility in his University of Durham Riddell Memorial

---

[43] See C. S. Lewis, "The Humanitarian Theory of Punishment," in *Contemporary Punishment: Views, Explanations, and Justifications*, ed. Rudolph Gerber and Patrick McAnany (Notre Dame, IN: University of Notre Dame Press, 1972), 194*ff* (originally published in *20th Century: An Australian Quarterly Review*, vol. III, no. 3 [1949] and, later, in *Res Judicatae*, vol. VI [June 1953]).

Lectures, published in 1951 under the title *Responsibility*.[44] The three lectures were a reflective meditation on psychology and law, and on the question of responsibility across both. Moberly's central concern was the "Christian" conception of responsibility in light of modern tensions between psychology and law, the subject of his first lecture. Neither psychologist nor legal theorist, Moberly was an ethicist who accepted the inherent imperfections of any system of human construct. For him, the object was not to distill *one* theory, *one* practice – but rather to arrive at a set of principles upholding the moral life of the individual and his or her consciously shouldered participation in the roughly hewn reality of social endeavor.

Moberly's first lecture, "Psychology and Law," demonstrates that he was well versed in the modern positivist's critique of traditional ideas of punishment-worthy, free-will-based responsibility: many – or all – offenders were not "responsible," and so punishment could not be justified on grounds of deterrence, reformation, or retribution. Where some held a "moderate" form of this view – that many, but not all, criminals are not responsible – others counted free will as an illusion, period. To take an extremist line, "ultimately, every one of us, and not only the social failure and outcast, is the product of the psycho-physical constitution with which he was born and of the society into which he was born." Moberly contrasted the psychologist's objection to "responsibility," in the sense of meaning "an actual condition of the delinquent's mind which justifies his being punished," to the view that the sense of responsibility might be used as a "weapon."[45]

Men may be called 'responsible' in a secondary sense; that is, they are liable to punishment simply because there is reason to believe that punishment will produce the desired effect upon them. The relevant question then is not whether punishment is just, in the sense of being merited, for analysis shows that such a question is meaningless. It is only whether punishment is likely to deter and so to prove a profitable investment. Liability to punishment is not dependent on the prior fact of moral responsibility. 'Responsibility' is only another name for the liability, and that is to be determined solely by expediency as tested by experience.[46]

As for the law as it existed, on Moberly's account, responsibility was rooted in a somewhat ambiguous notion of self-control, on which could be projected *either* a notion of free will or the substitution of the same by an ethic of social normality and lawful action, not willed but determined. In either view, where self-control was abandoned, fault, blame, and deserved punishment reasonably entered the language of formal and popular justice alike. On the level of underlying theory, the positivist admits that blame is merely a psychological artifact, where the legalist remains agnostic, constantly

[44] Sir Walter Hamilton Moberly, *Responsibility* (London: Oxford University Press, 1951).
[45] Moberly, *Responsibility*, 14–16.
[46] Moberly, *Responsibility*, 16.

moving back and forth between a positivist or utilitarian description and an endorsement of blame and punishment as truly justified – that is, the legalist left open the possibility of "free will." In practice, the contest between positivist and legalist was more concrete, and typically involved the limits of "self-control": When did the offender possess the capacity to respond to the threat of the law?

Although sensitive to the contributions of science, Moberly built on the legalist's answer to this question, which was more optimistic – or at least more constructive – with regard to the individual's power of self-control. In opposition to the psychiatric world's acceptance of the uncontrollable impulse test for insanity, for example, the legalist could consider whether such a test would weaken the resistance of individuals who might in fact exercise "self-control" if such a defense was not an option. In practical terms, the legalist concluded:

It is a lesser evil that here and there a man shall be punished for succumbing to an impulse which was genuinely irresistible than that the door should be opened for large numbers, who find such impulses very hard to resist, to hope for immunity if they succumb. In the words of Baron Bramwell: "If an influence is so powerful as to be termed irresistible, so much more the reason why we should not withdraw any of the safeguards tending to counteract it." Or, as a Canadian judge rather brutally expressed it: "If you cannot resist an impulse in any other way, we will hang a rope in front of your eyes and perhaps that will help."[47]

To this argument, which was essentially one of public utility, Moberly added his own take, by which he hoped to "appeal to the educator and moralist as well as to the jurist" while also speaking to the individual's "status in the community" and the imperatives of political liberty. In doing so, Moberly upheld the traditional authority of the law, but in terms that won compelling force through dialogue with social science and by way of the specter of midcentury fascism.[48]

Beginning with the insights of modern-day explorations into the disturbances of the human psyche, Moberly unequivocally recognized: "Men whose case is wholly pathological are disqualified for freedom. No man can contract out of his social obligations on the plea of moral incapacity without thereby abdicating his right to the direction of his own life." Where human reason ceased to function, there was no remittance possible, through punishment, to the dignity of the integrative self. But, that being so, Moberly did not accept a wholesale extension of the premises of psychiatry or behaviorism to offenders as a whole, to the detriment of their *moral* capacities. The jurist, the behavioral scientist, and the ethicist all must tread gingerly

---

[47] Moberly, *Responsibility*, 19–20 (quoting Baron Bramwell and Canadian judge Riddell in *King v. Creighton* [1908], as quoted in Henry Weihofen, *Insanity as a Defense in Criminal Law* [New York: Commonwealth Fund, 1933], 32, 59).

[48] Moberly, *Responsibility*, 20.

in the field of "individualization" whose allowances for cognitive incapacity or uncontrollable will, he advised, dangerously risked "a cruel kindness."[49] For moral life was, in part, social life. To exempt a person from moral life, in any degree, was to suspend – and possibly to exile – him or her from society, without the compensation of earlier ages that gave the exile at least the hospitality due the stranger in communities not his or her own. Nor was social exclusion under the tutelage of treatment necessarily an answer, as it still denied the person's *self-command* – that return benefit of society to its members for their allegiance to the collective whole.

Moberly defended criticism of the "rigid and impersonal character of the procedure of the Courts" as "indeed part of what we mean by the 'Rule of Law'": that rule could not be arbitrary for being the bulwark against an amoral social order and the divorce of citizenship from a code of ethics. What seemed to offer a kinder leniency – the introduction of individualized "factors at present legally irrelevant" – came much nearer to a tyrannical imposition of authority as it gave opening to essentially arbitrary, unconsidered prejudicial judgment. He cited as an example of that outcome – with its implicit ramifications – the Nazi proposal to abolish the rule *nulla poena* on grounds "that any attack on the interests of the community and any offense against the demands of the national life was wrong and therefore ought to be punished."[50] The law's proper role was to support a moral order based on notions of autonomy, and this was "in the highest interests of the offender himself." From the nursery on, individuals learned – to their benefit – "to conform to the requirements of the moral order," and the law, when it entered, was both tutor in and guardian over this school of social education:

Recite a delinquent's disabilities and handicaps in front of him in open court and you are doing something to confirm them; you are impairing that self-respect and sense of responsibility which is the chief incentive to effort. Treat him as sane and responsible and as a whole man and you give him the best chance of rising to this level.[51]

Thus Moberly's account of the legal perspective featured the inculcation of a sense of personal responsibility – a sense of autonomy – but did not amount to a thick description of the role of the illusion of freedom in psychological health or in the development of one's own potential. The jurist, no doubt, would equate the sense of freedom with the feeling of human dignity, but Moberly's emphasis was on political liberty, rather than free will. He reserved the fuller discussion of the human side of freedom for his final lecture on the "Christian" conception of responsibility.[52]

---

[49] Moberly, *Responsibility*, 20.
[50] Moberly, *Responsibility*, 21.
[51] Moberly, *Responsibility*, 23.
[52] "The Christian Conception Further Analysed," in Moberly, *Responsibility*, 44–62.

Moberly's Christian existentialism culminated in an observation that bears importantly upon themes of "Psychology and Law." The main character in Eliot's *The Family Reunion*, Moberly related, found "self-mastery and peace by whole-hearted acceptance of responsibility and of the need of expiation and by abandoning all attempt to excuse or mitigate, and so delimit, his liability." Here were dimensions of human growth not mentioned in the first two lectures, ones that pointed to a fuller psychological (perhaps spiritual) aspect of the experience of freedom.

In truth it seems to be the acknowledged masters of the spiritual life who are given to accusing themselves and to accepting responsibility for elements in their make-up, in regard to which, by the rules of moralistic critics, such accusation is superfluous or wrong-headed.... So far from being morbid and debilitating, this extended sense of guilt is a growing-point. On these lines, indeed, we are forced to widen our conception of responsibility. It no longer appears simply a liability arising out of a power. *It may also be a power arising out of a voluntary, and apparently quixotic, embracing of a liability that could have been disputed.*[53]

The Christian understood that "the mutual influence between him and others is ceaseless," accepting that "he *is* the whole of himself and not merely certain bits," that there is no "Urself."[54] While the "psychologist of the extreme school says that no men are guilty," and the "moralist says that some men are guilty of some of their actions, i.e., of those that are fully conscious and deliberate," the "theologian says that all men are guilty before God, for all have contributed to the corrupt environment which is a factor predisposing to particular sins."[55] Sin, then, was not what isolated one human being from another, driving some to crime. It was the liability under which all lived, because each individual was subject to the same burden of responsibility not to choose the wrong, in order to be a free individual in a world of human beings forever liable to wrongdoing.

Against the background of Moberly's Christian ethics, the words "power arising out of a voluntary, and apparently quixotic, embracing of a liability that could have been disputed" take on special meaning. This act of faith presumed a belief in God and in ultimate mysteries that dissolved all possibility of tension between science and law. Responsibility – free will (in a certain sense) – became a phenomenological reality. There is nothing more to be said, at this level. But if one treats Moberly's first lecture ("Psychology and Law") as a description of the real world (as some of Moberly's American juristic readers did), the matter appears differently. Here, there is no Christian phenomenology to dissolve the tensions between law and science.

From an "external" perspective, Moberly's legalist account was deterministic. Indeed, the law sought justification for itself on the basis of an

---

[53] Moberly, *Responsibility*, 53–54 (emphasis added).
[54] Moberly, *Responsibility*, 54.
[55] Moberly, *Responsibility*, 61–62.

understanding of human behavior. But, equally, he thought the law ought to address the public in the language of freedom – not the language of freedom-as-heuristic, but the language of freedom-as-reality. Jurists might admit to each other and to members of other elites – even to the educated public – the heuristic nature of the freedom-as-reality rhetoric, but that rhetoric must in the everyday course of things carry conviction. Inculcation of the sense of individual responsibility required that all the actors involved treat the notion of individual responsibility as resting on the individual's capacity to choose his course of action, to exercise true free will. Moberly did not investigate the implication of this dual voice of the law; there is in his account little hint of the tension that might accompany the modern juristic enterprise or of the disjunction between the "academic" understanding of law and that of the public at large. Nor did he turn his attention to how that tension conditioned, at least in the United States, the development and implementation of legal institutions and doctrine. The principles he outlined explained, he thought, a reasonable *resistance* to individualization. No doubt to some extent they did. But individualization was simultaneously attractive to a juristic caste that sought discretionary means to alleviate the tension between a literalist outward embrace of freedom and the determinist mind-set that underlay the decision to adopt that outward stance.

Like Knight, Moberly presented a moral-legal rule of responsibility, one that brought the law into conjunction with conventional morality. Both the scientist and the theologian sought to explicate the law in terms of the psychology of freedom, really to justify the law as they understood it. Neither adopted Hall's idealist or Arnold's realist language, but both also helped point the way from the debates of the 1930s to those of the 1950s and beyond.

Wilber Katz

Wilber Katz – an almost identical expositor of a criminal jurisprudence of responsibility that drew upon the convergences in postwar legal and behavioral science – was a professor of corporate law and former Dean at the University of Chicago Law School. Although he was not a criminal law teacher or scholar, in 1950 he taught a course on Psychology and Law that might have focused his attention on the issues raised here.[56] Katz shared Moberly's inspiration, but addressed more directly the potential for an unresolvable tension within the law, in all its secular reality. In June 1952, Katz addressed the Conference of Episcopal College Clergy, whose proceedings were devoted to "the problem of integrating religion with the field of study and teaching." His talk, "Responsibility and Freedom: A Difficulty in

---

[56] See *Association of American Law Schools Directory of Teachers in Member Schools, 1950–1951* (St. Paul, MN: West Publishing, 1950), 171.

Relating Christianity and Law," presented difficulties he had encountered over the years in attempting to make sense of the notion of free will. His experience and reading had led him to the view that freedom was very limited – indeed, he confessed, "I have often doubted the existence of even a limited freedom of choice" – and he had "speculated as to whether moral responsibility is limited in proportion to limited freedom." Yet Alexander and Staub's claim that freedom was an illusion, and one to be swept away, had left Katz uneasy: "My trouble has been that I have been unable either to take this approach or to let it alone."[57] Katz admitted to seeing "some glimmer of truth" in the view that "*reasoning about [free will] betrays itself as immoral, namely as an attempt to lull our bad conscience by escaping moral obligations.*"[58] The view "that the law is not concerned with the reality of free will, that the law simply treats people *as if* they were free," was difficult to support. "It is not comfortable," he remarked, "to regard the learning of one's profession as resting on a make-believe!"[59]

Katz reported that he had already induced Robert Knight to admit (in correspondence) to the paradox of the latter's fitting together in an uneasy alliance a theory of determinism in the formation of human psychology, and a method of therapy that encouraged the consciousness of free will. Knight had admitted he was cornered. The submission did not *admit* free will. Katz was not asking for so much. What it underscored was Katz's criterion for the "mature personality," which was "the capacity to endure, to accept frustration." For the problem of responsibility and freedom was singularly resistant to facile language or simple resolution. One took it up less "in faith," as Moberly argued, than with an acceptance that certain fundamentals would never be entirely comprehended.[60]

Katz enumerated five working definitions of freedom, which ranged from "freedom from" to "freedom to." The last was the most tendentious, by his own reckoning, and the most crucial for the development of his thought on a problem simultaneously spiritual and political. It was the "freedom to escape from the determining influence of defensive habits – freedom to increase [one's] capacity to endure." Christianity offered this freedom through divine grace, but in law grace was not at issue, and man in society lived under law, wherever the soul and spirit might abide. Social man, then, must come to understand and to live by the true relationship between freedom and responsibility:

Man's ultimate freedom is his capacity to assume moral responsibility. His ultimate responsibility is for the exercise of this freedom. A person who is morally mature

[57] Katz, "Responsibility and Freedom," 271–72.
[58] Katz, "Responsibility and Freedom," 275 (quoting Maximilian Beck, "Human Equality: The Essence of Democracy," *Common Cause*, vol. 1 [1948]: 468 [emphasis supplied by Katz]).
[59] Katz, "Responsibility and Freedom," 275.
[60] Katz, "Responsibility and Freedom," 275–78.

feels himself responsible for his actions regardless of the extent to which others have determined them. He does not pass the buck to those who molded his character. If he is conscious of their influence, he assumes vicariously a share of their responsibility.[61]

Katz recognized his debt to Moberly's articulation of the problem when the latter had ascribed to responsibility not simply or even mainly individual fault, but shared liability in what the individual might deny on his part.[62] But the law, of course, made no allowance for the voluntary taking up of responsibility. It commanded and enforced, with penalties for noncompliance. And here one faced the dilemma, related to the question of responsibility and freedom, of how to justify the retributive aspect of punishment. For Katz had concluded that punishment's retributive character was denied only by ignoring the law's intent and enforcement. "When we impose legal responsibility," Katz observed, "we necessarily assert that the penalty imposed is justified by the act done and not merely by objectives hoped to be accomplished."[63]

Law was a deterrent *based on* responsibility, indeed, a responsibility that the law explicitly helped to elicit and then foster in the individual and the community. It required of the citizen self-control and social responsibility. Said Katz:

If the idea of retribution thus cannot be avoided, I must revise my notion of moral responsibility. I need not recant my belief that responsibility is largely vicarious, but I must admit that this is not the whole truth. It is true that responsibility is something to be shouldered, but it seems also to be true that the responsibility is already ours to be shouldered. Moral development, increase of freedom, requires voluntary acceptance of responsibility, but refusal of responsibility leaves responsibility intact. My responsibility, including the vicarious component, is mine because of the very structure of relations among fallen men. The truth about responsibility is paradoxical because this structure of relations is not fully intelligible.[64]

Retribution must be justifiable as a corollary to legally affirmed responsibility, which in turn affirmed moral freedom.

Katz drew upon Moberly but enunciated a view that bridged Christian existential ideas and what he took to be implied by the

---

[61] Katz, "Responsibility and Freedom," 278.

[62] Katz, "Responsibility and Freedom," 278–79. Katz noted that, at the meeting at which he read the paper and upon which the present article was based, his attention was called to Moberly's lectures. He then quoted Moberly's statement about responsibility: "'It may also be a power arising out of a voluntary, and apparently quixotic, embracing of a liability that could have been disputed.'"

[63] Katz, "Responsibility and Freedom," 278–81. For an article (not cited by Katz) that had insisted upon just this point, see: D. J. B. Hawkins, "Punishment and Moral Responsibility," *Modern Law Review*, vol. 7 (1944): 205–08.

[64] Katz, "Responsibility and Freedom," 281.

criminal jurisprudence of his day. His exposition of the moral-legal idea of responsibility vacillated between a purely moral-legal conception of free will and a species of the reality of free will. If an "as if" view of free will continued to "infuriate" him, it was because he associated that view with an expression of crude instrumentalism, a reliance upon legal fiction. He would invoke instead a belief in what must really be, regardless of whether that truth was susceptible to human intelligence. For Katz, the "truth of responsibility" *was* a paradox. To deny that conclusion was to avoid the problem. He, like Moberly, included duality in the rationale of the criminal law.

By way of conclusion, Katz noted two other efforts "to heal the breach between lawyers and doctors," regarding both the insanity defense and a moral-legal concept of responsibility. As I have previously recounted, Jerome Hall had proposed the integration of the legal and medical, largely on the terrain of the former. The other opening had been given by a 1952 article by Edwin R. Keedy – then an emeritus law professor and former dean of the University of Pennsylvania Law School – that revived a recommendation in the 1913 report of the AICLC Committee on Insanity and Criminal Responsibility, chaired by Keedy.[65] This proposal, discussed further in the next chapter, advocated – in lieu of integration – a "separate but equal" approach to the spheres of psychiatry and law. Katz was more persuaded by the second and earlier formulation. He reiterated that "the criminal law is primarily retributive and that responsibility is rooted in the structure of human interconnectedness which remains a mystery." He maintained: "This affords little basis for reasoning as to the types of individuals who should be exempt." Katz noted that Keedy's approach "is perhaps more immediately promising since psychiatrists and lawyers share the human tendency which theologians call 'original sin.'" The search for medical language that would convey meaning useful to the determination of a legal concept of responsibility was a lost cause. Experts should testify based on their knowledge. The judge should instruct the jury solely that if it finds "'from such testimony that the defendant was [irresistibly] impelled, then the necessary volition was lacking and the defendant should be acquitted.'"[66] The legal instructions should include "'no medical or psychological theories'" and should not attempt "'any legal definition of insanity.'" The effect would be one that "'clearly separates the

[65] Edwin R. Keedy, "Irresistible Impulse as a Defense in the Criminal Law," *University of Pennsylvania Law Review*, vol. 100 (1952): 956–93, 989.
[66] Katz, "Responsibility and Freedom," 284–85 (quoting Edwin Keedy et al., "Insanity and Criminal Responsibility" [second report of AICLC Committee "B," chaired by Professor Edwin Keedy], *JCLC*, vol. 3 [1913]: 719–27, 720).

legal and medical functions of the trial.'"[67] It would also explicitly trust
the jury to draw a final conclusion in the face of the mystery of human
interconnectedness.

Katz's understanding of legal responsibility, then, had brought him to the
point of endorsing – resonances of Arnold – the inspirations of conventional
morality: "If it is agreed," he contended,

> that law is law and medical psychology is something else again, there can be a truce
> in which the doctors can keep to themselves their ideas about the relation between
> volition and responsibility. If they do so, the lawyers can suppress their concern for
> the "subversive" character of medical dogma. And in the doubtful cases, the juries
> can be relied upon to continue "doing what comes naturally," not too much puzzled
> by the gap between the medical evidence and the law.[68]

CONCLUSION

The new directions traced in brief here – through the thought and writings of Hall, Arnold, Knight, Moberly, and Katz – were each in their own
way attempts to reconnect with society and its precepts, lest the life of the
law lose relevance. The directions, and the varieties of freedom to which
they gave voice, if not without precedents were, nonetheless, new in their
objective to overcome, or narrow, the disjunction between law and popular
morality, and between science and freedom – even if that required, ironically, the acceptance of dualism. The trajectories constituted elite reassess-
ments of Western conventions of morality, humanly experienced freedom,
and Christian ethics but, of course, not yet a resolution between law and
social science.[69] These trajectories more concretely entered the criminal trial

---

[67] Katz, "Responsibility and Freedom," 284–85 (quoting Keedy, "Irresistible Impulse," 992 n. 213).

[68] Katz, "Responsibility and Freedom," 285.

[69] Many of the issues discussed in the text were raised – often in instructive and revealing
ways – in 1950 at the second New York University conference on "Social Meaning of Legal
Concepts" on the subject of "Criminal Guilt." For the transcripts of the conference, see
Social Meanings of Legal Concepts: No. 2. Criminal Guilt (New York: New York University
School of Law, 1950). The main speakers were a legal anthropologist (Karl Llewellyn), a
criminologist (Edwin J. Lukas), a psychiatrist (Frederic Wertham), and a philosopher (the
theologian, Joseph F. Fletcher). Fletcher's paper, "The Ethics of Criminal Guilt" (171–84),
is of particular interest for the terms in which he criticized modern positivism's denial of
free will (174) and, as he saw the matter, acceptance of moral relativism (178). "The jurist
and the moralist need not claim for men more than a 'limited' or 'conditional' freedom and
knowledge." Of "man," Fletcher concluded:

> he lives under the law, which he likewise struggles to make an instrument of his
> ethical vision. Sometimes it finds him innocent, sometimes it finds him guilty. When
> it finds him guilty it does so because he really *is* a man, a responsible person who
> exercised his humanity in an act of disobedience. It is, therefore, precisely because

and the jury's deliberations with the 1954 *Durham* decision and some of the responses to Judge Bazelon's famous opinion in that case, to which I now turn.

he can be guilty of crime that there is no dishonor to him or in the law when he stands before the bar of judgment. (183)

Paul Tappan, a criminologist and self-described "positivist," responded in his "Comments," that he denied, inter alia, "that the conception of a free will is a useful or accurate tool to employ in a system of human justice" (185). To which Fletcher countered: "The behavior sciences do not assert that a man's conduct is *entirely* conditioned. He has some choice (the attack on 'free will' is a red herring), otherwise he has no responsibility and all talk about justice is nonsense" (186).

6

Durham v. United States, the Moral Context of the Criminal Law, and Reinterpretations of the Progressive Inheritance: 1954–1958

INTRODUCTION

In practice, the insanity defense retained its role as a divisive touchstone for those concerned with identifying the proper underlying bases for criminal responsibility. Federal Court of Appeals Judge David Bazelon's landmark 1954 opinion regarding the insanity defense in *Durham v. United States*[1] can be understood as a prime example of the ongoing attempts to found a workable test upon the uneven ground where science, legal theory, and conventional morality met. *Durham* established a liberal new test for legal insanity, essentially leaving the determination to the jury but with almost unlimited input from scientific experts. On one view, an (implied) inevitable disjunction between conventional morality and science, and the resulting bifurcation of trials – commonly viewed as a major hurdle by positivist scholars – could become a useful tool rather than a disadvantage: where science could not definitively define the bounds of free will, the jury could step in by applying traditional (but evolving) social ideals of morality; at the same time, scientific testimony could itself influence the evolution of these ideals by educating jurors and, in turn, society at large. Thus law could remain socially relevant while incorporating advances in scientific understanding. But *Durham* was also vulnerable to criticism, especially by those concerned that psychological theory should not dominate the law and by those who rejected Bazelon's open-ended "product" test for insanity. A particularly strong (and perhaps initially surprising) critic on the former point

---

[1] *Durham v. United States*, 214 F.2d 862 (D.C. Cir. 1954). I initially developed my discussion of *Durham* in Thomas A. Green, "Conventional Morality and the Rule of Law: Freedom, Responsibility, and the Criminal Trial Jury in American Legal Thought, 1900–60," chap. 15 in *Transformations in American Legal History: Law, Ideology, and Methods – Essays in Honor of Morton J. Horwitz, Volume II*, ed. Daniel W. Hamilton and Alfred L. Brophy (Cambridge: Harvard University Press, 2010), 261–68.

was the emerging scholar Thomas Szasz, a psychiatrist who nonetheless defended the law on the law's own terms. Szasz urged that the tenets of modern psychiatry – and its exaggerated capacity to meaningfully classify the mind – were irreconcilable with the integral notion of human responsibility. Further, he did so on grounds not only of a freedom associated with psychological health, but of political liberty.

Herbert Wechsler, who was engaged in the task of formulating a test for legal responsibility to be included in the American Law Institute's Model Penal Code (MPC), provided the utilitarian counterpoint to *Durham*. Wechsler's preferred test was most reminiscent of earlier-period, consequentialist thinking about the aims of the criminal law. The MPC itself – and its ultimate formulation of the insanity test – was the result of hard-won compromise. Its aim, particularly by Wechsler's reckoning, was to achieve consequentialist ends by way of an eminently modern, scientific code that limited state incursion at the guilt phase by retaining the traditional (but now more clearly defined) focus on intent to prospectively define offenses. Although it effectively affirmed the jury's role as final arbiter of what would be understood as moral condemnation, it nonetheless tried to shape that role to buttress the goal of deterrence. The MPC influence is a testament to the enduring consequentialist aims that remain embedded in American law. Yet the compromises that underlay it may also embody the confusion and disagreement that persist to this day regarding the mixed – and therefore often muddied and, sometimes, even contradictory – goals and presumptions of the law.

Finally, I close this chapter by turning from *Durham* and the MPC to a discussion of Henry Hart's influential 1958 essay, "The Aims of the Criminal Law." Hart combined the growing traditionalism of the 1940s and 1950s with the focus on individualized treatment central to the positivist discussion of the 1930s. He contributed to reinvigorating the traditional premise that law, at its core, concerned moral condemnation. But his emphasis was on the psychological effects of a presumption that individuals are reasonable and responsible – that is, capable of moral action; under such a presumption, he posited, most people will rise to the occasion, to their own benefit and to that of society. Hart's contribution was an important bridge between consequentialism and a process of condemnation genuinely rooted in affirming individual autonomy. Yet the bridge would be temporary, owing to its shaky foundations: Hart still attempted to avoid the strong retribution associated with traditional notions of free will, and it was only a matter of time before his thin, essentially expressivist basis for criminal condemnation and punishment began to show wear. Thus, I employ this discussion of Hart to close Part II and bring us to Part III of this book, which explores the deep challenges to consequentialism – both in theory and in practice – that would shape American legal scholarship through the end of the twentieth century and into the twenty-first.

THE INSANITY DEFENSE AND *DURHAM*

Legal Insanity

By the 1950s, discussion regarding the freedom problem centered largely on the legal insanity defense. Of course legal insanity represented the most common exception to responsibility for non-positivists. At the other end of the spectrum, for those deterministic psychiatrists and other behavioral scientists who found the law's very concept of responsibility problematic – or even nonsensical – the insanity defense begged deeper questions and lagged hopelessly behind current medical research.[2] Yet it was these very medical and behavioral scientists who were called upon to testify as expert witnesses at trials involving the insanity defense. Thus, it was they who pressed hardest for reform of the prevailing rules. Acknowledging the practical need for a conventional legal theory of responsibility, they typically sought a significantly broader definition of legal insanity than the common law recognized, partly because they wished to minimize the compromise science had to make with the law and partly because the existing legal definitions of insanity seemed to them incoherent on those definitions' own terms. The so-called cognitive or right-wrong (*M'Naghten*) test, some charged, failed even to comport with the law's *own* conception of free volition. The irresistible impulse test, for its part, captured some who lacked (legal) volition, but not others whose symptoms were in the nature of deep brooding and compulsive yet calculated behavior. Accordingly, from the middle of the nineteenth century forward, medical jurisprudence experts had campaigned against the *M'Naghten* test and deemed the irresistible impulse test only a marginal improvement. For many, only the New Hampshire rule – which permitted the jury to deem an offender insane if it found that his act was, as a matter of fact, a product of mental disease[3] – met with approval; indeed, that rule had been adopted because of the influence that the medical scientist Isaac Ray exercised over New Hampshire Supreme Court Chief Justice Doe.[4]

After decades of efforts from various sources, the brief prospect of far-reaching reform of the legal insanity issue had been achieved in 1913 under

[2] Manfred Guttmacher and Gregory Zilboorg numbered among a small cadre of well-known and outspoken psychiatric spokesmen, but the ranks they led were substantial.
[3] See *State v. Pike*, 49 N.H. 399 (1869); *State v. Jones*, 50 N.H. 369 (1871).
[4] See John Reid, "Understanding the New Hampshire Doctrine of Criminal Insanity," *Yale Law Journal*, vol. 69 (1960): 367–420; Louis E. Reik, "The Doe-Ray Correspondence: A Pioneer Collaboration in the Jurisprudence of Mental Disease," *Yale Law Journal*, vol. 63 (1953): 183–96. The most comprehensive account of late nineteenth and early twentieth century medical-legal debate concerning the insanity defense is Janet Ann Tighe, "A Question of Responsibility: The Development of American Forensic Psychiatry, 1838–1930" (Ph.D. dissertation, University of Pennsylvania, 1983, available at http://repository.upenn.edu/dissertations/AAI8406727). A useful review of this background is in Thomas Maeder, *Crime and Madness: The Origins and Evolution of the Insanity Defense* (New York: Harper and Rowe, 1985), esp. chaps. 4 and 5.

the auspices of the AICLC, when the so-called Keedy Committee offered a radically new approach that went well beyond the recommendation that would be offered in the later 1916 Keedy report.[5] The 1913 formulation – which made possession of mens rea the central issue and "insanity" simply one possible basis for its absence – represented a compromise that many in the medical world much preferred,[6] but that was never adopted. Now, some forty years after its 1913 derivation (and two years before *Durham*), Keedy returned to the no-mens-rea formulation at the close of his 1952 article on the irresistible impulse test:

No person suffering from mental disease shall hereafter be convicted of any criminal charge, when at the time of the act or omission alleged against him, he did not have, by reason of such mental disease, the particular state of mind that must accompany such act or omission in order to constitute the crime charged.[7]

In a case where evidence of irresistible impulse was set forth, Keedy now wrote, the judge's instructions to the jury[8] would be:

A mental requirement of every crime is volition, which means that a person is able to exercise a choice either to act or not to act. In this case there was medical testimony that the defendant was suffering from mental disease and as a consequence was irresistibly impelled to commit the harm with which he was charged. If you find from such testimony that the defendant was so impelled, then the necessary volition was lacking and the defendant should be acquitted.[9]

That same year, the Keedy formulation was embodied in a proposed bill by the Medico-Legal Bar Association Committee of the Pennsylvania Psychiatric Society.[10] The bill (never adopted by the Pennsylvania legislature) met the psychiatric community's long-held preference that medical experts

---

[5] Edwin Keedy et al., "Insanity and Criminal Responsibility" (second report of AICLC Committee "B," chaired by Professor Edwin Keedy), *JCLC*, vol. 3 (1913): 719–27; Edwin Keedy et al., "Insanity and Criminal Responsibility" (report of AICLC Committee "A," chaired by Professor Edwin Keedy), *JCLC*, vol. 7 (1916): 484–91. See my discussion of the 1916 report in Chapter 3.

[6] Indeed, although William A. White signed on to the 1916 version, which he helped to craft, White may well have readily embraced the earlier approach, had it still seemed a viable option.

[7] Edwin R. Keedy, "Irresistible Impulse as a Defense in the Criminal Law," *University of Pennsylvania Law Review*, vol. 100 (1952):956–93, 992.

[8] When the Keedy Committee first proffered its recommendation, it was supposed on all sides that the issue would be resolved by a jury. Earlier bar association committees had divided on whether to resolve the legal insanity question through, instead, a panel of experts. But the 1910 *Strasburg* decision (ruling, mainly on due process grounds, that a jury must render a final decision with regard to legal insanity) pretty much laid that matter to rest. It remained open whether experts would testify only as part of an adversarial process, or as a single entity commissioned by the court. By 1952, however, the Keedy approach was envisioned in the context of a traditional adversarial process.

[9] Keedy, "Irresistible Impulse," 993.

[10] Keedy, "Irresistible Impulse," 992–93.

be allowed to testify in the language of their profession, unconstrained by legal or even specific medical definitions of mental disease. Medical science was fluid, and each case called for its own analysis; legal process ought to reflect that reality. The mental element required by law for the specific criminal offense charged should be central; jurors should assess whether, given medical testimony, that element ("state of mind") existed. As in Keedy's example, the jury would not focus on whether the defendant had been able to "exercise a choice," but on whether he or she had been "irresistibly impelled" (that is, motivated by a *non*-culpable state of mind). Nor would jurors undertake to assess the matter precisely in the terms of the New Hampshire rule, wherein the insanity defense was maintained and psychiatrists testified, but specific legal tests were abandoned, leaving jurors to find insanity (or otherwise) simply as a matter of fact. This reformulation of the New Hampshire rule served to underline the limits, nature, and purpose of expert testimony, as well as to keep jurors focused on that testimony.

By midcentury, the medical community may have recognized that it was unlikely that legislatures or courts would convert a test for legal insanity into a test for mens rea as Keedy proposed. Still, they hoped measures could be taken to adjust the existing legal insanity defense along the lines of the New Hampshire approach so as to reduce the tensions medical experts experienced when they testified. These measures would lessen the artificial linedrawing by those who testified as well as by those who based conclusions on that testimony: a closer approximation to the truth would be achieved. At the same time, the concept of "mental illness" would retain its salience, so that even as it expanded, the presumption would prevail that all those not mentally ill remained responsible. In this sense, "reform" would achieve, unintentionally or otherwise, "conservative" purposes: it would conserve the underlying presumption of the law.

Among positivist-leaning legal scholars there was little agreement on the insanity defense. Although a few shared the more extreme scientificdeterminist position on responsibility, most legal-academic positivists were merely skeptical about responsibility, sanctioning the concept as a necessary real-world device but supporting a broadening of the defense. Of those few who openly endorsed recourse to the concept of free will, Hall was the most prominent. Such "traditionalists" as there were, however, may well have deemed some form of the irresistible impulse test reasonable, departing from Hall's view that *M'Naghten* was sufficient because a true understanding of cognition incorporated all those with relevantly gravely impaired volition. It is not clear how many who were, roughly speaking, utilitarians adopted Wechsler and Michael's 1937 position that use of the cognitive test alone might well best serve the goal of overall efficiency.

From the traditional juristic perspective, change threatened to take a heavy toll. Precisely because the distinction between responsible and irresponsible had come to be widely viewed as a practical, moral-*legal* conclusion, reform was out of the question if it would be understood as premised on scientific notions that conflicted with the fundamental legal idea of responsibility. The basis for reform might embrace, for example, a broader definition of "irresistible impulse," but – and this psychiatrists would have to accept – the law could only outwardly accept such impulses as part of a finite field of excusing "causes" of criminal behavior, and a field of such causes that represented a rare condition at that. Although many psychiatrists might balk at the implication that all individuals *not* impelled by mental disease were effectively *un*impelled, the saving grace for all concerned was that this was not a matter on which medical experts were called upon to testify. And such a conservative reform still would serve important purposes from the medical perspective: the nonscientific term "irresistible impulse" could drop out, and something like the New Hampshire "product" test could be adopted in order to allow psychiatrists to speak in their professional tongue and jurors to hear all of the relevant psychiatric testimony. Again, this would always be within the context of a projected understanding, supposedly shared by all parties, that "mental diseases" or "defects" were the unusual exceptions to an otherwise defensible notion of legal responsibility.

Durham v. United States, David Bazelon, C.J.

In this light, then, Chief Judge David Bazelon's 1954 opinion for the U.S. Court of Appeals for the D.C. Circuit in *Durham v. United States*[11] appears as a far-reaching "liberal" reform *within* the "conservative" legal tradition. Bazelon adopted a near twin of the New Hampshire rule that fell well short of the mens-rea-based Keedy formulation, but that translated reform of the traditional legal insanity tests into terms that removed constraints on the conversation between medical experts and jurors. The agreed-upon boundary between responsibility and irresponsibility remained mental disease or defect, and these were (implicitly) understood to involve relatively rare conditions.

At issue in *Durham* was the defendant's claim that he was of unsound mind at the time he committed the charged crime of housebreaking. The appeals court, with Bazelon as its Chief, reversed the conviction, concluding in part that "existing tests of criminal responsibility are obsolete and should be superseded."[12] Bazelon commenced the main body of his opinion with an encapsulation of a century's worth of critique of the cognitive test. The test "requires court and jury to rely upon what is, scientifically speaking, inadequate, and most often invalid and irrelevant testimony in determining criminal responsibility," by virtue of "its misleading emphasis on the cognitive."

---

[11] *Durham*, 214 F.2d 862. For a useful summary of the defendant Monte Durham's psychiatric case history and of elements of Bazelon's decision not treated here, see Maeder, *Crime and Madness*, 80–87.

[12] *Durham*, 214 F.2d at 864.

Here, the insistence upon the integration of the human personality (the cognitive being but one part) – from Glueck through a recent report of the British Royal Commission on Capital Punishment[13] – formed the inevitable centerpiece. But Bazelon continued:

The fundamental objection to the right-wrong test, however, is not that criminal irresponsibility is made to rest upon an inadequate, invalid or indeterminable symptom or manifestation, but that it is made to rest upon *any* particular symptom.... In this field of law as in others, the fact finder should be free to consider all information advanced by relevant scientific disciplines.[14]

Such a perspective also made obvious the infirmities of the irresistible impulse test. In 1929, the D.C. Court of Appeals had adopted a version of that test, defining such an "impulse" as one where the offender's "reasoning powers were so far dethroned by his diseased mental condition as to deprive him of the will power to resist the insane impulse to perpetrate the deed, though knowing it to be wrong"; the impulse, the Court had declared, "must be such as to override the reason and judgment and obliterate the sense of right and wrong to the extent that the accused is deprived of the power to choose between right and wrong."[15] This apparently comprehensive language proved unsatisfactory to Bazelon, who observed that the term "'irresistible impulse'... carries the misleading implication the diseased mental condition[s] produce only sudden, momentary or spontaneous inclinations to commit unlawful acts," whereas – as the British Royal Commission had stated – a criminal act "'may be coolly and carefully prepared; yet is still the act of a madman.'" Thus, said Bazelon, the irresistible impulse test is "inadequate in that it gives no recognition to mental illness characterized by brooding and reflection."[16] And thus the need for a broader test.

The new "*Durham*" test was simply that "an accused is not criminally responsible if his unlawful act was the product of mental disease or defect."

---

[13] *Report* of the Royal Commission on Capital Punishment, 1949–53 (London, 1953) (reprinted London: Her Majesty's Stationary Office, 1973). The Royal Commission's recommendations and discussion regarding the difficulties of defining the insanity defense quickly became a reference point within the American debate about the defense. A majority of the Commission favored what might appear as the ultimate moral-legal position: it would abandon *M'Naghten* and simply "leave the jury to determine whether at the time of the act the accused was suffering from disease of the mind or mental deficiency to such a degree that he ought not to be held responsible" (276). The Commission's secondary recommendation, which was preferred by the dissenters (287), would have expanded *M'Naghten*, requiring the jury to "be satisfied that, at the time of committing the act, the accused, as a result of disease of the mind or mental deficiency, (a) did not know the nature and quality of the act or (b) did not know that it was wrong or (c) was incapable of preventing himself from committing it" (276).

[14] *Durham*, 214 F.2d at 871–72.

[15] *Smith v. United States*, 36 F.2d 548, 549 (D.C. Cir. 1929).

[16] *Durham*, 214 F.2d at 873–74 (quoting Royal Commission *Report*, 110).

The virtues of the test were that "the jury will not be required to rely on [selected 'symptoms, phases or manifestations' of disease] as criteria for determining the ultimate question of fact upon which [a] claim [of criminal irresponsibility] depends," and "the psychiatrist will be permitted to carry out his principal court function" to "inform the jury of the character of the accused's mental disease or defect."[17] It remained unclear how the jury was to get from the now-corrected process of assessing mental disease or defect to the question of whether the act charged was a "product" of mental disease or defect. What standard was either psychiatrist or juror to apply regarding causation, which implicitly lay at the heart of the "product" test?

Bazelon stated simply that an accused "would still be responsible for his unlawful act if there was no causal connection between such mental abnormality and the act," and again cited the Royal Commission, which stated that virtually every abnormality played "'some part in the causation'" and that the "'graver'" the abnormality, the "'more probable'" a "'causal connection.'"[18] These were not very helpful phrases: psychiatric testimony as to degree of seriousness of mental disease might yield a strong presumption of "a causal connection," but was that "causal connection" strong in the sense of the *main* cause? Was it less "resistible"? Apparently such questions should be left to the jury, which would apply standards of conventional morality as tested guides in answering them. As Bazelon memorably commented:

we permit [the jury] to perform its traditional function ... to apply "our inherited ideas of moral responsibility to individuals prosecuted for crime * * *." Juries will continue to make moral judgments, still operating under the fundamental precept that "Our collective conscience does not allow punishment where it cannot impose blame." But in making such judgments, they will be guided by wider horizons of knowledge concerning mental life. ...

The legal and moral traditions of the western world require that those who, of their own free will and with evil intent (sometimes called *mens rea*), commit acts which violate the law, shall be criminally responsible for those acts. Our traditions also require that where such acts stem from and are the product of a mental disease or defect as those terms are herein used moral blame shall not attach.[19]

Here, then, was the voice of tradition: Bazelon endorsed the underlying presumption of the criminal law and invoked the jury, which should, he thought, resolve cases in accordance with that tradition.

Notably, although Bazelon, in the main section of his opinion, followed the line of argument set forth by Abe Fortas and Abe Krash, the court-appointed attorneys for the appellant Durham – and although he effectively adopted the New Hampshire rule, which was one of the options

[17] *Durham*, 214 F.2d at 874–76.
[18] *Durham*, 214 F.2d at 875 (quoting Royal Commission *Report*, 99).
[19] *Durham*, 214 F.2d at 876 (quoting *Holloway v. United States*, 148 F.2d 665, 666–67 (D.C. Cir. 1945).

recommended in that brief – he gave no voice to what Fortas and Krash, by way of conclusion, termed a "radically different approach" to *all* criminal cases. Under that starkly positivist approach, for which Fortas and Krash drew upon Glueck and Cardozo:

> The courts would determine whether the defendant committed the act. The fact being ascertained, further disposition of the defendant would depend upon the judgment of trained personnel as to the rehabilitation or therapeutic possibilities rather than upon judgments as to "responsibility." Criminal administration would focus on prevention and therapy ... rather than upon conceptions of criminal "intent," which, however phrased, remain abstractions that are difficult to determine, awkward to administer, and often barren in results.[20]

Bazelon revealed no interest in thus restricting the role of the jury to mere determination of "whether the defendant has committed the act." Quite the opposite, however difficult judgments of "responsibility" and "intent," those judgments were quintessentially jury-based, albeit to be rendered in the light of the fullest possible psychiatric testimony. For Bazelon, the crucial point was that the traditional role of the jury should not be constrained by a legal process – and rules of legal responsibility – that artificially convinced them of a defendant's guilt. That is, the process should not induce them to create false positives – to convict in cases where, had they learned more about the defendant's mental condition, they would *in light of ongoing social understandings of the basis for blame* have acquitted.[21]

---

[20] Supplemental Brief for Appellant on Reargument, submitted to the United States Court of Appeals for the District of Columbia Circuit, *Durham v. United States* (1954), by Abe Fortas, Attorney for Appellant, by Designation of Court, and Abe Krash, of counsel, Arnold, Fortas and Porter. I am grateful to Laura Kalman for supplying me with a copy of the brief.

[21] In defense of the "product" test, Bazelon required no more of juries, he noted, than was commonly required in cases that raised the question whether a plaintiff had a good claim under an insurance policy that restricted recovery to persons with a total disability. In such cases, juries were "not required to depend upon arbitrarily selected 'symptoms, phases or manifestations' of the disease as criteria for determining the ultimate question of fact upon which the claim depends." *Durham*, 214 F.2d at 875. Although the free will claim would presumably not arise in instances of claimed total physical disability, it would arise where mental disability was at issue; there total disability because of mental disease required evidence of the plaintiff's inability to reason normally or to control his or her behavior. It might be supposed that the analogy to the jury's familiar line-drawing in civil suits regarding recovery under insurance policies might have sufficed for Bazelon's purposes in defending the *Durham* rule. Further advertence to the free will issue might thus have been avoided entirely. Why, then, the mention of free will? The issue in *Durham* was not simply presence or absence of total disability, but presence or absence of *criminal* responsibility. The notion that a person normally possessed the capacity to control his behavior in the insurance-recovery context could be expected to survive the claim that ultimately all behavior is determined; a concept of criminal responsibility premised on blameworthiness and deserved punishment (and possibly resulting in loss of life or liberty), however, might not. However far Bazelon personally subscribed to this blame-and-punishment-based view of criminal responsibility, he treated it as a central commitment of the criminal law. He must have recognized therefore that his analogy to insurance cases begged

Bazelon would defend the law's traditional response to questions about human freedom by following *Holloway*'s general propositions about free will ("moral responsibility" was Arnold's euphemism) and its related proposition about the role of the jury. In doing so, however, he turned Arnold's decision partway on its head. Bazelon would not have denied Arnold's observation that the ordinary man typically believes that reason overrides emotion and instinct, whereas science often treats reason as a post hoc "rationalization." Bazelon believed, however, that unconstrained psychiatric testimony would put conventional beliefs to an important (more scientific) test, leading to, as he later put it, "more sophisticated concepts of free will."[22] Again, in his later comments on *Durham*, Bazelon maintained that a scientifically informed criminal law beneficially tested society's deepest beliefs.[23] There was in this an inherent conclusion that society was (contrary to Arnold's view) up to the task, and that the task would not in itself be debilitating or corrosive of society's own self-protection. Law would not easily give way to the ordinary man's ordinary beliefs, but would ask the ordinary man whether he was sure he did not want to modify his ordinary beliefs in a given instance. Insofar as the ordinary man, having heard all that science could say, resolved that his ordinary view was right, there the line between guilt and innocence would – and should – be drawn.

Durham voiced a commitment to free will as a social belief – following *Holloway*, Bazelon referred to "inherited ideas of moral responsibility." We cannot say what Bazelon himself thought about the idea of free will. He might have accepted it as representing, under limited conditions, an actual truth, although one that society conventionally applied far too broadly. Or, like Hall, he might have seen free will as representing a "truth" not verifiable by science but obvious to the reasoning being, although again a concept that, in criminal law, required much greater testing and much more confined application. He might, in either case, have been personally deeply skeptical about resting "blame" on free will in the context of criminal responsibility, believing instead that the important matter was the determination of the best means to rehabilitate a person who manifested serious antisocial behavior. Whatever his personal beliefs, Bazelon recognized the existing criminal law's fundamental commitment to "inherited ideas of moral responsibility" and attempted to fashion a result that he thought best dignified that commitment.

crucial questions about conventional understandings of human behavior, and of course he well knew that psychiatrists (among others) had made those questions central to the debate over the insanity defense and over criminal responsibility more generally.

[22] David L. Bazelon, "The Morality of the Criminal Law," *Southern California Law Review*, vol. 49 (1976): 385–405, 391.

[23] Bazelon reflected on *Durham* at many points in his later work. Most important, in addition to "Morality of the Criminal Law," see David L. Bazelon, "The Concept of Responsibility," *Georgetown Law Journal*, vol. 53 (1964): 5–18; David L. Bazelon, "The Dilemma of Criminal Responsibility," *Kentucky Law Journal*, vol. 72 (1983): 263–277.

In *Durham*, he wrote in terms of social beliefs and of juries as representing those beliefs; he did not direct his attention to free will as truth or as something in fact experienced by the individual. Society – social practices – remained something of a "system" that was, as it were, truly out there, as it had typically been for jurists in the positivist tradition. Whereas Robert Knight, the scientist, Walter Moberly, the ethicist, and Wilber Katz, the legal academic, had gone inside the individual mind – had trained their light on the person who held and sought to justify belief in human freedom – Bazelon, like Arnold, looked to the patterns of thought in society at large.

Bazelon can best be read, I believe, as testing the rule of criminal responsibility as a moral-legal rule, not because free will definitely did not exist, but because the law was committed to it as a moral tradition despite the law's necessary agnosticism either about the truth of its actual existence or, if it actually existed, the bounds it existed within. Although he followed Arnold in addressing the social and moral beliefs that underlay the law's standard presumption, he differed greatly with Arnold's conclusion about how law and science ought to be situated in relation to each other. If he followed Arnold in imagining that the law stood for the proposition that a person might be subject to blame and punishment on the basis of social belief about human behavior, rather than on the basis of proof that the defendant could in fact have done other than he had done, Bazelon wanted to hem in this social belief – to test it as much as possible on the basis of scientific testimony. But ultimately, I speculate, *Durham* conceded that the guilty were defined by social belief that lay beyond the domain of scientific verification – although, presumably, in accordance with a belief that the guilty themselves shared as a general matter. On this view, Bazelon's essentially moral-legal rule of responsibility was an "as-if" rule – again not an entirely new idea, but one that legal scholars confronted more self-consciously in the century's middle years as free will ceased being considered merely a holdover belief that must temporarily be accommodated, and came to be accepted as central to the true (and appropriate) meaning of criminal responsibility.

Whatever Bazelon precisely considered as of 1954, he certainly did not suppose that lay jurors themselves would adopt an essentially philosophical perspective and, understanding free will as possibly no more than a beneficial fiction, then proceed self-consciously to apply that perspective to defendants in criminal cases. One cannot be certain that Bazelon understood that the criminal law instantiated and, in a certain sense, depended upon the disjunction between prevailing academic and social understandings of free will. He envisioned that juries would apply a conventional – but (he hoped) evolving – understanding of human behavior. Might he also have deduced from contemporary trends that, in place of the determinism of much early Progressive treatmentist thought, there was a new legal academic appreciation of the philosophical aspiration embedded in the idea of free will? If so, perhaps his opinion can be seen as an attempt of its own day to mediate between Progressive and post-Progressive visions of the relationship between conventional morality and a positivist-leaning rule of law. In this context, a moral-legal rule of criminal responsibility understood law neither from within the typical juror's understanding (as legal theorists imagined that understanding) nor in terms of the pristine analysis of the legal academic, but from the perspective of the disjunction itself: it gave place to a literal social belief in free will alongside an academic understanding of the idea of free will. And thus would have emerged the paradox that the very disjunction between conventional morality and the rule of law, which in the 1920s and 1930s threatened the theoretical viability of criminal jurisprudence, became by the 1950s a component essential to defining criminal responsibility. Juries would continue to attach blame where there had been free will, as they understood that concept. Outside that verge, the rule of law still held without a debilitating rupture between lay and scholarly perspectives on free will. Bazelon's broader, albeit less predictable (and ultimately unsuccessful), legal insanity formulation would have been all the more a rule of law for its goal of putting social intuitions regarding free will to the greatest possible test. Bazelon, on this reading, mirrored several academic conceptions of the day and optimistically brought them together: commonplace empirical observation about conventional understandings, a mainstream psychiatric perspective, and humane aspirations for a mixed notion of "as-if" individual, and true social, responsibility. For him, lines that legal academics had often seen as parallel met in relatively easy, if not entirely untroubled, overlapping coexistence. Bazelon's emphasis on the substance of free will, rather than on the idea of free will mainly as a handmaiden of political liberty, thus also distinguished *Durham* as a decision borne on midcentury currents that validated the consciousness of freedom, in both legal and political spheres. *Durham*'s importance lies in the affirmation of, as well as the search for, a moral-legal idea of responsibility; these aspects of the decision are arguably more significant than the specificities of its compromising solution to the insanity defense. For this reason, the focus here is not on *Durham* as a case precedent, but on the responses it inspired.

DIVERGENCE AND CONVERGENCE

Although overturned in 1972 – when the D.C. Circuit substituted the American Law Institute (or ALI) legal insanity test for Bazelon's by then much disparaged (and partly altered) "product" test[24] – *Durham* was the catalyst for an outpouring of comments, analyses, and empirical studies

---

[24] *United States v. Brawner*, 471 F.2d 969 (D.C. Cir. 1972). On the evolution of D. C. Circuit case law after *Durham* through *Brawner*, see Maeder, *Crime and Madness*, 87–97; Michele Cotton, "A Foolish Consistency: Keeping Determinism Out of the Criminal Law," *Boston University Public Interest Law Journal*, vol. 15 (2005): 1–48, 5–9.

on Bazelon's opinion as well as on prosecutorial decisions, jury verdicts, and judicial charges influenced by it. Most contemporary commentators – pro or con – directed their attention to the "product" test and its concomitant expansion of the legitimate domain of psychiatric testimony.[25] Some contemporaries, however, adverted to Bazelon's approach to the search for a moral-legal idea of responsibility; some welcomed it, some did not. Indeed, the D.C. Circuit itself was far from unanimous regarding the test and its ramifications. Bazelon's conservative antagonist, then Judge Warren Burger, led scathing disapproval of the product test on grounds both practical and theoretical. On the practical side, Burger urged that even the psychiatric community had not established meaningful, agreed-upon definitions of "mental disease" or "mental defect." The term "product," moreover, was "not used in relation to ordinary matters or subjects familiar to laymen or indeed even to judges," but "rather in a quasi-medical sense of being the causal link between the 'disease' and the criminal act charged." Yet there was no agreement concerning how, exactly, a crime may be *caused* by a mental disease; indeed, in this context, "product" was a "spurious term, neither wholly medical nor wholly legal but partaking of both" that simply invited conclusory testimony from competing experts.[26] More theoretically, Burger argued that, despite its protestations to the contrary, Bazelon's *Durham* opinion effectively eliminated jury consideration of the critical issue: "free will" or "man's capacity to make choices in regulating conduct." This was a dire mistake, for,

---

[25] See, e.g., "Symposium on Criminal Responsibility," *Kansas Law Review*, vol. 4 (1956): 350–95, a conference at the University of Kansas (December 1955) "sponsored by the Schools of Law and Medicine in cooperation with the Menninger Foundation" and heavily dominated by medical professionals; "Mental Responsibility," *Kentucky Law Journal*, vol. 45 (1956): 213–90, a series of articles by scholars in a variety of fields, including law (Roy Moreland, Professor of Law at the University of Kentucky and a critic of *Durham*); "Criminal Responsibility and Mental Disease," *Tennessee Law Review*, vol. 26 (1959): 221–46, a panel presentation at the Nineteenth Annual Law Institute of the University of Tennessee College of Law and the Knoxville Bar Association (October 1958), which featured an address by the prominent psychiatrist Philip Q. Roche – whose book, *The Criminal Mind* (New York: Farrar, Straus and Cudahy, 1958), had just won the Isaac Ray Award and who was supportive of *Durham* for its (as he saw it) limiting the role of medical experts to strictly medical, not legal, facts – followed by a vigorous response from several practicing lawyers.

These and many other works of the period provide a gold mine for historians who seek a fully interdisciplinary perspective on criminal responsibility in the 1950s. I have focused mainly on legal academics rather than on medical, behavioral, or social scientists, humanists (including writers of fiction) or, for that matter, on members of the bar. The far fuller story that the abundant writings of the day allow will, no doubt, throw the legal academic world into interesting relief; whether it will require substantial revisions of that world's story – the one I tell – remains to be seen.

[26] *Blocker v. United States*, 288 F.2d 853 (D.C. Cir. 1961) (Burger, J., concurring in result), 859–63.

while philosophers, theologians, scientists and lawyers have debated for centuries whether such a thing as "free will" really exists, society and the law have no choice in the matter. We must proceed, until a firm alternative is available, on the scientifically unprovable assumption that human beings make choices in the regulation of their conduct.[27]

University of Chicago law professor Harry Kalven appears not to have similarly concluded that *Durham*, in effect, had read free will – or, at least, genuinely *blameworthy* will – out of the law. In introducing a symposium on *Durham* published in the *Chicago Law Review*, Kalven more optimistically considered Bazelon's "careful and psychologically literate opinion," which, he said, "sparks many reflections about the ends of the criminal law, about the relationship today of law and psychiatry, about our dependence upon the jury to solve our most difficult questions." Kalven emphasized that "the decision fully retains the moral context of the criminal law," by which he clearly meant more than the matter of political liberty. For Bazelon, Kalven stated, "talks in terms of whom we can properly blame." He added:

It is here that I would find the source of much of the significance, perplexity and fascination of the issue of criminal insanity. For it would appear that we cannot in handling the marginally insane criminal readily avoid the profound and pervasive educating impact of the law. In deciding publicly whether Monte Durham goes to jail or goes to a mental hospital the legal system touches deeply our sense of where the blameworthy, and the praiseworthy begins and ends in our daily life.[28]

---

[27] *Blocker*, 288 F.2d at 865. Burger would continue in his opinions to criticize the Court's formulation of the *Durham* rule until his appointment as Chief Justice of the Supreme Court in 1969, three years before the D.C. Circuit would overturn *Durham* in *Brawner*. He also spoke widely about the history and current manifestations of the insanity defense. The gist of his views on the free will aspect of criminal responsibility was well conveyed in a 1964 article drawing on a string of his recent lectures to members of both the legal and the medical communities:

> For centuries all law has rested on and grown out of certain basic moral and ethical standards which are part of the fabric of Western civilization. But there are some very articulate spokesmen for psychiatry who insist they cannot function in the area of morals, ethics, and free will, and some state flatly that these factors have nothing to do with man's responsibility for his actions.... [E]ssentially they share a common, if unspoken, acceptance of determinism as the dominant force in human behavior. This view tends to ignore the fact that the very rules which may allow for exculpation of the mentally deranged delinquent are rooted in the Judeo-Christian concepts of morality and the recognition that Man has a will and is capable of making choices. Thus they overlook that it is this collective moral yardstick which may set the defendant free! (Warren E. Burger, "Psychiatrists, Lawyers, and the Courts," *Federal Probation*, vol. 28, no. 2 (1964): 3–10, 8)

[28] Harry Kalven, "Introduction" to "Insanity and the Criminal Law – A Critique of *Durham v. United States*," *University of Chicago Law Review*, vol. 22 (1955): 317–19, 318 (this symposium on *Durham*, composed of articles from several commentators, is referred to hereafter as "Insanity and the Criminal Law").

Neither a holistic positivist nor a strict utilitarian view met the demands of the quest for such beginnings and endings, at least not for many legal academics in the 1950s.

Such insistence on the value of blameworthiness was not shared by Judge Learned Hand, who declined to contribute to the symposium except by way of a letter of refusal. Hand characterized the disjunction between the rule of law and conventional morality in the bleak and resigned terms of the preceding decades. Bazelon's opinion was "perhaps ... all that can be said," but "it did not seem to [Hand] to give us any guidance that perceptibly would help."

> The truth appears to me to be that the question goes to the heart of whatever we choose to make our purpose in criminal punishment. It is only indirectly, or at second hand, a psychiatric question. My own ideas, insofar as I have any, are that there are two controlling factors to consider. One is how far imprisonment is effective as deterrent.... The other factor is that most people have a feeling that "justice" requires a law breaker to suffer, just as they think that sin should entail suffering in the sinner. Personally, I do not share that feeling, which is a vestige, I believe, of very ancient primitive and irrational beliefs and emotions. However, it would be unwise, and incidentally impracticable to disregard it as a constituent element: it is extremely strong in most people.[29]

Judge Hand's closing admonition – with its implied negative view of an all-too-necessary accommodation of the criminal trial jury's traditional role, as opposed to Bazelon's, Burger's, and Kalven's much more positive views of that role – struck a chord to which even Herbert Wechsler was just then proving responsive in his coordination of the efforts to produce a model penal code. In an indirect way, that admonition also took residence within – or at the periphery of – both the spirit of positivist accommodationism and the idea of a moral-legal, as opposed to a scientific, rule of criminal responsibility. Among some supporters and opponents alike, the *Durham* decision tended to underwrite the search for such an idea – in effect to convert Hand's terms of surrender into one or another more positive new demarche. Bazelon's invocation of an essentially moral-legal concept of free will, and his positioning of that concept in relation both to psychiatric perspectives and to real-world practices of blame and punishment, brought legal-academic discussion that much closer to the problem of free will in the criminal law, as Kalven's brief comment bore witness.[30]

---

[29] Kalven, "Introduction," 319 (letter from Hand quoted in editors' note).

[30] In an insightful article, Louis Seidman analyzes several midcentury attempts, including that of Bazelon, to transcend the disjunction between the criminal law's "formal" or traditional bases – including that of free will – and "realist" views rooted in determinism. Louis Michael Seidman, "Points of Intersection: Discontinuities at the Junction of Criminal Law and the Regulatory State," *Journal of Contemporary Legal Issues*, vol. 7 (1996): 97–163. Seidman generally concludes that such attempts unavoidably have the effect of reaffirming traditional views, for the criminal law can never become realist; if it did, "it would no longer be the

I have selected for more in-depth consideration a few responses to *Durham* that display the mid-1950s diversity of perspectives on criminal responsibility that directly opposed, sustained, or guardedly diffused the positivism of earlier years. Most legal academics continued to embrace a penology based upon some mix of deterrence and rehabilitation; that is, for most scholars (Hall excepted) consequentialist ideas continued to play a dominant or exclusive role. The distinctive character of the immediate post-*Durham* years consisted in the renewed vigor of academic attempts to reduce or constructively manipulate the disjunction between themselves and a lay public. The interrelated means at their disposal were twofold: the recrudescence of freedom even in positivist formulations of human behavior and the jury's garnering of greater respect among legal scholars. Whether or not the jury was educable, its responses were worthy of due consideration, as the very question of freedom and responsibility before the law was showing.

All in all, the legal-academic writings of the 1950s exhibit a number of subtle developments even while often remaining of a piece with the Progressive inheritance. They exhibit a new and different personality – or set of personalities – if one pays attention to the individual voices. It is the voices that count, if one is to understand not merely the trajectory of cultural "change," but the individual questioning and searching behind the broadly written narrative.

The Limits of Utilitarian Compromise: Herbert Wechsler and the Model Penal Code

Even as Bazelon was transforming the legal insanity defense in Washington, DC, the American Law Institute committee charged with the task of drafting a model penal code was hard at work. The result of their efforts – which, most notably, codified the elements of criminal offenses and formalized the notion of mens rea – would itself spur decades of scholarship and be called

criminal law," which "*is* that portion of our legal system defined by the practice of blaming" (160). *Durham,* regardless of its progressive inspiration, was no exception. Any test for insanity "posits some baseline, natural condition which is somehow distorted by a departure from normality, thereby ignoring the realist insight that no such 'natural' condition exists because *all* conduct is socially located and determined." At base, "Judge Bazelon's quarrel with *M'Naghten* was not that the distinction between the blameworthy and blameless was incoherent, but that the test slotted defendants into the wrong categories" (117–18). Seidman thus casts *Durham* as a realist failure (115). However that may be, my own interest has been to explore the full range of Bazelon's motivations, which appear aimed not just at a more scientifically enlightened law but, indeed, at what Bazelon conceived of as a necessary and justifiable compromise between science and the practice of blaming.

Seidman's article casts a wide net, covering many issues that I pass by, in part because he has already done them justice. My own approach gives fuller play to the *longue durée* and especially to the ambiguities long embedded in criminal jurisprudence (relative to the free will/determinism issue) – and to a less monolithic view of the "realists."

"the most consequential criminal law code in the history of Anglo-American law."[31] The code's distaste for strict liability and attention to criminal intent – categorized as performing a prohibited act purposely, knowingly, recklessly, or negligently – sharpened the legal conversation concerning culpable states of mind and avoided so-called moralistic notions of willfulness, maliciousness, and wantonness. My narrow focus here is on one of the MPC's central sections regarding criminal responsibility – and, in particular, on Herbert Wechsler's approach to the issue as the Chief Reporter for the MPC project.[32] Illustrating Wechsler's consequentialist bent alongside his commitment to political liberty, the MPC's formulation of the insanity defense (albeit not so called) melded theoretical and practical concerns in terms that would be, until events of the early 1980s, widely adopted.

A tentative draft of the section on "Responsibility" was issued in 1955. Section 4.01 of "Responsibility," covering "Mental Disease or Defect Excluding Responsibility," contained a main formulation and two alternative ones. The main formulation, ultimately adopted by the Council of the Institute (1962), combined a version of the cognitive test with something akin to the irresistible impulse test:

(1) A person is not responsible for criminal conduct if at the time of such conduct as a result of mental disease or defect he lacks substantial capacity either to appreciate the criminality of his conduct or to conform his conduct to the requirements of the law.

It further stated:

(2) The terms "mental disease or defect" do not include an abnormality manifested only by repeated criminal or otherwise anti-social conduct.[33]

---

[31] Sanford H. Kadish, "Fifty Years of Criminal Law: An Opinionated Review," *California Law Review*, vol. 87 (1999): 943–82, 948.
[32] For some recent work on the aims and innovations of the MPC more generally, see, e.g., Gerald Leonard, "Towards a Legal History of American Criminal Theory: Culture and Doctrine from Blackstone to the Model Penal Code," *Buffalo Criminal Law Review*, vol. 6 (2003): 691–832, 803–16; Seidman, "Points of Intersection," 107–15; Paul H. Robinson and Markus D. Dubber, "The American Model Penal Code: A Brief Overview," *New Criminal Law Review*, vol. 10 (2007): 319–41; Kadish, "Fifty Years of Criminal Law," 947–53. For a critique of the MPC as the embodiment of a larger "cult of positivism and neutral principles," see V. F. Nourse, "Hearts and Minds: Understanding the New Culpability," *Buffalo Criminal Law Review*, vol. 6 (2002): 361–88 (quoted material from 385). As is particularly germane to my inquiry, Nourse suggests that the mixed aims underlying the MPC – particularly its attempt to redefine crime and mens rea in what she views as mechanistic, behavioral, and ultimately *inhuman*, rather than normative, terms – did not clarify the law but obscured its unavoidable normative implications. I discuss related elements of Nourse's scholarship at length in Chapter 9.
[33] *Model Penal Code: Tentative Draft No. 4* (Philadelphia: American Law Institute, 1955), 27 (hereafter *Tentative Draft*). As Abraham Goldstein notes, the ALI "substitutes 'appreciate' for

The *Comment* on the tentative draft, no doubt written mainly by Wechsler, defended this essential use of the *M'Naghten* test in terms that stressed deterrence and, so far as possible, finessed the free will issue; the *Comment* asserted that the test for legal responsibility did not attempt to define insanity, but instead outlined the "cases in which reason can not operate and in which it is totally impossible for individuals to be deterred." And further: "Absent these minimal elements of rationality, condemnation and punishment are obviously both unjust and futile." Again, in terms Wechsler had long since made familiar: "the category defined by the rule is so extreme that to the ordinary man the exculpations of the persons it encompasses bespeaks no weakness in the law. He does not identify such persons with himself; they are a world apart." This was also the rationale used by those jurisdictions that employed the irresistible impulse test, the *Comment* stated. The draft opted for an explicit formulation regarding impairment of volitional capacity: "lacks substantial capacity ... to conform his conduct." This language acknowledged "the criticism of the 'irresistible impulse' formulation as inept in so far as it may be impliedly restricted to sudden, spontaneous acts as distinguished from insane propulsions that are accompanied by brooding or reflection."[34] In short, it addressed the problem of definition that had in large measure led Bazelon to alter the process of determination in legal insanity cases.

The debate about alternatives to paragraph (1) of section 4.01 that preceded the section's adoption, however, acknowledged the persisting difficulty of prescriptively pinning down both the circumstances under which free will is sufficiently compromised that the actor should be alleviated from legal responsibility and the process or decision maker to which the task should be delegated. Of the two proposed alternatives to paragraph (1), Wechsler and "a minority of the Council" favored alternative (a):

> (a) A person is not responsible for criminal conduct if at the time of such conduct as a result of mental disease or defect his *capacity* either *to appreciate the criminality of his conduct* or *to conform his conduct to the requirements of the law is so substantially impaired that he cannot justly be held responsible.*

Alternative (b) provided:

> (b) A person is not responsible for criminal conduct if at the time of such conduct as a result of mental disease or defect he *lacks substantial capacity to appreciate the criminality of his conduct* or *is in such state*

'know,' thereby indicating a preference for the view that a sane offender must be emotionally as well as intellectually aware of the significance of his conduct." Abraham S. Goldstein, *The Insanity Defense* (New Haven, CT: Yale University Press, 1967), 87.

[34] *Comment* to *Tentative Draft*, 156–57 (hereafter *Comment*).

> *that the prospect of conviction and punishment cannot constitute a significant restraining influence upon him.*[35]

Although the two alternatives were "to some extent, of course ... the same inquiries ... the latter asks a narrower and harder question, involving the assessment of capacity to respond to a single influence, the threat of punishment." Wechsler yielded to the psychiatrists by foregoing alternative (b), which required a judgment not simply on mental state, but a predicative assessment of deterrability before the prospect of punishment; he surrendered theoretical purism where it stymied collaboration between legal and medical experts, noting in the *Comment* that "in so far as non-deterrability is the determination that is sought, it must be reached by probing general capacity to conform to the requirements of the law."[36]

The disagreements over the language of paragraph (1) and alternative (a) hinged on a quantitative and a qualitative distinction, respectively, each with implications for a legal conception of responsibility. Regarding the quantitative issue, the language of paragraph (1) and of alternative (a) coincided. Both depended on the word "substantial": respectively, the accused must "lack substantial capacity" to appreciate the criminality of his conduct or to conform his conduct to the requirements of the law, or this capacity must be "so substantially impaired" that he cannot justly be held responsible. The quantitative shift away from the *M'Naghten* and irresistible impulse tests' demands that impairment be complete was intentional. The *Comment* stated: "The extremity of these conceptions is, we think, the point that poses largest difficulty to psychiatrists when called upon to aid in their administration."[37] "Substantial," a highly relative term, of course raised the problem of ambiguity. It also, however, rested the determination of responsibility with the law conceived of as a moral authority, asking *not* at what point did the individual cross over into the certifiably and irremediably insane, *but* at what point did the individual cease to be a responsibility-bearing human being.

Regarding the qualitative distinction, paragraph (1) and alternative (a) diverged. Here was a discrepancy in wording – between "capacity" and "impairment." Paragraph (1) – "lacks substantial capacity" – was a negative formulation of responsibility: the administration of justice does not apply where capacity is lacking. It required, first, evidence for that lack, followed by a decision, based on the facts, about whether traditional court justice pertained. Alternative (a) – "capacity to appreciate the criminality of his conduct or to conform his conduct to the requirements of the law is so substantially impaired" – was the positive obverse. Capacity was a given; it was

---

[35] *Tentative Draft*, 27 (emphasis added).
[36] *Comment*, 158.
[37] *Comment*, 158.

never expressly absent. There were, however, cases in which obstruction to the exercise of that capacity to bear responsibility outweighed its essential primacy.

Paragraph (1), therefore, put before the jury the determination of fact; alternative (a), the determination of justice. According to the *Comment*, Wechsler and others favored the alternative because they believed it would lead to a more precise (i.e., less generous to the defendant) application of the law:

> The proponents of the alternative contend that since the jury normally will feel that it is only just to exculpate if the disorder was extreme, that otherwise conviction is demanded, it is safer to invoke the jury's sense of justice than to rest entirely on the single word "substantial," imputing no specific measure of degree. The issue is an important one and it is submitted for consideration by the Institute.[38]

This attempted "utilitarian" compromise, in lieu of the more explicitly utilitarian alternative (b), perhaps ironically gave signal importance to the jury and, like Bazelon's decision, facilitated coordination of medical testimony, due process, and social justice. Although, whereas *Durham* left the terms of engagement to be set in the courtroom as defined by the arguments and broadly evaluated by the jury, Wechsler proposed to establish narrower terms prior to a case coming to court, insuring more effectively the undeflected aim of the law. Nevertheless, alternative (a) too foundered, this time from the juristic side.

The drafters of the MPC did not reserve their criticism solely for the predominating *M'Naghten* and irresistible impulse tests. Directing their attention to the British Royal Commission, they concluded that its recommendation – to have the jury decide if mental disease afflicted a defendant "to such a degree that he ought not to be held responsible"[39] – failed because it did not "focus on the *consequences* of disease or defect." That is, it made the medical factor of disease determinant, rather than the *self*, willing or unwilling. *Durham*'s open-ended "product" language hardly compensated.[40] The drafters of the MPC, in contrast, insisted upon language that addressed the connection between a mental disease and its consequences. That imperative motivated paragraph (2), which dealt with the mere psychopath. To look at consequences was also to focus on causes; the interest of the law was not in symptoms as they led back to mental disease, but in those springs of action

---

[38] *Comment*, 159.

[39] Royal Commission *Report*, 276.

[40] The ALI drafting committee enlisted the aid of three leading psychiatrists, all of whom favored adoption of the *Durham* rule, as they subsequently reported: Lawrence Z. Freedman, Winfred Overholser, and Manfred Guttmacher, "Mental Disease or Defect Excluding Responsibility – A Psychiatric View of the American Law Institute Model Penal Code Proposal," *American Journal of Psychiatry*, vol. 118 (1961): 32–34. See Herbert Wechsler, "On Culpability and Crime: The Treatment of Mens Rea in the Model Penal Code," *Annals of the American Academy of Political and Social Science*, vol. 339 (1962): 24–41, 38.

which evinced – to use the language of the MPC – either the capacity to conform to the law or the substantial lack of such.[41] The psychopath might be one who took to obsessive extremes behavior not inimical to the sane person, and to whom therefore paragraph (1) did not apply. But behavior symptomatic of "repeated criminal or otherwise anti-social conduct," according to paragraph (2), did not provide sufficient reason for suspending the rules and guidelines of legal causation.[42]

For Wechsler, the MPC's definition of responsibility under the criminal law was several degrees of separation from a utilitarian resolution of theoretical integrity. He had relaxed his grasp on alternative (b), then (a). Those jettisoned, the revised *M'Naghten* language at least still presented the virtue of a sentiment of certitude in identifying the undeterrable. Thus he remained an accomplice in the MPC formulation of "Responsibility," which (to his mind) had put force of law first by making proof of immunity to the threat of law, over proof of disease, primary for the insanity defense. He had compromised, yet the less-than-optimal code could still conceivably be means to a utilitarian end. In the process, he had also struck a certain truce with the lay jury. For his part, Wechsler deemed free will virtually a moot point for the law. The jury would no doubt (and unfortunately) translate "capacity ... to ... conform" into possession of free will, and it might interpret "substantial" in such a way that effective recourse to free will was precluded even where deterrability persisted. But so long as the priority was *legal causation*, the intermixture of free-will-based language, as understood by a jury, did not overly threaten the utilitarian intent of the law to deter.

Wechsler had compromised but he had not wavered. Positivist claims for human behavior exercised a far more deleterious drag on the law than notions of free will. Thus in his contribution to the *Chicago Law Review* "Symposium" on Bazelon's decision, Wechsler showed considerable frustration. He commented, deridingly, that the decision would "undoubtedly be hailed in many quarters as a welcome if belated step in the accommodation of the penal law to modern psychiatric knowledge, a milestone in the path toward a more scientific legal process." His confidence "with respect to both result and rationale" was minimal.[43] Significantly, *Durham* neglected

---

[41] *Comment*, 160. On this score, the drafters of the MPC and the members of the British Royal Commission were in accord: psychopathy was not synonymous with disease.

[42] This reading of psychopathy did not endear itself to the ALI psychiatrists who, regardless of whether the classification of disease extended so far, deemed the psychopath a worthy recipient of psychiatric treatment. *Durham* in this regard grated less harshly: they could better swallow a psychiatrically informed *legal* test than a legal presumption about where responsibility ended and their diagnostic assessments began. See *Comment*, 158–59 and Appendix B: Manfred S. Guttmacher, "Principal Difficulties with the Present Criteria of Responsibility and Possible Alternatives," 170–81. Cf. Cotton's perspective on the MPC's exclusion of psychopathy from its definition of insanity in "Foolish Consistency," 11–14.

[43] Herbert Wechsler, "The Criteria of Criminal Responsibility," in "Insanity and the Criminal Law," 367–76, 368.

the causal standard that the jury would have to apply, with the result that it would not be wrong for jurors to insist that "the test of 'a causal relationship' is satisfied on evidence of but-for cause alone." Wechsler expected Bazelon's answer to this objection would be that "the jury is to give the importance to causal relationships that satisfies its sense of justice in relation to a criminal conviction," as was suggested by Bazelon's well-known claim that juries "'will continue to make moral judgments,'" albeit while "'guided by wider horizons of knowledge concerning mental life.'"[44] Were one to leave the matter to "the jury's sense of justice," Wechsler retorted, better "to submit the question whether the capacity of the accused to control his conduct in accordance with the law was impaired so greatly that he cannot justly be held criminally responsible." This test – consistent with Wechsler's preferred alternative (a) to the test ultimately adopted by the drafters of the MPC – would meet the spirit of *Durham* and make it "perfectly explicit" that the "complete impairment" standard had been sacrificed in favor of impairment that was "less than total," the "precise degree demanded" being "governed by the [jury's] sense of justice." A broadly "just" interpretation of capacity to control one's conduct offered safer ground than a broad reading of causation. Wechsler ended his response to *Durham* by reiterating his deterrence-based view and then commenting: "This, to be sure, is not poetic justice. It is public justice, which in the interest of the common good prescribes a standard all must strive to satisfy who can, those whose nature or nurture leads them to conform with difficulty no less than those who find compliance easy." This stark landscape of the law – at the guilt-assessment stage – stood in contrast to the sentencing process, when there would be a place, Wechsler noted, for "finer distinctions," should they be "in order."[45] That is: bifurcation and treatmentism – controlled, of course, by the dominant goal of deterrence.

Wechsler considered two possible responses to his own approach. Some viewed the "condemnatory-punitive aspect of criminal conviction as unjust and irrational in any case," a stance that was "rooted in a kind of psychiatric crypto-ethics not uncommon in our culture."[46] Wechsler affirmed Moberly's invocation of the "'cruel kindness'" of excusing "'people who labor under handicaps.'"[47] He also granted that Bazelon had in fact held his own against the extreme positivist distortion of justice. The more relevant objection was that the distinction between "total impairment" and impairment of (only) "a very high degree" (Wechsler's gloss on "substantially impaired") was impractical, intrinsically difficult, or downright conjectural, and likely to

---

[44] Wechsler, "Criteria," 371 (quoting *Durham*, 214 F.2d at 876).
[45] Wechsler, "Criteria," 372–75.
[46] Wechsler, "Criteria," 375.
[47] Wechsler, "Criteria," 375 n. 22 (quoting Sir Walter Hamilton Moberly, *Responsibility* [London: Oxford University Press, 1951], 20).

lead to nullification of the law. "This," Wechsler conceded, "was an argument of weight." Wechsler's solution was that psychiatrists should "cast their opinions as to impairment of capacity in terms of judgments of degree," and the jury should be "admonished ... that only a very high degree of incapacity warrants finding irresponsibility," which would "exclude undifferentiated psychopaths who in the present state of psychiatric knowledge must ... be viewed as problems to be dealt with by conviction and correction."[48]

Wechsler's approach to utilitarianism placed a restraint upon the state by insisting that only criminal intent justified legal condemnation. Without this legal principle, Wechsler believed, the law would work an injustice. Indeed, as though reaching for an independent moral principle that lay outside of utility, he went so far as to assert: "Criminal law imports a condemnation, the gravest we permit ourselves to make. To condemn when fault is absent is barbaric. It is the badge of tyranny, the plainest illustration of injustice." Here, mainly with respect to strict liability, Wechsler addressed principles of culpability that seem to transcend utility and to presage the much more fully worked out ideas of Herbert Hart, who stressed the individual's expectations and sense of security. In developing his thought in terms consistent both with general principles of justice and the demands of deterrence theory, Wechsler ventured that we are "very properly" reluctant to assign criminality "merely because the actor should have known of its offensive quality." We want to be certain that the actor "really must have known."[49] If, by

[48] Wechsler, "Criteria," 375–76. Wechsler acknowledged that some jurisdictions disallowed impairment of capacity as grounds for mitigation on capital conviction. These doctrines, which limited the degree to which the sentencing process might compensate for the powerful presumption of human autonomy at the trial stage, made the case for "something less than total incapacity" persuasive. "But," Wechsler concluded, "whether the retention of the strict criteria, coupled with admission of the psychiatric evidence in mitigation, might yield a better result – puts for me a most perplexing question."

[49] Herbert Wechsler, "A Thoughtful Code of Substantive Law," *JCLC*, vol. 45 (1955): 524–30, 528–29. It is not clear precisely how Wechsler conceived of the relationship between justice and utility. At points, his work can be read to imply that justice to the individual is a principle of independent significance. In 1962, for example, in discussing the voluntary act requirement – where he focused almost exclusively on sheer deterrability – at one point, he introduced a notion of "personal security" in the interest of both society at large *and* individual actors, stating: "It cannot be expected that involuntary movement will be calculably influenced by threatened condemnation ... Moreover, the sense of personal security, so vital to both individuals and group tranquility, would be short lived in a society where such movement or inactivity could lead to formal social condemnation" ("On Culpability and Crime," 27). And similarly, in later interviews conducted between 1978 and 1982, he stated:

> I have always been exceedingly utilitarian in my views and approaches; but everybody knows that a social order that doesn't provide adequate protection for personal dignity and autonomy and bodily integrity is a defective social order. You don't have to count anything up in order to know that, nor do you need any sociological expertise or psychological expertise. Or any other kind of expertise. (Norman Silber and Geoffrey Miller, "Toward 'Neutral Principles' in the Law:

virtue of mental disease or defect, the actor could not have known either what he was doing or that it was wrong ("its offensive quality"), he was not responsible (he had, I infer, not truly been subject to the threat of the law). Moreover, Wechsler had come increasingly to acquiesce in the "so-called irresistible impulse test," where the "defendant is rendered incapable of self-control," although, as his post-*Durham* writings make clear, by this he meant near-total impairment of the capacity for self-control.[50]

More central to our current purposes, Wechsler's modest concessions regarding the proposed MPC's responsibility provisions were consistent with the reluctant accommodationist perspective he signaled on the eve of the code-drafting process. From the outset of that process he had recognized the practical impossibility of a purely deterrence-based approach – or perhaps he had recognized that the demand for "social justice" would itself have to be figured into the utilitarian calculus, with all that implied about the necessary impurity of the utilitarian project in the realm of actual practice. Never given to equivocation, he frankly stated: "Civilized social thought regards the penal law as the ultimate weapon for diminishing the incidence of major injuries to individuals and institutions, *with only such concessions to retaliatory passions as are practically necessary for a system to survive.*"[51] Wechsler's near-absolutism regarding deterrability thus greatly influenced the MPC, but did not prevent his endorsing MPC language that could be read as consistent with traditional notions of responsibility. The MPC would inevitably remain open to criticism from those who opposed such notions altogether, as well as from those who so strongly supported such ideas that the MPC's inexplicit commitment to them was a reverse anathema. Nonetheless, Wechsler had mediated what might have been thought unresolvable differences among retributivists, positivists, and utilitarians. From the perspective of the utilitarian, the "capacity to conform" wording could be read one way; from the perspective of the extreme positivist (the least satisfied of the three), it could be read from quite another against the background of expert testimony more constrained than by *Durham* (which, according to the *Comment*, was "warmly supported by psychiatrists"[52]) but less so than by the traditional tests; from that of the retributivist, the essence of free will – be it "real" or a mere consciousness – was implicitly retained. As for Wechsler himself, he remained confident that, so long as medical experts were held at bay, legal professionals could translate lay determinations rooted in the idea of free will into juristic understandings of

Selections from the Oral History of Herbert Wechsler," *Columbia Law Review*, vol. 93 (1993): 854–931, 869)

[50] Wechsler, "Thoughtful Code of Substantive Law," 528–29.

[51] Herbert Wechsler, "The Challenge of a Model Penal Code," *Harvard Law Review*, vol. 65 (1952): 1097–1133, 1105 (emphasis added).

[52] *Comment*, 159.

a specifically legal concept of responsibility based on the principle of utility. In the face of the popular, jury-based meaning of "social justice," utility – unlike Bazelon's approach to the jury's role relative to law and psychiatry – required not the acceptance, but the manipulation, of disjunction.[53]

The Voice of Traditionalism: Jerome Hall

Many academic jurists greeted *Durham* with enthusiasm.[54] Others endorsed it in principle, but preferred the MPC draft formulation to Bazelon's more open-ended "product of mental disease or defect" language. Others opposed *Durham* as far too broad.[55] A few opposed both *Durham* and the MPC on the grounds that *M'Naghten* was sufficient: it captured, they claimed, all that was necessary within a broad understanding of the operation of cognitive capacity. Among these was the irrepressible Jerome Hall. Hall was incapable of addressing the specific question of the legal insanity defense without commenting more broadly on the larger issue of responsibility. He eschewed legal formulations that signaled semantic accommodation with either scientific determinism or philosophical skepticism.

Hall's first criticism of *Durham* came in two 1956 articles;[56] the first built on a December 1955 conference paper and the second responded to praise for the decision from soon-to-be Chief Judge of the Fourth Circuit Court

[53] Seidman takes the position that ambiguous language employed throughout the MPC essentially resulted in a "muddle" as the drafters self-consciously attempted to graft progressive reform onto the criminal law's ineradicable traditional premises – particularly that of free will ("Points of Intersection," 107–15). He seems to view the MPC less as a successful compromise than as a testament to the ineradicability of the law's traditional premises. The drafters found themselves forced to use "weasel words" to "finesse the problem" posed by the disjunction between tradition and determinism; and, through their language and comments, they often "seem intent on deliberately advertising the incoherence of their own project ... as if they are signaling to the cognoscenti their powerlessness to make sense out of the formalist categories they are somehow compelled to use" (109–10). The task of drawing lines between the blameless and the blameworthy *while* accepting the tenets of determinism was theoretically impossible; so, as was also true under the *Durham* rule, the job was ultimately passed on to the court and jury (114).

My own account of responses to *Durham* dovetails with Seidman's perspective on the MPC at a number of points. Such differences as there may be result from the fact that I have adopted a different angle of vision, focused less on "the drafters" than on a number of the "cognoscenti" themselves, whose own pathways of reflection on the criminal law revealed – depending on one's point of view – muddle, compromise, finesse, or deep insight into the ineradicability of the human predicament.

[54] For a favorable but circumspect view, see Henry Weihofen, "The Flowering of New Hampshire," *University of Chicago Law Review*, vol. 22 (1955): 356–66.

[55] E.g., S. Oley Cutler, S.J., "Insanity as a Defense in Criminal Law," *Catholic Lawyer*, vol. 5 (1959): 44–60, 49–54; Ray Moreland, "Mental Responsibility and the Criminal Law – A Defence," *Kentucky Law Journal*, vol. 45 (1956): 215–35, 231.

[56] Jerome Hall, "Psychiatry and Criminal Responsibility," *Yale Law Journal*, vol. 65 (1956): 761–85; "Responsibility and Law: In Defense of the *McNaghten* Rules," *ABA Journal*, vol. 42 (1956): 917–19, 984–89.

of Appeals, Simon Sobeloff, in the September 1955 *ABA Journal*.[57] Hall insisted that Bazelon and Sobeloff were guilty of the common misconception that the great weight of psychiatric opinion ran against the *M'Naghten* rule, and in favor of the "irresistible impulse" test. He pointed to several medical-legal scholars (including Fredric Wertham, Hervey Cleckley, H. A. Davidson, and Norwood East) "who find much merit in [the law of criminal responsibility]," and he implied that relatively few of the country's "8500 practicing psychiatrists" were "represented by the extremist critics," noting that "no more than a handful of them have ever been consulted by members of the legal profession."[58] Moreover, "irresistible impulse" was "rejected by most psychiatrists as unsound!"[59] Taking advantage of the drift in some behavioral-science circles away from the positivist critique of the law, Hall quoted psychologist Edward Thorndike's observation that "'dealing as it does mainly with human behavior, the law very likely has more to teach psychology than to learn from it.'"[60]

Law and science differed, Hall once again explained; the latter takes a determinist position, whereas the criminal law,

> while it is also a science, is not a science whose sole concern is to understand and describe what goes on. It is, instead, a practical, rational, normative science which, although it draws upon theoretical science, also is concerned to pass judgment on human conduct. Its view of human nature *asserts the reality of free choice* and rejects the thesis that the conduct of normal adults is a mere expression of imperious psychological necessity. Given the scientific purpose to understand conduct, determinism is a necessary postulate. Given the additional purpose to evaluate conduct, some degree of autonomy is a necessary postulate.[61]

No one was more insistent than Hall about the importance of a distinctively legal, rather than scientific, concept of responsibility. For Hall, the idea of a "legal rule" did not convey instrumentalism, heuristics, or apologetics. If it mirrored social convention, it was not in order to be acceptable, or to do its work of guaranteeing order, or simply to instantiate humans' aspirations. The law *was* experience, and had as much a claim to reality as science.

---

[57] Simon Sobeloff, "Insanity and the Criminal Law: From McNaghten to *Durham* and Beyond," *ABA Journal*, vol. 41 (1955): 793–96.

[58] Hall, "Psychiatry and Criminal Responsibility," 761–62 (citing Dr. Philip Q. Roche's study, as reported in Keedy, "Irresistible Impulse," 989; a 1954 poll by the Committee on Psychiatry and Law of the Group for the Advancement of Psychiatry, Criminal Responsibility and Psychiatric Expert Testimony; and Manfred Guttmacher's poll, reported in "The Quest for a Test of Criminal Responsibility," *American Journal of Psychiatry*, vol. 111 [1954]: 428, 430).

[59] Hall, "Psychiatry and Criminal Responsibility," 762.

[60] Hall, "Psychiatry and Criminal Responsibility," 763 (quoting Edward Lee Thorndike, *Man and His Works* [1943], 133).

[61] Hall, "Psychiatry and Criminal Responsibility," 764 (emphasis added).

Hall's account of punishment proceeded along similar lines. He recognized that "from the view point of empirical science" one might analyze punishment in "cause-and-effect" terms: punishment could "be seen as an emotional reaction, the vengeance of an angry group"; it was also, instrumentally, a "condition which must be included among the causal factors of human behavior." But "for the purposes of law," punishment had also to be understood in terms of "a view of human nature that is both practical and ethical," and this meant that it must be seen in relation to the notion that one is "accountable, as a normal person, for voluntary conduct." Punishment, then, was "a corollary of responsibility, based upon the concept of man as capable, within limits, of making free moral choices." Furthermore, Hall continued, "if human beings are in any degree free moral agents, then treatment cannot be wholly substituted for punishment.... A dogma that equates normal adults with helpless victims of disease is incompatible with respect for personality and distinctive human traits."[62] On this point Hall might have quoted Moberly to good effect.

Hall added little to his earlier commentaries on M'Naghten and "irresistible impulse." His critique in the 1956 papers dwelt on the theory of integration of personality and the central role of rationality. With regard to M'Naghten, he cited Weihofen's concession in 1954 that "'if the word "know" were given [a] broader interpretation, so as to require knowledge "fused with affect" and assimilated by the whole personality ... much of the criticism of the knowledge test would be met.'"[63] The British Royal Commission offered rules that were no improvement. Its second preference (the primary preference of the minority) would retain M'Naghten and add, in place of "irresistible impulse," "incapable of preventing himself from committing [the act],"[64] which Hall viewed as little better. He also compared it with the MPC draft's language (inability "to conform his conduct to the requirements of law") and concluded: "With due deference, I submit that these proposals either amount to a merely verbal reformulation of the 'irresistible impulse' test, or else are so general and nebulous as to amount to the abolition of all rules."[65] Hall readily enlisted the English jurist Patrick Devlin's critique of the Royal Commission's second preference, that it was "'tantamount to inquiring from the jury whether the accused was so insane that he ought not to be regarded as responsible and thus leaving them in the end with the general question.'"[66] The Royal Commission's primary

---

[62] Hall, "Psychiatry and Criminal Responsibility," 764–66.

[63] Hall, "Psychiatry and Criminal Responsibility," 781 (quoting Henry Weihofen, *Mental Disorder as a Criminal Defense* [1954], 77).

[64] Royal Commission *Report*, 276, 287.

[65] Hall, "Psychiatry and Criminal Responsibility," 776–77.

[66] Hall, "Psychiatry and Criminal Responsibility," 779 (quoting Patrick Devlin, "Criminal Responsibility and Punishment: Functions of Judge and Jury," *Criminal Law Review*, vol. 1 [1954]: 661, 683).

recommendation – which simply left the jury to decide "whether at the time of the act the accused was suffering from disease of the mind or mental deficiency to such a degree that he ought not to be held responsible" – was, Hall pointed out, in fact designed to do just that.[67] It would please those psychiatrists who claimed they were unable to testify under *M'Naghten*; it "would allow them to testify in any way they pleased, and in support of any conceivable theory," but such testimony would be useless to the jury, which would be left "groping their way through a blizzard of scientific terminology and conflicting theories."[68] The result would be inconsistent with the requirements of stable, comprehensible classifications that could be applied consistently – it would, that is, defeat the rule of law.

Durham, then, was a failure. It "purports to offer the jury at least some guidance," yet its "product" test "vies in vagueness" with the Royal Commission's main offering, leaving the jury to "make determinations about degrees of impairment or disease that puzzle the experts" and to "speculate" regarding causation, on which *Durham* places its emphasis. Most of all, of course,

the *Durham* test ignores cognition; it ignores the rational element of purposive conduct, or at best insinuates it under a spacious mantle of verbal imprecision; it ignores the question that is crucial, from the perspective of the law – whether the accused was competent to make the relevant moral decision.

The criminal law is concerned with voluntary conduct, and the problem of "causation" is therefore quite different there from what it is in the realm of mechanics. To make sense of "causation" in the sphere of purposive conduct means to take account of the actor as a rational being.... [T]o say that he voluntarily brought [a harm] about is to say also that cognition was involved in the conduct. This is how

---

[67] Royal Commission *Report*, 276. Indeed, in urging that criminal responsibility "is essentially a moral question" that requires "reconcil[ing] the requirements of justice with the moral feelings of the community at large," a majority of the Commission had concluded that, although "medicine can bring valuable aid," the question is "one which is most appropriately decided by a jury of ordinary men and women, not by medical or legal experts" (100). Interestingly, the Commission's three dissenting members, who preferred the secondary recommendation that retained but augmented *M'Naghten*, had criticized the primary recommendation for reasons similar to those later advanced by critics of *both* recommendations. The question of responsibility was, the dissenters argued, still one that must be addressed through a legal rule defining, "as clearly as possible," the line between culpable and non-culpable behavior. Regardless that this line may be difficult to draw in a particular case, the jury needs, at least, "the guidance of a general principle or criterion": "to have no rule at all would be to leave the decision on which often a man's life depends to the uncertain variations of ethical standard and emotional reaction which may influence the minds of the members of a jury" (286–87). The dissenters charged that the primary recommendation allowed the law to "shirk its duty" in this regard (286); it "overlooks the individual accused" and primarily provided "a convenient escape hatch" for the majority, which "simply cast on a jury the identical problem that these Commissioners were unable to resolve with all the intellectual ammunition, skill and training ranged before them" (710).

[68] Hall, "Psychiatry and Criminal Responsibility," 779.

the problem of causation must be dealt with in analysis of purposive conduct; this, indeed, is the logic of the *M'Naghten Rules* and of integrative psychology.[69]

The assault on *M'Naghten*, Hall stated, "assumes that even the most thoughtful layman's experience with his fellow men and his sensitive insight into the functioning of his own personality in elementary acts for which persons are held responsible, are wholly fallacious."[70]

At times, Hall's words can be read consistently with a mere "as if" orientation to free will, but the dominant theme, which he passionately defended, remained "as is." For Hall, Western tradition and common sense testified to those perceptions of Everyman that were so palpable they could not reasonably be doubted. Thus he wrote that "only when responsibility is held in view, with its implications of moral obligation and *the significant, if limited, capacity of free choice by normal persons*, can the meaning of grounds of punishment be grasped."[71]

By the spring of 1957, Hall had coordinated the various elements of his defense of *M'Naghten* – and of the entire concept of responsibility – into a rousing campaign speech, which he delivered in the course of a panel discussion on "Mental Disease and Criminal Responsibility" at Harvard Law School. The discussants, with Hall, were Professor Abram Chayes of Harvard, who had submitted an amicus brief for the defendant in *Durham*, and Wechsler, who spoke for the MPC Tentative Draft. In his opening remarks, Hall laid it on the line:

The problem of criminal responsibility makes sense only if human responsibility makes sense…. Thus our problem is an aspect of the central question in any human being's life, his stand *vis à vis* the world, especially whether moral obligation, freedom and responsibility have meaning for him. For many reasons and because of major changes in certain cultural currents which I cannot elaborate here, we face a mounting wave of irrationalism which threatens to put out the spark of human understanding or so depreciate it that the age-old conception, at least in the western world, of man as a rational free being would disappear, and new ideas of human nature and new implications for criminal law and much else would prevail.[72]

Hall asserted that the "growing cult of irresponsibility" found expression in the "irresistible impulse" test and in "its recent reformulations," by which he meant *Durham* and the MPC draft. Those tests translated "irresistible impulse" into "terms of inability to conform to the law or to control one's conduct": his two "able opponents" stood "on common ground in representing an extreme wing of modern psychiatry's case for

[69] Hall, "Psychiatry and Criminal Responsibility," 780.
[70] Hall, "Responsibility and Law," 919 (Hall replied here to Judge Sobeloff).
[71] Hall, "Responsibility and Law," 984 (emphasis added).
[72] Jerome Hall, "Mental Disease and Criminal Responsibility – *M'Naghten* versus *Durham* and the American Law Institute's Tentative Draft," *Indiana Law Journal*, vol. 33 (1957): 212–26, 212.

irrationalism."[73] With the fate of Western civilization hanging in the balance, Hall pressed his case in the presence of the accused.

So far as the details of his position were concerned, Hall added little of note. *M'Naghten* he termed "the rule of reason," which reduced to the defendant's "competence to understand ordinary everyday things and actions and [their] ordinary consequences," to what psychiatrists referred to as "the reality principle." It embodied the wisdom of the ancient Greeks, indeed extended back "to the very dawn of civilization, during all of which time it was recognized that what distinguished men from other animals was human intelligence." As to the all-important "relationship between intelligence and the control of conduct," one should demand "a great deal of evidence before [accepting] the irrationalism that one's reason may be unimpaired and that nonetheless it exercises no control over … conduct." Hall then called upon his opponents to "tell us whether they are opposed to the rule of reason, whether they think it is a myth or vestige of some sort of superstition" – whether "they prefer a new world to come, perhaps that of 1984 or of other experts who exclude all blame and all praise from a mechanized world." For this is what rejection of *M'Naghten* signified – what preserving it but adding "irresistible impulse" to it implied. "How do you reconcile these matters, gentlemen?"[74]

The sole account of which I am aware of this momentous occasion – that of Hall himself – does not contain remarks by Chayes or Wechsler in defense of their apostasy, but implies that the former "criticized *M'Naghten* and discussed the *Durham Rule*" in fairly standard terms and the latter criticized both *M'Naghten* and *Durham* in the language of the MPC Tentative Draft comment. Neither replied to Hall in the terms he had set forth, and both might well have viewed Hall's opening statement as unnecessarily apocalyptic. For Chayes, the path was well-worn: the "'right-wrong'" test did "'not take sufficient account of psychic realities and scientific knowledge,'" etc., and "'the "irresistible impulse" test … gives no recognition to mental illness characterized by brooding and reflection.'"[75] Wechsler seems to have reiterated his claims (in defense of the Tentative Draft) that *M'Naghten* went too far in requiring *complete* impairment and to have rehearsed his argument that the *Durham* formulation contained fundamental ambiguity on the matter of proof of causation.[76]

Hall's response was as predictable as the positions he criticized, for all had been said before, and many times. But his account now took on sharper focus: "irresistible impulse" was more clearly than before the true villain of

---

[73] Hall, "Mental Disease and Criminal Responsibility," 213.

[74] Hall, "Mental Disease and Criminal Responsibility," 213–15.

[75] Hall, "Mental Disease and Criminal Responsibility," 215–17 (quoting *Durham*, 214 F.2d at 874).

[76] Hall, "Mental Disease and Criminal Responsibility," 218.

the piece. *Durham*, of course, suspended the rule of law, for it had left no clear guidelines. Here, Hall agreed with Wechsler that, as Hall put it, "the *Durham* rule may turn out to be cruel rather than opening the door to more lenient consideration," for the expert psychiatric witness was under no constraint and might "hold the jury at his mercy because they have no standard to help them appraise his testimony." Still, Hall believed that Wechsler's (MPC) "proposed 'irresistible impulse' [i.e., 'capacity to conform'] rule [was] equally vague and defective."[77] But the truly serious problem was not that of vagueness, uncertainty, or unfairness – as bad as those were. It was the necessary meaning of "irresistible impulse." If that test were indeed to stand on its own – if it were to add *anything* to *M'Naghten* – it then broke faith with the underlying wisdom of the ages, the product, and the definition, of human intelligence. To accept "irresistible impulse" – or its surrogate – as an addition to *M'Naghten* was to deny human responsibility; there could be no stopping point, only irrationalism, a deterministic abyss.

What the proponents of "irresistible impulse" are in effect telling us is that the most distinctive and potent function on earth – human understanding in its full amplitude – can be normal but nonetheless impotent even as regards killing or raping or robbing. That is the thesis they are advancing and do not forget that. It can only mean that intelligence is unrelated to the control of human conduct.[78]

The Vicissitudes of Positivism: Warren Hill and Thurman Arnold

Durham, then, faced opposition from at least two sides. The utilitarian queried the integrity of a decision that simultaneously wielded the language of free will and left legal causation to the vagaries of lay inference. Hall – did he lead a charge or make the last stand? – reared back at *Durham*'s seeming oath of fealty to behavioral science. In the lurch hung, as ever, the silently insistent question of a free will that set (or not) in motion the capacity to act and to know the consequences of the action. The scholarly lucubrations of the preceding decade and more had turned up no solution. They had, however, brought increasing attention to the role of human consciousness.[79] Bazelon did not mention it in his opinion, yet to respond to *Durham* was to acknowledge, in some form, the individual consciousness. For Wechsler, this consciousness was implicated in a concession to the idea of a capacity to conform to the law that was not simply the condition of deterrability; for Hall, it was in the persuasiveness of the *longue durée* of Western values. For

---

[77] Hall, "Mental Disease and Criminal Responsibility," 221.

[78] Hall, "Mental Disease and Criminal Responsibility," 223.

[79] See, e.g., Otto E. Guttentag, M.D., "Prison vs. Closed Ward: Their Philosophical Relationship," *Kentucky Law Journal*, vol. 45 (1957): 251–54; Dr. M. A. Sklansky, "Responsibility: A Psychiatrist's Point of View," *Kentucky Law Journal*, vol. 45 (1957): 270–75; and the previous discussions of Robert Knight, Walter Moberly, and Wilber Katz in Chapter 5.

the positivists the matter of consciousness of freedom brought some of their number back to the fundamentals not of "the West" but of people. But was freedom an instance of human myopia or people's way to clarity of vision?

The supposed primitiveness of widespread lay beliefs had driven the more extreme positivists of the century's early decades to distraction. For utilitarians such as Wechsler it was a reality that any effective calculus had to take into account. For each group (as, earlier, for Pound) both justice and the social defense required either reducing the influence of lay participation or – via the principles of penology – setting a different example for all to see and learn from. Those scholars (the majority) who eschewed the positivist or utilitarian extremes sometimes took a broader view. These positivist-*leaning* jurists (such as Katz and Bazelon himself) would gradually work to limit and, finally, eliminate primitiveness, trusting in a future society of persons who directed the consciousness of freedom to the combined ends of social defense, personal well-being, and justice.

If a utopian vision of "we are all existentialists now" was appalling to the convinced believer in the reality of human free will, it was perhaps not much less so to those who thought the existential perspective belied the angst of Hamlet and brought with it a self-defeating vulnerability to the more serious threats to the social defense. It was also a disturbing vision to those who thought it reflected grossly unrealistic assumptions about commonplace human behavior: society at large was far from prepared for such revolutions of internal spheres. Whatever Bazelon might have had in mind, if that utopia was accepted as the true lesson of *Durham*, one might well hesitate to greet the decision with enthusiasm – or even with equanimity.

The most prominent – yet offstage – *presumed* critic of such a utopian view was, of course, Thurman Arnold, whose writings of the two preceding decades Warren Hill, of the Ohio State law school, now recovered (for Hill's own purposes) in a remarkably original response to the *Durham* decision. Ultimately, Hill concluded, Arnold sided with the positivists in thinking that (in Hill's words) "there would be no progress in our treatment of the criminal problem until we cease regarding it as a moral one and adopt the same attitude toward criminals as we do now toward the insane,"[80] a view Hill himself shared. But Arnold would have seen *Durham* as counterproductive, Hill claimed, a false step induced by a faulty understanding of the nature of people – or of most people. Hill's analysis built upon Arnold's 1930s functionalist anthropology; it was, however, very much Hill's own response, for even as it inferred what Arnold would have said, it also struck its own fresh note.

Bazelon had drawn on Arnold's opinion in *Holloway*, inverting its logic, as we have seen, by offering legal justification and precedent for psychiatry's having its say in the workings of the susceptible terrain between mind and

---

[80] Warren P. Hill, "The Psychological Realism of Thurman Arnold," in "Insanity and the Criminal Law": 377–96, 387 (citing Thurman Arnold, *Symbols of Government* [1935], 167).

heart. But Bazelon had not addressed Arnold's theoretical presumptions. As Hill explained Arnold's position: "the basic premises upon which the jury operates are false in the light of the modern science of psychology. But erroneous as these legally supported assumptions may be, they are defensible as an institutional matter if they comport with the 'instinctive sense of the justice of the ordinary man.'"[81] The court must honor a popular (mis) understanding of free will that offered at least a rationale of enough internal consistency to insure the workings of social justice. And, Hill continued, a similar logic applied in Arnold's 1945 *Fisher* opinion. There, the defendant had clearly exhibited mental abnormalities, but had been "unable to satisfy the accepted tests of insanity," Hill explained, so he was convicted of first degree murder after his lawyer unsuccessfully asked for an instruction that the jury should consider whether his only "'partial responsibility'" negated the required deliberation and premeditation. Arnold affirmed the conviction: Fisher should be treated "'as if'" he were a normal person, for "'age old conceptions of individual moral responsibility cannot be abandoned without creating a laxity of enforcement that undermines the whole administration of criminal law.'"[82]

Durham, too, Hill now argued, might be read in light of Arnold's philosophy:

> A critique of the court's holding in the *Durham* case by one who professes Arnold's philosophy, then, might run as follows. By scrapping the old tests, the court has partially withdrawn legal sanction from the popular assumption that the cognitive phase of mental life is the most important factor in governing human conduct. The jury will no longer be indulged in their "folklore" of criminal psychology which regards "reasoning" as the real cause of behavior. Instead they will be told ... that deep-seated emotional currents may move men to act more often than their realistic reason and will would let them, ... and that "unhealthy" mental processes are only quantitatively different from normal ones.[83]

Although the jury was, according to Bazelon (quoting from Arnold's opinion in *Holloway*), to apply its "inherited ideas of moral responsibility," the new rule governing expert testimony, Hill surmised, made it likely that "the area of moral judgment will be greatly contracted." *Durham*, ran Hill's hypothetical Arnoldian critique, opened the door wide to modern psychiatry, which "has in fact partially undermined conventional morality."[84] If the jury is persuaded by expert testimony, "there will occur a substitution of understanding for censure. In what sense then is the jury free to apply its inherited ideas of morality? ... In transforming the tests of insanity from

[81] Hill, "Psychological Realism," 382.
[82] Hill, "Psychological Realism," 384 (internal quotations are from Arnold in *Fisher v. United States*, 149 F.2d 28, 29 [D.C. Cir. 1945]).
[83] Hill, "Psychological Realism," 385.
[84] Hill, "Psychological Realism," 385.

legal 'folklore' to questions of scientific fact, the institution of the jury has been deprived of its *raison d'etre*." And, finally, the displacement by modern psychiatry of the "out-moded belief in 'faculty psychology,'" which had long "furnished the theoretical substructure for the dramatization of the ideal of moral responsibility," was akin to "furnishing a primitive medicine-man with such modern diagnostic tools as an X-ray machine." Not only will the "primitive" misuse them, "but if perchance he gains by them some accurate knowledge of the human organism and how it functions, it will so contradict his mystical presuppositions that he will decline into torpor and pessimism."[85]

Thus did the Arnold of the 1930s and 1940s respond, in Hill's imagination, to the potential implications of Bazelon's mid-1950s decision. But Hill shifted ground when he proceeded to examine *Durham* for its more specific defects. Although he hastened to assure his readers that Arnold was dissatisfied with the effects of punishment on the individual, he submitted that Arnold's "greater concern [was] for the demands of society than for the individual offender," which led him to "part company with most of the medical critics of the law." According to Hill, one of the most significant social effects of "such a partial abolition or mitigation of punishment" as in *Durham* was the likely diminution of "the area within which the jury may vent its instinctual aggression as 'catharsis.'"[86] "Folklore" beliefs in free will and in the criminal as the "other" and as evil incarnate served usefully to underpin the "idea of vengeance against human wickedness."[87] Hill read Arnold in light of the literature on aggression and on social sublimation of aggressive instincts, citing works available to Arnold (Charles Mercier, Staub, and Alexander) and some influential in Hill's own day (J. C. Flugel and Paul Reiwald).[88] He thus conjoined Arnold's views and contemporary social behavior theory without following the same logic as Wechsler. Wechsler had insisted that the truly irresponsible person was someone with whom most people did not identify and therefore whose punishment lacked general deterrent force. But he had made no reference to the idea (extrapolated from Arnold by Hill) that enlarging the sphere of irresponsibility would deprive society "of one of

[85] Hill, "Psychological Realism," 386–87.

[86] Hill, "Psychological Realism," 387. Hill's treatment of Arnold in this regard was consistent with his gloss on Arnold's opinion in *Fisher*, which Hill read as revealing concern for the weakening of social and individual resistance to the commission of criminal acts. In his initial comments on *Durham* he placed Arnold's concern on a loss of "mystical presuppositions" vitiating the individual's sense of agency.

[87] Hill, "Psychological Realism," 389.

[88] Hill, "Psychological Realism," 386–88 (citing Charles A. Mercier, *Criminal Responsibility* [New York: Physicians and Surgeons Book Co., 1926]; Alexander and Staub, *The Criminal, the Judge, and the Public*; J. C. Flugel, *Man, Morals and Society* [1945]; Paul Reiwald, *Society and Its Criminals* [1950]).

its main outlets for the anti-social aggressiveness that it has so guiltily but effectively repressed."[89]

Although Hill himself believed that *Durham* risked committing that very error, he nonetheless thought it left "the jury free in most instances to practice the folklore of a retributive system." He thus concluded his essay by producing what might be called a scaled-down Arnoldian view, in accordance with which he cautiously defended *Durham's* failure to define "mental disease" and the court's allocations of functions between judge and jury. As to that all-important allocation of functions: "So long as there is retention of any of the 'metaphysics of moral responsibility' it makes sense to let the jury, as a microcosm of the law-abiding public, decide whether or not to impose the same standards of righteousness on certain of the maladjusted or nonconformists as they seek to impose on themselves."[90] With respect to "borderline types" there was likely to be "resistance to the imparted insights of psychiatry." The jury's own psychologically driven understandings of human behavior would prevail. Although Hill found great virtue in Wechsler's approach regarding general and special deterrence, he foresaw cases in which it made little sense to compel jurors "to report their prognosis, and prescription for mediating between the needs of society and the offender, in the crude and absolutistic terms of a primitive harsh morality."[91] As he saw the matter, *Durham* worked a "beneficial" change "if viewed as a transitional device toward a more realistic system of social defense."

> Jurors who serve in the courts of the District now have an enhanced opportunity to undergo a form of adult education in the dynamics of human behavior. While this may not produce greater juror competence it should eventually convince those whose minds are at all accessible that the problem of understanding the criminal and planning his therapy, so as to be able to return him ultimately to a world he can both accept and enjoy, is a problem of baffling complexity from whose attempted solution the amateur should respectfully withdraw. Such arrogance and moral superiority must vanish with the dawning of greater self-knowledge and insight.[92]

Hill, thus, was a gradualist, a positivist-leaning jurist who accorded due respect to *Durham* and who counseled neither "despair" nor "an overly heady optimism." The lesson Arnold taught him was that deep and pervasive attitudinal changes did not come effortlessly; intellectual grasp of the underlying causes of crime and of the "waste" and "cruelty" of the current system did not translate easily into "growth of our social conscience" or repudiation of the reliance on "the punitive system of control as a distraction from disturbing realities."[93] Hill took the Arnold of the 1930s and

[89] Hill, "Psychological Realism," 388.
[90] Hill, "Psychological Realism," 391.
[91] Hill, "Psychological Realism," 395.
[92] Hill, "Psychological Realism," 396.
[93] Hill, "Psychological Realism," 396.

1940s and domesticated him to the 1950s, draining him of his exaggerated terminology and of what he took to be Arnold's implicit assumption of a relatively nonmalleable human condition. He found in *Durham* some hope for a future in which the criminal trial would less often be a ritual enactment of sublimated aggression – some hope for an eventually kinder and gentler retributivism. He found in Bazelon's approach to the jury a device for, as it were, the partial containment of disjunction between elite conceptualizations of responsibility, whether scientific or legal, and those embedded in conventional morality. Indeed, he found some hope, even, for the eventual displacement of punishment by the more rational approach to criminal behavior that he and Arnold favored. The hiatus between positivism and utilitarianism abided but found its limits. And it was ironically the matter of human consciousness of freedom that prevented the hiatus from becoming a gulf. The consequentialist, whether reform- or deterrence-based, had to account for a common variable, the motivating power of a sense-reality of free will.

Hill's commentary on *Durham* found great favor with Arnold, who wrote him from his Washington law firm office that "it is the best article I have ever read on the subject." Arnold assured Hill that this was not sheer flattery by reason of Hill's having made Arnold his centerpiece: "I can inform you that everyone else in the office, including those who worked on the Durham case is most enthusiastic"[94] – presumably a reference primarily to Arnold's partner Fortas, who had been appointed as the indigent Durham's primary attorney before the Court of Appeals and had argued (as Arnold later put it) "that the right-and-wrong test was obsolete in the light of modern psychological knowledge."[95]

Arnold's realist-based Progressivism was emphatic:

So long as the issue to be tried is whether the defendant is to be blamed for his conduct and tried in a society which will not pay for the care of delinquents we are not going to get much difference in results. The great advance which the opinion will make lies in the fact that a priestlike tribunal has formally recognized mental disease as the controlling factor in an insanity case rather than sin.[96]

Thus, while Arnold commended Hill for understanding "that the criminal trial is a symbolic battle in which the state is protecting its citizens from their enemies and at the same time being just to them," he stressed that symbols nonetheless stood apart from realities. Juries, Arnold confidently

---

[94] Arnold to Hill, March 29, 1955, in *Voltaire and the Cowboy: The Letters of Thurman Arnold*, ed. Gene M. Gressley (Boulder: Colorado Associated University Press, 1977), 417.

[95] Thurman Arnold, *Fair Fights and Foul: A Dissenting Lawyer's Life* (New York: Harcourt, Brace and World, 1965), 233.

[96] Gressley, *Letters*, 419.

asserted, would continue to convict defendants such as Durham, the new test notwithstanding. The prediction proved correct with respect to Durham,[97] although incorrect to the extent that Arnold thought Bazelon's rule would not increase the flow of offenders to mental hospitals – a result that Hill had himself predicted.[98] Once convicted under the new rule, Arnold wrote, Durham would lose on appeal: "the Court of Appeals will not reverse the conviction in spite of the fact that the evidence as I view it shows an almost conclusive case." The Court would, Arnold opined, "have recourse to reasoning such as I used in the Fisher case" and not "put the rule to such a strain," which could only do "harm to the cause of those who advocate" it. "Durham, though unquestionably insane, is a menace to the community." Arnold went further: "I suspect that the new rule will make it *more difficult* to acquit, at least in cases of some emotional crimes," whereas a jury conclusion that the defendant "could not tell right from wrong" was unlikely to cause the kind of reactive "hue and cry" from the community that would, presumably, put juries on their guard. Despite this bleak view, Arnold fully appreciated the symbolic result Bazelon had achieved and even deemed it a step toward some eventual progress. He thus told Hill that he had not himself taken the same course because "I thought that the right and wrong test was more necessary to a public sense of justice than it appears to be now."[99]

Arnold read Bazelon's "radical"[100] opinion in *Durham* as many others did: it widened the door of the courtroom for the scientist and bespoke a more rational and just future for the criminal law, at least with respect to the legal insanity defense, if not necessarily to the matter of criminal responsibility more generally. Arnold's thinking (as of 1955) was both more forthright and less subtle than Hill's – and less optimistic as well. Hill was also in the positivist-leaning camp, as his skeptical reference to the "metaphysics of moral responsibility" suggests, and for him, as for Arnold, the jury would have an especially important role so long as those "metaphysics" of blame were retained. Arnold did not, however, advert in his letter to Hill's conjecture that, under the new rule, the jury might be further educated toward leaving difficult questions of science to experts, and this optimistic notion perhaps distinguished the two men. But, as mere accommodationists, neither fully understood Bazelon's quite different positivist-leaning point – or if they understood it, neither agreed with it – that the criminal trial was irreducibly about the (increasingly informed) jury-based testing of a metaphysics of

---

[97] On remand, a jury convicted Monte Durham under the *Durham* rule. The conviction was again overturned on appeal, this time because of an instructional error. Ultimately, Durham pleaded guilty. See Maeder, *Crime and Madness,* 84.

[98] Gressley, *Letters,* 417–18; Hill, "Psychological Realism," 387 n. 40.

[99] Gressley, *Letters,* 417–19.

[100] Gressley, *Letters,* 419.

blame that inevitably and rightly lay at its very heart. Two others, however, Wilber Katz and Thomas Szasz, did understand that point, although each in his own very different way.

Wilber Katz

Among *Durham*'s galvanizing effects was to reposition players in the scholarly fields of debate and dialogue so that a new panorama of voices was emerging without any individual one transmuting into another, or losing its own distinctive cachet. Thus, although Wechsler and Hall together stood aloof from Bazelon's decision, Hall would never count himself a utilitarian, and Wechsler would yield no more of social utility to Hall's particular brand of Western ethics than to psychiatry's bid for preeminent grace. For Wechsler, *Durham* gave too much weight to mental illness over the criteria for mental capacity and legal persuasiveness. For Hall, *Durham*'s bequest to criminal jurisprudence was potentially more disturbing. In attempting to mediate between a scientific perspective and retributivism, it sacrificed, in his view, the moral fabric of society.

Warren Hill, by way of Thurman Arnold, was, in contrast to Wechsler and Hall, an affirmative voice for Bazelon's new departure in *Durham*. *Durham* was a positive means to the end of "adult education." The jury became, perhaps ironically, its own educator (toward, perhaps, standing down in the face of scientific complexity) through participating in a process whose rationale was tacit, at least to the common man. Wilber Katz too welcomed *Durham*, and in more emphatic language than Hill, because for Katz *Durham* was a justifiable end in itself, a *method* of proceeding – whether successful or not in the particular instance – whereby law and psychiatry found common ground in the "as if" proposition.

Of all those American academic and professional diagnosticians to take up the problem of criminal responsibility, Katz aimed most directly for the underlying issue of free will. His 1952 address to the Conference of Episcopal College Clergy[101] had been as much soul-searching as scholarly commentary. Hall conveyed intensity of purpose, but his very certainty spared his writing from the anguish, ultimately, of extrapolating the moral tenets of human action and its consequences. Katz had known angst; *Durham* was a way past a plaguing dilemma. With Bazelon's decision in *Durham*, Katz was pleased to say, "the connection between free will and responsibility is explicit."[102] According to Bazelon, mental disease deprived a person of his free will. Therefore, where disabling psychoses were not in evidence, the defendant was morally responsible because – at least from the perspective of the common man – he was morally free.

---

[101] Katz, "Responsibility and Freedom."
[102] Wilber Katz, "Law, Psychiatry, and Free Will," in "Insanity and the Criminal Law," 397–404, 397.

In his 1955 assessment not simply of *Durham* but of the relationship it made possible between law and psychiatry, Katz reviewed the supposed decades-old stasis: psychiatry denying free will; law-in-practice upholding it, at least deductively in its working out of the retributive response to crime through guilt assessment and punishment. The law, however, did not emanate from free will as a metaphysical truth. "Indeed careful judges," Katz stated, "often speak of legal responsibility as based upon an *assumption* of free will," an idea Katz had struggled with in 1952 but now, in the light of *Durham*, positively welcomed. Both Justice Cardozo and Justice Jackson, he noted, used such language. And, from the psychiatrists' side, even the most deterministic of their profession still required an element of what bore resemblance to free will, if not the substantive phenomenon, for the necessary "effort" to respond to therapy; although they might cavil with inherent responsibility, they were not loathe to impose it for reformatory ends.[103] The antagonists – were they such – in their various soundings forth attested to the utility of free will as an "as if." The problem identified by *Durham* was where the "as if" became inoperative.

Katz anticipated psychiatrists' objections to the implication of *Durham* that culpability came down to "the presence or absence of free will." His confidence in *Durham* to transcend feuding factions, however, did not waver. Some overlap in their approaches seemed achievable. For example, the Group for Advancement of Psychiatry, Criminal Responsibility and Psychiatric Expert Testimony asserted:

Ego impairment would appear to be a direct measure of responsibility. Ego impairment implies lessened control in maintaining behavioral norms of social interaction. In law, such would be the basis of exculpation ... On this level of abstraction the lawyer and psychiatrist can agree. The psychiatrist can determine that ego impairment exists and the lawyer can transpose the fact into his terms of intent and responsibility."[104]

Here the psychiatrist deferred to the law after first delineating the responsibility-bearing ego *within* the law. The commonality was there, although on terms other than Katz, or Bazelon, finally argued. For Katz, the lawyer might retrieve from the psychiatrist a workable definition of responsibility and of that threshold where an individual ceased to exercise "'judgment, discretion, and control' in the conduct of his affairs and social relations." The psychiatrist, in turn, offered the professional insight that "most (if not all) human beings have a capacity to grow in responsibility." The lawyer thus won from the psychiatrist an admission of responsibility; the psychiatrist set the lawyer on a path of "self-questioning." Indeed, the lawyer "has

---

[103] Katz, "Law, Psychiatry, and Free Will," 398–99.
[104] Katz, "Law, Psychiatry, and Free Will," 399–400 (quoting Group for Advancement of Psychiatry, Criminal Responsibility and Psychiatric Expert Testimony, Report No. 26 [1954], 6 n. 2).

been unwilling to admit that free will is only an expedient assumption; but does he assert the reality of a freedom coextensive with that which the law assumes? Does he affirm anything broader than the limited power ... to accept or reject opportunities for growth in responsibility[?]"[105]

The efficacy of law did not derive from a judicial opinion on the metaphysics of free will. Rather, the lawyer had to recognize that the experience of free will as free choice occurred within the bounds of often painful necessity. Further, here Katz suggested that, where "common-sense morality" (and Katz used the term with all due respect) gave wider girth to free choice, it was the correlative of the law's doctrines of "*vicarious* responsibility"[106] – that is, broadly stated, responsibility rooted in certain relationships with and expectations of each other, if not in direct, personal causation. What in 1952 he had put forth as a philosophical truism, two years later was given pragmatic relevance by *Durham*. Vicarious responsibility, of course, did not cut through all ambiguity. Actual and vicarious responsibility resisted neat Aristotelian classification, and the mature individual tended to assume full responsibility, regardless of a qualifying circumstance. But it was not a case of contradiction, as vicarious responsibility, once shouldered, was of a piece with free choice: the free choice to act socially as well as individually.

Katz elegantly held a strictly utilitarian interpretation at bay. The lawyer looks to the morality of the criminal law and "he is shocked," Katz wrote, by Holmes's (mid-1920s, but only recently published) musing: "'If I were having a philosophical talk with a man I was going to have hanged (or electrocuted) I should say, I don't doubt that your act was inevitable for you but to make it more avoidable by others we propose to sacrifice you to the common good. You may regard yourself as a soldier dying for your country if you like. But the law must keep its promises.'"[107] Speaking for himself and for his generation, Katz stated flatly: "This is revolting." But did he – or his generation – have something better to offer? His alternative, based on the insights of his earlier paper, was subtle. "If ... the idea of retribution were to be abandoned," he presupposed without qualm, "the law's concept of responsibility might be stated in terms which are entirely forward looking. It might be said that the law summons all men to responsibility. It expects the relatively healthy, 'deterrable' individuals to respond with only the help which the common life affords."[108] Punishment was still a part of that summoning and help, but *not* by sacrificing the individual to the common good. Rather, punishment should be seen as implicating the offender and the rest of society's members together in an act that could not have occurred without

[105] Katz, "Law, Psychiatry, and Free Will," 400–01.
[106] Katz, "Law, Psychiatry, and Free Will," 401.
[107] Katz, "Law, Psychiatry, and Free Will," 402 (quoting Mark DeWolfe Howe, ed., *Holmes-Laski Letters* [1953], 806).
[108] Katz, "Law, Psychiatry, and Free Will," 403.

the constant sharing (as distinct from shifting) of responsibility that allowed the one and the many to achieve the ends of moral community.

The psychiatrist disconcerted by *Durham* had only to recognize that an "as if" conception of free will was entirely consonant with Bazelon's language. And the lawyer? Maybe the process of "adult education" needed to include him, which, understandably, *was* disconcerting, but not insurmountably so. The lawyer "has assumed that vicarious liability is exceptional; now he is asked to recognize that liability for 'fault' is also in large measure vicarious. Perhaps he may get used to this idea, particularly when he finds that it is not merely a creature of the dialectic of law and psychiatry." The precedent – and law accorded much to precedent – could be found in Christian ethics, and here Katz returned to the thought of Moberly, whose insights survived *Durham*: "It may be [that it is] by the acceptance of a moral liability greater than appears to be due that moral advance is made."[109]

The world post-*Durham* had indeed changed: "the possibility of profound understanding between psychiatrists and lawyers"[110] was more than a mirage on the horizon. And in that crucial evolutionary development, Katz had himself evolved. Two years previously he had counseled separate but equal spheres where law and psychiatry abutted. The "as if" legal definition of responsibility that Katz thought implied in *Durham* heralded, for him, their far closer collaboration, without the domains of either disappearing in the weave.

Thomas Szasz

Writing in the early 1960s as a member of the medical faculty of the State University of New York, the young psychiatrist Thomas Szasz could not be said to speak for any great number in his profession or in criminal jurisprudence. Yet the unapologetic boldness of his intervention on behalf of the law was itself a marker of how far unease with a pure positivism had disturbed the equanimity of the law's theoretical tradition at midcentury. Szasz, like Jerome Hall, dissented from what he took to be *Durham's* laxness before the hegemony of behavioral science. And, like Hall, his cri de coeur was to preserve the innateness of human responsibility. But Szasz did not fear for Western tradition so much as for the law itself. "Free will" was, he proclaimed, an essential postulate in order that justification for the law be honored. Behavioral science, Szasz believed, only exacerbated, rather than resolved, the disjunction between legal theory and popular understanding. So much for Katz's finding hope in *Durham* for a rapprochement between law and science.

Szasz emerged in his early work as a trenchant critic of the imperialistic tendencies of psychiatry, especially with respect to the law. He distinguished

---

[109] Katz, "Law, Psychiatry, and Free Will," 404.
[110] Katz, "Law, Psychiatry, and Free Will," 404.

between the psychiatrist as medical scientist dealing with physiological matters and the psychiatrist as psychoanalyst or psychotherapist dealing with moral matters. In the latter role, the psychiatrist ought to recognize the legal tenet that humans choose and are responsible for their acts. Mental disease should not remove legal responsibility. He distinguished between science and law in terms of their being two opposed disciplines. Science's function was to explain and classify: explain, where origins and causes were hidden; classify, where experience left the facts in too disordered a state. When science attributed behavior to mental illness, it merely produced an unverifiable theory. The supposition that humans could be divided as a matter of fact in the legal context between the mentally healthy and the mentally ill, in the way that they could be divided between male and female, was absurd.[111] The separate notion of free will was fundamental to the criminal law and to human endeavor. The view of humans as choosing beings rather than as machines, and the fundamental idea, if not reality, of free will (in the sense requisite for "responsibility") converged on political liberty, in which psychiatry had no inherently vested interest. For the law to set scientific order ahead of justice, theory ahead of experience, was for it to squander the very rights it was meant to defend – at least in the American context – of civil, political, and individual liberty.

In his early papers – as later in his frankly libertarian book, *Law, Liberty and Psychiatry* – Szasz endorsed the "classic traditions of Anglo-American legal thinking" that privileged "rules of irrelevance," and claimed that these rules regarding admissibility of evidence ought normally to include a person's mental status. "Except perhaps in cases of the grossest kinds of defect – which in practice would make it impossible for a person to participate in ... marriage, work or crime – people should be treated seriously."[112] He attacked psychiatry for inviting the state to "help" the "mentally ill," who supposedly did not know what was best for them and were a danger to society. He denounced the psychiatric tradition that included Alexander and Staub, Guttmacher, Overholser, Roche, Zilboorg, and even the jurist Bazelon for appropriating the law to the adventure of reconceiving crime as disease.[113]

But there was more to Szasz's argument than a critique of the concept of mental illness and his assertion that law and science critically differed. Szasz argued that psychiatry counterproductively deflected the feelings of anxiety and guilt that rightly accompanied the assessment of responsibility. In doing so, he claimed, psychiatry limited the opportunities for social and individual growth. The law, he said, functions both "to bring order into the realm

[111] Thomas S. Szasz, *Law, Liberty, and Psychiatry: An Inquiry into the Social Uses of Mental Health Practices* (New York: Macmillan, 1963), 135.
[112] Szasz, *Law, Liberty, and Psychiatry*, 246.
[113] Szasz, *Law, Liberty, and Psychiatry*, 327.

of human conduct" and to protect "people from a feeling of (unconscious, unexplained) guilt." The ascription of responsibility according to preset rules that mirror common patterns of identification with, or repudiation of, the offender functions to assuage guilt. The rule that one must not punish the insane requires a decision that is often fraught with anxiety however, and here the psychiatrist had come to play an increasingly problematic role.[114]

Again, "from the point of view of scientific determinism ... the notion of 'responsibility' is without any meaning whatsoever"; it "leaves no room for the possibility of 'choice' and 'free will.'"[115] Determinism thus bears no relation to human experience: man is a blaming animal and "criminal justice today is based on the ethical premise that only those persons to whom [blame] can be attached should be punished." Here his complaint: "It is this social and scientific gap into which the contemporary psychiatrist has projected himself." Whether psychiatrists testified under the *M'Naghten* rule or the *Durham* test, they resorted "in either case, to using the meaningless, or at best extremely polyvalent, notion of 'mental illness,' deluding themselves into believing that they have made a 'diagnosis' when in fact they are acting simply in the role of one of society's blame-assigning agencies."[116] In other words,

the "responsibility" (and the need to dispose of the possible feelings of guilt) is shifted to the psychiatrist. Thus, in effect, the psychiatrist is asked by the court to give it *assurance* that it can proceed with punishment *without feeling guilt*. I think it may be no exaggeration to assert that in many cases this may be the only real function of the psychiatrist in the legal handling of a criminal case.[117]

Law was enlisting the psychiatrist to sidestep the troublesome matter of blaming. The psychiatrist was deploying functionalist precepts to diagnose social dysfunction.

The consequence was "a serious problem for a democratic society" in which "each man" is not merely "'responsible' for his own conduct," but "society is 'responsible' for handling not only the criminal, but the sick and the poor as well." In this latter social context, "as individuals" we are responsible for "recogniz[ing] and tolerat[ing] our causal participation in

[114] Thomas S. Szasz, "Some Observations on the Relationship between Psychiatry and the Law," *AMA Archives of Neurology and Psychiatry*, vol. 75 (1956): 297–315, 309–10.
[115] Szasz, "Some Observations," 306.
[116] Thomas S. Szasz, "Psychiatry, Ethics, and the Criminal Law," *Columbia Law Review*, vol. 58 (1958): 183–98, 189. Szasz, while joining Jerome Hall in warning of the dangers of medicalizing the law (Szasz, *Law, Liberty, and Psychiatry*, 92), criticized Hall for his view that the *M'Naghten* rule tracked significant mental disease and could be relied upon for legal determinations (101–02). Szasz recognized Fredric Wertham as the only psychiatrist who generally shared his views on the dangers of "psychoauthoritarianism" (92, 101). See Fredric Wertham, "Psychoauthoritarianism and the Law," in "Insanity and the Criminal Law," 336–338.
[117] Szasz, "Some Observations," 310.

relationships that 'go wrong' and end in trouble." Szasz proffered this "sort of self-therapeutic view of responsibility" as "the only sure way to bring about self-change." Similarly, only through our participation in the difficult process of ascribing blame "by open recognition of the social participation in crime … can society come to a point where it will take adequate action to change itself." [118]

Szasz thought *Durham* "unadulterated nonsense." It not only made mental illness (or "disease") a matter of fact for the jury when it was no more than a theory, but it left to the psychiatrist and the jury the decision "whether the criminal act in question was committed as the result of such 'illness.'" [119] Moreover, *Durham* greatly expanded the guilt-assuaging role of the psychiatric expert. The jury was more active as well – that was Bazelon's point – as it assessed unconstrained psychiatric testimony in light of community understandings. But this activity, which Bazelon took to be (in a certain sense) democratic, Szasz understood as virtually its opposite – as sheer avoidance of responsibility.

In sum, Szasz attacked the conventional positivist position from inside the positivist camp, labeling *its* liberalism antiliberal and antihumanitarian despite good motives. He recognized the human need to believe in free will and the psychic health implications of that belief. But he would not restrict free will to a convenience for social control. And he certainly would not, by a real inversion of logic, turn the "belief" into a palliative while exchanging justice for treatment. Finally, he drew from the common experience of "guilt" some moral lessons about both the true role of the jury and the nature of social existence. Here, he proceeded in his "as if" perspective beyond issues of adjustment or psychic health. At the core of his libertarianism was a view of the purpose of human existence, an ethics of the experiencing and acceptance of responsibility. Moberly, we might conjecture, would have heartily agreed.

CONVERGENCE TRIUMPHANT: HENRY HART

Such was the state of debate in the immediate post-*Durham* years. Most commentators – academic and professional, legal and behavioral – focused narrowly on the appropriate limits of the insanity defense, sometimes revealing hints of their thinking about the more general question of human freedom, but mainly leaving the historian to speculate. With respect to the insanity defense, the friends of *Durham* outnumbered its detractors (at least in the pages of the law journals of the day), especially if one includes those who were comfortable with the proposed MPC formulation but (unlike Wechsler) preferred the product test to the traditional tests. The debate over

---

[118] Szasz, "Psychiatry, Ethics, and the Criminal Law," 195.
[119] Szasz, "Psychiatry, Ethics, and the Criminal Law," 190.

the defense, although it was only part of the story, was the part that counted because it involved rules for the resolution of actual cases. Nonetheless the further-reaching discussion of the principles of criminal responsibility continued, not only among legal and behavioral science scholars, but increasingly among academic philosophers as well. From the more skeptical perspective of positivist legal scholars, what mattered was fashioning a defense of a heuristic premise – of a way of talking about what Moberly had termed the "embracing of a liability that could have been disputed."

Harvard law professor Henry Hart's contribution to this project shifted the terms significantly from the existential to the pragmatic: from a concern to explain what free will could mean to an unexamined acceptance of the individual's susceptibility to blame; and from a main focus on the psychic health of the offender to an emphasis on his moral education. Hart took account of retributivism as a social fact, but adapted it to the criminal law's own consequentialist and expressivist purposes. He combined aspects of the mosaic of positivist and deterrence-based thought of the preceding decades with the language – although not the underlying premises – of traditionalism. In the process, Hart seemed to supply a rationale for the belief in human freedom, or, at least, for the suspension of disbelief. But in truth he never engaged with (or even took notice of) either idea. His was an ingenious and, perhaps, quintessentially pragmatic American solution.

Hart's 1958 article, "The Aims of the Criminal Law," came as something of a shot across the bow of the MPC, which was still only in tentative draft form. Terming his own approach "somewhat, but not widely, at variance with the statement of purposes and principles of construction" of the MPC, Hart produced an alternative statement of purposes. For the MPC's opening "general purposes of the provisions governing the definition of offenses" – namely, to "forbid and prevent conduct that unjustifiably and inexcusably inflicts or threatens substantial harm" – Hart substituted: "to foster the development of personal capacity for responsible decision to the end that every individual may realize his potentialities as a participating and contributing member of his community."[120] Whereas the MPC purported to put prevention and deterrence first and largely as ends in themselves, Hart stressed human individual growth and self-realization in the arts of social living, although these ends were to be achieved by means that accorded with substantive and procedural standards roughly identical to those of the MPC. Whereas the MPC spoke in the language of "fault," Hart invoked that of "blame-worthiness," stressing at every turn that the criminal law's

---

[120] Henry M. Hart, Jr., "The Aims of the Criminal Law," *Law and Contemporary Problems*, vol. 23 (1958): 440. For a significant (and differing) reading of Hart's famous article, see Richard A. Posner, "Henry Hart's 'The Aims of the Criminal Law': A Reconsideration," chap 5 in *In the Name of Justice: Leading Experts Reexamine the Classic Article "The Aims of the Criminal Law"* ed. Timothy Lynch (Washington, DC: Cato Institute, 2009).

special quality was its "*moral* condemnation" of offenders.[121] "What distinguishes a criminal from a civil sanction and all that distinguishes it, it is ventured, is the judgment of community condemnation which accompanies and justifies its imposition."[122] Hart allied himself with George Gardner's even starker evocation of this theme: "'It is the expression of the community's hatred, fear, or contempt for the convict which alone characterizes physical hardship as punishment.'"[123] And this perspective led directly to what Hart called his "central thesis": that the criminal law "is misused when it is ... applied to conduct which is not blameworthy"[124] and instead condemns one by "ill chance," as he stressed in his critique of strict liability.[125]

For Hart, the criminal law's legislating of moral condemnation served a variety of purposes. First and foremost was the "inculcation of a sense of social responsibility throughout the society." This "dominant aim" necessarily involved the "aim of deterrence of undesired conduct," and because "violators are to be condemned as defaulters in their duty to the community and treated accordingly, the aim can also be described as punitive." The legislative declaration would at the same time "constitute an important first step in identifying those whose behaviors show them to be in need of cure and rehabilitation" – an aim to be included – and it would identify those more serious offenders for whom the aim of "temporary or permanent disablement" is appropriate.[126]

Hart's characterization of the criminal law sounded in retributivist terms – moral condemnation (even "hatred") of the criminal – but the criminal law's dominant aim of "inculcation of a sense of responsibility" was overwhelmingly expressivist-consequentialist. This inculcation occurred at the points of legislation, charge, and trial, the trial judge's sentence, and punishment or treatment. Those last terms – "punishment" and "treatment" – were interchangeable, as the criminal law stood both for what was commonly understood as punitive (the instantiation of moral condemnation under the law) and for cure and rehabilitation, the two means by which the law achieved its main "positive" purpose "to foster the development of personal capacity for responsible decision" by, at least in part, teaching offenders that the behavior for which they had been convicted was morally blameworthy.

Hart paid particular attention to the process by which individuals learned their responsibilities and thereby attained the personal growth that all law took as its ultimate, "positive" aim. He firmly rejected not only the radical

---

[121] Hart, "Aims of the Criminal Law," 405–06, 408–09, 419–20, 424–25.

[122] Hart, "Aims of the Criminal Law," 404.

[123] Hart, "Aims of the Criminal Law," 404–05 (emphasis added; quoting George Gardner, "*Bailey v. Richardson* and the Constitution of the United States," *Boston University Law Review*, vol. 33 [1953]: 176, 193).

[124] Hart, "Aims of the Criminal Law," 405 n. 13.

[125] Hart, "Aims of the Criminal Law," 422–25.

[126] Hart, "Aims of the Criminal Law," 413.

positivist message that the offender "will merely be considered to be sick and subjected to officially-imposed rehabilitative treatment in an effort to cure [him]," but also the more conventional positivist-inspired reformationist message that the offender's "own personal need for cure and rehabilitation will be the predominating factor in determining what happens to [him]."[127] He pointed to the due process dangers of these variants of the "curative-rehabilitative theory" according to which a person is "punished, or treated, for what he is or is believed to be, rather than for what he has done." If, for example, a person's "offense" is minor but the possibility of his reformation is thought to be slight, the other side of the coin of mercy can become cruelty."[128] Moreover the normal safeguards of the criminal law, which "will appear to be appropriate" under a condemnatory system "would come into question under a purely rehabilitative theory."[129] But Hart's more revealing critique shared a vocabulary with his own "positive" perspective on the character-building virtues of condemnation. Hart here borrowed from Moberly:

Recite a delinquent's disabilities and handicaps in front of him in open court and you are doing something to confirm them; you are impairing that self-respect and sense of responsibility which is the chief incentive to effort. Treat him as sane and responsible and as a whole man and you give him the best chance of rising to this level.[130]

Thus, correct criminal process proceeded upon the proposition that the criminal law spoke to prospective offenders as follows: "If you violate any of these laws and the violation is culpable, your conduct will receive the formal and solemn condemnation of the community as morally blameworthy, and you will be subjected to whatever punishment, or treatment, is appropriate to vindicate the law and to further its various purposes."[131] And the method and goal of this condemnatory punishment, or treatment, Hart neatly encapsulated in terms that came as close as did any in the article to articulating his theory of human behavior as it related to criminal responsibility.

What is crucial in this process is the enlargement of each individual's capacity for effectual and responsible decision. For it is only through personal, self-reliant participation, by trial and error, in the problem of existence, both personal and social, that the capacity to participate effectively can grow. Man learns wisdom in choosing by being made aware that he must abide the consequences of his choice. In

---

[127] Hart, "Aims of the Criminal Law," 413.
[128] Hart, "Aims of the Criminal Law," 407. Hart cited the assertion of Barnes and Teeters that "'those who cannot be reformed ... must be segregated for life – but not necessarily punished – *irrespective of the crimes they have committed*'" (407 n. 19 [quoting Harry E. Barnes and Negley K. Teeters, *New Horizons in Criminology*, rev. ed. (1945), 953 (Hart's emphasis)]).
[129] Hart, "Aims of the Criminal Law," 411.
[130] Hart, "Aims of the Criminal Law," 410 n. 23 (quoting Moberly, *Responsibility*, 23).
[131] Hart, "Aims of the Criminal Law," 408.

the training of a child in the small circle of the family, this principle is familiar enough. It has the same validity in the training of an adult in the larger circle of the community.[132]

Although Hart never used the term "free will," we may safely assume that he associated some version of that idea with normal human behavior. Humans have a capacity for "choice" and, evidently, for "self-reliant participation." That they learn "wisdom in choosing" is more ambiguous; it could be read as positivist in its own way, as a sort of stimulus-response learning process that gave specific direction to the application of a preexisting capacity for choice. Hart's terms were, in general, consonant with a deterministic view of human development *and* actual choice. Such a view countered his central point, however, that "blameworthy choice" rested on something other than "ill chance." The reader was left to imagine just what that something other was. Indeed, much of Hart's essay reads as an argument for the adoption of a *social convention* of blameworthiness based on free choice, a convention that traded on the *sense* of personal responsibility and, presumably, of the consciousness of free will, but on little more. Hart, then, might be said to have offered his own interpretation of the idea of criminal responsibility as a moral-legal rule.

But alongside Hart's language of inducement and training, his later claim, that "individuals who are able but unwilling to comply" with "reasonably grounded appeal[s] to the citizen's sense of responsibility as a citizen" are "precisely the ones who ought to be condemned as criminals," lacks foundation – and even appears as a paradoxical circularity. What can "able to comply with" mean in this context? Hart set forth an ambiguous test. First, a due process consideration: the legislature will, in a just world, reflect "community attitudes and needs," so that "actual knowledge of the wrongfulness of the prohibited conduct will usually exist," or be fairly assumed to exist. And, second, the crucial substantive consideration: the "obligations of conduct fixed by a fair appraisal of the minimum requirements for the maintenance and fostering of community life will, by hypothesis, be obligations which normal members of the community will be able to comply with." As to "normal" and "able": "the traditional law provides materials for solution of the problem when inability negatives blameworthiness," for example, the "doctrines with respect to duress, as well as doctrines providing for the exculpation of those individuals who because of mental disease or defect are to be deemed incapable of acting as responsible, participating members of society."[133] Here Hart essentially fell back on the law as it existed, with no mention of the relationship among "able," "willing," and all the (determining) processes of family and social life (including the processes of the

---

[132] Hart, "Aims of the Criminal Law," 410.
[133] Hart, "Aims of the Criminal Law," 413–14.

criminal law itself) that, according to Hart, play a critical role in the shaping of human disposition, insight, and "responsible decision." The criminal law and its attendant processes help to determine behavior, but the proscribed behavior of the legally sane (not under duress) that neither the criminal law nor anything else has succeeded in preventing is criminal (hence subject to additional training with the inducement: better luck next time round).

There is, it would seem, a discrepancy here, because of Hart's determination not to engage in analysis of the underlying premises of criminal responsibility but, rather, simply to accept evolving social-legal standards in service of the overriding aims of the criminal law. Yet his essay possesses great rhetorical power regarding human potential, social conventions, and the purposes of the criminal law. By emphasizing a socially rooted blameworthiness, Hart, seemingly, had returned criminal law to its traditional roots, thus minimizing the disjunction between academic ideas and social attitudes that plagued the positivists. In placing personal growth for social participation ahead of prevention as the overriding goal of the criminal law, he avoided, too, the tensions between conventional blame and a headier utilitarianism that Wechsler had to confront, given the only very rough overlap between utility and mercurial social demands for revenge, mercy, or both. Most important, Hart provided a rationale for community-based condemnation. Out of something long characterized as negative, atavistic, immature ("primitive and irrational," Judge Hand had declared), came something positive, progressive, mature, something – one might even say – "curative-rehabilitative."

Indeed one might say just this, for Hart's discussion of "treatment" neatly allied the idea of condemnation – which was crucial to the grading of offenses and the predefined severity of treatment thus authorized for each offense – with a rehabilitative ideal: "Punishments," he asserted,

should be severe enough to impress not only upon the defendant's mind, but upon the public mind, the gravity of society's condemnation of irresponsible behavior. But the ultimate aim of condemning irresponsibility is training for responsibility.... Allowance for the possibility of reformation, or formation, of character in the generality of cases becomes at this point, in other words, an *overriding consideration*.[134]

This formulation was consistent with "eliminating capital punishment and minimizing both the occasions and the length of incarceration."[135] Where offenders were sentenced to prison, it followed that although "prison and parole authorities would receive prisoners from trial courts with sentences for predetermined, individualized maximum and, when appropriate, minimum terms," these correctional authorities would have primary responsibility for determination of "what kind of custodial treatment would best

[134] Hart, "Aims of the Criminal Law," 426 (emphasis added).
[135] Hart, "Aims of the Criminal Law," 426.

promote the individual prisoner's growth in responsibility."[136] Whatever the penal technique, the critical step was the offender's internalization of the community's strong disapprobation – and even condemnation. Hart's view thus lessened "bifurcation," that is, the distance between the trial stage and sentencing, for he emphasized the potential reformatory effects of both determination of guilt and the trial judges' expression of social condemnation as well as those resulting from punitive and rehabilitative treatment. Indeed, where the very fact of a conviction premised upon condemnation itself had a reforming effect, suspension of sentence was most often appropriate. Except in especially serious cases, general deterrence was, presumably, well accounted for in the very public condemnation of the individual offender. Reformation of the offender, then, was both preventative and a goal in itself, although in many cases the juncture of law and psychology argued for something closer to the stocks than the couch.

Hart's linking of moral condemnation and self-realization as a participating member of the community was a tour de force. It could be applied to Puritan penology, to the shaming practices sometimes recommended for the modern state, and to much that lay in-between. It resonated, ironically enough, with aspects of the juristic positivism of the 1930s: with the early Hall's prescription for gradual expansion of individualization, with Waite's emphasis on the offender's internalization of society's scorn and contempt, with Gausewitz's accommodationist program of reformation. Although it did not lead from the positivist perspective – but instead justified punishment via social condemnation – its ultimate ends were reformative rather than, strictly speaking, deterrence-based. Still, its stress on condemnatory conduct was meant in large part to vindicate political liberty against the threat of increasing (legal-positivist-based) strict liability.

Despite his focus on reform, however, Hart resisted portraying the offender as a victim of circumstances and therefore not fully responsible. Here he drew on Moberly, as had Wechsler, but whereas Wechsler focused on the "cruelty" of treating individuals as lacking the capacity for responsibility, Hart focused on the importance of maintaining the individual's "self respect" and "incentive to effort."[137] He did not, of course, adopt Moberly's metaphysics of personal responsibility. And, unlike Hill, Hart viewed lay participation in the criminal process as crucial to the offender's (rather than the juror's) moral education. The criminal trial was not, however, thereby a training in the scientific underpinnings of human behavior. Unlike Szasz, Hart stopped well short of equating moral education with the universalizing

---

[136] Hart, "Aims of the Criminal Law," 440.
[137] Accordingly, although Hart met Wechsler's requirements for special deterrence, he gave less emphasis to general deterrence; Hart offered a more conventional sounding account of guilt assessment than did Wechsler and he more fully embraced rehabilitation as an ultimate goal.

of the experience of guilt, although even Szasz could concur in Hart's portrayal of the criminal process as a public, educative ritual of moral condemnation. Although the terms in which Hart addressed guilt assessment risked exposing the infirmity of a bare invocation of "blameworthy choice," Hart's stress on rehabilitation carried forward Progressivism's partial compensation for that infirmity. Wechsler's approach, in contrast to Hart's, was to define criminal responsibility in terms of culpable mental states and the future danger of similar public injury that they implied – largely to replace personal guilt with society's need for protection. Wechsler's utilitarianism ultimately could not prevail against the widespread social conception of "justice" and insistence upon "personal responsibility." [138]

Hart's seminal essay, we shall see, foreshadows the retributivism of the century's last decades. Nonetheless, Hart had his eye on the past and the ideas he explored are most familiar when we approach his "Aims" from that perspective. Hart was strongly vested in the consequentialist debate between deterrence and cure. He was impatient with positivism's cure theory yet he found a compromise between rehabilitation and blameworthiness by adjusting the terms of prevention to those of conventional morality. To the extent that Hart put prevention ahead of cure, he did so, however, without endorsing a purely utilitarian theory of general deterrence.

What most separated Hart from the retributivism of the 1980s and beyond was his particular approach to the idea of blameworthiness. The determinist critique seems to have interested him not at all. His response to positivism rested on consequential grounds: treat people as having the capacity for responsible behavior and they will rise to the occasion; individual and social well-being – the point of *all* law – will thereby be best served. Hart's retributivism, if such it was, bore relation to the later idea of "the utility of desert," [139] but Hart never used the word "desert" or investigated the underlying premises of that core element of retributivism. The usefulness, *going forward*, of moral condemnation to the consequentialist aims of the criminal law – not the philosophical justification for that condemnation – was Hart's subject. And, as I illustrate below, in Part III, that united him more closely with his Progressive and post-Progressive forbears than with the retributivists who followed.

---

[138] In a private conversation (January 1997), Wechsler, by way of retrospection, described Hart's "Aims of the Criminal Law" as "the most important and insightful work of the day." I am indebted to Herbert Wechsler (and his wife, Doris) for providing reflections on the criminal jurisprudence of the 1930–1960 period.

[139] I touch on the "utility of desert" in Chapter 8, n. 8, and Chapter 9.

CONCLUSION

By the end of the 1950s, American legal scholars had developed an impressive range of nuanced answers – sometimes explicit, but more often implicit – to whether and where notions of free will had a place in the law. Their maturing scholarship, alongside a maturing nation, was beginning to move beyond the comparatively single-minded reformist bent of the Progressive Era. Postwar scholars offered a range of positions and concerns that cannot be classified in any simple manner. But, if they may be characterized in any way as a group, they should be said to have brought increasing depth and awareness to questions concerning what the rule of law *is* – or should be – and what part in that rule should be played by conventional morality. The Progressive, systems-based approach to the law – which focused on the needs of society, even if those needs also included some fostering of individual pursuits – was now making way for new attention to the individual. Not in the imposed sense of "individualization" related to post-conviction treatment, but in the senses both of the individual's internalization of freedom and of his external freedom-based relationship to the state. Indeed, for many commentators, the acknowledgment of the importance of the individual's experience of freedom overlapped with the imperatives of political liberty: each element of freedom could be said to require an orientation to the individual that, somehow, delineated the innocent from the guilty in a way that the public would understand as reinforcing both elements.

A primary difference among midcentury scholars ultimately came to be whether this particular freedom-girding role of the law was conceived largely as a conceit that could nonetheless serve consequentialist ends or, in fact, as the legal system's very (epitomized) essence. Scholarly acceptance of the jury ran along a similar spectrum. Most scholars presumed the jury would serve an ongoing role as final arbiter of close questions concerning legal responsibility on a case-by-case basis, particularly when judging legal insanity. But visions of the jury varied widely, from that of a perhaps regrettable, but necessary, cultural limit on the input of medical and behavioral experts, to that of the proper, ultimate decision maker on a matter that was inherently a question of morality.

Still, on balance, the Progressive inheritance had endured. In rescuing a sort of post-Progressive version of traditional culpability from the determinist critique, emerging moral-legal notions of responsibility continued to affirm the essence of that critique: consequentialist goals remained central and, where the idea of free will reentered scholarly discussion, it most often did so in a limited, instrumentally justified, "as if" form that implicitly accepted determinist premises for human action. For most progressive scholars, this "as if" orientation remained a loosely theorized nod either to conventional notions of agency or, at least, to the supportive role those notions could play in a centrally consequentialist legal regime. It was aspirational or

semantic. It existed in a psychological or ideological sphere separate from
the reality (or possibility) of determinism, and the interrelationship between
the two realms, if any, was rarely probed.

In light of this growing dual commitment to both "responsibility," in
some form, and determinism, at first glance it is puzzling that, before midcentury, more legal scholars did not directly resolve the free will problem
by forthrightly taking up fully compatibilist positions – by squaring legal
blame with humans' (determined) capacity for reason, deliberation, or volition, and thus urging either that "free will" should be (re)defined as consistent with determinism or, if understood in the robust, true-free-will sense,
simply jettisoned as unnecessary to human understandings of responsibility.
There was much earlier commentary in this vein to draw on, yet Hume,
Hobbes, and other early compatibilist thinkers were still rarely referenced
by legal scholars even as of the 1950s. I venture that, for the mainstream
consequentialist legal community, the hopeful allure of scientific-positivist
and/or utilitiarian principles had, for a time, lessened the need for a complete philosophical rubric justifying criminal responsibility in the face of
determinism: after all, if the goal of law might ultimately become cure or
nonpunitive repression, the deeper free will question – begged by the law's
retributive connotations – might fade away. Even if society required an "as
if" sense of personal freedom in order to function – whether temporarily or
in an ongoing sense – that "as if" need only support an instrumental notion
of our duties to each other and to society, and not a sense of personal desert
as the result of truly free choice.

But, the Progressive dream was shadowed by the realization that maintaining even an instrumental sense of personal responsibility required drawing
on traditional notions of culpability – indeed, barring a complete reeducation of society, these notions could not be divorced from a law enacted
and imposed, at least in part, by a populace committed to them. Hence
scholars' hope that this common morality with regard to culpability might
be integrated – perhaps semantically, or in a theoretically thinner form –
into a more progressive system of law, and perhaps even be transformed in
the process. Yet, scholars were discovering that, no matter how responsibility was semantically or theoretically circumscribed to remain consistent in
some way with consequential, non-retributive ends, it still invoked – tacitly
or otherwise – blame and moral transgression. Just as significant, no matter
how punishment was described as non-retributive or as a means to beneficial rehabilitation, it was still understood as punishment; this was true,
in particular, in light of the real-world critique of rehabilitation that was
slowly gaining steam and would come to a head in the early 1970s. In other
words, without an actual Progressive remaking of the law's processes and
tenets – a short-lived dream for some that had been quickly abandoned –
"as if" free will would have a difficult time carrying the weight of criminal
condemnation: it seemed incapable of justifying the punitive retribution that

began to seem inseparable from public understandings of – and practical ramifications of – the law, however condemnation and punishment might be euphemized by theorists.

In recognizing the need for some integration of "freedom" into the positivist/consequentialist enterprise, the scholarship of the 1930s, 1940s, and 1950s had helped create the conditions that necessitated – and enabled – its surpassing by scholars of the 1960s and beyond. For some of the latter, the "as if" would remain – but it clearly required fortification by increasingly complex and theorized justifications for the imposition of criminal responsibility, usually rooted in the imperatives of political liberty, the factual nature of the human capacity for reason, or notions of the dignity and autonomy inherent in personhood. For others in the century's last decades, "as if" simply would not suffice: it was these scholars who more often drew on both historical and modern formal philosophical compatibilism to redefine criminal responsibility – and sometimes, the notion of "free will" itself – in ways that did not, purportedly, conflict with determinism. Whatever the nuances of their approaches, all those who took up the responsibility question in these later years were faced with the task of again reconceiving responsibility in light not only of the determinist critique, but of the tenacity of ideas of freedom and retribution that increasingly appeared to be inseparable from the rule of law in America.

PART III

FREEDOM, CRIMINAL RESPONSIBILITY, AND RETRIBUTIVISM IN LATE-TWENTIETH-CENTURY LEGAL THOUGHT

INTRODUCTION

Harry Kalven's 1955 invocation of blameworthiness as a fundamental condition of criminal responsibility – emphasizing the "moral context of the criminal law" and opining that "the legal system touches deeply our sense of where the blameworthy, and the praiseworthy begins and ends in our daily life"[1] – at once possessed a formulaic quality and presented a challenge to long-standing conventions within American legal academic circles. Kalven had not been specific regarding the nature and implications of this foundational idea. And we have seen that although some other responses to *Durham* also bespoke a modern criminal jurisprudence that placed blameworthiness at the center of things, they too revealed that the connotations of the idea were various. Blameworthiness could be assimilated to utility or to a reformative ideal. It could underwrite an emergent retributivism. It might remain no more than a baseline, or threshold condition, insisted on in the interest of political liberty, or it might unite more broadly with human values (potentially expressed in the terms of conventional morality). And those values could be viewed as appropriate either because they represented social understandings that the law ought to reflect, or because they represented underlying *truths* that the law ought to reflect, regardless of whether such truths were consistent with social understandings.

Although the meanings and implications of blame varied significantly, legal scholarship was largely united at least in moving beyond attempts – whether centrally positivist or utilitarian in tenor – to define criminal liability in terms that minimized personal, blameworthy fault in light of the determinist critique. The shift was initially pragmatic. Concerns

---

[1] Harry Kalven, "Introduction" to "Insanity and the Criminal Law – A Critique of *Durham v. United States*," *University of Chicago Law Review*, vol. 22 (1955): 317–19, 318.

about political liberty or the integrity of the rule of law – as a historically and culturally embedded institution – had led to an increasing consensus that the threshold for criminal sanctions must lie squarely on individual conduct proscribed by law. Particularly in the postwar years, the core principle *nullum crimen, nulla poena sine lege* was reinvigorated, and it was commonly assumed that an individual's general dangerousness or need for treatment would never be sufficient, alone, to invoke intervention by the criminal justice system. But free will itself was most often treated in an "as if" fashion: conventional ideas about it might find a role in the legal process and provide foundation for the law as an essentially social institution, yet pervasive academic skepticism about true free will relegated it – along with traditional ideas of retribution-worthy individual blame or desert – to an instrumental, background position. The resulting "moral-legal" idea of responsibility was significant and, in an essential sense, enduring. But it would not be enough. Both theoretically and politically, initial formulations of this idea would provide too bare a framework for criminal condemnation on the basis of individual desert. The second half of the twentieth century witnessed the return among a significant number of legal academics to retributivism and to recovered ideas of a deserved blameworthiness. This theoretical development paralleled developments in national politics and in penal practice. But the academic shift cannot be simplified as a mere outgrowth of, or reaction to, external events. Rather, its route was complex and, to some degree, grounded in different concerns – and expressed in different terms – than those of politicians or the penal bureaucracy.

The period from about 1960 to 1975 is widely thought of as a time of national crisis with regard to crime and criminal justice. By many accounts, it is a crisis that never fully abated. The reasons offered for the crisis, however – and even the descriptions of factors said to constitute it – are complicated and often opposing. Crime rates rose dramatically during this period, which was also marked by waves of rioting not only as the result of urban racial conflict and opposition to the Vietnam War, but also within the nation's often violent prisons; the times were characterized by grave fears about crime, as well as about general social upheaval. Still, prison rates were initially relatively low in comparison with the unprecedented (and unparalleled, worldwide) high rates the nation would see beginning in the early 1970s and continuing through the end of the century. The initial low rates were in part associated with the impact of treatment- and diversion-based penal methods. On one side, faith in the possible success of such progressive methods was still widespread at least as of the early 1960s. On the other, the combination of high crime rates and low incarceration rates allowed for a mounting public impression that police, prosecutors, and penal officers were simply ill-equipped (because of, it was sometimes argued, progressive policies toward crime) to deal with the unrelenting reality of modern crime.[2]

At least, this latter explanation is how the conservative "law and order" movement – epitomized by the 1964 Goldwater presidential campaign – would characterize the problem. The Goldwater campaign injected into the national discussion a staunch crime control approach that gave new voice to the retributive urges that the reform community had long kept at arm's length. The strong political pull of this conservative emphasis on personal responsibility would ultimately infect both conservative and liberal appraisals of the sources of crime, as well as of the "welfare state," generally.[3]

The response of President Lyndon Johnson's Commission on Law Enforcement and Administration of Justice – or the President's Crime Commission, as it came to be known – presented the matter differently. The Commission's Report, issued in 1967, certainly reflected the nation's fear of crime and decried its deleterious effects on communities. But, in large part, the Report held fast to the liberal/progressive notion that the causes of crime were primarily environmental, and thus should be addressed through intensified social and economic programming, not only for prisoners and parolees, but for poor and minority communities, generally. The Report was a strong statement in favor of the rehabilitative regime but, in keeping with the times, its impact was more ambiguous; although it spawned a temporary highpoint in community services and expansion of probation and parole programs, it also resulted, for example, in significant federal expenditures on repressive, military-style law enforcement equipment.

So initial perceptions of and responses to the crisis in justice were conflicted. But, where the motives of some of the system's critics would remain opposed, their proposed solutions would begin to dovetail. Most critical in this regard is the fact that, by the 1970s, hope for the rehabilitative penal ideal began to give way even among its prior supporters.[4] On a basic empirical level, studies

---

[2] For statistical references and overviews of the state of criminal justice – and of criminal justice politics – over the period 1960–2000, with a focus on the crisis years 1960–1975 and the trends I discuss, see, e.g., Samuel Walker, *Popular Justice: A History of American Criminal Justice*, 2nd ed. (New York: Oxford University Press, 1998), chap. 6, "National Crisis Over Criminal Justice, 1960–1975," and chap. 7, "Crime and Justice in a Conservative Era, 1975–1995"; William J. Stuntz, *The Collapse of American Criminal Justice* (Cambridge, MA: Belknap Press, 2011), esp. chap. 9, "The Rise and Fall of Crime, the Fall and Rise of Criminal Punishment."

[3] For remarks on the evolution of the conservative view – and its transforming effects on national politics through the end of the century – see Stuntz, *Collapse*, 236–41; Walker, *Popular Justice*, chap. 7. David Garland offers a particularly full account of these issues in *The Culture of Control: Crime and Social Order in Contemporary Society* (Chicago: University of Chicago Press, 2001), noted further throughout this Introduction.

[4] The reluctant agreement of some progressive scholars to deprioritize rehabilitation in light of its real-world failures is candidly illustrated by the introductory statement accompanying

confirmed that, in practice, treatment programs were largely unsuccessful in preventing recidivism. From more theoretical and political standpoints, the rehabilitative ideal faced continuing postwar challenges from those who conceived of its tenets as authoritarian – or at least potentially so – and essentially inimical to a free society.[5] Whether they were perceived as resulting from deficiencies in implementation, gaps in the empirical premises of the rehabilitation movement, or other circumstances, the apparent failures of the rehabilitative method drew concern from all sides. Building toward the end of the century, political rhetoric increasingly emphasized personal responsibility and espoused "get tough" measures that were supported in vivid detail by crime rates and the legislated War on Drugs.[6] At the other end of the spectrum, the civil rights movement – institutionalized in part by rulings on due process and equal protection by the Supreme Court under Chief Justice Warren – challenged rehabilitation on the basis of both its real-world failures and its paternalistic, discriminatory assumptions about crime and

---

Andrew von Hirsch's *Doing Justice: The Choice of Punishments* (Report of the Committee for the Study of Incarceration) (New York: Hill and Wang, 1976), the significant 1976 report of an interdisciplinary scholarly committee regarding crime and incarceration. I discuss this statement at length in Chapter 7.

[5] The most thoughtful near-contemporary set of reflections on the various causes of the American justice system's turn away from its decades-long rehabilitative focus – including attention to the political-liberty ramifications of the rehabilitative regime – is Francis A. Allen's *The Decline of the Rehabilitative Ideal: Penal Policy and Social Purpose* (New Haven: Yale University Press, 1981). David Garland also offers a particularly in-depth and thought-provoking analysis of the collapse of the criminal justice system's central rehabilitative premises – and its aftermath through the end of the century – in *Culture of Control*, see, esp., the overview at pp. 8–14, and chap. 3, "The Crisis of Penal Modernism." Garland urges that the abruptness of the 1970s shift away from the "penal welfarism" that had been a central force in the justice system since the 1890s cannot be overstated (p. 3).

[6] In *Culture of Control*, Garland charts the political cooptation of crime policy – which moved from the hands of the professional penal bureaucracy to those of politicians – and discusses the particularly remarkable transformation in political rhetoric that started on the far right but would come to dominate much of the political spectrum by at least the 1990s: a resurgence of the sort of vengeful rhetoric that, until the 1970s, had been associated with punitive measures ubiquitously "criticized as anachronisms that had no place within a 'modern' penal system" (8–9). For more commentary on the political and penological transformations that manifested in end-of-century America, see James Q. Whitman, *Harsh Justice: Criminal Punishment and the Widening Divide between America and Europe* (New York: Oxford University Press, 2003); Jonathan Simon, *Governing through Crime: How the War on Crime Transformed American Democracy and Created a Culture of Fear* (New York: Oxford University Press, 2006). See also Robert A. Ferguson, *Inferno: An Anatomy of American Punishment* (Cambridge, MA: Harvard University Press, 2014). Various commentators assert that the end-of-century *political* preference for retributive crime policy tended to be more extreme than the public's shared sense of just sentencing. E.g., Paul H. Robinson and John M. Darley, "Intuitions of Justice: Implications for Criminal Law and Justice Policy," *Southern California Law Review*, vol. 81 (2007): 1–67, 42; Alice Ristroph, "Desert, Democracy, and Sentencing Reform," *JCLC*, vol. 96 (2006): 1293–352, 1307 n. 49. Ristroph cites studies suggesting that the public, while perhaps increasingly citing retribution or "just deserts" as the primary goal of sentencing, also supported utilitarian and reform-oriented goals (1306 and n. 45).

"criminals."[7] Although the pendulum swing in official jurisprudence toward individual rights would begin to reverse by the 1990s alongside other conservative political developments, constitutional protection of individual rights became a significant, permanent factor in criminal justice administration.

The initial result of this confluence of divergent factors was a relatively unified call for less discretion by criminal justice officials, particularly in sentencing. Fixed sentences – as opposed to indeterminate ones, with release dependent on the results of treatment – were advocated on all sides, although the presumed advantages of the change ranged widely: the law and order set favored the retributive/deterrent message of mandatory sentences; liberal/progressive groups sought to limit the discriminatory reach of official discretion in what they viewed as an essentially broken, clearly racially biased, and often abusive penal system. Later, visions for reform would again diverge, particularly as the more rights-oriented critics reacted to actual legislation implementing the changes: fixed sentences took the form of lengthy mandatory-minimum terms and "three-strikes-and-you're-out" laws that fed the sharp growth in prison populations and, especially in connection with the substantive law on drug crimes, disparately affected the poor and racial minorities.[8] But, through the 1970s, a range of voices all wanted the same thing: a less discretionary and less paternal justice system that clearly defined the rights and powers of citizens and officials alike. One result was an unavoidable focus on the individual as the responsible agent of his or her life and conduct.[9]

---

[7] In 1971, the American Friends Service Committee released its well-known report, *Struggle for Justice: A Report on Crime and Punishment in America* (New York: Hill and Wang, 1971), a searing evaluation of the justice system that exposed vast racial bias and challenged the paternalistic, rehabilitative premises of sentencing and penology still rooted in Progressive Era ideals. Generally, of course, the pervasiveness of the justice system's disparate impacts on citizens along lines of race and class – particularly its impact on African-American men – only increased over time. Statistics and commentary that touch on this particular complex and troubling topic, which is inseparable from any discussion of the American justice system, appear throughout the historical works I cite here.

[8] Early in the twenty-first century, the American Law Institute would propose a vast overhaul of its model sentencing recommendations in direct reaction to these realities of U.S. sentencing and penal policies. See my discussion in Chapter 9.

[9] A particularly noteworthy observation on the convergence of attitudes opposed to the justice system's rehabilitative focus concerns the drift away from the central notion that crime is a problem to be addressed by the state through the remediation of individual character. As Garland illustrates, new theories of criminology were substantially less united regarding the causes of crime than were the roughly "Progressive" theories that dominated the first two-thirds of the century, but many otherwise divergent theories overlapped in their emphasis on the criminal actor as an autonomous, rational individual not thought to be intrinsically abnormal or in need of cure. In this sense, the existence of crime was normalized – albeit on varying terms – and thought of less as an ultimately eradicable societal problem than as a social "fact" to be controlled or negotiated. On the Left, critical sociology reconceived criminality as, in part, a label arising from power relations and the imposition of "majority" values (themselves often manufactured by powerful elites). In keeping with the widespread application of economic and market theories to social issues, others emphasized the actor's

Freedom, Criminal Responsibility, and Retributivism

   The insanity defense, the definitive excuse from criminal responsibility,
also received its share of the public spotlight. The Model Penal Code
formulation – which included both a cognitive prong ("lacks substantial
capacity ... to appreciate the criminality (wrongfulness) of his conduct")
and a volitional prong (lacks substantial capacity ... to conform his conduct to the requirements of the law")[10] – was widely adopted both by state
legislatures and federal circuits after its official promulgation in 1962. In
1982, however, that standard (combined with a burden on the government
to prove sanity) was the basis for the jury's acquittal of John Hinckley, Jr.,
on grounds of insanity in the trial on his attempt to assassinate President
Reagan. The outcry (ripe from prior critiques of the defense's overuse) was
widespread and the reaction was swift. The Reagan administration immediately proposed abolishing the defense altogether for federal law, instead
permitting evidence of mental disease or defect only to negate the mens rea
element of a crime. Congress did not go quite this far but, in 1984, enacted
a strict version of the cognitive test, limited the testimony of experts, and
shifted the burden to the defense to prove insanity.[11] Many states followed
suit, at least with regard to the formulation of the test itself, and, soon, the
cognitive/*M'Naghten* standard replaced the MPC test as the majority rule.
Reversion to the cognitive test had been championed by, among others, the
American Bar Association and the American Psychiatric Association.[12]

---

rational cost/benefit analysis in choosing to violate the law. From a more political/rhetorical
angle, still others pressed the neoconservative view that some individuals simply choose to
be immoral or evil, and are best treated essentially as enemies of the state. See *Culture of
Control*, esp. 65–68, 127–38, 182–87. Although these approaches are often opposed in their
essential premises, each rejects the Progressive idea of the criminal offender as an unfortunate product of his or her environment or heredity who should become a charge of the state
and, if possible, treated and reintegrated into "normal" society.

[10] *Model Penal Code: Official Draft* (Philadelphia: American Law Institute, 1962), § 4.01.
[11] Insanity Defense Reform Act of 1984, Pub. L. No. 98–473, § 402(a) (1984); 18
   U.S.C. § 17.
[12] Neither association counseled total abolition of the insanity defense, which, they urged,
   would offend the "moral tenets of the criminal law" and the "moral intuitions of the community" because the criminal law is "rooted in beliefs about human rationality, deterrability and
   free will," which "represent articles of moral faith rather than scientific fact." Statement of
   the ABA in "The Insanity Defense: ABA and APA Proposals for Change," *Mental Disability
   Law Reporter*, vol. 7 (1983): 136–47, 210–11, 137. In the APA's words: "within the framework of English and American law, defendants who lack the ability (the capacity) to rationally control their behavior do not possess free will. They cannot be said to have 'chosen to do
   wrong.' ... Retention of the insanity defense is essential to the moral integrity of the criminal
   law" (144). In supporting the cognitive test, the ABA, in particular, disavowed the "wave of
   clinical optimism" that had dominated the 1950s (and was "reflected in the volitional portion of the [MPC] test"), concluding that "experience confirms that there is still ... no objective basis for distinguishing between offenders who were undeterrable and those who were
   merely undeterred, between the impulse that was irresistible and the impulse not resisted, or
   between substantial impairment of capacity and some lesser impairment" (138).

This is not to suggest that the MPC's general influence had simply run its course. Its codification of offenses and excuses became a touchstone for modern American criminal law. And the MPC as a whole undoubtedly changed the American conversation about the criminal law in the latter half of the century, spurring wide-ranging commentary not just about the Code's provisions themselves but, indeed, about the meaning and purposes of the law.[13] But the elements of the MPC that invoked deeper questions

The Idaho legislature effectively did abolish the insanity defense in the wake of the Hinckley trial. See, e.g., Brian E. Elkins, "Idaho's Repeal of the Insanity Defense: What Are We Trying to Prove?" *Idaho Law Review*, vol. 31 (1994): 151–72, esp. pp. 154–55. Idaho thus joined Montana, the only other state that had abolished the defense (Montana had done so in 1979). Utah's legislature would abolish the defense in 1993. Ibid., 155 n. 19. In upholding the legislation, the highest courts of these three states distinguished the reasoning of cases including *State v. Strasburg*, 110 P. 1020 (Wash. 1910), concluding that the Idaho, Utah, and Montana statutes did not offend due process because, unlike the statute at issue in *Strasburg*, the more recent statutes permitted admission of evidence of mental illness to rebut proof of mens rea. See, e.g., Andrew M. Levine, "Denying the Settled Insanity Defense: Another Necessary Step in Dealing with Drug and Alcohol Abuse," *Boston University Law Review*, vol 78 (1998): 75–104, 81–82, 85.

Many of the legal theorists I have discussed here who advocated for abolition of the insanity defense – or near-abolition, with a focus on culpable mens rea instead of on predetermined definitions of insanity – aimed at a range of goals generally informed by determinism, such as promoting detention of dangerous individuals regardless of whether they subjectively intended wrongdoing, increasing opportunities for rehabilitation of offenders, or, indeed, absolving large classes of individuals from criminal guilt altogether. Abolition thus had the potential to satisfy the strict deterrent goals of social defense theorists (and of course their allies in the larger political world) but, also, the goals of those either who favored benevolent medicalization of the criminal law (whether partial medicalization, e.g. perhaps Edwin Keedy or William A. White, or a more total medicalization, e.g. Barbara Wootton) or who sought to limit the state's reach in imposing condemnation and punishment (e.g. Norval Morris and David Bazelon). The debate spawned by the Hinckley trial and resulting in abolition of the insanity defense in Idaho seemed of a more clearly conservative bent, however, in line with retributive rhetoric and certainly contrary to hopes such as Bazelon's that abolition would encourage acquittal on progressive moral grounds thanks to a "broad inquiry into all forms of disabilities and motivations." David L. Bazelon, "The Morality of the Criminal Law," *Southern California Law Review*, vol. 49 (1976): 385–405, 397. The devil was in the details. Idaho's post-abolition law was cited, for example, as encouraging criminal condemnation and execution of those with severe mental illnesses because, although the statute nominally permitted evidence of mental illness to rebut mens rea, the law no longer meaningfully informed juries regarding how to assess such illness or its relationship to culpable intent. Elkins, "Idaho's Repeal of the Insanity Defense," esp. 152, 166–70.

On formulations of the insanity defense before and after the Hinckley trial, see "The Insanity Defense: ABA and APA Proposals for Change," generally; Lincoln Caplan, *The Insanity Defense and the Trial of John W. Hinckley* (Boston: D. R. Godine, 1984); Sanford H. Kadish, "Fifty Years of Criminal Law: An Opinionated Review," *California Law Review*, vol. 87 (1999): 943–82, 959–61; Michele Cotton, "A Foolish Consistency: Keeping Determinism Out of the Criminal Law," *Boston University Public Interest Law Journal*, vol. 15 (2005): 1–48, 14–18.

[13] As Sanford Kadish has commented, it "served to reorient scholarship from a preoccupation with chronicling the criminal law toward a critical legislative perspective" ("Fifty Years,"

concerning criminal responsibility – such as the threshold for the insanity defense and the Code's clear disfavoring of strict liability – were ultimately less influential on statutory and common law in practice. As practiced, the formal law often favored (or at least permitted) holding actors criminally responsible even at the margins, where culpability was most debatable. Legislatures continued to enact strict liability offenses – particularly in the realm of regulatory crimes – and the U.S. Supreme Court did not materially alter its conclusion, stated in *United States v. Dotterweich* (1943) and affirmed in *Morissette v. United States* (1952), that strict liability is a permissible basis for some crimes.[14]

Finally, for its part, the Supreme Court would decline to foray into larger questions of mens rea and culpability. In *Powell v. Texas* (1968) – a public drunkenness case in which the defendant argued that his alcohol addiction had destroyed his will to resist drinking – the Court, still under Chief Justice Warren, signaled in fractured opinions that it would not enter the free will debate by commenting on whether individuals may be punished for acts over which they arguably had no internal control.[15] The lead opinion's conclusion – that the "evolving aims of the criminal law and changing religious,

---

950). Cf. Peter W. Low, "The Model Penal Code, The Common Law, and Mistakes of Fact: Recklessness, Negligence, or Strict Liability?" *Rutgers Law Journal*, vol. 19 (1988): 539–68, 542 ("The fact is that the Model Penal Code defines the terms of debate on virtually every significant issue involved in the definition of crime and the recognition of defenses.").

[14] *United States v. Dotterweich*, 320 U.S. 277 (1943); *Morissette v. United States*, 342 U.S. 246 (1952); and see Kadish, "Fifty Years," 954–58 (discussing the persistence of what Kadish calls "liability without fault").

[15] *Powell v. Texas*, 392 U.S. 514 (1968); and see the discussion in Kadish, "Fifty Years," 964–66. *Powell* affirmed the public drunkenness conviction in three separate opinions, with a four-justice dissent written by Justice Abe Fortas – who had, of course, once advocated for the defendant in *Durham*. *Powell* drew a critical line beyond which *Robinson v. California*, 370 U.S. 660 (1962) – which had held that the Eighth Amendment precluded punishment for drug addiction (as a status or disease), without more – would not reach. Justice Thurgood Marshall's lead opinion, joined by three others including Warren, held itself out as based on "[t]raditional common law concepts of personal accountability and essential considerations of federalism." As a factual matter, the justices were "unable to conclude, on the state of this record or on the current state of medical knowledge, that chronic alcoholics in general, and Leroy Powell in particular, suffer from such an irresistible compulsion to drink and to get drunk in public that they are utterly unable to control their performance of either or both of these acts, and thus cannot be deterred at all from public intoxication" (*Powell*, 392 U.S. at 535, Marshall, J.). But, Marshall continued, "in any event, this Court has never articulated a general constitutional doctrine of *mens rea*":

> We cannot cast aside the centuries-long evolution of the collection of interlocking and overlapping concepts which the common law has utilized to assess the moral accountability of an individual for his antisocial deeds. The doctrines of *actus reus, mens rea,* insanity, mistake, justification, and duress have historically provided the tools for a constantly shifting adjustment of the tension between the evolving aims of the criminal law and changing religious, moral, philosophical, and medical views of the nature of man. This process of adjustment has always been thought to be the province of the States.

moral, philosophical, and medical views of the nature of man" essentially were beyond the Court's province[16] – left it to the scholars (those so inclined, anyway) to make sense of the human will's proper relationship to criminal culpability, although their conclusions thus were bound, in some regards, to remain as abstract commentaries on a law that, in practice, often appeared willfully untheorized.

This limited encapsulation of criminal justice in post-1960 America certainly oversimplifies a complex (and as yet unresolved) period in the nation's history. But it provides context for my study of the reemergence of retributivist responsibility theory among legal scholars – even if this context perhaps should raise more questions than it answers. On one hand, the convergence of desert theory, political rhetoric, and penal practice might appear to reflect the ultimate victory of conventional morality over positivist theory by the end of the century. Indeed, David Garland, for one, suggests that the "open embrace of previously discredited purposes" of punishment – and "explicit attempts to express public anger and resentment" through the criminal process – "transformed the more formal, academic discourse of the philosophy of punishment," leading philosophers to "create rationales for retributive measures that better express the cultural assumptions and political interests that now shape the practice of punishment."[17] On the other hand, although it is true that legal scholars did "create rationales for retributive measures," a close look at the nature of legal ideas and the manner in which those ideas unfolded belies any straightforward conclusion about the transformation to which Garland refers – that is, about the precise relationship between public discourse and legal-academic thought. If theorists sometimes made use of arguments from their real-world counterparts, they mainly stood apart from the practices of that increasingly harsh penal domain and inhabited an intellectual world of their own – and one (in a manner of speaking) of their own making.

In the first place, most retributivist legal scholars believed that real-world practices based on conventional morality represented an older, revenge-based version of retributivism that was very different from the one based on

> Nothing could be less fruitful than for this Court to be impelled into defining some sort of insanity test in constitutional terms.... [F]ormulating a constitutional rule would reduce, if not eliminate, ... fruitful experimentation, and freeze the developing productive dialogue between law and psychiatry into a rigid constitutional mold. It is simply not yet the time to write into the Constitution formulas cast in terms whose meaning, let alone relevance, is not yet clear either to doctors or to lawyers. (*id.* at 535–537)

In his dissent, Justice Fortas urged that, despite the lack of complete knowledge about alcoholism and its causes, authorities agreed "that alcoholism is caused and maintained by something other than the *moral fault* of the alcoholic, something that, to a greater or lesser extent, depending upon the physiological or psychological makeup and history of the individual, *cannot be controlled by him*" (*id.* at 561, Fortas, J., dissenting).

[16] *Powell*, 392 U.S. at 536 (Marshall, J.).
[17] Garland, *Culture of Control*, 9.

notions of desert rooted in the dignity and autonomy of the individual (or in the nature of "personhood") to which they themselves adhered.[18] Further, for many legal scholars, confrontation with the determinist critique yielded adoption of forms of philosophical compatibilism positing the compatibility of human responsibility with determinism and the lack of true free will. It was argued, for example, that the capacity and opportunity to exercise reasoned choice (itself often thought of as definitive of "personhood") – put otherwise, a person's "uncoerced" reasoned participation within the determined chain of physical and mental events – provided a sound basis for moral and legal responsibility even under conditions of universal causation. Although compatibilist scholarship often drew on conventional blaming practices, it nonetheless did so (perhaps ironically) in justifying theories of responsibility that denied – or announced agnosticism about – the very notion of free will on which, presumably, those conventional practices were premised. To be sure, legal academics who embraced compatibilism might have believed that their resolutions of the deep underlying issues regarding criminal responsibility accorded *in effect*, or in some other ultimate sense, with pervasive social attitudes (which is perhaps Garland's main point), but they no doubt – most of them – realized that the distance between conventional true-free-will-based understandings and their own way of thinking about the freedom issue remained very great. Finally, as I shall stress, the new retributivism was far from a monolith, and the "compatibilism" with which it is generally associated took varying forms and degrees, often occasioning doubts about – or even resistance to – the very idea that lay at its core. Thus,

---

[18] Alice Ristroph posits that, even with regard to terminology, "scholars began using the terms *desert* and *justice* to the increasing exclusion of *retribution*" in order to "dissociate retribution from revenge" and thus "allow[] punishment theorists to draw on a concept that has a more neutral philosophical status." Retributivism could therefore better accommodate utilitarian aims and egalitarian liberal ideals ("Desert, Democracy, and Sentencing Reform," 1300–01). It is also significant, of course, that roughly "retributivist" academic theories varied significantly, including with regard to whether, and by whom, they were best labeled "retributivist" or, instead, "mixed theories" combining consequentialist aims with notions of personal desert. My account intrinsically reflects this complexity and emphasizes the substance, rather than the labeling, of various theories. Douglas Husak, a leading philosopher of the criminal law, addresses the complexity and, in part, circumscribes "retributivism" by identifying those to whom the term should *not* apply, that is, one "does not qualify as a retributivist if he neglects desert altogether or awards it only a peripheral role in his rationale for criminal law and punitive sanctions." "'Broad Culpability' and the Retributivist Dream," *Ohio State Journal of Criminal Law*, vol. 9 (2012): 449–485, 450. Antony Duff illustrates the difficulty of labels, and the overlap between consequential and retributive or desert-based aims, in R. A. Duff, "Penal Communications: Recent Work in the Philosophy of Punishment," *Crime and Justice: An Annual Review of Research*, vol. 20 (1995): 1–97, esp. 7–9, 25–31. See also John Cottingham's oft-cited article, "Varieties of Retribution," *Philosophical Quarterly*, vol. 29 (1979): 238–46. Cf. Michael S. Moore's distinctions among theories justifying punishment in "Closet Retributivism," chap. 2 in *Placing Blame: A Theory of Criminal Law* (New York: Clarendon Press, 1997), 83–93 (originally published in *USC Cites* [1982]: 9–15) (arguing for a narrow definition of true "retributivism").

it seems to me, in considering common views and practices, scholars more often were seeking to work out a philosophically sound theory of criminal responsibility than they were attempting to reach a result that would fit contemporary political passions or please society at large. Whatever *effects* scholarly thinking might have had,[19] the relationship of legal compatibilist scholarship to real-world thought and practices was exceedingly complex.

Overall, I view the legal scholarship of the period discussed here in Part III – roughly 1960 through the century's end – as distinct from the legal scholarship that preceded it in many ways, but especially in two: it witnessed both a turn to retributivism within legal-academic circles that proceeded well beyond the nascent movement toward desert in scholarship of the immediate postwar years; and, relatedly, it exhibited an increasing influence of academic philosophy within legal-academic circles. As a result, it also faced the endemic challenges and ironies of the academic compatibilist enterprise. My intent in this Part is to allow these distinctions to unfold through the legal-academic writings of the period; as with Parts I and II, I intend Part III as a single, somewhat freestanding essay or study, my approach to which is guided by the nature of the scholarship that marked the historic era at hand. Many themes continue, of course. The insanity defense remains

---

[19] The law of unintended consequences loomed large here, as it had throughout the century with respect to legal-academic engagement with criminal responsibility. Some scholars thought their colleagues ought to have known better. James Whitman, for one, urged neo-retributivist scholars to examine their own influence. He argued that, even if a revived, purer retributivism arising from theoretical considerations had philosophical or logical appeal, its theoreticians could not escape the possibility that their approval of "retributivism" nonetheless fueled the inhumane, vengeance-based punishment that – for various historical and political reasons – befell the United States from the 1970s forward. James Q. Whitman, "A Plea against Retributivism," *Buffalo Criminal Law Review*, vol. 7 [2003]: 85–107, 89–90. See my note in the introductory section of Chapter 8 for David Dolinko's assessment along similar lines. Anders Kaye's related critique of late-twentieth and early-twenty-first century compatibilist legal scholarship represents a considerably more damning view. In a richly detailed, insightful, and passionately written article, Kaye argued that the claimed purity and neutrality of compatibilist theories of criminal responsibility masked conservative sociopolitical aims because their focus on the individual to the exclusion of social causes of behavior reinforced economic class divisions and hindered social change. Anders Kaye, "The Secret Politics of the Compatibilist Criminal Law," *Kansas Law Review*, vol. 55 (2007): 365–427. Although Kaye identified the many variations within modern compatibilist theory, his emphasis on (what he takes to be) their common aim to marginalize the effects of socioeconomic conditions leaves little room for examination of differences among compatibilists (and merely quasi- or, really, non-compatibilists) with respect to the strength of their convictions – even their skepticism about the compatibilist project. My own account captures fewer scholars as I keep my focus on legal academics; my essentially historical approach puts somewhat greater emphasis on "what happened" and how it unfolded – or came to pass. I do not take issue with Kaye's claim about the effects of compatibilism. I tend to think, however (although I do not argue the point in this work), that for many compatibilists the "secret" of their "politics" remained safely hidden from themselves. See also Anders Kaye, "Resurrecting the Causal Theory of the Excuses," *Nebraska Law Review*, vol. 83 (2005): 1116–77.

a touchstone. And, although it plays a less central role in this Part, the jury remains as a background, or offstage, motif.[20] As in the preceding Parts, my approach is designed not so much to be exhaustive with regard to the era's scholarship, but to provide representative works that illustrate the way in which perspectives on free will and political liberty influenced the manner in which modern (desert-based) criminal responsibility theory evolved. Perhaps most significant, when that evolution is marked not by conclusive answers, but by variations and unanswered questions, my hope is to present the scholarly conversation as it existed – that is, to show how the scholars themselves grappled with the responsibility question, purported to solve it, or identified aspects of it that they concluded must be left unresolved.

This study has two main chapters, the first of which, Chapter 7, focuses on the later 1950s to the mid-1970s, a period in which some leading

---

[20] Fuller treatment of the jury in modern American legal thought awaits its own day in court. In the main, I draw attention in this work to what I take to be a relatively positive view of the criminal trial jury in post-1960 criminal jurisprudence writings. Often that positive view is merely implicit. I do not pursue modern scholarship on the jury in its own right and outside of my principal focus on the freedom issue relative to criminal responsibility theory. The field of modern jury studies is vast, more than a mere cottage industry; it embraces the civil as well as the criminal jury, and the scholarly endeavor is shared by legal academics, sociologists, psychologists, and political scientists, among others – a great deal of it by members of the Law and Society Association and the Association for Law, Culture and the Humanities. No doubt, the large body of work on the modern jury influenced criminal jurisprudence scholars in significant ways. For example, the publication in 1966 of the founding work in modern jury studies, Harry Kalven, Jr., and Hans Zeisel, *The American Jury* (Boston: Little Brown, 1966), might well have lessened the sense of mystery about the jury as well as the (sometimes) outsized fears of the jury's disruption of the rule of law. And many ensuing, more particularized studies probably conditioned responsibility theory in one way or another. As I have indicated in the Introduction to this book (under the heading "Negotiating Determinism and Conventional Morality: The Jury, the Insanity Defense, and the Bifurcation of Criminal Process"), I intend to make a start – in the time I have left – at the integration of ideas about the jury and ideas about responsibility in Anglo-American criminal justice history.

A significant related area that I do not take up in this book involves how the free will/ determinism debate touches on the death penalty. Death penalty jurisprudence is of interest because it commonly mitigates the free will/determinism tension through a formally bifurcated process: at the trial stage, typical rules apply regarding the threshold for criminal responsibility; but, during the post-conviction inquiry into whether a death sentence will be imposed, juries are permitted to consider a range of influences and background conditions to conclude that a particular defendant – although culpable for the underlying death-eligible crime – does not truly deserve death. Bifurcation in this area thus gives the jury a unique opportunity to express both that an individual freely caused grievous harm *and yet* that he or she was sufficiently affected by causes beyond his or her control that death is not warranted. For discussion of the free-will-related issues this practice raises – and abundant citations to death penalty scholarship and jurisprudence – see Jeffrey L. Kirchmeier, "A Tear in the Eye of the Law: Mitigating Factors and the Progression toward a Disease Theory of Criminal Justice," *Oregon Law Review*, vol. 83 (2004): 631–730. On death penalty jurisprudence into the 1980s, see the classic article by Robert Weisberg, "Deregulating Death," *Supreme Court Review*, vol. 1983 (1983): 305–95.

legal scholars sought to come to terms with the abundant problems of consequentialism. I do not attempt a comprehensive reconstruction of the two-front battle that they (and other scholars) waged against both a sheer utilitarianism, identified with Bentham and his successors in the American academy, and a particularly robust rehabilitationism, identified with the Progressives' positivism and more recent experiments with a therapeutic approach to criminal justice. Aspects of both of these battles found a place in the legal academic writings I consider, but I treat them relatively briefly as I am more concerned with the roots – the underlying ideas – of a new retributivism. More precisely, I consider the evolution of the acceptance of individual desert as a foundation of the criminal law as a whole: importantly, my study is not of retributive penal theory per se,[21] but of a more basic role played by retributivism as a structural element of the law, with ramifications for how the law – including not just its theoretical purposes, but all its constituents from offenses to defenses to proper procedures – is defined and conceived. Notions of the proper role for individual desert had developed uncertainly (and sometimes defensively), we have seen, from the core *nulla poena* principle that had never entirely left legal-academic thought. Though it had received little focused attention in the early decades of the century, it had been foregrounded in the 1930s (by Sayre and Hall, among others) and had achieved a defining place in the 1955 Tentative Draft of the Model Penal Code. The characterization of desert as a limit on state intervention received increasing emphasis in the late 1950s and the 1960s. And, through the 1970s, the case for a moral basis for criminal responsibility was further developed. The central building blocks of the new retributivism took form as American legal scholars, motivated in part by a growing pragmatism, spelled out the virtues of a desert-based criminal responsibility. But they effected this turn to retributivism (or, perhaps, backed into it) without first either strongly rejecting rehabilitation or devoting much direct attention to the determinist critique (the latter project being one in which contemporary academic philosophers were, in contrast, already deeply engaged). Perhaps the hope for rehabilitation – and the less punitive, or at least less vengeful, incarceration and treatment it promised – was still alive in most legal scholars' minds. Or perhaps modern compatibilist philosophy simply had yet to penetrate their ranks. Whatever the reason, although most of the scholars I discuss in Chapter 7 departed from Henry Hart's relative silence about free will in defining blame, they still generally fended off confrontation with it by demonstrating how the free will problem could be gotten round, often by satisfying themselves with an enduring "as if" conception of free will that

---

[21] Retributive penal theory is, of course, the subject of much writing and debate in its own right. For a useful account as of 1981, which considers the reinvigoration of retributivist penal theory beginning in the 1960s, see D. J. Galligan, "The Return to Retribution in Penal Theory," in *Crime, Proof and Punishment: Essays in Honor of Sir Rupert Cross*, ed. C. Tapper (London: Butterworths, 1981), 144–71.

need not be opposed to – but also that need not unequivocally accept – the determinist assertion of universal causation.

Legal scholars would soon more directly confront determinism, however, by way of a more or less formal philosophical compatibilism that affirmed genuine responsibility despite an increasingly explicit acceptance of determinism and the lack of true free will. Chapter 8 records some of the sounds of the noisy new legal-academic world across the period I refer to as the "long 1980s," roughly 1978–1994. By this point, legal-academic thought had come, to some considerable extent, to reflect the crosscutting currents in academic philosophical work on the free will/determinism problem. On the surface at least, the distinction between the "legal" and "non-legal" academics sometimes even disappeared. Not entirely, of course: the law maintained its own imperatives, and even an individual who was both lawyer and philosopher might well have approached the concept of criminal responsibility in two distinct ways that both differed and overlapped. Although I refer to a few professional philosophers who were not (or not mainly) lawyers, my central interest remains lawyers who were not professional philosophers, albeit many were influenced by professional philosophical scholarship. In some instances, that influence was based on no more than a vague awareness of philosophical endeavors to deal with the free will problem; in others the influence reflected substantial knowledge of the sister field. The history of the relationship between the two fields (although an important subject in its own right) is not my concern. Rather, the resulting legal-academic perspective is, even as that perspective became increasingly difficult to isolate in terms of a separate, non-professional-philosophical point of view. In Chapter 8, I emphasize Michael Moore's injecting into twentieth-century American legal academic writing an explicit standard form of philosophical compatibilism based on the capacity and opportunity for practical reasoning[22] (and underpinned by a less common adoption of a reasoned moral realism). I place this emphasis alongside Lloyd Weinreb's partly overlapping but mainly contrasting approach, which stressed the mysterious aspects of a practical compatibilism that demanded consideration despite – or because of – its not

---

[22] As readers will recognize, compatibilism (in its various forms) has a longer history in twentieth-century American legal thought than is suggested here. I emphasize its "explicit" expressions, but even these – an earlier example being Wechsler and Michael's late 1930s compatibilism (see my discussion in Chapter 4) – themselves referred to a long-standing view mirrored in, for example, early statements such as that of Edward Lindsey in 1910 (see Chapter 2, n. 9). By "standard form," I refer to a compatibilism that was offered in support of desert-based responsibility, not mere deterrability – the line of course not always being clear, particularly when the underlying compatibilism was largely implicit (some may have understood the Model Penal Code, for example, in what were to become standard-form terms). What I call attention to is the relative absence of *explicit* legal-academic compatibilist analysis before the 1970s – as opposed to a possible unstated background assumption. The history of compatibilism in pre-1970s legal thought deserves the attention of future scholars.

being reducible to reasoned justification. This central chapter in Part III then brings to the fore variations upon these two ways of thinking about the freedom question relative to criminal responsibility, to conventional morality, and, especially, to the ideas of "person" and desert.

The resulting conversation of the long 1980s bookends the very different conversation among consequentialists of the 1920s and 1930s and it throws into further relief that of the 1940s and 1950s, which lay somewhere between the two with respect to the contours of legal-academic thought. Late-in-century criminal responsibility discourse centered on a "person" who was left all but invisible in the Progressives' socialized jurisprudence, despite – ironically – their devotion to a penology based on individuation. Reform for Progressives had invoked an individual to be acted upon, an object more than a subject. The subject had thereafter begun to take form against the background of a moral-legal idea of freedom, the development of which accompanied a reorientation among the aims of the law from a focus on the overall needs of society to emphasizing the individual actor as the locus of criminal responsibility. But the person as a subject became truly central only in light of the subsequent attempt to find a justification for desert. Still, in the pages of long-1980s writings, this "person" remained a wraithlike figure, and often enough the artist, filling out his canvas, seemed to know that both he and the "person" stood on shifting sands.

The conversation of the long 1980s thus also sets the stage for end-of-century criminal-responsibility scholarship, on which I offer some informal observations by way of an Epilogue (Chapter 9) that closes this final Part. There I consider some more recent alternatives that sought to overcome perceived infirmities of rational-choice-based compatibilism – but I foreground what might be thought of as the triumph of this compatibilism in mainstream criminal jurisprudence. Indeed, late-in-century compatibilism, in its various – and distinctly varying – forms, survived the turn of the twenty-first century and, I suggest, remains dominant for many of the legal scholars who continue to this day to worry the free will problem in the context of criminal responsibility. But some commentators, both within and outside the legal academy, now ask whether criminal responsibility will survive the deterministic implications of the *new* new sciences – neuroscience and gene-sequencing, among others – after apparently having finally won the battle against the Progressive sciences that had taken hold of the scholarly imagination at the beginning of the last century.

7

The Foundations of Neo-Retributivism: 1957–1976

INTRODUCTION

In concluding my study of the century's middle decades with a commentary on Henry Hart's 1958 article, "The Aims of the Criminal Law," I suggested that Hart placed special emphasis on the idea of blameworthiness yet revealed the influence of scientific-positivist thought in the course of privileging reformationist ideas over those of utility. At the same time, he was silent about the underlying question of free will. Although Hart's silence might have concealed an unspoken compatibilism, one senses that he deemed the matter a metaphysical issue best left to philosophers and, in any case, on commonsense principles, an issue unnecessary – or unwise – for the lawyer to explore. Accordingly the aims of the criminal law might mirror the ideas of the wider populace, including the assumption that we are freely willing beings – indeed they might reflect the notion that law *ought* to accommodate those ideas – but law could do so indirectly or perhaps by unspoken implication. It is not easy to say what Hart thought about this, and that in itself is of no little importance.

On my reading of the scholarship of the late 1950s to mid-1970s, many legal scholars followed Hart in examining the law's aims and connections to ideas of blame, yet they proceeded well beyond his 1958 undertaking in seeking more secure theoretical foundations for a notion of individual blame justifying criminal condemnation. The necessity of limits on state intervention into the lives of individuals to uphold political liberty was clear. But it was also increasingly recognized that the rule of law was – and indeed, depended on being – at least in part a social/political institution that must be responsive (whether rightly or necessarily) to general social attitudes; therefore, it could not be (or at least could not *entirely* be) divorced from conventional retributive associations, both to maintain legitimacy in the public mind and to act upon individuals as a deterrent. With regard to sentencing, although many, if not most, scholars remained committed to a legal regime that took rehabilitation and other consequentialist ends meaningfully into account; they recognized that, to the extent criminal sanctions unavoidably involved some element of punishment – or at least measures that would be experienced or viewed as such – a foundational idea justifying individual blame was all the more important. But if, for scholars, true free will was not to serve as the basis for blame, what would?

The focus was first on limits to rehabilitationism in the name of political liberty and then on limits to consequentialism more generally of a somewhat more philosophically sophisticated sort. I begin with Francis Allen, whose mid-to-late 1950s writings stressed the former. During this period, Allen took stock of criminal law and its administration on the eve of the modern era. He paid little attention to free will as such. But the values that he sought to safeguard through emphasis on political liberty included an "autonomy" that perhaps extended beyond freedom from control by the state. His early essays prefigured his classic synthetic work, *The Decline of the Rehabilitative Ideal* (1981) – indeed, they preceded the culmination of that decline by more than a decade. Even more than his later work, this early work emphasized the preservation of rehabilitationism by establishing its political, moral, and practical limits; only indirectly – and unintentionally – did Allen facilitate the emergence in legal academic circles of a displacement of rehabilitation by a translation of the bare invocation of blameworthiness into the more concrete idea of desert.

The 1957–1964 work of English legal philosopher Herbert Hart and his famous rationale for the legal excuses posited a more philosophically sophisticated moral constraint on consequentialism. The English Hart argued for the centrality of an offender's opportunity and capacity for choice while also invoking humans' irreducible *experience* of choice – and our reactions to each other based on this shared experience – as independently "true" and not dependent on metaphysical free will. I give a great deal of space to Hart, whose influence quickly reached American shores. Among those American legal scholars whose work reflected the influence of both Allen and Hart were Herbert Packer, Sanford Kadish, and Abraham Goldstein. All of these figures contributed to the preconditions for a turn to desert theory, although most eschewed that idea, and only one or two beckoned even tentatively toward it.

Then, in the third section of this chapter, I take up Herbert Morris's 1968 essay, "Persons and Punishment," which presented the most influential early exposition of a systematic theory of desert. That essay combined ideas of a neo-Kantian sort, which had recently reemerged in political philosophy in a turn against utilitarianism, with legal academic ideas of longer vintage and of a less overtly anti-utilitarian kind. Morris turned a corner that, by this time, was anticipated by the evolution of reactions to radical positivism through the 1960s. By valuing the "person" – as well as the rights and exercise of choice Morris believed were inherent to personhood – Morris bolstered the notion that punishment for wrongdoing could, itself, be a moral end of the law. But he did so without directly stating whether he held an "as if" or "as is" view of free will – or even whether he thought this distinction mattered.

I close this chapter by discussing two significant mid-1970s texts: the "Introduction" to *Doing Justice: The Choice of Punishments*, the Report of the Committee for the Study of Incarceration, and Stephen Morse's influential article "The Twilight of Welfare Criminology." These texts exemplify the tensions between the increasingly fragmented "Progressive" viewpoint (i.e., the scientific-positivist/consequentialist viewpoint that had bloomed in the Progressive Era) and the coming triumph of neo-retributivism. The introduction to *Doing Justice* is particularly striking, as it illustrates the Committee's remarkably self-conscious acceptance of the retributivist tide while expressing its authors' (not necessarily the entire Committee's) steadfast commitment to the underlying values of the Progressive movement.

Taken together, the scholars I discuss only sketchily fill out the gradual turn from a consequentialism of a mainly reformationist kind to the particular form of a neo-retributivism of the 1970s and beyond. As I outlined in the introduction to this Part, elements of this important transformation have been taken up by others; additional chapters of the story no doubt remain to be written and, when they are, the free will issue might recede into the background. Here that issue – really, efforts to avoid it – are foregrounded: legal scholars of the late 1950s to mid-1970s most commonly formulated blame in ways that implicitly or otherwise rendered irrelevant – or at least tried to render irrelevant – the potentially inherent problem with imposing blame in the absence of true free will. Direct confrontation with the free will problem would mostly come later, as I discuss in Chapter 8.

For the time being, reaffirmations of human dignity and "choice" complemented reaffirmations of the law's role in protecting liberty and dignity as an institution that, by its unique nature, might rightly provide some shelter from the winds of science. This combination of aims drew legal theory back toward conventional morality. But the relationship between theory and convention was difficult to sort out, and perhaps most difficult for the theoreticians themselves; this is evident in some of their work, from which I attempt to draw conclusions while maintaining, where possible, its searching, partly inconclusive tenor. Recognition of the role of conventional views implicitly conflicted with the fact that those views presumably assumed a true freedom of will that was not the basis for scholarly formulations of blame. But this conflict was rarely faced head-on. It was generally unclear, for example, how far the rediscovered respect for legal institutions, as important mediators between individuals and the state, extended to the institution of the jury as an explicit representative of conventional views. Where Bazelon, for instance, would continue forthrightly to favor the jury (albeit one increasingly educated by experts) as an ultimate line-drawer with regard to morality and freedom, others appeared to enlist the jury more pragmatically, as an instrumental or communicative representative of the fairness or other social values deemed necessary for law's proper function. This complicated relationship between legal theory and conventional morality was epitomized by Herbert Hart's reliance on conventional notions of responsibility alongside his seemingly contradictory rejection of retributive punishment. And this contradiction might be said to have foreshadowed later uses of Hart's themes to support the very recrudescence of retributivism he sought to avoid.

HERBERT HART AND THE AMERICAN CRIMINAL JURISPRUDENCE OF THE 1960S

In theorizing the link between criminal liability and the capacity and opportunity for choice, Oxford's Herbert Hart would become a significant influence on American legal theory in the latter half of the twentieth century. Before discussing Hart at length, I begin with Chicago law professor Francis Allen, whose own significant work reveals elements akin to the seminal – but quite different – concepts of both Herbert Hart and Harvard's Henry Hart. Allen's parallels to the American Hart are clearest. Still, although Allen did not cite the English Hart – particularly in Allen's 1964 essay on Holmes – the influence of Herbert Hart's articles of 1957–1961 on some of Allen's work seems unmistakable. Allen's attempts to preserve the benefits of rehabilitation while acknowledging meaningful limits on state intervention thus bridged important midcentury currents of thought and were influential in their own right.

A Critique: Francis Allen

Henry Hart's 1958 "Aims of the Criminal Law" can be read as of a piece with Francis Allen's own exhortation to emphasize the rule of law rather than behavioral science technique. Science would not be abandoned; Allen was generous in his assessment of its contributions to criminal justice administration over the preceding half century. But Allen, like Hart, worried that law would privilege the methods and values of science and lose itself in the process: "It is not too much to say that a great part of the criminological labors of the last half-century has proceeded with little consideration of the political and ethical values inevitably involved." These values law must embody, Allen argued in 1956; they underwrote the proper application of state force, the appropriate legal-procedural mandates, and, of course, the all-important definition of criminal responsibility. Allen's often searing critique of abuses incurred in the name of science was not accompanied, however, by naïveté – or by Henry Hart's relative confidence – about the ease of finding solutions. "The problems," Allen conceded, "of reconciling these political values with the advantages of individualized therapeutic treatment of those brought within the scope of state sanctions presents an intellectual challenge of major proportions."[1] Henry Hart wrote mainly from the perspective of the legislator who observed the imperatives of legality and the social values foundational to the state's implementation of criminal process and criminal sanctions. Like others before him, he drew attention to the message a curative-rehabilitative regime might send. As we have seen, he, like Allen, sought a media between such a regime – aspects of which he distinctly favored in the name of individual growth and development – and the political and social values inherent in a properly condemnatory criminal law. But neither Allen nor Henry Hart achieved a theoretical reconciliation of the political and the scientific values involved.

Although Allen's work as of 1959 appears cautiously aimed at preserving the most worthy elements of the rehabilitative ideal, he wrote even more emphatically than Henry Hart about the dangers inherent in a centrally rehabilitative regime. In 1956, Allen had called for the further application of medical and behavioral-science methods – especially with regard to persons subject to the overreach of traditional penal sanctions (e.g., alcoholics) – and had stated the problem mainly in terms of the lack of proper "medical care and social welfare."[2] But, in his 1959 article "Criminal Justice, Legal Values and the Rehabilitative Ideal,"[3] he leveled his gaze both at the abuse of those curative methods and at the infirmities of the underlying theory that had brought science into a dominant position within criminal justice administration. Allen never doubted that there was a place for scientific technique when it was applied with a humility appropriate to the limits of current knowledge and constrained by a rule of law that reflected political and social values. But the abuse of those limits and of that constraint now received his full attention.

In the 1959 piece, Allen noted that the rehabilitative ideal traced to deterministic ideas about human behavior – ideas that, he charged, "possess a delusive simplicity." The result had been the steady and uncritical development of the view that therapeutic measures "should be designed to effect changes in the behavior of the convicted person in the interests of his own happiness, health, and satisfactions and in the interest of the social defense."[4] In the preceding year, Allen had directed his attention to the overreach of sexual psychopath laws and to abuses of legality in the name of therapeutic treatment in juvenile courts.[5] Now his target was wider still. The several

[1] Francis A. Allen, "Law and the Future: Criminal Law and Administration," *Northwestern University Law Review*, vol. 51 (1956): 207–17, 209.

[2] Allen, "Law and the Future," 211.

[3] Francis A. Allen, "Criminal Justice, Legal Values and the Rehabilitative Ideal," *JCLC*, vol. 50 (1959): 226–32.

[4] Allen, "Criminal Justice, Legal Values," 226.

[5] Francis A. Allen, "The Borderland of the Criminal Law: Problems of 'Socializing' Criminal Justice," *Social Service Review*, vol. 32 (1958): 107–19.

problematic tendencies he criticized were a narrowing of scientific interests, a "disinterest in the definition of criminal behavior" that "has afflicted the lawyers quite as much as the behavioral scientists" (leading even criminal law scholars "to assume that problems of procedure and treatment are the things that 'really matter'"), and a debasement of the rehabilitative ideal in practice. The last tendency involved professionals in the penal bureaucracy justifying abusive custodial measures, and lengthening incarceration periods, on the pretext of therapeutic benefit, although these "benefits" were mere shams that the law failed to confront forthrightly.[6]

The brief 1959 essay did not elaborate on the substance of the "major challenges" that Allen, in 1956, had suggested would inhere in reconciling political values with the ideals of rehabilitative treatment. The 1959 piece largely just alluded to "the values of individual liberty and volition" and of "human dignity" that had been compromised by the "attitudes and measures" spawned by the rehabilitative ideal. And Allen now argued that the "most fundamental problems" lay not with the behavioral sciences but with political philosophy and political science. A generalized political liberty was mainly at issue; the threat posed by the perversion of, and over-concentration on, therapeutic technique undermined the "proper relations of the individual citizen to state power."[7]

Allen next turned to the shortcomings of well-meaning scientists and lawyers who had produced far from the rehabilitative "ideal" they had sought. In recounting one instance that manifested especially egregious abuse, he concluded that it perhaps reflected "that arrogance and insensitivity to human values to which men who have no reason to doubt their own motives appear peculiarly susceptible."[8] As to the "delusive simplicity" of determinism as a way of understanding the truths of human behavior, he now said practically nothing. He certainly did not take a specific stand on what those truths might be or whether they were, in fact, knowable. Rather the errors of the singularly deterministic view were manifested in an undermining of human values that apparently were either self-evident or were implicit in the principles of political philosophy. The law rested on such principles – whatever they might have been – which defined the appropriate limits to the state's application of the science of human behavior; or, perhaps they defined the very substance of an appropriate understanding of human nature. Allen did not say which of these perspectives he had in mind. If he believed that the ultimate truths regarding human nature remained beyond one's grasp – were metaphysical or simply as yet unknown – he did not say so. The "major challenge" was apparently to create a fit between a law based on political philosophy and political science and a law also responsive to

---

[6] Allen, "Criminal Justice, Legal Values," 228–29.
[7] Allen, "Criminal Justice, Legal Values," 230.
[8] Allen, "Criminal Justice, Legal Values," 232.

current scientific knowledge, not to defend political philosophy or political science against the science or philosophy of determinism.

Three years later, writing about the insanity defense, Allen explained the wisdom of the Model Penal Code formulation of responsibility, especially its language mandating substantial capacity "to conform [one's] conduct to the requirements of law." This, he said, reasonably left medical experts to testify as to conditions that might affect such a capacity – matters of fact that experts were competent to assess. The MPC's test marked a major improvement, Allen thought, over both the *Durham* "product" test and the similar "in consequence thereof" language advanced by the Group for Advancement of Psychiatry, for the MPC directed attention to the vitiation of normal capacity, that is, to an end result, as it were, not to a causal question. Whether the defendant had actually possessed or lacked a normal capacity was, further, a moral question for the trier of fact.[9] What was the precise nature of this "moral" issue? Was the question whether a particular individual possessed the crucial (and normally possessed) capacity, a question that was inherently a matter of intuitive judgment? Or was it whether, in a given case, it was just to assign responsibility in the face of unknown truths about human nature? Again, Allen did not say, although I assume he meant the former.

Further developing his themes, in 1964 Allen criticized Holmes's objective approach to criminal responsibility,[10] stressing instead a blameworthiness principle that linked law to social ideas. This was not the blameworthiness of revenge, he noted, but a principle that accorded with the human values that law ought to serve. It stood for a retributive element that drew part of its force from the fact that its concordance with conventional morality was necessary for law to achieve the consequentialist goal of prevention. And there was more: it served the ends of recognizable justice. Allen now forthrightly stated that rehabilitation, although it may remain as a goal, could not be the central end of the criminal law, for the rehabilitative process – whatever its consequentialist goals – still presumes an offender, and an offender presumes an offense. Thus, in defining offenses, legislators still must first look to an individual's mens rea in terms of blameworthiness; they were not justified in focusing primarily on prevention or cure. And in assessing blameworthiness, Allen observed, we are not disposed to simply exculpate those who are socially constrained; rather we "pragmatically" leave the enforceable legal limits of blameworthiness to the discretionary aspects of law, including the resolution of guilt or innocence by a jury.[11]

[9] Francis A. Allen, "The Rule of the American Law Institute's Model Penal Code," *Marquette Law Review*, vol. 45 (1962): 494–505, 500, 502–04.
[10] Oliver Wendell Holmes, *The Common Law*, ed. Mark DeWolfe Howe (Boston: Little, Brown, 1963) (Holmes originally published in 1881), chap. 2, "The Criminal Law."
[11] Francis A. Allen, "Criminal Law," *University of Chicago Law Review*, vol. 31 (1964): 257–62.

As I have said, Allen's 1964 article did not cite Herbert Hart, to whom I now turn. But Hart had recently produced an account of criminal responsibility with which Allen's 1964 piece clearly resonates. Perhaps in light of Allen's apparent primary aim to preserve the "advantages of individualized therapeutic treatment" by circumscribing its just application, however, his focus was more on describing the proper framework of a just legal regime than on detailing the specific values underlying such a regime. Hart set forth principles based upon "political and ethical values" as Allen had himself advised, and thereby filled gaps that Allen somewhat mysteriously left open.

A New Initiative: Herbert Hart

Herbert Hart forthrightly took the consequentialist principle of overall utility to be the general justifying aim of the institution of criminal law. He had little, if any, patience with either retributive or denunciatory rationales (although the latter might be understood as utilitarian, it unfortunately conjured up the former).[12] In this particular respect, Hart's view had much in common with those on the deterrence side of the Progressive tradition. Hart also denied that a criminal offense was necessarily a commission of a morally wrong act. It was the "voluntary" commission of a validly promulgated and presumptively noticed prohibited act, nothing necessarily more.

But Hart also insisted upon a principle regarding the distribution of punishment, which lay outside pure utilitarianism. This principle embodied an independent precept of justice: it is unjust to hold one responsible for an act he or she did not commit or committed without being able to choose otherwise. Thus the principle of distribution – the question of upon whom the state could bring its powers of enforcement (and the outer limit of how much it could bring)[13] – was an overriding moral constraint on

---

[12] Neil MacCormick, *H. L. A. Hart*, 2nd ed. (Stanford, CA: Stanford University Press, 2008), provides an excellent summary and analysis of Hart's criminal jurisprudence (chap. 12, "Sanctions, Punishment, Justice"). MacCormick's assessment of Hart's general justifying aim, and of Hart's resistance to retributivism with respect to that aim, is of special importance (pp. 172–79). See also Nicola Lacey, *A Life of H. L. A. Hart: The Nightmare and the Noble Dream* (Oxford: Oxford University Press, 2004), 179–83.

[13] "The further principle that different kinds of offence of different gravity ... should not be punished with equal severity is the one which like other principles of Distribution may qualify the pursuit of our General Aim and is not deducible from it." H. L. A. Hart, "Prolegomenon to the Principles of Punishment," chap. 1 in H. L. A. Hart, *Punishment and Responsibility: Essays in the Philosophy of Law* (Oxford: Clarendon Press, 1968), 25 (originally published in *Proceedings of the Aristotelian Society*, n.s., vol. 60 (1959): 1–26). With particular regard to Hart's principle of distribution, critics questioned whether this notion genuinely could be separated from an at least partially retributive account of the law. In one scholar's view, at a minimum, a demand for such proportionality requires "an uneasy alliance between the distinctively retributive notions of gravity and culpability on the one hand, and the competing claims of rehabilitation, deterrence and incapacitation on the other hand. The introduction

the general justifying aim of utility. In form, this constraint appeared to adhere to backward-looking retributive or blame-oriented principles: one was accountable for an act committed under circumstances in which it might reasonably be said he or she could have chosen not to commit it. Yet Hart – again more in line with his Progressive predecessors than with his successors – would steadfastly attempt to distance his approach from retributive connotations.[14]

Hart first enunciated the bare bones of his well-known rationale of the legal excuses in 1957, during a visiting year at Harvard Law School, in a paper delivered at a conference at New York University on "Determinism and Freedom in the Age of Modern Science." His contribution to the main subject of the conference was meager. The other conference participants discussed whether determinism was true – either in quantum physics or in other aspects of the material world, or in matters internal to human psychology – or discussed in depth whether responsibility might exist in a determined world. Hart, on the other hand, simply announced that, so long as one could not definitely say determinism *was* true – and no one who read the discordant views expressed at the conference could conclude that philosophers or scientists were agreed that it was, or even about what it meant to say that it was – one ought to proceed on the commonly experienced (and common-sense) conclusion that individuals did indeed choose and live their lives in accordance with the understanding that such choice was effective. A very rough summary of his early formulation is as follows: we have the ability – or conscious sense of and belief in our ability – to choose our actions. Because those choices determine our future, we thus have the ability to predict our liability to interference by the state. We derive satisfaction from knowing that our choices are effective in this way and that the pursuit of our interests is indeed our chosen pursuit. Hart thus pointed to a "choosing system" that is effective even if, as it happens, our choices are in fact determined. And the law, he said, must never take away the satisfaction and security we derive from this sense that we possess the power of choice, even if maintaining them involves a sacrifice of overall security for society.[15]

---

at the sentencing stage of deserts, based on the seriousness of the offence, as the primary principles makes most sense if the general aim includes some concern to punish wrong-doing." D. J. Galligan, "The Return to Retribution in Penal Theory," in *Crime, Proof and Punishment: Essays in Honor of Sir Rupert Cross*, ed. C. Tapper (London: Butterworths, 1981), 151–52. Galligan offers a range of important critiques – by himself and others – of this and other aspects of Hart's basic theory at 149–52.

[14] MacCormick, *H. L. A. Hart*, 182 (distinguishing Hart's approach to both "title" to punish and amount of punishment from retribution).

[15] H. L. A. Hart, "Legal Responsibility and Excuses," chap. 2 in *Punishment and Responsibility* (originally published in *Determinism and Freedom in the Age of Modern Science: A Philosophical Symposium*, ed. Sidney Hook [New York: New York University Press, 1958], 81–104.).

In this way, Hart neatly finessed the determinist critique. He did not pause to defend traditional philosophical compatibilist ideas or explicitly to deny or affirm libertarian ones. All that mattered, he said, was that we do not know, and perhaps can never know, the truth of determinism. Significantly, this was not a counterfactual "as if" position; it allowed, in a sense, for a presumption, a for-all-we-know (and probably all-we-ever-will-know) proposition. Hart expressed his own form of compatibilism: one between responsibility under the criminal law and any form of determinism that did not involve certain knowledge of scientific laws that precluded us from conceiving of our choices *as* our choices. He explained:

no form of determinism that I, at least, can construct can throw any doubt on, or show to be illusory, the real satisfaction that a system of criminal law incorporating excusing conditions provides for individuals in maximizing the effect of their choices within the framework of coercive law. The choices remain choices, the satisfactions remain satisfactions, and the consequences of choices remain the consequences of choices, *even if choices are determined* and even if other "determinants" besides our choices condition the satisfaction arising from their being rendered effective in this way by the criminal law.[16]

Hart thus had identified the values that characterized what he would term in his famous "Prolegomenon" of 1959[17] a moral constraint upon the utility that was the general justifying aim of the criminal law.[18] The law

[16] Hart, "Legal Responsibility and Excuses," 48 (emphasis added). For a philosopher's critique of Hart's conference paper, see Elizabeth Lane Beardsley, "'Excusing Conditions' and Moral Responsibility," in Hook, ed., *Determinism and Freedom*, 133–37. A brief and more supportive response to (and elaboration upon) Hart's central idea is Percy W. Bridgman, "Determinism and Punishment," Hook, ed., *Determinism and Freedom*, 143–45. Bridgman distinguished between "the level of daily life" and "the deterministic level" (143). As to the former, we develop a language to describe this situation, in which our own inability to foresee the future and that of our fellows is reflected in the concept of 'free will'" (144).

> It is in the nature of things impossible to erect a single consistent verbal structure, logically watertight in all respects. To insist on acting as if we could is in the first place self-defeating – for by what logic can the man who argues that punishment is unjustified expect his argument to affect the actions of his opponent, when both his argument and the response to it were already rigidly determined? ... At present the only technique we have for dealing with our fellows is to act as if they were the same sort of creature as we ourselves. (144)

Bridgman's particular version of "as if" of course potentially licensed justifications for punishment that went well beyond those Hart embraced.

[17] Hart, "Prolegomenon to the Principles of Punishment."

[18] I describe Hart's 1959 position as an elaboration of his position in 1957. (I read "free choice," as Hart employed that phrase in "Prolegomenon," p. 22, line 6, in light of his earlier formulation.) It may well be that Hart's overall theory underwent a significant shift, however, during these years, as has been suggested by Michael Moore. Moore, apparently following T. M. Scanlon, posited that Hart's rationale arguably began as rule-utilitarianism that essentially privileged the good of free choice over the good of crime prevention. Moore concluded that Hart did not rely on choice theory as a deontological or non-consequentialist moral side-constraint on utility until 1958. Michael S. Moore, "Choice, Character, and Excuse,"

should reinforce our exercise of choice by condemning only those offenders who "had, when they acted, the normal capacities, physical and mental, for abstaining from what [the law] forbids, and a fair opportunity to exercise these capacities." Conversely, "where these capacities and opportunities are absent, as they are in different ways in the varied cases of accident, mistake, paralysis, reflex action, coercion, insanity, etc.," the law must refrain from condemning the actor because we conclude, as a moral matter, that "'he could not have helped it' or 'he could not have done otherwise' or 'he had no real choice.'"[19] Hart's focus on constraint of the law under these latter conditions identified the legal idea of mens rea mainly with the absence of excusing conditions. Perhaps most significant in Hart's mind was the idea that culpability did not have to implicate blame, but corresponded to a jus-tice-based principle of responsibility: "the simple idea that unless a man has the capacity and a fair opportunity or chance to adjust his behaviour to the law its penalties ought not to be applied to him." Recognition of this principle of fairness and justice allows an individual "to predict and plan the future course" of his life, which is to say that it "maximizes his power to identify in advance the space which will be left open to him free from the law's interference." Moreover, such a principle, "which makes liability to punishment depend upon a voluntary act[,] calls for the exercise of powers of self-control" and rewards "the prime social virtue of self-restraint."[20] This last consideration united Hart's theory of criminal responsibility with his more general precepts regarding the concept of law, for it invoked his view that one's legal and moral obligations were social and thus reciprocal. One's liberty and the pursuit of one's objectives depended upon noninterference by others, and they thus raised a mutual obligation of noninterference with respect to others. This maximized individual satisfaction and, collectively, social welfare.[21]

Hart rebutted the "Benthamite explanation" of excusing conditions according to which such conditions identified not an independent moral principle but simply various bases for the inefficacy of the threat of the law, and thus circumstances in which enforcement of criminal sanctions was "inefficient" as not "securing the maintenance of law at the least cost

---

chap. 13 in *Placing Blame: A Theory of Criminal Law* (New York: Clarendon Press, 1997), 549–52 (originally published in *Social Philosophy & Policy*, vol. 7 [1990]: 29–58). If so, however, it did not implicate the meaning Hart gave to "free choice."

[19] Hart, "Negligence, *Mens Rea* and Criminal Responsibility," chap. 6 in *Punishment and Responsibility*, 152 (originally published in A. G. Guest, ed., *Oxford Essays in Jurisprudence* [London: Oxford University Press, 1961]).

[20] Hart, "Punishment and the Elimination of Responsibility," chap. 7 in *Punishment and Responsibility*, 181–82 (originally presented as a lecture in 1961 at King's College, London, and published in 1962 by the Athlone Press).

[21] See H. L. A. Hart, *The Concept of Law* (Oxford: Clarendon Press, 1961), esp. chap. IX.

and pain."[22] He rebutted as well the view that the excusing conditions in the criminal law derived from "the more fundamental requirement that for criminal responsibility there must be 'moral culpability,' which would not exist when the excusing conditions are present." Hart taxed Jerome Hall for this view, as Hart put it, that "moral culpability is the basis of responsibility in crime." Hall and others had wrongly concluded, Hart said, that criminal liability must either be strict "or *must* be based on moral culpability," whereas there was in fact a third possibility. Hart here introduced what was to become the basic idea of the "Prolegomenon": the system of criminal law must as a whole "produce more good than evil"; if it did, then enforcement, whether or not a particular provision identified a moral wrong, was justified – unless, of course, enforcement worked the particular independent moral injustice Hart associated with failure to recognize the presence of a (lack-of-choice-based) excusing condition.[23]

Overall, Hart's focus on choice linked the law's purpose to its proper structure – in terms both utilitarian and moral – by way of a premise that, even if it did not assert the reality of free will, could be seen as depending on a "real" subjective experience of free will. Still, he would not state his premise using the language of free will. His defense of a "choosing system" openly avoided analysis of the meaning of such phrases as "'He did it voluntarily,'" "'He acted of his own free will,'" or "'He could have done otherwise.'" He allowed that such statements might be shown "not logically incompatible with the existence of the type of laws the determinist

---

[22] Hart, "Legal Responsibility and Excuses," 40. On related grounds, Hart also took aim at Wechsler and Michael, whose 1937 "Rationale" he treated as one of the "modern extended forms of Utilitarianism." "Sometimes the principle that punishment should be restricted to those who have voluntarily broken the law is defended not as a principle which is rational and morally important in itself but as something so engrained in popular conceptions of justice in certain societies including our own, that not to recognize it would lead to disturbance, or to the nullification of the criminal law since officials or juries might refuse to co-operation in such a system" ("Prolegomenon," 20–21).
   As we have seen, by 1952 (if not earlier) Wechsler had concluded that "to condemn when fault is absent is barbaric. It is the badge of tyranny, the plainest illustration of injustice." Herbert Wechsler, "A Thoughtful Code of Substantive Law," *JCLC*, vol. 45 (1955): 524–30, 528–29. The claim appeared to stand outside of, and over and above, utilitarian practice. And Wechsler's 1962 article, "On Culpability and Crime: The Treatment of Mens Rea in the Model Penal Code," *Annals of the American Academy of Political and Social Science*, vol. 339 (1962): 24–41, at one point placed a Hartian emphasis on "the sense of personal security" that is "so vital to both individual and group tranquility" (27). Recall that Wechsler would later describe himself as "exceedingly utilitarian," but added "everybody knows that a social order that doesn't provide adequate protection for personal dignity and autonomy and bodily integrity is a defective social order" (Norman Silber and Geoffrey Miller, "Toward 'Neutral Principles' in the Law: Selections from the Oral History of Herbert Wechsler," *Columbia Law Review*, vol. 93 [1993]: 854–931, 869). See my discussion of Wechsler in Chapter 6.
[23] Hart, "Legal Responsibility and Excuses," 35–38.

claims may exist; if they do exist it may not follow that statements of the kind quoted are always false, for it may be that these statements are true given certain conditions, which need not include the non-existence of any such laws."[24] But this was a matter that Hart would not investigate, here or elsewhere. His compatibilism was entirely premised upon the experience of choice and the inferences humans draw from that experience, absent (in fact, probably impossible ever to obtain) certain knowledge and immediate awareness of the utter predictability yielded by determinism. Nothing more. In closing Hart conceded: "what I have written concerns only *legal* responsibility and the rationale of excuses in a legal system in which there are organized, coercive sanctions. I do not think the same arguments can be used to defend *moral* responsibility from the determinist, if it is in any danger from that source."[25]

This posture remained firm when, two years after the "Prolegomenon," Hart responded to magistrate and social scientist Lady Barbara Wootton's suggestion, launched in her 1959 book[26] and 1960 article,[27] that the mens rea element be forgone in trials where the legal insanity defense is raised. As Hart put Wootton's position, those convicted for having exhibited the "outward acts" prohibited by law should, instead, be subjected to a determination at sentencing regarding the best means of treatment. Wootton offered what could appear as a throwback to prewar American Progressivism, but with its own distinctions borne of 1960s humanism and her own skepticism of the bounds of science. She argued not for hard determinism, but for the proposition that, in the absence of any reliable scientific means of assessing whether a particular individual could actually have done other than he did, criminal law ought to be purely forward-looking – and ought to be that only in a strictly treatmentist or incapacitative sense. Treatment might be either therapeutic or a matter of punishment, but if the latter, then purely for remedial purposes (i.e., within the realm of treatment). This, as Hart stated,

[24] Hart, "Legal Responsibility and Excuses," 30. Hart specified: "I will not deal here with a determinist who is so incautious as to say that it may be false that anyone has ever acted 'voluntarily,' 'of his own free will,' or 'could have done otherwise than he did.'" Rather, he confront[ed] a more cautious sceptic who, without committing himself as to the meaning of those expressions or their logical or linguistic dependence on, or independence of, the negation of those types of law to which the determinist refers, yet criticizes our allocation of responsibility by reference to excusing conditions. This more cautious determinist says that whatever the expressions "voluntary," etc. may mean, unless we have reasonable grounds for thinking there are no such laws, the distinctions drawn by these expressions cannot be regarded as of any importance, and there can be neither reason nor justice in allowing punishment to depend on the presence or absence of excusing conditions. (30–31)

[25] Hart, "Legal Responsibility and Excuses," 53.

[26] Barbara Wootton, *Social Science and Social Pathology* (London: George Allen and Unwin, 1959).

[27] Barbara Wootton, "Diminished Responsibility: A Layman's View," *Law Quarterly Review*, vol. 76 (1960): 224–39.

meant the elimination of (the legal idea of) responsibility in the criminal law.[28] Indeed, two years after that, in her Hamlyn lectures of 1963, Wootton took the bait and applied her no-mens-rea principle more generally to all criminal defendants and offenses.[29]

But in Hart's 1961 response to Wootton, "Punishment and the Elimination of Responsibility," he also took his own ideas a step further – or a step deeper – by asserting an underlying general principle based on his understanding of the very nature of human beings. It is this assertion that ultimately proves most interesting in the context of my historical study of the delicate balances struck between theories of criminal responsibility and conventional understandings of human nature. For this move – by which Hart stressed the need for law to take into account how humans in fact behave in society – compromised his attempt to divorce liability from retribution and, in the process, made the necessity of embracing retributivism in any meaningful theory of law appear all the more inevitable.

Hart recognized that Wootton's objections to mens rea were not premised on a holistic determinism, but on a related scientific view that one could not determine precisely an individual's state of mind. Thus he directed his reply to this latter argument, although he found its plausibility to be limited at best. Even if determinations regarding the precise nature of mental and emotional states were necessarily subject to some doubt, Hart asserted, acting on that doubt in the way that Wootton recommended unreasonably sacrificed fundamental principles of fairness and justice. Because Wootton's critique was also aimed at the infirmities of retributivism, Hart further explained in 1961 – and again more clearly in his 1964 response to the Hamlyn lectures[30] – that there was a difference between retributivism and the fairness/ justice principle he had set forth. Again, he said, his principle was not in service of punishment premised upon blame, but went only to *liability* to punishment with the goal of prevention, and thus reduced to the moral principle of affording each person the opportunity to plan and live his or her life in a way that did not occasion interference by the criminal law.[31]

Hart then proceeded beyond the particular virtues of the basic principle he had thus far recorded. He continued: "Underlying these separate points there is I think a more important general principle." This principle rested on the nature of the "person," by which Hart meant human beings as they are in fact constituted. Persons, he said, "interpret each other's movements as manifestations of intention and choices," and thus in terms of whether harms visited upon them are deliberate or voluntary – a distinction that

[28] See Hart, "Punishment and the Elimination of Responsibility."

[29] Barbara Wootton, *Crime and the Criminal Law: Reflections of a Magistrate and Social Scientist* (London: Stevens and Sons, 1963).

[30] H. L. A. Hart, *The Morality of the Criminal Law: Two Lectures* (Jerusalem: Magnes Press, Hebrew University, 1964), esp. pp. 12–29.

[31] Hart, "Punishment and the Elimination of Responsibility," esp. 180–82.

affected the moral judgments passed upon those committing the harm. There were involuntary aspects of the person's response to one judged to have acted deliberately: the emotions of "fear, indignation, anger, resentment." But there was also a rational component (although one he doubtless thought greatly affected by those emotions): my judgment that you acted intentionally "will enter into deliberations about my future voluntary conduct towards you and will colour all my social relations with you," as would not be the case were we to perceive others' acts as involuntary.[32] From this Hart asserted:

This is how human nature in human society actually is and as yet we have no power to alter it. The bearing of this fundamental fact on the law is this. If as our legal moralists maintain it is important for the law to reflect common judgments of morality, it is surely even more important that it should in general reflect in its judgments on human conduct distinctions which not only underlay morality, but pervade the whole of our social life. This it would fail to do if it treated men merely as alterable, predictable, curable, or manipulable things.

For these reasons then I think there will be a place for the principle of responsibility even when retributive and denunciatory ideas of punishment are dead.[33]

Hart's particular observations about human nature – the nature of "persons" – bear obvious similarity to those of his Oxford colleague and close friend, Peter Strawson, whose seminal essay of the same year, "Freedom and Resentment," was to have an important impact in philosophical circles and, by the 1970s, in legal (including American) academic enclaves as well. In confronting the ramifications of determinism for moral condemnation and punishment – or, perhaps better said, in rendering a confrontation unnecessary – Strawson effectively asserted that determinism, even if true, was irrelevant as a practical matter to the human process of blaming. Instead, he invoked what he termed the "participant reactive attitudes" – such as "gratitude, resentment, forgiveness, love, and hurt feelings" – we naturally feel in the course of our normal relations with each other.[34] His account was based on his detailed observations concerning the social and psychological realities of human life. His conclusions were rooted in the "very great importance that we attach to the attitudes and intentions towards us of other human beings, and the great extent to which our personal feelings and reactions depend upon, or involve, our beliefs about these attitudes and intentions."[35] Our reactive feelings and beliefs – which follow our interpretations of the intentions motivating others' acts – underlie our "language of

---

[32] Hart, "Punishment and the Elimination of Responsibility," 182–83.
[33] Hart, "Punishment and the Elimination of Responsibility," 183.
[34] P. F. Strawson, "Freedom and Resentment," chap. 1 in *Freedom and Resentment and Other Essays* (London: Methuen, 1974), 4, 10 (originally published in *Proceedings of the British Academy*, vol. 48 [1962]: 1–25).
[35] Strawson, "Freedom and Resentment," 5.

morals" and account for our practices of blaming or excusing in a given case or circumstance.[36] Most critically, these subjective, "non-detached attitudes" to which we are *all* prone characterize the normal relationships central to human life and thus preclude the purely objective view of human acts seemingly required by a legal system based only on determinist/consequentialist principles; because such attitudes are so "deeply rooted" in "human nature" and in the "general framework of human life," we could not set them aside even if we thought them objectively ill-based.[37]

Thus, the approaches of both Hart and Strawson relied on the significance of what they deemed universal elements of human life *as it actually is*. But their intended implications differed. Focusing on acts understood as intentional, Strawson ingeniously naturalized *retributivism* via an appeal to those "reactive attitudes" he claimed we all share. Focusing on acts not so understood, Hart naturalized a *non-retributive* principle of a moral constraint upon utility via an appeal to universal human expectations and reactions. Although Hart recognized reactive attitudes as underlying conventional morality, he perhaps understood this morality as less fixed than did Strawson; Hart insisted that its retributive aspects were unnecessary to a moral theory of criminal responsibility. For Hart, where there was no basis for a legal excuse, there was, by definition, no constraint upon utility; *utility* was then the justification for punishment whatever the accompanying social understandings of punishment might be. But Hart's evolving attention to present conventional attitudes of moral blame and odium in reaction to lawbreaking would ultimately take a certain toll. His emphasis on such attitudes to rebut Wootton's notion of an ideal, noncriminalizing system for dealing with offenders left little room for Hart's vision of a truly non-retributive approach to criminal responsibility.

Hart, Wootton, and the Fate of Judgment without Blame

There can be no denying Hart's great contribution to the criminal jurisprudence of his day. The idea of a moral constraint upon utilitarianism would remain influential. As an ideal that promoted political liberty, human self-restraint and individual pursuit of interests, it rang true. But the "person," as defined by Hart, was not to be confined by a conception of fairness and

---

[36] Strawson, "Freedom and Resentment," 7–9, 23.

[37] Strawson, "Freedom and Resentment," 4–6, 11, 13, 16, and see 18, 25. Indeed, Strawson concluded that our capacity to view others objectively – and thus as proper subjects of mere "treatment" (or as mere "object[s] of social policy") – is generally limited to those situations in which we specifically deem them incapable of normal adult intentions and relationships – that is, if the actor is psychologically abnormal or is a child (8–9). With regard to the rationality of adopting a more objective stance toward all others' acts, Strawson went so far as to assert that "it is *useless* to ask whether it would not be rational for us to do what is not in our nature to do" (18). Here he adopted language that might have seemed deterministic to many readers, and surprisingly so in light of his insistence that he himself did "not know what the thesis of determinism is" (1).

justice that merely underwrote a moral constraint on utility. When Hart marshaled his (and perhaps Strawson's) insights regarding "how human nature in society actually is" against Wootton's campaign for eliminating responsibility, Hart himself introduced a discordant element that threatened to undermine his quite austere version of a responsibility principle.

For Hart, unlike for Strawson, "how human nature in society actually is" reduced to a fine residue technically severable from conventional retribution: because persons read one another in relation to whether behavior is deliberate or involuntary, a principle of responsibility that distinguished between those intentional states was necessary for the law, but such readings by others might ultimately no longer be accompanied by retributive or denunciatory ideas. Still, even in a future where such ideas were divorced from our notions of culpability, the basic moral constraint principle nonetheless should remain in favor of the actor (and his subjective experience of free will or choice), given the fairness and justice of meeting normal and justifiable expectations – that is, given the good that results from allowing individuals to plan their lives and pursue their interests free from unpredictable legal constraint. In other words, culpable choice could survive the demise of retributive desert.

Hart's principle might *logically*, as it were, have a place when ideas of retributivism and denunciation were dead, but these ideas would not easily die. And how could one separate Hart's reliance on conventional human experiences, judgments, and reactions from their retributive, free-will-based origins? When all was said and done, Wootton had induced Hart to state the very conditions of human life that would render Hart's formulation of a responsibility principle a somewhat abstract idea.

Wootton would also draw more direct concessions. She herself did not view Hart's principle as abstract. Indeed it seemed to her all too concrete, for, she thought, it safeguarded true "punishment" premised on a voluntary act, regardless that Hart placed it in the frame of an assertedly utilitarian system of criminal justice. Wootton, on the other hand, carried forward a version of radical positivist ideas wherein "punishment," if employed, was a form of remedial or incapacitative treatment within a system of criminal law that, *in essence*, had been decriminalized. In her 1963 Hamlyn lecture she observed of Hart:

Although rejecting many traditional theories, such as that punishment should be "retributive" or "denunciatory," he nevertheless seems wholly unable to envisage a system in which sentence is not automatically equated with "punishment." Thus he writes of "values quite distinct from those of retributive punishment which the system of responsibility does maintain, and which remain of great importance even if our aims in *punishing* are the forward-looking aims of social protection"; and again "even if we *punish* men not as wicked but as nuisances ..." while he makes many references to the principle that liability to punishment must depend upon a voluntary act. Perhaps it requires the naïveté of an amateur to suggest that forward-looking aims of social protection might, on occasion, have absolutely no connection with punishment.[38]

Predictably, Wootton's response to Hart's critique of the "elimination of responsibility" drew a counter-critique. This came in one of Hart's Lionel Cohen lectures delivered at Hebrew University in Jerusalem in 1964. "Changing Conceptions of Responsibility" forcefully restated Hart's earlier arguments for the principle of responsibility, but it contained both a major concession to Wootton and a further concession regarding the actual condition of things. The former did not affect Hart's basic principle, but the latter posed a further threat to that principle's viability in the world as it "actually is." Hart first observed that "the weakest of the arguments" adduced against those who opposed dispensing with the concept of mens rea is "perhaps the one most frequently heard": that "our concern with the concept of personal responsibility incorporated in the doctrine of *mens rea* only makes sense if we subscribe to a retributive theory of punishment."[39]

Lady Wootton falls a victim to it because she makes too crude a dichotomy between "punishment" and "prevention." She does not even mention a moral outlook on punishment which is surely very common, very simple and except perhaps for the determinist perfectly defensible. This is the view that out of considerations of fairness or justice to individuals we should restrict even punishment designed as a "preventive" to those who had a normal capacity and a fair opportunity to obey. This is still an intelligible ideal of justice to the individuals whom we punish even if we punish them to protect society from the harm that crime does and not to pay back the harm that they have done.[40]

Having restated the basic principle – and having noted what he took to be Wootton's basic misunderstanding – Hart nonetheless conceded the potential costs of applying his principle in terms of loss of social security: individuals who had lacked mens rea but who were in fact dangerous could be acquitted and discharged altogether. He dealt sympathetically, albeit skeptically, with Wootton's claim that an individual's capacity to resist temptation is something "'buried in [his] consciousness, into which no human being can enter'"[41] – a point Hart again distinguished from "philosophical arguments" made by others (in response to the determinist critique) that "pitch the case altogether too high" and "are supposed to show that the question whether a man could have acted differently is *in principle unanswerable*." Wootton's "best arguments," in contrast, were more practical and rested on the confusing nature of "forensic debate[s] before judge and jury" and of judges' charges to juries on "the question whether a mentally disordered

[38] Wootton, *Crime and the Criminal Law*, 50–51.
[39] Hart, "Changing Conceptions of Responsibility," chap. 8 in *Punishment and Responsibility*, 200 (originally published in Hart, *Morality of the Criminal Law*, 5–29).
[40] Hart, "Changing Conceptions," 201.
[41] Hart, "Changing Conceptions," 203 (quoting Wootton, "Diminished Responsibility," 232).

person could have controlled his action or whether his capacity to do this was or was not 'substantially impaired.'" These practical difficulties led to Hart's concession that "the 'moderate' form of the new doctrine" preached by Wootton and others was preferable to the existing law.[42]

Under the scheme Hart now proposed, mens rea "would continue to be a necessary condition of liability to be investigated and settled before conviction *except so far as it relates to mental abnormality*." The issue of mental abnormality would be raised – if at all – after conviction, would mainly pertain to the offender's present mental state, and would be relevant to the issue of appropriate post-conviction treatment. The offender's mental state at the time of the crime "would only be relevant so far as it provide ancillary evidence of the nature of his abnormality and indicated the appropriate treatment." Thus did Hart accede to abolition of the conventional form of the insanity defense, but with an important proviso that, post-conviction, "where the appropriate direct evidence of mental disorder was forthcoming the Courts should no longer be permitted to think in terms of responsibility and mete out penal sentences instead of compulsory mental treatment."[43] In effect, a post hoc dismissal of the guilt associated with the previously recorded conviction would prevail in some insanity cases – abolition in those cases was not to be so much of the defense itself as of the determination of mental abnormality by a jury.

Beyond this "moderate" form of the new doctrine, however, Hart would not go. Concerns of individual freedom of course loomed large in this preference for a distinctly restricted reform: otherwise, he warned, "occasions for official interference with our lives and for compulsion will be vastly increased." Moreover – and relatedly – Wootton's view "that what we now call punishment (imprisonment and the like) and compulsory medical treatment should be regarded just as alternative forms of social hygiene" posed difficulties. She accepted that where "'medicine has nothing to offer'" an offender may be sentenced to "'places of safety'" for purposes of specific deterrence, and to this Hart objected on two grounds, one "moral" and one "social or criminological."[44] In his expression of the moral problem, Hart slid – without discussion – from specific deterrence (Wootton's objective) to general deterrence:

If we imprison a man who has broken the law in order to deter him *and by his example others*, we are using him for the benefit of society, and for many people, including myself, this is a step which requires to be justified by (*inter alia*) the demonstration that the person so treated could have helped doing what he did.[45]

---

[42] Hart, "Changing Conceptions," 203–05.
[43] Hart, "Changing Conceptions," 205 (emphasis added).
[44] Hart, "Changing Conceptions," 206–07 (quoting Wootton, *Crime and the Criminal Law*, 79–80).
[45] Hart, "Changing Conceptions," 207 (emphasis added).

Hart's "sociological or criminological doubts" related to Wootton's faith that in time imprisonment for specific deterrent purposes would come to be understood socially as akin to detention for medical treatment. He noted that social safety required imprisonment for general deterrence and brushed aside Wootton's willingness "to forego this aspect of punishment" in light of her doubts that it was effective; he asserted that social needs now required – and perhaps would long do so – a basis for imprisonment (general deterrence) that was inherently different from that associated with medical treatment. Then came the "second feature distinguishing punishments from treatment," which responded to Wootton's scheme wherein conviction based on outward conduct would be retained, rather than a total decriminalization that dispensed with proof of an offending act:

unlike a medical inspection followed by detention in hospital, conviction by a court followed by a sentence of imprisonment is a public act expressing the odium, if not the hostility, of society for those who break the law. As long as those features attach to conviction and sentence of imprisonment, the moral objection to their use on those who could not have helped doing what they did will remain. On the other hand, if they cease to attach, will not the law have lost an important element in its authority and deterrent force – as important perhaps for some convicted persons as the deterrent force of the actual measures which it administers.[46]

In other words, even specific deterrence in the name of prevention might require the offender's internalization of an essentially *retributive* conventional morality. How, then, could Hart's basic responsibility principle ever come to function absent the present, retributive element?

Hart's exchanges with Lady Wootton replayed, yet significantly advanced, the debates of the Progressive Era and its aftermath. Hart's claims upon the social perspective resonated with those set forth in the 1910 *Strasburg* case in response to Progressive ideals. Wootton believed that imprisonment for general deterrence was ineffective, but her redefinition of imprisonment as a specific deterrent in the sheer sense of "treatment" would be similarly ineffective, Hart argued, for loss of the very statement that conviction represented in the social imagination.

Positivist and deterrence-based legal academics of the 1930s had circled round a set of problems that Hart thought could be resolved by combining a general justifying aim of utility with a moral principle that acted as a limit on utility. That principle took the conventional morality that Michael and Wechsler, in their rebuttal to the positivists, had assimilated to utility and transmuted it into a basic principle that stood outside of, and as a constraint upon, utility. Although Hart insisted that his basic principle did not necessarily carry retributive meaning, he clearly understood the early positivists' point – and made ready use of it for his own purposes – that *socially* it would nonetheless be taken to do so. At the same time, like the early positivists

[46] Hart, "Changing Conceptions," 208–09.

(but unlike Strawson), Hart imagined that the retributive and denunciatory elements he had identified might eventually fade away. Whereas for the positivists this would open the way to a purely treatmentist criminal law (not unlike that of Wootton), for Hart it left a residue of *non*-retributive principles of fairness and justice that precluded criminal liability for commission of a prohibited act that one could not have chosen not to commit, and that retained criminal liability for the remainder of "chosen" acts.

Hart invoked deep-seated human responses to the deliberate and involuntary acts of others in defense of his abstract – or abstracted – principle. But in doing so he came perilously close to recognizing the potential that this very human psychology – which many argued unavoidably included the retributive urge – held for destabilizing the principle itself. In his attempt to domesticate conventional attitudes to an ultimately non-blame-oriented vision of responsibility, he may have underestimated the central role blame and retribution played in conventional psychology – and perhaps even in the justifications he offered for his own approach. He never envisaged putting conventional psychology to the use that some others who followed him did – that is, they accorded it even more substantial scope while simultaneously (in a certain sense) defanging and ennobling it by redefining the very meaning of retributive punishment from a species of revenge to a species of deserved respect due a person as an autonomous agent. That neo-retributivist move would soon come, and some of those who made it would draw upon Hart, putting him to uses he thought philosophically indefensible, unwise, and perhaps even disreputable. Hart's basic principle was to become, despite his own intentions, one building block of a revised retributivism. His recognition of the realities of human psychology – rendered in greater detail and with far greater force by Strawson – was to become another. And the strands of thought about the salutary aspects of guilt and responsibility that were yielded by 1940s and 1950s confrontations with the determinist critique were to be yet others. At one point or another, all would figure in the slide, during the late 1960s and the 1970s, from Hartian moral-constraint jurisprudence to its close relative, "negative retributivism" (which holds that desert is necessary but not sufficient, alone, to justify criminal blame and punishment), and even, in some quarters, to its more distant relation, positive retributivism (which asserts that desert, alone is sufficient to justify – and indeed, may require – blame and punishment).[47]

---

[47] As I have indicated, "retributivism" defies clear categorization; we may debate where any one theory of desert lies on a spectrum from a moral side-constraint on consequentialism, to negative retributivism to positive retributivism. Antony Duff's helpful rough delineation classifies as "negative retributivism" those theories that root criminal condemnation and punishment in personal desert for wrongdoing (i.e., that do not impose punishment merely to serve deterrent or rehabilitative ends), but as a distributive principle or side constraint for a system primarily aimed at other consequential goals. In Duff's words, it is "negative" because it primarily "forbids the punishment of the innocent (and perhaps also the excessive punishment of the guilty)" and "provides no complete justification of punishment"; "it tells us that we

Sixties American Criminal Jurisprudence: Packer, Kadish, and Goldstein

The practical and the "metaphysical" were nicely balanced in pre-Herbert Morris 1960s American criminal jurisprudence. Herbert Hart's caution was observed: the domestication of conventional morality was achieved with aplomb and assurance, and with little postwar existential angst. Practical wisdom was the hallmark of the most important academic writings of the period, which emphasized the relationships among criminal responsibility, political liberty, and the individual's sense of well-being – albeit with various approaches to an instrumental idea of free will. In the main, there was little discussion of the victim's or community's reaction to the offender (that side of Hart was lost; Strawson had not as yet been noticed). Where such discussion did occur, moreover, it was most commonly broadly directed to achieving community stability. True to Kalven's and Henry Hart's admonitions, 1960s scholarship accepted the criminal law's role as a blaming institution. There were hints of a desert-based defense of punishment premised upon the criminal law's vindication of the offender's dignity and autonomy. But, as is illustrated by the selected scholars I discuss here in light of their specific attention to responsibility and punishment (I cannot claim that they necessarily represent the views – silent or otherwise – of all in their field), the vision of punishment appears to have remained consequentialist, and indeed mainly rehabilitational. For the most part, American legal scholars only gradually worked out a significant modification of Herbert Hart's basic position.

may punish the guilty (their punishment is not unjust), but not that or why we *should* punish them." (For obvious reasons, Herbert Hart's theory could be described this way, although I join those who place him in a separate, non-blame-based side-constraint category given his preference – ultimately realistic or not – for avoiding traditional notions of desert while imposing legal liability.) Positive retributivism, on the other hand, is commonly associated with the notion that desert is both necessary and sufficient to justify blame and punishment: it does not merely protect the innocent, but concludes that the guilty indeed "*ought* to be punished"; they *deserve* punishment, albeit for a range of overlapping reasons depending on the given theory. See R. A. Duff, "Penal Communications: Recent Work in the Philosophy of Punishment," *Crime and Justice: An Annual Review of Research*, vol. 20 (1995): 1–97, esp. 7. Michael Moore more pointedly defines what others call "positive retributivism" and urges that true "retributivism" inheres only in this category: true retributivists believe not just that the guilty deserve punishment, but that desert *alone* gives society the right and duty to punish them; indeed, says Moore, punishment of the guilty is "an *intrinsic* good" for a genuine retributivist. "Closet Retributivism," chap. 2 in *Placing Blame*, 87–91 (originally published in *USC Cites* [1982]). Compare, e.g., Douglas Husak, "'Broad Culpability' and the Retributivist Dream," *Ohio State Journal of Criminal Law*, vol. 9 (2012): 449–485, 450 n. 4 ("Nearly every retributivist finds room for consequentialist considerations – most notably, the prevention of crime – somewhere in his account. It is hard to know when an approach qualifies as a 'mixed theory,' blending backward-looking and forward-looking elements in a single view. But a theory need not be 'pure' to count as retributive; it need only regard desert and blame as central to attempts to provide answers to normative questions about criminal law and punishment.").

Herbert Packer

Like Herbert Hart, Stanford law professor Herbert Packer insisted on the principle of responsibility solely as a limiting condition. Packer followed Hart in his critique of an unfettered utilitarianism: "Punishment of the morally innocent does not reinforce one's sense of identification as a law-abider, but rather undermines it." But Packer also envisioned a more substantial role for the criminal law. The criminal law, Packer asserted, "must in a free society be judged ultimately on the basis of its success in promoting human autonomy and the capacity for individual human growth and development."[48] This sounded more like Henry than like Herbert Hart, but Packer nonetheless remained closer to the latter. Packer encapsulated something akin to Herbert Hart's minimalist position on accountability in Packer's own critique of the stark positivism of Wootton and her few legal-academic followers in the United States. Like Herbert Hart, he avoided the language of desert. But Packer did not rest accountability on an independent moral principle. Rather, he appealed to the "*instrumental* case for culpability": "People ought in general to be able to plan their conduct"; the criminal law ought to be "*seen to be* fair," which entails most of all that "no one should be subjected to punishment without having an opportunity to litigate the issue of his culpability." And although Packer appealed as well to the rehabilitative ideal, he denied that this ideal could stand as a justification for imposing punishment, and questioned whether the capacity currently existed to achieve reform or to avoid baseless differences in treatment. His compromise rested first on the conclusion that justification for conviction, that is, "culpability," must rest on preventive principles, but, of course, subject to the "instrumental ... limitation on the utilitarian position." Then, once a conviction has been thus justified, "the rehabilitative ideal should be fully used in deciding what kinds of punishment should be imposed."[49]

With specific regard to Packer's conception of desert, his instrumental and consequentialist concerns did not invoke desert in a traditional sense. Yet, his orientation toward desert was not always clear. At one point, for example, he introduced a significant ambiguity into his discussion, asserting:

It is wrong to say that we should punish persons simply because they commit offenses under circumstances that we can call blameworthy. It is right to say that we should not punish those who commit offenses unless we can say that their conduct is blameworthy.[50]

Here he seems to espouse negative retributivism, or what came to be a classic form of "mixed theory" combining retributivism with consequentialist ends, wherein blameworthiness is a necessary but not sufficient basis

---

[48] Herbert L. Packer, *The Limits of the Criminal Sanction* (Stanford, CA: Stanford University Press, 1968), 65.
[49] Packer, *Limits of the Criminal Sanction*, 67–69.
[50] Packer, *Limits of the Criminal Sanction*, 66.

for punishment. Yet, read in relation to his overall position, the statement appears to be closer to Hart's idea of a mere limiting condition upon consequentialist punishment not meant to genuinely endorse moral desert. The issue concerns the conceptualization of the limiting condition. Hart had been careful to avoid the term "blameworthy" and to write solely in terms of the requirement – on grounds of morality and justice – of a voluntary commission of an act that was prohibited by the criminal law (a "liability-triggering" act, we might say). Packer, on the other hand, would require an act that could be "characterized as blameworthy."[51] Still, Packer appeared to employ the word "blameworthy" only in the sense that it established legal culpability; it did not suggest a justified retributive element in the punishment that might follow. Indeed, he distanced himself from the "retributive position" and readily criticized the "moral ambiguity" of punishment as compared to rehabilitation, insisting that punishment, as a "social institution," was "necessary but lamentable." Further, he specifically asserted that "the role of culpability in the justification for punishment is an instrumental one"; because the actor is "blameworthy," the imposition of criminal liability appears "fair" (as it "ought"), not only to the actor but to society in general.[52] Such an instrumental consideration was consistent with Hart's limiting principle. But Packer's formulation aligned the principle – which, for Hart, was rooted in morality only in an abstract way – more closely with conventional morality. Thus Packer exposed the possibility – inevitability? – of slippage from a mere limiting principle to an at least partial justification for retributive punishment of the sort that ultimately came to flower within American legal academic criminal jurisprudence.

Packer's expression of a variant of Herbert Hartian jurisprudence otherwise left little disguised. It openly announced a departure from conventional morality's acceptance of true free will, an acceptance that Hart had attempted to fend off through indirection. Packer's version of an "as if" position on free will is, of course, well-known:

The idea of free will in relation to conduct is not, in the legal system, a statement of fact, but rather a *value preference* having very little to do with the metaphysics of determinism and free will. The fallacy that legal values describe physical reality is a very common one.... Very simply, the law treats man's conduct as autonomous and willed, not because it is, but *because it is desirable to proceed as if it were*. It is desirable because the capacity of the individual human being to live his life in reasonable freedom from socially imposed external constraints ... would be fatally impaired unless the law provided a *locus poenitentiae*, a point of no-return beyond which external constraints may be imposed but before which the individual is free – not free of whatever compulsions determinists tell us he labors under but free of the very specific compulsions of the law.[53]

[51] Packer, *Limits of the Criminal Sanction*, 62.
[52] Packer, *Limits of the Criminal Sanction*, 67–70.
[53] Packer, *Limits of the Criminal Sanction*, 74–75 (emphasis added); see also 132.

The "point of no-return" at which the attribution of "autonomous and willed" attached to conduct – the moment of truth for the "value preference" of the law's "idea of free will" – was (as it was for Hart) defined negatively. "By the use of the term 'voluntary' in relation to conduct … [t]he law is not affirming that some conduct is the product of the free exercise of conscious volition; it is excluding, in a crude kind of way, conduct that in any view is not." Packer gave as examples "conduct that occurs while the actor is in an unconscious state – sleepwalking, epileptic seizures, automatism," and he asserted that the law excluded such conduct from "voluntary" conduct

primarily in response to the simple intuition that nothing would more surely undermine the individual's sense of autonomy and security than to hold him to account for conduct *he* does not think he can control. He may be deluded, if the determinists are right, in his belief that such conduct differs significantly from any other conduct in which he engages. But that is beside the point. *He* thinks there is a difference, and that is what the law acts upon.[54]

In drawing the line at unconscious (or closely analogous) behavior, the "law" (here, Packer mainly had the Model Penal Code in mind) might more convincingly stake its claim on grounds of sheer deterrability than on those of the Hartian accountability principle to which Packer (on "instrumental" grounds) actually adhered. It is, perhaps, an empirical question, but it is not obvious that most people would define as "free" virtually *all* behavior short of that which Packer would define as unfree – that *any* broader exclusion of conduct from "voluntary" would necessarily "undermine the individual's sense of autonomy and security." Yet it is also not obvious where else one might draw the line in a way that would protect the individual against the erosion of that sense. If some social or psychological constraints (short of those that rendered one virtually unconscious or totally out of control) created unfreedom, why did not others just a bit removed? And if those others were added to the realm of the nonvoluntary, what about those just a bit more removed? Hence, presumably, the bright-line test for nonvoluntary conduct, which must remain at "conduct that in any view is not." A legal fiction – or a "value preference" – is not necessarily meant, I gather, to overlap with empirical reality, whether of the purely scientific sort or of the sort that accords with the actual bounds of human intuition.

    Alongside his strict view of nonvoluntary behavior, Packer also nonetheless accepted that "we must put up with the bother of the insanity defense" because it is critical to upholding the law's "contingent and instrumental posit of freedom": "to exclude [the insanity defense] is to deprive the criminal law of its chief paradigm of free will." To this end, regardless of whether it is in fact true that some mental illnesses create excusable volitional impairment – perceptions of such impairment itself being "a culturally conditioned matter" that is not "immutable" – "there must be some recognition

[54] Packer, *Limits of the Criminal Sanction*, 76–77.

of the generally held assumption that some people are, by reason of mental illness, significantly impaired in their volitional capacity." The point was that, to reinforce the important instrumental idea of freedom, "some kind of line must be drawn in the face of our intuition, however wrongheaded it may be, that mental illness contributes to volitional impairment."[55]

Packer thus accepted the law's test for culpability based primarily on voluntary conduct and a strictly limited, instrumentally defined absence of volitional impairment. The latter ought to reflect the law's "paradigm of free will" that the law adopted as a "value preference," but that – here Packer was ambiguous – society at large understood in true free will terms. Some elements in Packer's theoretical construct might seem to suggest insincerity in his claimed rejection of a pure "utilitarian ideal of prevention" – that is, his focus on conduct could be extended logically to imply no need for a culpable mental state beyond whatever was required for the prohibited conduct to be deterrable. On the other hand, Packer was unambiguous in his rejection of strict liability, which, he stated, is "denounced, and rightly so, as being incompatible with culpability limitations."[56]

Packer's restrictive conception of non-culpability must be understood in relation, first, to his liberty-based concern that the law not punish on the basis of "thoughts and emotions" or "personality patterns and character structures,"[57] and, second, to his views about punishment: his utter unhappiness with the practice, and – most of all – the importance he attributed to the rehabilitative ideal *when* that ideal was properly limited. Packer openly, even insistently, emphasized the "moral ambiguity" of punishment: "We cannot avoid punishment, nor can we ever feel entirely happy about it." This confronted the legislator with grave responsibilities at the outset; when defining criminal offenses he must "pay careful attention to the limits imposed by the rationale of the criminal law" and accept them "not grudgingly, as a nuisance or an interference with important practical goals, but willingly as a means of preventing this human agency from becoming

---

[55] Packer, *Limits of the Criminal Sanction*, 132–33. Packer was not particularly concerned about specific tests for the mutable concept of insanity, observing that it is not "too important how discriminating we are about drawing some kind of line to separate those suffering volitional impairment from the rest of us." Currently, insanity fell in the middle of a spectrum between, on one end, prohibited conduct occurring during epileptic fits (when we say there was no voluntary act at all), and, on the other end, such conduct committed under circumstances of "cultural deprivation of a kind associated with urban poverty," which, although they "restrict the individual's capacity to choose and make him more susceptible to engaging in antisocial conduct than the 'average' member of society ..., we regard ... as too remote to justify an excuse" (133). He appeared to believe that cognitive tests for insanity were sufficient because they encompassed a volitional understanding of culpable conduct: "We excuse a man who does not understand not because he does not understand but because his lack of understanding renders him incapable of making a meaningful choice. Cognition is not the complement of volition; it is its precursor" (134).

[56] Packer, *Limits of the Criminal Sanction*, 76.

[57] Packer, *Limits of the Criminal Sanction*, 73.

tyrannical." He must also look to the rationale of the criminal law for the "clues" it "conceals" regarding "the criteria that he should take into account in determining what kinds of behavior should be treated as 'criminal.'"[58] In other words, the law must limit the substance of its reach, guided by the "ultimate goal of law in a free society, which is to liberate rather than to restrain." This rationale was, however, transitional. Packer warned: "As we find ourselves gaining more nearly exact knowledge about the sources and control of deviant behavior, the pressure from the behavioral position upon this rationale will become very strong and may prove to be irresistible." We will be powerfully tempted "to relax the constraints that inhibit us at present from aggressively intervening in the lives of individuals in the name of crime prevention." Packer resisted the wisdom of such a transition – the "millennium," as he put it – toward which the behavioral school pointed. Echoing Herbert Hart, he concluded: "Skeptics about its advent may then as now find some merit in a limiting rationale for the criminal sanction."[59]

Overall, despite his stress on the promotion of "human autonomy and the capacity for individual growth and development," Packer couched his arguments mainly within the context of political liberty. His apparent disdain for the human impulse to punish based on a robust form of blameworthiness led him to reject (pace Henry Hart) "assertions that punishment on the basis of moral fault strengthens the moral fiber of the individual being punished, or constitutes education for good citizenship, or something of that sort." He neither insisted that such an impulse was inevitably part of the human makeup nor enlisted it as an ally in the struggle for political liberty, that is, against the tyranny that might well attend the behaviorist victory. Rather, Packer preferred benevolent rehabilitation, which might have served as an offset to his instrumental acceptance of culpability premised merely on the "value preference" of the "idea of free will" (a 1960s version, one might say, of the compensatory role that individualized sentencing had played for earlier positivists who had accepted *faute de mieux* a bifurcation of guilt assessment and post-conviction treatment). For Packer, punishment remained "lamentable," "not a virtue, only a necessity"[60] – the lonely job of the legislator even if carried forward as "treatment" in the transformed world that Pound and the positivists hoped would someday come. It might come, Packer thought, but, for reasons that Herbert Hart fully accepted, its siren song ought nonetheless to be resisted.

Legal philosopher Ronald Dworkin expanded on this theme in political liberty terms the following year in his discourse on rights:

Some philosophers think, on the basis of contemporary physiology and psychology, that this phenomenological distinction between choice and compulsion makes no sense. They believe that all human behavior is determined by factors beyond

---

[58] Packer, *Limits of the Criminal Sanction*, 69–70.
[59] Packer, *Limits of the Criminal Sanction*, 66.
[60] Packer, *Limits of the Criminal Sanction*, 67.

individual control, so that the feelings of free choice we have are just illusions. But the scientific evidence for this is far from conclusive, and even those who think it weighty must decide how the law should respond until the case is proved (if it ever is or can be). If we accept the view that all behavior is determined, for example, would it follow that we should abandon entirely the idea that human beings have rights that their government is morally bound to respect? If we chose not to go so far, either because the scientific evidence is inconclusive, or because we are reluctant to abandon the notion of rights in any event, would it not be inconsistent to abandon the mental defense in the name of science?[61]

Dworkin's reflections here, like Packer's, resonated with the view of Herbert Hart in his statement of "liberal" principles, although Dworkin developed his own defense of the principle of "equal respect as an individual."[62] Dworkin's suggestion that, in considering these weighty issues, we "must decide" and "cho[o]se" appears unself-conscious, as does Packer's implicit assumption about the choices of those "skeptics" who doubted the wisdom of the behaviorist approach. Both left open the possibility that the claims of science, although irresistible, might never be fully proven, and one infers the course of action they counseled could at least be thought about as other than determined. For if it was itself fully determined ...?

This unselfconsciousness about moral suasion in the face of a hypothesized determinism united 1960s criminal jurisprudence with its predecessor formulations. Of course, Jerome Hall had seen the point, noting of the more radical positivists that "it has never occurred to them to 'determine' what determines their Determinism."[63] But mainly the game was played, then as ever, with as little crippling self-reflexiveness as one, in the nature of things, is determined to indulge. The liberal and reformist criminal jurisprudence of the 1960s was especially free from debilitating self-conscious irony. Distinctly post-existential, it made few leaps of faith; true to its progressive tendencies, it privileged rationality without noticing – or if it noticed, without calling attention to the fact – that reason when applied to morality sooner or later bends back upon itself.

Sanford Kadish

Berkeley law professor Sanford Kadish was yet another commentator for whom Wootton's bold initiative largely framed the issue. Kadish's memorable "The Decline of Innocence" (1968)[64] first responded to a movement

[61] Ronald Dworkin, *Taking Rights Seriously* (Cambridge, MA: Harvard University Press, 1978), 11–12 (chap. 1, "Jurisprudence," originally published in *New York Review of Books*, 1969).
[62] Dworkin, *Taking Rights Seriously*, 12–13.
[63] Jerome Hall, "Mental Disease and Criminal Responsibility – *M'Naghten* versus *Durham* and the American Law Institute's Tentative Draft," *Indiana Law Journal*, vol. 33 (1957): 212–26, 712.
[64] Sanford H. Kadish, "The Decline of Innocence," essay 5 in *Blame and Punishment: Essays in the Criminal Law* (New York: Macmillan, 1987) (originally published in *Cambridge Law Journal*, vol. 26 [1968]: 273–90).

within the 1960s American legal and psychiatric worlds to abolish the insanity defense[65] and then turned to Wootton's proposal of total abolition of the mens rea requirement. His opening formulation of his objection tracked both Herbert Hart and Packer. "The essence of the proposal is that innocence [based on blameworthiness], moral innocence, if you will, should not disqualify a person from the consequences of the penal law."[66] Kadish demonstrated the practical impossibility of removing the admittedly vexing problem of mental abnormality from the criminal trial merely by abolishing the insanity defense, then noted the "fundamental objection" to such a move:

[Abolition of the insanity defense] opens to the condemnation of a criminal conviction a class of persons who, on any common-sense notion of justice, are beyond blaming and ought not to be punished. The criminal law as we know it today does associate a substantial condemnatory onus with conviction for a crime. So long as this is so a just and humane legal system has an obligation to make a distinction between those who are eligible for this condemnation and those who are not.[67]

All the more so, Kadish thought, with respect to the totalizing move – the rejection of the punishment system altogether, as in Wootton's "radical" proposal – which would "tear up, root and branch, all manifestations of *mens rea* toward the end of extirpating blame and punishment from the criminal law."[68] Kadish's response drew largely upon Herbert Hart but was more

---

[65] See, e.g., Justice Joseph Weintraub (New Jersey), "Insanity as a Defense: A Panel Discussion," 37 F.R.D. 365, 369 (1964); Seymour L. Halleck, *Psychiatry and the Dilemmas of Crime: A Study of Causes, Punishment, and Treatment* (New York: Harper and Rowe, 1967), esp. 341–42. University of Chicago Law and Criminology Professor Norval Morris was perhaps the best known of those who advocated abolition of the defense. See Norval Morris, "Psychiatry and the Dangerous Criminal," *Southern California Law Review*, vol. 41 (1968): 514–47; and, later, Norval Morris, *Madness and the Criminal Law* (Chicago: University of Chicago Press, 1982). Initially sounding like Wootton, Morris pointed to our inability to genuinely assess the impact of mental abnormality on the commission of an offense. But he was less doubtful than Wooten of our ability to gauge the actor's mens rea. Instead of abolishing mens rea, he would have retained it as a centerpiece; he would have abolished insanity as a special defense and allowed most issues concerning the accused's mental condition to figure into the question whether he or she possessed the intent necessary for him or her to be convicted for the relevant offense. For those convicted, the influence of any mental illness would then also be considered upon sentencing, most commonly as a factor that mitigated desert (see, esp., *Madness*, 61–65). With regard to the goals of sentencing, Morris again diverged from Wootton; he rejected rehabilitation – particularly the sort of medicalized, open-ended incarceration that Wootton espoused – as a *defining* goal of sentencing (although he did strongly encourage voluntary rehabilitation programs within prisons). See, esp., Norval Morris, "The Future of Imprisonment: Toward a Punitive Philosophy," *Michigan Law Review*, vol. 72 (1974): 1161–280. Instead, he advocated that individual desert must be employed to limit the bounds of state-imposed punishment (*Madness*, esp. 196–202). I touch on Morris and his influential notion of "limiting retributivism" further in Chapters 8 and 9.

[66] Kadish, "Decline of Innocence," 65.

[67] Kadish, "Decline of Innocence," 73.

[68] Kadish, "Decline of Innocence," 75.

expansive in its expression of the values to be defended and, like Packer, more frank in its recognition of the "as if" basis of free will within a system of criminal responsibility:

Much of our commitment to democratic values, to human dignity and self-determination, to the value of the individual, turns on the pivot of a view of man as a responsible agent entitled to be praised or blamed depending upon his free choice of conduct. A view of men "merely as alterable, predictable, curable or manipulable things" is the foundation of a very different social order indeed. The ancient notion of free will may well in substantial measure be a myth. But even a convinced determinist should reject a governmental regime which is founded on anything less in its system of authoritative disposition of citizens. Whether the concept of man as a responsible agent is fact or fancy is a very different question from whether we ought to insist that the government in its coercive dealings with individuals must act on that premise.[69]

Although Kadish referred to "the criminal law as we know it today," it is doubtful that he foresaw a different future, either with respect to the practical realities of governmental "disposition of citizens" or those of the "feelings of outrage and injustice over great wrongs" that were "human," and unlikely to be eradicated by "a non-punitive law."[70] As in Hart's 1961 essay (and, of course, as in Strawson's as well), the attribution of conventional morality had moved from the positivists' descriptions of judgments and feelings "out there" (in society at large) to assertions of judgments and feelings within us *all*. Kadish's formulation of what was at stake, however, was more robust. Political liberty, human dignity, and (universal) human nature regarding "feelings of outrage" dovetailed; together they grounded the very idea of criminal responsibility, which both reflected and vindicated commonplace human understandings. The "outrage" that generated the desire for revenge to a large extent had been cleansed, at least in theory, by its association with the idea of the dignity accorded to one deemed appropriately held responsible; it had not been cleansed of its association with the "substantial condemnatory onus" borne by criminal convicts. Here the maybe-myth of free will took its inevitable toll. Hart (echoed by Packer) had said: "This is how human nature in human society actually is and as yet we have no power to alter it." Yet he also allowed that "there will be a place for the principle of responsibility even when retributive and denunciatory ideas of punishment are dead,"[71] suggesting a possible change in human emotions but the ongoing correlative requirements of respect for normal expectations flowing from the experience of choosing and the vindication of political liberty. Kadish, however, was apparently more resigned

---

[69] Kadish, "Decline of Innocence," 77 (quoting Hart, "Punishment and the Elimination of Responsibility," 183).

[70] Kadish, "Decline of Innocence," 79.

[71] Hart, "Punishment and the Elimination of Responsibility," 183.

to permanence in human nature, and he more openly stated the virtues that attached to these realities. His "convinced determinist" ought to act not only on political liberty principles, but also to vindicate "human dignity," the "value of the individual," and the natural responses of humans – and ought to because doing so accorded with recognition of an ultimate human truth. There might be some room for closing the gap between law and science, but calm acceptance, even promotion, of some significant unbridgeable distance between the two lay at the heart of his criminal jurisprudence.

Kadish's "Decline of Innocence" can be read, one might nonetheless suppose, as consistent with Hart's basic principle: a side constraint on consequentialist punishment. But Kadish did not expressly refer to a merely limiting role for blameworthiness, and indeed his language regarding "blame" is open to a broader reading concerning both the attribution of responsibility and the imposition of punishment than was that of Hart (or of Packer). That is, Kadish appeared to favor a true "negative retributivism," according to which retribution – blameworthiness premised upon desert – was a necessary, but not a sufficient basis for punishment. Although utility – or consequentialism – remained as an important aim, Kadish allowed for the possibility of a respectable retributive element in punishment. Indeed, this is how he himself would later characterize his 1968 article, but, then, that was only after the turn to retributivism in the 1970s and beyond.[72]

Abraham Goldstein

It is more difficult to place Yale Law School professor Abraham Goldstein's pathbreaking book *The Insanity Defense* (1967) within the (Herbert) Hartian tradition. Goldstein never cited Herbert Hart, nor did he cite Henry Hart, which is surprising as the American Hart can be read in support of Goldstein's particular application of 1960s principles. Goldstein admitted to "the superficial plausibility" of the proposal to abolish the insanity defense, but he marshaled powerful reasons for maintaining it. "Most fundamentally," Goldstein argued (along with Kadish), "eliminating the insanity defense would remove from the criminal law and the public conscience the vitally

---

[72] In 1987, Kadish cited "Decline of Innocence" as supporting blame-based punishment; he made plain, however, that he did not "embrace the retributive view that responsibility for law violation itself requires punishment, only that responsibility is necessary, but not sufficient, for punishment." Sanford Kadish, "Excusing Crime," essay 6 in *Blame and Punishment* (also published in *California Law Review*, vol. 75 [1987]: 257–89), 88 n. 20. In 1994, he appeared even more to affirmatively embrace retributive urges, albeit with conceded ambiguities (which I touch on in Chapter 9). His overall formulation cast his views – as of 1994 and 1968 – as intended to uphold deserved punishment not in a positive retributivist sense, but to preserve the inverse of desert: "how long could the commitment that the innocent *should not* be punished," he asked, "remain vigorous once it was no longer believed that the guilty *should* be punished?" Sanford H. Kadish, "The Criminal Law and the Luck of the Draw," *JCLC*, vol. 84 (1994): 679–702, 700–01 (again citing "Decline of Innocence").

important distinction between illness and evil."[73] Like Packer, Goldstein pointed to the individual "who wished to contest his responsibility before the public and his peers," only to find he could not do so, for "he would be approached entirely in social engineering terms." This, he argued, "over-looks entirely the place of the concept of responsibility itself in keeping the mechanism in proper running order."

> That concept is more seriously threatened today than ever before. This is a time of anomie.... As [the "paternal" state's effort] gains momentum, there is a very real risk it will bring with it a culture which will not make the individuals within it feel it is important to learn the discipline of moderation and conformity to communal norms.
>
>   In such a time, the insanity defense can play a part in reinforcing the sense of obligation or responsibility. Its emphasis on whether an offender is sick or bad helps to keep alive the almost forgotten drama of individual responsibility.... [I]t becomes part of a complex of cultural forces that keep alive the moral lessons, *and the myths*, which are essential to the continued order of society. In short, even if we have misgivings about blaming a particular individual, because he has been shaped long ago by forces he may no longer be able to resist, the concept of "blame" may be necessary.[74]

Goldstein thus stressed communal order, and, echoing Henry Hart, he asserted that individuals needed to learn, and to act out, "conformity or ... a reasonable nonconformity."[75] He identified a value system absorbed through early training by parents as well as through enactment within community tribunals. He treated as instrumental not only the belief in individual autonomy and responsibility, but also the practice of blaming. Here he appears to have adopted some form of retributivism premised upon the idea of desert, but it was decidedly an instrumental acceptance. Perhaps he viewed desert mainly as a side-constraint on the application of either rehabilitative or utilitarian punishment, so that punishment itself would remain aimed only at traditional consequentialist ends. And here Kadish might have agreed – although neither scholar was clear about this. The implications of emphasizing the social idea of blame as a side-constraint on utility would

---

[73] Abraham S. Goldstein, *The Insanity Defense* (New Haven, CT: Yale University Press, 1967), 222–23. At a later point, Goldstein commented:

> the heart of the distinction between conviction and acquittal by reason of insanity lies in the fact that the former represents official condemnation. Yet the acquittal is in itself a sanction, bringing with it comparable stigma and the prospect of indeterminate detention. If the choice between the two sanctions is to be made in a way that will not only be acceptable to the larger community but will also serve the function we have noted, it is important that the decision be made by a democratically selected jury rather than by experts – because the public can identify with the former but not with the latter. (225)

[74] Goldstein, *Insanity Defense*, 223–24 (emphasis added).
[75] Goldstein, *Insanity Defense*, 224.

differ from the implications of Herbert Hart's emphasis on the individual's own sense of self-determination through simple deliberation and choice as a side-constraint; yet this difference remained clouded until a true revival of retributivism forced the distinction out into the open.

There were strong resonances in Goldstein of the as-if approach to 1960s jurisprudence embraced by Kadish, but Goldstein placed less emphasis than Kadish on ineffable passions and beliefs and more on the need to buttress the value system that makes communal living possible. Like Bazelon, Goldstein privileged the role of the jury in insanity cases, not so much, however, because the social view represented the appropriate version of the "truth" regarding what was, in principle, a matter that resisted clear definition. Rather, for Goldstein, the social view represented a version of the truth that would maintain respect for a necessary system of social values. Was that version – any version – simple "myth"? Goldstein's formulation – like Kadish's "may well ... be ... myth" and "fact or fancy," or Packer's "value preference" – was vague on this point: forces that one "may no longer be able to resist" substituted for a resolute determinism; the concession in such circumstances was only that "'blame' may be necessary." Goldstein's account, it would seem, was premised on the sort of agnosticism that Dworkin openly embraced.

Herbert Hart, Packer, Kadish, and Goldstein wrestled with the concept of responsibility, but only to a limited extent with the underpinnings of the idea of personal desert. For all of them, of course, the individual "deserved" to be *free* from liability unless the limiting conditions of liability had been met; for all of them the individual was subject to – and in *that* sense "deserved" – consequentialist-based punishment if those conditions had been met. Kadish and Goldstein perhaps imagined some role for deserved retributive punishment, addressing that role largely as a by-product of the need to maintain political liberty, social values, and individual values and needs. Only Kadish addressed the idea of respect for the dignity of the individual to the extent of at least implying that such respect in itself justified the imposition of retributive punishment for a criminal act. Neither focused on the individual's wrongdoing as an intrinsic basis of deserved (as opposed to justified) punishment. A merely "as if" or "maybe myth" approach to free will seems to have set limits on the embrace of a desert-based retributivism.

Although the jurisprudence of the 1960s (so far) mainly evidenced agnosticism about determinism, it opined that political, social, and individual values would require an idea of responsibility even in a determined world. That was a pregnant idea, but one that – for legal scholars – as yet lay undeveloped. The writers I have canvassed neither filled out the idea of the "person" in relation to desert nor responded directly to the determinist critique that the idea of desert could not survive causal analysis of the offender's behavior. The turn to neo-retributivism – that is, to a claimed liberal-egalitarian idea of deserved punishment – had only just gotten under way within the American legal academy.

HERBERT MORRIS: RETRIBUTIVISM REVIVED

The year 1968 marked the highpoint of what I have called 1960s American criminal jurisprudence, or legal-academic thought more or less in the (Herbert) Hartian vein. It also witnessed a new departure for the traditionalist (i.e., desert-based punishment) position within the legal academy, a more resolute turn to what might be called neo-retributivism: publication of UCLA Law and Philosophy professor Herbert Morris's essay, "Persons and Punishment."[76] This new departure dovetailed at points with Hartian notions, even substantially drew upon them. It also resonated with the somewhat indistinct chords of a new retributivism sounded in the writings of Kadish and Goldstein, but Morris's approach was less instrumental in nature than either of theirs. His own approach combined a view of human nature ("personhood") that can be read as a commitment to something close to true free will with natural rights theory. Together, these elements served to ground a distinctly positive form of just-deserts punishment. There were, however, limits to the affirmation of free will in Morris's foundational essay, a scaling down of the concept – or an envelopment of it in the idea of the "person" – that proved influential for many scholars in the succeeding decades. Morris appears as a neo-Kantian retributivist,[77] a seminal figure in modern criminal jurisprudence who translated 1950s existentialism into 1960s rights theory under the guise of a revival of a Hegelian notion of the person's "right" to punishment.[78]

[76] Herbert Morris, "Persons and Punishment," chap. 2 in *On Guilt and Innocence: Essays in Legal Philosophy and Moral Psychology* (Berkeley: University of California Press, 1976) (originally published in *The Monist*, vol. 52, no. 4 [October, 1968]).

[77] My reading of Morris is conventional in this regard. In a 2009 article, Michael Davis argued that Morris's seminal 1968 article "never discussed justification of punishment" and was widely misread to affirmatively support retributivism. "Punishment Theory's Golden Half Century: A Survey of Developments from (about) 1957 to 2007," *Journal of Ethics*, vol. 13 (2009): 73–100, 93. Although Davis offers a fair reading of Morris, I am, of course, mainly concerned with the way Morris was received in his own day and the influence Morris had as a result of that reception. Davis, who admits to having first read Morris in the way that Morris's contemporaries and I did (ibid., 93 n. 47), would, I assume, agree with my analysis of Morris's historical place and influence, at least down through the end of the twentieth century.

[78] See *Hegel's Philosophy of Right*, trans. T. M. Knox (Oxford: Clarendon Press, 1942), § 100: "Punishment is regarded as containing the criminal's right and hence by being punished he is honoured as a rational being.... [The criminal] does not receive this due of honour [if] treated either as a harmful animal who has to be made harmless, or with a view to deterring and reforming him." See also C. S. Lewis, "The Humanitarian Theory of Punishment," in *Contemporary Punishment: Views, Explanations, and Justifications*, ed. Rudolph Gerber

Morris's essay, like much 1960s criminal jurisprudence, was couched as a response to scientific positivism. In place of Wootton, however, Morris set up a row of mostly longer-standing positivist targets: Bertrand Russell, B. F. Skinner, Benjamin Karpman, and Karl Menninger. All favored a therapeutic response to criminal behavior instead of punishment, although in the quotes that Morris selected from each only Skinner indicated a totalizing determinism. Russell and Karpman equated crime with "disease" and "insanity" respectively. For Menninger the offender was "driven," whereas "we are not": we have the "knowledge" that derives the "power" to dispense with "the frightened vengeance of the old penology." Morris accepted the fact that some people (offenders or otherwise) were truly ill. One has a duty to treat them, and if possible, to restore them to the status of functioning persons. They have a right to be treated as persons, just as those who are not ill and who have done wrong "have a right to be responded to as persons who have done wrong."[79] One might have expected that Morris would focus directly on the concept of mental illness, that is, on the characteristics that separated the (relatively few) "ill" from the many persons who committed acts that were potentially criminal offenses. But his approach to that crucial matter was indirect. He set out instead to show that most persons had a right to punishment, and he strove to provide a definition of such persons and to persuade the reader that they in fact existed.

Morris's argument is lengthy and fairly complicated. It begins with a description of an imagined system in which the concept of punishment for wrongdoing is central, in contrast to an alternative system wherein "the central concepts are control of dangerous individuals and treatment of disease." In the former, humans typically possess – as, he asserted, they in fact do – "a rough equivalence in strength and abilities, a capacity to be injured by each offense and to make judgments that such injury is undesirable, a limited strength of will, and a capacity to reason and to conform conduct to rules." General compliance with rules yields to all individuals the benefits of noninterference and security. "Mutual benefit" thus involves "the assumption ... of a burden" of "self-restraint." Failure to exercise self-restraint involves renunciation of "a burden which others have voluntarily assumed and thus gains an advantage which others, who have restrained themselves, do not possess." Punishment of those who have gained such advantages is "reasonable and just": it "restores the equilibrium of benefits and burdens." Forgiveness would also be restorative, but only if resorted to sufficiently rarely that it did not destroy the incentive to exercise self-restraint. Defenses are provided, "each one of which can be said to have as

and Patrick McAnany (Notre Dame, IN: University of Notre Dame Press, 1972), 194ff, 194–95 (originally published in *20th Century: An Australian Quarterly Review*, vol. III, no. 3 [1949] and, later, in *Res Judicatae*, vol. VI [June 1953]).
[79] Morris, "Persons and Punishment," 57–58.

its object diminishing the chances of forcibly depriving a person of benefits others have if that person has not derived an unfair advantage." Morris defined such a person as one "who could not have restrained himself" or whom "it is unreasonable to expect ... to behave otherwise than he did." He then provided two examples that, if taken literally, would, by implication, close the bay window this definition seemed to leave open to the breezes of determinism: children, and those who "lacked the capacity to conform [their] conduct to the rules" (still open), including "someone ... in an epileptic seizure ... " (slam!). "Punishment in these [extreme] cases would be punishment of the innocent, that is, punishment of those who do not voluntarily renounce a burden others have assumed." Further, prescribed punishments are "publicized" and "defenses are respected"; the "rules are designed to benefit all." Thus, there is after all, Morris concluded, "some plausibility in the exaggerated claim that in choosing to do an act violative of the rules an individual has chosen to be punished."[80]

[80] Morris, "Persons and Punishment," 33–36. Critics would (and continue to) debate the elements of Morris's influential "benefits and burdens" approach. Just some of the important critiques of Morris's position (and later positions following Morris) are John Deigh, "On the Right to Be Punished: Some Serious Doubts," *Ethics*, vol. 94 (1984): 191–211; Jeffrie G. Murphy, "The State's Interest in Retribution," *Journal of Contemporary Legal Issues*, vol. 5 (1994): 283–98, 289–92; David Dolinko, "Some Thoughts about Retributivism," *Ethics*, vol. 101 (1991): 537–59, esp. 545–52; and see David Dolinko, "Three Mistakes of Retributivism," *UCLA Law Review*, vol. 39 (1992): 1623–57, esp. 1644, 1646–48. In particular, critics challenged Morris (and other theorists employing benefits-and-burdens or social contract approaches to desert) based on the presumption that such theories depend on the untrue empirical assumption that all law-abiding members of a society benefit equally from that society in terms of their actual welfare or circumstances. See esp. Jeffrie G. Murphy, "Marxism and Retribution," *Philosophy and Public Affairs*, vol. 2 (1973): 217–43, esp. 239–41. Murphy (otherwise initially a supporter of Morris) considered Marx's possible views on desert theory, including as suggested by Marx's 1853 query: "'Is it not a delusion to substitute for the individual with his real motives, with multifarious social circumstances pressing upon him, the abstraction of 'free will' – one among the many qualities of man for man himself?'" (218 [quoting Karl Marx, "Capital Punishment," *New York Daily Tribune*, February 18, 1853]). Morris himself had directly addressed this issue, observing: "To the extent that the rules are thought to be to the advantage of only some or to the extent there is a maldistribution of benefits and burdens, the difference between coercion and law disappears" ("Persons and Punishment," 48). But some would say he did so only superficially, "say[ing] nothing about whether real-life legal systems satisfy or even approximate an initial equal distribution" (Alice Ristroph, "Desert, Democracy, and Sentencing Reform," *JCLC*, vol. 96 (2006): 1293–352, 1343). Discussing Murphy's critique, Ristroph states that initial socioeconomic equality is important because "that is the only world in which people can exercise choice" *and* "in which we can fairly portray crime as a disruption of equal benefits and burdens" (1345 n. 207). Peter Westen rebuts such core criticisms in his recent explication of a "stronger interpretation" of Morris, "Fair-Play Desert for Retributivists," in *Legal, Moral, and Metaphysical Truths: The Philosophy of Michael S. Moore*, ed. Kimberly Kessler Ferzan and Stephen J. Morse (Oxford University Press: forthcoming). Westen urges, for example, that the relevant "benefits" are not "comparative" advantages or a fair initial distribution of welfare, but those "non-comparative" benefits that individuals derive from living in a state with legal protections against invasions of their "lives, personal security and property,"

The contrasting imagined system is a world apart from the familiar one just described. In this alternative world, all persons who have harmed are deemed to have manifested "some pathological condition"; "normal" actions are "assimilated to the normal and healthy functioning of bodily organs." Whereas, in our familiar world, "we draw a distinction between the operation of the kidney and raising an arm on request," the alternative system erases the "distinction between mere events or happenings and human actions." Abnormality – like normality – is understood as "a happening with a causal explanation rather than an action for which there were reasons" for which "institutions of social control respond, not with punishment, but with either preventive detention ... or therapy." In such a system, there is "compassion" for the offender and a "ministering to his illness"; the "conceptions of 'paying a debt' or 'having a debt forgiven' or pardoning have no place." Neither, of course, does "proportionality" in the sense implied by the notion of "'cruel and unusual punishments.'" The patient's burden will be proportional to social benefit and will be limited only by the idea of a "'cure being worse than the disease.'" Nor will it be clearly necessary in the alternative system "to wait until symptoms manifest themselves in socially harmful conduct" or to worry about the procedures that surround, and limit exposure to, punishment, such as double jeopardy and self-incrimination. Why prove conduct pathological beyond a reasonable doubt? Why substitute a lay jury for clinical experts?[81]

Thus did Morris argue for the attractiveness of a claim to a right to be punished, meaning "a right to all those institutions and practices linked to punishment." Like Herbert Hart, Morris invoked one's "ability to predict" state interference and one's preference both for being able to make choices and for "having the responses of others to us determined ... by what we choose rather than what they choose." Which is to say, the right to a punishment system is founded on a person's "right to institutions that respect his choices."[82] His particular invocation of choice, however, seemingly took Morris beyond Hart and others, and certainly beyond Packer's instrumentalism. Morris saw respect for choice as integral to treating individuals as "persons," and the "right to be treated as a person" as "a fundamental human right belonging to all human beings by virtue of their being human."

thus "escaping predatory states of nature." "One can perhaps imagine societies in which the benefits of escapes [from] such states of nature are questionable," says Westen, "but that is surely not the case within modern democratic societies" (Quotations from draft on file with the author, pp. 32–33). Cf. George Sher, "Deserved Punishment," in *Desert* (Princeton, NJ: Princeton University Press, 1987), 69–90 (drawing on Morris's benefits/burdens approach) and George Sher, "Deserved Punishment Revisited," in *Approximate Justice: Studies in Non-Ideal Theory* (New York: Rowman and Littlefield, 1997), 165–80 (clarifying and amending Sher's view in the wake of criticisms of benefits/burdens approaches).

[81] Morris, "Persons and Punishment," 37–40.
[82] Morris, "Persons and Punishment," 41.

It was "also a natural, inalienable, and absolute right."[83] With respect to the "natural"ness of the right, Morris drew close to defining "free," "choice," and "person":

[The right to be treated as a person] is linked to a feature of human beings which were that feature absent – the capacity to reason and to choose on the basis of reasons – profound conceptual changes would be involved in the thought about human beings. It is a right, then, connected with a feature of man that sets man apart from other natural phenomena.[84]

"The capacity to reason and to choose on the basis of reasons": Was there more? Speaking to the negative, Morris earlier had identified some of the "wide range of cases in which a person is used to accomplish the aim of another" and so "is less than fully free." These were cases of duress, hypnosis, deception, and some instances of coercion. In still other cases, some involving coercion, individuals with the capacity for choice were not "used" but had decisions made for them. But why was obedience to a law that was backed up by the threat of punishment *not* this final form of "coercion," or not being treated as a person? Because (speaking here to the positive), in the system overall "benefits and burdens are equally distributed," so that "it cannot be said that some are being subordinated to others"; accordingly, the "voluntary agent" who diverges his conduct from "what is expected or what the norm is, *on general causal principles, [is] regarded as the cause* of what results from his conduct."[85] This minimalist (perhaps merely compatibilist, although Morris never used that term) concept of what we might call "free choice" was central for Morris, as it underlay the "fundamental" right to be treated as a person. The denial of that right "entail[ed] the denial of all moral rights and duties," for "any framework of rights and duties presupposes individuals that have the capacity to choose on the basis of reasons presented to them." Again,

if individuals were incapable of controlling their actions we would have no notion of a legitimate claim that they do so.... In a system of rights ... there is a point in appealing to the rules in legitimating one's complaint. Implied, then, in any conception of rights [is] the existence of individuals capable of choosing and capable of choosing on the basis of considerations with respect to rules.[86]

In some respects, Morris's essay was of a piece with mainstream 1960s legal-academic thought. Morris never used the term "free will"; his account can be read as premised on agnosticism about "true" human freedom and as a reasoned analysis of the implications of a causally determined human consciousness of freedom – as, hence, an "as if" rejoinder to those who would

---

[83] Morris, "Persons and Punishment," 49.
[84] Morris, "Persons and Punishment," 50.
[85] Morris, "Persons and Punishment," 46–48 (emphasis added).
[86] Morris, "Persons and Punishment," 56–57.

attempt to make law consistent with deterministic premises. Moreover, Morris's declared "right to punishment" can be reformulated in negative retributivist terms – not, to be sure, as a mere side-constraint upon purely consequentialist punishment, but as a necessary although not sufficient consideration. Read in this fashion, Morris's contribution remained in the vein of mainstream 1960s thought although it also offered a significant departure from Hart and Packer and a considerable elaboration upon Kadish's position.

Nonetheless, with Morris, in essence a new foundation for positive (in-itself-sufficient) retributivism was achieved. This was owing both to his benefits-and-burdens argument and, especially, to his conceptualization of the "person." The extent to which the idea of the "person" relied upon a notion of true free will remains something of a mystery. Although Morris did not refer to free will, neither did he refer to the mere consciousness of freedom. Although nothing that he said necessarily goes beyond that mere consciousness (combined, of course, with the capacity to deliberate), he certainly believed that the freedom and voluntariness to which he did refer grounded a right and a correlative desert of a particularly strong sort. He felt it necessary to show why obedience ought not to be described as coercion by *the law*, but offered little beyond that with regard to outside influences on obedience. His most emphatic and most interesting claim, that "if individuals were incapable of controlling their actions we would have no notion of a legitimate claim that they do so," remains ambiguous with respect to the concept of free will, for it remains reducible to a claim of mere consciousness of the "capacity to reason and to choose on the basis of reasons," which capacity may be taken as Morris's definition of "capable" and "controlling." Yet Morris seems to have treated his idea of freedom as a species of reality, and as something more than the sheer power of capacity for determined deliberation and choice.

Whatever freedom meant for Morris, it surely meant that individuals who possessed the capacity to act upon reasons had a right to be thought of and treated as choosing beings for whom desert-based punishment, not therapy, was an appropriate (if not always a *required*) response. Morris's objections to therapy had mainly to do with its (alleged) denial that the individual under treatment was a "person." Punishment recognized personhood; it also restored a balance between the security that resulted from others' exercise of self-restraint and the sacrifice involved in one's own self-restraint. The right to punishment – of (metaphorically) chosen and actually *deserved* punishment – flowed from this idea of the person, including each person's obligation to respect the personhood of others. It seems at some remove from more conventional ideas regarding wrongdoing or evil and the justice inherent in being made to suffer for such behavior. This high-minded version of retributivism served to domesticate the harsh realities of conventional morality to which Hart referred at the cost of destabilizing his basic principle. Morris provided a means by which legal scholars could, at least in their own minds, translate everyday revenge into a "paying-back" that was premised on the desert demanded by notions of human dignity and autonomy.

We may read Morris's Kantian benefit/burden account as a natural rights theory, or as the sort of social compact idea that Herbert Hart had set forth in *The Concept of Law* (1961),[87] or again, as a construct that recognized and provided justification for conventional retributive responses in human psychology. Morris referred, it is true, to the "resentment" that is natural in the face of wrongdoing (in the sense of taking benefit while avoiding burden) – a term likely borrowed either from Hart or from Strawson – but the dominant tone of deserved punishment is punishment that is a "paying back" within a rights tradition. It is also a form of desert that accords with the very concept of human dignity, a concept of dignity that bore relation to Hart's notion of the fairness and justice inherent to a "choosing system," and all the more so to Kadish's specification of human values that must be respected. It was of course a very different concept of dignity than the one that positivists (in a misguided way, according to Morris) sought to vindicate.

Morris's essay marked the culmination of a slowly building counter to positivist-leaning jurisprudence. The first reaction against positivism was the utilitarian campaign of the mid-to-late 1930s, which took a heavy toll but suffered from the same weakness as 1930s positivism: it was too far removed from conventional notions of morality and justice. Some 1950s positivist-leaning scholars, we have seen, found the means to reach out to conventional ideas of freedom, but the tension between their determinism and their particular forms of "as if" freedom kept them on the margins. "As if" freedom fit a more modified consequentialism a good deal better, as Herbert Hart and his followers understood. The varieties of "negative" retributivism of the 1960s gathered strength as they marshaled elements of earlier critiques of positivism in their arguments for moral constraints on consequentialism. But how long could this new idea of personal liability remain either a mere side-constraint or a more robust yet still negative retributivism premised, not mainly on desert, but instead mainly on prescripts of political liberty, the need to maintain social values, and respect for the individual's sense of personal well-being? What Morris seems to have believed was that retributivism could be "positive" yet more thoroughly cleansed of the background ideas of evil and vengeance than even Kadish had imagined. It could be centered firmly on desert while appealing to the dignity and responsibility-bearing essence of the whole person. It could flow from the very nature of personhood itself rather than depend on essentially instrumental considerations regarding the way individuals ought to be viewed. It could be muscular yet high-minded, existential (or "natural") yet practical, and everyday in its approach to desert. That is, it need not merely

---

[87] See MacCormick, *H. L. A. Hart*, 170, 179.

invoke Moberly's idea that taking responsibility was founded precisely on the fact that it could have been disputed, but could seize on the capacity for deliberation, on the capacity for "self-control" through the making of choices, and, most of all, on that capacity to conceive of, and appeal to, rights that uniquely defined human beings. Morris thus returned honor to retributivism. In doing so, he effected – more fully than Kadish – the turn from a primarily political-liberty-based orientation to one centered on vindication of the idea of the human as an end in himself. By focusing on the natural, unique attributes of the "person" who was in Hart's (and Hart's followers') terms mainly the individual citizen in relation to the state, Morris might be said to have driven 1960s legal-academic criminal jurisprudence to its logical conclusion.

Yet the power of Morris's desert-based construct lay mainly in the purely intuitive appeal of this ethical vision of the "person." More technically, Morris might be said to have produced only a jerry-built approach to an ambiguous concept of human freedom. His concept of human autonomy largely reduced to "the capacity to reason and to choose on the basis of reasons" along with the possession of the consciousness of freedom, which positivists had long since claimed could be understood as a causally determined mental state, a matter that Morris did not directly confront as would compatibilists of the ensuing decades. His appeal to humans' unique capacity to conceive of rights did stand apart as a deeper insight, but as one that was baldly stated and not pursued. Morris's distinction between coerced or unreasoned behavior and normal acts ("freely" chosen for reasons) suggests something closer to a conventional compatibilism, but this also remained undeclared and undeveloped. And in legal-academic circles, at least, Morris's compatibilist argument for desert-based responsibility *and punishment* (if that is what it was) might as yet have seemed a thin brew. In time, however, the idea of the "person" – as Morris expressed it – proved thick enough for some among the many American legal scholars who came to form the various schools of neo-retributivism of the 1970s and beyond. Just how thick the idea of the "person" had to be may well have depended – it is hard to be certain about this – on the particular social justification for retributive punishment that one found persuasive.

CROSSROADS: THE EARLY 1970S

The full extent of Morris's contribution to the revival of retributivism remains difficult to assess. He was not alone in the project of breathing new life into long-dormant Kantian ideas. The separation of desert and vengeance had ancient roots and 1950s manifestations. And the focus on "unfair advantage" was not truly novel. Herbert Hart's essays on criminal responsibility had selected specific targets – holistic utilitarianism and Wootton's behaviorism – and suggested a minimalist form of attack: a merely limiting form of responsibility theory. But at least one of Hart's American followers, Kadish, went further by invoking a mainly political-liberty-based idea of human freedom in light of the oft-rehearsed claim that the criminal law was a "blaming" institution that might allow more room for the idea of desert than did Hart's formulation. One might conclude that the time was ripe for the articulation of a more robust desert-based idea of a responsibility-bearing form of human freedom. The appeal of Morris's elegant rights-based essay on persons, responsibility, and desert-based punishment was, perhaps (like the essay itself) overdetermined.

Moreover, there were other routes to the revival of desert. Chief among them was that of legal/moral philosopher Joel Feinberg, who instead attempted to justify retributive punishment in terms of "expressive justice"; that is, punishment has an "expressive function," or "*symbolic significance*," as a "conventional device for the expression of attitudes of resentment and indignation, and of judgments of disapproval and reprobation" that Feinberg concluded "must be part of the *definition* of legal punishment."[88] Otherwise, significant and "socially useful" purposes of punishment – authoritative disavowal, the public's symbolic nonacquiescence in crime, vindication of the law, and the absolution of others – would be left unfulfilled.[89] Implicit in Feinberg's theory – and more explicit in his other writings – was the notion that those properly condemned for crime genuinely could be deemed at fault for their acts according to any meaningful definition of freedom or voluntariness.[90] Feinberg thus deemphasized rights theory – as between offender and victim – and marshaled a version of Henry Hart's idea of social "condemnation," although one about to be more firmly grounded, thanks to Morris, by an (albeit mainly assumed, not argued) freedom-based theory of responsibility. Morris was, then, only one of several common cites and, increasingly, was noted mainly for his theory of responsibility rather than for his later theory of punishment.[91] Those who cited him were often

---

[88] Joel Feinberg, "The Expressive Function of Punishment," in *Doing and Deserving: Essays in the Theory of Responsibility* (Princeton, NJ: Princeton University Press, 1970), 95–118, 98 (originally published in *The Monist*, vol. 49 [1965]: 397–423).

[89] Feinberg, "Expressive Function," 101–05, 115. Feinberg also emphasized that disregarding the condemnatory function of punishment obliterates the necessary distinction between punishment and "mere penalties" – imposed, that is, for civil infractions – that are not meant to invoke the same kind of public reprobation (98, 105).

[90] See, e.g., Feinberg, "Expressive Function," 113 (it is "morally wrong ... to condemn a *faultless* man") (emphasis added); Feinberg, "Causing Voluntary Actions," in *Doing and Deserving*, 152–86 (asserting the compatibility of determinist principles and voluntary acts) (originally presented to the Oberlin Colloquium in Philosophy [1964] and published in the Proceedings of the Colloquium, *Metaphysics and Explanation*, ed. W. H. Capitan and D. D. Merrill [Pittsburgh: University of Pittsburgh Press, 1966], 29–47); and Feinberg, *Doing and Deserving*, generally.

[91] Herbert Morris, "A Paternalistic Theory of Punishment," *American Philosophical Quarterly*, vol. 18 (1981): 263–71.

influenced as well by the sea change in American penal theory of the early 1970s – the turn away from rehabilitation and individualization and back to an emphasis on the seriousness of the offense on grounds not only of desert, but also of deterrence. Hence also the enduring attractiveness of Feinberg's expressive theory (although it had emerged in the context of rehabilitation) and its later-appearing distant relative, communicative theory, which was intended as a moralized revival of rehabilitation and individualization (and to a version of which Morris himself had migrated by the early 1980s[92]).

Finally, although Morris addressed the free will problem more directly than some others, even he did not use that term. Some of those who followed, even if they adopted his view that persons were inherently responsibility-bearing, finessed the matter of free will, openly declaring it to be an insoluble problem and contending that one must simply proceed as though some substantial degree of freedom in fact existed. In the long run, as we shall see, to the extent Morris remained influential, it was in part because he made agnosticism more respectable, although that is hardly what he had intended to do.

Doing Justice and the Decline of the Rehabilitative Ideal

We may further assess the relationship between the free will problem and a newly emergent focus on desert in legal academic circles through examination of two important texts from the mid-1970s. As with Morris, in these writings desert led and freedom followed, guarding the flank as needed but only referred to obliquely; a straightforward response to the determinist critique would only later come to defend a hard-earned, settled conviction in favor of neo-retributivism. The first text is the Introduction to *Doing Justice: The Choice of Punishments*, the Report of the Committee for the Study of Incarceration (1976).[93] The Report itself represented the conclusions

---

[92] Morris, "Paternalistic Theory of Punishment." In essence, Morris's "Paternalistic Theory" urged that, to be morally acceptable, punishment should include the goals of communicating the reasons for punishment and allowing opportunities for repentance and the development of the offender's moral and intellectual capacities. Some commentators would suggest that the new formulation repudiated his former commitment to desert and instead, pace Morris's own claims about the theory (264), revived essentially positivist rehabilitative/reform-oriented theories of the law's purposes. E.g., John Braithwaite and Philip Pettit, *Not Just Deserts* (Oxford: Oxford University Press, 1990), 158–59; cf. Andrew von Hirsch, "Proportionality in the Philosophy of Punishment," *Crime and Justice: An Annual Review of Research*, vol. 16 (1992): 55–98, 65. David Dolinko, although critical of whether Morris's theory of punishment ultimately succeeded, provided a nuanced assessment concluding that Morris "recognizes a plurality of justifications for punishment, including both achieving retributive justice and promoting the offender's own moral good," thus advancing his "paternalism" "without repudiating his retributivist emphasis on depriving criminals of their unfair advantage." David Dolinko, "Morris on Paternalism and Punishment," *Law and Philosophy*, vol. 18 (1999): 345–61, 350.

[93] Willard Gaylin and David J. Rothman, "Introduction," in Andrew von Hirsch, *Doing Justice: The Choice of Punishments* (Report of the Committee for the Study of Incarceration) (New York: Hill and Wang, 1976).

(accompanied by several partial dissents) of a group composed mainly of academics – some legal, some from related disciplines – that met between 1971 and 1975. Its principal author was the group's Executive Director, Andrew von Hirsch, Associate Professor of Criminal Justice at Rutgers University.[94] As a whole, *Doing Justice* epitomized the sea change that signaled the waning of Progressivism in criminal justice nearly seven decades after that movement, already in full sway, had been heralded by the statement of the founders of the AICLC pursuant to the 1909 Chicago Conference. The Introduction by no means repudiated all of the premises of its forebear, but it certainly drew different lessons. Those lessons were aptly summarized by the Introduction's two authors, both positivist-leaning scholars who stood just outside the world of legal academics: Willard Gaylin, Professor of Psychiatry at Columbia University's medical and law schools, and David Rothman, Professor of History at Columbia and a leading authority on the history of penal and civil incarceration in the United States.[95]

---

[94] The Committee was charged by the Field Foundation with creating a guiding rationale for prison and sentencing reform in light of "growing disenchantment with prisons, and with the disparities and irrationalities of the sentencing process." Charles E. Goodell, "Preface," in von Hirsch, *Doing Justice*, xv. It was chaired by Goodell – a lawyer, author, and former U.S. senator and Chairman of the Presidential Clemency Board – and comprised of a broad range of professionals and scholars. Legal academics were represented by Alan M. Dershowitz of Harvard, Joseph Goldstein and Stanton Wheeler of Yale, and Herman Schwartz, who was then serving as Chairman of the New York State Commission of Correction. Other academics included Marshall Cohen (Philosophy), Samuel Dubois Cook (Political Science), Erving Goffman (Anthropology and Sociology), Simon Rottenberg (Economics), and Leslie T. Wilkins (Criminal Justice). Willard Gaylin, coauthor of the Introduction, was the Committee's only psychiatrist. The Committee also included human rights advocate Eleanor Holmes Norton, formerly of the ACLU, and Jorge Lara-Braud of the National Council of Churches. Von Hirsch's staff included David F. Greenberg, a sociologist who had coauthored the American Friends Service Committee's 1971 *Struggle for Justice* Report. *Doing Justice*, vii–ix. Goodell summarized their overall recommendations as calling for "stringent limitation on incarceration as punishment" especially for first offenders, more alternatives to incarceration, reduction of sentencing disparity, less sentencing discretion, and the end of indeterminate sentencing. A central idea was to base sentencing on the seriousness of the offense itself – "on what he *did* rather than on what the sentence expects he will do if treated in a certain fashion." "Preface," xvii–xviii. The Committee's recommendations in this regard (and in others) bear notable similarity to those underlying proposals that the American Law Institute would make thirty years later in revising the Model Penal Code sentencing provisions (see my discussion in Chapter 9).

[95] In 1971 Rothman had released *The Discovery of the Asylum*, his book on Jacksonian Era American penology. He was in the process of writing what would become his 1980 book, *Conscience and Convenience: The Asylum and Its Alternatives in Progressive America*, which reflected both the ideals of the Progressive Era and how those ideals were undermined by indeterminate sentencing in practice, which was marked by long-term incarceration that was rarely accompanied by effective treatment. His resulting perspective was illustrated in his contributions to the Introduction to *Doing Justice*, which summarized the ongoing failures of the rehabilitative ideal.

Yet Gaylin and Rothman's Introduction reads more like an apologia than an announcement of a breakthrough or a confident pronouncement of faith – or even than a progress report. It stated that *Doing Justice* "distinguishes between vengeance and desert, and shows that desert is a rich and important concept, grounded in ideas of fairness."[96] It left the task of explicating "fairness" to von Hirsch (in chapter 6 of the Report), who combined Morris's "restatement of the Kantian argument" regarding "unfair advantage" with the principle of "reprobation" that is "implicit in punishment" (here citing Feinberg on the ascription of blame) in explaining why Kant's theory of the "imposition of *some* kind of deprivation" should "take the peculiar form of punishment."[97] There were, von Hirsch acknowledged, countervailing reasons for not punishing a person who "deserved" to be punished – for punishment deliberately causes avoidable human suffering, which certainly should not be an end in itself. In answer, however, he deftly (if necessarily briefly) invoked the utilitarian goal of deterrence, asserting that punishment, when properly limited by desert, "may prevent more misery than it inflicts" – and make the "distribution" of misery "more acceptable" – because "fewer innocent persons will be victimized by crimes" and suffering will be imposed on wrongdoers, instead. Punishment, *Doing Justice* concluded, was based on – and indeed required – both desert and deterrence principles.[98]

Gaylin and Rothman summarized the group's stance in terms faithful to the Report, but with a poignancy all their own as they conceded the failure of the "rehabilitative model," which

despite its emphasis on understanding and concern, has been more cruel and punitive than a frankly punitive model would probably be.... Under the rehabilitative model, we have been able to abuse our charges, the prisoners, without disabusing our consciences. Beneath this cloak of benevolence, hypocrisy has flourished.... Finally, to sentence people guilty of similar crimes to different dispositions in the name of rehabilitation – to punish not for act but for condition – violates, this book argues, fundamental concepts of equity and fairness. And so we as a group, trained in humanistic traditions, have ironically embraced the seemingly harsh principle of just deserts.[99]

This embrace of just deserts, the authors of the Introduction continued, meant the abandonment of a "primary reliance upon a utilitarian rationale" and the adoption of a different justification for punishment – not simply as an instrumental move given its political-liberty-based dangers in practice,

---

[96] Gaylin and Rothman, "Introduction," xxix.

[97] Von Hirsch, *Doing Justice*, 48–49.

[98] Von Hirsch, *Doing Justice*, 52–54. Galligan, "Return to Retribution," analyzes this argument at 161–63. For an important contemporary assessment of *Doing Justice* that pays little attention to the Introduction to the Report, see Martin Gardner, "The Renaissance of Retribution – An Examination of Doing Justice," *Wisconsin Law Review* (1976): 781–815.

[99] Gaylin and Rothman, "Introduction," xxxviii.

but also "because it is right.... Certain things are simply wrong and ought to be punished. And this we do believe."[100]

Gaylin and Rothman dwelt on the "irony" to which they had called attention. The rehabilitative model "was a scheme born to optimism, and faith, and humanism. It viewed the evils in man as essentially correctable, and only partially the responsibility of the individual." This view, taken to its extreme (they claimed) by Menninger, was "always under attack from the conservative community," and "now we find ourselves, for different reasons, with different motives, joining the argument for its abandonment." Abandonment of the "therapeutic model" was not easy or pleasant. ("To some members of the Committee, it still may hold the highest ideal, and they abandon it with great reluctance.")[101] And, faithful to the positivist vision that had long dominated behavioral and legal-science scholarship on criminal responsibility, the authors found a redeeming aspect in this abandonment, that is, the possibility that "when we honestly face the fact that our purpose is retributive, we may, with a re-found compassion and a renewed humanity, limit the degree of retribution we will exact." Nonetheless they openly stated their feelings of profound defeat:

And still we are not happy. Our solution is one of despair, not hope. We recognize ... we abandon not just our innocence but perhaps more. The concept of deserts is intellectual and moralistic; in its devotion to principle, it turns back on such compromising considerations as generosity and charity, compassion and love.[102]

The authors admitted that the Committee could offer only "partial solutions, while awaiting more insights, greater knowledge, and more complete answers in some hoped-for future"; the determinative factor in their thinking was the "commitment to the most stringent limits on incarceration." Better to ignore the Committee's recommendations entirely, they insisted, than "to accept any part of them without that focus on *de*carceration about which all its other parts pivot."[103]

The program the Committee offered, Gaylin and Rothman concluded, "holds the promise of workability," but little more. It reflected a "shift, forced by our own [i.e., society's] limitations, our narrowness, our meanness, our sense of the other as alien and the alien as enemy." And further: "we will pay a price," as each "retreat from individualism ... make[s] it progressively easier to abandon it elsewhere." Gloomier still: "More and more, in the push for space, food, and pleasures, we are progressively being reduced and regimented, homogenized and dehumanized."[104] There was here (as in the Report itself) no mention of the dignity of being conceived

---

[100] Gaylin and Rothman, "Introduction," xxxviii–ix.
[101] Gaylin and Rothman, "Introduction," xxxvii–viii.
[102] Gaylin and Rothman, "Introduction," xxxix.
[103] Gaylin and Rothman, "Introduction," xxxix–xl (emphasis added).
[104] Gaylin and Rothman, "Introduction," xl–xli.

of as autonomous, but simply a concession to an abstract "wrong"ness that threatened to affirm, rather than to domesticate and transmute into something positive, the harshness of conventional morality – and this despite the hope for a return to a nonjudgmental model that challenged that unfortunate forming morality. No wonder the authors of the Introduction wrote with so profound a tone of regret. Could the body of the Report to follow survive its introduction? Even the final sentence of the Introduction looked beyond the Report to a reversal of what the Report itself represented. The resonances of the Pound of the 1920s are unmistakable: "Perhaps we can anticipate a time when with new insights, and new institutions, a different group of individuals in a different social setting will reconvene and once again discover the *amoral, non-judgmental* world of the rehabilitative model."[105]

The Committee Report itself was, we are not surprised to learn from the Introduction, a compromise presented without "the recriminations, the cries of accusation, the sense of frustration, the internal tensions, the pleas, and the remorse that led to a final compromise position."[106] Thus, chapter 6 enunciated the desert theory of the new order without the context that the Introduction revealed. In the main body of *Doing Justice*, Morris's and Feinberg's revival of Kant stood on its own terms, not as a second-best theory of justice that ranked first only in the exigent circumstances of real-world practicalities. And, as we have seen, even the Introduction treated von Hirsch's bare assertion of the desert principle with respect: "There is the feeling of a Kantian imperative behind the word 'deserts.' Certain things are simply wrong and ought to be punished. And this we do believe."[107] This expression of belief, however, sat uncomfortably alongside the invocation of "the amoral, non-judgmental world of the rehabilitative model" that seems most consistent with the central argument of the Introduction. For whom – one wonders – did Gaylin and Rothman speak, and to what extent had "compromise" produced an internally contradictory introductory statement?[108]

There was also a hint of contradiction in their treatment of free will. Early on in the Introduction, the authors adverted to the free will problem (a matter not explicitly discussed in *Doing Justice* itself, perhaps because the

[105] Gaylin and Rothman, "Introduction," xli (emphasis added).
[106] Gaylin and Rothman, "Introduction," xxvi. The four partial dissents (Goldstein, Rottenberg, Schwartz, and Wilkins) all took issue with one or another aspect of the Report's stress on desert. See von Hirsch, *Doing Justice*, 171–79.
[107] Gaylin and Rothman, "Introduction," xxxix.
[108] I am grateful to David Rothman for discussing with me the matter of authorship of the Introduction to *Doing Justice*. Von Hirsch invited Rothman and Gaylin to write the Introduction; in doing so, they primarily expressed their own opinions. Rothman affirmed that the references to "charity" and "love" reflected Gaylin's influence – the critique of rehabilitation in practice coming mainly from Rothman. The two were united in their characterization of "the amoral, non-judgmental world of the rehabilitative model." (David Rothman, personal communication, August 19, 2004.)

official Report focused primarily on the details of punishment schemes and treated justifications for punishment very briefly). They did so in the course of explaining the Committee's methodology and the practical realities of interdisciplinary study of criminal justice issues, which included "at times ... sacrific[ing] an ideal or a 'truth' fundamental in one's professional practice, in order to serve the purposes of the group effort." As an example, they observed that the psychoanalytically trained psychiatrist adheres to "psychic determinism," but "determinism is antithetical to the social concept underlying criminal law, which must assume free will, or choice in action." The authors continued:

It really is not important which concept is true, or if either is true. For certain purposes, either assumption may be useful or necessary; but to assume both at the same time is logically impossible. Obviously, if a psychiatrist is going to work within a system that requires personal responsibility, he must learn to draw distinctions from his experience about the nature of human beings and the nature of choice that are useful to those responsible for enforcement of law. He must find a way to accommodate his concept of psychic determinism with the free will necessary for assigning responsibility.[109]

The presumption that "a psychiatrist is going to work within a system that requires personal responsibility" could seem odd in light of the authors' hope, presumably on behalf of some others on the Committee, for rediscovery of "the amoral, non-judgmental world of the rehabilitative model." What, one wonders, was going on?

Such potential contradictions may make more sense if the Introduction is read in the light of the long-standing bifurcation of guilt assessment and post-conviction disposition of offenders. As to guilt assessment, one had, as ever, to concede the dominance of law's reliance on the desert principle. Indeed, the Introduction, like the Report itself, took the law's traditional presumption of personal responsibility as a fait accompli and did not stress the point. As to sentencing, there was general agreement on the goal of an "equitable and fair" system of incarceration. Now, however, as a practical matter most (although not all) thought that might best be achieved through sentencing that was less discretionary and that focused on the seriousness of the offense under a desert principle – thus through the abandonment (at least pro tem) of the largely failing rehabilitation model. This was a regrettable but practical necessity that also had the effect of eliminating the need to move from a desert-based approach to guilt assessment to a "nonjudgmental" rehabilitative sentencing model (traditional Progressive "bifurcation"). The result was a unified system wherein both phases of criminal justice were premised on desert. Yet some legal and other academics were therefore bound to be concerned about a potential exaggeration of offense-based desert relative to individualized guilt assessment. Indeed, the authors

[109] Gaylin and Rothman, "Introduction," xxv–vi.

of the Introduction implied that their central concern was how to treat convicted offenders in the most humane and equitable way *relative to the only partial responsibility they actually bore*. But, in compromising the rehabilitative ideal in light of the realities of the rehabilitative regime, the idea of only partial responsibility (one might conclude) was now in danger of being subsumed by the desert principle inherent in an offense-based, rather than offender-based, sentencing scheme.

On this reading, support for the desert principle might coexist with hopes for a nonjudgmental future, but the balance was delicate: placing too much pressure on desert drew the elements (and perhaps the Committee) into conflict. The desert principle could be useful, even necessary, when translated into the way a healthy person ought to think about himself *within the rehabilitative model*. But, as that model fell out of favor, desert was more clearly revealed as a potentially damaging fiction: it could stand on its own as justification for the punishment that many Committee members perhaps reluctantly accepted as a lesser of two evils only if that punishment were kept to a minimum. That is, even if, at its core, the desert principle expressed a truth ("And this we do believe"), it was a fragile truth that could bear only the most modest weight in terms of guilt and punishment. Some (perhaps many) Committee members – including the legal academics – were bound to regret basing punishment on so fragile a principle, and one so vulnerable to misunderstanding. Further, with regard to free will itself, they might agree to disagree about the truth of free will so long as post-conviction sentencing translated "personal responsibility" into the healthy person's perspective on himself in a world generally understood as involving only partial responsibility. And they probably all agreed that, whatever "free will" meant, it could not support a desert principle that stood for more than a practical defense of minimal punishment qua punishment. So long as that (and nothing more) was the goal, and so long as it promised no exaggeration of the idea of true guilt at guilt assessment, the implied invocation of free will need not be at issue. (Indeed, it was the rehabilitative model that was more likely to provoke disagreement about free will, as its more positivist proponents were inclined to criticize the apparent contradiction between guilt assessment and sentencing.) But, for obvious reasons, the return to desert-based sentencing threatened to turn terms of compromise (often based on an untheorized, instrumental use of free will) into terms of conflict.

As for the *Doing Justice* Report, its position on free will was rendered entirely opaque by its particular use of Kant and Morris. Desert depended, in large part, on "unfair advantage" and inherent wrongfulness, and that was that. Von Hirsch made no effort to analyze the human behavioral underpinnings of those ideas. Presumably the former idea was premised on a "choice" not to exercise a restraint others "chose" to exercise, but for all that the Report made of it, that choice might well have amounted, as Jeffrie Murphy had argued, to an objective displacement of an unregulated *ex ante* unfair distribution.[110] Morris had himself avoided the term "free will," and had grounded desert on rationality and capacity and, especially, on the correlative right attaching to personhood. That approach was, of course, consistent with agnosticism about *true* free will, but for Morris what mainly mattered was a particular *idea* of freedom that was grounded on the phenomenon of personhood. For the neo-retributivist legal academics who claimed to follow Morris, on the other hand, "desert" was rapidly becoming something of an untheorized mantra, especially for those who, like von Hirsch (and presumably many of the legal scholars on the full Committee), avoided the mysteries of "personhood" and focused mainly on the formal displacement aspect of a taking of "unfair advantage." For them, the premises that underlay the substantive idea of a wrongful – that is, truly blameworthy – act did not create the background disturbance that such premises so obviously created for the positivist-leaning nonlawyers who authored the Report's somewhat doleful Introduction.

The Capacity to Conform: David Bazelon and Stephen Morse

Our second text, "The Twilight of Welfare Criminology,"[111] is the reply of Stephen Morse, then a young law professor at the University of Southern California Law Center, to Judge David Bazelon's J. Edgar Hoover Foundation lecture at that school in 1976. Morse exuded a degree of confidence that the authors of the Introduction to *Doing Justice* neither possessed nor, under the circumstances, wanted to display. He embraced the new departures of the day, justifying them with an eclectic and wide-ranging series of arguments. There was, in Morse's tract, no backing into a future that had already arrived. His was a courteous but firm declaration, at the nation's bicentennial, that Bazelon's form of liberalism – and certainly the "amoral and nonjudgmental" vision of a strict (or even quasi-) positivism – was passé.

Bazelon's lecture, "The Morality of Criminal Law," rehearsed his earlier battles on behalf of a "social-justice" perspective in the assessment of criminal responsibility, especially those centered on the insanity defense that he had waged in cases from *Durham* (1954) until *Brawner* (1972).[112] The latter case saw the abandonment of the *Durham* rule in favor of the American

---

[110] Murphy, "Marxism and Retribution" (I touched on Murphy's view earlier in this chapter, n. 80.). Von Hirsch himself would later come to doubt the benefits-and-burdens or "unfair advantage" approach in part for this reason. See Andrew von Hirsch, *Past or Future Crimes: Deservedness and Dangerousness in the Sentencing of Criminals* (Manchester: Manchester University Press, 1985), esp. 58 ("I have since come to doubt the force of this and similar arguments ... [in part because] they require a heroic belief in the justice of the underlying social arrangements."); and see Andrew von Hirsch, *Censure and Sanctions* (New York: Oxford University Press, 1993), esp. 7–8 (further criticizing unfair advantage theory).

[111] Stephen J. Morse, "The Twilight of Welfare Criminology: A Reply to Judge Bazelon," *Southern California Law Review*, vol. 49 (1976): 1247–68.

[112] *United States v. Brawner*, 471 F.2d 969 (D.C. Cir. 1972).

Law Institute's Model Penal Code test. Bazelon had himself concurred in the rejection of the *Durham* "product test" (which he continued to think had done good service), but had dissented from the majority's MPC substitute and proffered instead something "akin to the A.L.I. minority proposals ... or to one of the recommendations of the British Royal Commission."[113] Under Bazelon's suggested test, the defendant would be found not responsible "'*if at the time of his unlawful conduct his mental or emotional processes or behavior controls were impaired to such an extent that he cannot justly be held responsible for his act.*'"[114] In the several years since *Brawner*, Bazelon now reported, he had come to favor abolition of the insanity test. Instead, he concluded, the question of responsibility

should be explored when the Government seeks to discharge its burden of establishing, beyond a reasonable doubt, the existence of *mens rea* or intent.... I see abolition as a way of broadening the inquiry beyond the medical model.... [M]*ens rea* offers the opportunity and hope of proving more hospitable to a broad inquiry into *all forms of disabilities and motivations.*[115]

Bazelon's liberal version of positivist-leaning criminal jurisprudence had not greatly altered in the two decades since *Durham*. He presupposed some distinct measure of, or potential for, free will but mainly drew attention to the myriad constraints that limited – or altogether eliminated – it in practice. The criminal law, he argued, should not look to the social defense and adopt a "law-as-external-constraint" approach, for that would be to deny the moral imperative of premising guilt upon free will. Where a person's actual freedom had been compromised, the reach of the criminal law should be restrained. "The real question, it seems to me, is how we can afford *not* to live up to our moral pretenses, and *not* to excuse unfree choices or non-blameworthy acts."[116]

But the 1960s had not left Bazelon completely unchanged. Liberal social policy, reflected in heightened concerns about the links among poverty, race, and crime, encouraged him to expand his view of constraints upon the freedom that the law presumed. The "war on crime" deepened his sense of the fragility of legalism, that is, of the moral essence of law embodied in its assertion that criminal guilt is premised on "*free*" behavior and nothing less. Political liberty required that free will had existed in a given case, but demanded a thorough investigation of whether it had truly existed; this meant a restrictive reading of free will, one that allowed, even, for a "rotten

---

[113] David L. Bazelon, "The Morality of the Criminal Law," *Southern California Law Review*, vol. 49 (1976): 385–405, 395.

[114] Bazelon, "Morality," 396 (emphasis in original) (quoting *Brawner*, 471 F.2d at 1032 [Bazelon, C.J., concurring in part and dissenting in part]).

[115] Bazelon, "Morality," 397 (emphasis added).

[116] Bazelon, "Morality," 398.

social background" defense.[117] Thus, for Bazelon, the trial became ever more a moment at which the community might both learn about the determinants of human nature and express itself accordingly; the legal process could be educative as well as informed by deep social and human understandings.[118] It could supply a solvent to the rigors of an uninformed conventional morality that the law's standard endorsement of freedom and responsibility otherwise likely – if unwittingly – encouraged. Bazelon's reactions to early 1970s politics and political science thus ran counter to those of many others, who had given up hope for the rehabilitative ideal and had come, quite to the contrary, to see the state's "intrusiveness" with respect to penological methods as dehumanizing. There is nothing of Morris in his writings, nothing that suggests he even considered the possibility that punishment was an offender's "right" or that enforcement of the law was a sign of respect for the offending "person." Although Bazelon apparently endorsed the presumption of some capacity for the exercise of free will, he focused mainly on the "unfree." Even with respect to the free he opposed retributivism and shied away from the language of desert, except, of course, to suggest that the guilty deserved rehabilitation. His views were liberal, positivist-leaning, optimistic (within distinct limits), and not uncomplicated.

Morse considered Bazelon's lecture liberal, overly positivist, in an important sense pessimistic, and decidedly simplistic. He objected to Bazelon's characterization of the "law as external constraint" position as amoral and utilitarian; this, Morse countered, was "unfair and incorrect." Both positions – Bazelon's "social justice" position and the "law and order" position with which Morse associated himself – were "moral," Morse insisted; both adhered to "the fundamental moral principle" and concept of justice that Bazelon outlined based on the idea that "'the law should not convict unless it can condemn.'" The difference between the positions, Morse asserted, lay in their models of human behavior. The "social justice advocate, evidently, is willing to believe that large numbers of persons have little choice regarding their behavior and should not be held responsible for it," whereas "the law-and-order advocate believes that most persons do choose their behavior and should be held accountable for it."[119] Not morality, but the accuracy of basic assumptions about human behavior, was at issue.

[117] *United States v. Alexander*, 471 F.2d 923, 957–65 (D.C. Cir. 1973) (Bazelon, C.J., dissenting).

[118] In his dissent to *United States v. Dougherty*, 470 F.2d 1113 (D.C. Cir. 1972), moreover, Bazelon stood in strong support of the jury's traditional "right" to nullification; although *Dougherty* was a Vietnam protest case involving civil disobedience, Bazelon clearly believed that nullification also properly extended to cases in which the jury concluded that a defendant's free will was constrained despite that his or her act and mens rea otherwise met the official legal criteria for conviction. I discuss this point further in Thomas A. Green, "The Jury and Criminal Responsibility in Anglo-American History," *Criminal Law and Philosophy*, vol. 8 (forthcoming 2014) (also available at http://dx.doi.org/10.1007/s11572-013-9267-0), at n. 27.

[119] Morse, "Twilight," 1248–49.

Morse briefly examined "the Judge's analysis of 'free will,'" noting that Bazelon "does not enter into the metaphysical and unresolvable complexities" of the concept, but instead adopts "along with lawyers in general, an intuitive, common sense approach to free choice." Bazelon had produced examples of situations, Morse conceded, wherein "the reasonable person" would probably "agree that there was a high likelihood that the particular crime in question would be committed." But, he pursued, does this mean that "the actor was unfree?" The same "common sense analysis of free choice" also produced a very different perspective, said Morse:

A common sense and intuitive view would hold that although all of us choose our behavior, we are all the victims of various pressures affecting our choices. All environments affect choices and make some choices easy and some choices hard.... On the average, it will be harder for the person who lives in a "criminogenic" subculture to obey the law.... Yet it is clear that the environment is not all-determinative: it interacts with intra-personal factors. The majority of persons in the most criminogenic subculture are law-abiding.... [B]ehavior *is* a matter of choice.[120]

At this point, Morse paused – time for a clarifying footnote: "This statement is, of course, a statement of belief and values rather than a statement of fact.... In any case, the belief that behavior is a matter of choice is a necessary foundation of the criminal law."[121] With this age-old caveat in mind, Morse proceeded to the observation that there is "no bright line between free and unfree choices.... Nor is there a higher moral authority which can tell society where to draw the line." Society is left to draw the line "that comports with our collective sense of morality," although "by whom it should be drawn" remains an issue. This was also, of course, Bazelon's view, and the jury had long been his choice of institution for the necessary line-drawing. Morse criticized Bazelon for characterizing the law-and-order position, in contrast, "as claiming that the *unfree* offender ought to be condemned and punished so that the law may [as Bazelon put it] 'maintain a stern visage of uncompromising force ... to encourage those with impairment to exercise that amount of free will which they do possess.'" To the contrary, the law-and-order adherent "is simply not convinced that those Judge Bazelon considers unfree are, in fact, faced with sufficiently hard choices to justify acquittal." Indeed, Bazelon failed to "explore the possibility that reasonable persons could differ about who is unfree." The proper litmus was "general social consensus" regarding when "an actor's choice to obey the law was too difficult to allow just condemnation of the actor," and this consensus was represented by legislative choices regarding the doctrines of excuse and justification. Morse disagreed with Bazelon's assertion that individual juries, each with its own potential prejudices, were best positioned to draw the necessary societal lines.[122]

---

[120] Morse, "Twilight," 1251–52.
[121] Morse, "Twilight," 1252 n. 18.
[122] Morse, "Twilight," 1253–54.

The law-and-order position, then, rested on its assumption (which, Morse stressed, was not contradicted by available science[123]) that most people, even most people in difficult circumstances – toward the hard-choice end of the spectrum – are "free." And this with full knowledge that the statement, "behavior *is* a matter of choice," is one that "cannot be empirically proven ... [or] disproven," but is "a statement of belief and values."[124] Morse believed there were deterrent grounds for running the risk of erring on the side of the restrictive view of unfreedom, but he wanted to emphasize that, even for persons at the *relatively* unfree end of the spectrum, "the decision to offend is still a result of the actor's choice, and thus he deserves to be punished on retributive as well as deterrent grounds." The desert attending a choice to do wrong was effectively presumed. Proceeding in this fashion, Morse insisted, was "both moral and respectful to the actor."[125] Here, of course, Morse marshaled a variety of arguments against Bazelon's relatively restrictive reading of "free." Morse not only cited Morris, but also reached beyond him to C. S. Lewis, when he noted that Bazelon's "program would lead to disrespect for personal autonomy, to massive invasions of privacy, and to the 'tyranny of the normative.'"[126] He drew support from Herbert Hart as well. Having claimed (contra Bazelon) that, "broadening the class of persons who are considered not responsible for their behavior seems dangerous to public order and disrespectful to the personal dignity of individuals," Morse (with Hart) argued that such "broadening" required "broad social consensus for such a change" or clear scientific evidence on behavioral choice showing that "only prejudice" prevents change from being implemented.[127] It was important for society to make clear that it "views [people] as responsible persons who are in control of their lives and who are accountable for their actions; ... the law's presumption of responsibility will encourage the internalization of control." Here Morse cited Johannes Andenaes's very recent and

[123] Morse, "Twilight," 1255. Addressing the fruits of determinism, Morse observed that not only had the century's social and psychological sciences failed thus far to identify the causes of crime with any useful specificity, but the social reform programs favored by Bazelon had not succeeded in reducing crime (1258–67).

[124] Morse, "Twilight," 1252, and n. 18 (citing James Q. Wilson, *Thinking about Crime* [1975], 43–51).

[125] Morse, "Twilight," 1253, and n. 20 (citing Ernst van den Haag, *Punishing Criminals* [1975]).

[126] Morse, "Twilight," 1256 n. 30. Indeed, just as the rehabilitation model came to appear intrusive and ineffective for offenders, "intrusive and repressive interventions into families ... are authorized in the name of social justice" and yet had not reduced crime rates (1262). Morse emphasized the various moral ends at stake, including not just personal autonomy, but also public safety. He urged that, in light of our lack of definitive answers regarding the causes of (and remedies for) crime, the law-and-order view offered the most effective means to achieving multiple moral goals – including crime prevention, even if by way of mandatory, admittedly punitive sentences – and it was most just to impose the burdens of the system "on the person convicted beyond a reasonable doubt of a dangerous offense" (1266).

[127] Morse, "Twilight," 1267.

influential article, "The Moral or Educative Influence of Criminal Law,"[128] a sort of halfway house on the road from Feinberg's "expressive" justice to Antony Duff's and others' "communicative" theory.[129] Finally, returning to C. S. Lewis (and hence to Morris), Morse argued for treating "all persons as autonomous and capable of that most human capacity, the power to choose. To treat persons otherwise is to treat them as less than human."[130]

Morse's "Twilight of Welfare Criminology" represents one particular – and perhaps the dominant – trajectory of legal-academic thought in the early-to-mid- 1970s. Unlike the Introduction to *Doing Justice*, it did not back into its position or pine for a future in which even Judge Bazelon might appear as a moderate. Morse melded the noble ends of retributivist thought with the realities of a conventional morality, harnessing encouragement of the latter for the goal of deterrence. He was reassured by the general law-abidingness of those who visited harsh judgment on offenders – and he was unbothered by what might be thought a contradiction between that socially based harshness and the legal academic's focus on the dignity inherent in the idea of capacity for responsibility. To be sure, in contrast to the Introduction, Morse dealt mainly with the problem of responsibility – the assessment of guilt – and its relationship to the structures and strategies of enforcement of the criminal law; he contributed little in any direct sense to the theory of punishment, instead endorsing a mixed theory in which deterrence and retributivism lay side by side but without offering specifics as to how the two interrelated. But there is little reason to suppose Morse would have disagreed with von Hirsch's encapsulation of that relationship in the body of *Doing Justice*, which was published in the same year as Morse's article and epitomized the thought of a broadly representative group of leading legal and other academics. Unlike von Hirsch, Morse stressed the dignity/autonomy aspect of retributivism, rather than the restorative benefit/burden aspect. But, otherwise, Morse's approach neatly complemented the neo-retributivist theory of punishment embodied in *Doing Justice*. Gaylin and Rothman's Introduction, on the other hand, mainly considered the treatment of convicted offenders, a stage at which behaviorism died hard for many in the Progressive tradition, including those who accepted the traditional lip service to autonomy at the guilt assessment stage. The authors of the Introduction shared Bazelon's doubts about the practical realities of "choice," but they also worried about the hardship and unfairness that accompanied rehabilitative punishment *in practice*. That worry – rather than the concerns of Lewis or Morris (or, indeed, of proponents of 1960s "negative" retributivism) regarding the "dehumanizing" implications of the

[128] Morse, "Twilight," 1267 and n. 70 (citing Johannes Andenaes, "The Moral or Educative Influence of Criminal Law," in *Punishment and Deterrence* [1974]).
[129] I discuss Duff's approach in Chapter 9.
[130] Morse, "Twilight," 1268.

"non-judgmental" model itself – moved the authors of the Introduction and, presumably, much of the full Committee as well.

Morse followed Lewis and Morris, but did not adopt the latter's methodology. Morris had argued that the uniquely human traits of reason and capacity to choose *tout court* defined personhood, which in turn logically implied a form of human freedom. Morse took a more conventional social-scientific (rather than phenomenological) approach and conjoined it with arguments from practical policy and Kantian values. Morse never distinguished simply between compulsion and deliberation, but placed even apparently deliberate choices on a spectrum of "easy" to "hard." On the other hand, with a bow to the law's dependence on causal analysis regarding the relationship between the quality of choice and the ascription of criminal responsibility, he employed current social science studies showing that, even in criminogenic areas, most obeyed the law – and he did so in order to justify the presumption that most choices were in fact free. He then buttressed this restrictive view of unfreedom with the moral idea (borrowed from Morris) of treating others as "persons." Driven by the failure of 1960s social reforms, by the widespread critique of rehabilitation, and by doubts about the incapacity of the poor (freely) to choose to obey the law, Morse opted for the "fairer" approach to the crime problem: "get tough" measures that were cost-effective, deterrent, *and* yet respectful of personal dignity. This, he argued, would minimize recourse to truly repressive measures – that is, the intrusively therapeutic measures that, he implied, Bazelon's reading of the "choice" spectrum would ironically encourage.

"Freedom" for Morse (as of 1976) was thus both a practical and a moral conclusion, one drawn in the face of its own ultimate unprovability. It was a choice of conceptualization based in part on social- and behavioral-science studies of behavior patterns and of the process of internalization of control, as well as on common-sense and intuitive ideas about the nature of human beings. It was not a merely internalist position: Morse admitted free will was unverifiable, but the choice to believe in it was a choice to believe in it as factual, that is, a choice to affirm it as an external reality. In time, Morse (like some other legal academics) would concede that determinism governed all human thought and action, but this was a "soft determinism" that allowed for the compatibility of rationality (absent compulsion) with criminal and moral responsibility. This would bring him (and others) closer to an internalist account of free will that reflected the attraction of an essentially subjective idea of personhood wherein the belief in freedom would be understood simply as an aspect of human consciousness. By implication this belief was understood as held only because humans were determined to hold it, and could not make sense of themselves except by doing so. But that way of thinking about human freedom – whatever its roots in earlier philosophical and psychological circles – was only just beginning to find its way into what had already emerged as an essentially retributivist American academic criminal jurisprudence.

CONCLUSION

By its very title, Morse's "Twilight of Welfare Criminology" portended the passing of the rehabilitative ideal in real-world practice and its subordination in mainstream legal-academic thought.[131] Morse's focus, instead, on criminal desert attaching to an actor's reasoned choice, carried forward the central tenet of Herbert Hart's jurisprudence – but, of course, took it beyond the role it played for Hart as a mere side-constraint on consequential aims. Granted, what might be termed rational choice – or the opportunity and capacity for deliberation – had long been a mainstay of much criminal jurisprudence. It was the particular orientation toward rational choice, and the evolving uses to which that orientation was put, that counted. Rational choice had grounded classical forms of compatibilism for, among others, Hobbes and Hume, and had undergirded the Benthamite utilitarian association of responsibility with deterrability. So, too, it had underwritten Jerome Hall's traditionalist free will position that mirrored social understandings, and it thus brought the law in line with conventional morality. This traditionalist perspective had fallen prey to positivist legal scholars of the late-nineteenth and early-twentieth centuries who brought behavioral and medical science to bear in their support for the reform side of consequentialism. For them, rational choice was a determined – or highly conditioned – phenomenon (or, perhaps, a rationalization of underlying psychological impulses), whose alleged compatibility with responsibility invoked a metaphysics that, with rare exception, they appear to have believed did not reward serious consideration. Further, most people – and the official law – adhered to a true or presumed free will, or so the positivists claimed, and thus the utilitarian gospel of choice-based deterrence was problematic because it ran interference, even if unintentionally, for the traditional free-will-based socio-legal understanding. The Model Penal Code served to pave over those competing perspectives, but only superficially. On the one hand, the MPC attempted to meld choice-based deterrence with treatmentist principles. On the other, it squared rational choice – or a schematization of levels of intentionality – with the requirement of a baseline for mens rea that most legal scholars increasingly understood in terms of "blameworthiness." Still, where the MPC's – and the criminal law's – attachment to the baseline *nulla poena*

[131] But see Michelle S. Phelps, "Rehabilitation in the Punitive Era: The Gap between Rhetoric and Reality in U.S. Prison Programs," *Law & Society Review*, vol. 45 (2011): 33–68 (demonstrating that funding for, and participation in, rehabilitative programming continued in the 1970s and 1980s despite widespread desert-based punishment rhetoric).

doctrine was clear enough, its commitment to a genuinely blame-oriented form of responsibility remained deeply ambiguous.

Herbert Hart's criminal jurisprudence involved an attempt to reinvigorate rational choice in a post-Progressive world where responsibility survived the determinist critique. The idea was to head off the association between choice and traditional desert by draining responsibility of desert-based blameworthiness; that is, by defining desert solely in terms of the limits to imposing utilitarian-based punishment on a particular offender. In the course of his exchanges with Wootton, however, Hart recognized the role played by a conventional morality based on ordinary human psychology without directly examining the implications of this role – which he rooted in individuals' expectations and satisfactions, but hoped to distance from conventional retributive urges – for his own moral principle governing the distribution of *non*-retributive punishment.

Several of the most prominent American criminal law scholars of the 1960s reflected Hart's influence to one degree or another, although none adopted his approach holistically. In common with Hart, they brushed aside deep philosophical concern with the free will/determinism problem; like him they expressed impatience with what they regarded as a metaphysical issue that lay beyond resolution. But, as we have seen, Kadish and Goldstein (unlike Packer) adopted language that suggested acceptance of a retributivist element in punishment. This acceptance – if that is what it was – remained untheorized, as they focused on responsibility rather than on punishment. Nonetheless, root ideas about responsibility soon became, in the hands of Herbert Morris and those who followed, central to the justification for retributive punishment. Hart had supplied materials for Morris's conceptualization of the "person," a conceptualization that in turn supplied a more direct response to the determinist critique than Morris's contemporaries had offered. Morris's idea of the "person" drew on a variety of sources: a rights theory that bore close relation to John Rawls's[132] and Hart's concepts of fairness and justice relative to the individual and the individual's concomitant social obligations, as well as insights into human psychology that Morris drew from intuition, empirical observation, and literary evocations of human nature regarding guilt and remorse. From a certain perspective, there was a kind of circularity in Morris's theory of personhood: the "person" was by definition free (or, at least, not unfree); yet he was free precisely because he possessed the capacities that justified and underlay the values Morris and his predecessors had identified. Morris's benefits-and-burdens theory provided a somewhat more formal defense within the prevailing rights tradition and contributed importantly to the rebirth of retributivism.

Morse paid no attention to Morris's benefits-and-burdens argument. He came closer to Morris's invocation of the person, but for Morse, we might

---

[132] John Rawls, *A Theory of Justice* (Cambridge, MA: Belknap Press, 1971).

say, it served only as a justification for punishment in the sense also implied by Kadish: quite simply, it treated individuals with the dignity they deserved. The idea of the person, in this scaled-down view, did not resolve the freedom issue – that issue Morse, in this stage of his scholarship, resolved via a combination of more conventional grounds and sheer faith in the capacity for choice. Thus the historian-turned-anthropologist might view the 1970s Morse as a member of an American tribe that treated free – or responsibility-bearing – choice simply as a moral way of viewing human beings. Vindication of conventional social and individual values led and the affirmation of free will followed, whether as a matter of working hypothesis, of agnosticism trumped by the demands of human consciousness, or of sheer "faith." As we shall see, this tribal response endured. It was the default position even for many of those who, in ensuing years, raised doubts either about Morris's phenomenology or about the philosophical compatibilism that some leading academics – by then Morse included –found a convincing response to the determinist critique. The position was beyond testing in any ultimate sense. The test it passed was that it made sense of the ultimate: the very possibility of responsibility. That is to say, like Morris's concept of the "person," it no more than affirmed the values invoked in its own defense.

While grappling with justifications for blame in light of doubts about the truth of free will, the emerging legal-academic perspective also enobled the very idea of retributivism that had rendered blame problematic in the first place; the notion that dignity or respect for personhood underlay blame could distance the scholarly picture of responsibility from the more traditional revenge-based retributive version embedded in conventional morality, although at times (as in the case of Morse) it seemed the two versions might be squared. In contrast, the more grudging orientations toward conventional morality of Gaylin and Rothman, on the one hand, and of Bazelon, on the other, appeared increasingly out of the mainstream. Such orientations – rooted more in a cautious deference to, rather than a newly theorized acceptance of, societal values – might well have squared with Kadish's invocation of basic values, but they evidenced little, if any, concern with Morris's identification of person and desert. For commentators such as Gaylin, Rothman, and Bazelon, a future rebirth of rehabilitation or a revision of the law that remade the trial into an instrument of education regarding the limits of personal responsibility remained the solvents of conventional morality; they did not favor the theoretical reworking of that morality via a reworked desert theory.

Overall the relationship of 1960s and early 1970s American legal scholarship to conventional morality was almost pointedly ambiguous. The expanding affirmation of social attitudes ranged from pragmatic to embracing, but theory always stood at least one step apart from the retributivist notions of blame presumed to remain in the hearts and minds of the actual public. And it was, perhaps, no mere coincidence that many scholars failed to directly address exactly what considerations the jury, as representative of that public, was thought to – or supposed to – take into account in judging responsibility. Of course the jury was enlisted by some – such as Bazelon and perhaps Allen – as a seemingly positive (or, at least, potentially positive) element in the evolution of blaming practices as ultimate moral judge. But the question whether the jury was a positive element, or merely a necessary one, was more commonly avoided. As scholars distanced themselves from the state overreach associated with positivism and pure consequentialism – and thereby reaffirmed more traditional notions of liability – the jury was accepted as a component of a legal system that took seriously its historical role as protector of individual liberty. But scholars cannot have thought that their carefully circumscribed theories of individual blame – in Herbert Hart's case, indeed, of a hoped-for eventual liability *without* traditional blame – genuinely comported with the actual decision-making process as jurors understood it. Rather, the jury's return to favor seems largely instrumental, an inescapable element of a legal system premised on political freedom and rational choice. The jury thus also conveniently continued to serve as a black box from which responsibility judgments emanated without required explanation, thereby obscuring the relatively untheorized and sometimes contradictory-seeming enlistment of conventional attitudes to support the retributive brands of blame that were gradually reemerging among some scholars. This aspect of the jury's significant, but often invisible, role indeed may have portended the clearer turn toward a more confident and robust retributivism that soon followed although, ironically, the rift between the jury's presumed notions of blame and that of many neo-retributivist scholars would appear wider than ever.

8

Rethinking the Freedom Question: 1978–1994

INTRODUCTION

By the mid-1970s, the academic tide had begun to turn: for the first time in the twentieth century, retributivism was coming to be a dominant mode of legal-academic thought.[1] Retributivism had made its first major inroads in penology and sentencing policy, an ironic reversal of late-nineteenth-century and Progressive Era trends, where penological theory led the movement toward a scientifically informed, treatment-based approach. As a practical matter, rehabilitation based upon a positivist model had largely failed. And theories of punishment that invoked a (somewhat disembodied) Kantian concept of desert were attractive to legal academics who at first had drifted toward retributivism mainly for political liberty and other, largely instrumental, purposes. Yet a philosophically grounded retributivist theory of criminal responsibility – one that directly responded to the determinist critique – proved more difficult to work out. Morse's response to Bazelon represented an eclectic approach, one that combined Herbert Morris's ideas regarding human values with rough-and-ready common sense regarding the capacity for effective (i.e., blameworthy) choice. The latter, barely theorized, drew upon empirical studies of behavior and recognition of the sheer consciousness of human freedom. Both might be considered weak reeds: the fact that most people who experienced "criminogenic" conditions were law-abiding (as Morse had observed in asserting that most people possess the capacity for relatively free choice) could be explained by abundant intra-cultural

[1] See, e.g., D. J. Galligan, "The Return to Retribution in Penal Theory," in *Crime, Proof and Punishment: Essays in Honor of Sir Rupert Cross*, ed. C. Tapper (London: Butterworths, 1981),; Michael Davis, "Recent Work in Punishment Theory," *Public Affairs Quarterly*, vol. 4 (1990): 217–32; Michele Cotton, "Back with a Vengeance: The Resilience of Retribution as an Articulated Purpose of Criminal Punishment," *American Criminal Law Review*, vol. 37 (2000): 1313–62.

conditions, preserving the hypothesis that all behavior is fully determined. As for the consciousness of freedom, it had long since been explained away; as Morse himself conceded, the assertion that it corresponded to an actual capacity to choose to do other than what one has chosen to do was no more than a matter of "belief and values."

The decade-and-a-half following upon the exchange between Bazelon and Morse witnessed a flowering of interest in substantive criminal law doctrine and especially in the theory underlying legal excuses. Clearly, the maturation of the retributivist turn accompanied – one ventures to say required – grappling with fundamentals. For the most part, legal academics who spoke to the matter remained within, or close to, the determinist camp (broadly defined). Thus, the free will problem loomed large as a megalith to be surmounted, gotten round, or simply come to terms with. This had, of course, been true on some level for (Herbert) Hartians and, before them, for most positivist-leaning academics. Yet for the new retributivists the stakes were higher, given their heightened commitment to desert theory – that is, their movement beyond a limiting moral principle in the context of a system centered on utilitarian and/or rehabilitative forms of mainly *non*-retributive punishment. Where retributive punishment was said to be genuinely justified by criminal blame, they could no longer settle for merely heuristic ways of thinking about human responsibility mainly in the interest of political liberty.

Many thus became attracted to philosophical "compatibilist" approaches to the problem of free will, which postulated that moral and legal responsibility (and, for some, even variously defined "free" will) is entirely compatible with determinism. By the mid-to-late twentieth century, the free will/determinism problem had become the subject of intense debate among Anglo-American philosophers. Although that important debate (and its continuation into the new century) will not receive systematic treatment here, it often overlapped with legal scholarship, and some key points of influence will be noted.[2] A wide range of thinkers expressed variants of compatibilism (or "soft" determinism), building on classical compatibilist ideas to argue that moral and legal responsibility

---

[2] Robert Kane provides a helpful introduction to twentieth-century scholarship on the free will problem in *A Contemporary Introduction to Free Will* (New York: Oxford University Press, 2005). See also the introduction and compilation of essays in Gary Watson, ed., *Free Will*, 2nd ed. (New York: Oxford University Press, 2003). I offer only broad outlines of some main strains of later-twentieth-century academic philosophy concerning free will and determinism in order to provide some context for the legal academic theories that in part – and often only vaguely or unsystematically – drew on this burgeoning field of philosophical study. Particularly apt summaries of the major positions regarding the relationship of free will to criminal responsibility within both philosophical and legal academic circles include Peter Westen, "Getting the Fly Out of the Bottle: The False Problem of Free Will and Determinism," *Buffalo Criminal Law Review*, vol. 8 (2005): 599–652, 609–20, and Anders Kaye, "The Secret Politics of the Compatibilist Criminal Law," *Kansas Law Review*, vol. 55 (2007): 365–427, 368–79.

can – and should – be defined in humanistic terms that effectively avoid the determinist critique. Instead of basing responsibility on the conventional idea of a truly "free" will, many argued for the relevance of an actor's capacity for rational choice, of one's ability to engage in morally responsive reasoning, or of one's "character."[3] Compatibilist approaches thus offered legal scholars a concrete theoretical avenue to accommodate their determinist concerns about the existence of free will alongside their concerns that the rule of law should reinforce the dignity and liberty inherent in notions of personal responsibility. Certainly compatibilism faced its share of criticism within philosophical circles. Some scholars still forthrightly rejected determinism[4] or, conversely, rejected desert-worthy moral responsibility.[5] Others remained more explicitly agnostic about compatibilism, positing that the implications of a still-possible

[3] Prominent works by later-twentieth-century thinkers described as compatibilists include Daniel Dennett, *Elbow Room: The Varieties of Free Will Worth Wanting* (Cambridge, MA: MIT Press, 1984); Harry Frankfurt, "Alternate Possibilities and Moral Responsibilities," chap. 8 in Watson, *Free Will* (originally published in *Journal of Philosophy*, vol. 66 [1969]: 829–39); Harry Frankfurt, "Freedom of the Will and the Concept of a Person," chap. 16 in Watson, *Free Will* (originally published in *Journal of Philosophy*, vol. 68 [1971]: 5–20); Gary Watson, "Free Agency," chap. 17 in Watson, *Free Will* (originally published in *Journal of Philosophy*, vol. 72 [1975]: 205–20); Susan Wolf, *Freedom within Reason* (New York: Oxford University Press, 1990). Kane describes in detail various strands of compatibilism in his *Contemporary Introduction*, esp. chaps. 2, 9, and 10. P. F. Strawson's "Freedom and Resentment" (originally published in 1962) was, of course, also particularly influential. See, e.g., Michael McKenna and Paul Russell, eds., *Free Will and Reactive Attitudes: Perspectives on P. F. Strawson's "Freedom and Resentment"* (Farnham and Burlington: Ashgate, 2008), which mainly collected work published between 1980 and 2004; R. Jay Wallace, *Responsibility and the Moral Sentiments* (Cambridge, MA: Harvard University Press, 1994), which greatly extended Strawsonian thought and proved influential among some legal academics.

[4] A subset of philosophers continued to argue that, at a minimum, determinist principles do not apply to the human will. These libertarian theorists often maintained dualist approaches such as that classically associated with Kant's distinction between the "phenomenal" and "noumenal" spheres, according to which human freedom simply cannot be reduced to scientific terms. Although many legal academics would continue to trace ideas about desert inhering in "personhood" to Kant, fewer accepted the centrally dualist, libertarian thrust of his account. Representative works by modern incompatibilist libertarian thinkers include Roderick M. Chisholm, "Human Freedom and the Self," chap. 1 in Watson, *Free Will* (originally published by the University of Kansas Department of Philosophy, 1964); Carl Ginet, *On Action* (New York: Cambridge University Press, 1990); Randolph Clarke, *Libertarian Accounts of Free Will* (New York: Oxford University Press, 2003). Kane discusses a range of libertarian views in *Contemporary Introduction*, esp. chaps. 4–6.

[5] A comparatively rare strain of philosophers – often called skeptics or pessimists about free will – continued to challenge the notion of ultimate morally responsible action. Some – the hard determinists – accepted the truth of determinism and concluded that it rules out free will and moral responsibility. Others argued that "true" free will – at least of the sort posited by libertarians – is impossible regardless of whether determinism is true. Perhaps most prominent among the latter group is Galen Strawson (Peter's son, but not in the same philosophical camp) who claimed that the libertarian notion of free will rests on the impossible concept of one being a *causa sui* – that is, being the cause of oneself. See Galen Strawson, *Freedom and Belief* (New York: Oxford University Press, 1986); Galen Strawson, "The Impossibility

metaphysical free will were as yet beyond resolution.[6] But for legal academics who gave sustained attention to the free will problem, the reemerging importance of individual desert as a justification for attributing criminal responsibility (and imposing criminal sanctions) naturally rendered compatibilism most attractive.

In effect, two dominant strains of what I term "neo-retributivist" thought emerged among legal scholars. The formal compatibilists – led by Michael Moore and by Morse, who moved beyond his earlier, less explicitly compatibilist approach – expressly relied on philosophical argument for the compatibility of determinism with moral and legal responsibility. Others (perhaps the majority) stayed closer to the more amorphous commitment to blame common to the late 1960s by professing agnosticism about the truth of free will or determinism (or both). Instead, they premised desert on a looser compatibilism – or on a compatibilism-in-effect – rooted in arguments directly from dignity, autonomy and the attributes of the person (and, often, the imperatives of political liberty), all features to which true or formal compatibilists also appealed, but over and beyond the philosophical argument for compatibilism. The attempts to found retributivism on modern adaptations of centuries-old philosophical principles that explain why most individuals' capacity for criminal liability remains unaffected by a (conceded or at least possible) determinism indicate the extent to which positivism survived as a

---

of Moral Responsibility," *Philosophical Studies*, vol. 75 (1994): 5–24 (reprinted as chap. 11 in Watson, *Free Will*). Strawson claimed that the opposite of determinism, "indeterminism," at best supports a form of freedom – a consciousness of freedom – that serves well enough in the daily pursuit of one's life-hopes, but that does not provide a basis for the more definitive kind of "buck-stopping" responsibility we commonly seek in matters of praise or blame. Galen Strawson, "Consciousness, Free Will, and the Unimportance of Determinism," *Inquiry*, vol. 32 (1989): 3–27, 21–24. Some skeptics emphasized the importance of an illusion of free will to human well-being. Others stressed, as in the English philosopher Ted Honderich's formulation, the importance of pursuing our "life-hopes" despite rejecting the illusory elements of free will. Honderich, *A Theory of Determinism: The Mind, Neuroscience, and Life-Hopes* (New York: Oxford University Press, 1988). (Honderich gave special attention to the implications of determinism for retributive punishment in *Punishment: The Supposed Justifications* [London: Hutchinson, 1969].) On the nature and role of illusion in this context, see, above all, Saul Smilansky's important book, *Free Will and Illusion* (New York: Oxford University Press, 2000). Smilansky places the phenomenon of illusion in relation to compatibilism, which inevitably falls short of providing an ultimate "up-to-usness." For his part, philosopher Thomas Nagel – who asserted the apparent impossibility of reconciling our internal sense of autonomy with external views that acknowledge the background factors that influence our formation and actions – claimed to "change [his] mind about the problem of free will every time [he thought] about it." Nagel, *The View from Nowhere* (New York: Oxford University Press, 1986), esp. chap. VII, "Freedom" (quoted material from p. 112). Other skeptical approaches toward free will include Derk Pereboom, *Living without Free Will* (New York: Cambridge University Press, 2001). Kane offers an overview of hard determinism and other skeptical theories in *Contemporary Introduction*, esp. chap. 7.

[6] For a later and particularly robust statement of this view, see Jerry Fodor, "Why Would Mother Nature Bother?," review of *Freedom Evolves*, by Daniel C. Dennett, *London Review of Books*, March 6, 2003, 17–18.

theory of the causes of human behavior, even as its program for reform of penal theory and practice had largely been eclipsed.

This retributivism of our own recent past (and present) – what I call neo-retributivism, to distinguish modern desert theory premised upon the dignity and capacity of the "person" from a harsher (vengeance-based) desert theory premised upon a more conventional belief in true free will[7] – was (and remains) still very much a work in progress. It is too early to say just how the conditions of the twenty-first century will determine our thinking about it. My own tentative and generalizing historical account of the century's closing decades fades at points into a thematic and nearly presentist assessment of the vicissitudes attending legal-academic worrying of the freedom problem in the context of criminal responsibility. This chapter – the main section of my third study – recreates the "conversation" of what I call the long 1980s (1978–1994), first through a discussion of several especially important and quite different approaches, and then in terms of a fuller account of the interplay among some of the American commentators of that period. I am – as I have been throughout these essays – quite selective. I point to main trends, or variations upon evolving main themes, and I focus on the language and turn of mind of those whose work seems to me to express concerns that played a significant part in the particular twentieth-century story of the free will problem I tell.

Although my account of ideas regarding criminal responsibility dovetails at points with contemporaneous ideas regarding punishment, I continue to treat the latter subject only very partially, at a few points where it directly affected thought regarding the freedom question. But it is worth noting, at the outset, one particular point of overlap that complicates the scholarship of the long 1980s, when signs of unease with desert-based punishment lay all about (albeit, for some, unease was a virtue, a condition one ought to experience in doing what Packer had described as the inevitable and unpleasant work of judging and punishing). For some scholars the (perceived) inherent weakness of modern desert theory was to some extent compensated for by the symbiotic relationship between neo-retributivism and utilitarianism. Most late-twentieth-century legal scholars espoused a mixed retributivist-utilitarian penal theory, and some scholars managed to satisfy their unease

---

[7] I use the term "neo-retributivism" to distinguish post-1960s American retributivist thought premised on ideas about dignity and autonomy from an earlier or more commonplace retributivism that most legal scholars associated with revenge. Of course, original philosophical or Kantian retributivism is generally thought to have been premised on dignity and autonomy, with revenge-based retributivism thought to be a perversion of the real thing. Some might therefore prefer that I use "retributivism" where I have used "neo-retributivism" and "faux-retributivism" where I have used "retributivism." For recent commentary on modern retributivist theory and its reclamation of retributivism's original Kantian and Hegelian roots, see Mark D. White, ed., *Retributivism: Essays on Theory and Policy* (New York: Oxford University Press, 2011).

with the basis for retribution by adjusting the mix: they might pay homage to near-universal intuitions about personal responsibility while resting punishment largely on utilitarian grounds or, indeed, might fully envelope retributivism within utilitarianism in accordance with the idea of the "utility of desert."[8] Such scholars thereby implicitly subordinated desert, and thus relieved a degree of pressure from the free will problem. Each perspective – utility and desert – reinforced the other; although both received attention, neither seemed to require independent justification, especially by those whose agnosticism about the ultimate basis for retributivism made them more comfortable with a version of utility that no more than traded upon widespread acceptance of the desert principle. This was not the Progressive "compensation" of "amoral, non-judgmental" rehabilitation. Rather, it was an offset of utility, wherein punishment premised on desert was felt to be justified in part by – or was simply made easier to accept because of – the fact that something very like it would in any case have been imposed within a scheme premised solely upon overall social welfare. As a result of the pervasiveness of these mental maneuvers, it is not always easy at this remove to tell a neo-retributivist from a utilitarian – or, more to my point, to measure the intensity of the unease that the concept of desert occasioned over the last decades of the century, particularly among those scholars who found it unnecessary, or unfruitful, to confront the free will problem directly.

---

[8] Paul Robinson and John Darley, whose late-1990s work I touch on again in Chapter 9, exemplified the ingenious melding of retributivism with utilitarian goals: their central claim was that harnessing common notions of desert is the most effective means to general deterrence; they urged that the distribution of punishment must be rooted in desert in order to maintain the social respect for the law that led to law abidingness. See Paul H. Robinson and John M. Darley, "The Utility of Desert," *Northwestern University Law Review*, vol. 91 (1997): 453–99; and Robinson and Darley, *Justice, Liability and Blame: Community Views and the Criminal Law* (Boulder, CO: Westview Press, 1995). Others, most famously represented by Richard Posner, viewed desert, and, in particular, the underlying assumption of human autonomy, as reflecting a form of hardwired consciousness that had evolved to suit the end of maximizing social well-being: "There is no mystery about the survival value of the illusion (if that is what it is) of freedom, and thus no mystery about why it may be hard-wired into our brains. The feeling of freedom forces us to act deliberately, in the sense of gathering as much relevant information as possible concerning the pros and cons of alternative courses of action before we act." Richard A. Posner, *The Problems of Jurisprudence* (Cambridge, MA: Harvard University Press, 1990), 178. There were also, of course, utilitarians who rejected retributivism *tout court*. Among those, David Dolinko – a respectful critic of Herbert Morris – stood out. Dolinko perceived in post-Hart retributivists a less-than-salubrious, if often subconscious, taking pleasure in the administration of punishment, and he read mainstream criminal jurisprudence in light of harsh real-world practices that, he claimed, retributivists either legitimated or in any case unintentionally facilitated. Punishment, he said, was a social necessity, and nothing more; it was to be lamented – here resonances of Packer, whom Dolinko apparently read (correctly) as a consequentialist regarding punishment. See David Dolinko, "Some Thoughts about Retributivism," *Ethics*, vol. 101 (1991): 537–59; and see David Dolinko, "Three Mistakes of Retributivism," *UCLA Law Review*, vol. 39 (1992): 1623–57.

I begin the substance of this chapter with four commentators of the late 1970s to mid-1980s: George Fletcher, Michael Moore, Stephen Morse, and Lloyd Weinreb. Each scholar was concerned with the freedom question, and each resolved it (or proclaimed its non-resolvability) in differing ways. For Fletcher, the possibility of universal causation remained a problem: it seemed to him to disable moral theory regarding responsibility. His 1978 account took little notice of the compatibilist arguments that had, long since, emerged in philosophers' discussion of determinism. Instead, he made a feint toward character theory, which others developed in the ensuing decades. Moore, by contrast, was already in the process of building an approach that, by 1984, had matured into a remarkable statement of compatibilist theory. In the following year, his "Causation and the Excuses" took criminal jurisprudence a critical step forward beyond both Herbert Hart and Morris, upon whom he effectively built, and, crucially, beyond the merely implicit compatibilism of the early Morse. Retributivism now responded more fully than ever before to the determinist critique. Urging that the law had a strong, but misunderstood, footing for desert, Moore dissected and rejected the causal theory that many scholars had presumed the law enlisted to impose and excuse guilt: the law did not excuse whenever harmful conduct was caused by forces beyond the actor's control, as causal theory would have it;[9] in light of determinism, said Moore, such a theory of excuse leads to utter contradiction, given that *all* conduct is, at bottom, caused by such forces. In other words, either the strict positivists were right, and causation negates all responsibility, or causation is not the key to responsibility. Moore, of course, took the latter position, arguing that the law (and, indeed, humans generally) actually imposed and excused guilt based on the actor's capacity and opportunity for practical reasoning at the time of the harmful act. In many ways, Morse followed suit, embracing the clearer lines drawn by Moorean compatibilism. But Morse did not adopt Moore's moral realism, which situated moral and legal responsibility as logical truths. Rather, Morse attempted to found responsibility on an avowed moral pragmatism.

Although compatibilism – explicit or implicit – came to dominate much late-twentieth-century American retributivist thought, its paradoxes were legion, not the least being that the conventional morality to which it sometimes looked for verification might in fact have rested upon the traditional causal understanding of responsibility that Moore charged was internally contradictory (because it was only *selectively* deterministic – accepting some causes, and not others, as excuses) and that was inconsistent with the very *universal* causation that compatibilism assumes. This irony was turned to account in 1986 by Lloyd Weinreb, whose response to Moore's choice-based compatibilism I juxtapose with Moore's more influential essay. Not that Weinreb's way of viewing the world lacked adherents. Indeed, the ineffability of causal theory was sometimes evidenced even in the writings

[9] For a thorough encapsulation (and defense) of causal theory, see Anders Kaye, "Resurrecting the Causal Theory of the Excuses," *Nebraska Law Review*, vol. 83 (2005): 1116–77.

of opponents of that theory, whose invocation of Morris's idea of "personhood" had as much in common with Weinreb's way of thinking as it had with Moore's. This last point comes into clearer focus when I turn to a somewhat broader – albeit still selective – account of the discussion of the long 1980s. That discussion possessed several important features. First, some scholars who proclaimed agnosticism regarding the compatibility of determinism and responsibility at least appear to have continued to combine the idea of blameworthy choice with a causal theory of responsibility and excuse. Sanford Kadish, for example, seems to have adhered to a causal view, yet he also recognized the debilitating force of the principle of universal causation. Between 1985 and 1987, however – and perhaps as a result of Moore's work – Kadish gravitated toward a compatibilist choice theory. Toward, but not entirely to, that theory: ambivalence remained. Second, some leading choice scholars (I focus on Joshua Dressler) accepted the free will problem as, in principle, unresolvable, but nonetheless premised responsibility upon a concept of choice that at least implied something close to true free will. Dressler defended his position in terms of respect for the "person." Indeed, respect for the person (usually, via Morris) in the face of agnosticism regarding free will was (and perhaps remains) central to much neo-retributivist theory. Third, many legal academics attempted to relocate the baseline for responsibility in some aspect of the offender's "character," rather than in choice per se. For some, this was in part a response to perceived infirmities of the traditional baseline of freely willed action. Yet character theory itself foundered on the determinist critique: what made the offender responsible for his character? Legal scholars confronted this problem in a variety of ways. Here I take up Peter Arenella, who admitted the near-intractability of the problem in his important character-based response to straightforward rational choice theory. Finally, some legal scholars who accepted retributivism premised upon capacity and opportunity for choice (or practical reasoning) sought to limit the reach of that idea either by contesting the underlying assumptions of Moore's compatibilism (Richard Boldt) or by redefining the conditions required for such choice (R. George Wright).

My resulting "story" of the long 1980s largely defies any attempt to construct a linear plot, thanks to the period's very nature. The often wide-ranging conversation had no clear theme – beyond, that is, the unease and debate that centrally characterized it. Most notably, the end of this period marked a point when neo-retributivism appeared here to stay, in one form or another, as a dominant rationale underlying substantive criminal law theory. It was also a time when many vocal legal scholars – the more philosophically inclined Moore and Morse being notable exceptions – acknowledged but left off trying to resolve the still-nagging contradictions arguably inherent in their more or less compatibilist theories of desert; ultimately they were content, or perhaps resigned, simply to accept an unprovable compatibilism as the only available way to promote political liberty and acknowledge personhood within a workable legal system.

Finally, this sometimes content, sometimes grudging, but increasingly commonplace acceptance of compatibilism evidenced, as always, the heavy hand of (presumed) conventional morality. Although legal scholars of the long 1980s varied in their orientations toward the common notions of justice to which the rule of law must pay homage, they were united in their desire to embrace – even foster – their scholarly version of these notions. So far had the wheel turned since the Progressive Era, when in the United States, as in the West in general, scientific-positivist criminal jurisprudence reformers sought to free the law from its anchorage in the prevailing popular morality. Scholars of the modern era reconfigured, naturalized, and universalized the conventional. In doing so, they built upon, but far outstripped, midcentury forms of accommodation. Desert theory, it seems to me, often reflected scholars' evolving interpretations of conventional morality and blaming practices; scholars thus relied heavily on their understandings of common retributivist intuitions, albeit absorbing those intuitions while simultaneously sanctifying retributivism in theory, rediscovering its original philosophical roots in the dignity and autonomy of the person and downplaying its vengeance-based adulterations. It was not that modern scholars either overlooked or sanctioned the abuses of desert – as criminal incarceration increased in record numbers, a harsh spirit of revenge colored quotidian politics, and actual incarceration practice often elided dangerousness and desert. Rather, the scholarly, truth-seeking world continued its search for the Holy Grail of a justifiable theory of responsibility and state-imposed punishment, not (from its own perspective) in order to run interference for real-world practices, but to lay the basis for a reform of those practices that could withstand theoretical critique. Perhaps particularly for the formal compatibilists, cooptation of conventional morality for the ends of a respectable rule of law seemed not only possible, but probable, once one separated the "true" morality embedded in the conventions to which we all supposedly adhere from the false-consciousness of free will that might justify desert conventionally, but could not rightly do so morally. There remained, of course, the question whether such cooptation ultimately allowed for a theory of desert that unified scholarly and conventional approaches or, instead – by altering the very terms of responsibility beyond those assumed to be accepted by the public – embodied an ultimate irony.

FOUR PERSPECTIVES ON FREEDOM AND RESPONSIBILITY

George Fletcher

George Fletcher's *Rethinking Criminal Law* (1978)[10] signaled the rejuvenation of American substantive criminal law scholarship. The time was ripe for such an enterprise, Fletcher said; he pointed directly to the revival

[10] George P. Fletcher, *Rethinking Criminal Law* (Boston: Little, Brown, 1978).

of retributivism in penal theory and to the "growing concern that moral culpability function as a necessary condition of liability." Identifying the central task of legal theory as "justifying the use of the state's coercive power against free and autonomous persons," he continued: "If the rationale or a limiting condition of criminal punishment is personal desert, then legal theory invariably intervenes with philosophical claims about wrongdoing, culpability, justifying circumstances and excuses." Thus, revived notions of desert required careful consideration of the theory underlying the criminal law and, in particular, underlying our definitions of criminal liability. Fletcher was undertaking a task from which others had been deflected, he claimed, by utilitarianism ("this emphasis on goals has distracted our attention from the problem of justice to the individual accused"), by the concern "to identify and confine potentially dangerous offenders" (which "betokens a movement to merge criminal law with an administrative process of civil commitment"), and by "the progressive legitimation of discretionary judgments" (which left "fine discriminations in the level of punishment" to prosecutors, judges, and parole boards, rather than to criminal law doctrine). From this neglected theoretical landscape Fletcher set out on a broad quest to "rework[] the apparatus with which we think about criminal liability" by examining its pattern of oft conflicting postulates[11] and encouraging "reflect[ion] upon claims of justice in subjecting fellow citizens to condemnation and imprisonment as criminals."[12] Like Herbert Hart and Morris, Fletcher was building on the change of tide toward a "revival of normative ethics," which he identified with the work of Rawls, Robert Nozick, Dworkin, and Roberto Unger, and their "sustained critique" of the "calculus of utility."[13] He built, too, on the evolving critique not only of indeterminate sentences (in practice) but also of the rehabilitative ideal (in theory). Von Hirsch's *Doing Justice*, Fletcher posited, was a turning point in this readjustment toward the embrace of desert theory, one reflection of "disillusionment" with Progressive benevolence.[14] Fletcher's monumental *Rethinking* was indeed a brainchild of the late 1960s and 1970s.

A central theme of Fletcher's volume – in a reversal from the forward-looking Progressive focus on the mental or moral health of an offender, as well as from the utilitarian attention to deterrence – was an emphasis on the critical backward-looking component of actual harm caused by wrongdoing. Mounting a robust claim for compatibilism – or, conversely, for freedom of the will – was not his goal. But any deep discussion of desert ultimately led

[11] Fletcher, *Rethinking Criminal Law*, xix–xxii.
[12] Fletcher, *Rethinking Criminal Law*, 875.
[13] Fletcher, *Rethinking Criminal Law*, xx. I have touched on Dworkin's influence and noted Rawls's widely cited work. The relevant works by Nozick and Unger are Robert Nozick, *Anarchy, State, and Utopia* (New York: Basic Books, 1974), and Roberto Mangabeira Unger, *Knowledge and Politics* (New York: Free Press, 1975).
[14] Fletcher, *Rethinking Criminal Law*, 416 and n. 21.

to the question of determinism, which Fletcher faced with a fairly agnostic mix of attention to an offender's character and, when all else failed, transparent pragmatism.

In his discussions of desert, Fletcher deemed Morris important, but less for Morris's particular "imbalance of benefits and burdens" theory – which Fletcher greeted with some diffidence – than for Morris's closely related grounding of "the duty to suffer punishment in the act of wrong doing and its consequences" (and, above all, in the fact of harm) rather than in the offender's "having wicked thoughts or even in his acting in a way properly subject to blame." Herbert Hart's contribution, by way of synthesizing consequentialism and retributivism, was also of great significance, but it "fails to develop a thesis about distributing the burden of punishment in particular cases." Hart's moral-constraint brand of desert would not do, for "the emphasis is on the injustice of punishing someone who has not had a fair chance of avoiding liability, rather than on desert, wrongdoing or culpability as affirmative rationalia for distributing the burdens of the punitive system."[15]

It was here that Fletcher introduced the concept of character, albeit while embedding that concept within an overall perspective on choice that retained the concept of the individual's capacity to shape his own character. Retributive punishment, Fletcher began, "is just only if punishment is measured by the desert of the offender." But, contrary to most others' formulations, desert depended upon the offender's character. "Therefore, a judgment about character is essential to the just distribution of punishment." He acknowledged that the "principle of legality" induces us to "accept the artificiality of inferring character from a single deed," rather than from the "full range" of an offender's deeds; this is "the price of maintaining the suspect's privacy." But the critical question should be "whether a particular wrongful act is attributable either to the actor's character or to the circumstances that overwhelmed his capacity for choice."[16]

Fletcher recognized that this formulation begged the question: Is character caused or chosen? But he did not provide a concept of character that offered invulnerability to the determinist critique. Rather, at base, he offered an alternative method to identify the place on the causation spectrum where legally culpable acts end and excusable acts begin. Most significant, he posited that creating such a distinction between culpable and excusable acts was necessary for any meaningful legal system to function; as though confessing his own failure to isolate character from the contingencies of choice, Fletcher essentially asserted that the cultural requirement of a meaningful system of accountability presently trumped the logical ramifications of determinism. Indeed, he counseled the importance of keeping character and choice separate precisely to avoid "the cul-de-sac of environmental

[15] Fletcher, *Rethinking Criminal Law*, 418–19.
[16] Fletcher, *Rethinking Criminal Law*, 800–01.

determinism." He expressly conceded that "it may be the case that all human conduct is, in fact, compelled by circumstances," but concluded that "if it is, we should have to abandon the whole process of blame and punishment." Fletcher sought refuge against this possibility by appealing to "moral and institutional" arguments "against excusing too many offenders," and, in something like a (Peter) Strawsonian move, he posited that the "moral or philosophical argument is difficult to resolve except by noting that we all blame and criticize others, and in turn subject ourselves to blame and criticism, on the assumption of responsibility for our conduct." This assumption does not require introducing "freighted terms like 'freedom of will'"; rather,

the point is simply that the criminal law should express the way we live. Our culture is built on the assumption that, absent valid claims of excuse, we are accountable for what we do. If that cultural presupposition should someday prove to be empirically false, there will be far more radical changes in our way of life than those expressed in the criminal law.[17]

Thus, Fletcher's character theory constituted a relatively untheorized rejection of traditional (i.e., causal) choice theory, safeguarded in part by an appeal to conventional beliefs and cultural practices and in part by the dire implications of the determinist critique:

The only way to work out a theory of excuses is to insist that the excuse represents a limited, temporal distortion of the actor's character. Social deprivation and particular forms of social interaction might conceivably fashion a person's character to be heedless of the rights of others. If that should be the case, the influence of experience would be too pervasive to constitute an excuse. The circumstances surrounding the deed can yield an excuse only in so far as they distort the actor's capacity for choice in a limited situation.[18]

This seems but an elegant restatement of Morse's 1976 position.

Fletcher undertook a sensitive discussion of what he deemed an alternative (non-character-based) route to the "rationale of excusing conditions" – namely, voluntariness. He found appealing Herbert Hart's argument that it was "ideologically desirable for the government to treat its citizens as self-actuating, choosing agents," to incorporate a "principle of respect for individual autonomy." Throughout, Fletcher evidenced an awareness that the concept and language of voluntariness was mainly supported by its pervasiveness within the web of ideas internal to legal thought, and he never insisted upon an "objective" – or external – foundation for it that resided outside of human consciousness. He recognized that embracing the idea of voluntariness exposed his version of character theory to the conclusion that it necessarily rested upon the Aristotelian claim that, at some level, "people

---

[17] Fletcher, *Rethinking Criminal Law*, 801–02.
[18] Fletcher, *Rethinking Criminal Law*, 802.

choose to develop the kind of character that they have." Yet he conceded that "it is difficult to maintain that all our vices are traceable to prior acts of choice and that therefore character is ultimately linked to a way of life we are free to perpetuate or reject."[19] This did not, however, lead Fletcher back to Hart's position, wherein, it might be said, the very infirmity of voluntariness or the choice theory of character accounted for a distinctly mitigated invocation of retributivism. Nor did it lead Fletcher forward to strict internalism. Certainly Fletcher voiced doubts about the reality of free will and seems to have approached internalism; that is, he seems to have taken subjectivity as support for acting upon the assumption of accountability for one's character, a perspective that differed from Morse's more conventional "statement of belief and values" in support of the (external) reality of free will. Yet Fletcher did not rest his idea of accountability simply on the basis of the universality of the psychology of freedom or on the implications of that phenomenon for the concept of a "person." Instead, illustrating the difficulty and ambiguity often inherent in – and, indeed, the creativity often required of – theories of responsibility in an age of both determinism and desert, Fletcher seems to have justified proceeding on the basis that humans, although not necessarily "free," nonetheless choose in a manner that makes them genuinely "accountable" as though they were indeed factually free.

The retributivist drift had occasioned Fletcher's impressive attempt at a rethinking of the substantive criminal law. In his introduction of character, even the response to the determinist critique was tentatively rethought, although ultimately only to be pronounced as, at present, mainly beyond rethinking. In the end, law must follow life; beyond our everyday intuitions and practices lies the abyss. This was well-aged wisdom that had for long been invoked within the context of positivist-leaning, or only weakly retributive, criminal jurisprudence that kept faith with consequentionalist – and therein, mainly rehabilitationist – penology. Just how much weight would the legal academy be inclined to rest upon this wisdom in this new age of "personal responsibility"?

Michael Moore

Two imposing essays of the mid-1980s that proceeded beyond Fletcher's discussion and avoidance of the determinist critique manifested markedly contrasting approaches to the free will problem and bore witness to the deep disturbance occasioned by the academic embrace of desert-based responsibility and punishment. Both Michael Moore, then of the University of Southern California Law Center, and Lloyd Weinreb, of Harvard Law, accepted the truth of determinism – at least insofar as humans had access to truth. Moore confidently denied the relevance of this truth to moral and legal responsibility whereas Weinreb considered its compatibility with the

---

[19] Fletcher, *Rethinking Criminal Law*, 805.

idea of desert undeniable yet fundamentally mysterious. Although neither of these two approaches resolved the matter for all those who followed, many of those who immediately followed worked within the spaces that Moore and Weinreb opened up. I discuss their approaches here along with Morse's developing compatibilism; Morse traced Moore in many ways, but Morse's approach remained essentially pragmatic. Moore's sweeping "moral realism," on the other hand, purported to connect proper legal responsibility judgments with metaphysical truths.

Moore's 1985 "Causation and the Excuses,"[20] applying principles he had stated in greater detail the previous year in his important book *Law and Psychiatry*,[21] gave the deficiencies of causal theory, and the correctness of a compatibilist rational choice theory, what was to become a locus classicus for legal academics. A man of his time, Moore unapologetically accepted punishment for wrongdoing as an inescapable foundation of the law. Neither purely utilitarian nor purely rehabilitative schemes were viable; moreover, it was merely an "easy out" to "say[] that involuntary treatment does not constitute punishment." Thus, we must want a "legal system that punishes at least some offenders" – indeed, it was "absurd" to conclude otherwise. Here a crucial premise: liability to punishment for violating the law meant that "moral culpability is necessary for legal liability."[22] In other words: desert matters. The problem was our mistaken acceptance of causal theories of excuse, which rendered genuine desert untenable.

Moore explained that his target, causal theory, "regards causation as the core of both legal and moral excuse," thus asserting that "when an agent is caused to act by a factor outside his control he is excused" and "the criminal law is morally right in excusing all and only" such persons.[23] In light of the truth of determinism – according to which "all events, including all human behavior, are caused" – Moore urged that causal theory thus logically requires the conclusion that "moral responsibility is an illusion on which liability to criminal punishment cannot be built." The widespread yet mistaken adherence to causal theory plagued the criminal law and had led to "our unfortunate cynicism" about its moral basis. Moore claimed that this "cynicism" led in turn to a retreat to "a purely utilitarian theory of punishment and of legal excuse" or a "deeper skepticism" of the sort voiced by Mark Kelman a few years earlier in his seminal critical-legal-theory article, "Interpretive Construction in the Substantive Criminal Law."[24] Evidence of causal theory

[20] Michael S. Moore, "Causation and the Excuses," *California Law Review*, vol. 73 (1985): 1091–1149.
[21] Michael S. Moore, *Law and Psychiatry: Rethinking the Relationship* (New York: Cambridge University Press, 1984).
[22] Moore, "Causation and the Excuses," 1113.
[23] Moore, "Causation and the Excuses," 1091.
[24] Moore, "Causation and the Excuses," 1094 (citing Mark Kelman, "Interpretive Construction in the Substantive Criminal Law," *Stanford Law Review*, vol. 33 [1981]: 591–673).

and of its own self-annihilating logic lay all about, in contemporary and traditional legal- and behavioral-science theory, in judicial thought (Judge Bazelon's environmental determinism was, for Moore, a prime example), and in "the common sense beliefs of many educated laypersons." Moore cited the "folk wisdom" of the French proverb, "*tout comprendre c'est tout pardonner*," to epitomize the wrongheadedness he endeavored to eradicate.[25] His answer was to relocate the baseline for responsibility not in the notion of "free will" or action free of causation, but in the idea of "choice" marked by the presence of "the capacity and opportunity to exercise the practical reasoning that is distinctive of [one's] personhood."[26]

The intricacies of Moore's potent argument trace to the mid-1970s, when Moore began playing a leading role in introducing developments in the philosophy of mind and action into criminal jurisprudence. His early work, beginning with "Mental Illness and Responsibility" (1975)[27] and culminating in "Responsibility and the Unconscious" (1980),[28] established the rich body of ideas that he continued to elaborate upon across the 1980s and 1990s. Moore began with mental illness as a basis for legal excuse, with the intention of demonstrating that psychiatry had an important but widely misunderstood role to play in the criminal law. The misunderstanding was shared by most psychiatrists and many legal scholars alike: the latter had not been clear regarding the true requisites for criminal responsibility; the former, in part misled by jurists, had concluded that there existed an impassable gulf between the law's selectively deterministic causal theory of excuses and science's totalizing determinism. Moore's 1975 article cleared away the misunderstanding in broad and, from the juristic perspective, transformative strokes. His aim was largely to reframe the law as it existed – to redescribe and clarify it in philosophically defensible terms. Drawing upon some of the same sources that Morse was to rely upon in his response to Bazelon the following year, but adding crucial ingredients from academic philosophy and cognitive psychology, Moore set the terms of much of the legal-academic discussion of criminal responsibility for the remainder of the century.

The chief basis for the legal excuse of insanity, Moore argued in 1975, was irrationality, or lack of capacity or opportunity for practical reasoning. Absence of intentionality could not be that basis, as many mentally ill persons who merited an excuse intended their behavior. Nor did ignorance of the law or compulsion per se explain all cases, both because many of the mentally ill well understood that their behavior was morally and legally proscribed and because legally excusable compulsion typically related to motivating factors

[25] Moore, "Causation and the Excuses," 1092–93.
[26] Moore, "Causation and the Excuses," 1149.
[27] Michael S. Moore, "Mental Illness and Responsibility," *Bulletin of the Menninger Clinic*, vol. 39 (1975): 308–28.
[28] Michael S. Moore, "Responsibility and the Unconscious," *Southern California Law Review*, vol. 53 (1980): 1563–1675.

outside of the normal formation of desires and the will to act upon them. As
to the absence of free will, Moore took on the determinist critique directly,
and did so in a manner that implicated the legal excuses generally, not simply
the excuse of legal insanity. All behavior was caused, he readily agreed, but
that could hardly be the basis for legal excuse – here, the theme that was to
be central to the 1985 article – as that would apply to all human actions and
nullify entirely the concepts of moral and legal responsibility. Psychiatrists
who concluded that their understanding of human behavior was at odds
with law's idea of responsibility missed the point – which most legal scholars had missed as well – that there were two entirely opposite yet totally
compatible and equally true ways of thinking about human behavior: "As
persons we are both complicated bits of dumb clockwork and intelligent,
purposive moral agents."[29] The latter view reflected everyday thought and
language about ourselves and others, as well as the simple fact that, as persons, we act upon reasons. As he would put it in 1979:

Intentionality [i.e., as "a characteristic of mental *language*, not of underlying mental
phenomena"] is *the* distinguishing mark of our talk about persons and minds and
further ... this kind of talk cannot be reduced to talk of an extensional kind [i.e., as
rendered in the vocabulary of the natural sciences].... One result of this irreducibil-
ity is that determinists who rely on physiological or other hypotheses formed in an
extensional language must necessarily pass like ships in the night those who speak
(in the Intentional idioms) of agents being responsible for intentional actions.[30]

In the immediately ensuing years, Moore would defend this tenet of compatibilism, which was of long vintage in academic philosophy and had been
more recently articulated by, among others, Daniel Dennett[31] and Anthony
Kenny.[32]

The job of the psychiatrist, Moore argued, was to inform the jury with
respect to its role: the determination of whether a particular defendant had
possessed the capacity for rational thought and behavior. About this, he
said, the psychiatrist had much to offer, both as a matter of science and in
terms of deep insight of a more intuitive nature. Moore, at this early stage in
his thought, brought the psychiatrist and the juror together much as Bazelon
had attempted to do. And he claimed, as Bazelon did, that the jury's role
was ultimately a moral one, meaning that the line to be drawn regarding
possession of the crucial capacity was, ultimately, a matter of intuition and
personal judgment. By shifting the focus from the possession of criminal

[29] Moore, "Mental Illness and Responsibility," 315.
[30] Michael S. Moore, "Responsibility for Unconsciously Motivated Action," *International Journal of Law and Psychiatry*, vol. 2 (1979): 323–47, 342 n. 50.
[31] Daniel Clement Dennett, *Content and Consciousness* (New York: Humanities Press, 1969), esp. chap 2; Daniel Clement Dennett, "Mechanism and Responsibility," in Ted Honderich, ed., *Essays on Freedom of Action* (London: Routledge & Kegan Paul, 1973).
[32] Anthony Kenny, *Freewill and Responsibility* (London: Routledge & Kegan Paul, 1978).

intent, in the sense of a capacity for self-control (or "free will"), to the possession of capacity and opportunity for practical reasoning, however, Moore
had taken a very different path from that trod by Bazelon and many others.
Moore did adopt Bazelon's view – a view shared, Moore noted, by the 1953
British Royal Commission – that the jury must decide whether the defendant may "justly be held responsible" for the act. But Moore argued that
his own test – "Was the accused so *irrational* that he cannot justly be held
responsible?" – was precisely the basis on which jurors, and all of us, in fact
determine whether moral and legal responsibility exist.[33]

Moore's reliance on his understanding of our everyday responsibility
judgments would become a foundation of the moral theory he developed in
the ensuing years.[34] He had identified himself in 1975 as a negative retributivist: "We do not punish someone *because* he is morally culpable; but we
will not punish him *unless* he is."[35] Five years later, however, Moore claimed
that moral blameworthiness was not only a necessary basis for legal punishment, but was sufficient in and of itself.[36] By then he was convinced that our
everyday thought, our "moral intuitions in particular cases ... together with
the intuitive plausibility of the principle being defended" (here Moore drew
an analogy to Rawls's approach to ethics in general) provided a basis for
moral judgment that could not be gainsaid.[37] This "moral realism" would be
a tenet of "Causation and the Excuses" and would take Moore well beyond
much of the mainstream compatibilism among legal scholars that he nonetheless helped to inspire. It also purported to root correct responsibility
judgments in conventional practices, thus apparently reconnecting moral
and legal theory with the very blame-oriented conventions that earlier-in-
century legal theorists sought to escape.

---

[33] Moore, "Mental Illness and Responsibility," 322 (emphasis added).
[34] In his 1979 article, "Responsibility for Unconsciously Motivated Action," and his more fully
developed piece of the next year, "Responsibility and the Unconscious" (both noted previously), Moore continued his critique of psychiatrists' mistaken understanding of the nature
of moral and criminal responsibility. Moore reiterated his argument that a mechanistic view
of human thought and behavior was simply one perspective; the proposition that responsibility inhered in the intentional acts of persons – when those acts met the test of rationality – grounded a second equally valid such understanding. Moore articulated a concept of the
"person" in relation to this second view and provided a learned discourse on the problem
of unconscious thoughts and desires. With respect to the latter, Moore argued vigorously
against the position that conscious behavior is ruled (determined) by the subconscious and
concluded that the idea of the compatibility of the two realms of "persons" and mechanisms
easily survived commonplace psychiatric criticisms as well as that of philosophers (Moore
focused on John Hospers) who drew upon the psychiatric view (see Hospers, "Free Will
and Psychoanalysis," in *Freedom and Responsibility: Readings in Philosophy and Law*, ed.
Herbert Morris [Stanford, CA: Stanford University Press, 1961], 463–72 [originally published 1950]).
[35] Moore, "Mental Illness and Responsibility," 310.
[36] Moore, "Responsibility and the Unconscious," 1586 n. 68.
[37] Moore, "Responsibility for Unconsciously Motivated Action," 332 n. 19.

Moore's argument in his seminal "Causation and the Excuses" (1985) was straightforward, thoroughgoing, and relentless. Urging that "we must reject the causal theory of excuse," he sought to establish that causal theory neither accurately described the existing law of excuses nor provided a "morally acceptable basis" for defining legal excuses.[38] Rather, he claimed, his own approach offered a better fit with both the existing doctrine of excuses and "the mass of our judgements about where it is just to praise and blame."[39] His own approach was, thus, more descriptively accurate, bore more normative force, and, ultimately, was more morally defensible. Moore's attack began with his reductio ad absurdum: if determinism is true, then all behavior is caused and thus, if only *uncaused* behavior is responsible, no behavior qualifies for moral responsibility or legal punishment. Causal theorists had thus either to give up determinism or to give up causal theory – or, of course, to give up responsibility. The first would be to fly in the face of science; the last was an absurdity, as causal theory was itself a theory of responsibility.[40] Moore shored up his premises by demonstrating that determinism, by definition, did not admit of degrees or any other kind of selectivity.[41] And he rejected dualism distinguishing between natural

---

[38] Moore, "Causation and the Excuses," 1091.

[39] Moore, "Causation and the Excuses," 1147.

[40] Moore, "Causation and the Excuses," 1112–14.

[41] Moore, "Causation and the Excuses," 1114–20. In rejecting "degree determinism" (1114–18), Moore criticized Norval Morris (among others, including Bazelon and Glueck), whose call for abolition of the special defense of insanity arose from a causal analysis of the law of excuses. Morris's renowned scholarship on desert was persuasive in its own right, and its contrasts with Moore's work exemplify the many internal disagreements among legal scholars who, nonetheless, jointly contributed to the reintroduction of desert as a critical element of criminal law theory. I do not treat Morris separately in the text, in large part because of his focus on theories of punishment, as opposed to underlying questions of free will or ontological bases for human responsibility. Morris had asserted that "freedom of choice" exists on a "continuum," the poles of which – choices that are "entirely rational" and those that are "pathologically determined" – are never reached in practice. Thus, he said, "the moral issue sinks into the sands of reality." Norval Morris, *Madness and the Criminal Law* (Chicago: University of Chicago Press, 1982), 61. His proposed response – elimination of the insanity defense – was based, first, on his acknowledgment that we cannot, with certainty, measure the degree to which a crime was caused by factors outside the actor's control, and, second, on his claim that we currently do so arbitrarily and unjustly: we offer an excuse if mental illness may be said to have caused the crime at issue, yet we do not excuse when crime is caused by "gross social adversity," although the latter is "more potent in its pressure toward criminality ... than is any psychotic condition" (63). Moore, of course, rejected the notion that relative degrees of causation are relevant to any analysis of responsibility, a point he iterated in more detail with regard to Morris's theory in a 1985 review of Morris's book. Michael S. Moore, "The Determinist Theory of Excuses," review of Morris, *Madness and the Criminal Law*, *Ethics*, vol. 95 (1985): 909–19. In the 1982 book, Morris had not taken up the issue of free will in any deep sense. He acknowledged that the fields of law and psychiatry employed different concepts and language (*Madness*, 54–55), and he referred to the "pervasive moral sense that when choice to do ill is lacking, it is improper to impute guilt" (57).

causation and causation in the realm of human behavior.[42] Reiterating his recent arguments that caused behavior could – in fact, did – constitute human action (and appearing to turn aside his earlier (1975 and post) references to "separate systems"), he argued that caused human actions existed in the same frame as caused natural events.[43] Dualism he exploded as an artifact of a now-discredited linguistic turn.[44]

But, then, why *not* treat the infirmities of causal theory as proof of the impossibility of *any* theory of moral and legal responsibility? Here, Moore relied on the essential relationship of responsibility to "personhood." And in a classic statement of the proposition that the idea of "personhood" was itself premised on some logically consistent basis, he appealed to the domains of universal reasoning, settled intuitions, and commonly held judgments in particular instances; in the stuff of everyday practice, he found the ultimate affirmation of a philosophically "real" moral and legal responsibility. On these grounds, he concluded that the true basis for responsibility was the presence of "both the capacity and opportunity to exercise the practical reasoning that is distinctive of [one's] personhood."[45] This, he argued, allowed for a concept of "choice" that was compatible with determinism and still accorded with the great mass of our settled intuitions about responsibility.

In defending this position Moore first continued a line of argument that reflected the crucial moment – from the late 1970s forward – of penetration of American legal-academic criminal jurisprudence by longer-term developments in analytic and moral philosophy. Moore rejected Harry Frankfurt's 1969 (and immediately famous) arguments against the principle of alternative possibilities, that is, the principle that one may be morally responsible for

---

But his overall goal – although expressed in carefully considered theoretical terms – was, in many senses, primarily practical: Morris revealed inconsistencies in the application of the law's presumptive premises in order to urge internal reform of the injustices he believed were currently visited (during both the guilt assessment and the sentencing stages) upon the many defendants who clearly suffered from varying degrees of inadequately treated mental illness. His accompanying prescription for "limiting retributivism" – according to which all sentences must be limited by desert for the crime (or series of crimes), and thus which precludes the state from using the criminal law to indefinitely detain offenders for treatment or because of vague notions of their future dangerousness (see, esp., 31–32, 148–52) – remains influential, as I discuss briefly in Chapter 9.

[42] Moore, "Causation and the Excuses," 1120–28. Here, Moore made short shrift of Jerome Hall's two realms of understanding human behavior (1121–22).

[43] Nonetheless there was something "special" about human agency, even if its specialness simply lay in its relative uniqueness or complexity. "Persons are autonomous [regardless] that everything they do is caused by some set of factors external to their will." Thus "human action is a natural kind of event about which we should seek more and more knowledge" because "the unique attributes of human action suggest that there is a deeper nature to such events in terms of underlying causes" (Moore, "Causation and the Excuses," 1132–34).

[44] I discuss this further later in the chapter in connection with Richard Boldt's critique of Moore.

[45] Moore, "Causation and the Excuses," 1149.

(or have "freely willed") one's acts only if one could have done otherwise.[46] Instead Moore adopted G. E. Moore's early-twentieth-century gloss of the "principle of responsibility," that "an actor is responsible for his actions only if he could have chosen to do otherwise": it does not mean, "could, no matter what," but instead that "he could have if he had chosen (or willed) to do otherwise."[47] According to Michael Moore:

The consequence of [G. E.] Moore's conditional interpretation of the principle of responsibility is to make responsibility for an action compatible with causation of that action. For the only freedom the principle of responsibility now requires is the freedom (or power) to give effect to one's own desires. One's choices, or willings, in other words, must themselves be causes of actions for [G. E.] Moore's interpretation of the principle to be satisfied; it is not required that such choices be uncaused.[48]

Having thus identified "these capability/opportunity senses of 'could,'" Moore declared them to be "so perfectly ordinary that one might doubt whether ordinary speech has the sense of 'could' required by the causal theorist." But he rejected the proposition – to which he concluded G. E. Moore, himself, adhered – that linguistic analysis could resolve "the meaning of the word 'could' as used in the principle of responsibility."[49] Here entered Michael Moore's moral realism, the contours of which he had developed in a lengthy 1982 article on "Moral Reality."[50] Only a *moral* argument, he claimed, was sufficient to establish a meaningful interpretation of "could" that properly circumscribed the principle of responsibility.

The "only moral argument" Moore was able to "imagine that would establish one interpretation over the other is one that appeals to the totality of our moral experience involving praise and blame." He thus appealed to "that range of emotions and attitudes partly described by P. F. Strawson and Herbert Morris – the attitudes of resentment, moral indignation, condemnation, approval, guilt, remorse, shame, pride and the like – and [here going beyond Strawson] that range of more cognitive judgements about when an actor deserves moral praise or blame."[51] Such an appeal to Strawson's seminal ideas, in particular, had become common among compatibilist and compatibilist-leaning scholars at least as of the mid-1970s; Strawson's "Freedom and Resentment" was first published in 1962, and then reprinted in 1968 and 1974, by which latter date he was coming to have an influence on American legal-academic scholarship. Indeed, Moore had cited Strawson in both 1975 and 1980 in defense of his own views regarding the distinction

---

[46] Moore, "Causation and the Excuses," 1141 (citing Harry Frankfurt, "Alternate Possibilities and Moral Responsibility," *The Journal of Philosophy*, vol. 66 [1969]: 835).
[47] Moore, "Causation and the Excuses," 1142 (citing G. E. Moore, *Ethics* [1912], 84–95).
[48] Moore, "Causation and the Excuses," 1142–43.
[49] Moore, "Causation and the Excuses," 1143.
[50] Michael S. Moore, "Moral Reality," *Wisconsin Law Review*, vol. 1982 (1982): 1061–1156.
[51] Moore, "Causation and the Excuses," 1144.

between, as Moore put it in the latter piece, the vocabulary of the sciences and the language of "intentionality" we use to "talk about persons and minds" or "agents being responsible for intentional actions."[52]

Yet Moore consciously proceeded beyond Strawson. Both Strawson and Moore argued that a proper understanding of the nature of persons rendered the determinist critique irrelevant. And Moore could, to a point, be understood as building his ethical theory on something like conventional "reactive attitudes." But Moore insisted that conventional attitudes and judgments revealed a test for responsibility that existed as an independent moral truth grounded on philosophical reasoning whose essential propositions included, but hardly reduced to, Strawson's observations about the sheer naturalness of interpersonal understandings. That is, Moore described an approach that aimed at identifying moral truths underpinned in part by the responsibility attributions that Strawson implicitly suggested could not – and need not – be affirmed by demonstrating their independent metaphysical "truth." Moreover, although Moore also drew on Rawls's tools for reasoning toward correct ethical principles, Moore reached beyond Rawls's essentially constructivist approach to understanding moral rules and toward a pure moral realism.

Moore's own work on moral realism rejected the moral skepticism that suggests there are "no right answers to moral questions" but only our own subjective "feelings, thoughts or attitudes."[53] Just as causal theory created "debilitating cynicism," he urged that moral skepticism was psychologically "devastating" because it caused the skeptic to "devalue his own values." Indeed, it was particularly devastating to the judge whose "daily task is to impose values on others," and led judges and legal scholars alike to favor "purely formalistic," valueless, "scientific," or blindly majoritarian approaches to law.[54] Moreover, it ruled out any consideration of the important concept of criminal desert or retributive punishment because desert could never be premised on an essentially empty, valueless system. Instead, we are left to purely utilitarian justifications for the law, which are themselves impossible for the skeptic to truly justify because they required the ordering of values – a task that the relativist moral skeptic cannot achieve.[55]

Although I do not pretend to recount the full extent of Moore's moral realism here, the kernel at the center of his approach was his demonstration that moral facts are akin to physical facts; the two are not identical, but neither is more or less observable or justifiable, particularly in light of our scientific understanding that no beliefs – even those about the world's physical properties – are mere "inferenceless readoffs of reality."[56] Rather,

---

[52] Moore, "Responsibility for Unconsciously Motivated Action," 342 n. 50.
[53] Moore, "Moral Reality," 1066, 1075.
[54] Moore, "Moral Reality," 1063–65.
[55] Moore, "Moral Reality," 1067–71.
[56] See, generally, Moore, "Moral Reality," 1105–1116. Quoted material from 1110.

any belief, moral or factual, is justified only by showing that it coheres well with everything else one believes. In factual matters as well as moral matters, the best one can do in the way of justification is enter into what Rawls calls "reflective equilibrium," whereby one matches one's own particular judgments with one's more general principles without presupposing that one group must necessarily have to yield where judgments and principles contradict each other.[57]

Thus, there is no reason to discount our perceptions of moral "fact" as compared to our perceptions of physical fact; indeed, "there is a moral reality described by the use of moral language."[58] Further, there are causal relationships between moral facts and our moral beliefs and judgments:

We "see" that an action is wrong by applying the best moral theory we have about wrongfulness to the action before us. The sensory equipment that need be accounted for here is no more and no different than that required for the account of perception itself. To judge an action as cruel is already to have made certain inferences from certain perceptions. To judge the act to be wrong involves but a further inference. Because we regularly make such inferences, one is entitled to say that there are causal relations between the qualities of wrongfulness and cruelty, on the one hand, and the corresponding beliefs, on the other. This is, no doubt, such an ordinary explanation of the causal relation between moral reality and moral beliefs that it is a disappointment to some, who expected something more magical.[59]

It was by this logic that Moore asserted the truth-value of our moral perceptions and judgments. He then explained that our reactive emotions are one method of perception: "Emotions have causes, and they have objects." For example, an "insult causes me to be angry, and the object of that anger is the person who insulted me." Further, because

it is not true that any emotion can be felt for any situation[, t]here is ... a structured connection between the emotions we feel, and how the world is. There are causal regularities that lie behind our various emotional reactions to various situations, and there are norms of appropriateness that we employ, however implicitly, in selecting the objects of our emotions.[60]

For these reasons, emotions are "connected to the real world in a sufficiently structured way that one may use one's emotional reactions as the basis for legitimate inferences about how the moral world really is." For example, one "may form an intuition that some action is wrong by the inference one draws from one's emotions of revulsion." In other words, our patterns of

---

[57] Moore, "Moral Reality," 1113.
[58] Moore, "Moral Reality," 1117. Moore admitted he thus established the objective nature of our moral beliefs or intuitions only for those who accept the objective nature of our perceptions of facts; but he suspected that most moral skeptics were not factual skeptics and rather believed in the objective nature of factual perceptions (1152–53).
[59] Moore, "Moral Reality," 1133.
[60] Moore, "Moral Reality," 1135.

reactions do not underlie justifiable responsibility judgments *only* because the patterns are identifiable and inevitable (essentially as Strawson would have it). Such patterns also reveal an objective truth that genuinely – not just descriptively or pragmatically – justifies desert in the same way, say, that seeing what we perceive as the color "red" justifies believing that an object is, in truth, red. Moore was careful to point out that emotional reactions are not a *sole* basis for blame, however; rather, we might overreact to an action or might not react to an action that we later conclude was wrong. Thus our moral theory based on our past perceptions also enters the picture and, in a process of ongoing cognitive appraisal, our theory should be "turned back on the range of emotions that generated it in order to judge their moral worth."[61] Put otherwise, and again clarifying his usage of the word "intuition": "one does not want to identify intuitions with emotions. Intuitions include dispositions to believe as well as actual beliefs because one does not always believe what one first intuits about the moral qualities of some act, just as one does not always believe one's eyes."[62]

So, what does the totality of our experiences tell us about the true moral basis for blame? Returning now to "Causation and the Excuses," Moore asserted that our experiences root an objective morality that has nothing to do with "free will" or excuse for "caused" acts. Rather, all our experience tells us that we constantly give "praise and blame for actions and choices *we know to be caused by factors external to the actor's free will.*" Indeed, if we doubted there were causes of someone's behavior, we would "be in doubt about as to whether a person really deserved praise or blame."[63] Our everyday intuitions confirm our comfort with basing praise and blame not on free will, but on a person's capacity and opportunity for practical reasoning, which reasoning Moore defined as "(1) the ability to form an object we desire to achieve through action, (2) the ability to form a belief about how certain actions will or will not achieve the objects of our desires, and (3) the ability to act on our desires and our beliefs so that our actions form the 'conclusion' of a valid practical syllogism."[64]

And, Moore urged, his analysis of the law bore out his argument. The legal excuses were all best explained in terms of a compromised capacity/opportunity for practical reasoning. Insanity and infancy deal with

---

[61] Moore, "Moral Reality," 1136, and see 1115–16. In this vein, Moore did not discount the "anguish" we may feel when faced with seeming moral dilemmas. Despite his claim that there are correct answers to moral questions, he acknowledged that, as with the hard sciences, we may not know all the moral facts relevant to a particular question or situation. Thus one is still left to the "process of deciding what one ought to do, and of justifying the choice one makes" by attempting to "cohere all one's particular judgments with one's more general principles into a system of moral beliefs that best fits both one's considered judgments about particulars and one's intuitively plausible principles" (1150–52).

[62] Moore, "Moral Reality," 1134 n. 164.

[63] Moore, "Causation and the Excuses," 1144–45 (emphasis added).

[64] Moore, "Causation and the Excuses," 1148. Moore's capacity/opportunity formulation bore obvious similarity to Herbert Hart's choice theory, on which Moore would rely heavily in

"profound defects in practical-reasoning capacities"; involuntary intoxication "involves a temporary derangement of the critical capacities"; mistake of fact or of law deprives one of the "opportunity to avoid evil that he would have if he knew what he was doing and still violated the law." Duress and necessity were similarly opportunity-based: "External compulsion by threats or natural necessities presents an even less extreme case of lack of opportunity ... still it excuses [the actor] because we recognize that his opportunity to conform to the law is severely restricted compared to that of persons who are not compelled to break the law."[65]

Moore had established the logical inconsistencies of the causal theorist's position. He demonstrated through ingenious argument the disjunction between the analytical purity reflected in his analysis of the law of excuses and the "impure" philosophy[66] that sometimes characterized commonplace but uncritical professional and lay causal-theory assumptions about the determinants of responsibility. He argued that we often mistakenly believe we are applying principles of causation based on free will or "control" whereas, in fact, we truly associate responsibility with the opportunity and capacity for practical reasoning *tout court* and do so even when we recognize that the actor's behavior is determined. Thus, Moore painstakingly established the compatibilist principles that (he believed) the law *actually* assumes undergird our truest moral intuitions, as opposed to what most lawyers, laymen, and even most criminal jurisprudence scholars mistakenly believe the law assumes about those intuitions.

Moore acknowledged, however, that such mistaken beliefs were a very powerful and prominent aspect of twentieth-century American legal-academic criminal jurisprudence. On this point, he took note of "a very isolated class of moral experience that speaks for [the causal theorist's] interpretation of the principle of responsibility," namely, "the sympathy we may feel for wrongdoers whose wrongdoing was caused by factors such as social adversity or psychological abuse during childhood." But he discounted such sympathetic feelings as outliers resulting from "extraneous factors" and warned that their apparent moral goodness proves deceptive. They likely belied "an elitism and a condescension" that "betokens a refusal to

---

his 1990 article, "Choice, Character, and Excuse," chap. 13 in *Placing Blame: A Theory of Criminal Law* (New York: Clarendon Press, 1997) (originally published in *Social Philosophy & Policy*, vol. 7 [1990]: 29–58), wherein Moore urged that only the choice theory of excuse – and not the character theory – "captures the kind of moral responsibility relevant to *retributive* punishment" (548–49, emphasis added). As I have suggested, this is a move that Hart himself – who eschewed retributive desert and rejected a necessary connection between legal culpability and *moral* culpability (see, e.g., H. L. A. Hart, "Legal Responsibility and Excuses," chap. 2 in *Punishment and Responsibility: Essays in the Philosophy of Law* [Oxford: Clarendon Press, 1968], 35–38, 53 [originally published in *Determinism and Freedom in the Age of Modern Science: A Philosophical Symposium*, ed. Sidney Hook (New York: New York University Press, 1958), 81–104]) – would firmly resist.
[65] Moore, "Causation and the Excuses," 1149.
[66] Moore, "Causation and the Excuses," 1119.

acknowledge the equal moral dignity of others" and "a sense about one's self – as the seat of subjective will and responsibility – that one refuses to acknowledge in others." Most important, such causal sympathies, like the causal theorist's overall interpretation of the principle of responsibility, are "inconsistent with the mass of our judgements about where it is just to praise and blame."[67] If we realize this,

> the result is to reject any requirement that, before we say an actor "could have acted otherwise," we establish that his choice to act was uncaused. Put another way, the result is to affirm the proposition ... that one is responsible for actions that result from one's choices, *even though those choices are caused by factors themselves unchosen.*[68]

Moore's formal compatibilist discourse provided a comprehensive justification for the reemergence of retributivism as a worthy aim of the law. Moore did not just postulate the "dignity" and "personhood" of human beings despite their being wholly vulnerable to causal forces. Rather, in the vein of much academic philosophy, he articulated an idea of responsibility that rendered determinism irrelevant. And he did so by rejecting the mere "as if" accommodation of conventional attitudes common to American legal jurisprudence, instead purporting to found his moral realism directly on such attitudes and thereby justifying genuine moral and legal desert in a determined world. So was there a role for the conventional belief in free will, which would seem antithetical to Moore's approach?

Most determinist scholars had presumed a broad conventional belief in free will that conflicted with determinism. Moore apparently perceived the same conflict, accepting that "common sense" is "philosophically impure."[69] But he does not appear to have urged, at least for the time being, that the concept of a "free will" is better (or actually) equated with or conceived of as the capacity/opportunity to exercise rational choice. Rather, he seemed to equate "free will" with the sort of uncaused origination that he rejected;

---

[67] Moore, "Causation and the Excuses," 1145–47. Moore pointed out, significantly, that one rarely hears the same arguments made to excuse criminals because of their happy childhood, their parents' wealth, or the advantages they may have enjoyed – even though such factors my well cause someone (for example Loeb and Leopold) to become a criminal. This asymmetry could evidence a connection between our sympathy for the disadvantaged defendant and either (1) our own guilt at not having done enough to alleviate "unhappy" causes of crime, or (2) our sense that those who became criminals because of adverse circumstances have "already suffered enough." (1146)

Moore's observation was intended to throw "our" sympathetic responses into relief – to give dimension to "the mass of our judgements." He likely considered that we commonly attribute capacity and opportunity for practical reason to the socially and economically well-off, rather than that we commonly attribute to them the power of self-origination of thoughts and behavior (i.e., true free will).

[68] Moore, "Causation and the Excuses" (emphasis added).

[69] Moore, "Causation and the Excuses," 1115.

indeed, he chided agnostics who "waffle on determinism" and those who "adopt an 'as if' strategy whereby we lawyers can pretend that people are free *even though they really are not.*"[70] In other words, Moore rejected free will *while* relying on conventional belief, yet *while* recognizing that, conventionally, we often presume that responsibility requires acting via an uncaused (i.e., self-originating), *free* will. Such reliance on a body of belief that includes free will in order to justify a moral theory that expressly rejects free will may appear to require rather significant unpacking.

Moore's professed offering of the "most coherent account of our moral experience"[71] may, at first, seem puzzling given that he admitted inconsistency between his description and our intuitions. Resolving the inconsistency in favor of his theory, moreover, he suggested that it is the *community* that misunderstands its own moral sentiments, not Moore. Where common sense allows only for some degree of – but not universal – causal explanation, Moore insisted, common sense is simply "wrong."[72] At the same time, he chastised the causal theorist who might "claim that most of our moral experience is just false in light of the truth of *his* interpretation of responsibility."[73] And this despite the strong intuitive appeal of causal theory that Moore admitted is evident in the cases that cause us to experience sympathy for a wrongdoer's past adversity.

The presumptive resolution to the puzzle lay in Moore's oft-stated admonitions that "no area of human knowledge is perfectly coherent" and "any moral theory will have to reject some of the emotions that generate the theory in order to maintain overall coherence."[74] Presumably "free will" is an intuition that – like our sympathy for those "whose wrongdoing was caused by factors such as social adversity or psychological abuse during childhood" – we may agree simply to give up once we understand that the *mass* of our judgments is not actually rooted in the impure logic of causal theory. In comparison, Moore reassured the reader that "any systematic exposition of our sensory experience, for example, has to disregard certain visual experiences because they give us inaccurate information about the world. (The perception of a 'bent' stick partially immersed in water is a good example.)"[75] Other scholars would, of course, question whether common perceptions of free will are akin to – and as easily dismissed as – the optical illusion of a straight stick that appears bent in water.[76]

---

[70] Moore, "Causation and the Excuses," 1114 (emphasis added).
[71] Moore, "Causation and the Excuses," 1144.
[72] Moore, "Causation and the Excuses," 1119.
[73] Moore, "Causation and the Excuses," 1145–46 (emphasis added).
[74] Moore, "Causation and the Excuses," 1145–46 and n. 150 (citing his more comprehensive explanation of this point in Moore, "Moral Reality," 1136).
[75] Moore, "Causation and the Excuses," 1145–46.
[76] E.g., Boldt, discussed later in this chapter, would urge that Moore "ought not be allowed to deny so easily that portion of our experience that fails to comport with his revised principle of

On one hand, Moore appeared to think that, at a minimum, we should strive to dismiss such perceptions, for example, by objectively considering our "practices of assessing merit and responsibility" and realizing they "are consistent with the proposition that persons are responsible for their (determined) choices, inconsistent with its negation."[77] He similarly observed, in the context of rejecting the ordinary-language view of meaning, that "inferences from patterns of ordinary usage cannot replace scientific insight about the true nature of the things to which words refer." Thus, the correct "meaning of words like 'intention' is given by the best scientific theory that one can muster about the true nature of intentions, even though that theory may involve knowledge that most ordinary speakers do not have and that, accordingly, is not reflected in their ordinary usage."[78] In other words, truth trumps ordinary understanding (at least when that ordinary understanding conflicts with the mass of our ordinary understandings) and, ideally, we are capable of revising our (outlier) ordinary understandings when they conflict with the truth. So, I gather, we should aim to overlook the perhaps inevitable emotional experiences tied to our presumptions about free will and to judge based not on our emotions alone, but based on the ongoing cognitive appraisal of true responsibility to which Moore importantly contributed.[79]

---

responsibility." Richard C. Boldt, "The Construction of Responsibility in the Criminal Law," *University of Pennsylvania Law Review*, vol. 140 (1992): 2245–332, 2268–69. Of course, such criticisms are not uniquely aimed at Moore, but also more generally at formal compatibilists' attempts to reconcile, in Gary Watson's words, "the disparity between what they offer and what we naturally believe in our daily lives about our agency" ("Introduction," in Watson, *Free Will*, 24). In a later, direct attack on compatibilist retributivism (that of Moore, in particular) and defense of causal theory, Anders Kaye – in part resurrecting ideas espoused by Lloyd Weinreb (whom I discuss in depth later in this chapter) – would exploit the apparent disparity in contending that our blaming intuitions inarguably are, in fact, only partially (or "provisionally") deterministic – and for good reason, regardless that the result inevitably defies pure logic. He has accused Moore and others of "reverse-engineering [their] criteria for blame and excuse from provisionally determinist causal moral judgments" and then supporting their own implausible approaches with "artificial criteria for excuse and blame, criteria that – like simulated sweetener – disguise their lack of substance by mimicking the taste of something else familiar and substantial." Kaye, "Resurrecting Causal Theory," 1167. In an opposing spin on the potential problems with formal compatibilists' reliance on common views, Victor Tadros – who claims to espouse (an arguably weak) compatibilism but to reject retributivism – has recently challenged *retributivists'* reliance on our "intuitions about desert" where there is "good reason to doubt the veracity of our intuitions about desert" given that they are underpinned by false conceptions of free will. Victor Tadros, *The Ends of Harm: The Moral Foundations of Criminal Law* (New York: Oxford University Press, 2011), 63.

[77] Moore, "Causation and the Excuses," 1144.
[78] Moore, "Causation and the Excuses," 1126.
[79] Interestingly, on its surface this appears similar to a more recent claim by psychologists Joshua Greene and Jonathan Cohen (which I discuss further in Chapter 9) that advances in

Or perhaps Moore would not find it necessary to go this far. He may be better read as offering a sound theoretical (and "true," under his metaphysical analysis) underpinning for desert, meant primarily to reassure that small group of his contemporaries who were the only ones to worry (at least out loud) about determinism's implications for retributive punishment in the first place: those legal academics, philosophers, and jurists concerned about the generally unspoken foundations of the legal system. On this view, it may matter less that the intuition of free will is conventionally pervasive: if his audience could at least *conceive of* revising the basis for judgment in the way Moore urged – and presuming he convinced them that the capacity and opportunity for rational choice, not causal sympathies, in fact underlie human judgments *most* of the time – then they might be more *theoretically* comfortable attributing criminal desert despite the reality of determinism.

Yet it is possible that other theorists who were, in the abstract, as deterministic as Moore had retreated to an "as if" position regarding free will (and to one degree or another of a "causal theory") precisely because doing so accorded with their own everyday psychology as well as with their perceptions about the widespread, albeit "impure," social understanding of the basis of responsibility. For many scholars, "as if" might well have been a response to their own recognition of the very logical impossibility Moore claimed made their approach untenable. Moore refused to believe that "impure" philosophy was as pure as philosophy could – or should – be with respect to the idea of "ought" (that is, the idea of when desert is prescriptively justified and thus ought to be imposed). He did not consider that generations of legal academics – who might not have put it quite this way – suspended belief in holistic (incompatibilist, or "hard") determinism even while accepting that holistically *logical* belief in prescriptively justified desert was not possible in principle. It remained to be seen whether Moore, the ultimate compatibilist, could convince them definitively to drop the "as if," that is, to espouse a retributivist form of responsibility based entirely on *causally determined* capacity/opportunity grounds, without their reinterpreting those very grounds in "as if" terms in pragmatic recognition

---

neuroscience will finally be capable of convincing us – or at least some of us – to "reject[] free will as it is ordinarily conceived" because it "will vividly illustrate what until now could only be appreciated through esoteric theorizing: that there is something fishy about our ordinary conceptions of human action and responsibility." Joshua Greene and Jonathan Cohen, "For the Law, Neuroscience Changes Nothing and Everything," *Philosophical Transactions of the Royal Society of London B*, vol. 359 (2004): 1775–85, 1775–76. But Greene and Cohen draw a very different conclusion than does Moore, arguing that the result will be a rejection of retributivism. Moore, at least as of 1985, urged to the contrary that retributivism would survive even "an advancing, mechanistic science" because "to explain the mind in terms of the brain, or even to identify the mind with the brain, is not to explain the mind away": "persons can be agents who act for reasons even in a world in which all mental states and all physical events are caused" ("Causation and the Excuses," 1127).

of the ineffability of the conventional psychology of contra-causal human freedom.

Stephen Morse

Moore had an important influence on Morse, who, by 1982, had adopted something close to Moore's view that the capacity for practical reasoning and the absence of compulsion were the requisites for criminal liability.[80] By then, Morse had turned away from his 1976 formulation – still evident at points in his 1978 and 1979 articles[81] – that behavior existed on a continuum from easy to difficult choices, relative to the law's acceptance of the "commonsense" understanding of free will. Evidently following Moore, Morse now accepted the view that "causation" and the ascription of moral or legal responsibility were different systems, and he adopted a philosophical compatibilism that accorded with the philosopher Anthony Kenny's influential 1978 book, *Freewill and Responsibility*.[82] Like Moore, Morse argued:

The language of the *prima facie* case in criminal law is one of actors acting for reasons.... It is possible to redefine all behavior including the formulation of mens rea, as events or effects ... with such a redefinition, however, one is no longer talking the language of persons, reasons, choices, and responsibility. Instead, one is talking about persons and their behavior as objects and events. The two realms of discourse should not be confused, because if causation is equated with excuse, it leads to the reductionist conclusion that no one is responsible – presumably all behavior has causes.[83]

Morse applied his adopted principles of responsibility to a searching – and searing – critique of mental health experts' assumptions about the relevance of their science to the law. He suggested guidelines for expert testimony, which, he argued, extended only to "observations about thoughts, feelings, and actions," the application of this data being a matter for the trier of fact

---

[80] Stephen J. Morse, "Failed Explanations and Criminal Responsibility: Experts and the Unconscious," *Virginia Law Review*, vol. 68 (1982): 971–1084.

[81] Stephen J. Morse, "Crazy Behavior, Morals, and Science: An Analysis of Mental Health Law," *Southern California Law Review*, vol. 51 (1978): 527–656, esp. 561–64; Stephen J. Morse, "Diminished Capacity: A Moral and Legal Conundrum," *International Journal of Law and Psychiatry*, vol. 2 (1979): 271–98.

[82] Morse, "Failed Explanations," 1037 (citing Kenny, *Freewill and Responsibility*, 22–45).

[83] Morse, "Failed Explanations," 1029. Morse's prior "continuum" and "hard choice" language bore obvious similarity to that of Norval Morris in works including Morris's 1982 *Madness and the Criminal Law*. In his review of the 1982 book, however, Morse (again like Moore, see Moore's criticism of Morris, footnoted previously in my discussion of Moore) took issue with Morris's call for abolition of the insanity defense, in part based on Morse's newer formulation of responsibility rooted in an actor's capacities for rationality and self-control. Stephen J. Morse, "Justice, Mercy, and Craziness," review of Morris, *Madness and the Criminal Law*, *Stanford Law Review*, vol. 36 (1984): 1485–515. While criticizing

and thus ultimately a matter of social and moral judgment. Morse restated his new position in 1984 in "Undiminished Confusion in Diminished Capacity,"[84] and again at a symposium the following year in "Psychology, Determinism and Legal Responsibility."[85] In the latter piece – the culmination and most systematically articulated of his pre-1990s writings on the underlying principles of criminal responsibility – Morse's focus was again the relationship between psychology and the law with particular regard to the insanity defense. But, in this twin to Moore's 1985 "Causation and the Excuses," he also exhaustively criticized causal theories of legal excuse and the presumption by hard determinists that moral responsibility requires a species of nonexistent "free will." Expressly crediting Moore's influence[86] – and acknowledging a similar *reductio* and opposition to selective and probabilistic determinism – Morse argued (as he has essentially continued to do since) that there exists in law and "common morality" a "deep consensus that there are two criteria for moral and legal responsibility: the actor must be reasonably capable of rational behavior and reasonably uncompelled."[87] The argument, although it was "compatible with consequentialist justifications for punishment," was self-consciously "written from a nonconsequentialist vantage point and thus directly support[ed] retributivist justifications for punishment."[88]

Morse's particular approach adopted philosopher Daniel Dennett's 1984 compatibilist stance, including Dennett's seemingly paradoxical proposition that "'we can imagine a rational *and deterministic* being who is not deluded when it views its future as open and "up to" it. Yes, we can imagine a responsible free agent of whom it is true that whenever it has acted in the past, it could not have acted otherwise.'"[89] The invocation of Dennett was

Morris's formulation as "confus[ing] causation with excuse" (1488), Morse did not take up his own former language in this piece or discuss whether it had been similarly flawed. The crux of Morse's criticism exemplified one major distinction among the various scholars who contributed to the retributivist revival: Norval Morris's essentially negative retributive approach – while giving desert a role beyond its *mere* use as a limit on utility – steadfastly emphasized desert as a constraint on punishment and thus as a tool of justice to be employed once the minimal requirements of criminal conviction had been met; Morse much more clearly advanced desert affirmatively, as an element of liability that imbued the conviction itself with justice.

[84] Stephen J. Morse, "Undiminished Confusion in Diminished Capacity," *JCLC*, vol. 75 (1984): 1–55.

[85] Stephen J. Morse, "Psychology, Determinism and Legal Responsibility," in *Nebraska Symposium on Motivation 1985, Volume 33: The Law as a Behavioral Instrument*, ed. Gary B. Melton (Lincoln: University of Nebraska Press, 1986), 35–85. See also Stephen J. Morse, "Excusing the Crazy: The Insanity Defense Reconsidered," *Southern California Law Review*, vol. 58 (1985): 777–837.

[86] Morse, "Psychology, Determinism and Legal Responsibility," 35 n. 1.

[87] Morse, "Psychology, Determinism and Legal Responsibility," 59.

[88] Morse, "Psychology, Determinism and Legal Responsibility," 56.

[89] Morse, "Psychology, Determinism and Legal Responsibility," 70 (quoting Dennett, *Elbow Room*, 170).

intended to explain why each of us should feel (and believe we are) free in a determined world. Much of Morse's discussion, however, was an attempt to justify legal and moral responsibility on grounds that were not set forth, or implicit, in the quotation from Dennett. These grounds Morse described as conceptual, empirical, and normative.

The "conceptual" grounding tracked Herbert Morris's distinction between persons and things: "Morality is concerned with persons who characteristically act with consciousness that they are doing so for reasons and are accountable." It adopted Moore's elaboration in his early writings: "the language and conceptual apparatus of morality cannot be reduced to that of the natural scientific world without losing its moral meaning." We can describe a person's behavior "in the language of neurophysiology" – or any other scientific language – but "moral evaluation makes sense only if we view this person as an agent who [behaved] consciously, rationally, and without compulsion."[90]

Morse next leaned heavily on what he termed Peter Strawson's "empirical observations," here capturing and universalizing, rather than remaining aloof from, conventional morality. He asserted that our viewing persons as we do is both natural and well-nigh inevitable: "When others injure us, we resent it and blame them unless there is a good reason not to." Presumably, there is good reason not to when we sense that they are unconscious, irrational, or compelled.

All these reactions, which are embedded in the very nature of personhood and human interaction, would be irrelevant to the incompatibilist. There would be no resentment, no blame; all persons would be viewed entirely objectively. For Strawson, such an approach is logically possible but probably humanly impossible.... Strawson's point, of course, is neither conceptual nor normative; it is based on empirical observations and assumptions. Still, I think it is so obviously correct that it would be folly to try to create and impose a normative, moral and legal system that contradicts it. Such a system would not work, whereas a compatibilist system does work.[91]

What did "work" mean to Morse in this context? Avoidance of the logical contradiction ("impure" philosophy) of causal theory spoke to the negative; what spoke to the positive? We come finally to Morse's "normative" basis for the principles of compatibilism. He asserted what he described as

an article of faith, a fundamental value I hold. I believe we ought to treat persons as persons ... I offer this assertion baldly, however, in the belief that it is widely shared among almost all persons in Western cultures and that it would be impossible to understand their behavior unless they did share this value. Intellectual posturing aside, human interaction worth having is almost inconceivable unless people do have this value.[92]

[90] Morse, "Psychology, Determinism and Legal Responsibility," 56–57.
[91] Morse, "Psychology, Determinism and Legal Responsibility," 58.
[92] Morse, "Psychology, Determinism and Legal Responsibility," 58–59.

Again, conventional morality had become central to the affirmation of a retributive form of responsibility. Was Morse's formulation any better equipped than Moore's to justify his reliance on conventional, often causal or free-will-based, attitudes to underpin a compatibilist, free-will-*denying* version of responsibility?

Both Moore and Morse had drawn upon Strawson's naturalization of conventional responsibility attribution, and both also sought to establish a consistent, logical basis for that attribution. For Moore, "the totality of our moral experience involving praise and blame" revealed that the crucial determinant for responsibility was a capacity and opportunity for practical reasoning; for Morse, our "deep consensus" on these matters was that the responsible actor must have been "reasonably capable of rational behavior and reasonably uncompelled." Their responsibility formulations and integration of conventional attitudes were thus substantially the same, but their methodology and moral theory differed. For Morse, this broad social "consensus" justified the law's approach as a practical, rational, and conventionally moral matter; for Moore, it demonstrated that the law's approach was itself morally compelled, that it – and his gloss on conventional morality – reflected a metaphysical truth.

Moore's strong claim in this regard arguably necessitated his discussion of what, exactly, one should do with one's causal intuitions when faced with the reality of determinism: one should acknowledge they are inconsistent with the totality of our moral experiences and discard them – or, at least, allow one's cognitive judgments to override one's impure sympathies and thus refrain from affirmatively judging on the basis of the latter. I have suggested it is unclear whether Moore truly believed that the conventional belief in free will could itself thereby be effectively rooted out of our considered responsibility judgments or, indeed, whether this was even necessary in practice so long as the theoreticians – and, ultimately, the legislators and jurists – could accept and apply the purer logic of his approach.

Morse argued for the relevance of conventional attitudes and practices along lines more similar to Strawson's: they were relevant precisely because "blaming and excusing are interpersonal, social activities"; indeed conventional attitudes and practices essentially *constitute* the very idea of responsibility.[93] This approach, based on Morse's bald assertion of the importance of personhood – of treating "persons as persons" – relied less on pure logic, instead bolstering his underlying compatibilist theory with some of the very values that others might say are inextricable from the ineffable belief in free will. In contrast to Moore, Morse directly discussed the fate of "free will," although it is not entirely clear whether Morse believed, like Moore, that we should revise our notions of freedom (and its necessity) or, instead, that Morse felt his own formulation essentially described, in precise terms,

---

[93] Morse, "Psychology, Determinism and Legal Responsibility," 59.

what we already think of as free will. Claiming that he had "no idea what is typically meant by free will" or "the relationship of this ill-defined term to determinism," his preference was to "exorcise" all "talk of free will or free choice."[94] At times he at least implied that any seeming difference between conventional belief and his rubric for responsibility attribution was merely a matter of semantics; all excuses were premised on "nonculpable irrationality or compulsion" regardless that "all persons in all contexts might not use exactly these terms."[95]

In this vein, Morse also came out overwhelmingly on the side of the jury. Trusting the finder of fact as "the moral representative of society," he urged that "twelve persons good and true are quite sufficient" to make the "commonsense moral and legal judgments" necessary even in cases alleging insanity.[96] Again emphasizing that legal and moral responsibility are defined by a "moral and social standard," the bounds of legal responsibility must be set according to those institutions empowered to make "individual moral and social decisions": in the United States, therefore, "substantive standards for legal insanity should be set largely by the legislature and interpreted by the courts, and individual cases should be decided by juries and judges."[97]

Morse's confidence in such commonsense judgments could give the impression that, all along, the presumption that the law relied on contra-causal "free will" was the result of misunderstandings on the part of causal theorists and psychiatric experts – conventional morality was not to blame, despite that it made use of imprecise free will terminology. Indeed, one almost begins expecting Morse to profess that the very disjuncture between determinism and conventional morality that preoccupied decades of American legal scholars had been invented by Progressives who, in their zeal for the new behavioral sciences, vastly underestimated public opinion. But obviously the whole picture is not so simple. Through his heavy reliance on Dennett, Morse ultimately acknowledged his assumption that we "persons" habitually assume our freedom inheres in a fairly robust notion of free will even if perhaps, on examination, we might agree that we do not lose much by accepting the compatibilist version. Here, asking us to revise our conventional attitudes in a manner somewhat different from Moore's – and revealing his true compatibilist stripes – Morse optimistically repeated Dennett's invitation to consider "'just what variety of free will is supposedly jeopardized'" by the reality of determinism. As long as we feel we are "'in control of ourselves, and not under the control of others'" – or feel we have "'the power to decide our courses of action and to decide them wisely, in the light of our expectations and desires'" – does determinism really threaten

[94] Morse, "Psychology, Determinism and Legal Responsibility," 44, 54.
[95] Morse, "Psychology, Determinism and Legal Responsibility," 59.
[96] Morse, "Psychology, Determinism and Legal Responsibility," 78, 80.
[97] Morse, "Psychology, Determinism and Legal Responsibility," 69.

anything we genuinely care about? Albeit admitting we will have to "'try hard,'" Morse, via Dennett, indeed urged

"we can imagine a being that listens to the voice of reason and yet is not exempted from the causal milieu. Yes, we can imagine a being whose every decision is caused by the interactions of features of its current state and features of its environment over which it has no control – and yet which is itself in control and not being controlled by that omnipresent and omnicausal environment."[98]

Together, Moore and Morse had, by the mid-1980s, become legal academia's leading opponents of causal theory and proponents of compatibilism between universal causation and moral and legal responsibility. Although their methods and underlying theory differed, they each contributed to the establishment of rational choice as a defensible alternative to *free* choice as the foundation for desert despite determinism. But still not all were convinced that our causal sympathies, or our sense of *contra*-causal free will, were revisable – or, indeed, were unnecessary to desert-bearing responsibility.

Lloyd Weinreb

Among those who remained unconvinced was Lloyd Weinreb, whose profoundly humanistic essay, "Desert, Punishment, and Criminal Responsibility,"[99] appeared the year after Moore's "Causation and the Excuses." Fully aware of the problems determinism posed for desert in light of our association of desert with free will – and, like Moore and Morse, giving weight to the "conventional pattern of our thought" – Weinreb nonetheless rejected the very premise that our causal intuitions could be separated from ideas of desert, either in fact or in theory. Only a "normative ontological perspective" that accounts for intractable contradictions can be relied on, as a practical matter, to help make sense of doctrinal problems concerning desert and punishment in the criminal law. Yet, he admitted, *even* such a perspective, does not – cannot – "put[] the matter beyond debate" or "make sense of the claim that 'what is, because it is, ought to be.'"[100] Weinreb's essay, then, was mainly an accounting for (rather than a resolution of) the familiar contradiction that Moore had declared should – and could – be remedied.

Weinreb fully accepted Moore's argument that (as Weinreb paraphrased it) "the basis of excuses cannot be simply that a causal explanation has been

---

[98] Morse, "Psychology, Determinism and Legal Responsibility," 69–70 (quoting Dennett, *Elbow Room*, 169, 172).

[99] Lloyd L. Weinreb, "Desert, Punishment, and Criminal Responsibility," *Law and Contemporary Problems*, vol. 49 (Summer 1986): 47–80. See also Lloyd L. Weinreb, *Natural Law and Justice* (Cambridge, MA: Harvard University Press, 1987), chap. 7, which addresses most of the overarching philosophical issues discussed in the article, but does not focus on them relative to criminal law.

[100] Weinreb, "Desert, Punishment, and Criminal Responsibility," 53.

found for the conduct in question," for that would make "all our conduct –
in principle – excusable and individual responsibility would be eliminated
altogether." Weinreb agreed as well that "our experience of ourselves and
others conclusively contradicts any such simple dichotomy" as that between
pure causal explanation, on the one hand, and meaningful responsibility, on
the other. But, he continued, "we disagree, however, about what to do next."
For, "pervasively," our general experience suggests that "a causal explanation
does count." That is, we *do* draw lines – and lines, moreover, that are intrinsically meaningful to us – on the basis of background causes leading up to
a particular act. Accordingly, the "price of validating our moral experience
in the manner that Moore chooses is, at least without further explanation,
a deep rupture in the framework of our general experience of the world."
Weinreb further expressed doubt about Moore's attempt to "unify our
excuses by reference only to practical reasoning capacities," observing that
the "apparent ground of unification, surely, is that some other, presumably
causal, process has taken over and wiped out those capacities."[101]

The fact that "causal explanation does count," Weinreb conceded, does
not mean that it can be shown just how or why it does, or even precisely what
it means. Rather, this very fact raises intractable contradictions. In describing
the ways in which we seem to attribute responsibility, Weinreb observed that
we generally require "that a person have exercised a capacity to direct his
actions for himself." Our conception of self-determination, moreover, seems
to imply an autonomous self. But our ineradicable habit of causal explanation reduces such a self to a mere abstraction; there is no logically identifiable line between where causation ends and the "self" begins. Still, we attach
desert to a concrete self, a "personal" self, and not to an abstraction. Weinreb
noted that "we reject immediately vicarious liability for the acts of another."
The result is an "autonomous self, a self-determining, individual entity – a
person in the ordinary sense, with concrete attributes and an actual history"
whose "non-autonomously acquired attributes are implicated in the actual
exercise of the capacity for self-determination that calls forth the attribution
of desert." And yet, "non-autonomous factors in a situation are just what
we regularly allow as excuses."[102] We can observe and catalogue our resulting feints and retreats and our adoption of a dual perspective – all mental
maneuvers that cannot resolve, Weinreb implied, the familiar contradiction
he had exposed in a strikingly sensitive and probing fashion. The contradiction might be observed, comprehended, accounted for, but it could not be
resolved either in the logical sense that legal analysis typically requires or in
the reassuring sense that our own minds seem restlessly to seek.

To illustrate the logical inconsistencies in our line-drawing between personal responsibility and harms thought to be caused, at least in part, by

---

[101] Weinreb, "Desert, Punishment, and Criminal Responsibility," 60 n. 27 (emphasis added).
[102] Weinreb, "Desert, Punishment, and Criminal Responsibility," 56–57.

circumstance, Weinreb focused on a range of problem cases that he claimed we commonly are inclined to think wrongly decided, at least on first glance. In felony murder, for example, a "discordant emphasis on normatively separable faults" is, he observed, "understood to be a response, 'human' but theoretically misconceived, to our grief and anger at the harm itself – an irrational 'striking-out' at someone without whose wrongful conduct the harm would not have occurred." Similarly, the "doctrines about provocation and defense of a third person likewise are presumed to reflect a strongly felt 'intuitive' response to the situation, rather than a reflective judgment." Weinreb posited that, although the results in these cases – in which we attach fault to acts that are related to the harm only by "but-for" causation – contradict our usual understanding of the necessary conditions for responsibility, the settled legal doctrines underlying such results are not simply mistakes. Rather, they reflect a "deep ontological assumption that human experience is contained within, or composes, a normative order" that assigns responsibility when harm is connected in certain ways with wrongdoing. Indeed, this assumption is a "structural element of human experience as we know it." And, here, his point: although this assumption may be most obvious in such troubling cases "because it is extended beyond its conventional limits[,] ... it is just as essential to our resolution of untroubling cases and, except as a matter of convention, no better validated in the latter than the former." [103]

"The heart of the matter," Weinreb insisted in explanation, "is the problem about desert," a problem with which, he thought, both Strawson and Moore ultimately failed to deal. "We know persons are (sometimes) free and responsible," but we cannot account for their freedom within a determined natural order. Thus the problem "concerns the conditions of freedom itself." Freedom requires desert in order to have normative significance, but desert "seems to require that a person's acts be *both* free *and* determinate": a person is not said to be morally responsible – and thus worthy of desert – unless he is free. But, "unless the conditions in which a person acts are fully determined according to his desert [and themselves determine his acts], they are arbitrary from a moral point of view." We typically avoid the problem by simply assuming the "reality of freedom, arbitrary or not," and tying desert to it. This approach, he noted, departs from the classical Greek view, in which "the deservedness of our natural condition, determinate or not, was assumed; and freedom was tied to it." But, either way, "both are indemonstrable, unanalyzable assumptions that rest finally on our recognition of human beings as morally responsible: persons rather than things." Ultimately we are inclined, Weinreb argued, to "think of desert as dependent on freedom" but to require, "from the ontological perspective," no more than normatively significant causal connections between harm and

---

[103] Weinreb, "Desert, Punishment, and Criminal Responsibility," 73.

certain kinds of acts. In practice the critical normative factor appears to be whether harm seems most related to "what we think of as a humanly (that is, self-determined) wrongful act" rather than a natural occurrence. Hence the troubling cases (where harm is a mere but-for result of an act that is wrongful for other reasons), which may conflict with our understanding of desert or justice from an ethical perspective, but, which from the onto-logical perspective, restore the normative order through punishment of the "responsible person." The liability that follows – whether in troubling cases or more straightforward ones – "is not more fortuitous than the combina-tion of personal factors that account for the conduct itself. (The victim of the felony had a bad heart; the felon had a bad upbringing.)." Thus, under some circumstances, the criminal law breaks with settled conventions about how far "out" liability will go "in order not to undermine the conventional basis of desert altogether, by calling into question whether a person can ever truly be said to have acted with freedom and responsibility despite the deter-minate conditions of his existence." Indeed, Weinreb added, "if, as Nozick says, desert does not have to go all the way down, why should it have to go all the way out?"[104] And finally, as Weinreb put it the following year in *Natural Law and Justice*: "As a fact about the human condition, free will and cause are compatible. Both are part of our experience, and we are not torn asunder. Rationally, they are not compatible. The fundamental opposi-tion is between experience and reason."[105]

Taking the point further, Weinreb asserted that there is "in principle no answer" to the question "How far down is desert." Thus one might sim-ply "conclude that a satisfactory general theory of criminal responsibility is unattainable." And so with theories of punishment: "Retribution fails from the utilitarian perspective because desert cannot be demonstrated and punishment for desert alone seems futile. Utilitarianism fails from the retributive perspective because desert cannot be dismissed and punishment for its utility alone seems unjust." Resolution lies in moving "a step further back." Desert is simply assumed, and it is unnecessary to justify punishment otherwise. This follows because "only if desert is fulfilled can we be fully regarded as persons – free, morally responsible, and deserving." Weinreb conceded once again that desert may thus be called "morally arbitrary" and that normative natural order thus may appear "unintelligible." But he reit-erated that "only our awareness of ourselves as persons, acting freely and morally responsible, concludes the issue to the contrary." Finally, in answer to the utilitarian's objections, Weinreb concluded:

The utilitarian avoids that response by driving a wedge between desert and pun-ishment and focusing his attack on the latter. But there is no space between them.

[104] Weinreb, "Desert, Punishment, and Criminal Responsibility," 74–77.
[105] Weinreb, *Natural Law and Justice*, footnote at p. 201.

Punishment or a failure to punish for utilitarian reasons defeats the conditions of desert on which freedom itself depends. It regards persons as things, fit for whatever purposes are acceptable. The utilitarian does not really believe that. If he did, he could not object to the retributive position, as he does, on moral grounds.[106]

Thus the "intuitions" about desert that Moore thought commonly attached to capacity and opportunity for practical reasoning Weinreb located much farther back, as it were, in "our awareness of ourselves as persons, acting freely and morally responsible." Our understanding of the world, moreover, forces us to conclude that something causes (or precludes) the very capacity to which Moore pointed; "a causal explanation does count." The reach of excuses in particular cases rests on conventions that respond to our need for maintaining the central understanding of ourselves as "persons" rather than "things." This fully internalistic account of criminal responsibility involved much thicker analysis of law-following-culture-and-human-nature than Fletcher provided. It was less rationalistic than Morris's assertion that humans' "capacity to reason and to choose on the basis of reasons" grounded their right to be treated as persons, and it explicitly departed from Strawson's relatively formal dual perspective, reducing all, instead, to a single point of view. Yet, by its very terms, it was (as with Strawson's account) sheer explanation – or empiricism – not justification at all, except in the transcendental (or, perhaps, simply natural, i.e., Strawsonian) sense that one is "justified" in being the being that one is, a perspective that for Weinreb seems to have grounded a natural-law-based idea of the oughtness of desert. Weinreb's point about foundations was that desert went "all the way down" in the only sense in which one *could* speak of desert, and that freedom attached to desert, at least in human psychology. And yet, Weinreb's deconstruction of desert stopped short, for although it allowed the inference that the distinction between persons and things was solely an artifact of human psychology, it seems not to have allowed that persons might be no more than a special sort of thing, or "things" with a (determined) human consciousness and a (determined) capacity for reasoning. Somehow, for Weinreb (as for us all), in the natural world (as well as in the human mind) a meaningful dualism between persons and things was determined to prevail.[107]

CHOICE, CAUSATION, AND CHARACTER – VICISSITUDES OF THE IDEA OF THE PERSON: 1985–1992

The important contributions of Fletcher, Moore, Morse, and Weinreb defined much of the terrain of American neo-retributivist legal-academic

---

[106] Weinreb, "Desert, Punishment, and Criminal Responsibility," 80.
[107] Weinreb offered a particularly succinct summary of these themes eight years later in *Oedipus at Fenway Park: What Rights Are and Why There Are Any* (Cambridge, MA:

commentary of the 1980s and beyond. The foundational influence of Herbert Hart is also evident throughout that commentary: capacity and opportunity for choice was invoked on all sides. Of course, Hart spoke for only an especially thin, or limiting, form of desert. His formulation was based on considerations of political liberty and the moral requirement of respect for the justified and settled expectations of individuals, and it worked within an overall justifying goal of utility. A neo-retributivism that grounded punishment in substantial part on desert demanded a good deal more from the notion of capacity and opportunity for choice; and the more it demanded, the greater the urgency to answer the determinist critique – or so it appears to have seemed to many scholars.

Fletcher accordingly endeavored to shore up the traditional reliance on voluntaristic choice with a character-based theory of responsibility. He worried about the problem of how one gets the character he or she possesses, but concluded one could test the presumption of personal responsibility only so far: law must remain in accord with the deepest understandings of the culture in which it was embedded. It is not clear, however, what he believed was gained by an emphasis on character, other than a corresponding (but not total) de-emphasis on voluntarism. But, then, much of Fletcher's account was couched in terms of only a curt and conclusory response to the determinist critique: (hard) determinism was simply not proven and currently not acceptable. Moore and Morse met the determinist critique head-on: they conceded (soft) determinism. For them, reasoned choice was fundamental to responsibility, and responsibility was compatible with determinism. Moore found Fletcher's relative denial of determinism puzzling. As of 1985, he had nothing to say about character theory – he would provide a sustained critique of that theory some five years later[108] – and instead rested his moral-realism-based case for capacity and opportunity for practical reasoning on near-universal intuitions and particular judgments about one's own behavior and the behavior of others. Moore employed Herbert Morris's appeal to human dignity as further evidence of the ultimate truth of these embedded notions despite determinism, rather than, like Fletcher, as a reason for taking a stand against the determinist perspective itself.

Moore and Morse have had an important impact upon American legal-academic criminal jurisprudence. In particular, the manner in which they conjoined choice theory and philosophical compatibilism conditioned the nature of much commentary of the long 1980s. By no means, however, did all who participated in the conversations of those years work within the general framework they presented. For Moore's and Morse's approaches also shared the inevitable vulnerabilities of compatibilism. By accepting universal

---

Harvard University Press, 1994), esp. chap. 2, "Human Responsibility" (further noted below in the Conclusion, n. 17).

[108] See, generally, Moore, "Choice, Character, and Excuse."

causation, and thus accepting that the capacity and opportunity for rationality are themselves ultimately caused, it was difficult for them to fully fend off the hard determinist argument that their theories of responsibility reduced to mere "as if" positions with regard to responsibility-bearing choice – that is, mere descriptions of human beliefs and behavior that could not truly justify desert, no matter how much we (are determined to) value them. Hence, perhaps, the attractiveness of Weinreb's refusal even to attempt to describe a coherent external justification for responsibility, instead embracing the contradictions in our ways of thinking about human motivation and essentially satisfying himself with the notion that it is valuable to value our personhood and the traits – including rationality and responsibility – that define it. Though his fully internal account was thus logically circular, it was self-consciously so, and there is some satisfaction in simply taking it on its own terms (and being unconcerned that any such satisfaction may nonetheless be determined). In this way, Weinreb proceeded beyond Fletcher, who similarly avoided any attempt to fully justify desert logically in the face of determinism, but did so on pragmatic grounds, effectively by accepting a descriptive accounting for choice-based desert that he believed inhered in the systems necessary for society to function.

Like Weinreb, other neo-retributivists, rather than taking up formal compatibilism, preferred some degree of agnosticism and imprecision in part in order to take more nuanced – and often more ambiguous – views of responsibility attribution. These scholars, including Sanford Kadish and Joshua Dressler, were not unconcerned with determinism. But their formulations avoided the formal compatibilists' counterintuitive reliance on conventional morality alongside an explicit rejection of free will. I have broadly associated them with a second dominant strain of neo-retributivist, loosely compatibilist thought that sacrificed a certain philosophical purity in attempts to root blame more directly in concepts of personhood, political liberty – or, indeed, even of "free will." Of course others, such as Peter Arenella, attempted to more thoroughly sidestep the pitfalls of ascribing blameworthy choice despite the (potential) lack of free will, by recasting responsibility as an aspect of character, rather than of choice per se. Each approach might be said to have provided a satisfying picture of the roots of responsibility on some levels, while providing less clarity on others. One result was that, especially during the period 1985–1992, one significant feature of legal-academic writing was an unfolding of ideas that revealed frustration and puzzlement, unsettlement alongside the expression of settled convictions.

Sanford Kadish

By the 1980s, Sanford Kadish's views on criminal responsibility more clearly went beyond a sheer Hartian moral-constraint view to a more robust version of negative retributivism.[109] "The Decline of Innocence" (1968) had reflected Kadish's concerns about a totalizing criminalization – for that is how society was bound to view the policy of a state that operated along purely treat-mentist lines, eschewing conventional notions of condemnable behavior.[110] Political liberty concerns loomed large in the 1968 essay, yet something more than Hart's moral limits upon utilitarian punishment appeared as well. Kadish implied a role for deserved punishment, a hint of the neo-Kantian idea announced in the "Introduction" to *Doing Justice*. There, you will recall, Gaylin and Rothman had declared: "Certain things are simply wrong and ought to be punished. And this we do believe."[111] Kadish invoked the *popular* view to that effect even as he stated his own agnosticism regarding the concept of free will that, it was generally assumed, commonly underlay this position. Of course Kadish mainly adhered, vis-à-vis punishment, to the rehabilitational ideal. But he nonetheless accepted punishment-viewed-in-terms-of-condemnation – the popular view – and even marshaled that idea against the threat of an all-powerful state, while never justifying doing so in purely utilitarian terms.

In the two decades after his 1968 essay, Kadish continued to emphasize a socially derived – as opposed to factually free-will-based – moral element in criminal responsibility. In 1976 he set forth a rights-based theory of jus-tification and, correlatively, of blameworthiness.[112] And four years later, in an imagined "Dialogue" with a law student who supposes that the first-year course in Criminal Law is a waste of time, Kadish invoked a concept of "personal responsibility" that, he confirmed, "is no artificial construct of the criminal law." To the contrary, it "is deeply rooted in our moral sense of fitness that punishment entails blame and that, therefore, punishment may not justly be imposed where the person is not blameworthy." The "notion of the injustice of blame when the person could not have done otherwise is central."[113]

[109] And see Sanford H. Kadish, "The Criminal Law and the Luck of the Draw," *JCLC*, vol. 84 (1994): 679–702, wherein, in 1994, Kadish confirmed his invocation of "negative retributivism" (698), albeit in a framework that appears to retreat somewhat from his 1980s agnostic compatibilism to a most holistic agnosticism. I discuss further the 1994 article in Chapter 9.
[110] Sanford H. Kadish, "The Decline of Innocence," essay 5 in *Blame and Punishment: Essays in the Criminal Law* (New York: Macmillan, 1987) (originally published in *Cambridge Law Journal*, vol. 26 [1968]: 273–90), 75–79 (see my prior discussion of Kadish in Chapter 7).
[111] Willard Gaylin and David J. Rothman, "Introduction," in Andrew von Hirsch, *Doing Justice: The Choice of Punishments* (Report of the Committee for the Study of Incarceration) (New York: Hill and Wang, 1976), xxxix.
[112] Sanford Kadish, "Respect for Life and Regard for Rights in the Criminal Law," essay 7 in *Blame and Punishment* (originally published in *California Law Review*, vol. 64 [1976]: 871–901).
[113] Sanford Kadish, "Why Substantive Criminal Law – A Dialogue," essay 1 in *Blame and Punishment*, 12–13 (originally published in *Cleveland-Marshall Law Review*, vol. 29 [1980]: 1–15).

For Kadish, what did "could not have done otherwise" entail? In "Complicity, Cause and Blame" (1985), he appeared to endorse a view of the law that straddled compatibilism and libertarianism without fully committing himself to philosophical justification of compatibilism. Significantly, he initially noted the law's essentially social and psychological foundations, but maintained that "we need not take a position on whether the concepts presupposed by the criminal law are, in the final analysis true."[114] I quote Kadish at length:

The notion of responsibility that underlies the concept of blame is an elusive one. Without attending to a variety of subtle complications that inhere in the concept, or arguing any particular philosophical position, we may say generally that blame imports the notion of choice. We perceive human actions as differing from other events in the world. Things happen and events occur.... Human actions stand on an entirely different footing. While man is total subject under the laws of the natural world, he is total sovereign over his own actions. Except in special circumstances, he possesses volition through which he is free to choose his actions. He may be influenced in his choices, but influences do not work like wind upon a straw; rather they are considerations on the basis of which he chooses to act. He may also be the object of influence in the larger sense that he is the product of the forces that have shaped him. But his actions are his and his alone, not those of his genes or his rearing, because if he had so desired he could have chosen to do otherwise. This is the perception that underlies the conception of responsibility which, in turn, is central to the conception of blame. ...

The justification for this view of human action is the subject of the controversy over free will and determinism. The incompatibilists argue that this view of human action requires a conception of the will as uncaused – a singular exception to an otherwise determinate world. On the other hand, some compatibilists argue that this view of responsibility may adequately rest on our certain knowledge that we can do as we choose so long as no physical force compels our action. Is freedom of will grounded in reality, or is it an illusory by-product of our prejudices and ignorance? Is it enough that it is rooted in our subjective experience of ourselves not as straws in the wind, but as agents with our own identities who define and act to achieve our own purposes? Since my task is to identify and trace the effect of this perception in legal doctrine, I need not enter this controversy.[115]

The evident ambiguities in Kadish's view survived to plague his well-known article of two years later, "Excusing Crime." By then, however, Kadish gave way – at least to some considerable extent – to Moore, whose 1985 "Causation and the Excuses" he cited at several points.[116] In "Excusing Crime," Kadish "propose[d] to examine the rationale and functioning of

[114] Sanford Kadish, "Complicity, Cause and Blame," essay 8 in *Blame and Punishment*, 137 (originally published in *California Law Review*, vol. 73 [1985]: 323–410).
[115] Kadish, "Complicity, Cause and Blame," 140–41.
[116] Sanford Kadish, "Excusing Crime," essay 6 in *Blame and Punishment* (also published in *California Law Review*, vol. 75 [1987]: 257–89), 81, n. 1, 99, n. 62, 103, n. 80.

excuses in the legal system and to consider how far the law does and should follow ordinary moral conceptions in its definition of excusing conditions."[117] But his thinking remained elusive, as he primarily appealed to cultural norms rather than set forth a theory regarding the nature of human freedom. "Blame and punishment," he asserted, "give expression to the concept of personal responsibility, which is a central feature of our moral culture."[118] In an accompanying footnote, however, he cited "The Decline of Innocence" and clarified that "of course" he did not "embrace the retributive view that responsibility for law violation itself requires punishment"; rather, "responsibility is necessary, but not sufficient for punishment."[119] He did not tell us what else is required. And although he might have viewed retributivist goals primarily as being in the nature of a side-constraint upon consequentialism – as not requiring being acted upon with regard to punishment in any particular case – he nonetheless appeared to view the retributivist element, when acted upon, as having legitimate force of its own.

What appears to be a shift in Kadish's approach to the legal idea of criminal responsibility came in a discussion of "irresponsibility," where Kadish first addressed the "practical" considerations that explain why insanity is an excuse under the criminal law "only if it is the result of a mental disease." Kadish noted matters of proof and incentive (mere personal incapacity not triggered by mental disease or defect would provide "less incentive" for "potential violators to make every effort to comply").[120] But this, Kadish suggested, was "not the heart of the matter." Now he concluded:

Neither in moral judgments nor in legal ones do we ask of a person who wrongs another whether he could have helped choosing to do so. Being responsible for our characters means that we are responsible for our choices *even if in some sense they have their causes like any other events in the world.*[121]

Kadish's insertion of the idea of responsibility for character perhaps reflected acceptance of the view that Moore had taken in seeking to bring resolution to the two unresolved lines of argument in Fletcher's *Rethinking Criminal Law*. In any case, despite the cautious language ("even if in some sense"), Kadish appeared to take a step beyond the agnosticism that characterized his 1985 essay; the influence of Moore, whose 1984 book and earlier articles Kadish had not cited in 1985, was now unmistakable.

But how far had Kadish drifted toward Moore's compatibilism, and away from a compatibilism that rested on dual (natural and human) understandings of causation, in his attempt to state the meaning of the *law* (against the background of his own self-professed agnosticism)? The evidence

---

[117] Kadish, "Excusing Crime," 81.
[118] Kadish, "Excusing Crime," 88.
[119] Kadish, "Excusing Crime," 88 n. 20.
[120] Kadish, "Excusing Crime," 98.
[121] Kadish, "Excusing Crime," 99 (emphasis added).

remains unclear, but Kadish appears to have adopted the essence of Moore's choice-based theory and yet assimilated it to the essence of his own earlier-expressed agnosticism. Indeed, Kadish unself-consciously implied what Weinreb had made explicit, that choice theory inevitably reduced to a form of causal theory – a form that maintained the baseline of causation, but simply declared that the threshold for exculpatory causation had not been met when the conditions of rational choice were present. Unlike Weinreb, however, Kadish did not trace the element of causal theory that pervaded one's everyday thought.

Kadish's adoption of a somewhat agnostic compatibilism is evident in his response to arguments that the law should adopt the "rotten social background" (RSB) defense associated with Judge Bazelon,[122] and recently revived in UCLA Law Professor Richard Delgado's well-known 1985 article, "'Rotten Social Background': Should the Criminal Law Recognize a Defense of Severe Environmental Deprivation?"[123] Delgado sought to test the viability of the defense, which had been debated by Bazelon and Morse in 1976. This debate had been continued by others, Delgado observed, but without "careful review of the social science literature on environmental crimogenesis."[124] Delgado first located the baseline for criminal responsibility in the "voluntary choice model as formulated by [Herbert] Hart," which, he said, "is widely accepted as the principle of justice limiting imposition of punishment." Significantly, however, Delgado also seemed to assume a causal theory of excuse and referred, without caveats, to "free choice" or "free will" as the basis of responsibility. Voluntary choice was the salient factor, he further asserted, because "a criminal act that is external to and dissociated from the individual tells us nothing about the individual's character; in Aristotle's words, were it not for such externalities, the actor 'would not choose any such act in itself.'"[125] Delgado concluded that, under the law's existing rubric, the multiple external forces to which those who live in extreme poverty are subjected – such as constant stress, violence, malnutrition, and lack of economic and educational opportunities – should often be said to have caused involuntary behavior or a lack of free choice. The RSB defendant could thus arguably fit his or her claim into typical excuse categories given that extreme poverty caused, for example, involuntary rage, deprivation of knowledge of majority norms effectively resulting in mistakes of law, and insanity-like physiological conditions leading to non-culpable

[122] *United States v. Alexander*, 471 F.2d 923, 957–65 (D.C. Cir. 1973) (Bazelon, C.J., dissenting); David L. Bazelon, "The Morality of the Criminal Law," *Southern California Law Review*, vol. 49 (1976): 385–405, 395.

[123] Richard Delgado, "'Rotten Social Background': Should the Criminal Law Recognize a Defense of Severe Environmental Deprivation?", *Law and Inequality*, vol. 3 (1985): 9–90.

[124] Delgado, "'Rotten Social Background,'" 11–12.

[125] Delgado, "'Rotten Social Background,'" 16–17, and see 55 ("blame is inappropriate when a defendant's criminal behavior is caused by extrinsic factors beyond his or her control").

lack of self-control.[126] But RSB could also function as a special defense more generally, given the various ways that extreme poverty had been shown to result in conditions that, in a given case, precluded voluntary behavior as that behavior is commonly understood.[127]

Delgado then proceeded to a number of other, justice-based premises that could be used either to support recognition of an RSB defense within the existing law of excuses or, potentially, as freestanding reasons to exculpate a range of socially deprived defendants. Key among these premises was his discussion of the theory underlying retributive punishment. Here he drew on Herbert Morris who, in Delgado's words, had established that "from the society's perspective, the wrongdoer has taken unfair advantage of the agreed-upon sharing of benefits and burdens"; "from the criminal's perspective, punishment is fitting because it recognizes his or her autonomy," and so reflects a "right to be punished," an idea that Delgado traced to Kant, Hegel, and Marx,[128] and associated with Morris's argument that the right to be punished "derives from a fundamental right to be treated as a person."[129] Accepting this justification for punishment, Delgado urged (alongside Jeffrie Murphy) that liability to criminal punishment depended on background conditions that allowed the actor to benefit from social life; legal condemnation was unjust if applied to one who broke the law while possessing (in effect) the capacity and opportunity for practical reasoning, but who never had access to the benefits of social life. Indeed, "more traditional retributivist theories – not based on the notion of benefits and burdens – could simply punish the RSB defendant for breaking the law, whether or not the defendant benefits from social life at all. Such a theory of punishment amounts to little more than the assertion of force."[130]

Kadish's response in "Excusing Crime" focused on the general arguments that RSB conditions might, themselves, constitute a defense – that is, he did not address isolated claims that RSB conditions cause mental or physiological disturbances that satisfy preexisting definitions of legal insanity.[131] Kadish argued that, although "social deprivation may well establish a credible explanation of how the defendant has come to have the character he has,"

it does not establish a moral excuse any more than a legal one, for there is a difference between explaining a person's wrongful behavior and explaining it away.

---

[126] Delgado, "'Rotten Social Background,'" 85–89.
[127] Delgado, "'Rotten Social Background,'" 63–68.
[128] Delgado drew much of this point from John Harris, "The Marxist Conception of Violence," *Philosophy and Public Affairs*, vol. 3 (1974): 192–220.
[129] Delgado "'Rotten Social Background,'" 68–69 and n. 385.
[130] Delgado, "'Rotten Social Background,'" 70–71 n. 397.
[131] Kadish did acknowledge, however, "the strongest case for the social deprivation defense," which Delgado indeed had raised: "that a state which fosters or tolerates such deprivation

Explanations are not excuses if they merely explain how the defendant came to have the character of someone who could do such a thing. If it were otherwise, there would be no basis for moral responsibility in any case where we knew enough about a person to understand him. And that would mean every case, because ignorance about a person could hardly stand as a justification for blaming him [citing Moore, "Causation and the Excuses"].

The reason the argument fails to make out a moral excuse, as insanity does, is that it fails to establish the breakdown of rationality and judgment that is incompatible with moral agency. It may be conceded that cultural deprivation *contributed to* making the defendant what he is (though, of course, only some so brought up end up committing crimes [here, citing Morse, "Twilight of Welfare Criminology" (1976)]). He is a person with the wrong values and inclinations, not a human being whose powers of judgment and rational actions have been so destroyed that he must be dealt with like an infant, a machine, or an animal. Those who propose this defense are plainly moved by compassion for the downtrodden, to whom, however, it is nonetheless an insult [again citing Morse, who drew upon Morris].[132]

Here Kadish appeared to reject causal theory in favor of a Moorean insistence upon the salience of rational choice – of "powers of judgment and rational actions." True causal theory, Moore had pointed out, aimed at establishing that one who was caused to commit a prohibited act should, on that basis alone, be excused from liability for that act – that because he was subject to causal forces he was not free enough to retain his own independent power of causation. This, it appears, is something close to the line Kadish took in 1985 when he purported merely to identify the *law's* idea of responsibility, and that is indeed the way in which the law had conventionally been understood. Moore sought to sever responsibility from causation. He insisted that we do (and ought to) hold persons responsible for acts we *know are caused* when we believe they acted under conditions of capacity and opportunity for practical reasoning. He recognized that we often (wrongly) associate such acts with non-caused (self-originated) behavior. But he insisted that our deep intuitions tell us that such acts, though caused, are nonetheless in and of themselves responsibility-bearing. It is not clear that Kadish ever fully accepted this way of thinking about the law. Kadish drew on Moore's rubric, but never wholeheartedly endorsed the totality of Moore's reasoning. Tellingly, Kadish never explicitly employed Moore's ultimate justification – that basing responsibility *tout court* upon possession of the critical capacity conditions accords with the great mass of our intuitions. Kadish's failure to

---

forfeits its right to condemn its victims." "But," said Kadish, "the question 'Who has the legitimate authority to judge and punish?' is a different question from 'Who should be blamed for individual crimes?' The social deprivation defense may be a fair vehicle for accusing the society responsible for the deprivation. But it is not a ground for excusing the deprived defendant, because by itself it fails to establish the defendant's lack of responsibility" ("Excusing Crime," 103).
[132] Kadish, "Excusing Crime," 103 (emphasis added).

adopt a formal explanatory theory for his practical compatibilism resulted in the implication that, on some level, he resisted claims for the truth-value of a formal compatibilism rooted in commonly held intuitions. He left open the possibility that Weinreb, ultimately, was correct: humans systematically make responsibility judgments in terms of an ineffably causal way of understanding themselves, others, and the world about them.[133]

Joshua Dressler

It was becoming increasingly common in jurisprudence, as in academic philosophy generally, to accept compatibilism. But some loosely compatibilist scholars, although sensitive both to the determinist critique and the attractions of formal compatibilism, remained unpersuaded by strict rational-choice-based approaches. Where some, such as Kadish, offered ultimately ambiguous accounts rooted in rational choice (alongside other values the law was thought to uphold), others conceded agnosticism regarding the reality of free will and relied heavily not on the capacity and opportunity for practical reasoning, but on the universal intuition of freedom to choose. The latter move has sometimes taken the form of a self-conscious recognition of the infirmities of all possible positions and an endorsement of "free choice" as the best of all possible (if imperfect) ways of conceiving of responsibility. Joshua Dressler has stated this position well. His 1988 article, "Reflections on the Excusing of Wrongdoers: Moral Theory, the New Excuses and the Model Penal Code,"[134] navigated between the perspectives of Moore and Weinreb. It reflects the instability of criminal jurisprudence at a particular moment in time, and perhaps reflects, too, the sometime ambiguities and ambivalences of Dressler's erstwhile mentor, Kadish. Like Kadish, Dressler drifted in the direction of a Moorean compatibilism without ever entirely escaping the gravitational pull of causal theory. In Dressler's case, however, this had less to do with the logic of causal preconditions for the status of practical reasoning and more to do with the attractions of the metaphysical notion of "free choice." Dressler was interested primarily in demonstrating that the Model Penal Code and the actual law of excuses rested on a species of the idea of "free choice," a demonstration that hovered between declaring that determinism is irrelevant in principle and observing that, although a relevant determinism is impossible to disprove, it should be treated as false in practice.

But let us back up a moment and consider Dressler's route, over nearly a decade, to the position he espoused in 1988 in the wake of the recent contributions by Moore and Weinreb. Writing in 1979, in response to Delgado's

---

[133] And, indeed, in 1994 Kadish stepped through the door he had thus left open. See my comments on Kadish's article "The Criminal Law and the Luck of the Draw" in Chapter 9.

[134] Joshua Dressler, "Reflections on the Excusing of Wrong-Doers: Moral Theory, the New Excuses and the Model Penal Code," *Rutgers Law Journal*, vol. 19 (1988): 671–716.

recommendation that the law adopt a "brainwashing defense"[135] (that is, a defense based upon "coercive persuasion"), Dressler argued that such a move would play havoc with the law's fundamental premise of free will.[136] On one hand, Dressler, himself, shared more than a little skepticism about this premise. On the other, he recognized the critical role free will played in current legal doctrine. Thus, Delgado's recommendation (as Dressler understood it[137]) either went "too far or not far enough": "Either we reject [Delgado's brainwashing] defense," said Dressler, "or we revolutionize the criminal law." The latter was not unthinkable. Indeed, Dressler expressly said of himself: "The present author is a philosophical determinist. He would therefore, probably, although not certainly, choose the path of revolutionizing the law." But he would not advocate revolution on the present occasion. Rather, the purpose of his reply to Delgado was "more modest":

> to demonstrate that the question Delgado asks ... is an incorrect inquiry. Instead, society must ask a more difficult question: whether to reject entirely the premise of free will and the criminal law doctrines based on it, or leave unchanged the current exculpatory concepts of the criminal law.[138]

Dressler stressed that, given the law's premise of free will, the excuses were currently structured in such a way that the "morally relevant factor is choice reduction, not exposure to 'abnormal influences.'"[139] And his approach to "choice reduction" was, throughout, consistent with causal theory – as was still common enough in the legal-academic conventions of the day.

Two years later, in 1981, Dressler continued to mediate between his own professed determinist tendencies and an apparent acceptance of responsibility premised on (relatively free) choice by again purporting mainly to describe the *law's* existing perspective. He drew upon Herbert Morris in his discussion of the law's premise that, as Dressler put it, "we have free will. We are not programmed to act as we do." He also adopted Morris's terms in

---

[135] Richard Delgado, "Ascription of Criminal States of Mind: Toward a Defense Theory for the Coercively Persuaded ('Brainwashed') Defendant," *Minnesota Law Review*, vol. 63 (1978): 1–33.

[136] Joshua Dressler, "Professor Delgado's 'Brainwashing' Defense: Courting a Determinist Legal System," *Minnesota Law Review*, vol. 63 (1979): 334–60.

[137] In a reply to Dressler, Delgado asserted that his test was narrower than Dressler had understood, stating that "Dressler's argument constitutes a convincing refutation – but not of my position." Delgado explained that his test distinguished those whose "behavioral and mentational patterns have been forcibly altered through terror, confinement, physical and psychological debilitation, and assaults on the self" and all others. "Specifically excluded [are] criminal acts resulting from ordinary solicitation, voluntary membership in a criminal subculture, *whole-life conditioning*, or simply giving in to temptation." Richard Delgado, "A Response to Professor Dressler," *Minnesota Law Review*, vol. 63 (1979): 361–66, 361 (emphasis added).

[138] Dressler, "Delgado's 'Brainwashing' Defense," 337 and n. 15.

[139] Dressler, "Delgado's 'Brainwashing' Defense," 358.

his own explication of Anglo-American law's reflection of the fact that "we tenaciously hold to the ethical view that we, as human beings, are unique entities" whose difference from "other animals" and "inanimate objects" results in a view of "human rights" that "may be identified in the law as the 'principle of personhood.'"¹⁴⁰ Dressler noted that the "principle of personhood and the resultant concept of distributive justice cannot stand if the initial premise that we differ from animals and objects is wrong" – that is, "if the determinists are correct." For "theologians, philosophers, and scientists," this remained a matter of debate, but not for the law: "It conclusively rejects determinism." The law does so, however, not necessarily because it insists we are in fact free. That might once have been the case, but now some view the rejection of determinism as "an acceptable legal fiction," for we recognize that determinism would spell the end of "'the principles that make our free society possible.'"¹⁴¹ Dressler cited Packer's famous passage regarding free will as a "value preference" for his own conclusion that "we [i.e., the law] accept the premise that humans possess autonomy because that is what we want to believe."¹⁴²

Was free will, then, merely the law's own "acceptable legal fiction" for Dressler, or was it coming to be yet more when, in 1984, Dressler contested Morse's critique of the doctrine of diminished capacity?¹⁴³ On the one hand, Dressler observed: "like Professor Morse, I value a legal system that treats the criminal actor with dignity by emphasizing the criminal's free will."¹⁴⁴

¹⁴⁰ Joshua Dressler, "Substantive Criminal Law through the Looking Glass of *Rummel v. Estelle*: Proportionality and Justice as Endangered Doctrines," *Southwestern Law Journal*, vol. 34 (1981): 1063–130, 1073.
¹⁴¹ Dressler, "Substantive Criminal Law," 1074–75 (quoting Melvin Nord, "The Mental Element in Crime," *University of Detroit Law Journal*, vol. 37 [1960]: 698).
¹⁴² Dressler, "Substantive Criminal Law," 1075.
¹⁴³ In "Reaffirming the Moral Legitimacy of the Doctrine of Diminished Capacity: A Brief Reply to Professor Morse," *JCLC*, vol. 75 (1984): 953–62, Dressler took issue with Morse's objections, in "Undiminished Confusion," to any defense involving diminished capacity – that is defenses involving provocation or less than "substantial" mental/emotional impairments that mitigate responsibility but are not full defenses leading to acquittal. Their debate can be characterized as a disagreement about what disposition of offenders best vindicates the notion of personal dignity that both scholars concluded must figure into responsibility judgments and the law of excuses. Where Morse preferred a bright-line test that equalizes moral responsibility for harm among all except the truly impaired, Dressler argued that personal dignity is best affirmed by recognizing the partial culpability of one whose will was relatively constrained – for, said Dressler: "If all people, as a species, possess free will, not all people command an equal degree of free will" ("Reply to Morse," 959). Morse would later change his stance, advocating for a generic partial responsibility excuse as "a moral imperative for a just criminal law that attempts never to punish defendants more than they deserve," in "Diminished Rationality, Diminished Responsibility," *Ohio State Journal of Criminal Law*, vol. 1 (2003): 289–308, 290.
¹⁴⁴ Dressler, "Reply to Morse," 957 and n. 35. Here he cited his own 1981 article, in which he had remained ambiguous about whether he merely explicated the law's view, and not necessarily his own.

Dressler now positively endorsed the principles of criminal responsibility that he had come to understand in Morris's terms. The personhood principle and the conferral of dignity perhaps argued against a revolution in our thinking about criminal law in the face of the arguments of the determinists. There was, on the other hand, little indication that Dressler had as yet reacted to recent compatibilist responses to the determinist critique. He did not cite Moore's 1984 book (or the articles that preceded it); as for Morse's diminished capacity article, it did not articulate fully the distinction between causal theory and strict rational choice theory that Morse set forth with greater clarity the following year. Four years later, however, in his 1988 article – his first major work on excuse theory – Dressler did indeed react to the new departures of the early to mid-1980s; his attempt to integrate them with his own evolving enactment of faith in law's underlying premise produced an instructive document of neo-retributivism's coming-of-age.

In "Reflections on Excusing Wrongdoers," Dressler asserted that his argument "assumes that hard determinism, with its conclusion that we must excuse all wrongdoers or develop a criminal justice system not based on concepts of desert, is wrong."[145] Still, although Dressler, the erstwhile professed "philosophical determinist" and proponent of "as if" free will, now accepted Moore's critique of causal theory[146] and rejected character-based theories of responsibility, in part because they were vulnerable to a similar reductio,[147] he seems not to have identified his own version of "free choice" theory with "soft-determinism" or "compatibilism." Perhaps Dressler meant only to reject any form of determinism that wasn't compatible with choice theory, but it is not clear that he imagined an acceptable form of determinism existed. Claiming that he refused to take sides, he noted the arguments of hard determinists against the conventional arguments of "'compatibilists' or 'soft' determinists," and asserted that he did "not intend to enter the debate." He stood aside, he informed readers, because

no matter how logically compelling the case for determinism may seem, and although people do not generally deny the determinist teachings of modern science, we also intuitively *feel* that we ordinarily have freedom of choice, and we develop our rules of criminal responsibility on the basis of this feeling. To borrow from Professor Weinreb's … description of the autonomous will being pushed into a corner[,] … no matter how far the human will *is* pushed into a corner, our faith in human nature always wins out. Determinists can tell us, of course, that these feelings are themselves determined (as are, of course, the determinists' own beliefs), and that a view of human will that rejects logic and science for intuitions is suspect. Ultimately, however, if determinism is correct, there is no independent way to determine its accuracy, since we are determined to believe whatever it is we believe.[148]

---

[145] Dressler, "Reflections," 688 n. 91.
[146] Dressler, "Reflections," 686–87.
[147] Dressler, "Reflections," 695–96.
[148] Dressler, "Reflections," 688 n. 91.

This last argument against the determinist critique, apparently drawn from a 1969 article by Nathaniel Branden,[149] represents, so far as I can tell, a rare departure among late-twentieth-century legal scholars. Taken to its logical conclusion (as applied by Dressler), it would seem to counsel a pragmatic rejection of the application of any theory of causation to the workings of the human mind – it would seem to advise, *faute de mieux*, suspension of disbelief in Kant's conception of the "noumenal sphere." Perhaps this is what Dressler had in mind; although much of his article seems to concede the truth of Moore's recognition of universal causation, much also appears (contra Moore's view) to distinguish law from other realms of moral inquiry – that is, to search for a moral/legal conception of responsibility in a particular realm of human activity that, reason tells us, cannot be governed by our understanding of scientific fact.

After rejecting causal and character-based theories, Dressler offered a new formulation that imposed responsibility when an actor's "choice" to violate the law was "free" in the sense that the actor had "substantial capacity and fair opportunity to: (1) understand the pertinent facts relating to his conduct; (2) appreciate that his conduct violates society's moral or legal norms; and (3) conform his conduct to the law."[150] The MPC (and, especially, the control prong of the section on responsibility) thus was, at least in Dressler's mind, close to the ideal.[151] Significantly, the new theory also bore obvious similarity to Moore's; apparently, the practical difference between accepting determinism as compatible with responsibility and rejecting determinism solely on grounds of its unverifiability (and of our inability consciously to adhere to it) need not, it turned out, be very great. Indeed, however Dressler himself viewed the matter, it might be said that he had actually adopted a compatibilist notion of freedom.

Yet there were important differences from Moore that underlay Dressler's reasoning. Dressler's agnosticism, however fragile, allowed him to focus on capacity and opportunity for "*free choice*," whereas Moore stressed capacity and opportunity for "*practical reasoning*," a mental process that does not conjure up so directly the background idea of true free will. Critically, Dressler translated this language of "free choice" into "the personhood principle." This principle fits our ineradicable concept of blame, he asserted (in line with Kadish), which "is predicated on our view of persons as autonomous agents, whose 'actions stand on an entirely different footing' from other

---

[149] Nathanial Branden, "Free Will, Moral Responsibility and the Law," *Southern California Law Review*, vol. 42 (1969): 264–92 (cited by Dressler, "Reflections," at 688, n. 91). Ted Honderich discussed this point in his 1969 book *Punishment: The Supposed Justifications*. For some doubts about whether determinism is any more threatening than is indeterminism to "our attitude to ourselves as knowers," see Galen Strawson, "Unimportance of Determinism," 12–13.

[150] Dressler, "Reflections," 701.

[151] Dressler, "Reflections," 703.

events in the universe."[152] Dressler noted that this concept of a "person" by its very nature "assumes the inaccuracy of 'hard determinism.'"[153] Moreover, he seems to have deduced that it also did not require the compatibilism of "soft determinism," for it assumes "the capacity and fair opportunity to function in a uniquely human way, *i.e.*, freely to choose whether to violate the moral/legal norms of society."[154] His "personhood principle," in other words, dovetailed with Weinreb's theory; Dressler adopted an internalistic *human* conception of the difference between "persons" and "things." This was a conception that, for all we know, humans might have been determined to hold, but that was in any event so natural and inescapable that it required recognition. Whereas Moore stressed universal intuitions and judgments in particular cases that led one to the conclusion that humans in fact possessed a responsibility-bearing power of choice (despite universal causation), Dressler stressed an internal consciousness of freedom that in and of itself grounded human responsibility (despite universal causation).

Although Dressler's somewhat opaque argument did not alter the more traditional parameters of twentieth century legal debate regarding the free will problem, his contribution was nonetheless of great interest. The article was, all in all, an act of inspired quasi-Kantian mediation of those who had gone immediately before. He attempted to bridge the causation-based idea of responsibility that Weinreb claimed is inescapable and the status-or activity-based idea of practical reasoning that Moore claimed accounts for the idea of responsibility. Dressler's derivation of "free-choice"-based responsibility focused on an activity, or status (capacity for reasoned choice), to which the law pays close attention even as that law (including, as we have seen, the MPC) is silent about the underlying implication – the background idea. In confronting the silence, one might recognize, as Moore had insisted, that there must be causes that explain the existence of that activity. But, as Weinreb had countered, one equally might acknowledge that the strong common association of that activity with the "person" demands attention of a distinctive, non-causal sort. Although Dressler did not directly confront the difference between Weinreb and Moore, his approach suggests that he largely agreed with Weinreb: our intuition that choosing/practical reasoning grounds responsibility is (pace Moore) related to our not fully accepting universal causation; yet we intuit the inability to conform to the law – the inability in a particular instance freely to choose – as the result of a background cause that "determined" the actor. For Weinreb the law's silence about the source of a responsibility-bearing status had worked to conceal this actual, inevitable, and pervasive contradiction, which amounted – in law as in our lives – to selective, essentially illogical recognition of causation.

[152] Dressler, "Reflections," 701 (quoting Kadish, "Complicity, Cause and Blame," 330).
[153] Dressler, "Reflections," 701 n. 137.
[154] Dressler, "Reflections," 701.

Dressler's acceptance of some of Weinreb's premises thus suggests a similar, implicit point about his own attempt to escape causal theory: contradictory, and selective although it may be, causal theory could in fact mirror the very activity-based theory that Dressler – and perhaps other "free choice" theorists who outwardly rejected causal theory – employed to bootstrap the concept of responsibility.

Peter Arenella

Some late-in-century theorists preferred an end run to a bootstrap. Especially in the 1980s and beyond, a significant number of American legal scholars sought to sidestep the problem of "choice" through an embrace of one or another form of "character theory." The question to be asked was what was the relationship between the defendant's act and his character, motivation, or disposition; this, rather than an assessment solely of whether the defendant had possessed the capacity and opportunity for choice, was key to whether he or she was legally responsible.[155] The offender was responsible if his or her act raised the inference that it reflected or expressed an overall bad character or a settled inclination to violate the law; or, in another version, if the act was "caused" by or attributable to the offender's bad character.[156] As George Vuoso put it: "What an actor does is relevant to a moral evaluation of him only to the extent that it reflects on the sort of person he is."[157] At home in utilitarianism (the idea descended from David Hume to Richard Brandt), this approach to responsibility was increasingly taken up by neo-retributivists of the long 1980s as well. Fletcher, you will recall, placed weight upon it in his defense of retributivism, though he did not employ it to fully displace a more traditional voluntarism.

In its furthest-reaching versions, character theory embraced a language that was implicitly freighted with free-will imagery yet stood apart as a quasi-determinist or, as with Vuoso, fully determinist account of human behavior. Its strongest critics included Dressler, who focused on the problem of what "causes" one's character and who relegated character to mere "corroborating evidence,"[158] and Moore, whose classic attempt at deconstruction of the idea in 1990 sought to demonstrate that it in fact reduced

---

[155] For a useful discussion of the distinction between choice and character theories, see Claire Finkelstein, "Excuses and Dispositions in Criminal Law," *Buffalo Criminal Law Review*, vol. 6 (2002): 317–60, 321–27.

[156] See, e.g., Benjamin B. Sendor, "The Relevance of Conduct and Character to Guilt and Punishment," *Notre Dame Journal of Law, Ethics and Public Policy*, vol. 10 (1996): 99–136, esp. 102–03.

[157] George Vuoso, "Background, Responsibility, and Excuse," *Yale Law Journal*, vol. 96 (1987): 1661–86, 1673. See also Moore, "Choice, Character and Excuse," for discussion of leading character theorists and their views.

[158] Dressler, "Reflections," 695.

to the different, and (as he saw the matter) better, idea of choice.[159] It was nonetheless, at least for a time, a powerful form of mediation, one to which Peter Arenella, in 1992, would give an imposing formulation.

In 1990, Arenella had addressed character in relation to the capacity for moral agency. His "Character, Choice and Moral Agency" was a resounding critique of Moore's (and others') "rational choice" approach, an approach that Arenella characterized as a "thin theory of rationality" that "permits choice theorists to define the moral agent's capacities for rational and uncompelled action in the abstract without tying those capacities to the unique character of the individual possessing them." Such commonplace rational choice theory avoided asking the truly relevant questions, thereby permitting us to blame "without ever asking whether the actor can fairly be held accountable for the goals, desires, values, and emotions that motivate his rational choices." A moral agent – according to choice theorists – was simply one whose acts could be *"fairly attributed"* to him or her because he or she "had the power to have acted otherwise."[160] This was "a very narrow conception of the moral self,"[161] Arenella charged, and constituted a fundamental misstep. Responsibility, in Arenella's character-based formulation, depended not on rational choice *tout court*, but upon the logically prior matter of one's possessing the capacity for "moral responsiveness" or the "ability to exercise moral judgment" which, in turn, determined the nature of one's rational choices. Responsibility, then, depended upon aspects of one's character, one's moral psychology, and the nature of one's emotional life, for these are what determined his all-important capacities for "self-reflection" and "self-revision."[162]

Despite his distancing responsibility from the notion of choice, Arenella was well aware that his theory was not immune to skepticism about free will.

---

[159] Moore, "Choice, Character, and Excuse."

[160] Peter Arenella, "Character, Choice and Moral Agency: The Relevance of Character to Our Moral Culpability Judgments," in *Crime, Culpability, and Remedy*, ed. Ellen Frankel Paul, Fred D. Miller, Jr., and Jeffrey Paul (Cambridge, MA: Blackwell, 1990), 59–83, 64.

[161] Arenella, "Character, Choice and Moral Agency," 78. Arenella cited, as an example, Dressler's 1988 article, "Reflections on the Excusing of Wrongdoers." He also noted that Moore had, in 1990, conceded that "'some emotions will necessarily have a place in'" the "'formation of the intentions and beliefs that guide and motivate the doing of the basic actions.'" But Arenella claimed that Moore "does not see the implications of this shift for his theory of culpability ... Moore appears to believe that once emotions are no longer seen as 'alien' to the moral agent's choosing self, their mere inclusion into the choosing self domesticates them." Arenella doubted that individuals could "control [emotions'] impact on [their] choices simply by choosing to act inconsistently with them. Nor does their inclusion into a broader definition of the choosing self prevent some emotions, like hatred, from completely overwhelming our practical reason" ("Character, Choice and Moral Agency," 80 [quoting Moore, "Choice, Character, and Excuse," text at notes 33–34]).

[162] Arenella, "Character, Choice and Moral Agency," 82. Arenella anticipated that a separate essay would be necessary in order to explain the "powers and self-understandings" that

Indeed, by way of concluding the 1990 piece, he alluded to the ever-present "specter of determinism," which, he acknowledged, equally threatened his own character-based approach. For, "few of us" believe we can "control how [our] motivational traits initially develop" and, further, proof that we then have any "power to revise relatively established features of our personality" is "fraught with difficulties that both soft and hard determinists are eager to point out." The article, then, concluded on a note of irresolution and self-doubt: Arenella expressly conceded that, although belief in "the existential claim that what we are is always up to us" may be "ennobling," "the evidence supporting this strong version of human autonomy will always be open to serious question."[163] Yet he – like many other legal academics – knew how to make use of the self-doubt that the free will question engendered; for, indeed, there was a certain ennoblement in the belief in an "existential claim" that one knew was no more than that. "To be sure," Arenella concluded,

it is difficult to defend the ways we lend moral stature to ourselves, and puzzles surround the meanings we create when we blame and excuse. But if we minimize the role of character in that story ... we will create a moral theory that neither describes nor justifies our blaming judgments. Better that we see the story we are telling ourselves.[164]

And without pausing to question the "ought" embedded in this recognition of the doubts one ought to have about the concept of ought, Arenella elaborated upon just why it is "better": "Perhaps the discrepancy between our vision of why we qualify as moral agents and the real-life conditions that make it so difficult for some criminal defendants to develop into full moral agents might motivate us to do something about those conditions."[165] Shades of Bazelon: doubts about free will themselves grounded the only morality we may affirm with confidence.

Two years later, in "Convicting the Morally Blameless,"[166] Arenella substantially developed his discussion of what the capacities for legal accountability involved in light of the "retributivist's intuition" that "equates justice to the individual with some showing of the offender's moral desert."[167] Yet he continued to admit the vulnerability of retributivism to the determinist critique. He remained agnostic about whether humans truly possess the autonomy required for desert-based liability, thus conceding the fragility of

---

"moral agents must possess before we can hold them morally responsible for failing to control how their character defects motivate their rational choices."
[163] Arenella, "Character, Choice and Moral Agency," 82–83.
[164] Arenella, "Character, Choice and Moral Agency," 83.
[165] Arenella, "Character, Choice and Moral Agency," 83.
[166] Peter Arenella, "Convicting the Morally Blameless: Reassessing the Relationship between Legal and Moral Accountability," *UCLA Law Review*, vol. 39 (1992): 1511–1622.
[167] Arenella, "Convicting the Morally Blameless," 1621.

his own position even as he rendered it in greater detail and with greater force. Here Arenella initially focused on cases of individuals who had been convicted of murder and found eligible for the death penalty despite low IQs and other pervasive cognitive, emotional, and social impairments.[168] His aim was to illustrate his claim that our criminal law, as it stands, "does not always honor its promise to exempt the morally blameless from criminal liability," because of its reliance on the rational choice model.[169] His own model, on the other hand, would lead to convictions more in keeping with "our most considered judgments of moral blame."[170]

For purposes of the article, Arenella accepted "the basic premises of the liberal paradigm for moral responsibility" – which "requires actors to have some form of knowledge, reason, and control of their actions before they can be fairly blamed for what they have done" – and the law's "putative link" between these conditions and "criminal liability for *mala in se* crimes."[171] But he sought once again to counter the version of the paradigm articulated by rational choice theorists – whom he now termed "conduct-responsibility theorists"[172] – who offered only a "very thin account of a moral agent's necessary attributes."[173] In place of this approach Arenella set forth "a far more robust account of knowledge, rationality, and control," one that looked instead to specific "character-based moral agency attributes":

the capacity to care for the interests of other human beings; the internalization of others' normative expectations, including self-identification as a participant in the community's blaming practices; the ability to engage in moral evaluation of one's character and acts, the capacity to respond to moral norms as a motivation for one's choices; and the power to control those firmly entrenched aspects of character that impair one's ability to act in accordance with one's moral judgments.[174]

In laboring to demonstrate that his own account was more consistent with our "most considered" moral judgments, Arenella drew upon Peter Strawson's identification of our participant-reactive attitudes of resentment and blame, which, Arenella said, stressed not simply the actor's breach of a moral norm, but our interpretation of the actor's lack of concern or respect for the norm breached. In Arenella's gloss on Strawson: "We require moral agency and fair attribution conditions before making deserved attributions of moral blame because their satisfaction supports our interpretation of the

---

[168] Arenella, "Convicting the Morally Blameless," 1513–16.
[169] Arenella, "Convicting the Morally Blameless," 1525.
[170] Arenella, "Convicting the Morally Blameless," 1544.
[171] Arenella, "Convicting the Morally Blameless," 1517–18.
[172] Arenella, "Convicting the Morally Blameless," 1522.
[173] Arenella, "Convicting the Morally Blameless," 1524.
[174] Arenella, "Convicting the Morally Blameless," 1525. Arenella recognized that "individuals clearly differ rather markedly in how effectively they exercise these threshold capacities," and "some moral agents appear to possess far greater moral potential than others." He

actor's conduct as evidence of the appropriate bad attitudes that sustain our blaming judgments." Still, there were significant limits to Arenella's agreement with Strawson who, Arenella stated, deployed his "naturalized model of moral responsibility" to insulate the "legitimacy of our moral responsibility judgments" from the "threat of determinism." In Arenella's words: "Strawson insists that we have little choice but to express and impose our basic natures in our moral blaming practices." Arenella countered, first, that our participant-reactive attitudes do not "fully constitute our moral responsibility judgments." Rather, as is illustrated by differences in blaming practices across cultures and by instances in the law when we decline to express our immediate reactive attitudes in the name of the overall social good, we have greater freedom than Strawson supposed "to construct different stories about the normative significance of human nature." Second, our participant-reactive attitudes themselves are vulnerable to causal accounts of human action: "our responsibility judgments are affected by how much we know about the person's ability to control those aspects of her character that motivate her choices." Indeed, if our participant-reactive attitudes are "insulated from the threat of determinism," Arenella asked, "why is there so much disagreement about whether these attitudes can be justified given what we know about the ultimate causes of human action?"[175]

Thus Arenella proceeded to use participant-reactive attitudes as "interpretive guides" that yielded the set of character-based determinants for culpability judgments that he counterposed to those of the conduct-attribution model.[176] But, in contrast to Strawson, his characterization of these attitudes was somewhat more complex – and, importantly, was less conclusive with regard to whether determinism might indeed undermine the moral soundness of our judgments. His method thus tracked Moore's in its domestication of conventional morality: Arenella, too, had recourse to our universal intuitions. But, in substance, Arenella's formulation dovetailed with Weinreb's focus on our irreducible tendency to think in causal terms. Recognition of this tendency guided us to an understanding of what it was in our reactions

---

emphasized that, although "serious deficiencies in the actor's ability to exercise these moral capacities support a full excuse," basic possession of the threshold capacities generally allows for culpability. This moral agency "continuum" was significant to his claim that his theory tracked our actual moral judgments better than theories offering a more "'all or nothing'" approach: his scheme clearly would not excuse typical moral psychopaths (who might be excused as insane under conduct-responsibility models), who privately exhibit many moral agency attributes including the "capacity to make moral choices" regardless that "they rarely d[o]" so (1613). Compare Robert Weisberg's discussion of Arenella on this point in "The Values of Interdisciplinarity in Homicide Law Reform," *Michigan Journal of Law Reform*, vol. 43 (2009): 53–78, 73–74.

175 Arenella, "Convicting the Morally Blameless," 1536–38 (also noting Gary Watson, "Responsibility and the Limits of Evil: Variations on a Strawsonian Theme," in *Responsibility, Character, and the Emotions*, ed. F. Schoeman [1987], 258).

176 Arenella, "Convicting the Morally Blameless," 1539–44.

to others that truly counted. And what *did* truly count was our interpretation of an actor's moral agency – that is, whether the actor's (caused) background and personal attributes had permitted him or her to become a genuine participant in our moral discourse capable of internalizing others' normative experiences and responding appropriately; we react to *this* sort of actor as one who *culpably* violated an agreed-upon norm. Arenella thus denied that our universal intuitions associated blameworthiness with the capacity and opportunity for practical reasoning and nothing more. He insisted instead that those intuitions involved an interpretation and assessment of a complex set of motivations and capacities that constituted moral agency and, contrary to Moore's view, that directly implicated ideas about causation.

As he had in 1990, Arenella recognized the difficulties that determinism posed for character-based theory. Indeed, in the conclusion to "Convicting the Morally Blameless," Arenella stated that, by virtue of its very nature, character-based theory reminds us that "'desert' does not 'go all the way down'":

> We neither choose nor control the process that determines whether we become moral agents. For the most part, our status as moral agents is a matter of constitutive and social luck. Moreover, we do not voluntarily take on the burdens and obligations of being a moral agent; they are thrust upon us.[177]

That is, determinism still has unavoidable implications for those character-based capacities upon which we in fact insist. Here Arenella hinted at, but did not fully embrace, ultimate and entire dissolution of all moral-agency theory. Yet, somehow, he still managed to come to terms with the threat determinism posed to his own theory. Just how he did so remains a puzzle – at least on my reading of the 1992 article – but it would appear that the "existential claim" of 1990 lived on. How did Arenella situate and affirm this claim?

Arenella's concluding discussion constituted a speculation "about why the criminal law has offered an impoverished account of moral agency," about why "few criminal law scholars appear interested in subjecting the law's account of moral responsibility to serious 'internal scrutiny' or in offering a revised version of the liberal model." He suggested that the answer, at least in part, itself "lies in the impact of determinism": "Having spent so much time worrying about whether we have any meaningful control over our behavior, many compatibilists and incompatibilists have unduly slighted questions about what a moral actor should be doing and feeling if he had such control." Hard determinists, he asserted, "adopt a utilitarian stance towards moral blame" – considering it a mere "social regulatory device" – because "they do not take the concept of moral desert seriously in

[177] Arenella, "Convicting the Morally Blameless," 1609–10.

a deterministic universe." As for Arenella's primary target – compatibilists who have adopted "some version of a 'just deserts' retributivist account of the criminal law" – some adhere to the "thin" account of moral agency offered by the rational choice model "because it *appears* easier to defend" from the onslaughts of determinism.[178] "Appears" was the all-important word: as Arenella had previously observed, the incompatibilist defeats this model simply by arguing that, because the nature of one's rational choices arises from "deeply embedded character traits" and one cannot control the development of these traits, one cannot be meaningfully responsible for the resulting choices.[179] Here the interesting move: Arenella then claimed that his character-based model "meets this part of the incompatibilist's challenge head-on" – yet he stated that it did so by concession. That is, he *conceded* that, if determinism is true, "then character motivates rational choices and that character is not chosen or deserved," and that his own model "assumes that whether we develop into fully accountable moral agents is fully determined by constitutional and environmental factors that we neither deserve nor control."[180] Had Arenella – at least within the confines of a lengthy foot-note – thus given up the ship? Not really, for, as he hastened to explain:

once someone has become a moral agent, she has the requisite abilities and capacities to make moral choices about what to do and how to be. Thus, moral agents merit moral blame for their immoral choices because they possess the moral capacities needed to make the morally correct choice. In essence, I align my self with soft deter-minism *once* moral agency attributes are present. Moral agents do not have contra-causal freedom but their moral capacities give them morally significant control over what to do and how to be.[181]

This was the crux of Arenella's particular brand of compatibilism – his way of meaningfully defining responsibility despite causation. He realized that the hard determinist could *still* deny that this account provided a basis for the possession of "morally significant control" over how we exercise these moral skills; in the end, desert *still* does not go all the way down in a literal, causal sense. We still punish – impose the stigma of criminal-ity, deprive of liberty, even take life – for aspects of character for which one is not ultimately responsible. Yet there remained, first, the conditional understanding of the freedom of human action, which did not require that the responsible actor "'could have done otherwise,'" but instead the "more modest 'could have done otherwise *if* the actor had wanted to act differently' conditional account relied on by many soft-determinists."[182] It appears that it was mainly this "conditional" (*choice-based*) account that was the thread by which Arenella – like Moore and other rational-choice theorists – hung.

[178] Arenella, "Convicting the Morally Blameless," 1610–12 (emphasis added).
[179] Arenella, "Convicting the Morally Blameless," 1612 n. 118.
[180] Arenella, "Convicting the Morally Blameless," 1612 n. 118.
[181] Arenella, "Convicting the Morally Blameless," 1612 n. 118.
[182] Arenella, "Convicting the Morally Blameless," 1612 n. 118.

Second, however, there remained those aspects of character theory that distinguished it from rational-choice theory: for those determined to possess what Arenella had termed in 1990 a person's capacity for "self-revision," the "soft-determined" choice nonetheless to act "criminally" in a particular instance grounded responsibility, not an ultimately non-determined responsibility, but a sufficient – a "morally significant" – one, the only one humans may be said to possess. Even though all aspects of character were subject to the determinist critique, some features of character involved relatively greater mediation by the individual's internal thought process, and, of these, some involved mediation that mimicked our (admittedly false) idea of human autonomy. These last features, he perhaps believed, we *ought* to reinforce, and by reserving attribution of responsibility for them alone we create the least (or least obvious to us) dissonance. Although he did not put the matter quite this way, Arenella's argument effectively conceded that the free will problem reduced responsibility-talk to the embracing of a paradox we are doomed to live with, an embracing of the counterfactual quality of our own consciousness. And character trumped rational choice (regardless that, as Arenella admitted, it would make only marginal differences in actual outcomes[183]) because it was *character* that tracked our deepest moral intuitions about just deserts.

Thus, in what was, at base, an entirely internalistic "defense" of character theory, Arenella stripped that theory of most of its mystification and came perilously close to concluding that one could achieve no more than pure description of the attribution of criminal responsibility, that there was no ground to stand on with respect to prescription. In the end, his internalism was self-conscious and even self-refuting. The footnoted discussion of the determinist critique placed a gloss upon his concluding intricate and seemingly confident statement of the nature and implications of his own moral capacity character-based theory of criminal responsibility. As he had promised, he remained true to the "liberal" tradition; indeed, he took the blameworthiness principle to what he deemed its logical moral conclusion. But the gloss remained: the footnoted aside was so integral to the article as a whole that it placed the concluding prescription in a certain light – that of a heuristic and ultimately existential claim regarding justified moral (and legal) retributivist condemnation. It was a prescription Arenella defended as the best that humans could achieve, but he never firmly concluded that the best was good enough.

VARIATION AND DEPARTURE: THE EARLY 1990S

Despite ongoing doubts about the plausibility of an increasingly widely accepted compatibilism and, hence, doubts about a convincing response

---

[183] Arenella, "Convicting the Morally Blameless," 1615–17.

to the determinist critique, the writings of the early 1990s nonetheless attested to the durability of neo-retributivism – of a desert-based form of criminal responsibility founded, ultimately, on the idea that humans were "persons," that is, that they acted upon reasons. But within this widely accepted frame there were endless variations, repetitions of familiar arguments, and – my main subject here – noteworthy departures. I focus mainly on two accounts that responded vigorously to the preceding interchange that had defined modern criminal jurisprudence's coming-of-age. Richard Boldt and R. George Wright sought, in very different ways, to confront and make use of the determinist critique. Both contextualized the legal academic's search for truth within the evolving (and roughly determinist) ideas of sister disciplines, producing accounts that were uncommonly rich resources in that regard. The ideas from outside the law that they employed had received some attention from proponents of mainstream compatibilist responsibility theory, but those theorists had striven to contain these ideas – to domesticate them – despite their unsettling implications. Boldt and Wright gave these ideas wider berth and to an important extent registered their potential limiting effect on notions of criminal responsibility.

Each in his own way, Boldt and Wright separated off offenses – those related, for Boldt, to chemical dependency, and for Wright, to severe social deprivation – to which responsibility should not attach. Boldt began with philosophy – whose new definitions of human freedom he examined but largely fenced off – and then settled into the burgeoning field of social construction, from whose essentially descriptive enterprise he drew prescriptive legal lessons. Wright drew from an eclectic mix of philosophy and social and behavioral science (although skirting social construction), while purporting to defend the law's central premise against all comers on the basis of ideas from within and outside of the law. Most interestingly, each approach, although aimed at *limiting* the realm of blameworthy behavior, was positioned as a defense of the law's conventional understanding that blameworthiness required moral responsibility; the idea was to shore up the range of genuinely blameworthy behavior and thereby allow the law to retain legitimacy – and avoid internal contradiction – by better aligning it with conventional morality or, at least, with that morality as rendered internally consistent from a critical standpoint. The law, each suggested, would be all the stronger for its being limited to the truly deserving.

Both Boldt and Wright thus endorsed retributivism, where it pertained, as a necessary but not exclusive goal of the law; both attempted to lay the determinist critique to rest (although in radically different ways). Yet it is tempting to view these recommendations for limitation of blameworthiness as a partial return to the tenets of positivism, indeed as a selective application of the Progressive agenda and its explicit commitment to social reform. But this was a positivism at peace with retributivism, not one that was *solely* in league with a reformationist-based consequentialism. From one perspective, Boldt and Wright breathed new life into the project that Bazelon (since the 1950s) and Delgado (as of 1985) had pursued. From another, they assimilated that project to the terms of the new retributivism. And from yet a third perspective, their efforts might someday be understood as (unwitting) steps beyond Bazelon and Delgado, along the way toward what John Hill, writing in 1988, had predicted would ultimately characterize the idea of responsibility in modern society: a hard-determinism-based denial of individual responsibility, *rejection* of retributivism, and externalization of responsibility to society at large. Accordingly, to frame my discussion of Boldt and Wright, I begin by introducing Hill.

John Hill

John Hill squarely confronted the determinist critique in his 1988 *Georgetown Law Journal* student note and declared it unanswerable. He counseled – or perhaps merely predicted – the ultimate abandonment of mainstream retributivist principles. Hill began by juxtaposing the "legal paradigm," according to which man is "a free, autonomous agent who makes deliberate choices," to modern psychiatry's understanding that man is "a product of the laws of nature." The legal perspective, he claimed, although typically viewed as "descriptive in nature," was in fact "an evolving prescriptive concept" serving to "delineate the boundaries" between responsible and nonresponsible behavior. This evolving concept, he argued, reflected an ongoing process of "externalization of attributes once considered to be properties of the individual *per se*. Law advances this process through steady expansion of the category of excuse, so that increasingly responsibility reflects an attribution of once-thought individual properties to society at large."[184]

Hill's account of the free will/determinism debate in philosophy was conventional enough. He focused especially on compatibilism and the proposition (which he associated with Hobbes, Locke, Hume, and the modern scholar, Charles Stevenson) that "while everything is determined, an action may be said to be 'free' when it is in accord with the desires and motives of the agent." This proposition was, he noted, disputed by the philosopher John Hospers, who had famously pointed out that a person's character – including, of course, desires and motives – was itself determined. Most important, Hill claimed that the disagreement between hard and soft determinists (i.e., compatibilists) was not "metaphysical," but was instead "semantic" and ("perhaps more interestingly") "normative." The semantic disagreement came down to the opposition between what Michael Moore had (drawing upon G. E. Moore) posited as conditional – "had [one] chosen

[184] John L. Hill, Note, "Freedom, Determinism, and the Externalization of Responsibility in the Law: A Philosophical Analysis," *Georgetown Law Journal*, vol. 76 (1988): 2045–74, 2045–46.

otherwise he could have acted in accordance with his choice" – and the hard determinist's insistence that "true freedom must be 'categorical'" – that the agent "must be able to choose his motives, propensities and inclinations." The normative disagreement inhered in the soft determinist's view that persons *should* be held responsible for their desires, motives, and choices although such mental states "may themselves be determined." "No empirical issue remains in dispute," Hill observed; rather "the question is value-laden and the answer given depends as much on one's conception of the role of responsibility and punishment as on one's definition of freedom."[185]

Hill agreed entirely with Moore's critique of "degree determinism," "ignorance determinism," "selective determinism," and "dualistic determinism." And, like Moore and Morse, he refuted Packer's "as if" view, which was "fundamentally unjust" from a "backward looking perspective" insofar as it admitted determinism as an underlying factual reality. From a "forward-looking perspective," however, "as-if responsibility is more a function of social utility [i.e., a strategy of behavior inducement] than a property or capacity of the individual" – a very different concept of responsibility from that held conventionally.[186]

Critically, however, the distinction between causal theory and compatibilism, traced by Hill from Moritz Schlick to A. J. Ayer to Moore, also failed in Hill's eyes. Hill focused in particular on Moore's claim that, although mental states, physiological events, and environmental influences were causal influences, they did not amount to compulsion insofar as they did not interfere with the agent's practical reasoning, as opposed, for example, to addictions, which did so interfere. This was, Hill said, a "noble attempt at reconciling determinism, responsibility, and the modern legal theory of excuse," but he contested Moore's claim that the first set of causal influences were not compelling. "Quite the contrary, the social conditions associated with growing up in a bad environment may undermine the very formation of the practical reasoning which Moore relies upon as constitutive of moral autonomy." The same applied to "physiological disturbances" (e.g., premenstrual stress syndrome) and "brainwashing" (Patty Hearst was invoked).[187]

Hill then noted that "the capacity for practical reasoning appears to pertain as much to willpower as to rationality." In Hill's rendition, Moore had asserted that "only loss of the capacity or opportunity to will is sufficient to excuse." Yet in law, excuse often centered on the notion *not* that the agent lost the power to will, but that he was caused "to will and act, in accordance with the will, *in a way different than he otherwise would have*," as in instances of provocation, duress, and the excuse of necessity. Hill illustrated

[185] Hill, Note, 2052–54.
[186] Hill, Note, 2057–58.
[187] Hill, Note, 2059–60.

that the excused "addict, the hothead, and the victim of duress all will their subsequent acts"; yet, so too does "the victim of poverty, the XYY male, and the psychopath, who are not accorded legal excuses." Further, causation and compulsion are not, Hill concluded, "qualitatively distinct, but rather fall on a continuum." Thus, Moore's theory – which drew a line between responsibility and excuse on the basis of a "purportedly metaphysically relevant distinction" – failed "not only prescriptively, as a theory of how law should excuse, but descriptively, as a theory of how it does in fact excuse." One must look for "some other value or consideration" to explain how policy makers draw the lines circumscribing our law of excuse.[188]

Although the larger part of Hill's article was devoted to what he took to be the contradictions inherent in the traditional individualized concept of moral responsibility, the more significant thrust of the piece came in his closing discussion of this "other value or consideration" traceable in an evolving law: the "externalization" of responsibility. Hill certainly recognized that, at its core, criminal responsibility continued to be governed by traditional ideas and that leading legal theorists continued to accept and defend those premises. Yet he seems to have believed that legal theory ran increasingly counter to the views of those professional elites outside of the law that grappled with social policy in relation to human behavior. In the main, he was engaging in purely descriptive legal sociology: modern society externalized responsibility as a result of its increasing understanding of the true sources of human behavior, which ultimately mandated a totalizing idea of excuse. This evolution in social thought necessarily involved a reconceptualization of responsibility – a shift from moral blame to scientific cause – and it presaged corresponding moves in the administration of the law, especially regarding criminal law's delineative, emotive, and allocative functions. Positive effects of this shift included individuals' "greater self-acceptance without moral anxiety" when their behavior violated social norms and, correspondingly, more attention paid by society "to those larger conditions which cause, and become manifest in, individual deviant acts." But there were also negative consequences, including the "reduced effectiveness of blame as a causal determinant in preventing socially harmful behavior." Thus, in assessing the "social and legal implications of modern society's trend toward externalization," Hill set forth two main presumptions regarding the course that society must undertake. To ensure "a level of adherence to its laws and to the social norms commensurate with that of traditional society ... modern society must compensate for waning individual psychological constraints" through new forms of social control. This required an understanding of "the causes of negative behavior," and then a reorganization of social institutions and a reform of the social environment accordingly. Further, responsibility

[188] Hill, Note, 2060–62.

in modern society will have to be "spread out over the whole society as a 'socialism of redress' becomes the status quo."[189]

Hill at last brought his analysis of what "must" (would inevitably) happen in modern society to bear on his discussion of current legal debate over the excuses. This debate, he postulated, was "really a debate about something more fundamental. In its own way the legal system is attempting to use the traditional, though outdated, notions of individual responsibility and excuse to fashion a form of rough justice which approximates the transition to a more modern view of human behavior." The "philosophically naive" positions of "degree determinism" and the like, Hill now declared, were the "most workable attempts" to square traditional ideas of freedom with the deterministic message of science. In the end, however, these "intermediate positions" must fail: "Man either is free or he is determined." Still, the inevitable shift in perspective would be slow in coming; an immediate and totalizing paradigm change would be "socially and legally disastrous, if not impossible." Here Hill stood back from his analysis of the inevitable to forewarn that "the process of externalization is not intrinsically good." It must be guided by "the normative principles of utility" and thus allowed to proceed only as far and as fast as is consonant with a net maintenance "in social utility, however utility is defined."[190] Hill's "normative principles" of a presumably determined adoption of utility remained, of course, undefended.

Richard Boldt

Richard C. Boldt's 1992 article, "The Construction of Responsibility in the Criminal Law," historicized and analyzed the mainstream criminal jurisprudence literature of the long 1980s in relation to the development of social construction theory within many sectors of the academy.[191] Social construction had found a home in critical legal studies scholarship, beginning at least with Roberto Unger's 1975 *Knowledge and Politics*. In Mark Kelman's 1980s writings, the two strains – social construction and critical legal analysis – combined in a natural and powerful fashion.[192] Social construction theory also influenced many of those legal scholars who, beginning in the

---

[189] Hill, Note, 2070–72.

[190] Hill, Note, 2073.

[191] Boldt carried forward principles set forth in his enterprising 1986 study, where he had examined a restitution-based approach to criminal law in light of social construction's critique of "the ideology of individuality." Richard C. Boldt, "Restitution, Criminal Law, and the Ideology of Individuality," *JCLC*, vol. 77 (1986): 969–1022. In the earlier piece Boldt drew extensively upon social theory writings from midcentury down to the mid-1980s, tracing a body of thought whose resonances can sometimes be located in mainstream legal scholarship but whose anti-individualistic premises had not been assimilated to the prevailing paradigm regarding criminal responsibility.

[192] Kelman, "Interpretive Construction"; Mark Kelman, *A Guide to Critical Legal Studies* (Cambridge, MA: Harvard University Press, 1987).

late 1970s, counseled understanding the construction of criminal responsibility in terms of "narrative," Delgado, Jack Balkin, and Robin West being only a few of the best known and most widely cited among them.[193] Social construction theory was often explicitly, and nearly always at least implicitly, deterministic. In the main, it was descriptive, but in the hands of some scholars – especially those in the legal academy – it waxed prescriptive, as it was commonly deployed not only to explode ("deconstruct") but also to contest the ideology that underwrote law's legitimation of prevailing patterns of political, social, and economic hierarchy.[194]

Boldt's 1992 "constructionist" intervention was itself strongly prescriptive. He argued that the chemically dependent – both alcoholics and drug addicts – ought to be removed from the domain of the criminally responsible (not via legal excuse, but via partial decriminalization). But, otherwise, that domain ought to remain premised upon the long-standing idea that criminal responsibility required moral responsibility – upon the idea, if not the objective fact, that the offender could have chosen not to commit the offense with which he was charged. Boldt's strikingly original argument departed from both causal theory and Moorean compatibilism. As to the former, Boldt accepted universal causation. More significantly, as to the latter, he aimed to show the infirmities of Moore's moral realism, and, by implication, of Morse's understanding of the nature of near-universal moral perceptions. Boldt accepted in principle Moore's claim that moral and legal responsibility depended upon the individual's possession of the fair opportunity and capacity for practical reason. But he argued that the perception that a particular individual possessed these prerequisites was itself a function of socially constructed notions about the behavior of particular persons in particular contexts. He further claimed (in Weinreb-like fashion) that we are all fundamentally two-minded – and thus internally contradictory – in our thinking about moral and criminal responsibility. When the deterministic side of our minds trumped what Boldt termed the "intentionalist" side – that is, when the sense that an actor was caused was simply too great for most people to maintain the paradigm of intentionalism without undermining the sense of law's coherence that gave the idea of responsibility its necessary force and effect – we ought, he argued, not to assign responsibility, both for the criminal law's sake and for our own. Boldt's social-constructionist engagement with Moore thus stood in stark contrast to Arenella's embattled attempt

[193] E.g., Richard Delgado, "Storytelling for Oppositionists and Others: A Plan for Narrative," *Michigan Law Review*, vol. 87 (1989): 2411–441; Jack M. Balkin, "The Rhetoric of Responsibility," *Virginia Law Review*, vol. 76 (1990): 197–264; Robin West, "Jurisprudence as Narrative: An Aesthetic Analysis of Modern Legal Theory," *New York University Law Review*, vol. 60 (1985): 145–211.
[194] Compare Kelman's candid querying of what his work accomplishes in "Interpretive Construction," 669–673, and Boldt (adding to Kelman's query) in "Construction of Responsibility," 2282.

of the same year to supplant Moore's rational choice with an ultimately individualist character theory aimed at surviving the determinist critique.

The centerpiece of Boldt's article was a proposed dualism according to which it was plausible to say that "both the determinist and intentionalist descriptions of the offenders' conduct are in some fashion true."[195] Boldt countered Moore's objections to such "linguistic dualism," arguing that, if one looks at language usage not (as Moore would have it) in relation to a background scientific truth, but instead in relation to social beliefs and practices that ground meaning for one who uses the language in question, the "dualist's claim no longer depends upon sterile linguistic rules." The meanings of the words in question are "real to the speakers of this language." Moore's account of the law regarding excuses was accurate, Boldt conceded, in that it made sense of the requirements of voluntariness and mens rea, which "are described as doctrinal instruments designed to test the capacity and opportunity of the defendant to engage in practical reasoning." But why should one conclude, Boldt queried, that practical reasoning "is *really* what matters ... if by 'really' one means that practical reasoning has some sort of independent epistemological significance?" At base, Boldt claimed that Moore was able to predict correctly who would be held responsible but failed to grapple sufficiently with the manner in which people "actually experience the *practice* of assigning or withholding responsibility." Commonly, Boldt asserted, in such cases as those involving chemical dependency, where cognitive capacity frequently is not erased, the legal outcome (accurately predicted by the presence or absence of such capacity) is totally aside from the social understanding; this understanding does not draw a line based on practical reasoning, but reduces to the view that "the conduct of addicts and alcoholics is the product of a struggle between nonautonomous factors inclining them toward abuse and an autonomous free will that could, and should, resist such a craving."[196] Thus, even if the law was premised upon choice, actual (jury-based) determination of the existence of blamable choice was premised upon causal theory.

Boldt also challenged Moore's distinction between the absolute and the conditional meanings of "could have done otherwise," the latter meaning (Moore's preference) requiring a counterfactual – or merely hypothetical – opportunity and capability to do otherwise. The result was that the "basis of responsibility [Moore] adopts depends upon a practical reasoning process which itself may be unfree." In other words, "Moore's theory does not require that desert go 'all the way down.'"[197] Accordingly, Moore must, in

[195] Boldt, "Construction of Responsibility," 2270.
[196] Boldt, "Construction of Responsibility," 2273–74.
[197] Boldt, "Construction of Responsibility," 2274–75 (Boldt cited Nozick, *Anarchy, State, and Utopia*, 225, and Weinreb, "Desert, Punishment, and Responsibility," 74–75, for the idea that desert does not go "all the way down").

effect, retreat to a theory of moral desert that makes freedom independent of desert, a theory that, as Weinreb posited, holds that "human actors deserve the conditions which determine their choices."[198] Again, this accorded with actual legal results, but not with conventional morality. For,

> most members of the community are not philosophers capable of an expansive detachment from deeply inscribed social convention.... Our experience of blaming requires that we understand human choices to be truly autonomous, in the sense that they are free from the determining force of factors beyond the control of the agents. That we accept outcomes inconsistent with such a normative posture means that both truths contained within the intentionalist/determinist dualism must obtain and both must be managed within the context of daily practice.[199]

In similar fashion, Boldt rebutted Moore's claim that dualism failed because it did not identify "boundaries between the determinist and intentionalist notions of human conduct" that were both "clearly defined and permeable." This claim was true enough at "the level of theoretical criticism," he said, and Moore's theory accurately predicted "our occasional shift from [in Strawson's terms] the participant to the objective viewpoint." But this hardly demonstrated that the shift was *experienced* in the terms that Moore set forth – as the offender's opportunity and capacity to engage in practical reasoning. Rather, Boldt claimed (once again drawing upon Weinreb), "people 'see' or 'understand' or simply 'live' through one or the other of Strawson's perspectives as a consequence of deep social convention."[200]

Dualism, then, allows the causal theorist to avoid Moore's *reductio* argument by describing human conduct as simultaneously free and determined. These seemingly inconsistent truths persist because the divide between actions and causes is ideological; it is a social construction which derives from collective activity.[201] Contrary to Moore's claim, this dualism does not depend upon the metaphysical or linguistic manipulations of theorists. It is a necessary creature of social life.[202]

Boldt's social constructionism thus appears to have operated in relation to built-in features of human psychology. Like Weinreb, Boldt adopted the view that humans both conceive of themselves and others as autonomous and simultaneously "share an instinct to search for causal explanations for occurrences in our environment." These mental moves were universal, natural, inevitable, and necessary for society to function; they were, evidently,

[198] Boldt, "Construction of Responsibility," 2275 (citing Weinreb, "Desert, Punishment, and Responsibility," 75).
[199] Boldt, "Construction of Responsibility," 2276.
[200] Boldt, "Construction of Responsibility," 2276–77.
[201] Boldt here cited Delgado's 1989 article, "Storytelling for Oppositionists and Others," 2414 n. 14.
[202] Boldt, "Construction of Responsibility," 2278 (citing Percy W. Bridgman, "Determinism and Punishment," in *Determinism and Freedom in the Age of Modern Science: A Philosophical Symposium*, ed. Sidney Hook [New York: New York University Press, 1958], 143–45).

not themselves socially engendered. The specific perception of freedom or non-freedom that individuals experience in particular cases was, on the other hand, produced by social conventions. Building upon Strawson, Boldt argued that we can identify "examples of social practice that instill in members of the community the ability unconsciously, yet purposefully to shift between the participant and objective viewpoints."[203]

And here, of course, "the criminal law is the most visible and explicit institutional setting for the working out of questions of individual responsibility."[204] Drawing extensively upon Kelman's 1981 "Interpretive Construction" article, Boldt suggested that one might add to Kelman's analysis the crucial proposition that "interpretive constructs function as mechanisms by which a determinist/intentionalist dualism is managed within the criminal law, and by extension, within society generally." This effect was achieved through the construction of "stories" that fit either the participant or objective perspective, stories that "are translated into legal narratives molded by the criminal law doctrines that define offenses and excuses." As a result "we acquire a generalized ability to attend to some information we encounter in daily life and to filter out other data we confront, so that we are able to maintain a line of separation between the two perspectives."[205]

Finally, Boldt continued to insist that there remained a gap between Moore's "abstract description of responsibility" and "our everyday experience in assigning responsibility." While Moore instructs the legal theorist as to an appropriate outcome, "as a community generally employing fixed rules corresponding to a dominant social consciousness, we are merely likely to conclude that an individual is or is not responsible."[206] In effect, Boldt attempted to strip Moore's universal moral perceptions (affirmed by deep intuitions and particular judgments) of an alignment with abstract metaphysical truth and instead to ground them firmly in (changing and internally contradictory) social conventions.

We need not rehearse in detail Boldt's incisive demonstration of the manner in which the majority and dissenting opinions in a 1973 drug possession case exemplified the law's fumbling as it sought, against all odds, to achieve a principled and coherent resolution along either intentionalist (the majority) or determinist (the dissent) lines.[207] Nor need we treat his

---

[203] Boldt, "Construction of Responsibility," 2279.

[204] Boldt, "Construction of Responsibility," 2280 (citing Robert W. Gordon, "Critical Legal Histories," *Stanford Law Review*, vol. 36 [1984]: 109, for a more general version of this claim about the function of "lawmaking and law-interpreting institutions," and John O. Cole, "Thoughts from the Land of And," *Mercer Law Review*, vol. 39 [1988]: 925, for a specific application of this claim to the criminal law).

[205] Boldt, "Construction of Responsibility," 2282–83.

[206] Boldt, "Construction of Responsibility," 2283–84.

[207] Boldt, "Construction of Responsibility," 2285–94, discussing *United States v. Moore*, 486 F.2d 1139 (D.C. Cir. 1973). *Moore* considered the criminal responsibility of a heroin addict

discussion of the debate over chemical dependency as a disease, or that of the "fundamental incompatibility of [deterministic] medical and [intentionalist] legal models of behavior."[208] Boldt's main point was that, with respect to chemical dependency, reform was required because society at large, simply put, was not guided by consistent "stories" that managed individuals' dual perspectives in a way that allowed them to adhere unself-consciously to one perspective or the other. Moreover, Boldt imaginatively analyzed current judicial practice in drug cases to suggest that courts, rejecting the medical position but unable to maintain a plausible focus on individual free action, had moved dangerously, if unself-consciously, toward the construction of invidious (and effectively deterministic) generalized tests (race and class, he claimed, were being read back into the question of intentionalism) as to a defendant's supposed individual responsibility.[209] There was more to Boldt's argument than even this important claim, but the claim largely grounded Boldt's recommendation of an alternative policy "that would recharacterize the vast majority of addicts and alcoholics as patients to be treated rather than as criminal offenders to be punished," a policy of "partial decriminalization" (*not* "legalization") aimed largely at possessory and public intoxication offenses.[210] Significantly, there was, as well, the objective of safeguarding the conventional assumptions of the law in all other instances, where, as he thought, social conventions allowed for reasonably consistent stories regarding the attribution of responsibility.[211] Boldt thus concluded his call for reform with the observation that legal policy in drug possession and public intoxication cases was unfortunately undermining the criminal

---

for heroin possession in the wake of the fractured U.S. Supreme Court opinions in *Powell v. Texas*, 392 U.S. 514 (1968). In *Moore*, a majority of the D.C. Circuit judges, sitting en banc, affirmed the defendant's conviction (*id.* at 1141–59, Wilkey, J., joined by MacKinnon and Robb, JJ.; 1159–206, Leventhal, J., joined by McGowan, J.), in part rejecting his argument that, as a heroin addict, he had no power of self-control or free choice with regard to the use of heroin and, therefore, should not be held responsible because "the common law has long held that the capacity to control behavior is a pre-requisite for criminal responsibility" (*id.* at 1145, internal quotations omitted). Chief Judge Bazelon largely joined Judge Wright's dissent (*id.* at 1208–60, Wright, J., joined by Bazelon, C.J., and Tamm and Robinson, JJ.), in which Wright concluded that common and statutory law recognized that addiction is a disease and addicts cannot freely control their behavior; therefore, addiction should exist as a defense, limited to "only those acts which, like mere purchase, receipt or possession of narcotics for personal use, are inseparable from the disease itself and, at the same time, inflict no direct harm upon other members of society" (*id.* at 1257). Bazelon preferred a broader version of the defense, permitting the jury "to consider addiction as a defense to a charge of, for example, armed robbery or trafficking in drugs, to determine whether the defendant was under such duress or compulsion, because of his addiction, that he was unable to conform his conduct to the requirements of the law (*id.* at 1260, Bazelon, C.J.).

[208] Boldt, "Construction of Responsibility," 2295–2307.
[209] Boldt, "Construction of Responsibility," 2317–20.
[210] Boldt, "Construction of Responsibility," 2313–14.
[211] Boldt, "Construction of Responsibility," e.g., 2316–17, 2282–83.

justice system's necessary role of maintaining a socially navigable system of "intentionalist ideology."[212]

In this way Boldt reinforced the conventional, free-will-based view of responsibility while simultaneously accepting the opposing truth of the scientific/determinist perspective. For him, as for Weinreb, the contradictions between the two views were inherent in all humans' perceptions of their world; the socially constructed notions of justice expressed through the criminal justice system operated to mediate – that is, to obscure from our conscious attention the contradictions between – these universally held yet opposing worldviews. Thus, for Boldt, the central question did not concern an abstract notion of "free will," but its consistent application within the stories the criminal law tells about responsibility. I venture to say that he advanced a functional compatibilism: despite the pull of determinism, responsible conduct existed when it was socially understood to be intentional. And, although society and the law might understand such action as truly free, at the same time the theorist might accept this freedom only on "as if" terms. The overall result was both conservative and critical: to uphold the conventional, retributivist aspects of the law, Boldt would render them largely inapplicable to a large group of offenders based on their relative lack of intentionality. This absolution for conditions beyond an offender's control – although certainly not Boldt's accompanying retributive premise – was a move that Progressive Era determinists might have heartily endorsed.

R. George Wright

R. George Wright's contribution to what could be seen as a renewed (albeit only partial) Progressivism was as direct as Boldt's was oblique. In his 1994 article, "The Progressive Logic of Criminal Responsibility and the Circumstances of the Most Deprived,"[213] Wright, like Boldt, effectively adopted Herbert Hart's baseline of fair opportunity and capacity for choice and – like Boldt – sought to defend it in the retributivist terms that many post-Hart scholars (unlike Hart himself) had come to set forth. Wright cited Moore as an exponent of Hart's basic idea but, unlike Boldt, did not seek to counter Moore's moral realism. Instead, he purported straightforwardly to ground his retributivism on the underlying principles of the Western liberal tradition and on widely accepted ideas about moral responsibility without attempting to defend or rebut claims about metaphysical truth. Although Wright responded to the determinist critique, he mainly admitted the unknowability of the truth of determinism and – like

---

[212] Boldt, "Construction of Responsibility," 2331.
[213] R. George Wright, "The Progressive Logic of Criminal Responsibility and the Circumstances of the Most Deprived," *Catholic University Law Review*, vol. 43 (1994): 459–504.

Kadish and Dressler – left the matter to philosophical speculation.[214] Of such speculation Wright was acutely aware: in addition to his consideration of much of the legal scholarship I have discussed here, his text and notes extensively detailed many contemporary philosophical moves in the direction of defining free will in usable human terms and a slew of works in political and social theory that assessed the dire implications of determinism for a coherent theory of responsibility.[215] But nothing deflected Wright from a defense of a moral responsibility standard essentially premised on capacity and opportunity; he simply assimilated to that defense as much as he possibly could from contemporary literature within and outside the law and declared that all speculative threats to such an idea of responsibility yielded no better – by which he seemed to mean both no more workable and no more preferable – theory.

Wright's initial aim was to circumscribe what he claimed were the essential preconditions for moral and legal responsibility, that is, freedom, knowledge, and control: preconditions that, he asserted, were reflected in existing law and generally accepted in society. His argument was that the law in practice deviated from its essential preconditions, and that many defendants – Wright focused on the severely socially deprived – were convicted despite their lack of one or more of the basic requirements for responsibility. Thus, Wright claimed, the law was regularly beset by contradictions that both worked injustice to individuals *and* posed a significant threat to law's vindication of widely accepted principles regarding criminal responsibility. It was this effort to save the law in theory from its impurities in practice that defined the 1994 article as a partial retreat to positivism and to something like the Progressive agenda even as it endorsed the essence of late-twentieth-century retributivism.

The article's discussion of freedom was far-ranging and, in a sense, fundamentally elusive. Attempting to synthesize a broad agreement about freedom's preconditions, Wright melded political liberty with conventional notions of opportunity and capacity for rational choice, which were themselves intertwined with the two other basic requirements of responsible action: knowledge and control. These latter two requirements gave structure

[214] Kaye, "Secret Politics," 381 n. 71, notes Wright's claim ("Progressive Logic" at 463, 475–76) that compatibilist responsibility inquiries "truncate the inquiry into moral responsibility" by (Kaye's phrase) "drawing the line at social conditions."

[215] A small selection of the notable philosophical work that Wright's extensive research took into account includes Richard Double, *The Non-reality of Free Will* (Oxford: Oxford University Press, 1991); J. R. Lucas, *Responsibility* (New York: Oxford University Press, 1993); Nancey Murphy, "Truth, Relativism, and Crossword Puzzles," *Zygon*, vol. 24 (1989): 299–314; Robert Nozick, *Philosophical Explanations* (Cambridge, MA: Harvard University Press, 1981); Michael Slote, "Ethics without Free Will," *Social Theory and Practice*, vol. 16 (1990): 369–83; Bruce N. Waller, *Freedom without Responsibility* (Philadelphia: Temple University Press, 1990).

to Wright's argument and led him to define opportunity and capacity in a fashion that gave limited scope to his notion of the freedom that accorded with a true measure of responsibility. Positing that the knowledge prong of responsibility requires, in part, "a reasonable and realistic opportunity to grasp or absorb the majority's relevant legal and moral norms," Wright urged that "persons subject to the most serious oppression" may faultlessly lack this knowledge as the result of "governmental and societal failure to provide [them] with knowledge of what the law requires or adequate opportunity to acquire such knowledge." With regard to control, he argued there was broad agreement that "persons may lack relevant control over some of their own personal characteristics, external facts and events, their own substantive choices or process of choice, and their own lives, and in relevant respects therefore bear reduced or no moral responsibility." "At least some subset of the most deprived lack such control," he concluded. Yet "the legal system generally has avoided this conclusion by insisting that only a discrete set of nonsystemic, essentially personal, idiosyncratic, transient, or episodic excuses" – mostly commonly those falling under the category of legal insanity – "exhaust the conditions capable of negating moral responsibility."[216]

Here Wright appears to have returned in his own mind to the Bazelon-Morse debate of 1976 as though it were the moment at which modern retributivist theory had gone wrong. Morse's position failed, Wright implied, because of its instability and its adoption of conclusory arguments to ward off the seeming threats both to workability and to political liberty posed by Bazelon's defense of a "rotten social background" excuse. Morse, we have seen, had subsequently attempted to reinforce his position with a thorough-going compatibilism centered on law's adherence to rationality and absence of hard choice, but had, or so Wright apparently believed, adopted reductionist understandings of both. Thus, rationality existed for Morse – and others of the long 1980s – even where severely socially deprived defendants lacked either the practical knowledge about the law and its workings or an understanding of the reasons for law-abiding behavior that were required for a true capacity for responsibility-bearingness. As to control, Wright adduced a theory of excuse that flowed from his attempted synthesis of commonplace assumptions regarding an individual's freedom of action. The result bore the marks of causal theory: the severely deprived should be excused because they were exposed to background/environmental conditions that caused them to lack meaningful control over their choices. But Wright suggested that this sort of environmental "constraint" on meaningful control was no more vulnerable to the determinist critique – or to Moore's *reductio* – than was Moore's own practical-reasoning-based formulation. The relevant responsibility-bearing capacity of either theorist ultimately arose from past

---

[216] Wright, "Progressive Logic," 473–75.

causes (as Weinreb had effectively pointed out with regard to Moore's formulation), and thus the difficultly of drawing a line between (irrelevant) causation and (relevant) constraint of the relevant capacity posed no less problem for Moore than for Wright.[217] Most important to Wright's formulation, of course, was his conclusion that the mere rationality to which Moore pinned responsibility was inconsistent with our – and the law's – overall notions of responsibility: one may act rationally within circumstances so constrained – and so beyond one's control – that responsibility is not present. In this respect, Wright urged that the logic of duress applied equally to situations in which deprived actors were so lacking in meaningful choice and opportunity that they should not be held responsible, despite the ability to "act conscientiously and intentionally to maximize their values."[218]

Wright thus strove to systematize and give logical separation to the two perspectives – intentionalism and determinism – that Boldt argued made simultaneous claims upon human consciousness and required mediation by socially constructed notions of responsibility. Although Wright was conversant with all strands of contemporary theory, his argument stood unaffected by critical legal studies or social construction. It appears as something of a throwback, a retrieval of attempts by Bazelon and Delgado to make the law live up to its purported "liberal" principles. But for Bazelon a commitment to rehabilitationism had compensated for acceptance of the community's responsibility to determine who may morally be held responsible and who may not; and Delgado had accepted Herbert Hart's basic principle as no more than a moral constraint upon the attribution of responsibility and had then focused his attention on features of non-responsibility. Wright, on the other hand, robustly defended retributivism, sometimes drawing none-too-generous lines between the responsible and non-responsible. To be sure, Wright at times employed language that resonated with Bazelon's, as when he argued that the refusal "to recognize the possibility of nonresponsibility due to severe social deprivation" was "to fail to recognize the profound moral importance of reforming conditions of social life." But he then married this with his claim that a central purpose of such reform was "to maximize the percentage of persons who can genuinely and correctly be considered fully and morally responsible."[219]

There was, then, no Progressivist pining in Wright's article for a future in which criminal law comprehensively employed positivist principles. Although Wright brought something of the positivist approach into conjunction with retributivism, he viewed the criminal law as an instrument

---

[217] Wright, "Progressive Logic," 476 n. 49 (here citing the discussions of Moore I have recounted previously by Weinreb, Boldt, and Hill), 489.

[218] Wright, "Progressive Logic," 478–79. Wright responded to the fact that most members of deprived social groups are law-abiding with the observation: "Certainly the ability to cope with genuine lack of freedom does not show that one is free" (484).

[219] Wright, "Progressive Logic," 488.

for bettering social conditions precisely in order to maximize a retributivist responsibility-bearingness, not as a carrier of ideas that might someday erode that particular moral vision. Yet, for Wright, the principles that were to be maximized were rationally deducible from what was, ultimately, a merely practical, commonsense defense of the premises of humans' capacity for autonomy. In his attempted rescue of what he termed the "Progressive" logic of criminal responsibility, Wright developed a distinctly heuristic argument against the potentially debilitating "progressive" logic of the determinist critique.

Well aware of the critique, Wright had specified: "It is hardly the intent of this Article to show that any conception of genuine moral responsibility is viable, beyond briefly suggesting below the unattractiveness of supposing otherwise." His goal, rather, was to demonstrate that "useful and plausible distinctions can be drawn" with regard to responsibility, "apart from the broader issue of the viability of responsibility in a world apparently ruled by causal determinism and inherent randomness."[220] Yet, toward the end of his article, Wright directly took up the determinism he viewed as increasingly prevalent in contemporary philosophical accounts of human nature. Remaining agnostic about the truth of determinism, he fashioned a response that privileged the value of the "dignity" inherent in the hypothesis that humans in fact possess the capacity for autonomous action. Drawing upon others' explorations of the paradoxes of a deterministic perspective, Wright turned arguments premised on determinism back on themselves. If determinism were true, he parried, there could be no "embarrassment" in our having thought, or in our continuing to act – indeed, in our choosing "to pretend, contrary to fact" – that moral responsibility exists, for "there is certainly no reason for an organic machine to be embarrassed because it is only a machine, if it thought otherwise." Beyond this, we might "admit our incapacity for moral responsibility" and still prefer a political regime ("democracy") that would more likely allow us to satisfy "our mere tastes and interests as organic machines."[221] "In any event," he concluded, there remained this prospect:

whatever moral world that could survive the demise of any familiar notion of moral responsibility would strike us now, with our current attitudes, as variously debilitating, terrifying, reducing the quality of our human relationships, or simply a great loss of value. ... Abandoning, rather than reforming, the judicial use of the familiar concept of moral responsibility seems unattractive. ...

If [instead] we hold persons genuinely responsible for their acts, we thereby implicitly assert the dignity of the offender, and avoid a system of trial, sentencing, and incarceration that implicitly denies that dignity.[222]

---

[220] Wright, "Progressive Logic," 489.
[221] Wright, "Progressive Logic," 496–98.
[222] Wright, "Progressive Logic," 498–99.

Wright was well aware that his prescription for reform – expanding the legal excuses – might be seen both as dangerous to society and as undermining the very dignity to which he appealed. He thus emphasized that he did not counsel returning those found severely socially deprived to the community. Rather, they should be confined until they could safely be set free. "It is hardly vindictive or improperly punitive to regrettably confine actual offenders who impose unreasonable dangers to their neighbors for as long as they demonstrably pose such a danger."[223] As to dignity, Wright distinguished "therapy or rehabilitation," which he would not impose, from "developing the conditions and capacity within society in order to foster moral responsibility." He was not counseling "making the offender morally good," about which he said we know little, but was instead counseling enhancing "persons' capacities to possess moral responsibility for their actions." The latter, of course, involved the inculcation of "relevant sorts of freedom, control and knowledge," a kind of reform that we are, Wright supposed, better prepared to achieve. The "coercion" such a regime of reform might involve was "coercion for the sake of autonomy," which would undermine true dignity far less than the current policy of "engaging in … [the] self-serving metaphysical flattery of defendants that has obscured the effects of long periods of undeserved severe deprivation."[224]

Like Boldt, Wright had presented an elaborate rationale for retributivist theory and sought to defend that theory against the potentially debilitating effects of its supposed internal contradictions. Where, for Boldt, those contradictions were inherent in all humans' perceptions of their world, for Wright they inhered in the misapplication of an admittedly hypothetical but internally coherent conventional worldview (human autonomy). Although Wright conceded that this autonomy principle was hypothesized – and was opposed by a counter-hypothesis (determinism) whose truth or falsity was either in principle, or simply as yet, unknowable – he posited that consistency afforded legitimacy to the retributivist criminal law, which, itself, Wright forthrightly endorsed and concluded was mandated by current attitudes and understandings.

Despite Boldt's and Wright's divergent premises, their common prescription was to shore up mainstream theory's basic principle by shearing away that which threatened to undermine it. For both, the shearing-off process involved a commitment to a system of reform that would exist outside of the current system of punishment of the criminally responsible. For Boldt this had involved medicalization, that is, treatment outside of the criminal justice system; for Wright it involved participation by the criminal justice system in an essentially rehabilitationist (although Wright would not call it that) enhancement of offenders' "capacities to possess moral responsibility for

---

[223] Wright, "Progressive Logic," 499.
[224] Wright, "Progressive Logic," 500–01.

their actions." Both thus sought a partial externalization of responsibility, but one that would coexist with a remedy – treatment for engendering responsibility-bearingness – that betokened a future in which traditional retributivist principles of criminal responsibility would be maximized. In effect, they counseled a mitigated form of Progressivism that was aimed, in the long run, at that Progressivism's withering away. It remains impossible to say whether their recommended solutions, if implemented, would ultimately prove to be mere halfway stopping points – partial externalizations characterized by compromised adherence to retributivism's personal responsibility – of the sort that Hill believed would, instead, mark criminal jurisprudence's halting but inevitable march to total externalization of responsibility.

CONCLUSION

Despite their Progressive-seeming prescriptions for reform, the efforts of Boldt and Wright – who each sought to reinforce the notion of desert by limiting its attribution to the truly deserving – at base reflected the dominance in legal-academic circles, by the century's last decades, of what I have called a neo-retributivist orientation to criminal responsibility. Of course, it is worth restating that, although retributivism had risen to the fore among theoretical discussions, most academics adopted a mixed theory of punishment: consequentialist justifications resided alongside retributivist ones, although in some instances that remains a matter of inference. But it was retributivism that received special attention both because it was increasingly understood as a sine qua non and because, in light of the determinist critique, it was retributivism that was thought to require a defense.

In tandem with much compatibilist philosophy of the time, some legal scholars – particularly the formal compatibilists led by Moore and Morse – directly confronted that critique and found it answerable: by the 1980s both Moore and Morse had fully enunciated compatibilist positions asserting that the opportunity and capacity for rational choice grounded legal and moral responsibility despite universal causation. Many other scholars who addressed the free will problem espoused what I have called loose or informal (or agnostic) compatibilist positions – that is, they affirmed desert despite the possibility (or unknowability) of determinism – regardless of whether we would say they effectively answered the determinist critique or, perhaps, confronted it and declared it either unanswerable or (in light of the nature of personhood and conventional attitudes) no longer in need of an answer.

I began this chapter with Fletcher's 1978 undertaking – to "rethink" criminal law – which proceeded beyond midcentury scholars' common avoidance of the determinist critique and toward the scholarship of the 1980s that more self-consciously grappled with that critique. Fletcher acknowledged the problems that determinism posed for responsibility. Yet, continuing recent criticism of the rehabilitational ideal (and essentially anticipating some of the informal compatibilism that would follow), Fletcher was more concerned by the threat posed by the state overreach that he associated with sheer consequentialism. In the end, although he admitted that his loosely theorized version of character theory was itself vulnerable to the determinist critique, he concluded that it was most important to affirm responsibility – and for the state to treat its citizens as autonomous actors – lest we give up blame altogether along with the culture from which our criminal law arose.

Arenella would later develop a more detailed approach rooting responsibility in character – specifically, in those actors whose characters suggested the capacity for moral agency. He, too, did not discount the vulnerability of his theory to the determinist critique. But, given the alternatives, Arenella (much like Fletcher) privileged legal and social systems that fostered individual autonomy in keeping with common understandings of responsibility. In a somewhat more critical vein than Fletcher – and leaning toward the more overtly critical-legal work of Boldt and Kelman – Arenella urged that, despite the possibility of determinism, a coherent theory of legal and moral responsibility is central to our ability to consistently, fairly judge each other. Although he conceded that such a theory would nonetheless unavoidably contain contradictions and imperfections, his answer was not to reject autonomy. Rather, he hoped that the inevitable contradictions might lead us to remedy the social conditions that raise the most difficult questions concerning the line between relatively uncoerced moral agency and acts that evince, instead, a lack of moral capacity likely because of the background conditions of the actor.

Such character-based approaches had their place and would continue to evolve through the turn of the next century. But it is fair to say that much of the more and less formal compatibilism of the long 1980s accepted responsibility based roughly on the capacity for rational choice – a capacity that accorded with, and paid homage to, an imagined universal aspect of human nature, what since Morris's 1968 essay was widely said to define the human being, the "person." Herbert Hart's particular expression of this line of thought had, ironically, become a kind of foundation stone for American neo-retributivists; what Hart had proposed merely as a limit upon liability and the duration of *consequentialist* punishment, Morris and those who followed him accepted as a chief rationale for both deserved liability and punishment.

Beyond this core of rough agreement, however, there were differing perspectives regarding the relationship between the objective fact of that essential human nature and a normative legal order. Where Moore and Morse concluded that rational choice was the linchpin of a comprehensive response to the determinist critique, others incorporated choice in more amorphous approaches that relied on various aspects of personhood and social relationships. These latter, more open-ended and broadly humanistic approaches accommodated a degree of agnosticism about the extent of the determinist threat. Weinreb went the farthest, rejecting the notion that there could be any clear-cut resolution of the intractable tension between our senses of autonomy and our causal intuitions. His answer was to acknowledge the universally accepted link between personhood and desert in an essentially descriptive account of the law. Kadish similarly continued to find it difficult to commit solely to either causation or autonomy in describing human action. Although he expressed doubts about the true nature of free will – and certainly about sheer retributivism – he pragmatically defended the legal and social notions of freedom and responsibility that were integral to our moral culture. Dressler, too, openly expressed agnosticism about the truth of free will while affirming responsibility. His account hovered between a compatibilist declaration that determinism is irrelevant to an at least partly retributivist criminal law and a conclusion that the universal human experience of free choice – of personhood – is, _tout court_, sufficient to underpin our blaming practices and to reject determinism in practice. In keeping with this array of neo-retributivist approaches common to the 1980s and 1990s, neither Boldt nor Wright viewed the truth, or possible truth, of determinism as a barrier to desert. Indeed, for each of them, compatibilism – if that is a term either would have embraced – was largely a foundation from which they proceeded to set themselves apart through attempts to confront what they saw as fault lines within mainstream retributivist legal theory; each offered a defense of that theory by endeavoring to expose, and to remedy, its internal contradictions.

Thus, throughout the 1980s and early 1990s, much legal scholarship on the free will problem coalesced around reaffirmations of desert that more directly acknowledged the determinist critique. Scholars' responses to the critique varied. But a compatibilist bent was not the only thing that many of them shared. Almost universally, they also expressed a shared sense that conventional attitudes about personhood and responsibility were integral to understanding – and to justifying – criminal condemnation. Over the course of the century, conventional free-will-based and other retributive modes of judgment had risen from denunciation by some Progressives, to increasing instrumental acceptance, to apparent relegitimization by the neo-retributivist tide. By the end of the century, responsibility scholarship was marked by claims on conventional attitudes and the incorporation of these attitudes in ways that inherently appeared to reduce the distance between theory and conventional morality. Concomitantly, it would seem that the role of the jury was increasingly less controversial. Sometimes explicitly, but more often implicitly, the jury saw approval not just for its instrumental role in protecting political liberty, as was commonly the case at least post–World War II, but also for its role as a litmus of conventional morality. In Morse's words, the jury was "the moral representative of society," and "twelve persons good and true are quite sufficient" to make the "commonsense moral and legal judgments" required by our criminal law.[225] Still, this was not Bazelon's comparatively full acceptance of the jury and its presumption that free behavior was possible. Rather, particularly for the more formal compatibilists, the jury's role – and theory's articulated acceptance of conventional moral views – appeared tightly circumscribed by the theoretical constructs that justified applying such views even in a determined world.

Accordingly, a clear tension persisted between responsibility scholarship's increasing acceptance – or at least incorporation – of conventional morality and the scholarship's *description* of that morality.[226] Formal theory's blameworthy, rationally choosing "person" operating in a world of universal causation was not precisely the same freely willing figure that earlier-in-century scholarship had assumed was the subject of conventional blame. Those who were more agnostic about formal compatibilism appeared to offer a better fit between theory and the actual contours of conventional morality, perhaps precisely because their aims were in part to justify blame attribution in ways that more holistically resembled the human act and experience of blaming. Weinreb was clearly motivated in part by the apparent distance between theory and real-world judging evident in formal legal compatibilist thought. And this seemingly unbridgeable distance may well be in part what underlay the increasingly common, ongoing rough use of compatibilist language as a loose and vaguely theorized foundation for retribution rooted in little more than the idea of personhood, Kantian dignity principles, and sheer resistance to the absurdum to which the reductio inexorably led.

By the 1990s, then, optimistic Progressive ideals, initially girded by science and humanist concerns, had faced significant erosion both from outside philosophical and practical forces and from latter-day Progressives' own questioning of rehabilitation in practice and of the limits of state power. But Progressivism had left formative marks on twentieth century criminal jurisprudence. The determinist critique had remained a central point of debate – or, at least, departure – for scholars concerned with the question of legal responsibility; indeed, the critique had generated much of the concern. And, for many, although hopes of a truly revolutionized legal regime based on Progressive ideals had passed, the social truths revealed during the height of Progressive thought remained as a critical means for softening or circumscribing the reach of blame-oriented responsibility and punishment. This interplay between Progressivism and determinism practically appeared to come full circle as scholars such as Boldt and Wright endorsed retributivist notions while attempting to limit blame and punishment along what

---

[225] Morse, "Psychology, Determinism and Legal Responsibility," 78, 80.

[226] Recall Michael Moore's view that, conventionally, we all associate capacity and opportunity for practical reasoning, *tout court*, with the capacity for moral and legal responsibility.

might be seen as something akin to classically, albeit selectively, Progressive/ determinist lines.

But the heyday of Progressivism was long since over, at least among legal scholars, who were, of necessity, more directly concerned with the real-world consequences of determinism than were philosophers or those in the field of psychology, who could be more concerned, respectively, with deep truths or with mere description than with the administration of a far-reaching – and, many would say, unavoidably punitive – criminal justice system. This pragmatic orientation of legal scholarship was evidenced in part by the shift away from the direct engagement with determinism exemplified by Moore and Morse, and toward the resilient agnosticism of, inter alia, Weinreb, Kadish, Dressler, and Wright. The latter scholars sometimes appeared more concerned with salvaging the practical (and perhaps psychological) virtues of blame-attribution than with dispelling the inconsistencies (and mysteries) Moore claimed were inherent in causal theory. Neo-retributivism had heightened the stakes and appeared to demand a response to the determinist critique. And the resulting desire of scholars to root desert in something more than mere utility or social convention naturally led them to compatibilism. But compatibilism's own conceptual difficulties led it to become a sort of mantra for many instead of a fully theorized position.

9

Epilogue

Competing Perspectives at the Close of the Twentieth Century

INTRODUCTION

The legal-academic conversation of the long 1980s yielded both a formal philosophical compatibilism that directly confronted determinism and alternative, less formal, implicitly compatibilist approaches to desert-based responsibility that subordinated – or even gave up on – a response to the determinist critique. Generally, compatibilism premised largely on humans' capacity for rational choice, and/or on the respect for the "person" inherent in recognizing such a capacity, persisted as the dominant rationale underlying attribution of guilt and imposition of punishment in the criminal law. But myriad concerns, whether scientific, philosophical, humanist, or political – many drawing in some way on midcentury Progressive Era-inspired thought and experiments – continued to challenge mainstream notions of desert from both inside and outside the legal academy. The unease – which some would say is, and indeed *should* be, inherent in our judging and punishing others – remained.

The last decade of the century saw the continued development of alternatives to rational-choice-based compatibilism that both responded to the arguably sterile claims on conventional morality made by formal compatibilism and elaborated on the personal and social aspects of responsibility. Some of these alternatives built on compatibilism but considered it as only a starting point. Others seem to have rejected not only compatibilism but the very premises underlying the ever-closer alliance between legal academics and professional philosophers; in truth, that alliance was unstable from the outset, as academic philosophy was itself splintered, providing more (and often radically differing) perspectives on the free will issue than the central (compatibilist) one to which mainstream legal academic thought had attached itself.

Some lines of legal thought centered either on an evaluation of the defendant's motivations – or "virtue" – or on the ritual of inculpation itself. I begin this final chapter by introducing variants along these lines of what legal scholar Victoria Nourse in 1998 termed "The New Normativity." Although these effectively character-based approaches retained a focus on the "person," they mostly eschewed the formal compatibilist emphasis on rational choice. Nourse and others posited the impossibility of logically categorizing culpable and non-culpable behavior using typical self-control or rational choice models. A common claim of many such approaches was, rather, that the phenomenon of judging is unavoidably normative and this must be admitted – and the process must be self-reflexive – in order to achieve real justice by way of an internally consistent legal system capable of treating citizens equally.

I also touch on the approaches of others who stepped aside from the reasoned choice/causation dichotomy by focusing even more directly on the cultural or discursive aspects of blamable behavior in attempts to marginalize traditional notions of individual choice without rejecting the idea of responsibility. Here I discuss the scholarship of the British academic Alan Norrie as a counterpoint to late-twentieth-century American scholarship, which, as a whole, emphasized the individual person's rationality or character as the focal point for responsibility attribution. Norrie emphasized the social and dialectical nature of criminal judgment. Like the American "new normatives," he rejected the notion that culpability can be meaningfully circumscribed by considering the isolated notion of an individual actor's apparent capacity for rational choice.

But I ultimately subordinate these various departures to *fin de millennium* manifestations of mainstream theory, represented in its most formal state by Moore and Morse. My suggestion is that, within legal-academic criminal jurisprudence circles, virtue or "normative" theory was epiphenomenal and quickly ran its course – and other alternatives, including social constructionism and communicative theory, appear not to have taken hold – while the various forms of rational choice theory, premised on the unique human capacity to act upon reason, have proved the century's lasting, if embattled, bequest to our own time.

In our own time, of course, mainstream compatibilism's more and less formal iterations of rational choice theory face new challenges, whether from neuroscience, sociobiology, gene sequencing, or some currents of academic philosophy. Beyond offering Morse a brief final word on the deterministic implications of neuroscience, in particular, I do not treat these twenty-first-century scientific challenges in any depth, but leave them to others better able to explicate them and to assess their implications. Mainstream thought regarding the bases for criminal responsibility in light of the determinist critique also faces the claim that both determinism and free will are incoherent ideas that legal scholars (and all others as well) ought simply to leave aside.[1] Whatever the wisdom of this last bit of advice, I suspect that many will not readily accept it, although I venture no opinion as to whether this is because they are determined to plod on as before or will freely choose to do so.

TOWARD A NEW NORMATIVITY

I begin my epilogue with a commentary on mid-1990s character-based accounts that sought to marginalize the causation problem that continued to bedevil modern criminal jurisprudence. Approaching the responsibility issue – and, derivatively, the freedom issue – in differing and particularly instructive ways, these accounts directed their attention primarily to virtue as the crucial aspect of the "person" – rather than to the capacity for reasoned choice, per se. They thus retained the idea of the individual as the locus of responsibility – indeed, they fought to shore up that idea against contemporary currents of the more broadly "socialized" notion of responsibility captured in 1992 in both Robert Weisberg's insightful non-retributivist essay, "Criminal Law, Criminology, and the Small World of Legal Scholars," and Meir Dan-Cohen's seminal essay, "Responsibility and the Boundaries of the Self."[2]

I channel my limited review through University of Wisconsin law professor Victoria Nourse, who, in her penetrating 1998 critique of *Moral Judgment*, James Q. Wilson's book on abuse of the "abuse excuse,"[3] drew on several

---

[1] See Peter Westen, "Getting the Fly Out of the Bottle: The False Problem of Free Will and Determinism," *Buffalo Criminal Law Review*, vol. 8 (2005): 599–652. Westen provides a challenging analysis of both free will and determinism and finds each incoherent on its own terms, concluding that the "supposed problem of free will and determinism" is a "[false] problem that we have created for our selves by posing questions in terms that are inconsistent with the presuppositions that we must necessarily invoke in addressing them." "The proper response," he admonishes, "is to recognize that nothing can possibly come of it and, hence, that nothing can possibly turn on it. Just stop thinking about it. Just think about something else!" (652). Westen does not reject responsibility itself, however, as an incoherent idea. Rather, he believes that, according to his own "attitudinal theory of excuse," we may assign "normative blame" – without, I infer, any inquiry into the concept or existence of free will – to one who "acted with an attitude of selfish or self-indulgent disregard for what the state, speaking in its criminal statutes, regards as the legitimate interests of persons under the circumstances." Peter Westen, "An Attitudinal Theory of Excuse," *Law and Philosophy*, vol. 25 (2006): 289–375, 373.

[2] Meir Dan-Cohen, "Responsibility and the Boundaries of the Self," *Harvard Law Review*, vol. 105 (1992): 959–1003.

[3] Victoria Nourse, "The New Normativity: The Abuse Excuse and the Resurgence of Judgment in the Criminal Law," review of *Moral Judgment: Does the Abuse Excuse Threaten Our Legal System?*, by James Q. Wilson, *Stanford Law Review*, vol. 50 (1998): 1435–70. For an elaboration of Nourse's ideas regarding a "new normativity," see Victoria Nourse, "Hearts and Minds: Understanding the New Culpability," *Buffalo Criminal Law Review*, vol. 6 (2002): 361–88.

representative accounts, including those of legal scholars Samuel Pillsbury, Kyron Huigens, Dan Kahan, and Martha Nussbaum. These authors oriented themselves in relation to the freedom problem, but each was also – to differing degrees and in differing ways – pushing it aside, striking out for another way of seeing the matter of responsibility. They looked to the nature and quality of the defendant's motivations as exhibited by the act in question and, as with all versions of character theory, their approaches implicitly invited the determinist's challenge: How can we fairly hold a defendant liable for failing to meet standards he was not provably able to meet? Should one wish to hypothesize a response to such a challenge, the work of Kahan and Nussbaum, in particular, could be taken to signal an important new departure within neo-retributivism, a move not only away from causal theory and its surrogates, but also toward ascription of responsibility based solely on one's failure to possess the attitudes that one "ought" to possess.

Highlighting the adoption of an Aristotelian concept of virtue, Nourse aptly described the particular offshoot of postmodernism within which she identified herself as in search of a "new normativity." She heralded the maturation of a school of thought that privileged "judgment" rather than "explanation" of the offender's behavior, a move she interpreted as greatly reducing concern with the idea of "self-control." That long-standing concern had, Nourse concluded, ultimately run its course. Advocating the abandonment of mechanistic/behavioral theories of responsibility, she sought criteria that resolved the attribution of responsibility problem in a manner that severed the determinants of responsibility from causal theories of criminal law defenses. In drawing out what she (with some reason) took to be the implications of late-twentieth-century retributivist theory, Nourse produced a pioneering essay, itself an historical moment perhaps more than she knew or was prepared for. Her late 1990s work and that of others who informed it, although not producing the broad scale theoretical sea change she called for, provided discerning reflections on the central premises of legal responsibility scholarship at the end of the century.

Nourse's review of Wilson presented a head-on challenge to Michael Moore and to rational choice theorists, generally. Wilson had drawn heavily on Moore, whose critique of causal theory Nourse thought clearly right. But, for Nourse, Moore's approach was fatally incomplete. "Even assuming a causal theory is wrong," she countered:

how do we know when we should or should not demand self-control? Moore's response is that excuses depend upon defendants' capacity for practical reasoning rather than self-control. That answer may prove better than causal explanations, but it does not clearly resolve the problem. If, as Moore would have it, we excuse in the case of compulsion because compulsion interferes with "practical reasoning," we are still left asking when defendants are "compelled" in this sense. Why is it, for example, that law and society frequently see men who kill their cheating spouses as at least partially incapable of reason and "compelled" to act, whereas they are quick to question whether women who kill their battering husbands in fear are similarly "compelled"?[4]

It was in this supposed explanatory gap left by Moore between responsible and excused behavior, Nourse posited, that Wilson inserted (albeit, in her view, ultimately unsuccessfully) his notion of "judgment" – of the moral *evaluation* of conduct thought to have gone missing from our conceptions of the law as the result of wrongheaded overreliance on (causal) social scientific *explanation* of conduct.[5] Nourse therefore tentatively located Wilson among other recent proponents of the "new normativity" in legal theory – those who "relied upon the evaluative voice in critiquing particular doctrines."[6] But Wilson's version apparently suffered from "one of the great dangers of evaluative theories": "that they simply reaffirm the valuations of those who create and apply them."[7] Wilson, on Nourse's reading, defined appropriate judgment in traditional, essentially historically bound terms, leading him to make unprincipled distinctions between, for example, male-centered ideas regarding provocation, which he endorsed, and some newer – and female-centered – notions associated with battered spouses, which he deemed abuses of legal excuse theory.[8]

The inability of either Moore or Wilson to draw a principled line between responsible and excused behavior, said Nourse, illustrated her central thesis: the problem was with the law's underlying mechanistic/behavioral theory of responsibility and excuse – what she termed the "self-control" model – which, she concluded, neither Moore nor Wilson successfully escaped.[9] Here, citing with approval Pillsbury, Huigens, Kahan, and Nussbaum (among others), Nourse turned hopefully to evaluative approaches and sought a substantive basis for "judgment" that would avoid the twin charges of arbitrariness and traditionalism that she leveled at Wilson. Nourse readily admitted that a theory of judging responsibility on grounds other than that of self-control had yet to be fully worked out. But she examined possible models for judgment – "by community," "by character," and "by critique." Her discussion of judgment by character relied on Aristotelian ideals and the work of Huigens, who enlisted Aristotle's *Ethics* to posit that inculpation based on character "has intrinsic value as part of the good life for human beings." According to to the "republican theory of inculpation" advanced by Huigens, the very practice of inculpation was valuable because it was among the features of a life directed toward the attainment of the "good," including participation

---

4 Nourse, "New Normativity," 1449 (citing Michael S. Moore, "Causation and the Excuses," *California Law Review*, vol. 73 (1985): 1091–1149, 1129–32).
5 Nourse, "New Normativity," 1436.
6 Nourse, "New Normativity," 1456.
7 Nourse, "New Normativity," 1466.
8 Nourse, "New Normativity," 1437–38, 1449–56.
9 Nourse, "New Normativity," 1467.

in political life and the development and evaluation of virtuous character through our unique ability to reason – and was itself constitutive of a kind of human freedom.[10]

Each potential model for judgment drew upon "republican" notions of virtue and consensus theory. Rather than focusing on the "behavioral aspects of crime," they presumed "individuals should be judged by the quality of their choices, not simply their capacity for choice."[11] Primarily, each – when properly applied – reduced the risks of inconsistency and arbitrariness through application of legally embedded and widely shared cultural norms regarding behavior that complied with meta-norms regarding equality: the golden rule, we might say, as applied to _all_ members of the community.[12] The obvious questions arise: What roots such judgments, if not an arbitrary value system such as the one Nourse attributed to Wilson? And what of the free will?

Early in her critique, Nourse implied that the causal/mechanistic model itself created the free will/determinism problem: "It is well-accepted within the criminal law academy," she asserted, "that if one takes the self-control argument to its logical conclusion, the theory 'has no limit.' Once we accept some reasons for a lack of self-control, why not accept all reasons?" In rejecting the self-control model, she rejected excuses "based on defendants' inability to freely choose a course of action."[13] She thus avoided the determinism question without expressly taking sides as to its truth, much as did Kahan and Nussbaum, who rejected a concept of "voluntary" that limited "the class of voluntary acts to those that are 'freely willed' or 'chosen.'"[14] Theirs was effectively a side-constrained consequentialist account that minimized the relevance of the free will issue to legal responsibility by identifying specific externally verifiable characteristics of human psychology – cognitive appraisals expressed by one's emotions – as the main legally meaningful determinants of the concept of "agency." Adhering to a form of character

---

[10] Kyron Huigens, "Virtue and Inculpation," _Harvard Law Review_, vol. 108 (1995): 1423–80, 1425, 1444–54.

[11] Nourse, "New Normativity," 1458.

[12] Perhaps most illustrative of this point is Nourse's discussion of judgment as critique, which in part incorporated the work of Kahan and Nussbaum, whom Nourse describes as "unearthing evaluative claims from behaviorist trappings. They do not pick and choose defenses that reflect 'judgment' and those that do not; they employ judgment as an intellectual method to explain and critique inconsistencies within contemporary doctrine." This sort of judgment "demand[s] not that we resolve first premises about criminal defendants' identity, but that we proceed from the more modest position that a just criminal law must, at a minimum, make consistent evaluative claims": it "does not appeal to an inarticulate or privileged sense of that which is 'common'; it relies, instead, upon the law itself as the measure of what we share" (Nourse, "New Normativity," 1466–67).

[13] Nourse, "New Normativity," 1446–48.

[14] Dan M. Kahan and Martha Nussbaum, "Two Conceptions of Emotion in Criminal Law," _Columbia Law Review_, vol. 96 (1996): 269–374, 341.

theory – the "evaluative view" of emotions[15] – Kahan and Nussbaum posited that "an act is 'voluntary' when it is sufficiently engaged with a person's agency to bear moral assessment." Their view "assumes that this condition is satisfied so long as a person's conduct can be comprehensibly explained in terms of her beliefs about, appraisals of, and desires for good essential to her well-being." They freely admitted that theirs was "a relatively modest view of human agency,"[16] and remained largely ambiguous about the role of free will to their primarily "descriptive" account.[17] Focusing on innate capacities of "critical assessment and reflection" – capacities already observable in early childhood and developed through moral education – they implied, but did not precisely state, that humans are born with the capacity for free will; instead (essentially in contrast to Huigens) they simply declared that they would "not embark on the metaphysical question … of what the contribution of the individual must be in order for [critical] assessment to be appropriate."[18]

The behavioral norms that Nourse (and Kahan and Nussbaum) suggested should underlie responsibility judgments might well preclude the condemnation of what one might call "determined" acts, but self-control was nonetheless somehow not at issue. Or was it? There is nothing to say that the behavioral norms to which the "new normativity" looked did not, in law as well as *in practice*, embed within themselves widespread and oft-applied principles – or intuitions – regarding the capacity for self-control. Where Huigens asserts that virtue is a jury question,[19] for example, might scholars still assume – and accept – that jurors conceive of themselves as assessing not virtue, as defined by Aristotle, but the defendant's capacity for self-control or blameworthy choice? In other words, it is not clear how much the exact nature of the subjective judgment mattered as long as the result (perhaps not coincidentally) could also be viewed as consistent with a particular scholarly brand of morally acceptable normative judgment. The distance between Bazelon's conception of the appropriate role of the jury with regard

---

[15] Kahan and Nussbaum presented the evaluative view – in contrast to the mechanistic conception – of emotion as the best explanation for the law, for its actual application, and for widespread social understandings of just deserts. The "mechanistic conception," they explained

> sees emotions as forces that do not contain or respond to thought; it is correspondingly skeptical about both the coherence of morally assessing emotions and the possibility of shaping and reshaping emotional lives. The evaluative conception, in contrast, holds that emotions express cognitive appraisals, that these appraisals can themselves be morally evaluated, and that persons (individually and collectively) can and should shape their emotions through moral education. (Kahan and Nussbaum, "Two Conceptions," 273)

[16] Kahan and Nussbaum, "Two Conceptions," 341.
[17] Kahan and Nussbaum, "Two Conceptions," 273.
[18] Kahan and Nussbaum, "Two Conceptions," 301 and n. 126.
[19] Huigens, "Virtue and Inculpation," 1462–67.

to the responsibility issue and conceptions of responsibility determination in 1990s (non-self-control) scholarship might not have been very great.

But let us try to take Nourse's understanding of the new scholarship on its own terms. We have, after all, nothing to say here about true law or pure logic; our interest is entirely a matter of the history of scholarly reflection regarding the responsibility question. The sole point for us is that Nourse and, in her view at least, some criminal jurisprudence scholars of our recent past urged – or toyed with, or unwittingly proposed – the view that the individual is "responsible" purely for failure to meet standards other than those centered on self-control. Or (here I am taking liberties) simply for failure to do unto others as he would have them do unto him – or perhaps for acting in ways for which the failure to blame is universally deemed unacceptable as a matter of simple humanity. We must imagine that none of these formulations is applicable simply because it might be – or might commonly be supposed to be – premised upon the idea that the retributively blamable offender could in fact have done other than he did; nor are they tests of whether he could have. But would these formulations have appealed to Nourse had she been absolutely convinced that offenders could *not* in fact have done otherwise? Or did they appeal only on grounds of an unargued-for compatibilist position or, alternatively, upon the belief that we can never know for certain whether the offender could not have done otherwise?

I suspect the latter. Although Nourse's formulations of the new normativity were not self-control tests, they appear to have emerged out of 1980s and 1990s character-based scholarship as a kind of surrogate for those tests. They responded to her view that Moore's conception of the determinants of responsibility fell short, that specification of thicker substantive norms of justice was required. More important, Nourse's formulation traded at least in part (or so I infer) on the justice of judgment under conditions of the unknowability, in principle, of life's ultimate secret. They were not meant in some other way to *answer* the ultimate question, for it was at least implicitly conceded that the answer is unknowable.

Pillsbury's 1992 essay, "The Meaning of Deserved Punishment," mediated between rational choice and Nourse's approach. Pillsbury offered a very self-conscious response to the determinist critique, accepting the possibility even of hard determinism but focusing on the centrality to human life of the search for meaning. His approach was premised on what he admitted was an initial leap of faith in the face of the unknown: "Like most people," Pillsbury asserted, he "live[d] in the faith that life has meaning and t[ook] that as [his] starting point." And "moral responsibility," he continued, "provides one of our most important ways of finding meaning in life." Holding responsible one who has broken the law affirms our experience of ourselves as autonomous, rational beings and expresses our commitment to the defense of values. Pillsbury thus invoked a search for meaning on behalf of a "commitment to choice and moral responsibility" in the face of profound doubt.[20] Process constructs meaning rather than insists upon a theory of true responsibility as a predicate.[21] Nourse's rich and inspired formulations appear similarly aimed at telling us how to proceed in this life (where there is no final answer) in accordance with our deepest convictions about what it means to be human. They announced, in effect (again, I am taking liberties), through their proclaimed neutrality and consistency, a standard that, one might say, all rational people would accept behind a veil of ignorance with respect to the question of the existence of free will, if they were to know that the world they would inhabit would itself be behind such a veil.

Nourse's last rubric, "judgment as critique," well describes some defining aspects of the ritual of "critical dialogue" and "reflection" rooted in "particular situations and cultures" (here drawing on Hanna Arendt) that would effectively replace our current mode of guilt attribution. This process avoids "an unthinking acceptance of the status quo" and instead embodies an ongoing, constantly revised conversation whereby we render judgments

---

[20] Samuel H. Pillsbury, "The Meaning of Deserved Punishment: An Essay on Choice, Character, and Responsibility," *Indiana Law Journal*, vol. 67 (1992): 719–52, 735.

[21] The presence of doubt, moreover, did not preclude traditional punishment, in Pillsbury's view. The fact that an offender has "challenged the very idea of human value ... require[s] a strong, punitive response," but this "deserved punishment" is not necessarily retributive in the conventional sense:

> We punish offenders not because they stand outside of society, not because they are alien enemies, but because they are fundamentally like the rest of us. The argument from meaning illustrates the way in which all humans are engaged in a struggle to become moral. The argument supports the common belief that persons like [the convicted murderer, John] Dobbert, Jr. deserve [capital] punishment, but not the belief that they lack value. (Pillsbury, "The Meaning of Deserved Punishment," 752)

Huigens went further than either Pillsbury or (on my reading) Nourse in an attempt to set the free will/determinism problem to rest by insisting on the individual's factually becoming a cause of his own personal self. Huigens was willing to concede that, of course "everything about our world is arbitrary in the same sense, down to all our basic physical existence." His answer to the determinist inhered in his conclusion that, nonetheless, such arbitrariness is not "relevant to moral and legal judgments," but simply constituted "the non-controversial framework within which those judgments are made" ("Virtue and Inculpation," 1470–71). With Aristotle, he believed: "I am responsible for my character to the extent I am responsible for the decisions I make about the ends and effects that shape it" (1448). It was a matter of line drawing: "With regard to inculpation, the determinist places the line farther back in the personal history of the accused than would one who affirms existing judgments about criminal responsibility" (1471). For Huigens (and Aristotle), who affirm such judgments,

> at some point the connection between my origins and my present self is so attenuated that my starting point falls into the background.... At that point my origins drop out of the question of responsibility.... [R]ecent influences on my character ... are the products of my particular choices.... I have made those choices – not in an ultimate sense, but in the only sense that is morally relevant.... [M]y arrival at a point at which my character and circumstances are such that I commit a criminal act is not a random occurrence, is not beyond my control, and is not an arbitrary basis of responsibility. (1472)

"with the fear and knowledge that they may be wrong." We judge "warily, without certainty or joy, and with a humility that requires [us] not only to evaluate but also to identify with the defendant as a member of the human community."[22] And we may add other defining aspects – if only as a historian's surmise about the unarticulated assumptions that informed this powerfully expressed legal-academic feeling-one's-way to a theory of criminal justice and criminal responsibility. Justice, according to Nourse, requires self-consciousness; self-questioning; open admission of doubts and difficulties; honest conversation with the about-to-be-condemned; (by implication, I infer) the belief that such condemnation would be just were one, oneself, in the offender's place; and – above all – humility. One inquires, in an evenhanded way, about relevant *and uncontroversial* norms in existing criminal law – thus, crucially, norms *other than* the law's underlying assumption of humans' capacity for self-control. It is then, or so I again infer, inappropriate (except in the extreme cases identified in existing law) for the offender to say: "I could not have done other," or "You can't prove I could have done other"; for he must say: "Whether or not I could have done other, what you do in judging me is what I would myself do, and think just, were I in your position." Nourse thus began – I sense – with worries regarding the determinist critique but, ultimately, with acceptance of the condition of unknowability of the truth of that critique, and she attempted to found an ethics upon that very condition. By implication, she acknowledged that those ethics might themselves be determined, but presumed that whether they were was itself unknowable, and argued (implicitly) that those ethics were just within a human frame, even if it should be the case (as only an all-knowing outside observer could know) that all human life is in fact determined. In sum, on this reading of Nourse and the new normatives, the determinist critique had been blunted – as it had been by Dressler and others who focused on the personhood principle – by appeal to an agnosticism that (it was believed) could not be gainsaid.

CULTURE, CRITIQUE, AND COMMUNICATION: BEYOND INDIVIDUAL FREEDOM AND DESERT?

It is fair to say that agnosticism permeated much late-twentieth-century legal scholarship on the responsibility question; many legal academics seemed to conclude (at least publicly) that neither the truth of determinism nor the existence of free will could be proved or disproved. Most seem to have accepted some mitigated form of determinism, adopting – unwittingly or otherwise – some version of what might be called "legal compatibilism": adult humans typically possess capacities or qualities that justify

---

[22] Nourse, "New Normativity," 1463–65, in part discussing Hanna Arendt, *Lectures on Kant's Political Philosophy*, ed. Ronald Beiner (Chicago: University of Chicago Press, 1982).

the attribution of criminal responsibility – free-will-based or otherwise – in an only *possibly* non-determined, or even in a fully determined, world. But any particular compatibilist position seemed fragile, either from a philosophical perspective or a conventional moral one. Thus I suggest that compatibilism became a sort of partially theorized mantra for many, as had the idea of responsibility as an aspect of personhood. Indeed, the two mantras were often barely separable from one another.

Nourse and the new normatives were not the only ones who offered new attempts at moving beyond the seemingly intractable tensions inherent in compatibilism. Other important lines of thought emphasized the dialogue within culture, and between society and the "self," in order to marginalize traditional notions of individual autonomy without rejecting a normative idea of responsibility. These approaches – I include both social construction theory and communicative theory – blunted the impact of critical legal theory's adoption (and adaptation) of the positivist critique of law's traditional underlying presumption. Indeed, critical theory had itself evolved in this very direction. Having "trashed" free will and (via Kelman's seminal article of 1981[23]) line-drawing on the basis of "free" and "unfree" behavior, critical theory had now largely made its peace with the idea of legal enforcement of responsibility – albeit socially constructed responsibility.

At base, these socialized approaches called for a rethinking of what is at issue when we speak of criminal responsibility. Although they gained more traction among legal theorists overseas, there were some parallel elements on the American side – there are reflections, for example, in Huigens's Aristotelian dialectic and in the primacy placed on internal societal coherence by Nourse, Kahan, and Nussbaum. Others, including Robert Weisberg of Stanford Law School, expressly asserted the centrality of culture. In 1992 Weisberg raised the challenge:

In a *Miranda* case, as well as in a Bernhard Goetz case or a cultural defense case our abstract debates over whether to apply subjective or objective tests of reasonable homicidal behavior are really masked political and anthropological debates over competing individualist and group models of human volition. Cast too often by legal address in terms of two denatured choices – free will or determinism – the question is more complicated: How many parts of an individual's volition are owed to his social duties to others? Culture is the element between denatured free will and scientific determinism which almost all of criminal law now treats as an exotic footnote, precisely because law only recognizes the phenomenon of culture when it manifests itself in an exotic way.[24]

[23] Mark Kelman, "Interpretive Construction in the Substantive Criminal Law," *Stanford Law Review*, vol. 33 [1981]: 591–673.

[24] Robert Weisberg, "Criminal Law, Criminology, and the Small World of Legal Scholars," *Colorado Law Review*, vol. 63 (1992): 521–68, 543.

"Culture" here appears to have borne close relation to the perspective on the responsible person to which the English legal scholar Jeremy Horder[25] and the Israeli-born British philosopher Joseph Raz[26] appealed, and the ideas that lay behind Weisberg's invocation of culture were well developed in the same year by Meir Dan-Cohen in terms of the "boundaries of the self."[27]

English legal scholar Alan Norrie provides a further example of the socialized understanding of responsibility. Norrie evidenced in the 1990s a turn to a search for a defensible realm of criminal responsibility via social construction theory. In so doing, he modified the critique of the free will doctrine that was central to his seminal critical-legal writings on the theory of responsibility in the 1980s and early 1990s.[28] Focusing on the problem of punishment, he now endorsed an approach that

would emphasize the ambivalence that accompanies our sense of judgment as a result of the ambiguous moral character of human agency as *both* social and individual. Only a *dialectical* account of punishment can take us beyond the antinomial understandings that structure criminal justice thought. Viewed in this light, the free will/determinism debate can be seen as one more false antimony which reflects, but cannot capture, real social and moral issues. [Michael] Moore's knockdown of the "determinist challenge" is so convincing that one might wonder why anyone could

[25] Horder denied that one need choose between a view of the individual as a "free chooser ultimately divorced from social and biological forces and other circumstances" and/or as "nothing more than a link in the chain of causation." The question was not precisely whether one's character causes behavior, but whether (here resonances of Arenella) in a given case "character [has shaped] conduct through evaluative guidance, whatever the conduct's cause."

> What matters to responsibility, then, is that one can maintain an adequate distance between the causes of conduct, and morally evaluative control over conduct in relation to the cause.... Sometimes there is no such distance. In insanity and diminished responsibility cases, as with very young children, defendants lack the evaluative control that would enable them to give moral shape to their conduct in the light of its cause ... everything depends on whether [one] was able adequately to revise or reassess his values at the relevant time: had he been exposed to moral influences for the good of a kind that could reasonably have informed and generated in him the basis of a moral capacity to conform his conduct to the law? (Jeremy Horder, "Criminal Law: Between Determinism, Liberalism, and Criminal Justice," *Current Legal Problems*, vol. 49 [1996]: 159–86, 170–72)

Horder invoked Thomas Nagel's objection that the idea that one is identified either with his subjectivity or his objectivity rests on a false opposition, and he drew upon Raz to support the proposition that the "relationship between conduct and character is reciprocal, not a matter of one-way causation" (171 nn. 35, 37).

[26] E.g., Joseph Raz, *Ethics in the Public Domain: Essays in the Morality of Law and Politics* (Oxford: Clarendon Press, 1994).

[27] Dan-Cohen, "Responsibility and the Boundaries of the Self." For discussion of these and related themes, see John T. Parry, "The Virtue of Necessity: Reshaping Culpability and the Rule of Law," *Houston Law Review*, vol. 36 (1999): 429–34.

[28] See especially Alan Norrie, *Crime, Reason and History: A Critical Introduction to Criminal Law* (London: Weidenfeld & Nicolson, 1993).

have been taken in by it in the first place. Free will/determinism is a straw issue which diverts attention from the much more difficult and conflictual questions of moral and political dialogue that are central to questions of punishment.[29]

Norrie nonetheless criticized Moore for failing to understand the implications of the mixed "social and individual" nature of human agency. In 1998, Norrie set forth his own (modified) views at length in "a social constructionist account of subjectivity" that acknowledged the "social and moral conflict behind the individualist categories." Borrowing from Rom Harré's "constructionist" concept of "selfhood,"[30] Norrie concluded that one is able "to rationalize the resonance that concepts of individual justice possess while insisting on their intrinsically problematic character.... Individual agents are always more and less than the individuals that liberalism sees and invokes."[31]

Norrie's "turn" involved a historicizing of the free will/determinism problem. He cited the work of Gareth Stedman Jones and David Garland, "who have shown the way in which determinist ideology was taken up historically as the basis for the resolution of social problems within welfare capitalist societies at the turn of the present century." Norrie continued:

Historical practice overdetermined the significance of the free will/determinism antinomy, but as an inadequate means to discuss the real social and individual, moral relations that are invoked by the problem of crime. The debate thus occupies the site of a real practical problem, but its true parameters cannot properly be grasped through this ideological, antinomial, optic.[32]

Thus, the free will/determinism "antinomy" had transmuted in Norrie's work into an individual/social antinomy. The latter, unlike the former, was, he thought, resolvable in everyday legal practice: the law must take account of the dialectical relationship between the social and the individual, must adopt a concept of "selfhood" that embodies that dialectic and, thus, the "ambiguous moral character of human agency."

---

[29] Alan Norrie, "Michael Moore's Deviation," review of Moore, *Placing Blame*, *Oxford Journal of Legal Studies*, vol. 19 (1999): 111–32, 123–24.

[30] E.g., Rom Harré, *Social Being* (2d ed.) (Oxford: Blackwell, 1993). For a thoroughgoing analysis along these lines, see Norrie *Punishment, Responsibility, and Justice: A Relational Critique* (Oxford: Oxford University Press, 2000).

[31] Alan Norrie, "'Simulacra of Morality'? Beyond the Ideal/Actual Antinomies of Criminal Justice," chap. 3 in *Philosophy and the Criminal Law: Principle and Critique*, ed. Antony Duff (New York: Cambridge University Press, 1998), 149–50.

[32] Norrie, "Moore's Deviation," 124 and n. 15 (citing Gareth Stedman Jones, *Outcast London: A Study in the Relationship between Classes in Victorian Society* [Oxford: Clarendon Press, 1971], and David Garland, *Punishment and Welfare: A History of Penal Strategies* [Aldershot, Hants: Gower, 1985]). Norrie added (n. 16) that this "would be the nub of [his] response to Jeremy Horder," who had criticized Norrie's earlier discussion of the free will/determinism problem in Horder, "Criminal Law: Between Determinism, Liberalism, and Criminal Justice."

Something akin to Norrie's approach was exemplified in the work of the British philosopher Antony Duff, whose ideas proved influential on a number of fronts. Duff responded to the problem posed by the attenuation of personal responsibility by positioning personal responsibility as a kind of potential that the law, through both trial and punishment, should seek to bring forth. Communicative justice, as Duff defined it, is something other than purely retributive; although it employs the idea of blameworthiness, it functions mainly as a ritual of instruction, of leading the offender to self-awareness, self-criticism, and the capacity for responsible self-assertion. Norrie shared much of Duff's inspiration, but he criticized Duff for his subordination of the social to the individual – that is, for Duff's alleged failure to embrace the dialectics of the person and the social. Duff responded with his own criticism of Norrie's particular expression of the idea of a social/individual "antinomy" in the law. The problem is not in the law, Duff argued, but in the relationship between the law and its "preconditions," in particular that the legal system "can claim the moral standing to apply the law to all those on whom it is supposedly binding." Duff claimed to avoid this problem because, on his account,

the courts can properly say it is not their responsibility to judge the extent to which such preconditions are satisfied.... On a minimalist view the most that is needed to give us such moral standing is that we have not (directly or maliciously) denied [the defendant] such rights or benefits as the law assigns her.... On a more ambitious view, we must (collectively or institutionally, if not individually or personally) have treated her as a member of the community in a richer sense than this: We must have treated her as a full and respected participant in our common life.[33]

Duff argued that an autonomy-based idea of criminal responsibility is internally "principled," not fundamentally "contradictory," as Norrie would have it. Respect for autonomy is an element of law's goal of "control": "the notion of 'control' is then itself understood in a way that respects the moral standing of those whose conduct is to be 'controlled.'"[34] Duff elaborated upon this in part in relation to the "abstraction" of "normality" that "is a necessary feature of a system like ours."[35] Contradictions within the law are not best understood as irresolvable; rather, the meeting of the necessary preconditions reduces them to the status of mere inevitable tensions that one must expect in any system of justice.

Duff's account of the law's "respect for autonomy," which I have very barely sketched, remained faithful to his elaborate and influential mid-1980s version of a theory of communicative justice. That theory had deep and familiar American roots, among them Henry Hart's 1958 "Aims of

---

[33] R. A. Duff, "Principle and Contradiction in the Criminal Law: Motives and Criminal Liability," chap. 4 in Duff, *Philosophy and the Criminal Law*, 195–97.

[34] Duff, "Principle and Contradiction," 170.

[35] Duff, "Principle and Contradiction," 190.

the Criminal Law," and Herbert Morris's 1981 "Paternalistic Theory of Punishment." Still, although communicative theory (as well as benign, non-retributive expressivism and Jean Hampton's "moral education" theory[36]) occupied a significant place in late-twentieth-century U.S. punishment theory, it did not receive the comprehensive theoretical treatment accorded it by Duff, in 1986, in the United Kingdom.[37] This, despite the fact that, stateside, the preconditions for such a new form of "compensatory" *penal* theory emerged in essentially retributivist writings on *responsibility* that transmuted the free will question into one of self and culture.[38]

---

[36] E.g., Jean Hampton, "The Moral Education Theory of Punishment," in *Punishment*, ed. A. John Simmons et al. (Princeton, NJ: Princeton University Press, 1995), 112–42 (originally published in *Philosophy and Public Affairs*, vol. 13 [1984]: 208–38).

[37] R. A. Duff, *Trials and Punishments* (Cambridge: Cambridge University Press, 1986).

[38] I am not addressing a norm-based theory of punishment that emerged in the United States in the late 1990s and that promoted relatively non-harsh shaming practices as a substitute for incarceration and fines, at least in less serious criminal offenses. See especially Dan M. Kahan, "Social Influence, Social Meaning, and Deterrence," *Virginia Law Review*, vol. 83 (1997): 349–95; Lawrence Lessig, "The Regulation of Social Meaning," *University of Chicago Law Review*, vol. 62 (1995): 943–1045; Dan M. Kahan and Tracey Meares, "Foreword: The Coming Crisis of Criminal Procedure," *Georgetown Law Review*, vol. 86 (1998): 1153–84; Lawrence Lessig, "The New Chicago School," *Journal of Legal Studies* (1998): 661–92. Although shaming practices might be taken to imply desert-based responsibility, the expressivist theory of punishment propounded here seems to reside within a consequentialist – deterrence-based – approach. Moreover, the principal contributors to this new departure in the field of punishment do not grapple with the problem of inculcating a sense of responsibility against a background of doubt about true personal autonomy, as do the proponents of communicative justice on whom I focus. For a lengthy study of this movement – which is still in the process of development – and a critique of its underlying conception of social norms, see Robert Weisberg, "Norms and the Criminal Law, and the Norms of Criminal Law Scholarship," *JCLC*, vol. 93 (2003): 467–591.

Yet another – and somewhat older – theory of punishment bloomed in the 1990s and beyond, one that occupied a central place in the movement for "restorative justice." Restorative justice "involves the victim, the offender, and the community in a search for solutions which promote repair, reconciliation, and reassurance." In doing so, restorative justice moves away from the traditional Statist model of criminal law that "determines blame and administers pain in a contest between the offender and the state directed by systematic rules." Howard Zehr, *Changing Lenses: A New Focus for Crime and Justice*, (Scottdale, PA: Herald Press, 1990), 181. Here too, the objectives of this movement appear to be consequentialist in nature although, as one leading proponent has claimed, restorative justice aims to find an alternative to punishment "for a future in which punishment is marginalized." John Braithwaite, "A Future Where Punishment Is Marginalized: Realistic or Utopian?," *UCLA Law Review*, vol. 46 (1999): 1727–50, 1729. A full account of the ideas of this movement appears in *Utah Law Review*, vol. 2003 (2003). Also marginalized is any discussion of traditional theories of responsibility as a predicate for restorative justice. For a critique of this feature of restorative justice, see David Dolinko, "Restorative Justice and the Justification of Punishment," *Utah Law Review*, vol. 2003 (2003): 319–42.

Although I do not take up the matter, it is possible that both the social-norms approach and the movement for restorative justice are – in differing ways – in part responding to perceived infirmities in traditional theories' reliance (whether via negative or positive

Duff emphasized, in his contribution to an at least seemingly retributivist theory of communicative justice, respect for the "autonomy" of the defendant: all the "preconditions" must be met and enacted by both trial and sentencing through open communication with the defendant regarding both the fact of his moral autonomy and the respect accorded him for that autonomy.[39] By contrast, Norrie, we have seen, imagined an approach to "selfhood" that reflected – and, indeed, openly announced – the very limits of the individual self, even the incoherence of that idea. His defendant could be understood as one who has been led to internalize his own situation as being only ambiguously an "individual." Unlike Duff's defendant, Norrie's was to be "communicated" with in terms of all those factors that rendered his "self" only ambiguously a responsible self. Yet, might not an understanding of those factors, when internalized, one wonders, have destabilized not only the individual's sense of "autonomy" but also his sense of personal well-being and the meaningfulness of life? Might not Norrie's version of the communicative process thus become, at least from the American perspective, the ultimate punishment? Duff's response to Norrie was itself free from the "self"-annihilating aspects of Norrie's "constructionist" theory, a theory that was a step too far both for those late-twentieth-century American legal academics whose own discourse of virtue, culture, and social construction sought a surrogate for true autonomy, and for those more mainstream theorists committed to using the idea of "capacity and opportunity" in relation to "personhood" to ground an acceptable neo-retributivist form of individual criminal responsibility.

Viewed in the overall context of my twentieth-century frame, Norrie purported to come full circle by moving beyond the free will/determinism debate, the centrality of which Norrie characterized as a historical artifact. Yet, on some level, one is tempted to think that a species of hard determinism had reappeared accompanied by a theoretical/philosophical softening agent that might or might not, especially from the perspective of conventional morality, look much different from the American Progressive experiments of the century's outset: the social process was again central, free will was by no means assumed, and the individual was to be engaged with by a state interested in his personal development. Social construction theory could also appear, however, as one of the innumerable forms of compatibilism that the late twentieth-century mind constructed in its determined search for a place to stand and to judge – that is, to derive prescription from what might be

retributivism) upon an underlying theory of personal responsibility. If so, my final remarks regarding Americans' attachment to free will (and its surrogates) might well prove overdrawn – at least with respect to the early twenty-first century.

[39] Duff, *Trials and Punishments*. See also R. A. Duff, *Punishment, Communication, and Community* (New York: Oxford University Press, 2001). For a review of this latter work, see Leo Zaibert, "Punishment, Liberalism, and Communitarianism," *Buffalo Criminal Law Review*, vol. 6 (2002): 673–90.

taken to be little more than (often astute) exercises in description – and thus to save the critical human notion of responsibility from (alleged) scientific realities of human existence.

COMPATIBILISM AND THE DETERMINED AFFIRMATION OF RESPONSIBILITY

It is too early to say whether approaches such as Norrie's could prove influential among American retributivist legal scholars other than those who have latched onto the mediating ("constructionist") concept of "culture" and, derivatively, the idea of "selfhood" as a profoundly liminal, yet responsibility-bearing, state. This despite the fact that some language of culture, social construction, and normativity appears even in more formal compatibilist accounts. For, at the century's end, it was the roughly compatibilist idea of *individual* responsibility premised upon the capacity and opportunity for reasoned choice that mainly grounded neo-retributivism in the domain of legal scholarship, which marks one of the endpoints of our story.

In the last decade of the closing century, to a large extent, criminal jurisprudence based upon an offender's deliberative choice had fallen in line with much contemporary compatibilist philosophical thought. Universal causation (it was commonly thought) could not be denied, but the individual's (determined) participation in the process of reasoned determination of his behavior yielded responsibility along varying conceptual lines. Certainly, as I outlined previously in the Introduction to Chapter 8, some philosophers – whether libertarians or skeptics – saw the matter differently. Legal scholars were also divided in their thinking, although not always attentive to new departures in philosophical or scientific thought. And some of them privileged character over choice, or tried to. But if any main trend can be identified within a neo-retributivism in the domain of legal scholarship, it was the compatibilist idea of responsibility premised upon the capacity and opportunity for uncoerced reasoned choice, as opposed to choice free from causation.

This compatibilism's most fully theorized expressions among American legal scholars remained those of Michael Moore and Stephen Morse. We have seen, nonetheless, how difficult it was to maintain the core position upon which both Morse and Moore insisted. The same conventional morality that they claimed identifies responsibility with reasoned choice might well posit that the actor chooses by utilizing a capacity for – in Galen Strawson's phrase – "uncaused origination"[40] (an idea that Morse and Moore, like Strawson fils, rejected), despite Moore's heroic labors to demonstrate that we truly accept the idea of responsibility for caused behavior. From the

---

[40] Galen Strawson, "Consciousness, Free Will, and the Unimportance of Determinism," *Inquiry*, vol. 32 (1989): 3–27, 23.

late 1970s through the 1990s, Moore and Morse steadfastly advanced full defenses of responsibility while expressly accepting determinism and eschewing libertarian notions of free will. Although their approaches nearly overlapped, the differences between them became all the clearer in the late 1990s. While Moore continued to invoke a moral realism premised upon what he deemed to be near-universal intuitions in an argument that left no room for a concept of hard determinism, or incompatibilism, Morse increasingly melded his defense of compatibilism with frank admissions of his own hard determinist anxieties that, on some level, he seemed to admit were ultimately unanswerable. From this uneven ground, however, he continued to defend compatibilism from all comers, and in ways the defense could appear all the more appealing for his willingness to press forward in the face of the unknowable, instead of retreating to a more holistic agnosticism.

Few legal scholars actually joined Moore or Morse (in print) in the attempt to demonstrate logically that responsibility for choice based on capacity for practical reasoning can be affirmed solely by reflection upon our particular judgments (and those of others) and upon our more general perceptions. And fewer still adopted Moore's view that this reflection yielded a metaphysical moral truth. Yet such philosophical grounding seems not to have mattered; many (I conjecture) were content with a sort of untheorized mantra of compatibilism accompanied by notions of personhood and a disinclination to comment directly on the free will question. Some – Sanford Kadish comes readily to mind – even backed away from prior seeming alignment with formal compatibilism, stepping down from the initial attractions of the 1980s compatibilist bandwagon and back toward a less theorized, more holistic, affirmation of responsibility despite the potential truth of universal causation.[41]

Michael Moore and Sanford Kadish on "Moral Luck"

In 1994, Moore maintained his self-professedly "nonfoundationalist" (i.e., non-natural-law-based) approach,[42] building a case for the "independent moral significance of wrongdoing" from, once again, "our particular

---

[41] Sanford H. Kadish, "The Criminal Law and the Luck of the Draw," *JCLC*, vol. 84 (1994): 679–702; see my discussion immediately below.

[42] As early as 1985, Moore had pointed out that the theory he was sketching need not be a natural law theory: "a connection to morality is not *necessary* for our criminal laws to be laws, as a natural law theory would assert." He continued to claim, however, that "as it happens ... our criminal law does reflect [an] underlying moral theory about when it is fair to ascribe responsibility to a person." Michael S. Moore, "The Moral and Metaphysical Sources of the Criminal Law," chap. 1 in *Nomos*, vol. 27, ed. J. Roland Pennock and John W. Chapman (New York: New York University Press, 1985), 14. The "underlying theory," we have seen, seemed to track conventional morality, as it was constructed from observations of the particular moral judgments of most people and out of an ingenious probing of the fit between those particular judgments and more general moral perceptions.

judgments, from our accompanying emotional experience" and (crucially) from the "reductio" of the impossibility of responsibility that is implied by the alternative view.[43] The article – which responded explicitly to the philosopher Thomas Nagel's examination of "moral luck,"[44] and implicitly both to John Hill's 1988 critique of compatibilism[45] and to Galen Strawson's views – was of a piece with Moore's earlier pronouncements against the moral and legal relevance of a notion of lack of control that proceeds from universal causation.

In 1986, the year after Moore published "Causation and the Excuses," Nagel had thrown down a gauntlet, challenging compatibilism and opining that "nothing approaching the truth has yet been said" on the free will/ determinism problem.[46] Moore's target in 1994 was Nagel's assertion that a paradox inheres in our inclination to hold actors responsible (or to absolve them) for the accidental results of their intentional acts. Nagel had posited that, "prior to reflection," we conceive of praising and blaming as rooted in an actor's fault, and thus not dependent on "what is due to factors beyond [the actor's] control"; but, in practice, we commonly judge culpability based on the ultimate results of intentional acts *even if* those results appear to be outside the actor's control. The driver who negligently failed to have his brakes checked is more culpable if, by happenstance, a child wanders into the street and cannot be avoided. The would-be murderer is less culpable if a bird flies into the path of her bullet, thereby preventing a human death. Acknowledging reasoning similar to that of Moore's *reductio*, Nagel had accepted as a matter of logic that, if we consider factors outside an actor's control *at all*, there is no basis for considering only *some* such factors; we should consider them all – down to the uncontrolled natures of our characters and circumstances – and conclude that, because "ultimately, nothing or almost nothing about what a person does seems to be under his control[,] ... most or all ordinary moral judgments are illegitimate."[47] Yet, of course, we *do* draw lines on the basis of some uncontrolled factors and not others. We do believe that the actual results of our actions count, often even when they appear caused by mere chance: this, said Nagel, is the unresolvable

---

[43] Michael S. Moore, "The Independent Moral Significance of Wrongdoing," *Journal of Contemporary Legal Issues*, vol. 5 (1994): 237–82, 280.
[44] Thomas Nagel, "Moral Luck," chap. 3 in *Mortal Questions* (New York: Cambridge University Press, 1979) (originally published in *Proceedings of the Aristotelian Society*, supp. vol. 50 [1976]: 137–51).
[45] John L. Hill, Note, "Freedom, Determinism, and the Externalization of Responsibility in the Law: A Philosophical Analysis," *Georgetown Law Journal*, vol. 76 (1988): 2045–74 (see my prior discussion of Hill in Chapter 8).
[46] Thomas Nagel, *The View from Nowhere* (New York: Oxford University Press, 1986), 137. In 1987, Nagel shed further doubt on compatibilism as a way out of the problem in *What Does It All Mean? A Very Short Introduction to Philosophy* (New York: Oxford University Press, 1987), esp. chap. 6, "Free Will."
[47] Nagel, "Moral Luck," 25–29.

problem of moral luck that is inextricably connected to our sense of human agency.[48]

In rejecting the notion that there is any "problem" of moral luck, Moore centrally urged that culpability for harm *never* depends on, as Nagel would have it, ultimate "control" of all potentially relevant factors. Rather, Nagel's notion of control, like the incompatibilist's claim that moral and legal responsibility depend on the absence of external causation, ran counter to how we actually conceive of the criteria for responsibility. Asserting that Nagel failed to offer an argument for "*his* notion of control" – really a lack of control – Moore suspected "that the only arguments available here are the same arguments as have been trotted out by incompatibilists on the free will issue for centuries." That is, they

have long sought to show that we must be in control over all factors that cause our choices in order for us to be responsible for both those choices and the wrongdoing such choices initiate. The question for incompatibilists has always been how they can support this demand for control, since it is not built into our ordinary notions of control. By our ordinary notions, we control our choices whenever such choices are not subject to threats or other coercion and when we have enough information to make them. There are no beachheads within our ordinary moral criteria for the incompatibilists' alien idea of control.[49]

In other words, the baseline for morally relevant "control" lay in the opportunity and capacity for rational choice. In turn, the baseline for increased desert due to increased harmful consequences – as was similarly evident in our ordinary notions and codified by legal concepts of proximate causation – lay in our everyday concepts of the normalcy (or lack of "freakishness") of the "causal route" between the rationally chosen act and the result. Thus,

---

[48] Nagel, "Moral Luck," 37–38. Nagel's description of the resulting insoluble paradox was rooted in his general position that we are essentially incapable of considering moral judgments from the "external" point of view associated with determinism, but instead render such judgments from an "internal" vantage point that accepts the reality of human agency and from which we are simply unable to conceive of human "actions being events, or people being things" (37). In part for this reason, of course, he questioned whether anything intelligible could be said about the free will/determinism problem and found "compatibilist accounts of freedom ... even less plausible than libertarian ones" given the failure of such accounts to "allay the feeling that, looked at from far enough outside, agents are helpless and not responsible" (Nagel, *View from Nowhere*, 113).

[49] Moore, "Independent Moral Significance," 257–58. Moore did not address the sort of beachheads in our ordinary moral experience that, a decade before, he had granted to the causal theorist: "the sympathy we may feel for wrongdoers whose wrongdoing was caused by factors such as social adversity or psychological abuse during childhood" (Moore, "Causation and the Excuses," 1145). Presumably Nagel's assertion that we question responsibility in the face of an actor's lack of control of his or her background conditions is similarly dismissed as in conflict with "the mass of our judgements about where it is just to praise and blame" and as deficient for not according individuals "equal moral dignity" and thus ultimately amounting to "condescension" (1147).

for example, one who intentionally throws a lit cigarette into some bushes is deemed fully liable for a resulting fire that spreads to a forest only if the causal chain of events is reasonably foreseeable: if the fire is carried by a "normal evening breeze," the actor is fully liable; but if the fire is carried by "a gale force wind never before seen at this time of year, which wind uproots the burning bushes and carries them to a distant forest, which ignites and burns," the actor is not fully liable. And we agree on different degrees of liability in these situations despite the actor's lack of actual "control" over the wind in either case. Moore concluded: "There undoubtedly is some luck involved in whether we cause the harms we intend or risk, but there will be *moral* luck only *vis-a-vis* some moral baseline of the normal that places all such luck on the side of the extraordinary."[50] Such a baseline is not what we employ in making ordinary moral judgments. So the so-called problem of moral luck is not truly a problem at all.[51]

For Moore, again, our "ordinary moral criteria" were the litmus and, again, his claims on those criteria purportedly were most correct. But, as before, it is not clear that Moore's methodology allowed him to fully consider that other feature of our ordinary moral experience to which Nagel held fast: the "freedom" – or "idea of agency," or sense of an "active self"[52] – that, we might hypothesize, most people read into the possession of rationality, that they subjectively experienced in choosing, or – perhaps most germane here – that they presumed underlay decisions that risk the predictable, "nonfreakish" harms for which we assign culpability based on principles of proximate causation. As before, Moore did not expressly hypothesize the response of the average person who has been informed that "could have chosen to do otherwise" means no more than "could have if [one] had chosen (or willed) to do otherwise," where choices themselves are caused and any sense of *ultimate* control is ephemeral.

Shortly before the publication of Moore's article, Sanford Kadish had also addressed the "problem" of moral luck, posing his own questions regarding the potential disjuncture between desert in principle and as understood conventionally.[53] Kadish did not attend to the issue of free will as such. Yet – although never a full-blooded formal compatibilist despite his earlier reliance on Moore[54] – Kadish now, on my reading, signaled a retreat even from

---

[50] Moore, "Independent Moral Significance," 254–56.
[51] See also Moore 's recent restatement of his views on the moral luck issue, in a brief and mainly introductory chapter in his monumental *Causation and Responsibility: An Essay in Law, Morals, and Metaphysics* (New York: Oxford University Press, 2009), chap. 2, "Causation and Moral Blameworthiness."
[52] Nagel, "Moral Luck," 37.
[53] Kadish, "Luck of the Draw" (1994).
[54] See Sanford Kadish, "Excusing Crime," essay 6 in *Blame and Punishment: Essays in the Criminal Law* (New York: Macmillan, 1987) (also published in *California Law Review*, vol.

his near-compatibilist position of the late 1980s and more clearly embraced the ambiguities that had been implicit in his earlier works.

Like Nagel, Kadish perceived irrationality in our inclination to hold actors responsible (or absolve them) for accidental results; he found the inclination to be inconsistent with our general acceptance of the notion "that punishment is deserved if persons are at fault, and that fault depends on their choice to do the wrongful action, not on what is beyond their control."[55] For Kadish, the moment of choice was critical: because "the settled moral understanding is that what you deserve is a function of what you choose ... chance occurrences that follow after you have made your choice" do not "determine what you deserve, for that is to rest desert upon factors other than what you chose to do. Fortuity prior to choice, therefore, may be accommodated to our notions of just desert; fortuity thereafter cannot."[56] He thus claimed a meaningful distinction between causal factors outside our control based on whether these factors preceded or succeeded choice.

It is not precisely clear just how Kadish conceived of "choice" such that it gave different logical relevance to events in the causal chain depending on whether they preceded or succeeded the act of choosing. Did he now accept that choice represented a qualitatively different sort of event – a "free" or self-originating act? In 1987, he had appeared to accept some version of the compatibilist premise that "we are responsible for our choices *even if* in some sense they have their causes like any other events in the world."[57] But, by 1994, he asserted that he found the prospect of determinism with regard to human action "highly contestable" and, in any event, inconsistent with the criminal law, which, "with its concepts of personal responsibility and desert, plainly rejects it."[58]

Still, Kadish did not necessarily view "free" choice as existing in fact or in some logically provable manner. As was true in his earlier work, in 1994 he relied heavily on our conventional attitudes – our "settled moral understanding[s]," our "intuitions," and "sense of justice."[59] But he now more deeply embraced the ambiguities and illogic of such attitudes, thereby not clearly endorsing any particular element of them. Instead, he concluded that "sometimes the law must defer to people's irrationalities to maintain the acceptance needed to govern."[60] That is, sometimes the law must inevitably

75 [1987]: 257–89), 81, n. 1, 99, n. 62, 103, n. 80, and my discussion of Kadish's work in Chapter 8).
55 Kadish, "Luck of the Draw," 688. Moore dismissed Kadish's emphasis on control (as representative of the "standard educated view" regarding moral luck) alongside Moore's response to Nagel ("Independent Moral Significance," 240, 276–79).
56 Kadish, "Luck of the Draw," 690.
57 Kadish, "Excusing Crime," 99 (emphasis added).
58 Kadish, "Luck of the Draw," 690.
59 E.g., Kadish, "Luck of the Draw," 679, 690.
60 Kadish, "Luck of the Draw," 680.

track conventional attitudes although they are inconsistent or logically indefensible. With regard to "moral luck," he admitted: "While in principle it's difficult to find good reasons for making desert turn on chance, here's the rub: most of us do in fact make judgments precisely of this kind.... That's the way our unexamined intuitions run."[61] The same was true with regard to the sort of positive retribution urged by Moore but not advocated, at least as a matter of principle, by Kadish: "I freely confess," Kadish admitted, "that, like most people, I have a feeling in my bones that it is right to punish wrongdoers even where no good comes of it. Yet I can find no persuasive justification for my feelings; that they are widely shared tells me that it is human, not that it is right."[62]

In this vein, Kadish closed the 1994 piece with a series of questions that spoke to the overlap between our moral aspirations and a sort of pragmatic instrumentalism inherent in legal theory as practiced. Although he still did not take on the free will problem directly, the shadow of the persisting questions it posed for a theory of criminal responsibility that might be both rationally defensible and conventionally acceptable hung over his remarks. "The doctrines of criminal liability and punishment represent a system of assessing legal blame which the law models upon the principles that govern assessing moral blame in our everyday social life," said Kadish. "If I am right that some of the law's doctrines are not rationally defensible, that is because, as Adam Smith observed, it is our moral judgments that are irregular."[63] Kadish continued:

On the one hand, it seems to me there must be a place for critical morality – for correcting moral mistakes, for weeding out mere prejudices, for maturing our moral vision. On the other hand, by what standards are we to judge which of our intuitive moral beliefs are prejudices and mistakes and which are worthy of keeping? If what we think is rational clashes with what we feel is right, must the lesson be always to try to change our feelings? If inconsistencies appear in the patterns of our beliefs, as they surely do, how quick should we be to assume that something has to go, and how do we know which should be rejected? I have no very good answers to these questions. Moral philosophers, I find, have too many. ...

Why, after all, must a worthwhile morality always be shaped by the pursuit of purposes, and why must it be transparent to reason? May I not be troubled that too rigorous a critical stance toward our moral intuitions might threaten what is most particular about our moral beliefs, namely their remarkable power to make us want to do what is right, even when doing so disserves our interests? Might it not, moreover, transform the nature of our moral experience in radical and undesirable ways? If people ceased to feel, for example, that wrongdoers should be punished, how would that affect the pattern of our beliefs with regard to right and wrong, to what is

---

[61] Kadish, "Luck of the Draw," 688.
[62] Kadish, "Luck of the Draw," 688.
[63] Kadish, "Luck of the Draw," 699 (referring to Adam Smith, *The Theory of Moral Sentiments*, ed. D. D. Raphael and A. L. Macfie [1976], 100).

deserved and what is not, to praise and blame? Perhaps disastrously, if it is the case, as John Stuart Mill argued, that the desire to punish the wrongdoer is an essential ingredient in the sentiment of justice.[64]

Stephen Morse

One might read the 1990s (and post) scholarship of Stephen Morse as agreeing with elements of the work of both Moore and Kadish. Indeed, in Morse's own study of "moral luck," he straddled the two viewpoints: he agreed with Moore that there is no "problem" of moral luck because there is no logical distinction between events in the universal causal chain based on whether they precede or succeed our choices; yet he agreed with Kadish that, in determining desert, the emphasis must be on intentional acts or forbearance, and not on consequences.[65] Conversant in the many theories of excuse and variations on compatibilism produced in the last decades of the century – from David Bazelon to Richard Boldt, Richard Delgado and R. George Wright[66] – Morse, perhaps more than any of his contemporaries, was steadfast in his ongoing consideration of the deeper questions surrounding criminal responsibility.

In 1998, in an extension to his analysis of the "new excuses" set forth in his probing 1994 article, "Culpability and Control,"[67] he continued to dovetail with Moore in identifying unexcused criminal responsibility with behavior that evidenced both "rationality" and the absence of "hard choice," or virtual compulsion. Neither responsibility nor the excuses, he continued to argue alongside Moore, rested on free will or the lack thereof, as many commentators over the years had wrongly supposed.[68] The basic building blocks

---

[64] Kadish, "Luck of the Draw," 700.

[65] See Stephen J. Morse, "Reason, Results, and Criminal Responsibility," *University of Illinois Law Review*, vol. 2004 (2004): 363–444, esp. 365–66 (proposing that "intentional action and forbearance are the only aspects of human conduct that potentially can be fully guided consciously, explicitly, and effectively by moral or legal rules" and thus are "the only proper objects for moral evaluation and the ascription of moral and criminal desert"; "the consequences of action cannot be fully guided and are thus not appropriate predicates for desert"). See also Stephen J. Morse, "The Moral Metaphysics of Causation and Results," *California Law Review*, vol. 88 (2000): 879–94, esp. 881, responding to Michael S. Moore, "The Metaphysics of Causal Intervention," *California Law Review*, vol. 88 (2000): 827–78.

[66] See, e.g., Stephen J. Morse, "Deprivation and Desert," chap. 5 in *From Social Justice to Criminal Justice: Poverty and the Administration of Criminal Law*, ed. William C. Heffernan and John Kleinig (New York: Oxford University Press, 2000), esp. 140 and n. 56.

[67] Stephen J. Morse, "Culpability and Control," *University of Pennsylvania Law Review*, vol. 142 (1994): 1587–1660. Morse later vowed to continue his repeated defenses of compatibilism as long as commentators persisted in advancing the errors of causal theory. Stephen J. Morse, "Addiction, Genetics, and Criminal Responsibility," *Law and Contemporary Problems*, vol. 69 (2006): 165–208, 174 n. 25 (citing, among others, Anders Kaye, "Resurrecting the Causal Theory of the Excuses," *Nebraska Law Review*, vol. 83 (2005): 1116–77).

[68] Stephen J. Morse, "Excusing and the New Excuse Defenses: A Legal and Conceptual Review," *Crime and Justice*, vol. 23 (1998): 329–406, 353–55.

of Morse's approach continued to appear nearly identical to Moore's, and the critical differences again inhered in the lack of any claim to independent metaphysical moral truth on Morse's part. In this sense, Morse's approach could be described as quintessentially "is/ought" – that is, he urged that human actions invite praise or blame precisely because desert-worthiness, or at least potential desert-worthiness, is *definitive* of human action. Still, based on this very proposition, he restated his intricate argument for why his account was not purely descriptive or pragmatic, but had its own "truth value." Morse reemphasized that blaming is not merely rooted in breach of a pragmatically agreed upon expectation; rather, appropriate normative judgments arise both from rationality and – here again aligned with Moore and Peter Strawson – the "reactive emotions" to wrongdoing that inherently accompany blaming. Blaming thus "involves a complex of emotions and their expression that have the force of a judgment." Morse further urged that our resulting patterns of blaming are internally coherent, are consistent with his litmus of rationality and the absence of compulsion and, crucially, entirely describe "real" responsibility. Moreover, from this base, we may indeed speak prescriptively about "when it is fair to hold people responsible, to blame them, and to express our blame through sanctioning responses."[69]

In making these claims, Morse maintained a unified challenge to both the determinist critique and the concept of free will. Drawing on contemporary compatibilist philosophy – and on the work of R. Jay Wallace, in particular – Morse rejected the strand of argument (relied on by Moore) that parsed the meaning of "could have done otherwise" as "strained" or dependent on "incredibly refined, technical logical distinctions."[70] Most important, such argument was unnecessary. Striking at the very foundation of the determinist critique, he asked: Why do we assume, in the first place, that "responsibility requires strong freedom"? Indeed, he asserted: "if determinism is true and responsibility requires strong freedom, I concede that responsibility is a myth." But, he urged, hard determinists begin from a misconception of the natures of both responsibility and freedom, thereby manufacturing the apparent need for a defense of responsibility, when it is they – the hard determinists – who should be on the defensive. Here, dramatically departing from Moore's metaphysics, Morse posed (and answered) the question from which the purported problems of determinism arise:

Is responsibility a metaphysical construct that is part of the inherent structure of the universe, or is it a social construction for which good, consistent reasons can be given? The described attack is an external critique that puts in doubt the entire practice of holding people responsible and blaming them. It seems to assume that there are preexisting metaphysically true moral facts – such as that strong freedom is required – with which our practices must correspond to be fair. What would

---

[69] Morse, "Excusing and the New Excuse Defenses," 342–45.
[70] Morse, "Excusing and the New Excuse Defenses," 345 (citing R. Jay Wallace, *Responsibility and the Moral Sentiments* [Cambridge, MA: Harvard University Press, 1994]).

these facts look like, however? Can sense be made of this type of critique? Ordinary language and our practices surely suggest, in contrast, that responsibility is a socially constructed practice. The shoe should be on the other foot. Critics should have to produce a positive account of why strong freedom is required.[71]

Next, instead of deflecting the common assumption that responsibility is presumed to be based on "free will," Morse probed the very idea of human "will" and its relationship to our practice of blaming. He urged that blaming and excusing never hinge on the effectiveness of one's "will" (or "volition" or "executory mental functioning"): our everyday intuitions tell us that people generally affirmatively *will* their actions, even when their behavior is excused because it is marked by irrationality or constrained by compulsion. Thus, defining a responsible act as one that is a product of a "free" will results merely in a "conclusory label" or "tautology" that, in reality, indicates that some other criteria for (or intuition of) responsibility is present.[72]

In this way, Morse renewed his stance that determinism is irrelevant to the normative, uniquely human realm of responsibility and responsibility-talk – a fact that had been obscured by confusing terms such as "free will." He implied that conventional morality boils down *not* to a belief in free will per se, but to a commonly shared "folk psychology" that presumes a "reason-giving explanation accounts for human behavior as a product of intentions that arise from the desires and beliefs of the agent."[73] And he appeared unconcerned that there could be disparities between his theory and morality as conventionally applied: as before, he expressed utter faith in society, its "community norms," and its institutional representatives (including the jury, which, "as the community's representative," should make culpability determinations at the "highly visible trial stage"[74]) to carry out just blaming practices, albeit perhaps with some tweaks to doctrine – particularly in the realm of the excuses and how we define them[75] – in order to better conform the letter of the law to the community's intuitions and overall practices.

Still, Morse acknowledged that not just theoreticians, but "many people," had the belief or intuition that responsibility depends on "strong" or "'contracausal'" freedom.[76] In the end, like Moore, he seems to have

[71] Morse, "Excusing and the New Excuse Defenses," 346.
[72] Morse, "Excusing and the New Excuse Defenses," 353–55.
[73] Morse, "Excusing and the New Excuse Defenses," 338.
[74] Morse, "Excusing and the New Excuse Defenses," 398–99.
[75] A central element of "Excusing and the New Excuse Defenses" was Morse's proposal that "the criminal law should adopt two generic excuses: the general incapacity for rationality or normative competence and hard choice," thus "enabl[ing] the law more rationally to consider any reasonable claim and relevant evidence that might satisfy the underlying reasons for excusing" and "permitting defendants to avoid the unreasonable strictures of existing excusing doctrine, which is generally tied to a medical model of abnormality" (390).
[76] Morse, "Excusing and the New Excuse Defenses," 345.

acknowledged that conventional morality or intuitions *as subjectively conceived of or experienced* did not precisely reduce to beliefs about persons acting on reasons. Yet – like Moore, and consistent with Morse's own earlier work – Morse did not directly take up any potential problems inherent in the distinction he acknowledged between intuitions about free will and folk psychological evaluations of mere rationality. It is possible that Morse presumed that the former, when applied from the jury box, mirrored the latter *in result* to an extent that made the distinction insignificant in practice. He may also be read to suggest that, despite a sort of disembodied conventional belief in contra-causal freedom, the rubric we actually employ in the moment of judging is best described as an estimation of the actor's rationality, even if we then *translate* the result into terms of freedom or a lack thereof. Either way, he appeared unworried about the distance between the compatibilist mode of judgment that rendered determinism irrelevant and conventional freedom-oriented beliefs about, or experiences of, judging.

Particularly interesting, then, is the fact that Morse *did* concede worries about hard determinism in a more global sense, although he freely admitted the paradoxical nature of his position. "The incompatibilist intuition that motivates critics of responsibility," Morse confessed, "exerts a powerful hold on us, a hold that I am prey to and worries me." He asserted that consequentialist responses to the determinist critique "make[] the world entirely too 'safe for determinism'" in their attempts to divorce responsibility from individual desert: they "do[] violence to our conceptual concerns" and to "current practice" because they do not "prohibit blaming and punishing innocent people if doing so would maximize the good." Here positing a "fundamental[]" and inseparable relationship between current blaming practices and their expression of "retrospective disapproval," Morse concluded: "A full, satisfying account of responsibility and blaming, paradoxically, should be subject to [hard] determinist worries."[77]

In the face of this paradox, however, Morse staunchly defended his internalist compatibilism. For our determinist worries are relative to an external account of responsibility that, critically, we can never have. Rather, we can proceed only from an *internal* perspective, from the vantage point of which we cannot know whether (hard) determinism is, in fact, true, and – most important – from which we must conduct our lives, and organize our societies, despite our position of ultimate ignorance. For, *even if* determinism is true, Morse now stated,

it is not clear what moral rules follow, and we cannot passively wait for determinism to "happen," to somehow indicate to us what rules, institutions, and practices we should adopt. *We have no rational alternative* but to deliberate, using our best moral theories and understanding of human behavior to devise and to justify a system that good reason tells us is likely with justice to promote human flourishing. This

[77] Morse, "Excusing and the New Excuse Defenses," 348.

internalist mode of proceeding ignores determinist worries when trying to explain and justify our rules and practices unless the truth of determinism somehow renders them inconsistent, incoherent, or unfair. But it does not.[78]

To this he added his claim for why we should not err on the side of eliminating responsibility in the face of hard determinist doubts. Interestingly, he sided with Nagel in concluding that "no conceptual or scientific analysis will ever resolve such doubts." But this conclusion did not lead Morse to Nagel's unresolved view of responsibility. Rather, in light of the ultimate unknown, Morse reminded us that the only evidence we have weighs in favor of responsibility: a requirement of "strong freedom" – and our intuitions about "free will" – are (at least when boiled down to their essentials) inconsistent with our blaming practices and understandings of the "will." He thus urged:

When deterministic anxieties cause us to consider from the external point of view whether to abandon responsibility and blaming practices as entirely incoherent and unjust, *we are entitled to a full-blown metaphysical and moral theory rather than an intuition.* No account sufficiently persuasive to require such a radical move has been given.[79]

In the end, then, Morse expressed his own brand of agnosticism alongside the carefully articulated logic of his compatibilism. He essentially conceded that we have no place from which to stand and judge – but such is a matter of external metaphysics. As an internal practical matter – and as a matter of personhood – we do stand, we do judge, and we are committed to ourselves as deserving. Morse's approach thus bore obvious similarities to the more agnostic and normative theories of the century's end. But, although on some level he accepted normative and socially constructed aspects of the law, he labored to show that he was no mere pragmatist or descriptivist – and certainly no mere consequentialist. Indeed, his work was perhaps most distinctive in its emphatic confidence that we *can* attach desert to our and others' rational choices not only because we *do,* but because we have every reason *to* do so, and (thus far) no convincing reason not to.

So why not simply give up defending against the determinist critique, like other *fin de millennium* legal scholars who affirmed responsibility in a roughly compatibilist vein while remaining comparably agnostic about the precise basis for responsibility in the face of the unknowable? Indeed, why not simply concede determinism's irrelevance to the law, and possible irrelevance to human behavior as humans understand it, as Kadish impliedly did? These others left more room for the innate *sense* of freedom we humans may find difficult to ignore, even in the interest of cognitive coherence. But

---

[78] Morse, "Excusing and the New Excuse Defenses," 348–49 (emphasis added).
[79] Morse, "Excusing and the New Excuse Defenses," 347 (citing Nagel, *View from Nowhere*; emphasis added).

Morse's unwillingness to finally give up the ghost – to move beyond his battle against hard determinism – might suggest the extent to which we find it equally hard to ignore threats to this innate sense of freedom, whether such threats originate from our conceptions of God, from Progressive Era scientific-positivism, or from the scientific promises of the twenty-first century. In other words, perhaps a part of us demands a direct response to the determinist, even if the response is not perfectly unassailable – and even if, ironically, that response must take the potential lack of true free will as its premise.

Fin de Millennium

Of course, it is possible to resist the urge to put such a response into print. And toward the century's end, few legal scholars spoke to the issue. Perhaps the free will debate within legal academia had run its natural course. Or, perhaps because of the apparent philosophical fragility of formal compatibilist approaches – or because of their failure to fully capture our *experience* of free will – most legal scholars who considered the issue at all simply continued, I infer, to hold a de facto compatibilist perspective by hewing silently to an internalism based on a resilient, doubtful agnosticism about the existence of free will. So far as one can guess from their limited comments, most legal scholars persisted in rooting responsibility in the ineffability of the consciousness of human freedom and its implications for the idea of "personhood" – and, perhaps, in the sheer rejection of the hard determinist alternative. Few spoke for causal theory[80] (or for a purely Kantian view of the "noumenal" sphere). More evident were hints at the capacity to conform via reason to the rules of law, an idea that is unique to humans, that is: "persons." This is to say that, although few legal scholars explicitly adopted the formal compatibilism of scholars such as Moore and Morse, I gather that most were de facto compatibilists in the sense that, in common with Moore and Morse, they privileged the capacity for reason in their search for the individual's ability to be a responsibility-bearing agent despite the at least possible truth of determinism.

[80] Anders Kaye (albeit writing in the early years of the new century) was the most prominent exception. Having taken critical aim directly at compatibilism, Kaye concluded that its variations had so failed logically and politically that we would be better off embracing our inclinations toward causal theory, expressly acknowledging its contradictions instead of unsuccessfully fending them off via one of the many versions of compatibilism. See Kaye, "The Secret Politics of the Compatibilist Criminal Law," *Kansas Law Review*, vol. 55 (2007): 365–427; Kaye, "Resurrecting Causal Theory." Kaye's aim was not to shore up traditional free-will-based retributivism, but rather to leave the way open for determinations of non- (or mitigated) responsibility on the basis of social and economic conditions that had a very substantial distorting impact on the offender's decision making, while yet not stripping him or her of the capacity and opportunity for practical reason that served as the responsibility threshold for compatibilists. This strategy might (as Kaye probably recognized) have the

454   Freedom, Criminal Responsibility, and Retributivism

Thus the differences among essentially compatibilist legal scholars, whether they accepted the moniker or not, proved less important than their shared emphases on choice, reason, and the special attributes of personhood – on affirming the relevance of an actor's capacity for participation in the choosing process despite the determinist critique. For some late-twentieth-century choice-based commentators, this dominant strain of thought seemed virtually beyond attack as a statement of fair attribution of responsibility, especially with respect to the criminal law, an allegedly earthly enterprise that need not meet the demands of natural-law theory.[81] But such differences as there were (not to mention the increasing silences) also suggest a fundamental ambiguity in end-of-the-century criminal jurisprudence – perhaps, even, a significant residue of unspoken acceptance of causal theory. They suggest, too, that the fracturing of perspectives in academic legal thought was as important as the seeming dominance of choice theory.

I leave the scholarship on criminal responsibility of this new century to others. But I venture to say that, so far, the landscape is much the same. The determinist torch is carried forward by the new sciences of the twenty-first century, and some commentators appear as optimistic as Speranza was, a century ago, that "the kingdom of scientific law is [now, *finally*] at hand."[82] Indeed, some seem to think that advances in our abilities to observe and correlate brain activity, genetic makeup, or other physical attributes to behavior will finally cause us to reconceive ourselves in deterministic terms. In one oft-cited article, for example, psychologists Joshua Greene and Jonathan Cohen urged that developments in cognitive neuroscience – particularly advances in functional neuroimaging it is hoped will reveal the precise, determined mechanical processes that underlie human decision making – will soon cause us to reject our "common-sense conceptions of free will" in light of determinism. The result? Although we may retain moral and legal responsibility, we will reject retributivism once and for all, with an "ensuing shift towards a consequentialist approach to punishment."[83]

Of particular interest is Greene and Cohen's claim that the transformation they predict can come to pass because the premises of formal compatibilism

---

effect of legitimating conventional morality (and its in-court outcomes) as much or more than compatibilism. Or it might work to reinvigorate Progressive ideas, at least with respect to sentencing practice if not guilt assessment.

[81] See Christopher Kutz, "Responsibility," chap. 14 in *Oxford Handbook of Jurisprudence and Philosophy of Law*, ed. Jules Coleman and Scott Shapiro (New York: Oxford University Press, 2002), 574. Kutz makes this point in purporting to summarize turn-of-the-century perspectives on criminal responsibility.

[82] Gino C. Speranza, "Natural Law versus Statutory Law," *Albany Law Journal*, vol. 59 (1899): 400–405, 404.

[83] Joshua Greene and Jonathan Cohen, "For the Law, Neuroscience Changes Nothing and Everything," *Philosophical Transactions of the Royal Society of London B*, vol. 359 (2004): 1775–85, 1775–76.

are, in one critical sense, simply wrong. On one hand, the authors accepted that "there is more than a grain of truth in compatibilism," which allows for a "derivative notion of free will" that we can accept – and put to good use – in the name of consequentialism[84] (perhaps Herbert Hart's use of rational choice as a side-constraint on consequentialist goals had it right). But, going straight to the heart of neo-retributivism, they argued that conventional morality ineradicably *does* premise desert on free will, not on a compatibilist notion of rational choice; thus, "retributivism, despite its unstable marriage to compatibilist philosophy in the letter of the law, ultimately depends on an intuitive, libertarian notion of free will that is undermined by science." And neuroscience's unprecedented ability to reveal the determined nature of the mind will "highlight and widen" this "gap between what the law officially cares about and what people really care about" when assigning blame; it will therefore "undermine people's common sense, libertarian conception of free will and the retributivist thinking that depends on it, both of which have heretofore been shielded by the inaccessibility of sophisticated thinking [or "esoteric theorizing"] about the mind and its neural basis."[85] And, once the mind is no longer a "black box," we will no longer have anywhere to pin our intuitive "commitment to some kind of magical mental causation." Thus humbled, this "belief in our specialness is likely to meet the same fate as other similar narcissistic beliefs that we have cherished in our past," such as "that the Earth lies at the centre of the universe."[86]

We should not be surprised that Morse, in particular, continues to meet such challenges head-on and well-equipped with the latest insights in both compatibilist philosophy and the relevant sciences. "Neuroscience," Morse insisted in 2008, "is simply the newest 'bogey' in a dispute about the general possibility of responsibility that has been ongoing for millennia."[87] While bluntly conceding that "Greene and Cohen are right about ordinary peoples' intuitions, of course," Morse nonetheless simply asserted that this "is a sociological observation and not a justification for thinking causation or determinism does or should excuse behavior." The fact remains that causal theory "is inconsistent with the positive doctrines and practices of

---

[84] Greene and Cohen, "Neuroscience Changes Nothing," 1783.

[85] Greene and Cohen, "Neuroscience Changes Nothing," 1775–76.

[86] Greene and Cohen, "Neuroscience Changes Nothing," 1780–81. Greene and Cohen nonetheless allow that, "for most day-to-day purposes it may be pointless or impossible to view ourselves or others in this detached sort of way." But, they urge: "Even if there is no intuitively satisfying solution to the problem of free will, it does not follow that there is no correct view of the matter" (1783–84). Here they sound much like Moore, and they differ only with regard to results: for Moore, the correct view *affirms* desert.

[87] Stephen J. Morse, "Determinism and the Death of Folk Psychology: Two Challenges to Responsibility from Neuroscience," *Minnesota Journal of Law, Science & Technology*, vol. 9 (2008): 1–36, 14. Morse has remained outspoken in his defense of challenges to responsibility from the newest scientific developments. See, e.g., Stephen J. Morse, "Avoiding Irrational NeuroLaw Exuberance: A Plea for Neuromodesty," *Mercer Law Review*, vol. 62 (2011):

law and morality," according to which we do not require contra-causal free
will to be "conscious and intentional creatures who act for reasons that play
a causal role in our behavior."[88] At base, consciousness and intentionally are
all we require. And all that the arguments from neuroscience have offered,
thus far,[89] are additional claims for what determinism of any stripe already
assumed: that our actions are subject to causal factors. "At present," Morse
concluded, we remain "justified in believing that we are agents and can be
responsible."[90]

As the new century takes shape, claims about the impact of neuroscience and other developing sciences on our ideas of responsibility may reinvigorate legal scholars' direct confrontation with notions of free will and
desert.[91] For the moment, I suspect that Morse (roughly) speaks for many
of them on these issues, at least with regard to his results. As was true at

---

837–60; Stephen J. Morse, "Genetics and Criminal Responsibility," *Trends in Cognitive Sciences*, vol. 15 (2011): 378–80; Stephen J. Morse, "Lost in Translation? An Essay on Law and Neuroscience," *Law and Neuroscience*, vol. 13 (2010): 529–62; Stephen J. Morse, "The Non-problem of Free Will in Forensic Psychiatry and Psychology," *Behavioral Sciences & the Law*, vol. 25 (2007): 203–20.

[88] Morse, "Death of Folk Psychology," 19.

[89] Morse's informed discussion of the present state of neuroscience expressed skepticism about (among other recent scientific claims) Greene and Cohen's predicted "'extremely high-reso-lution scanners that can simultaneously track the neural activity and connectivity of every neuron in the human brain'" (Morse, "Death of Folk Psychology," 22 [quoting Greene and Cohen, "Neuroscience Changes Nothing," 1781]). In addition to questioning the implicit "(barely) plausible computational ability" of such technology, he more fundamentally urged that "assum[ing] the validity of a complete reduction of mind to mental states at the level of (apparently) neural networks" is itself "controversial ... even among monists who believe that the brain produces the mind, which is realizable in the brain" (24–25). More promising for the hard determinist's cause, Morse admitted, would be empirical evidence to support a "No Action Thesis" (or "NAT") proving that our conscious intentions are not just caused, but in fact are not *causal* (24). "What if, for example, reasons for actions and intentions, agents' conscious understandings of their world and themselves do not explain actions but are simply post-hoc rationalizations that 'make sense of' the bodily motions or non-motions that brains produce?" (21). *This* sort of discovery could impugn the commonsense notion of agency on which law and morality depend. But, after addressing the most promising sources of such a discovery – including neuroscientist Benjamin Libet's well-known study on elec-trical activity in motor areas of the brain preceding a subject's conscious awareness of the intention to act – Morse remained convinced that, as of yet, we have no compelling proof that our reasons and intentions do not, in fact, cause our actions (25–31). Still he urged (here again speaking from a last-resort pragmatism that, I have suggested, serves as the first resort for many legal compatibilists): even upon (unlikely) proof of NAT, "human beings will find it almost impossible not to treat themselves as rational, intentional agents.... Moreover, if one uses the truth of pure mechanism as a premise in deciding what to do, this premise yields no particular moral, legal or political conclusions. It will provide no guide to how one should live or how one should respond to the truth of NAT" (32–33).

[90] Morse, "Death of Folk Psychology," 35.

[91] A growing cadre of scholars have directly addressed – and generally rejected – the hard de-terminist implications of twenty-first century science, often themselves drawing heavily on Morse and noting the parallels between current scientific claims (including their institutional,

century's end, prominent legal scholars are often less direct in their responses to the determinist critique, satisfied for the time to rest on a mantra of compatibilism, apparently finding it unnecessary or unwise to address the intricacies of the more formal philosophical debate. Of course the tones of the mantra vary and the term "compatibilism" itself can be lost in the fray. Some seem convinced that some version of compatibilism must be right, but only a limited sort, such as that between determinism and, for example, in Victor Tadros's 2011 rendition: "treating choice as morally significant in determining our liabilities, permissions, and duties."[92] For Tadros, this sort of thinner "compatibilism" (many would dub it incompatibilism) may justify punishment, but not *retributive* punishment. More familiar – and, I venture to speculate, more common – are commentaries such as that of Mitchell Berman who, in defending retributivism vis-à-vis Tadros, "skip[s] past" incompatibilist arguments against desert, which "prove too much by throwing into grave doubt not only our backward-looking agent evaluations but also our forward-looking acting-guiding moral norms." Indeed, "conceivably," the incompatibilist alternative "threatens all of morality, not just judgments about desert and the like."[93] Thus proceeds Berman, undeterred, to his defense of retributivism.

A particularly useful and likely typical exemplar of the way the field addresses itself to today's readership is the several-page explication (and disposal) of the free will/determinism debate in the Introduction to the

financial, and media support) and the turn-of-the-last-century claims advanced by scientific-positivists. See, e.g., Steven K. Erickson, "Blaming the Brain," *Minnesota Journal of Law, Science and Technology*, vol. 11 (2010): 27–77; Michael S. Pardo and Dennis Patterson, "Philosophical Foundations of Law and Neuroscience," *University of Illinois Law Review*, vol. 2010 (2010): 1211–50; Amanda C. Pustilnik, "Violence on the Brain: A Critique of Neuroscience in Criminal Law," *Wake Forest Law Review*, vol. 44 (2009): 183–237; Peggy Sasso, "Criminal Responsibility in the Age of Mind-Reading," *American Criminal Law Review*, vol. 46 (2009): 1191–244. Compare Thomas Nadelhoffer and Eddy Nahmias, "Neuroscience, Free Will, Folk Intuitions, and the Criminal Law," *Thurgood Marshall Law Review*, vol. 36 (2011): 157–76 (explicitly discussing Morse and highlighting legal policy implications of the confusion about responsibility that neuroscience may engender for lay-persons). Contrast, however, an earlier discussion by Andrew E. Lelling extensively reviewing developments in cognitive science and concluding that the law should take seriously the eliminative materialist claim that we do not act on the basis of unified mental states and volitions. Lelling, Comment, "Eliminative Materialism, Neuroscience and the Criminal Law," *University of Pennsylvania Law Review*, vol. 141 (1993): 1471–564. Lelling thus counsels partial reconciliation, offering various methods by which the law might gradually accommodate new neuroscientific findings into the law's preexisting "fictional system of intentionality" (1539) – albeit while also predicting a "long and arduous process of legal stubbornness combatting scientific progress" (1564).

92 Victor Tadros, *The Ends of Harm: The Moral Foundations of Criminal Law* (New York: Oxford University Press, 2011), 64.

93 Mitchell N. Berman, "Rehabilitating Retributivism," *Law and Philosophy*, vol. 32 (2013): 83–108, 93.

2009 volume *Crime and Culpability*, by Larry Alexander and Kimberly Kessler Ferzan, with contributions from Morse himself. The section on "Questions about Retributivism" outlines the three basic views regarding responsibility – hard determinism, libertarianism, and compatibilism – in standard forms, provides standard cites (mostly from academic philosophers), and closes with the authors' own views, Ferzan and Morse being traditional compatibilists, and Alexander remaining agnostic as to compatibilism.[94] Despite their studied consideration of the subject, the authors nonetheless conclude: "We need take no stand on the freewill-determinism issue." For, although Alexander, in particular, concludes that "as a metaphilosophical position, ... the freewill-determinism puzzle is one of those antinomies of thought that we are incapable of resolving, along with the mind-body and infinity puzzles" – indeed, although "the freewill-determinism puzzle will always dog practices of holding people morally responsible" – the three authors could agree that these are "practices that we nevertheless cannot imagine dispensing with." And "because we cannot dispose with such practices, a retributivist regarding criminal punishment need not resolve or even take sides on the freewill issue."[95] Such finessing of the free will/determinism issue, while nonetheless acknowledging the ever-present cloud of universal causation, suggests, perhaps, that compatibilism's greatest gift will ultimately prove to have been its licensing of the attribution of desert-based responsibility without totally debilitating concern with the determinist critique, rather than its actually having affirmed any particular alternative

---

[94] Larry Alexander and Kimberly Kessler Ferzan, with Stephen J. Morse, *Crime and Culpability: A Theory of Criminal Law* (New York: Cambridge University Press, 2009), 13–15. Moore's lighthearted formulation: "Two of them, at least, are good, level-headed compatibilists on the free-will issue. Dragging the agnostic on this issue (Alexander) along ..." (*Causation and Responsibility*, 27).

[95] Alexander et al., *Crime and Culpability*, 15. I defer to a later occasion (see the reference in my Conclusion to the book, at footnote 15) further discussion of the ways in which the reductio figured in late twentieth century criminal jurisprudence. Here I no more than call attention to the authors' apparent claim that "holding people morally responsible" in the retributive sense is the only possibility in the world we know, in the life we lead.

To the historian, this might appear to be a particularly strong and surprising claim. With respect to the criminal law, at least, why not hold one another criminally liable, though not "blameworthy," as such, and subject to one or another form of consequentialist (non-retributive) punishment and/or treatment? This was the dominant idea throughout the first half (or more) of the twentieth century; it had its proponents in the second half and still does in the current century. The authors might think this a poor or impractical idea, but they write in terms of what is humanly possible, a very different matter. Possibly they believe the idea, although sincerely held, in fact assumes a measure of belief in "moral responsibility," whether its proponents recognize that or not.

It is important that the authors address "moral" responsibility in pointing to what they understand as ineffable in human nature and thus a sine qua non for human society. Criminal responsibility seems to follow naturally and inevitably from this, which is another way of saying that the pure consequentialist is mistaken about his or her own underlying motivations or is, as it were, in a state of denial.

to the older and more traditional idea of such responsibility based on a presumption of true free will.

Perhaps so licensed, some thoughtful late-twentieth-century and early-twenty-first-century scholarship on desert declined to comment at all on the free will/determinism issue, and instead took the factual nature of conventional retributive attitudes on its own terms, often using those attitudes as instruments to other ends. The parallels to early-in-century utilitarian efforts and to midcentury quasi-positivist theory – which more forthrightly employed conventional beliefs in *free will* for instrumental purposes – are palpable. The difference (one difference, at least) was in tenor: the entirely practical approach of these particular later-in-century desert scholars did not even take time to finesse the initial question of criminal *responsibility*, which, evidently, some concluded had simply run its course. Instead, in a fashion we might dub "neo-utilitarian," that question was simply rolled into issues of sentencing, penology, and the law's overall effectiveness.

Particularly illustrative is the ongoing work of the legal scholar Paul Robinson and the psychologist John Darley, which was at the forefront of a version of what one might equally dub neo-retributivism or neo-utilitarianism that eschewed philosophers' "deontological desert" in favor of the notions of "empirical desert" rooted in public sentiments. Their work both employed social science to measure conventional reactions to wrongdoing, especially with regard to the extent of punishment for particular crimes, and posited that retributivist intuitions are deeply embedded not just in human social arrangements, but in human biology itself. A resulting central premise was that the law's effectiveness – and therefore its goals, including general deterrence and rehabilitation – depends on the legal system's maintaining a sense of moral authority by conforming to the public's intuitional sense of justice. Even if one has theoretical reasons for doing away with retributive punishment, they argued, such reasons must thus often give way to the conventional – and, indeed, evolutionary – desire to punish wrongdoing. For them, the conventional sense of desert was thus the initial gateway even to any *non*-retributive purpose one might wish to effect through a democratic legal system.[96] These scholars thereby confronted the realities of retribution – and its historical (perhaps definitional) relationship to the law – with rubrics for using retribution to such beneficial ends that, I gather, we need not worry (or at least not worry too much) about the soundness of its underpinnings.

> The argument, then, is not simply that the disjunction between an elitist determinist theory and broadly social conventional morality renders pure consequentialism an inevitable failure, but that conventional morality – or, I should say, at the least either a compatibilist-(Ferzan and Morse) or an agnosticism-based (Alexander) version of it – unites us all. At base, on this view, there is no disjunction. The "progress" across the century, the historian might thus conclude, involved the gradual casting off of false consciousness.

[96] See Paul H. Robinson and John M. Darley, "Intuitions of Justice: Implications for Criminal Law and Justice Policy," *Southern California Law Review*, vol. 81 (2007): 1–67; Robinson

A somewhat similar – and perhaps surprising, but certainly not unworried – turn toward desert appeared in the American Law Institute's revised 2007 Model Penal Code sentencing provisions, which newly listed retributivism as the first goal of sentencing, albeit not in so many words. Revised MPC § 1.02(2)(a)(i) would now state that individuals shall be sentenced "within a range of severity proportionate to the gravity of offenses, the harms done to crime victims, and the blameworthiness of offenders." Aims including "rehabilitation, general deterrence," and "incapacitation of dangerous offenders," which were significant elements of the original mid-century draft, were now secondary goals to be pursued only "when reasonably feasible" and "within the boundaries of proportionality" established by subsection (a)(i).[97] The new focus on blameworthiness was not without hesitation. Still clearly concerned, at heart, with utilitarian and rehabilitative goals, by 2007 the ALI's members were nonetheless focused on the unprecedented rate of imprisonment in the United States – and its disparate impact on racial and ethnic minority groups – that they believed had followed in part from the political and scholarly return to affirmative retributivism beginning in the 1960s. Thus, in their own spin on post-twentieth-century retributivism, revised § 1.02(2) became the centerpiece of a call for widespread sentencing reform employing Norval Morris's notion of "limiting retributivism," which prescribed sentences in a range proportional to individual blameworthiness as a limit on whatever other goals the state might also wish to effect.[98]

The ALI's hope, like Morris's, was that the conventional understanding of desert as proportional to the crime or harm done would work to reduce inappropriately lengthy and otherwise unjustly biased prison sentences. But the drafters explicitly avoided use of the word "retributivism,"

and Darley, "The Utility of Desert," *Northwestern University Law Review*, vol. 91 (1997): 453–99; Paul H. Robinson and John M. Darley, "Intuitions of Justice: Implications for Criminal Law and Justice Policy," *Southern California Law Review*, vol. 81 (2007): 1–67; Robinson and Darley, *Justice, Liability and Blame: Community Views and the Criminal Law* (Boulder, CO: Westview Press, 1995); Paul H. Robinson, Robert Kurzban and Owen D. Jones, "The Origins of Shared Intuitions of Justice," *Vanderbilt Law Review*, vol. 60 (2007): 1633–88; Paul H. Robinson, *Intuitions of Justice and the Utility of Desert* (New York: Oxford University Press, 2013).

[97] *Model Penal Code: Sentencing, Tentative Draft No. 1* (Philadelphia: American Law Institute, 2007), §§ 1.02(2)(a)(i)-(ii) (hereafter "2007 *Draft*"). For background on the 2007 *Draft* and the ALI's later work on specific sentencing guidelines recommendations, see Christopher Slobogin, "Introduction to the Symposium on the Model Penal Code's Sentencing Proposals," *Florida Law Review*, vol. 61 (2009): 665–82.

[98] See the Forward to the 2007 *Draft*, xiii–iv; the Reporter's Introductory Memorandum, xxvii–xxxvii; the Comment to § 1.02(2), 3–24; and the Reporter's Note on § 1.02(2), 24–45. Morris's formulation had arisen from his conviction that desert was not a *definitive* element of just punishment; although punishment should conform to a community's moral intuitions about desert, those intuitions, he asserted, are inexact. In his well-known phrase, we lack the "moral calipers" to establish just desert with precision. Rather, "all we

explaining that the term had become "ideologically charged" and that "limiting retributivism" was too easily "conflated" with "just-deserts theory, or with other theories that posit the derivation of penalty severity from indices of retribution standing alone."[99] Thus did the ALI appeal to the community's "moral judgments" or "instincts"[100] in reintroducing a minimal notion of desert as a side-constraint on punishment – a formulation drawn from ideas that had remained relatively unchanged since Norval Morris's origination of them in the 1970s.

Whether the MPC's compromise between desert and consequentialist values had the prospect of success was a matter of debate, the outcome of which depended on both how one defined success and the lens from which one viewed the conventional moral judgments that the ALI now relied on to protect individual offenders from state overreach. Commenting on the new MPC sentencing provisions during the drafting process, Paul Robinson urged that, in practice, the centrality of desert to § 1.02(2) would not result in broad possible ranges of "not unjust" punishment with sentences then fine-tuned based on utilitarian values, as the drafters hoped. His challenge was essentially factual: as a basic empirical matter, he argued, our intuitions

---

can with precision say is: 'As we know our community and its values, that does not seem an unjust punishment.'" Therefore, sentencing should be "within a range of not unjust punishments," which "limits the range within which utilitarian values may operate." Norval Morris and Marc Miller, "Predictions of Dangerousness," *Crime and Justice: An Annual Review of Research*, vol. 6 (1985): 1–50, 37. See also, generally: Norval Morris, *Madness and the Criminal Law* (Chicago: University of Chicago Press, 1982 (discussed previously in Chapter 8, n. 41 and n. 83); Norval Morris, *The Future of Imprisonment* (Chicago: University of Chicago Press, 1974). In § 1.02(2)(a)(iii) the ALI also explicitly employed Morris's emphasis on the principle of parsimony; sentences were to be "no more severe than necessary to achieve the applicable purposes in subsections (a)(i) and (a)(ii)" (2007 *Draft*, 1). And see Morris, *Future of Imprisonment*, 61 ("This principle is utilitarian and humanitarian; its justification is somewhat obvious since any punitive suffering beyond societal need is, in this context, what defines cruelty").

[99] Reporter's Note on 2007 *Draft* § 1.02(2), 30–31. Indeed, the Comment to the draft exhorted: "The revised Code does not codify a 'just deserts' philosophy of criminal penalties" (Comment to § 1.02(2), 17). Rather, it established "proportionality limitations" that "legitimate[] investment in a strong utilitarian agenda" (ibid., 8). The ALI's hesitance and careful wording is reminiscent of the apologetic return to desert evident in the Introduction to the Committee for the Study of Incarceration's 1976 Report, *Doing Justice* (discussed earlier, in Chapter 7). Indeed, as von Hirsch had stated in the Report's chapter on "Desert": "We prefer the term 'desert,'" and "do not find 'retribution' a helpful term"; it is "burdened with pejorative associations" and "there are other explanations of deserved punishment which do not rely on this notion of requital-of-evil" (von Hirsch, *Doing Justice: The Choice of Punishments* [Report of the Committee for the Study of Incarceration] [New York: Hill and Wang, 1976], 45–46). The ALI expressly rejected the approach to sentencing embodied by the 1976 Report, as a "'just deserts' model of sentence severity, which apportions degrees of punishment exclusively on retributive grounds" (Reporter's Note, 31).

[100] Reporter's Note, 31.

about desert are "quite specific" in light of the "demand of ordinal ranking" and the outer limits that given societies assign to all punishment.

Desert demands that a case of greater blameworthiness receive greater punishment than a case of comparatively less blameworthiness. Given the limited range of punishments a liberal democracy ought to be willing to inflict, distinguishing cases of distinguishable blameworthiness means that the deserved punishment in any given case will fall within a narrow range on the punishment continuum.[101]

Accordingly, desert would generally control the actual punishment imposed under the new MPC scheme; the secondary consequential goals nearer the hearts of the drafters would rarely actually come into play. This presumed reality about the MPC draft suited Robinson fine; he supported the result and offered his comment at the risk of "undermin[ing] its support among the 'limiting retributivism' advocates" but, as he put it, "comforted in the fact that people are commonly unpersuaded by what I say."[102]

Less content was James Whitman, trenchant critic of neo-retributivist philosophy, who asserted that the well-intentioned MPC drafters failed to thoroughly confront the questionable connection between retributivism and proportionality (along with other problems of retributivism), and instead "decided to ratify, if with caveats and hesitations, the orthodoxies of the last generation." Whitman challenged the notion that conventional American vengeance could be harnessed in the service of humane punishment. And, critically, he urged that elite constructors of the revived, purer retributivism of the legal academy – here he singled out Michael Moore and Jean Hampton but also invoked others who relied on desert to provide proportionality in sentencing – had to confront the possibility that their emphasis on desert supported the vengeance-based, mass imprisonment that blighted the United States by the end of the century.[103]

Another especially astute critic was Alice Ristroph, who voiced skepticism about recent attention to "empirical" desert as an end run around the sort of "metaphysical mysteries" of responsibility with which scholars had become

---

[101] Paul H. Robinson, "The A.L.I.'s Proposed Distributive Principle of 'Limiting Retributivism': Does It Mean in Practice Anything Other than Pure Desert?" *Buffalo Criminal Law Review*, vol. 7 (2004): 3–15, 10.

[102] Robinson, "A.L.I.'s Proposed Distributive Principle," 4.

[103] James Q. Whitman, "A Plea against Retributivism," *Buffalo Criminal Law Review*, vol. 7 [2003]: 85–107, 87–88. "Retributivism," said Whitman,

> is a form of admirable and elegant reasoning, to be sure, founded in what seem like unimpeachable moral certainties, and our neo-retributivist literature is a superb corpus. But it does often seem weirdly blind to the nasty realities of the American world around it, with its otherworldly discussions of abstractly conceived autonomous actors.... Whatever the humane intentions of retributivist philosophers, however certain they are that a retributivist system is one that honors principles of proportionality, it may be that crying "blame!" in the current American atmosphere does more harm than good. (89–90)

"increasingly impatient."[104] Ristroph suggested that limiting retributivism such as that embraced by the MPC "is very widely accepted and may be "'the consensus model.'"[105] Indeed, if she is correct on this point, one might speculate that this consensus explains, in some part, the pervasiveness of a less theorized compatibilist mantra with regard to criminal responsibility itself: a less formal, less complete response to the determinist critique may seem sufficient if individual desert is thought primarily to function as a *limit* to retributive punishment. Just as resolving the question of desert at all may have seemed less critical to those early and midcentury scholars who assumed that the result of criminal condemnation would be, not retributive punishment, but humane treatment or segregation, modern-day limiting retributivism arguably need not carry the burden of justifying retributive punishment in the positive sense advocated, for example, by Moore; it need not satisfy us that punishment of the guilty is "an *intrinsic* good, not [a] merely *instrumental* good."[106] Still, in response to the separate notion that sheer conventional understandings of desert might circumscribe the bounds of a more limited retributivism, Ristroph asserted that public conceptions of desert are both more "opaque" and more "elastic" than the hopeful empiricists had claimed. Notions of desert are rather, at bottom, normative. Thus, she urged, we cannot escape our unease about desert by simply contenting ourselves that it is sufficiently static or objective to supply meaningful limits on punishment.[107]

Even in the partially isolated context of sentencing, then, the meanings and implications of "desert" remained embattled even if the role of desert, on the whole, maintained the preeminence it had gained during the late twentieth century. Put otherwise, despite the empirical studies, supposed practical necessities, or optimistic pragmatic uses of desert, precisely what the law should *do* with conventional notions of desert and responsibility – and how strongly such notions should be relied on – certainly was not beyond debate, particularly for those who were determined to offer deeper,

---

[104] Alice Ristroph, "Desert, Democracy, and Sentencing Reform," *JCLC*, vol. 96 (2006): 1293–352, 1294.

[105] Ristroph, "Desert, Democracy, and Sentencing Reform," 1302.

[106] Michael Moore, "Closet Retributivism," chap. 2 in *Placing Blame: A Theory of Criminal Law* (New York: Clarendon Press, 1997) (originally published in *USC Cites* [1982]: 9–15), 87–88.

[107] Ristroph attempted to illustrate that, in practice, judgments about desert are "opaque" in the sense that they obscure – often even from the decision maker him- or herself – "arbitrary factors" including "racial bias, fear," and "disgust." Such judgments are also "elastic" in the sense that they are quite broad and malleable: "desert is hard to quantify and easy to stretch." Further, desert "has proven more illimitable than limiting": as sentences lengthen in practice, we seem to reach successive conclusions that "offenders deserve just as much punishment as they get" (Ristroph, "Desert, Democracy, and Sentencing Reform," 1295–98). Ristroph devotes additional focused attention to the 2007 MPC *Draft* in "How (Not) to Think Like a Punisher," *Florida Law Review*, vol. 61 (2009): 727–50.

philosophically defensible justifications for state practices (or the reform thereof). And, of course, the debate was all the more pressing for those who still felt that the threshold question of liability for wrongdoing must first be answered before any punishment might be imposed justly. Accordingly, formal compatibilist formulations of the bases for criminal responsibility – still spearheaded by Morse through his individual scholarship – would continue alongside the large body of legal scholarship that seemed to acknowledge the responsibility question but, instead of dwelling on the question at length, commonly (albeit implicitly) repeated (or silently accepted) some form of a post-twentieth-century compatibilist mantra. Compatibilism at the edges of legal scholarship – where that scholarship overlapped with philosophy – continued as well. Indeed, the free will question remained quite current for many academic philosophers, although it was not always clear how legal academics ought to translate ethical theory regarding one's own, individual sense of responsibility into prescriptions for blaming and punishing others. The question remains whether today's compatibilist philosophy has the potential to further settle the matter for criminal law scholars by convincing them that there are, indeed, logically defensible ways to speak about human actions and motivations without ultimate resort to the causal terms that so often have left them – or so they have thought – in gray and uncertain territory.

In the spirit of this question, I close my epilogue with brief attention to Ronald Dworkin's noteworthy 2011 contribution – in a chapter plainly entitled "Free Will and Responsibility"[108] – which played out an innovative version of the conventional philosophical compatibilist position by relying on ethical principles and the sheer quality of consciousness to link our (presumably) determined choices to responsibility for those choices. In his broad volume, *Justice for Hedgehogs*, Dworkin continued his quest to address political morality via a notion of the unity of value, according to which he took up the law "as a branch of morality."[109] Dworkin had come some distance from his 1969 political-liberty-based response to the determinist critique, in which having treated the free will/determinism problem as unresolved and perhaps unresolvable, he, like Kadish and Packer, defended limits to governmental coercion that were premised on an openly avowed as-if freedom.[110] Dworkin's 2011 position reflected, to a considerable degree, the arc of development in philosophical compatibilism over the period 1970–2010. In Dworkin's words, his shift was necessitated by his "emphasis on the importance of the distinct virtue of moral responsibility," which – as he

[108] Ronald Dworkin, chap. 10 in *Justice for Hedgehogs* (Cambridge, MA: Harvard University Press, 2011).

[109] Ronald Dworkin, Keynote Address to the 2009 Symposium *"Justice for Hedgehogs*: A Conference on Ronald Dworkin's Forthcoming Book," *Boston University Law Review*, vol. 90 (2010): 469–77, 472.

[110] See my brief discussion in Chapter 7.

stated in his opening address to a 2009 symposium on the then-forthcoming book – required him "to try to face up to the question of free will." He proceeded to "approach that issue by separating the two ideas of free will and responsibility and defending a compatibilist position through an ethical rather than a metaphysical argument."[111] Sounding like others who revived a sense of Aristotelian virtue, Dworkin now moved from a focus on political liberty to consideration of the individual moral "person," confidently asking, and answering: "Can we do a better or worse job of making decisions even if, unknown to us, the decisions we make are inevitable? I believe we can."[112]

In his chapter on free will and responsibility, Dworkin started by positing the utter untenability of actually living from a hard determinist standpoint. He dubbed as "recursive nonsense" the incompatibilist suggestion that we must abandon traditional criminal law in favor of therapeutic treatment: for (enter Dworkin's version of the *reductio*), if no one is responsible, "then officials who treat accused criminals as responsible for their actions are not responsible for their own actions, and it is therefore wrong [for criminologists] to accuse them of acting unfairly"; "of course," then it is also wrong for us to accuse the criminologists, yet wrong for us to accuse ourselves of this wrong. Given the impossibility of believing hard determinism in our day-to-day lives, Dworkin centered his inquiry on the inevitable first-person experience of "judgmental responsibility" for one's own decisions.[113] His resulting compatibilist description of responsibility fully separated the notion of desert from physics and metaphysics by denying entirely the relevance of "causal control"; he thus rejected not just causal theory, but also the idea that rationality is the critical factor. For Dworkin, it appears, we need not be concerned even with whether our conscious decisions are the causes of our actions. Indeed, we may disregard the very neuroscientific epiphenomenalism that worried Morse (the hypothesis that our conscious decisions do not cause our actions, which actually originate in our nervous and muscular systems[114]) for, Dworkin asserted, responsibility stands aside, as solely "an ethical or moral matter: it attaches to final decisions whether or not these are causally effective."[115] The sense of control relevant to responsibility is, instead, sheer "capacity control," which (he claimed) is consistent with our ordinary views of responsibility and according to which "an agent is in control when he is conscious of facing and making a decision, when no one else is making that decision through and for him, and when he has the capacities to form true beliefs about the world and to match his

---

[111] Dworkin, Keynote Address, 476.
[112] Dworkin, *Justice for Hedgehogs*, 241.
[113] Dworkin, *Justice for Hedgehogs*, 222–25.
[114] See n. 89, earlier in this chapter.
[115] Dworkin, *Justice for Hedgehogs*, 232.

decisions to his normative personality – his settled desires, ambitions, and convictions."[116]

This is only to barely sketch Dworkin's commitment to human responsibility as an ethical and moral matter, which illustrates the continuing scholarly effort to describe and justify what responsibility is and where it comes from, if not from free will. Well aware of the shifting scientific and metaphysical terrain on which we inevitably seem to find ourselves, Dworkin was convinced that we could find meaning and dignity in our choices – that we could find a certain "independence from the natural order" despite our lack of independence from causation. "The universe may know what we will decide," conceded Dworkin, "but we do not." Thus, he urged, for now, let us "think that the fact of our consciousness itself, together with the phenomenal challenge of lives to lead, itself gives us all the dignity we need or should crave."[117]

Could this admirable ethical stance be *all* we need? Dworkin argued that our ordinary beliefs, upon examination, are indeed consistent with his approach. But a legal historian, once again, is bound to wonder whether, when it comes to blaming and punishing individuals for the choices they have made, this version of control – Dworkin's "capacity control" – perhaps fits our ordinary views only insofar as that capacity assumes an underlying causal one. That is, the historian cannot help but wonder whether philosophy's appeals to the "ordinary" can ever – in our culture, at any rate – truly finesse the determinist critique.

---

[116] Dworkin, *Justice for Hedgehogs*, 228. In rejecting the causal control view of responsibility, Dworkin asserted that Nagel's concern with the external or "impersonal perspective" was essentially unrelated to "ethical and moral questions about responsibility (as distinct from scientific or metaphysical questions about freedom)." Dworkin clarified that he did not deny the relevance of this objective perspective merely (as per Peter Strawson) because we are unable to abandon our internal sense of responsibility: "We need a defense of our ordinary judgments," said Dworkin, "not just a confession of our inability to doubt them. We need to show that we have no reason to doubt them" (220 n. 4).

[117] Dworkin, *Justice for Hedgehogs*, 230.

Conclusion

The contours of the story told in Part III represent a quite tentative historicization of the free will problem as that problem manifested itself in the world of modern American criminal jurisprudence. Turn the kaleidoscope a few degrees and a different pattern appears, but one has to start somewhere, and if the point is to provoke others to join in, better if the first player has stopped at a point where the image can yield interesting and satisfying results by nearly any alternative adjustment. I would venture to say, however, that my pattern shares certain important characteristics with nearly any other likely to be produced.

Begin with the fact that the sheer volume of late-twentieth-century criminal jurisprudence writings beggared that of the pre-1960 decades. American criminal law scholarship on freedom and responsibility came of age at mid-century, partly as a result of *Durham*, largely as a result of the Model Penal Code, and definitively as a result of the reinvigoration of moral and political theory in various fields of Anglo-American scholarship. We think (often) of the influence of Rawls's *Theory of Justice* (1971), but it seems clear that the return to a kind of Kantianism regarding human values began earlier and attracted not only Rawls but many others, including criminal law scholars both before, and especially during, the post–World War II flirtation with existentialism. The flight back to freedom and to the dignity and responsibility of the individual within a social context was in part a reaction against strict utilitarianism. And, at the same moment, domestic currents of thought were fed by reactions to Continental authoritarian practices, even if they were not always produced directly by those reactions. Moreover, Americans' modern replay of the age old "war on crime," together with – and often at odds with – the post-World War II efflorescence of rights jurisprudence, brought criminal law and procedure into the public eye and into the law school curriculum as never before. The history of the transformation, both in scope and quantity, of the entire field of criminal jurisprudence awaits its chroniclers. Even if those who attempt such a history find little of lasting use in these pages, they might nonetheless be drawn by my account to some aspects of the free will theme that would otherwise have remained in the background.

Of course the concern with, and approach to, the free will question in the modern period differed from – even as they shared some characteristics with – those of the Progressive Era and its immediate aftermath. The earlier periods evidenced a degree of confidence in the "truths" revealed by scientific positivism that all but vanished in the legal thought of post–World War II America. Still, among legal academics, that earlier confidence was never more than partial. I focused on Pound because, as I have suggested, for all his much-vaunted sociological jurisprudence, he revealed the lingering metaphysical concerns that so clearly took their toll in later times. Although Pound never fully abandoned his tendency to locate the freedom problem as a distinctive artifact of an American historical experience subject to dramatic change, his exploration of social-interest theory (derivative as that exploration was) ultimately led him to speculate about the ineffability of the psychology of freedom.

From the perspective of the present, the criminal law scholars of the 1920s and 1930s who succeeded Pound might seem comparatively naïve. Yet most of them were well aware of the gulf between law and its conventional moral underpinnings, on the one hand, and empirical sociology and behavioral science, on the other. And they recognized the special requirements of the law and were attentive to widespread social understandings of human behavior, as well as to constitutional and other limitations on the importation of science into law. So they sought to maximize the lessons of science within those limitations, albeit often while anticipating the gradual erosion of conventional notions of responsibility and revenge. If these scientific positivists experienced a crisis of confidence, that was more a matter of doubt about the real-world possibility of the victory of science over social attitudes, and about the fit between scientific rationality and rights-based justice, than it was a matter of doubt about the freedom question. Some during what I have called "the forgotten years" were quite sophisticated, when viewed from the modern perspective, in their recognition of both the limits of scientific insight and the unique role of law. It sometimes seems that the bifurcation of the trial and sentencing processes was accepted in just this spirit. But others held out hope for a rational legal system rid of the "myths" and "metaphysical jargon" of freedom of the will[1] or, at least, sought to transform vengeance-based retribution into less objectionable social shaming practices.

[1] Henry Weihofen, "The Metaphysical Jargon of the Criminal Law," *ABA Journal*, vol. 22 (1936): 267–70, 267.

Wechsler and Michael's 1937 reaction against the main trend of scientific positivism marshaled ideas that were not entirely new; as early as the 1920s, for example, Wigmore – recognizing the growing split between apostles of "cure" and proponents of "repression" – had called attention to the mainstream Progressives' failure to put deterrence ahead of science-based reformation of offenders, but his increasing shrillness left little room for the possibility of a fit between the two. Wechsler and Michael achieved a version of such a fit with remarkable – and influential – clarity and force. Their contribution ensured the durability of the utilitarian end run of the freedom problem and so has to be considered an important part of the foundation of modernism. But modernism proved to be so much more. The reaction against both Wechsler and Michael's holistic utilitarian-ism and a scientific positivism that left no room for a moral-legal idea of criminal responsibility was due to so many features of the 1940s–1960s American experience that its (as yet unwritten) history is as daunting as it is intriguing.

I have presented the legal scholarship of the mid-1940s through the late 1960s in part as providing an essential emphasis on the other aspect of freedom – political liberty. Political liberty certainly had never fully dropped out of the discussion of criminal responsibility, but its centrality reemerged in the World War II period largely in light of events abroad. The dangers of an overreaching state loomed large and were clearly implicated by both scientific-positivist and utilitarian accounts of the law. In this context, the *idea* of free will – if not the wholehearted acceptance of its truth – found its way back into responsibility theory more squarely as an instrumental guarantor of political liberty, not simply as a concession to social conven-tion. The American legal system was now increasingly understood not as an instrument of scientific progress, but as an evolving, historically embedded social institution concerned both with political liberty and morality. The latter, of course, conventionally embodied notions of free will, which some legal scholars perhaps accepted as little more than mere myth or social con-vention. Others – the majority by my surmise – accepted the belief in free will as a social fact or universal subjective experience that reinforced the political and individual liberty, and the personal responsibility, necessary for individuals' well-being and a well-functioning society. Legal scholars did not speak with one voice as they struck varying balances among consequential-ist goals, liberty interests, and a growing recognition that, to be relevant and effective, the law was – at least for the moment – inextricably connected with conventional morality. But scholars did therefore share an increasingly apparent common goal: to meld twentieth-century scientific insight with a moral-legal notion of responsibility that necessarily stood somewhat apart from science. And, in doing so, collectively they effected an important change of focus, away from the workings of the overall "system" and toward the nature of the individual offender's moral responsibility.

As the legal academy now puzzled over the question of what, exactly, to do with conventional morality, the answer often involved the jury. Ever entwined with the law's complex relationship to conventional ideas of free will, the jury had often been greeted with little more than reluctant acceptance by early-in-century scholars within and outside the academy. By the 1950s, however, legal academics (and others) more commonly viewed the jury either as a positive contributor to a moral-legal idea of responsibility or – whether optimistically or grudgingly – as a mediator between such an idea and essentially consequentialist goals. In either event, the jury's role was epitomized by its judgments regarding legal insanity, which most visibly marked the line between responsible and non-responsible behavior and, since the 1910 *Strasburg* decision, were widely deemed to be secured to the jury as a constitutionally guaranteed protection of the individual's liberty interests.

Accordingly, Judge Bazelon's 1954 decision in *Durham* provoked discussion regarding not only the relationship between law and science, but also the interplay between scholarly and lay notions of free will. *Durham* offered both commentary on the jury's role and consideration of the relevance of scientific testimony to judgments of legal responsibility. Specifically, it invited consideration of "'our inherited ideas of moral responsibility'"[2] including free will – or at least our consciousness of free will – as more than an instrumental guarantor of political liberty. And although Bazelon openly hoped that our inherited ideas would be guided – courtesy of psychiatric testimony – to "wider horizons of knowledge concerning mental life"[3] and (as he later said) to "more sophisticated concepts of free will,"[4] he seemed optimistic that the jury could ultimately be trusted with the critical line-drawing between responsible and non-responsible behavior.

Bazelon clearly remained among the positivist-leaning jurists of his day. But his faith in the social and moral importance of facing the issue of responsibility through use of the jury, his apparent recognition of the irreducible consciousness of free will, and his acceptance of a (properly tested) attribution of blameworthiness anticipated – to his own great regret – the sharper turn away from consequentialism that soon became evident on a broader scale. *Durham* was thus consistent with the growing focus on the role of human consciousness in endeavors to quilt practical *and* philosophically defensible bases for responsibility from sometimes disparate elements, including a still predominantly determinist perspective regarding serious criminal behavior alongside consequential goals and political liberty

---

[2] *Durham v. United States*, 214 F.2d 862, 876 (D.C. Cir. 1954) (quoting Thurman Arnold's 1945 opinion in *Holloway v. United States*, 148 F.2d 665, 666–67 (D.C. Cir. 1945).
[3] *Id.*
[4] David L. Bazelon, "The Morality of the Criminal Law," *Southern California Law Review*, vol. 49 (1976): 385–405, 391.

concerns. As of the mid-to-late 1950s, to judge from the commentary on *Durham,* the result was still a rough patchwork. But most attempts shared a characteristic: it was clear that, to one degree or another, criminal law theory would have to make its peace with traditional conventional morality – as always, as that morality was understood by theorists – which, for reasons both instrumental and moral, clearly could not simply be rooted out of responsibility attribution. Henry Hart's 1958 "Aims of the Criminal Law" can be seen as epitomizing the culmination of these attempts, as he adapted the law's conventional notions of social condemnation (albeit without explicitly invoking free will) to consequentialist and expressivist ends. He accepted the law's essential moral role in assigning blame for the good both of the community and of individuals, who should be encouraged to develop a "personal capacity for responsible decision to the end that every individual may realize his potentialities as a participating and contributing member of his community."[5]

But most legal scholars of the 1950s still distanced themselves from the retributivism that would characterize much end-of-century responsibility theory. At most, they co-opted retributive urges for expressivist purposes or simply recognized the conventional notion of blame as a social fact – and perhaps still (they hoped) as a temporary one. It was Jerome Hall who, nearly alone among the audible voices, urged an inseparable connection between a moral-legal concept of responsibility and retributive blame. His mid-1950s writings were ahead of their time, anticipating both Herbert Morris's late-1960 contributions and later compatibilist thought, to the extent that he emphasized the links among political liberty, blame rooted in the "rational element of purposive conduct,"[6] and the respect for individual autonomy associated with desert-based punishment.

Attempts to accommodate conventional morality to an essentially consequentialist legal regime, often by exploiting the bifurcated trial/sentencing process, increasingly betrayed themselves as philosophically unstable, particularly in light of the apparent real-world limitations of the rehabilitative ideal. To be sure, Herbert Hart's influential acceptance of meaningful choice alongside an unknowable determinism offered the possibility of a more successful accommodation, but it also begged questions that helped frame the evolution of a non-Hartian, desert-based responsibility theory in the ensuing years. Although Hart appears to have been unconcerned that the choice we believe to be free might, unknown to us, actually arise from causes outside our ultimate control, this might have been owing to his insistence upon a non-retributive form of morally constrained consequentialism – a view

---

[5] Henry M. Hart, Jr., "The Aims of the Criminal Law," *Law and Contemporary Problems,* vol. 23 (1958): 401–41, 440.
[6] Jerome Hall, "Psychiatry and Criminal Responsibility," *Yale Law Journal,* vol. 65 (1956): 761–85, 780.

that, all in all, was more consistent with past ideas about punishment than with those on the near horizon.

By the early 1960s, the Model Penal Code offered a different blueprint for a moral-legal rule, one ushered largely by Wechsler himself. Like Bazelon, Wechsler viewed the jury as an instrument of compromise between consequential ideals and the imperatives of both political liberty and traditional social beliefs and practices. The MPC's legal insanity standard – according to which an actor was not responsible if he lacked substantial capacity to appreciate the nature of his behavior *or to conform his conduct to the requirements of the law* – was Janus-faced from the outset. For Wechsler it was acceptably consonant with the minimum requirements of sheer deterrability. But for others, as I believe he well knew, it invoked ideas inherent in the act of choosing in accordance with a notion of (relatively) autonomous decision making. Certainly a jury would typically register its own response in terms of the latter potential meaning, in accordance with its own "social" – and free-will-based – sense of justice. Thus, the MPC's inherently ambiguous language proposed an institutional mechanism for managing the disparate goals and premises of post-Progressive legal theory.

In practice, the MPC's method would remain an influential model for absorbing the disjuncture between traditionalism and consequentialism. But what could be seen as an elegant solution to the seemingly conflicting ends of a moral-legal rule could also be seen as an unsustainable attempt to have it both ways. Scholars of the 1960s, within the legal field and otherwise, sought sounder – or at least more transparent – justifications for the sort of conventional blame that seemed unavoidably to result from a choice-based moral-legal rule of responsibility. The resulting, and increasingly sophisticated, conversation evidenced a revived concern with defensible bases for blameworthy choice without losing the insight gained from social science, psychology, and other fields throughout the first half of the century. The conversation was also marked by a renewed, more direct confrontation with free will – both as a concept and as a fact, the contours and nature of which nonetheless remained elusive. The resulting interplay of consequentialism and, for lack of a better shorthand term, Kantianism, established the enduring textures of modernism.

Perhaps the most salient feature of modern scholars' rediscovery of "freedom" lay in the varied nature of the efforts to rest much upon that idea while yet acknowledging the shifting sands upon which their belief in freedom stood. Herbert Packer's seminal invocation of a strictly legal idea ("value preference"[7]) of human free will encapsulated one version of what I have loosely termed 1960s criminal jurisprudence, a midway point between an earlier, relatively untheorized suspension of disbelief with regard to true

---

[7] Herbert L. Packer, *The Limits of the Criminal Sanction* (Stanford, CA: Stanford University Press, 1968), 74.

free will and the formal compatibilism of the 1970s and beyond. Packer's argument regarding human freedom at times reduced to the blunt and practical. The legal system required the presumption of freedom, but this had little to do with the metaphysics of freedom, for Packer had great doubts about what that entailed. Like Kadish and others, Packer both invoked political-liberty-based limits to consequentialism and understood the psychology of freedom in a general way as an attribute of the healthy and well-integrated person, but he was perhaps singular in openly portraying freedom as a mere "value preference." He may have meant to say no more than Kadish, who conceded that free will might well be a "myth"[8] but left the free will question a choice between two possible perspectives, rather than one answered by a plenary assertion of a purely instrumental sort. Among Packer, the early Kadish, and Goldstein, none actually probed the psychology of freedom more than was necessary, perhaps because all feared the potential of such an investigation, or perhaps because all were committed in principle to a blaming yet non-retributive system of criminal justice.

The parameters of 1960s criminal jurisprudence become clearer in the light of Herbert Morris's foundational contribution to neo-retributivism. Here, mere presumption, maybe-myth, and instrumentality gave way to fuller consideration of how humans actually behave and to the way in which they think about themselves. Morris worked backward from the phenomena of acting upon reason and of the consciousness of freedom, which together defined the "person," as well as forward from the virtues of political liberty. His approach amounted to a claim that limits to utility were empty and fruitless unless premised upon the correlative concepts of the person and of human worth, upon the realities of human psychology that justified responsibility and desert as ends in themselves even when disutilitarian. The Kantian idea that every person possesses a right to be conceived of as autonomous, hence responsible, survived into the ensuing decades as a necessary premise of deserved punishment, but it was hardly universally understood as sufficient. Morris's deep insight appeared to some to require further defense against the scientific-positivism (i.e. determinism) that survived the decline of rehabilitationism. Neo-retributivism's answers to that positivism dared to seize upon a compatibilism that emerged more explicitly than before in twentieth-century legal-academic circles as post-Morris retributivists sought to explain when, and how far, the particular Kantian premises they adopted were philosophically defensible. It was, as we have seen, a long and arduous quest – and one whose ultimate success remains as yet a matter of some conjecture.

---

[8] Sanford H. Kadish, "The Decline of Innocence," essay 5 in *Blame and Punishment: Essays in the Criminal Law* (New York: Macmillan, 1987) (originally published in *Cambridge Law Journal*, vol. 26 [1968]: 273–90), 77.

Recall that the dominant rhetorical guideline of the century's last four decades (bridging 1960s jurisprudence and neo-retributivism) was Herbert Hart's formulation that the criminally responsible actor had possessed "a normal capacity and a fair opportunity" for choice.[9] This was not proposed as a scientific measurement, but as a generalized standard that met an individual's reasonable expectations regarding freedom from legal coercion. Some scholars took the further step of defining "capacity and opportunity" in a manner that identified a concept of choice that yielded moral and legal desert-based responsibility – that is, one that could, purportedly, withstand the determinist critique while narrowing the gap between the standard's various theoretical justifications and conventional morality. By the 1980s, the attempts of legal-academic neo-retributivists to justify choice-based desert most commonly proceeded along one of what I have characterized as two roughly defined compatibilist paths: formal philosophical compatibilism, such as that of Moore and Morse, and a broader path trod by de facto compatibilists who, although assertedly agnostic about compatibilism, nonetheless affirmed personal desert in some form while acknowledging, at the very least, the possibility of determinism. The primary point of disagreement among neo-retributivists was essentially about what degree of philosophical purity, on the one hand, and genuine individual freedom, on the other, was required to justify meaningful and fair responsibility attribution. They avoided the determinist critique alternately by presuming that something ineffable in the nature of human action rendered – indeed *had* to render – the critique irrelevant in practice, or by asserting that it was logically irrelevant when addressed from the correct philosophical point of view. As a whole, they represented a variety of perspectives ranging from Moore's avowed positive retributivism to an almost reluctant limiting retributivism, such as that embodied by Norval Morris's scholarship on punishment, later adopted by the American Law Institute in revising the Model Penal Code, or the professed negative retributivistm of, e.g., Kadish.[10]

---

[9] H. L. A. Hart, "Changing Conceptions of Responsibility," chap. 8 in *Punishment and Responsibility: Essays in the Philosophy of Law* (Oxford: Clarendon Press, 1968), 201 (originally published in Hart, *The Morality of the Criminal Law: Two Lectures* [Jerusalem: Magnes Press, Hebrew University, 1964], 5–29).

[10] Alice Ristroph is probably right that such negative or limiting retributivism became the consensus model in punishment theory, and thus it is not surprising that the more common legal-academic view regarding criminal liability itself was relatively parsimonious with regard to deserved punishment. There was, I speculate, a range of possible explanations for this result, which were not always expressly given by the scholarship and which might or might not have reflected scholars' irresolution regarding the question of free will. Prescriptions and intuitions in favor of constraints on punishment might have arisen from many considerations – certainly from doubts about responsibility because of a determinism that one can finesse only so far, but also from the fear of one's own capacity for feelings of revenge and the concomitant fragility of one's sense that one is acting on "high" principles of human dignity,

Still, despite their differences and reservations, these neo-retributivists – the formal compatibilists as well as the less formal desert theorists – generally shared a range of commitments that came to define mainstream legal-academic theory on responsibility. Regardless of whether they would term themselves positive or negative retributivists, they endorsed the limiting notion of blame that was securely rooted within well-defined boundaries against the incursion of state-imposed punishment, thereby upholding political liberty and, in Hart's rendition, the ability to "identify in advance the space which will be left open ... free from the law's interference" so that one can enjoy the satisfaction of "predict[ing] and plan[ning] the future course" of one's life.[11] Also in line with Hart's fundamental ideas on the subject, these scholars saw the criminal law not as an institution capable of scientific perfection, but as a creature of social life that must "reflect in its judgments on human conduct distinctions which not only underlay morality, but pervade the whole of our social life."[12] Hence the relevance of the law's according respect to the consciousness of freedom, regardless of the extent to which a given scholar may have rejected in theory the idea of true free will underlying that consciousness: the consciousness of freedom, experienced by legal scholars as by all others (and who can say with what influence on "pure" theory), underlay the concept of desert, which many scholars had come to see as natural and inescapable. This consciousness was also intimately connected with the cherished sense of personhood that underlay not just our capacities for self-respect and respect for others, but the very idea of human dignity that lent meaning to our individual lives and justice to our institutional practices. And finally, of course, neo-retributivists could agree on the essential unacceptability of hard determinism, which, taken to its logical conclusion, required rejecting these senses of personhood and dignity and, ultimately, yielded absurdity, meaninglessness, paralysis, and an unsustainable denial of human nature. Thus, despite the doubts, ambivalences, ambiguities, and sometimes contrasting certainties, overall, the post-1970 discussion resounded, on one level, with a certain confidence: personal desert, it turned out, counted. And despite the disparate methods for justifying this desert, the near-unity of effort to salvage desert from determinism suggested that the hundred-years' war over the freedom question had (apparently) been won. All that was left to determine was just how and why it had been won – what the soldiers should tell their children when they returned from the front.

---

and perhaps even the sense that Herbert Hart's version of a limiting principle on utility is, overall, just, but that its practical implementation is highly imperfect.

[11] Hart, "Punishment and the Elimination of Responsibility," chap. 7 in *Punishment and Responsibility* (originally presented as a lecture in 1961 at King's College, London, and published in 1962 by the Athlone Press), 181–82.

[12] Hart, "Punishment and the Elimination of Responsibility," 183.

It may be, however, that, as is often true of war, the reasons we give for the outcome are not just various and contested, but will fade into obscurity in favor of more present questions. Indeed, the varied reasoning underlying the resurgence of desert is easily overshadowed by the appearance of *fin de millennium* unity on the subject, which was enhanced in practice not just by political rhetoric and sentencing policy, but by broad scholarly recourse – whether explicit or, more often, implicit – to the jury as arbiter of criminal responsibility.[13] On the ground, points of disagreement or disjuncture underlying the affirmation of desert – whether within a given approach, between approaches, or between the scholarly world and the world of legal practice and policy – could be almost universally subsumed into the black box that is the jury. By almost any measure the result was ironic: despite several decades of academic machinations reaffirming desert in the face of the determinist critique, the jury – as representative of a conventional morality historically presumed to be rooted in a belief in free will – was reinforced as the locus for responsibility judgments, despite the fact that it was hardly thought to proceed self-consciously on the basis of any compatibilist (or other theoretical) conceptualization of the freedom problem that transcended determinism. The jury's approach might have appeared to theorists to mirror one or another such conceptualization with regard to results, and scholars could accept the jury as reinforcing the ineradicable *psychology* of free will, which theory had come to recognize as an element not just of personhood and personal well-being, but as a general good that encouraged the taking of responsibility in everyday life. Most critically – or at least most unanimously, among theorists – *political* liberty seemed to require statist respect for the idea and *practice* of free will. Perhaps Sanford Kadish expressed this particular element of agreement as well as anyone (in words already quoted):

> The ancient notion of free will may, in substantial measure, be a myth. But even a convinced determinist should reject a governmental regime which is founded on anything less in its system of authoritative disposition of citizens. Whether the concept of man as responsible agent is fact or fancy is a very different question from whether we ought to insist that the government in its coercive dealings with individuals must act on that premise.[14]

Where free will as a *fact* remained ephemeral, political liberty took up the slack and, for some, became all the justification needed to entrust the jury with the ultimate judgments. Theory might endorse these same

---

[13] Of course, the bulk of criminal cases are in fact resolved by guilty pleas. But might not the small minority of cases resolved by jury (or bench) trial have become defining, as the institutional mechanism of trial remains the reigning paradigm for resolution of criminal cases? I plan to pursue this question in future work on the relationship between ideas about responsibility and ideas about the criminal trial jury. My comments here are quite tentative.

[14] Kadish, "Decline of Innocence," 77.

judgments in result, but the theoretical reasoning – with its inherent variety and, oftentimes, irresolution – was easily obscured (or absorbed) by practice.

At the height of the Progressive movement, of course, some scholars (albeit mostly outside of legal academia), conceiving of an ever-expanding system modeled on the principles of juvenile justice, would have sacrificed the jury – *and* free will – to a more enlightened future presided over by a scientifically guided state. For them, state coercion in accordance with the assumption of free will – the myth licensing retributive punishment – was anathema; state coercion absent the myth – reformation-based treatment of corrigibles and permanent incapacitation of incorrigibles – accorded with the dictates of reason and humane impulses. But, true to the American jury's heritage, midcentury scholarship significantly reconceived the jury's role – as well as the concept of the responsibility-bearing person – in part precisely because of fears of lost liberty in the face of an overreaching state. By the end of the century, the jury had again risen to a secure place in the academic mind, although that mind had, at least in part, been put at ease by exactly the sort of abstract theorizing one would assume jurors would reject outright: although compatibilists comfortably enough ceded responsibility-attribution *in practice* to the jury, presumably scholars still assumed that jurors' judgments arose from a conception of free will that theorists had now spent a hundred years debunking and reframing.

In the end, despite the significant divergences and disagreements of many end-of-century approaches to the responsibility question, American legal scholars' prescriptions seemed to blur at the point of their emphasis on protecting individuality and liberty from the state and in their axiomatic use of the jury – intentionally or incidentally – to smooth out the rough edges where our sometimes conflicting beliefs and aspirations about freedom meet. Perhaps, to some degree, this should be viewed as reflecting our historical national commitments to individualism, political liberty, and trial by jury. And perhaps Pound was right in suggesting that our attachment to the idea of free will is a particular result of American history. But on a broader scale, if viewed from a vantage point far above the fray, twentieth-century American criminal-responsibility jurisprudence seems to reveal an intrinsically human neurosis regarding individual freedom in the context of human society.

For my part, at least thus far, I have taken my stand as of the end of the twentieth century and cast my gaze backward. Although that is the perspective of a historian, I readily admit that my account is less a history, as that term is now conventionally understood, and more a sketchbook for criminal law scholars and teachers and for those American historians who will perhaps seek to contextualize and elaborate on the ideas I have traced.

By century's end, American criminal jurisprudence had produced a rich and insightful commentary on the free will problem that Speranza had identified a hundred years before. Whether it had located the "Great Pacificator" for which Speranza had yearned remains a more difficult question. Daring fate, American neo-retributivist legal academics had abandoned the early-in-century search for a purely consequentialist approach to criminal responsibility premised, at least in large part, on the denial of free will and had reworked the particular midcentury version of a (largely instrumental) moral-legal idea of free will. They had, many of them, embraced a form of desert theory premised upon the idea of an irreducible human capacity for responsibility and sought to explain how that idea was compatible with determinist notions. Or, failing that, others simply identified either the aspects of the person to which blame might be said to attach or the values in our culture that made the capacity for deserved responsibility a necessary and natural attribute of the person. Or, in a few instances, they suggested that the very fact that the free will problem was insoluble made the attribution of culpability meaningful – that is, made it central to what being human was distinctively about: participation in a never-ending search for meaning. This last move, which carried forward existential themes evident in the immediate post–World War II period, might be read as a response to Speranza: he had seen the problem but had failed to recognize that the problem contained its own (and its only form of) solution. But this particular reinterpretation of the idea of freedom might well be seen as little more than renaming defeat a victory.

All this is to say that we – we legal scholars of this new century – well know how central the problem that Speranza addressed in "Medico-Legal Conflict" remains to our law and, more generally, to our lives. For most of us, I venture to say, whether we are always or only occasionally conscious of it, the search for a "pacificator" goes on. And although our deepest worries about the matter (when we have them) might be evidenced at the margins as they come to influence the minds of some judges, lawyers, and penologists, given their inevitable distance from our current politics and from the essence of (what we reasonably take to be) conventional morality, they are perhaps as foreign to society at large as were the ideas of fin de siècle criminal anthropologists or interwar realists and scientific positivists, especially with regard to the core issue of personal responsibility – the assessment of criminal guilt.

Indeed, "we" as individuals well know that academic concern with the mysteries of human free will remains just that: academic. Both in our private and many of our public capacities, if not always in our teaching and our theorizing in print, we too mainly indulge the presumption that underpins the law. As a group, we may express more skepticism about free will than other elements of the legal caste, but – perhaps out of allegiance to the consciousness of human freedom – when we act in the real world we are, most of us, not so very far from society at large. Like Pound, we leave the working out of the most difficult problems to the future. We play a role defined for us by our culture and our psychology, as generations of legal academics have before us and as those that follow probably will as well. Although I have contrasted academic views of responsibility with scholars' presumed picture of the conventional morality embodied by the jury, in the end of course the distinction is not so simple. Within the legal world of bench, bar, and academy, as in society at large, the traditional and fundamentally unstable view prevails: just as bifurcation of the legal process persists, so also does the division in our minds between the competing urges to explain causally and to affix blame.[15]

From the Progressive Era forward, the rhetoric of the social and psychological causes of crime have vied – in the law, in the media, in ourselves – with the rhetoric of, and ineradicable belief in, human freedom. This ceaseless

---

[15] My observation here is drawn from the Epilogue to Green, "Freedom and Criminal Responsibility in the Age of Pound: An Essay on Criminal Justice," *Michigan Law Review,* vol. 93 (1995): 1915–2053, 2047. For other evocations of this theme, as it applies to legal academics as well as others, see, e.g., Richard A. Posner, *The Problems of Jurisprudence* (Cambridge, MA: Harvard University Press, 1990), 178; Michael Corrado, "Addiction and Causation," *San Deigo Law Review,* vol. 37: 913–58, 917–18 (2000); Anders Kaye, "Resurrecting the Causal Theory of the Excuses," *Nebraska Law Review,* vol. 83 (2005): 1116–77, 1139; Louis Michael Seidman, "Points of Intersection: Discontinuities at the Junction of Criminal Law and the Regulatory State," *Journal of Contemporary Legal Issues,* vol. 7 (1996): 97–163, 162; Lloyd L. Weinreb, *Oedipus at Fenway Park: What Rights Are and Why There Are Any* (Cambridge, MA: Harvard University Press, 1994), 48.

These expressions of the implications of one's own consciousness of freedom are, no doubt, ubiquitous in scholarly literature, and presumably all the more so in scholars' everyday thought, even when not reflected upon in their writings. As the references here indicate, the theme, when expressed, is not confined to any one perspective on the basis for criminal responsibility and punishment. But different theorists might mean different things by it. The formal compatibilist, for instance, might claim to understand this everyday consciousness of "freedom" in the sense of freedom within a determined human order, that is, the freedom he or she associates with the capacity and opportunity for practical reasoning, and nothing more – not a consciousness of true free will, or "self-origination." To affirm this compatibilist freedom might, I suppose (and reasonably so, for all I know), suffice for some to escape the reductio, the abyss of the "absurd."

Even conceding that, the historian is nonetheless left with the question whether the psychological need to feel "free," on whatever terms, is itself a driving force for academics as they go about the chore of doing criminal responsibility work. That is, for example, when a scholar invokes the *reductio* as a reason for adopting a freedom-based (or at least, responsibility-based) perspective, the historian is left with the question whether that claim is simply a claim of reason or, although experienced by the claimant as such, is in fact a determined human response that, for all we know, is programmed into us. Or whether it is both (it is sometimes claimed that two plus two would in fact equal four even if we were determined to think so).

The philosophical issues here are well beyond my reach (although perhaps not beyond that of other historians, to whom I readily bequeath such matters). My subject extends only so far as the observed phenomena: the ubiquity among modern criminal justice scholars of open recognition of the universality of the consciousness of freedom; and the role this

battle is only partly contained by our explanations to ourselves and others for the consciousness of freedom or by the view that, although determining factors exist, they are either compatible with moral and legal responsibility or are typically not all-encompassing: that we – and those whom we blame – have the wherewithal to resist, even if we often lack the ability to draw the line between the resistible and the irresistible with certainty. Wharton's pact with the angels survives,[16] albeit often in an attenuated form. Nor have the values associated with the traditional view altered: political liberty, human dignity, and freedom of the will remain intertwined.

As has been the case for generations and perhaps centuries, we (all of us) sometimes reflect these uncertainties in our tendency to soften the rigors of the sanctions to which we subject those whom we judge.[17] We may also at times be partly appeased by the thought that a central goal of imprisonment is – or still could be – rehabilitation. Especially "limited-retributive" punishment might then be viewed as at least largely benign and responsive to the determinist aspect of human life. Indeed, on the very long view, one might conclude, society at large has grown increasingly aware of the fragility of human autonomy and become increasingly concerned that punishment

---

recognition might have played in the revival and development of justifications for desert-based punishment. If this particular recognition was an important factor for neo-retributivist academics, why was it not so for Progressives, if it was not? And, if it was influential in Progressives' everyday lives, why was it not more frequently evidenced in their criminal responsibility writings? My own sense is that it played a greater role than at first meets the eye. I reserve further discussion of this theme for future work that engages a question I have elsewhere posed regarding the relationship between conventional morality and legal-academic thought: "Do we take control of conventional morality as we make use of it? Or does it hold our thought in place (even shape it), control and make use of us?" Green, "The Jury and Criminal Responsibility in Anglo-American History," *Criminal Law and Philosophy*, vol. 8 (forthcoming 2014) (also available at http://dx.doi.org/10.1007/s11572-013-9267-0), quoted material from the text following n. 30. Some discussion of this theme is currently planned for a paper, coauthored with Merrill C. Hodnefield, to appear in the *American Journal of Legal History*, January 2015. Also note my observations in Chapter 9, n. 95, regarding recent scholars' embracing the *reductio*'s impact on legal theory.

[16] See Chapter 1, pp. 35–36.

[17] For a particularly effective evocation of this theme, see Weinreb, *Oedipus at Fenway Park*, chap. 2, "Human Responsibility." Weinreb states that "human responsibility is a structural fact of our experience. By 'structural fact' I mean a proposition that cannot be contradicted without altering the nature of our existence, not merely in some concrete particular(s) but in a fundamental way, making it a different experience entirely" (45). He then deftly notes the ways in which we also order our experiences in accordance with the natural world, concluding:

> The antinomy of freedom, the opposition between the natural order and the moral order, is complete and unavoidable. As an idea of reason, freedom is not within our grasp. If abstract reason thus fails decisively, there remains an issue that is all the more pressing: how within our experience the antinomy is resolved. For, perforce, it is resolved. (55)

With respect to finding resolution with regard to criminal responsibility, he suggests that "in practice, we often split the difference, our uncertainty whether the person is truly responsible at all mitigating the punishment" (54).

conjoin a good deal of cure for "illness" – or, perhaps, remediation for social conditions – with a moderate degree of deterrence and retribution.

Up close, however, the path of real-world ideas about criminal justice has hardly been linear. It has, rather, been either subject to moments of atavism or downright cyclical. The United States is, as I write, at an especially tense moment – and a lengthy one at that: for several decades now, the ideal of rehabilitation has been under significant pressure. To some large extent we have responded as a society to the observation (right or wrong) that the indeterminate sentence does not work. Our calls for fixed sentences and our critiques of rehabilitation are thus premised in part on the view that a return to older ways is fairer to those we hold responsible and even accords them a greater degree of human dignity. To some extent, too, we simply express our anger and our natural fears of crime. Not least, however, we seem to remain captive to the notion that we have gone too far in the direction of absolving one another of personal responsibility. It seems entirely plausible that the due-process and equal-protection based arguments for fixed sentences and for guidelines that supposedly ensure that such sentences will not vary much from judge to judge reflect in part a desire to strain out, to a large degree, consideration of background causal factors that "led" to the crimes for which the fixed and fair sentences are imposed.

The current widespread obsession in the political realm with personal responsibility, it should be noted, reflects a reaction not only against deterministic rhetoric regarding the causes of criminal behavior, but also against what are taken to be the deterministic assumptions that pervade the welfare state generally. These assumptions relate both to noncriminal and criminal concerns, as government initiatives affect existing concepts of just deserts regarding entitlements as well as those regarding retributive justice, the traditional domain of the criminal law. Progressivism is carried forward, but it is also under profound attack across much of the spectrum of political and social thought.

From a certain perspective, our politics have produced a macrocosmic reflection of the microcosmic experience within each of us. Just as legal scholars must mediate between their academic selves and themselves as members of society at large, and just as each of us mediates between our tendencies both to blame and to absolve, society as a whole is deeply divided between the heirs to Progressivism and those who have now rejected, or who never accepted, its message for criminal justice. Disagreements on responsibility not only track, in the large, religious, social, and other alignments, including movements along racial, ethnic, and gender lines, but are also, of course, internal to them. This is not the place for a rehearsal of the multifaceted role of the free-will/determinism issue in modern American society. Nor – even if it were – am I well suited to undertake such a task.[18] I want

---

[18] But some of the American historians among you might be well suited – and perhaps even interested. One of my hopes for this book is for it to encourage engagement with the historical

only to say that the issue is still very much with us and that, with respect to criminal justice, we – including legal scholars – are sometimes as conflicted as ever. Conflicted to the point that our attitudes defy generalization. The main direction of our present thought and behavior depends entirely on the eye of the beholder. If we tend to speak with greater confidence about main scholarly directions in the past, that may well be because of the increased perspective that a historical view affords. Which is to say that we know relatively little about the past and too much about the present.

About the inscrutable present we might nonetheless venture some final commentary along the lines marked out many pages ago by our discussion of Speranza and Pound. Speranza was an American lawyer, but at the start of his career he looked at American law from the outside with ties to, and an understanding of, the Continental tradition, and with the sympathies of the scientist. Pound was well inside the common law tradition, albeit among its more progressive spirits and trenchant critics of its "excesses." Although each urged that the law must take account of the determined aspects of our nature – aspects of which we are all more and less aware depending on the circumstances, and thus that make us either more or less forgiving of ourselves and each other in specific instances – we are confronted daily with evidence that seems to confirm Pound's insistence upon a particular form of American exceptionalism (our "frontier attitude") regarding the intensity of our attraction to human free will and individual rights and regarding the depths of our suspicion of the state. What Pound deemed a largely unhealthy, "held-over" attachment to will theory probably strikes some as Americans' ongoing embrace of the deepest truth, others as recourse to a useful belief (conducive both to the preservation of political liberty and the cultivation of a sense of personal well-being), and still others as too great a rejection of what – like it or not – we have come to know about the nature of our selves.

---

problem of the concern – or relative lack of concern – during the twentieth century with the free will issue in areas outside of criminal jurisprudence and criminal justice administration. That is, I hope to encourage consideration of the historical question whether, during the last century, we in fact see relatively little direct confrontation with the free will problem in most areas outside the criminal law. Even legal academics have less often confronted the determinist critique in *noncriminal* matters; some have raised the issue generally (e.g., some realists, critical legal scholars, social constructionists) but not not many have focused on it in the way that criminal jurisprudence scholars have. Of course, deterministic rhetoric of social, economic, racial, and gender disadvantage has been plentiful, and often in terms similar (or identical) to those expressed regarding the causes of crime. But as I noted with respect to civil law in the Progressive Era (see Chapter 2), in noncriminal matters *relative* unfreedom (in the sense of unequal bargaining power) was more often at issue. The presumption of a general capacity for freely willed action (at least under conditions of equal opportunity) prevailed – or at least for the most part went unchallenged. Not only ideas about the free will problem, but also the fact of their relative absence, are part of history. Yet, such ideas – and particularly their absence – are less often the subject matter of historians than one might expect. Or perhaps it is precisely what one would expect. If so, the reasons for that expectation are, themselves, a part of history – a part of the history of who we have been as well as a part of the principles of psychology regarding who we are.

Among even these last there may be some who nonetheless believe that an appropriate balance between the "religion" of free will and the "science" of determinism is struck in the rituals by which we now live. And among these rituals inherent to our particular concept of the rule of law are the practical and symbolic aspects of jury-based determination of guilt – in some cases, of punishment – in accordance neither with pure legal abstraction nor with supposed scientific precept, but, as we are wont to say, with the "common sense" and the "conscience" of the community.

Decisions, after all, must not only be made, they must also be lived with. So, too, must incoherence be lived with, and – evidently – its lessons allowed to temper our judgment as we, case by case, see fit. This is true not only with respect to our everyday lives, but in the domain of criminal justice administration as well. Perhaps there more than anywhere. For it is one thing to observe *academically* that we cannot prove beyond a reasonable doubt that the defendant was a free agent – or, even, an unfree but nonetheless responsible one; it is another to resist passing judgment upon persons who society has agreed must be held responsible – indeed, who are said to have a right both with respect to human dignity and as against overweening political authority to be conceived of as personally responsible. The resulting tension can be very great, and the ritual of judgment is indeed sometimes no less than an act of faith. One feels a certain truth – shall we say, a certain consolation? – in the observation that, after all (let Speranza's words be my last): "Law is one of the Humanities."

Index of Persons and Sources

This index includes all persons and cases. Other primary sources, listed by author, are included only if they receive specific attention as subjects in the text (or, albeit more selectively, in the footnotes); full citations to sources generally appear in footnotes accompanying the first mention of the source.

Hart, Herbert (H. L. A.) (and "Hartian"
  ideas), 236, 285, 287–325 *passim (but
  esp.* 291–304), 337, 340–41, 343, 345,
  350, 351, 353, 354, 355–56, 366n64,
  382, 383, 387, 414, 417, 421, 455,
  471–72, 474n10
  "Changing Conceptions of Responsibility"
    (1964), 301–3, 474
  The Concept of Law (1961), 10n7,
    294, 323
  "Legal Responsibility and Excuses"
    (1958), 292–96, 366n64
  "Negligence, *Mens Rea* and Criminal
    Responsibility" (1961), 293–94
  "Prolegomenon to the Principles of
    Punishment" (1959), 291n13, 293,
    293n18, 295, 295n22
  "Punishment and the Elimination of
    Responsibility" (1961), 294, 296–98,
    313, 475
Hartsfield, Larry K., 25n13
Haskell, Thomas L., 62n16, 63n18
Hatch, Henry, 47n34
Hawkins, D. J. B., 210n63
Hegel, G. W. F., 178, 317, 317n78, 348n7, 388
Herget, James E., 62n17, 67n30, 77n74,
  80n82
Hershey, O. F., 38
  "Criminal Anthropology" (1893), 27n18,
    38–39, 44n30
Hill, John L., 405–8, 417n217, 420
  "Freedom, Determinism, and the
    Externalization of Responsibility in the
    Law" (1988), 405–8, 443
Hill, Warren P., 245–51, 263
  "The Psychological Realism of Thurman
    Arnold" (1955), 245–48, 250n98
Hinckley, John, 274, 274–75n12
Hobbes, Thomas, 12, 58n8, 201, 340, 405
Hodnefield, Merrill C., 479n15
Holland, Thomas Erskine, 66
Holloway v. U.S. (D.C. Cir. 1945), 196–97,
  223, 245–46
Holmes, Oliver Wendell, 39n16, 41, 62n17,
  63n18, 143, 173, 191, 253, 290
Honderich, Ted, 346n5, 394n149
Hoover, J. Edgar, 24n4, 127, 182
Horder, Jeremy, 436
  "Criminal Law: Between Determinism,
    Liberalism, and Criminal Justice"
    (1996), 436n25, 437n32
Horwitz, Morton J., 61n15, 84n89

Hospers, John, 360n34, 405
Hovenkamp, Herbert, 25n9, 25n13, 49n40,
  100n6, 113n44
Howe, Mark DeWolfe, 51n42
Huigens, Kyron, 428–33, 435
  "Virtue and Inculpation" (1995), 429–31,
    433n21
Hull, N. E. H., 62n17
Hume, David, 12, 58n8, 82n86, 172, 178,
  201, 340, 396, 405
Husak, Douglas, 278n18, 304n47
Hutchins, Robert Maynard, 167n103, 196
  "The Law and the Psychologists" (1927),
    111n37, 149, 167n103

Jackson, Robert H., 252
James, William, 77n74, 80n82, 82n87
Johnson, Lyndon, 271
Jones, Gareth Stedman, 437
Jones, State v. (N.H. 1871), 216n3

Kadish, Sanford H., 285, 311–14, 315–16,
  322, 323, 324, 325, 341–42, 351,
  383–90, 415, 422, 424, 445–48, 452,
  464, 473, 474
  "Complicity, Cause and Blame" (1985),
    385, 389, 394
  "Excusing Crime" (1987), 314n72,
    385–90, 445n54, 446
  "Fifty Years of Criminal Law"
    (1999), 230nn31–32, 275nn12–13,
    276nn14–15
  "The Criminal Law and the Luck of the
    Draw" (1994), 314n72, 384n109, 442,
    445–48
  "The Decline of Innocence" (1968),
    311–14, 384, 386, 473, 476
  "Why Substantive Criminal Law"
    (1980), 384
Kahan, Dan M., 428, 429, 430n12, 435,
  439n38
  "Two Conceptions of Emotion in Criminal
    Law" (1996) (with Martha Nussbaum),
    430–31
Kalven, Harry, 227, 280n20, 305
  Introduction to "Insanity and the Criminal
    Law" (1955), 227, 269
Kane, Robert, 345n2, 346nn3–5
Kant, Immanuel (and "Kantian" ideas), 8,
  9n5, 178, 317, 323, 324, 328, 330, 332,
  339, 344, 346n4, 348n7, 384, 388, 395,
  453, 467, 472, 473

Subject Index

For central recurring themes, only primary or definitional discussions are referenced.

CPSIA information can be obtained at www.ICGtesting.com
Printed in the USA
LVOW12*0118130615

442371LV00001B/1/P

9 780521 854603